Sustainable Finance

Series Editors
Karen Wendt, CEO. Eccos Impact GmbH, President of SwissFinTechLadies, President Sustainable-Finance, Cham, Switzerland

Margarethe Rammerstorfer, Professor for Energy Finance and Investments, Institute for Finance, Banking and Insurance WU Vienna, Vienna, Austria

Sustainable Finance is a concise and authoritative reference series linking research and practice. It provides reliable concepts and research findings in the ever growing field of sustainable investing and finance, SDG economics and Leadership with the declared commitment to present the theories, methods, tools and investment approaches that can fulfil the United Nations Sustainable Development Goals and the Paris Agreement COP 21/22 alongside with de-risking assets and creating triple purpose solutions that ensure the parity of profit, people and planet through choice architecture passion and performance. The series addresses market failure, systemic risk and reinvents portfolio theory, portfolio engineering as well as behavioural finance, financial mediation, product innovation, shared values, community building, business strategy and innovation, exponential tech and creation of social capital. Sustainable Finance and SDG Economics series helps to understand keynotes on international guidelines, guiding accounting and accountability principles, prototyping new developments in triple bottom line investing, cost benefit analysis, integrated financial first plus impact first concepts and impact measurement. Going beyond adjacent fields (like accounting, marketing, strategy, risk management) it integrates the concept of psychology, innovation, exponential tech, choice architecture, alternative economics, blue economy shared values, professions of the future, leadership, human and community development, team culture, impact, quantitative and qualitative measurement, Harvard Negotiation, mediation and complementary currency design using exponential tech and ledger technology. Books in the series contain latest findings from research, concepts for implementation, as well as best practices and case studies for the finance industry. This book series is indexed in SCOPUS

B Rajesh Kumar

Green Finance

Navigating the Sustainable Investment Landscape

Springer

B Rajesh Kumar
Shiv Nadar University
Chennai, Tamil Nadu, India

ISSN 2522-8285 ISSN 2522-8293 (electronic)
Sustainable Finance
ISBN 978-3-032-03332-1 ISBN 978-3-032-03333-8 (eBook)
https://doi.org/10.1007/978-3-032-03333-8

This Springer imprint is published by the registered company Springer Nature Switzerland AG
The registered company address is: Gewerbestrasse 11, 6330 Cham, Switzerland

To
Appu and Lakshmi

Preface

The green economy is driving a global transformation, with sectors like renewable energy and eco-friendly infrastructure now surpassing traditional industries. This shift highlights the rising importance of sustainable practices in shaping the world economy. Several environmental systems have exceeded sustainable limits, threatening ecological balance. However, achieving global sustainability goals across key sectors such as food, cities, energy, and health presents a $12 trillion market opportunity, covering 60% of the tangible economy.

Innovative policies and carbon pricing play a key role in advancing a low-carbon, inclusive economy by cutting emissions, promoting green investments, and supporting the post-Paris Agreement transition. Globally, financial centres are seeing the rise of the "green fintech" market, which focuses on environmental objectives. Valued at an estimated $500 billion by 2025, green fintech integrate technology into financial services to align with Sustainable Development Goals and address sustainability risks. During the first half of year 2023, the cumulative issuance of green bonds amounted to USD 3.46 trillion. The market size of allocated capital to impact investment was estimated to be $1.164 trillion by 2022. The global sustainable finance market was valued at US$ 519.88 billion and is expected to grow at a compound annual growth rate (CAGR) of 22.6 percent during the period 2023–2030. Institutional investors, such as public pension funds (PPFs) and sovereign wealth funds (SWFs), are in a pivotal position to address sustainability challenges and finance sustainable energy investments.

As part of the UN GSFO's initiatives, UNCTAD, in partnership with the Principles for Responsible Investment (PRI) and the UNEP Finance Initiative (UNEP FI), has been tracking recent trends in sustainable finance policies and regulations across 35 countries and economic groupings. The development of sustainability reporting standards is supported by several key international initiatives, including the Task Force on Climate-related Financial Disclosures (TCFD), the Task Force on Nature-related Financial Disclosures (TNFD), the Sustainability Accounting Standards Board (SASB), the Global Reporting Initiative (GRI), and the International Financial Reporting Standards (IFRS).

This book aims to provide a comprehensive overview of the fundamentals of the global green economic landscape. It focuses on emerging trends in climate finance and highlights innovations in climate finance initiatives. The significance of impact investing is also explored in length. The book covers developments in sustainable debt markets and financial instruments, as well as trends in sustainable market finance. It examines climate transition initiatives undertaken by various institutions and discusses relevant policies, regulations, and standards in sustainable finance.

A dedicated section focuses on sustainable finance investments across different regions of the world. Additionally, the book analyses sustainable finance trends across various industry sectors, including chemicals, finance, energy, materials and construction, transportation and logistics, agriculture, food and forestry, technology, and consumer goods.

The second part of the book presents case studies of sustainable investments by companies across different sectors. It features more than 90 companies that have adopted green investment initiatives, highlighting real-world examples of sustainable finance strategies.

Chennai, India B. Rajesh Kumar

Acknowledgements

I gratefully acknowledge the invaluable contributions of numerous resources that informed the development of this book. In particular, I extensively reviewed reports prepared by the G20 Sustainable Finance Working Group, the Task Force on Climate-related Financial Disclosures (TCFD), the United Nations Environment Programme Finance Initiative (UNEP FI), the International Sustainability Standards Board (ISSB), and the Climate Bonds Initiative. I also drew insights from reports prepared by leading financial advisory and consultancy firms.

I would like to thank Ms. Rocio Torregrosa, Editor at Springer Nature, for her excellent support and encouragement throughout the projects I have been involved in with Springer. I also extend my sincere thanks to Ms. Sneha Arunagiri and her production team for their timely assistance in completing this project.

Competing Interests The author has no competing interests to declare that are relevant to the content of this manuscript.

Contents

Part I
Principles and Practices of Green Finance

Chapter 1
Fundamentals of Green Economy

The world is witnessing a transformational change on account of the trends in the green economy concept. The collective market value of sectors comprising the green economy such as renewable energy, energy efficiency, clean water supply, sustainable forestry and fishing, plastic and waste recycling, green infrastructure and eco friendly urban development have become the dominant economic sector worldwide. This sector has surpassed many traditional sectors which had historically dominated the global economic landscapes. This trend has underscored the growing significance of sustainable practices.

The green economy represents a pivotal pathway forward which offers a new frontier for high tech advancements, value added growth and employments opportunities for millions of people across the global. The adoption of the 2030 Agenda for Sustainable Development Goals (SDGs) and the Paris Agreement on climate change signified a new global consensus for sustainable development through green solutions. The major chunk of the current growth within the green economy market is primarily centered in a handful of developed and emerging nations. Consequently, a significant hurdle lies in ensuring that the transition to green economies extends its benefits globally. One approach to achieving this is by bolstering cooperation among countries in the Global South and fostering the exchange of green development models and solutions. Such collaboration holds promise in yielding dividends across the Sustainable Development Goals (SDGs), addressing both poverty alleviation and environmental preservation. Urgent acceleration of the green economy transition is imperative due to the escalating challenges of climate change, water scarcity, pollution, land degradation, and biodiversity loss, necessitating increased partnerships with the private sector, innovative green finance, and supportive public policies to facilitate greater investment and trade in environmental solutions. The transformation to a green economy is a function of innovations in technologies, products, services, business models, management practices, collaborative initiatives etc. Green economy is central to the response for climate change which is projected to reach 9.8 billion by the year 2050.

B. R. Kumar, *Green Finance*, Sustainable Finance,
https://doi.org/10.1007/978-3-032-03333-8_1

Several environmental systems are beyond the sustainable limits such as loss of biodiversity, nitrogen and phosphorus cycles, land use change and climate change. The achievement of global goals for sustainability offers a huge $12 trillion market potential across four key economic systems such as food and agriculture, cities, energy and materials, health and well-being. These four sectors comprise approximately 60% of the tangible economy and play a pivotal role in advancing the global goals agenda related to sustainability. The Solar Job Census report of 2016 suggest that one in every 50 new jobs in the United States were accounted by the solar industry. Notably, the growth in solar employment outpaced the overall U.S. economy by a staggering 17-fold, resulting in an increase of over 51,000 jobs. The collective workforce in the U.S. solar sector now stands at 260,000, surpassing the combined employment figures of 190,000 individuals in coal, oil, and natural gas power plants. This growth is particularly significant as various sectors of the U.S. job market face automation-related pressures, with estimates ranging from 10% to 53% in certain regions. Amidst the rise of automation, this expansion occurs during a period where numerous conventional roles face the threat of displacement. The World Bank projects that in China, two-thirds of jobs are vulnerable to automation, while in certain nations, up to 84% of jobs are potentially at risk.

Challenges to Green Economy

Scientists have detected plastic in tap water across the globe. Pesticides from intensified farming have built up in rivers spanning Germany, France, the Netherlands and the US, posing a significant threat to biodiversity. Arid areas in countries such as Pakistan are heavily burdened with dust particles contaminated by heavy metals from industrial and agricultural activities which lead to severe health repercussions among the populace. Transitioning to a green economy involves more than incremental changes. It requires fundamentally reshaping entire systems of production, distribution and consumption to address global challenges in a comprehensive manner. Prioritizing financial performance and shareholder value often overshadows the significance of environmentally responsible corporate stewardship, with short term gains often overshadowing the long-term interests and sustainability of a company.

There exists a business case for the adoption of sustainable practices throughout supply chains as it results not only in immediate savings but also fosters innovation. Companies such as Walmart and KKR have achieved profitability by reducing energy consumption and adoption of renewable energy. According to the Better Business, Better World report, sixty sustainable and inclusive market opportunities across four sectors -energy, cities, food and agriculture, and health and wellbeing are forecasted for economic expansion. This expansion is expected to outpace average GDP growth by two to three times over the next 10–15 years, resulting in a minimum of US$ 12 trillion in revenue and the creation of 380 million jobs by the year 2030.

Key Trends in Green Economy Transformation

World Economic Forum have emphasized on the fourth industrial revolution at the technology level. The field of Information and Communication Technology (ICT) has witnessed significant transformation over the past decades across various domains including robotics, artificial intelligence, nanotechnology, quantum computing, biotechnology, Internet of Things, 3D printing, and autonomous vehicles. The industrial revolution presents both opportunity and disruption. Crucial technological advances are reshaping management processes, business models, and industry structures, transcending sectoral boundaries and manifesting in various innovations. Basically, there are three key trends related to firms' focus on technological innovations which are relevant for green economy. The first key trend observed is that companies are adopting "servitization," where products are utilized for their services rather than owned outright. This trend is expanding across various sectors such as car leasing, tool hire, and sharing platforms. The production landscape is evolving with respect to ways in which products are produced. There is a fundamental shift towards decentralized, regional manufacturing, aided by emerging technologies such as 3-D printing. Digital platforms play a significant role in enabling easier reuse, recycling and remanufacturing processes and serves as pivotal components in the circular economy framework. Another trend observed is related to change of key inputs into industrial processes. Innovative materials often employing nano- or biotechnology are in the process of development which offer potential for longer lasting industrial products thereby decreasing waste and enhancing sustainability and productivity.

There are concerns regarding the economic repercussions on livelihoods and earning potential due to the adoption of these technologies. While past transitions typically create new jobs, they often disadvantage lower skilled workers unable to readily reskill. This scenario highlights the need for caution as businesses and policy makers harness these technologies for economic and environmental progress, necessitating attention towards social inclusion implications.

Management practices are also undergoing changes in the context of transition to green economy. Businesses are experimenting across different aspects such as changes in organizational structures (centralized versus distributed teams); implementation of strategies for gaining competitive advantages; reconfiguration of supply chains and sectors through peer collaborations, certifications, and other means. For example, in the year 2017, Hammerson, the UK's largest property group became the pioneer real estate firm to establish a goal of becoming a net positive company for net positivity in carbon emissions, resource consumption, water usage and socio-economic impacts by the year 2030. Another trend observed is the emergence of Science-Based Targets as a powerful initiative to boost companies' competitive advantage for the transition to the low -carbon economy. This initiative is a collaboration effort between the Carbon Disclosure Project (CDP), World Resources Institute (WRI), the World Wide Fund for Nature(WWF), the United Nations Global Impact (UNGC) and a We Mean Business Coalition commitments. During the period 2016–2018, about 305 companies have used Science-Based Targets. These companies are targeting to achieve 30–40% cuts in greenhouse gas emissions over the next 13 years and over 80% reductions by the year 2050. The pressure on governments to enact national policies backing corporate objectives will escalate, driven by corporations which seek clean power procurement. Governments will face heightened demands to bolster national plans in line with the Paris Agreement.

Achieving a green economy necessitates companies' long-term commitments integrated into their core purpose, with alignment between business purpose, corporate governance, shareholder behaviour, and corporate culture crucial for success. By 2017, over 2200 companies across 50 nations and 130 sectors were certified as B Corporations. These companies certified by the non-profit B Lab, adhere to stringent criteria for social and environmental performance, accountability, and transparency despite being for profit enterprises.

Corporate governance mechanism can be used as a tool to enhance green economy pursuits. Many investors and financial regulators are concerned about climate related financial risks and environmental impact of corporate activities. Organizations such as Client Earth and Share Action have directed their efforts towards corporate accountability, transparency, and responsibilities with significant implications for corporate governance. For example, Client Earth pursued legal action against Commonwealth Bank for inadequate disclosure of climate change risks to its business and took legal action against oil companies in California on behalf of affected communities for the expenses related to climate impacts on the state. The Earth on Board Initiative comprising of leading organizations focusses on sustainability as the fulcrum of business strategy. The organization supports Boards to create long term value based on principles of sustainability.

Energy Generation

Energy generation for decades relied on cheap, reliable energy sourced from fossil fuels driving industrial growth and societal advancements. Despite their environmental costs, fossil fuels persistently receive substantial public subsidies, obscuring the true social and environmental tolls of their extraction and usage. Net zero carbon economy is the need of the hour for sustainable green economy. To achieve this goal, the new strategy requires a recalibration of the existing economic, energy and industrial agendas and remove environmentally harmful subsidies. In order to achieve net zero economy, the fossil fuels have to be phased out and the use of renewable energy need to be increased to decrease greenhouse gas emissions. Another strategy would be to develop the capacity for "negative carbon" emissions in order to extract some greenhouse gases from the atmosphere and store them. In 2015, the global subsidies amounted to US$5.3 trillion which amount to 6.5% of global GDP. The Paris Agreement commits countries to "holding the increase in the global average temperature to well below 2 °C above pre-industrial levels and to pursue efforts to limit the temperature increase to 1.5 °C above pre-industrial levels".

Paris Agreement has far reaching effects on innovation in business and a significant game changer. The International Energy Agency (IEA) had estimated that US$ 16.5 trillion will need to be invested by the year 2030 to achieve the ambitious target of the 2 °C levels.

Countries committed to the Paris Agreement by outlining their Intended Nationally Determined Contributions (INDCs), later transformed into Nationally Determined Contributions (NDCs) upon ratification. These contributions delineate nations' strategies to mitigate emissions, adapt to climate change, and specify necessary support.

The fundamentals of energy generation are undergoing transformational changes. By 2017, in Germany coal and nuclear power account for only 15% of the country's total energy. Innovations in energy sector include wind and solar energy. Creative products, services and business models often leverages novel uses of technology or innovative company strategies for transition to zero carbon world.

Some trends are observed with respect to innovations in the energy sector. One of the trends observed is the dramatic fall in the prices of renewable generation technologies. In the UK, the price of off-shore wind has reduced by half during the period 2015–2017. Offshore wind, onshore wind and solar are cheaper than new gas and new nuclear projects in UK. Bloomberg New Energy Finance report 2016 suggest that solar costs have fallen by over 99% since 1976 and 90% since 2009. The Mohammed bin Rashid Al Maktoum Solar Park, the 16 square-kilometre 5000 MW photovoltaic plant when completed in 2030 will be the largest solar plant in the world with generation capacity of 2.5 million MWh of electricity per annum. The third phase completed in year 2017 set a world record -low tariff for solar power generation in terms of 2.99 US cents per kilowatt-hour. Huainan, the Chinese city had opened the world's largest floating solar farm which was built atop a former coal mine that had become a lake after being flooded with ground water. This 40 MW power plant consisting of 120,000 solar panels covers an area of more than 160 American football fields. The solar plant built at a cost of $45 million investment has the capacity to generate power for 15,000 homes. Freiburg's Solar Settlement features 59 homes with the world's first positive energy balance, generating $5600 annually per home. Hitachi Europe aims to transform the Scilly Isles into 'Smart Energy Islands', serving as a pioneering site for testing smart grid innovations.

Storage plays a crucial role due to the intermittent nature of renewables. In June 2017, approximately six giga factories for batteries were announced in regions such as Germany, Thailand, USA and Australia. Tesla is also in the forefront to develop storage capabilities. Currently research initiatives focus on development of low cost, less toxic and safe technologies which would revolutionize energy storage. Moixa have developed an all -in -one battery and inverter system for homes. Arriba Technologies battery energy storage technology adapts latest Internet of Things functionality which is designed for "Near Zero Carbon Buildings and Cities".

In the context of products, services and business models, renewable technologies integrated with aspects of the fourth industrial revolution are fostering the emergence of novel business models. For example, Electron, a platform devised by blockchain and energy trading experts are enhancing innovation in energy markets. The company Electron crafts resilient, innovative systems for industry's shift to smart grids, embracing decarbonization, decentralization, and digitization norms. Origami Energy uses smart technology to manage demand and supply through intelligently managing distributed energy assets via remote controls in order to assess future opportunities.

The Solar Home System offers "Pay As You Go" renewable energy for households, predominantly adopted in Africa and Bangladesh. These regions historically faced challenges in grid accessibility and financing for individual solar panel investments. The concept of Pay-As-You-Go financing enable customers to pay for what they need for bank accounts. ElectraSeed is an integration project which aim to deliver microgrids for facilitating the energy needs of millions of people.

M-Kopa Solar finances home solar installations and enables affordable mobile based electricity payments and monitors payment. Bangladesh based Bright Green Energy Foundation integrates Solar Home Systems, Solar Irrigation Pumps, Biogas Plants and improved cook stoves. The company also trains women entrepreneurs and technicians.

China based EQuota offers real time analytics, energy management systems and carbon services. The services offered by the company enabled a Chinese steel company to achieve 10% energy savings and $1 million cost reduction along with reduction of carbon emissions by 5000 tons. The JuiceNet Energy Services Platform aims to control 2 gigawatts of Virtual Power Plant which were assembled from over 250,000 electric vehicles' aggregated charging load.

Open source standards are used to drive energy efficiency investments. OpenEEmeter, is such an open-source software which calculates energy efficiency from smart meter data, promoting transparency, replicability, and accessibility based on open standard method.

A number of collaborative initiatives are being developed to stimulate innovation in the business sector. RE100 is a global, collaborative initiative consisting of companies which are committed to use 100% renewable electricity. Sustainable Energy for All's energy-based accelerators encompass diverse areas such as appliances, industrial energy, lighting, building which are tailored for innovative business models. The Global Off-grid Association is an independent, not for profit industry association consisting of over 100 members with the objective of offering sustainable growth through focus on policy environment, quality assurance and consumer protection. The new technologies of the 4IR are aiding the transition to the green economy.

Circular Economy and Green Economy

The relationship between the circular economy and the green economy advocates shared goals of promoting sustainability and reducing environmental degradation. The circular economy contributes to the green economy by reducing resource consumption, minimizing waste generation and fostering of efficient use of resources. The green economy concepts provide the framework and incentives for businesses and industries to adopt circular practices and technologies which align with sustainability goals. The push for the circular economy has been motivated by policy directives, input expenses and concerns with respect to supply security. Countries are implementing policies which compels firms to address waste, such as landfill, incineration taxes and extended producer responsibility. In response, many cities are increasingly adopting zero waste and circular economy strategies. The fourth industrial revolution have made adoption of the circular economy easier. Digital platforms enable multi-sided markets, facilitating the reuse of waste and the utilization of underutilized assets. Businesses like ZipCar and Airbnb exemplify both the circular and sharing economies.

New innovative methods are being evolved for commercialization of carbon capture technology. American company, Newlight developed a technology which combines air with methane-based greenhouse gas emissions to produce a plastic material which can match the performance of oil-based plastics. This carbon negative material plastic is composed of approximately 40% oxygen from air and 60% carbon and hydrogen captured from carbon emissions. It is observed that innovative materials can emerge from the reclamation of "waste" through novel processes. It is necessary that material innovation ought to ensure that products maintain their performance throughout the usage phase while also being readily recyclable for subsequent cycles. Jaguar Land Rover (JLR)seeks light weight aluminium for carbon, but energy intensive bauxite risks low carbon transition. JLR is pioneering RivAlloy, new alloy capable of accommodating higher impurity levels from recycled aluminium reducing landfill waste and transport emissions by utilizing UK-sourced materials instead of imports.

Maersk enhances ship recycling with Triple-E class and 'Cradle-to-Cradle Passport', detailing materials for efficient disassembly and recycling. Maersk offers financial incentives for responsible ship recycling, tying contract terms to vessel value at sale. If scrap value is less than 25%, vessels are recycled as per 'cradle-to-cradle' standards. The Dutch firm Bundles installs high-quality washing machines in households. Customers pay monthly or per use while Bundles retains ownership, providing IoT connectivity for usage tracking and maintenance. Sanergy constructs Fresh Life Toilets sold to residents turned franchise partners. Waste is collected daily, transformed into organic fertilizer, animal feed, and renewable energy centrally.

In 2017, the British Standards Institute established the world's first circular economy standard, BS 8001:2017, facilitating shared expectations and coordination across value networks. The Open Source Circular Economy (OSCE) fosters a knowledge common, akin to open-source software, to unlock circular manufacturing's potential.

The transition to a circular economy is gaining momentum, offering economic opportunities and carbon reductions. Businesses must shift from a waste-led perspective to embracing closed-loop value chains and new business models. Regulatory pressures, such as extended producer responsibility legislation, are driving action and incentivizing innovation.

Agriculture and Green Economy

The UN's Food and Agriculture Organization estimates that annual food production is required to increase from 8.4 billion tonnes to 13.5 billion tonnes to sustain a projected population of 9.7 billion in year 2050. There exist significant interconnections among food, energy, water and the environment. Irrigation impacts drinking water, aquatic ecosystems and hydroelectricity. Government policies significantly influences food, agriculture and land use dynamics. The fourth industrial revolution have facilitated the emergence of a new generation of "smart agriculture equipment". In 2017, Blue River Technology which can detect, identify and take management decisions using computer vision and artificial intelligence was acquired by US agricultural machinery manufacturer John for US$305 million. In the same year Netafim, the global leader in drip irrigation launched the NetMaize app. Utilizing farmer inputs and global weather data, the system tailors drip irrigation programs for corn growers, enhancing irrigation precision. Precision agriculture involves usage of satellite data, remote sensing devices and proximal data gathering technologies to optimize returns on inputs. Precision agriculture enables a 'per plant' or 'per animal' approach, made feasible by the digital technology boom. Blockchain technology is used to track produce from farm to fork. Provenance, a British tech startup secures funding from strategic investors to transform consumer trust by offering supply chain integrity and transparency. Provenance had successful pilot projects which track tuna in Southeast supply chains and fresh produce from origin to supermarket with the world's largest consumer cooperative. Provenance has secured $800,000 in private investment to complement ongoing grant funding and enabled a market launch in UK. The company Sundrop harnesses solar energy for irrigation, powering greenhouses and cooling systems which aims to promote sustainable agriculture and conservation. Sundrop cultivates fruits and vegetables without depleting local groundwater and diminishes greenhouse gas emissions. The Brazilian company Procomposto provides reverse logistics for urban organic waste, combating landfill emissions by promoting composting, thus fostering sustainable agricultural practices in Brazil. In Brazil, only one per cent of Brazil's organic waste is treated biologically or composted and the rest are disposed of in landfill or informal dumps. In a scenario of scaling up technology to cover 25% of the urban waste produced in Brazil, the Procomposto's model aims to create more than 10,000 jobs and help to reduce carbondioxide emissions by the equivalent of approximately 10,000 tonnes per day. Italian food major Barilla promotes a green economy by advocating for foods with low environmental impact, aiming for its products to prioritize sustainability by the year 2020. Spencer (M&S) incorporates sustainability into its Supplier Scorecard enhancing collaboration among suppliers and incentivizing best practices, thereby fostering a more sustainable supply chain while promoting business growth.

Many collaborative initiatives are focusing on collaboration to enable green economy in agriculture sectors. The Consumer Goods Forum facilitates collaboration among major brands to advance green economy goals, focusing on areas like deforestation, refrigeration, food waste reduction, and standardized environmental impact measurement. Protein Challenge 2040 is a global collaboration consisting of major players such Ahold Delhaize, Evonik, Firmenich, Hershey, Quorn, Seeding the Future, Target, Volac, Waitrose and WWF. It is the pioneering platform which brought together the global animal, plant, and novel protein industries together to accelerate progress towards sustainable production and consumption of protein to facilitate impactful solutions.

Innovations in Finance and Green Economy

Finance fuels the economy, facilitating payments, managing wealth, allocating capital, and mitigating risks of modern life. For sustainable development, investment in new infrastructure, retrofitting existing ones, deploying scalable technologies, fostering new business models and companies is the need of the hour. The lifespan of many infrastructure projects ranges from 25 to 50 years. Unlocking capital from high carbon economies is essential for sustainable development in the context of the long-term impact on climate goals and SDGs. According to World Bank estimates, the cost of adapting to a 2 °C increase in global average temperatures will be US$ 85–121 billion per year till the period 2050.

The People's Bank of China initiated a "green finance task force" with the UNEP to green China's financial system. Initially composed of 40 members, it expanded to over 100 institutions. The task force aims to align green economy priorities with financial policies, requiring significant investments, mainly from domestic and international markets. The UK government launched a Green Finance Taskforce in September 2017 to enhance the country's global leadership in the sector. Comprising senior financial sector leaders, it aims to collaborate with industry to expedite green finance growth and facilitate investments for achieving UK's carbon reduction goals. The Catalytic Finance Initiative (CFI) involves banks, asset managers, supranational agencies, and foundations, striving to boost financing for impactful global projects.

Many green specific products and services are in the financial offering which aids the development of green economy. In 2013, the US State of Massachussetts sold the first municipal green bond. In the same year, the city of Gothenburg, Sweden issued green bond worth SEK500 million. Further issuance of green bonds of value SEK 1.8 billion was made in year 2014, SEK 1 billion, each was made in 2015 and 2016 respectively. Green bonds were issued by the City of Johannesburg, the transport authorities of New York City, Seattle, and London as well as the water authority of Washington DC. The largest ever renewable project bond worth €978 million was used to refinance Meerwind in the North Sea. National Bank of Abu Dhabi issued the Gulf region's first green bond to raise US$ 587 million for projects to fight climate change. Investment grade loans are provided for clean infrastructure in OECD and emerging markets. New York Green Bank have made over $800 million in investments aimed to reduce carbon emissions by approximately 575,000 tons. The institutions involved in the transactions included Ameresco, Bank of America Merrill Lynch, BQ Energy, Citi, Deutsche Bank, First Eastern Investment Group, First Niagara Bank, Green City Power, M&T Bank, Renewable Funding, Sustainable Development Capital, and Tulum Management. Philanthropic funds are also supporting sustainability initiatives. Catalytic First loss offered a US$20 million fund to support the Global Alliance for Clean Cookstoves. IFC had issued IFC Forestry bond valued at $152 million which was a world first for forestry.

There are other noteworthy practices related to financial innovation in green economy. In Rabot, a complementary currency, Torekes, promotes a greener local economy by incentivizing ecofriendly activities like volunteering and carpooling. Citizens earn Torekes to rent allotments for growing food and use them for various local services, thereby fostering pride and sustainable behaviors in the community. The example of Rabot's Torekes exemplify the potential for a green economy. The modern trend suggests that emerging digital technology tools like blockchain enables innovative payment systems. Despite past regulatory concerns, more accessible tools will foster experimentation with complementary currencies. Several innovations are shaping up in the insurance sector to mitigate environmental risks. Africa Risk Capacity Insurance (ARC) provides index-based parametric risk transfer to countries like Kenya, Burkina Faso, and Malawi, safeguarding against reduced rainfall. ARC enhances climate risk understanding and fosters resilience through risk modeling and operational plans. The Centre for Agriculture and Rural Development Mutual Benefit Association, Philippines established the first non-life micro insurance company to specifically address climate risks and natural hazards.

Asset managers and investment houses are increasingly sensitizing the investment risks of climate change. Blackrock, one of the world's largest asset manager have focused on understanding how climate change presents market risks and opportunities. Major asset managers view climate change as a material risk and opportunity to their portfolio. Emerging indices are shedding light on the green economy's visibility. Standard and Poor's Long-Term Value Creation Index, co-founded by the Canadian Pension Plan Investment Board (CPPIB) promotes a shift from quarterly to sustainable capitalism fostering the green economy. Legal & General Investment Management had introduced a multi factor global equities index fund to address the investment risks associated with climate change. HSBC Bank UK Pension scheme has selected the fund for its equity default option which was valued at £1.85 billion. This was one of the first schemes to adopt a multi factor investment strategy which incorporates a degree of climate change protection. Osmosis Investment Management had introduced a number of resource efficient funds. In 2017, the Swedish state pension fund introduced the "Osmosis MoRE World Resource Efficiency Fund" which includes low volatility stocks that are considered efficient for their use of natural resources. The fund aims to improve the carbon footprint, water efficiency and waste management of investments.

Public development banks have become the single biggest providers of green asset finance. In the renewable energy sector, the development banks account for 15% of the total asset finance. Chinese Development Bank have been funding the largest deployment of wind and solar photovoltaic parks globally. Asian Development Bank focusses on environmentally sustainable growth as a key strategic development agenda. In 2016, 11 development banks consisting of African Development Bank, the Asian Development Bank, the Asian Infrastructure Investment Bank, the European Bank for Reconstruction and Development, the European Investment Bank, the Inter-American Development Bank Group, the International Finance Corporation, the Islamic Development Bank, the New Development Bank, the World Bank, and the International Monetary Fund jointly committed to the Sustainable Development goals 2030. These institutions have formed a collaborative climate action partnership to assist countries in implementing their Nationally Determined Contributions to the Paris Agreement and enhancing their adaptive capabilities. Focus includes scaling up low-carbon, climate-resilient investments, particularly in energy transition. Efforts involve improving access to funds like the Green Climate Fund and mobilizing private finance. IMF and World Bank provide technical support for carbon taxation implementation. In 2017, World Bank announced its withdrawal of financing of projects related to oil and gas extraction. The bank had also stopped lending for coal fired power stations. The Natural Capital Protocol provides a framework for businesses to incorporate the value of natural goods and services into decision-making processes.

The World Benchmarking Alliance (WBA) aggregates company data to aid investor decision-making, intending to produce publicly accessible corporate sustainability rankings. Modeled after existing benchmarks, it aims to encourage a "race to the top" in sustainability integration for future-ready investments. The Banking Environment Initiative and the Consumer Goods Forum aims to achieve zero net deforestation. The "Soft Commodities Compact" signed by banks basically ensure the commitments of financing the transformation of supply chains and raising industry wide banking standards. The banks which have adopted the Compact account for approximately 50% of global trade finance. The Global Innovation Lab for Climate Finance is a market accelerator for climate finance in developing countries. One specific innovation is Climate Investor One, the first financing facility introduced by Climate Fund Managers (CFM) which is developed by Global Innovation Lab. Renewable energy projects in developing nations encounter challenges of expertise gaps, financial negotiations, high capital costs, and attracting new investors. Climate Investor One aids projects by offering expertise, support through various stages, and equity financing, while unlocking capital through a pooled refinance fund appealing to institutional investors.

Energy Savings Insurance (ESI) addresses investment hurdles in energy efficiency by offering an insurance product for anticipated energy savings in projects conducted by small and medium-sized enterprises. With the endorsement by the Global Innovation Lab for Climate Finance, the Inter American Development bank has led the implementation of Energy Savings Insurance and has projects in seven countries. In 2016, ESI was launched in Columbia for energy efficiency in hospitality and healthcare sectors. It is expected to support about 104 firms in the hospitality and healthcare sectors. In Mexico, ESI have associated with FIRA, a rural development bank with an investment stimulus of US$ 25 million in the agro industry sector with over 190 energy efficiency projects. ESI schemes are deployed in countries such as El Salvador, Nicaragua, Brazil and Peru. One of the most significant initiatives related to climate change was the establishment of the Taskforce on Climate Related Financial Disclosure (TCFD). The taskforce was set up by the Financial Stability Board to develop recommendations for voluntary climate related financial disclosures. According to the recommendations, many companies and investors will have to work through the specific climate risks faced by them. Though the recommendations are voluntary, many countries have a requirement that companies disclose material risks.

Innovations in Policy Related to Green Economy

Innovations are required to generate a low carbon, climate-resilient resource efficient and socially inclusive economy. Innovative policy have the potential to stimulate investments and reduce costs in emerging technologies. Establishing a carbon price policy measure aims to mitigate the effects of climate change. Setting up of appropriate carbon tax can incentivize companies, households and reduce carbon emissions. Along this, there is potential to raise revenues to support the transition to the green economy.

After the Paris agreement, eight new carbon pricing initiatives have been implemented. Australia has launched a baseline and offset system as the safeguard mechanism to the Emissions Reduction Fund. China had introduced a pilot Emissions Trading Scheme in year 2016 to cover greenhouse gas (GHG) emissions. In 2017, China had set emissions quotas for firms in power sector which emits 3.3 billion tons of carbon dioxide annually. Carbon pricing initiatives were introduced by Canada. Alberta introduced a new carbon tax for large emitters which cover all GHG emissions from combustion. A baseline and credit system was introduced in British Columbia. The State of Ontario have implemented an ETS to cover GHG emissions from industry, electricity generators and for firms, importers, natural gas distributors and fuel suppliers. Chile has introduced a carbon tax for carbon di oxide emissions from large emitters from power and industrial sectors. Colombia had introduced carbon tax on all liquid and gaseous fossil fuels used for combustion. Washington State have established the Clean Air Rule related to baseline and credit system which covers fuel distributors and industrial companies which are not energy intensive. The member states of the International Civil Aviation Organization (ICAO) have initiated sector carbon pricing initiative-carbon offsetting and reduction scheme for international aviation. In the year 2017, China announced that a deadline for automakers will be in place to end the sales of fossil fuel powered vehicles. In 2019, Singapore imposed a tax on carbon. In 2017, India approved a new coal linkage policy which emphasized shift in energy policy from fossil fuels to renewable energy. The government of India committed to selling electric cars in the year 2030.

One of the major collaborative initiatives is the establishment of Under2 Coalition consisting of a total of 177 jurisdictions, representing 37 countries and six continents. The signatories of the coalition commit to reduce their GHG emissions by 80–95% compared to 1990 levels or to two metric tonnes of carbon dioxide equivalent per capita by the year 2050. Together, the Under2 Coalition represents a population exceeding 1.2 billion individuals and a GDP totalling $28.8 trillion. This translates to 16% of the world's population and 39% of the global economy. Nordic countries such as Denmark, Finland, Iceland, Norway and Sweden have collaborative green initiatives. Examples include Nordic Food Policy Lab which promotes policies on nutrition, food waste and new Nordic food, Nordic sustainable Cities which focusses on building networks and export of sustainable solutions for urban development; Nordic Climatic Solutions which focuses on Fossil Fuel Subsidy Reform and progressive Nordic Solutions in environmental economics, green technology etc.

References

Arriba Technologies. (2017). Arribatechnologies.com. https://www.arribatechnologies.com/

B Corporation (N.D.). 2017. http://bcorporation.uk/.

Bloomberg New Energy Finance. (2017). *New energy outlook 2017*. https://about.bnef.com/new-energy-outlook/.

Bloomberg News. (2017). China fossil fuel deadline shifts focus to electric car race. *Bloomberg*. https://www.bloomberg.com/news/articles/2017-09-10/china-s-fossil-fuel-deadline-shiftsfocus-to-electric-car-race-j7fktx9z

Blue River Technology. (2017). Bluerivertechnology.com. www.bluerivertechnology.com/

Brodie, C. (2017). India will sell only electric cars within the next 13 years. *World Economic Forum*. https://www.weforum.org/agenda/2017/05/india-electric-car-sales-only-2030/

Business and Sustainable Development Commission. (2017a). *Better business, better world*. https://report.businesscommission.org/uploads/BetterBiz-BetterWorld.pdf

Business and Sustainable Development Commission. (2017b). *Better business, better world*. http://report.businesscommission.org/uploads/BetterBiz-BetterWorld.pdf

Carbon Pricing Leadership Coalition. (2017). *Report of the high-level commission on carbon prices*. https://static1.squarespace.com/static/54ff9c5ce4b0a53decccfb4c/t/59244eed17bffc0ac256cf16/1495551740633/CarbonPricing_Final_May29.pdf

CCP Investment Board, Sustainable Living. (2017). http://www.cppib.com/en/how-we-invest/sustainable-investing/

Ceballos, G., Ehrlich, P. R., & Dirzo, R. (2017). Biological annihilation via the ongoing sixth mass extinction signalled by vertebrate population losses and declines. *Proceedings of the National Academy of Sciences, 114*(30), E6089–E6096. Retrieved from: http://www.pnas.org/content/114/30/E6089.full.pdf

Charlotte England. (2017). *Germany breaks renewable record with coal and nuclear power responsible for only 15 per cent of country's total energy*. https://www.independent.co.uk/

news/world/europe/germany-renewable-energy-record-coal-nuclear-powerenergiewende-low-carbon-goals-a7719006.html
Chestney, N. (2017, March 30). *National Bank of Abu Dhabi raises $587 million in green bond debut.* http://www.reuters.com/article/nbad-green-bond/national-bank-of-abu-dhabi-raises-587-million-in-green-bonddebut-idUSL5N1H732D
Chopra, D. (2009). *Who's who in microfinance: Center for Agriculture and Rural Development (CARD) Inc. of the Philippines.* https://www.microcapital.org/who%E2%80%99s-who-inmicrofinanc-center-for-agriculture-and-rural-developmentcard-inc-of-the-philippines/
Clearfleau. (2018). Clearfleau.com. http://clearfleau.com/
Coady, D., Parry, I., Sears, L., & Shang, B. (2017). How large are global fossil fuel subsidies? *World Development., 91*, 11–27. https://doi.org/10.1016/j.worlddev
Dalal, A. (2017). *Case brief: Pioneer microinsurance.* http://www.impactinsurance.org/sites/default/files/CaseBrief_june2017_web_version.pdf
Das, S., & Bera, S. (2017) Govt approves new coal linkage policy, pushes nuclear power plants. *Live Mint.* http://www.livemint.com/Politics/Fi0qKIKoK6Qcj3uTvioWpJ/Union-cabinet-approves-newcoal-linkage-policy.html
Deign, J. (2017) Battery gigafactories are now in the works and Elon Musk may add 4 more. *Greentech Media.* https://www.greentechmedia.com/articles/read/10-batterygigafactories-are-now-in-progress-and-musk-may-add-4-more#gs.OpStABM
Ellen MacArthur Foundation. (N.D.). Internet enabled pay-per-wash: A model offering multiple benefits. https://www.ellenmacarthurfoundation.org/case-studies/internet-enabled-pay-per-wash-a-modeloffering-multiple-benefits
European Commission. (2015). *Paris agreement.* https://ec.europa.eu/clima/policies/international/negotiations/paris_en
Fixsen, R. (2017). *AP1 invests $250m in low-vol 'resource-efficient' equities fund.* IPE. https://www.ipe.com/news/esg/ap1-invests-250m-in-lowvol-resource-efficient-equities-und/10018320.article
Global Alliance For Clean Cookstoves. (2017). Cleancookstoves.org. http://cleancookstoves.org/
Global Off-Grid Lighting Association. (2017). https://www.gogla.org/about-us
H2GO Power. (2017). H2gopower.com. http://www.h2gopower.com/
Hammerson. (2017). *Hammerson launches Net Positive strategy.* Retrieved from: https://www.hammerson.com/media/press-releases/hammersonlaunches-net-positive-strategy/
Harvard Business Review. (N.D.). *Future economy, we believe in climate change and we're taking action.* https://hbr.org/2017/08/future-economy.
Herman, G. (2011a, April 30). Alternatieve buurtmunt kent groot succes, Rabot houdt van Torekes. *NieuwsBlad.* http://www.nieuwsblad.be/cnt/f839i9vt
Herman, G. (2011b, April 30). Alternatieve buurtmunt kent groot succes, Rabot houdt van Torekes. *NieuwsBlad.* http://www.nieuwsblad.be/cnt/f839i9vt
International Finance Corporation. (2016). *Forests bond.* Retrieved from: https://www.ifc.org/wps/wcm/connect/5299a595-721b-41ef-90fa-2cff3d50982c/FI NAL+Forests+Bond+Investor+Presentation+10-5_pdf.pdf?MOD=AJPERES
Jun, M., Zadek, S. (2015, May 11). *Greening China's financial system. Project syndicate.* https://www.project-syndicate.org/commentary/chinasustainable-development-finance-by-ma-jun-and-simonzadek-2015-05?barrier=accessreg
Kay, J. (2017, June 24). *Technological change and the future of financial intermediation.* https://www.johnkay.com/2017/06/24/technologicalchange-future-financial-intermediation
Kortman, S., & Piller, F. (2016). Open business models and closed-loop value chains: Redefining the firm-consumer relationship. *California Management Review, 58*(3), 88–108.
Marks and Spencer. (2017). Sustainability scorecard. https://corporate.marksandspencer.com/plan-a/our-approach/food-andhousehold/capacity-building-initiatives/sustainabilityscorecard
Mazzucato, M., & Semieniuk, G., & Watson, J. (2015). *What will it take to get us a green revolution? Policy paper.* University of Sussex. https://www.sussex.ac.uk/webteam/gateway/file.php?name=what-will-it-take-to-get-us-a-green-revolution.pdf&site=264

Mohammed bin Rashid Al Maktoum Solar Park. (2017). https://www.dewa.gov.ae/en/customer/innovation/renewable-energy/mohammedbin-rashid-al-maktoum-solar-park

Moixa. (2017). Moixa.com. http://www.moixa.com/

Natural Capital Coalition Protocol. (2017). Naturalcapitalcoalition.org. http://naturalcapitalcoalition.org/protocol/

Nesta. (2017). *Leave behind one man and his dog, enter one man and his drone*. www.nesta.org.uk/news/precision-agriculture

Netafim.com. (2017). Maize irrigation App – Netafim. http://www.netafim.com/maize-irrigation-app

Nordic Energy Solutions. (2017). *Norden.org*. http://www.norden.org/en/theme/nordic-solutions-to-global-challenges/nordicenergy-solutions

OECD. (2015, January). What have we learned about extended producer responsibility in the past decade? A Survey of the recent EPR economic literature.

Origami Energy. (2018). Origamienergy.com. https://origamienergy.com/

Pro Composto. (2017). Procomposto.com.br. www.procomposto.com.br/

Provenance. (2017). Provenance.org. www.provenance.org/

S&P Dow Jones Indices. (2017). *Introducing the S&P LTVC Global Index*. Retrieved from: https://us.spindices.com/documents/additional-material/introducing-the-spltvc-global-index.pdf

Smart Energy Islands. (2017). Smartenergyislands. http://www.smartenergyislands.net/

Stern, N. & Ishii, N. (N.D.) Only green growth can bring prosperity. *The Guardian*. www.theguardian.com/the-gef-partner-zone/2017/jun/05/greengrowth-prosperity-world-environment-day-paris-agreement.

Stockholm Resilience Centre. (2017). *How far are we pushing chemical boundaries?* http://www.stockholmresilience.org/research/research-news/2017-06-09-how-far-are-wepushing-chemical-boundaries.html

Sustainable Energy For All. (2017). http://www.se4all.org/accelerators

The Banking Environment Initiative (BEI) & the Consumer Goods Forum (CGF). (2016, March). *'Soft commodities' compact*. University of Cambridge Institute for Sustainability Leadership. https://www.cisl.cam.ac.uk/business-action/sustainable-finance/banking-environment-initiative/pdfs/the-bei-and-cgfs-softcommodities-compact.pdf

The Lab, Driving Sustainable Investment. (2017). *Energy savings insurance scales across Latin America and beyond.* The Lab, Driving Sustainable Investments. http://cpilabs.wpengine.com/news/energy-savingsinsurance-scales-across-latin-america-and-beyond/

The Solar Foundation. (2016). *The national solar jobs census*. The Solar Foundation.

The World Bank. (2016). *Statement by multilateral development banks: Delivering on the 2030 agenda*. The World Bank. http://www.worldbank.org/en/news/press-release/2016/10/09/delivering-on-the-2030-agenda-statement

The World Bank. (2017) *World Bank Group announcements at one planet summit*. http://www.worldbank.org/en/news/press-release/2017/12/12/world-bank-groupannouncements-at-one-planet-summit

United Nations Environment. (2017). UNEP.org. http://web.unep.org/inquiry

University of Cambridge Institute for Sustainability Leadership (CISL). (2016). *Business compendium: How the private sector is building Europe's climate ambition*. Cambridge Institute for Sustainability Leadership.

University of Cambridge Institute for Sustainability Leadership and Energy Policy Research Group. (2017). *Market design for a high renewables European electricity system*. The Cambridge Institute for Sustainability Leadership.

Webb, M., & Power, C. (2016). Epic 100, the emerging businesses transforming energy systems. *Energy Unlocked*. https://static1.squarespace.com/static/556c3a68e4b056fbbd35d60c/t/58deb2a61b10e379 caba9034/1490989735952/EPIC100ReportWeb.pdf

World Green Economy Report. (2018). *Inspiring innovations in business, finance and policy*. Institute for Sustainability Leadership.

Zenghelis, D. (2016). Decarbonisation: Innovation and the economics of climate change. In M. Jacobs & M. Mazzucato (Eds.), *Rethinking capitalism*. Hoboken.

Chapter 2
Understanding Climate Finance

Trends Related to Climate Finance

In the year 2020–2021, the total climate finance flows amounted to $632 billion. In 2020, the climate finance mobilized by developed countries for global south countries amounted to $83.3 billion. About 273 asset managers are signatories to the net zero asset managers initiatives. Approximately 74 asset owners are signatories to the net zero asset owner alliance. There are 115 commercial bank signatories to net zero banking alliance with 70,000 billion of banking assets. There are twenty insurer signatories to the net zero insurance alliance. In 2021, an amount of $742 billion of financing for fossil fuels were undertaken by the 60 largest global banks. In 2021, $1100 billion of green and sustainable financial products were issued.

During the period between 2017–2018 and 2019–2020, the climate finance increased by 10%. In 2021, climate bonds increased by 19% compared to the previous year 2020. In 2021, the number of new green bond instruments issued were 2089 from 839 issuers. The value of these bond issued amounted to $522.7 billion.

Organizations such as the International Platform on Sustainable Finance (IPSF) and the Network for Greening the Financial System (NGFS) have intensified the mobilization of private capital towards sustainable environmental investments. The IPSF established by the European Union consisting of 18 members which included China represent more than half of the world's greenhouse gas emissions and half of the global population. NGFS established at the One Planet Summit in 2017 represent a group of central banks and supervisors with over 100 members across five continents aims to accelerate the implementation of green finance.

ESG investments in specialist funds amounted to $ 649 billion in the year 2021. According to Refinitiv, ESG funds account for 10% of global assets under management. According to Bloomberg, the total value of ESG assets under management could exceed $50 trillion by the year 2025.

B. R. Kumar, *Green Finance*, Sustainable Finance,
https://doi.org/10.1007/978-3-032-03333-8_2

According to the law firm White & Case firm, which analysed reports of 50 Fortune 100 companies, climate related disclosures are increasingly be made by these companies. According to Forest 500, about 58% of commodity firms exposed to forest risk supply chains have made commitments for issues of deforestation. Approximately 93 financial institutions have provided $2.6 trillion in financing to firms with highest deforestation risk.

In 2017, the Task Force on Climate related Financial Disclosures (TCFD), an initiative of the G20's Financial Stability Board(FSB) had proposed a series of recommendations on how to address financial risks related to climate issues. The TCFD is structured on basis of four aspects of business operations consisting of governance, strategy, risk management and performance indicators and targets.

United Nations Environment Programme Finance Initiative (UNEP FI) has developed a reference framework to ensure the strategic alignment of banks with the Sustainable Development Goals(SDGs) and Paris Agreement. The Principles for Responsible Banking (PRB) empower banks to make positive societal impact. The six major principles for Responsible banking are as follows:

- Define targets and positive impacts
- Include customers and consumers to promote sustainable practices
- Consult and engage with relevant stakeholders to achieve societal objectives
- Establish effective governance and a responsible banking culture
- Monitor individual and collective implementation of principles to ensure transparency and accountability for both positive and negative impacts.

PRB signatory banks are obligated to periodically show how they meet social expectations through structured reporting and standardized disclosure of extra financial performance indicators and targets. Over 270 banks representing about 45% of the world's banking assets are signatories to PRB.

Risks Related to Climate Finance

Financial institutions are exposed to climate risks. Three types of climate related financial risks can be categorized. Transition risks are attributed to the implementation of a low carbon economic model on economic actors. Physical risks arise from the uncertain economic effects of climate change on environment. Liability risks arises due to litigation against financial players for climate related issues. The insurance industry is exposed to the physical risks due to climate change. Swiss Re report suggest that natural catastrophes generated $112 billion worth of insured losses in the year 2021. Property related lines of businesses are expected to be impacted by the physical climate change risk. In the year 2020, approximately 80% of business losses due to natural calamities were accounted by damages to building.

The transition risks is visible through divestment movements in which financial institutions exit from activities which are incompatible with the climate objectives of the Paris Agreement such as exploration/extraction of oil or gas fields and establishment of coal fired power plants. According to the Fossil Fuel Divestment Commitments Database, approximately 1550 institutions have made commitments to some type of fossil fuel divestment for total value of $40.48 trillion. In the year 2021, La Banque Postale became the first financial institution to announce complete withdrawal from the oil and gas sector by the year 2030. In 2019, the largest sovereign wealth fund, Norwegian Government Pension Fund with $1.2 trillion in assets made largest ever divestment from fossil fuels which amounted to $ 13 billion. The International Energy Agency estimates that for carbon neutral energy sector by 2050, the investments in any new fossil fuel extraction project required to be stopped as of now.

They are two main forms of liability risks for financial institutions and the non-financial companies which are financed by the financial institutions. There have been increasing number of climate related lawsuits against private entities in countries such as US, Europe and Australia. In the year 2021, approximately 193 climate lawsuits were filed in the year 2021. One of landmark conviction was the ruling against Shell Company by a Dutch court. Another form of liability risk arises from shareholder activism. Activist hedge fund Engine No 1 was successful in placing its preferred three directors on ExxonMobil's board. Approximately 61% of Chevron's shareholders voted to reduce the company's emissions. According to data, approximately 172 environmental resolutions were proposed at general meetings to control GHG emissions. About 14 resolutions were adopted by companies to end financing for fossil fuels. The report by the Financial Stability Board (FSB) Task Force on Climate related Financial Disclosures (TCFD) in the year 2017 proposed the first step to assess climate risks by financial regulators.

Supervisors Tests for Assessing Climate Stress

Using the principles of stress testing, regulatory authorities are focussing on creating awareness of climate risks. These tools such as microprudential stress tests are used to analyse the impact of external shocks on the solvency of a financial institution. Macroprudential stress tests are carried out to assess the solvency of the financial system as a whole. Pilot climate stress tests have been carried out in countries such as Netherlands, France, Canada, Singapore and European Banking Union.

Three climate stress tests were carried out in Netherlands, France and the United Kingdom. The first comprehensive and climate change risk assessment exercise was conducted by the Banque de France (BdF) and Autorité de Contrôle Prudentiel et de Résolution (ACPR) with the voluntary participation of nine banking groups representing 85% of the combined French banking balance sheet and fifteen insurance groups representing 75% of French insurers' cumulative balance sheets. In the year 2021, the Bank of England and the Prudential Regulation Authority conducted their climate stress test with voluntary participation of the country's seven largest banking groups and five largest reinsurers. In the UK, the Bank of England designed the stress test with assistance from the Financial Stability Department and the PRA through the banking committees.

The French and English stress testing employed three of the four scenarios from the NGFS recommendations which extended to a 30-year horizon. The Netherlands' central bank conducted a stress test in 2018 with the voluntary participation of three banking groups, 50 pension funds and 29 insurance companies. Netherland's central bank conducted this exercise using a top down approach without the involvement of private sector participants. The stress test exercises are based on the National Institute Global Econometric Model (NiGEM) which represent a large-scale structural macro econometric model of the world economy. The NiGEM focusses on OECD countries and emerging countries like India, Brazil and South Africa. Using the NiGEM model, the economic impacts of climate scenarios are converted into macroeconomic impacts on factors such as GDP, interest, inflation and unemployment rates. The Integrated Assessment Models(IAM) are used to link GHG emissions, carbon prices and other economic factors using BoF/PRA pilot tests. The European Central Bank's climate stress test was conducted on 104 significant financial institutions in the year 2022. In terms of internal stress testing capacity, about 60% of banks have no stress testing framework for climate risk and only 20% consider climate risk in their loan process. Most banks earn most of their revenues from non-financial firms in high greenhouse gas sectors. Emissions breakdown reveals diversity, with significant shares from lower intensity sectors like construction.

Case Studies on Climate Finance Initiatives by Financial Institutions

World Bank report suggest that Kenya is required to build 250,000 homes on annual basis to overcome its housing deficit of two million homes. In 2017, the Kenyan government had launched the Big 4 Agenda, the development program with four objectives of food security, affordable housing, manufacturing and affordable healthcare. This development program aimed to build 500,000 homes by the year 2022 which was set to be sold at prices in the range $6000–$30,000. Kenyan government had also launched the Green Bonds Programme Kenya in partnership with Financial Sector Deepening Africa, the Kenya Bankers Association (KBA), the Nairobi Securities Exchange, the Climate Bonds Initiative and the Dutch development bank FMO. This program aimed to support the green bond market in Kenya through tax exemptions.

In Kenya, Acorn Holding a property developer, operator and manager of housing assets in Sub-Saharament company issued East Africa's first ever green bonds. The company issued green bonds worth $35.7 million in the year 2019 for the construction of 50,000 low carbon student lodgings. The bonds were listed on the London Stock Exchange and the Nairobi Securities Exchange and raised $35.7 million. The bonds were certified by the UK Climate Bonds Initiative for the potential for emission reduction from residential buildings. The designs are made according to green building standard certified to the Excellence in Design for Greater Efficiencies (EDGE) which are promoted by the International Development Finance Club(IDFC). This was the first Kenyan green bond to be certified by an international agency.

Net zero emissions occur when the amount of human caused carbon dioxide (CO2) emissions is equal to the amount of human caused CO2 removals over a defined period. Dutch bank, ING Group are among the few bank-based stakeholders who have set science based targets and initiated efforts to decarbonise its portfolio and operations. In 2015, ING made commitments to net zero. During 2019, ING Group joined the SBTi Expert Advisory Group to focus on climate goals. The advisory group aims to develop a methodology for verifying net zero targets set by members of the financial sector. Through this strategy, ING had aligned its loan portfolio of over €500 billion with the objectives of the Paris Agreement. To operationalize this strategy, ING group developed "Terra approach". This approach utilizes science-based scenarios and asset-level data to align the loan portfolio with the goals of the Paris Agreement, either through customer engagement or the bank's investment decisions. This approach incorporates various methodologies including PACTA (Paris Agreement Capital Transition Assessment) and the SBTi SDA (SBTi Sectoral Decarbonization Approach). The Terra approach includes sector-specific management of the portfolio. ING divides its portfolio activities into sectors such as power generation, fossil fuels, automotive, aviation, etc., each with its own transition scenario. Consequently, each sector has unique methodologies, scopes, portfolio targets, and metrics. A four-stage process is then applied to each sector. These stages not only clarify the commitment underlying decisions but also provide context by outlining the sector's challenges. As a result, each sector establishes its own decarbonization targets that contribute to achieving the overarching portfolio objective. As a part of shareholder communication strategy to inform the progress of this methodology, ING publishes an annual report which includes a Climate Alignment Dashboard. Two primary approaches have been identified to advance progress and reduce emissions: supporting existing customers in transitioning towards low-emissions technologies and redirecting investment choices towards low-emissions technologies. According to its 2021 report, five out of its nine portfolio sectors have successfully reduced the carbon intensity of investments below the relevant market or climate scenario standards. ING is working to decarbonize its asset portfolio and achieve net zero in its operations, reducing Scope 1, 2, and 3 emissions, and transitioning to 100% renewable energy. Additionally, ING participates in the voluntary carbon market to offset business travel emissions through REDD+ projects.

Thematic funds aim to understand the links between biodiversity and climate change by focussing on the protection and restoration of biodiversity and natural capital. Althelia Climate Fund was launched by Mirova in the year 2013. The fund's original liquidation date in June 2022 was extended to May 2023. Althelia uses innovative financial approach to slow deforestation and protect biodiversity by giving importance to ESG impacts of its projects.

Althelia have made investments in REDD+ projects like Tambopata-Bahuaja in the Peruvian Amazon, conserving 570,000 hectares of forest and restoring 4000 hectares for cocoa. AIDER oversees with a €12 million investment, repaid through agroforestry product sales and carbon credits. The 12-million-euro investment in AIDER aims to restore degraded land into agroforestry systems. The sources of loan repayment involve diversified income streams such as commercialisation of agroforestry products and certified environmental services such as carbon credits. The credits generated by the Tambopata REDD+ Project constitute a guarantee for Althelia in case of default. The project involved providing technical assistance to producers rather than direct funding. Projects face REDD+ challenges, using diverse indicators for success, supporting local communities with technical assistance. Other projects, like Novo Campo in Brazil, combat deforestation through sustainable cattle breeding and forest protection, managed by PECSA. The B-Corp labelled assistance facility ensures quality support, though income for local communities remains a challenge. Future goals include scaling up and adapting financial strategies to local needs.

Innovations in Climate Finance Initiatives

Globally financial centres have witnessed the emergence of "green fin tech market "which focusses on environmental goals. The overall fintech market is estimated at $500 billion by the year 2025. Green fintechs encompass technology-driven innovations integrated into financial processes and products, explicitly aligned with Sustainable Development Goals or mitigating sustainability risks. They offer seven key categories of green solutions: digital payment and account services, investment platforms, ESG-data and analytics tools, crowdfunding platforms, risk analysis and insurtech services, deposit and lending platforms, asset management solutions, and regulatory technology (regtech) solutions. In the year 2021, the UK Financial Conduct Authority (FCA) renewed the "Green FinTech Challenge' to encourage new product development with selected start-ups. The Monetary Authority of Singapore (MAS) promotes €35.81 million innovation program for green finance solutions. Initiatives such as Finance for Tomorrow in France aims to bolster the Fintech for Tomorrow Challenge by fostering market growth through prizes and partnerships.

The concept of the "green neo bank "is also gaining traction around the world. These streams of fintech offers the services of online banks along with commitments of responsible banks. In Germany , the first "green" financial institutions named "Tomorrow "was launched in the year 2018. Tomorrow contributes a percentage of fees from payments to climate projects particularly compensation projects involving tree plantation. During 2021–2022 period, three green techs -Helios, GreenGot and OnlyOne launched banking and savings product offerings which exclude fossil fuels and finance ecological and energy transitions. These Greentech firms don't have banking license and have to rely on banks such as Solarisbank, Crédit Mutuel Arkéa and Treezor to accept deposits and manage customers' funds. In the United States, GoodMoney, a banking platform, directs 50% of its profits towards environmental and social justice initiatives via impact investments and charitable contributions.

With respect to supervision, green bonds have become the new priority for central banks. The European Central Bank (ECB) Governing Council has decided to reorient its portfolio of corporate bonds held for monetary policy and guarantee purposes, implementing climate criteria. Aligned with its roadmap and action plan adopted in July 2021, the ECB will prioritize bond purchases from issuers with low greenhouse gas (GHG) emissions, ambitious emission reduction goals, and strong climate reporting. The ECB aims to decrease the proportion of high-carbon assets used as collateral for Eurosystem borrowing. Similarly, since November 2021, the Bank of England has adjusted its asset purchase program to support UK's net-zero targets. Additionally, Sweden's central bank, the Riksbank, has been investing in green bonds since January 2021.

Neo insurance companies dematerialize traditional insurance services and facilitate customers to finance virtuous projects with savings through life insurance. Goodvest, a French insurtech launched in year 2020 emphasizes transparency in its investment strategy by prioritizing non financial criteria over financial criteria and implement stringent exclusion policies specifically related to fossil fuels. In partnership with Generali Vie, Goodvest has created the Goodvie life insurance product. Their primary criterion involves conducting a carbon footprint analysis (including Scopes 1, 2, and 3) of companies and projects, ensuring portfolio alignment with the Paris Agreement and Sustainable Development Goals (SDGs). The insurtech closely monitors asset management companies' decisions and voting at AGMs to uphold alignment with the 2 °C trajectory. Goodvest's investment strategy has earned three labels—SRI, Greenfin, and Finansol—promoting confidence, and the company recently secured a €two million investment from Super Capital VC.

Impact finance have become the centre theme of financing and investment. During the period between 2015 and 2019, the total value of investments with focus on impact investment rose from $4.1 billion to $9.4 billion. Europe and Asian region accounted for the strongest growth. The UK based Impact Management Platform is involved in bringing together sustainable finance leaders since 2021. The Impact Task Force, supported by the UK government (former G7 chair), promotes global impact-driven economies. The world's top 300 impact investors managed $404 billion in impact assets in the year 2020.

Thematic funds select assets based on societal themes such as global warming, water management etc. During the period 2019–2021, the global thematic fund assets tripled to $806 billion. In the year 2021, the focus of thematic funds was on themes such as water treatment, security and robotics. For example, Pictet Water P focuses on water related firms. Investors seek climate funds aligned with SDGs, climate solutions, and renewable energy. IDIA Capital Investment launched France's first wood industry fund. J.P. Morgan AM's Climate Change Solution Fund, aligned with European regulations, invests in climate-related sectors such as energy, transport and construction.

The rapid rise of carbon neutrality as a goal backed by financial players has spurred sector-specific 'Net-Zero' alliances to establish shared objectives and methodologies, like the Net-Zero Asset Owner Alliance (NZAOA) founded in 2019, uniting 74 institutional investors overseeing $10.6 trillion in assets. The Net Zero Asset Manager Initiative combines more than 270 investment funds such as Blackrock, Macquarie or Mirova which represent assets of value $ 61.3 billion. The Net Zero Banking Alliance (NZBA) which was launched in 2021 has more than 100 signatory banks and includes tops banks such as JPMorgan Chase, BNP Paribas and Bank of America. The Net Zero Insurance Alliance (NZIA) established in 2021 has more than 20 members and include insurance majors such as AXA, Scor and Munich Re. During COP26, the Glasgow Financial Alliance for Net ZERO(GFANZ) published its inaugural progress report. NGOs are playing an active role related to climate Finance. Reclaim Finance have developed a tool the Oil Gas Policy Tracker to monitor the implementation of commitments made by financial companies. Shareholder activism is also showing increasing trend. About 172 environmental related resolutions were proposed in the year 2022 which included 71 related to GHG emissions tracking and 14 on ending financing for fossil fuels.

Significance of Climate Transition Finance

Governments aim for net zero emissions to limit global warming to 1.5 °C, outlined in Nationally Determined Contributions (NDCs) under the Paris Agreement. Corporates must decarbonize and scale climate solutions to align with these targets. Climate transition finance enables corporates to mitigate regulatory risks, capitalize on new opportunities, and adapt to market trends, crucial for sectors like heavy industry, agriculture, and energy which generate the largest global GHG emissions.

Regulatory shifts propel corporate focus on climate transition, prompting access to specialized financing. As nations codify net-zero commitments, regulations increasingly mandate ESG disclosures, climate impact assessments, and facilitate climate finance flows. By April 2022, the Principles for Responsible Investment (PRI) counted around 900 policy interventions. These interventions can be segregated into four broad categories. The first one involves corporate disclosure requirements on ESG and climate transition. Mandatory or voluntary corporate ESG disclosures have been adopted by developing countries. For example, Thailand adopted the disclosures in the year 2017 while India and Vietnam adopted the disclosures in year 2022 and 2013 respectively. United Kingdom and European Union have additional requirements such as firms to disclose climate transition plans by the year 2024. Another intervention is related to financial disclosure requirements. The initial recommendations of the Taskforce on Climate related Financial Disclosure (TCFD) have been made mandatory in countries such as UK and Japan. In 2023, International Sustainability Standards Boards (ISSB) had set a voluntary global baseline and have been advocated by countries from G7 and G20 countries. ISSB disclosure standards propose organizations to list out its exposure to significant climate related risks and transition plans. Sustainability or climate taxonomies are another set of intervention which provide the basis for assessing if a financial asset is deemed sustainable. Examples include the taxonomies related to European Union, South Africa, Mexico, Georgia and different development banks. Carbon border measures, tax incentives and credit facilities incentivize investment in climate aligned technologies. In 2022, the European Commission introduced a carbon border adjustment mechanism (the CBAM regulations) which aims to equalize the price of carbon between domestic products and imports. US government have increased the number of tax incentives to accelerate the transition such as the US Inflation Reduction Act (IRA). Likewise, China have introduced "Credit against tax payable" for investments in certain environmental equipment.

Sustainability Linked Green Bond Market Trends

The global green sustainability linked bond market growth rate have been registering strong demand from investors. During the first half of year 2023, the cumulative issuance of green bonds amounted to USD 3.46 trillion. The average deal size of non-financial corporates have been USD 200 million over the past five years. In the year 2022, approximately 78% of SLB volume were originated by non-financial companies with deal value in the range of USD 100 million to USD 500 million. Although the bulk of the deal came from developed countries, number of deals from middle- and low-income countries are showing an increasing trend. The concept of greenium -cheaper pricing for bonds which bear the green, sustainable label are gaining traction. Green bonds typically experience greater book cover and spread compression in the primary market when compared to their conventional counterparts on average. About 66% of green bonds were allocated to investors with green or socially responsible objectives. It is perceived that green label assist deal placement in volatile market. Even in market with increasing yields, green, sustainability and sustainability linked bonds can secure more favourable pricing.

Climate Finance Bond Issues by Corporations

Air Liquide SA, a French Multinational specializes in industrial gases and services. The company has established a sustainable financing framework applicable to green, social or sustainability bonds. The eligible project categories for green use of proceeds (UoP) include anaerobic digestion of bio-waste, landfill gas capture and utilization, CO2 capture and transport, hydrogen production and storage, as well as the manufacture of O2 and N2 for climate mitigation purposes, and green buildings. In the year 2021, Air Liquide issued a EUR 500 million(USD610 million) green bond with a fixed coupon of 0.375% maturing in 10 years. By May 2022, the funds from this bond had been allocated to 17 green projects.

Tokyu Fudosan Holdings, the Japanese real estate company focusses on urban development, strategic investment and property management. In the

(continued)

(continued)

year 2021, the company issued a JPY 10 billion (USD 73 million) Sustainability Linked Bond (SLB) with an interest rate of 0.3% linked to two SPTs. SPT1 aims to reduce GHG emissions by 46.2% by 2030(KPI1). KPI2 and SPT2 aims to achieve carbon negative status by the year 2025. If either of the SPTs is not met, penalties will be incurred at the bond's maturity as follows: A penalty of 0.25% of the issuance amount for SPT1 and SPT2. The penalties will be directed to the organization's conservation-focused foundation, the Midori wo Tsunagu Project, or other entities with similar objectives.

Autonom Services SA headquartered in Romania is a privately owned car leasing company which focusses on offering leasing services. In the year 2021, Autonom Services issued a USD 54 million Sustainability-Linked Bond (SLB) with an interest rate of 4.1%, tied to a single Key Performance Indicator (KPI) of the average CO2 intensity measured in grams per kilometre (gCO2/km), calculated based on the Worldwide Harmonized Light Vehicles Test Procedure. The firm has set ambitious Sustainability Performance Targets (SPTs) which aims for a 25% reduction in the carbon intensity of its fleet by year 2025 and 51% reduction by the year 2030.

Financing the Corporate Climate Transition with Bonds

The Climate Bonds Initiative (Climate Bonds) operates internationally to galvanize worldwide capital for climate initiatives. Its Climate Bonds Standard and Certification Scheme serve as a labelling mechanism for bonds, assets, and entire entities. This scheme enjoys global adoption by bond issuers, governments, investors, and financial markets, guiding them to prioritize investments that authentically combat climate change.

Financing the transition to a climate-friendly economy holds crucial significance in corporate transition strategies aimed at achieving comprehensive decarbonization. Basically, there are three thematic debt labels namely green, sustainability and sustainability linked bonds used for climate transition financing. These bonds possess identical financial traits to comparable standard products concerning seniority, maturity and credit rating. They stand on equal footing (pari passu) with other instruments of the same seniority from the same issuer in case of bankruptcy.

Transition Linked Bond Financing

Climate transition finance funds decarbonization efforts within entities, a subset of green finance, contributing to environmental improvement by financing the dynamic process of climate transition.

Corporates can utilize transition-linked bonds to finance climate transition, either as Use of Proceeds (UoP) bonds or Key Performance Indicator (KPI)-linked general purpose bonds. Example of UoP bonds include green or sustainability bonds which fund projects with specific and dedicated environmental and /or social benefits. KPI linked bonds also include sustainability linked bonds (SLBs) which are used by issuing firms to set sustainability targets for the firms. These bonds include penalties or rewards tied to meeting or not meeting pre-defined, time-bound sustainability performance targets (SPTs) for each predetermined Key Performance Indicator (KPI).

The transition plan starts with a visionary outlook with details of the envisioned state of net zero entity. The extent of its vision is defined by its selection of a science based 1.5 °C-aligned decarbonization pathway which stipulates the pace at which the company should reduce its carbon emissions.

The first step involves is the creation of the transition plan and its thematic label. The plan involves setting the organization's decarbonization goals in terms of key performance indicators (KPIs) and sustainability performance targets (SPTs). The company's climate and sustainability targets aligned with the goals of the Paris Agreement are integrated with the firm's strategy and governance. Further activities related to decarbonization levers are identified along with corresponding KPIs and SPTs. The next steps involved are bond issuance and post issuance reporting.

Regulations influence financial markets with transition linked bonds aiding investors in decarbonizing portfolios and meeting ESG reporting needs. Growing investor needs demand worldwide investment alignment with climate goals. Glasgow Financial Alliance for Net Zero which represent about 40% of global private financial assets have commitments to set near zero targets also influence capital allocation.

Climate Transition Plan

A climate transition strategy is a structured plan with clear timelines that details how an organization will shift its current resources, practices, and overall business approach to align with the most up-to-date and ambitious climate science goals. This includes objectives such as reducing greenhouse gas emissions by 50% by 2030 and achieving net zero emissions by 2050, ultimately aiming to cap global warming at 1.5 °C.

Grupo Bimbo S A B is a Mexican multinational food company with global presence in the bakery sector. Bimbo's transition plan aims to target a 50% emissions reduction in scope 1, 100% in scope 2 and 28% in scope 3 and net zero by the year 2050. Bimbo aims to reduce on scope 1 emissions through investment in zero carbon vehicles and electric solutions in its factory. The company aim to shift towards renewable energy sources to cut scope 2 emissions. The company aims to reduce waste and invest in regenerative agriculture to cut scope 3 emissions. In the year 2023, Bimbo published sustainability linked bond framework and had issued an MXN 12 billion bond.

Boliden is a Sweden based multinational metal, mining and smelting company. The company produces zinc, copper, lead, nickel, silver and gold with operations in Sweden, Finland, Norway and Ireland. The company is involved in the entire value chain from exploration and mining, to smelting and recycling. The year 2023 transition plan of the company targets a 40% reduction of absolute CO2 emissions in scope 1 and 2, and 30% reduction in scope 3 by 2030. The company aims to achieve its long-term goal of reaching net zero carbon emissions by the year 2050. As part of its medium target goals, Boliden invests in various alternative reduced carbon intensive technologies. In 2022, Boliden established a green finance framework. The company had priced five green bonds with a cumulative value of USD 344 million.

Guidelines for Thematic Labels

The issuance of a transition linked bond follow a standard and/or ICMA principle. ICMA principles have been integrated in the EU Green Bond Standard and the Climate Bonds Version 4.

Different Types of UoP Bonds

Green Bonds

Green Bonds encompass bond instruments where the funds, or an equal sum, are dedicated solely to finance or refinance new and/or existing eligible green projects. These projects adhere to the four fundamental components outlined in the Green Bond Principles. The standards for green bonds differ based on reference to regional or international taxonomy such as the Climate Bonds Taxonomy and Certification scheme, the EU Green bond standard, Green bonds guidelines issued by China and ASEAN green bond standards.

Sustainability bonds are bond instruments where the issue proceeds are applied to finance green and social projects.

General Purpose Bonds

SLBS

The financial and structural characteristics of these bond instruments vary depending on if the issuer achieves predefined sustainability or ESG objectives. SLBs is performance-based instrument.

Issuance Processes

The leadership team must guide the transition process in consultation with a broad range of stakeholders along with multiple teams focussing on sustainability, strategy, risk and audit, Information technology, communication and legal aspects. The transition plan depends on size, extent of climate materiality and complexity of its business model. For the transformation process, firms must assess its GHG emissions in terms of scope 1 and 2 emissions and derive a decarbonization or low carbon pathway. Like the issuance of conventional bonds, the issuance process of transition linked bonds involves the appointment of underwriters along with financial and legal advisors. Disclosures related to sustainability related standards and Global Reporting Initiative must be structured to overview the firm's social and environmental impacts and commitments. Air Liquide's GHG emissions accounting focus on six GHGs which are highlighted by the Kyoto Protocol and is carried out in line with the GHG Protocol's carbon accounting method.

Gfanz and SBTi have published guidance on science-based decarbonisation pathways. Approximately a third of all SLB issuers of projects linked to a GHG emissions reduction or transition to low carbon activities have been SBTi certified.

Heildeberg Materials is a global integrated manufacturers of building materials and solutions with representations in over 50 countries. Heildeberg have market leadership position in cement, aggregates and ready mixed concrete. The company is a signatory of the global initiative Business Ambition for 1.5 °C commitment which aims to limit global warming to 1.5 °C and achieving net-zero carbon emissions by 2050. The company aims to reduce its GHG emissions linked to cement production to 400 kg per tonne of cementitious material by the year 2030. Its target has been validated by the Science Based Targets initiative (SBTi) and is in alignment with the Transition Pathway Initiative (TPI) sectoral decarbonisation pathway.

Strategic Perspective of Action Plans

The strategy must ensure an inclusive transition which engages workers, suppliers and communities. It should align with UN SDGs and sustainability metrics. The plan must have detailed granular timelines to justify asset eligibility and decarbonization efforts. For short term to midterm, the reliable timeline would be to use 3–5 year interval and 5 to 10 year intervals thereafter as part of long term plan to achieve the target of net zero.

The Italian multinational company Enel is a global manufacturer and distributor of electricity and gas. The company is involved in the business of green and thermal power generation, electricity distribution and retail electricity and gas. The company have integrated a transition strategy into its overall business strategy with the focus on reduction of scope 1 emissions by shifting its power generation from thermal to 100% renewables. Scope 3 emissions involves the promotion of the electrification of final energy consumption and gradual exit from the gas retail business.

Enel has outlined precise strategies for a fair transition, including retraining affected workers. It delineates short-, mid-, and long-term actions to decarbonize each business line effectively.

The strategy adopted must cover all material sources and factors in a broader environmental framework. Each action's expected impact must be revealed and connected to the evolving trajectory of greenhouse gas emission reductions. The company must provide cost estimates for delineating capital expenditures(capex) and operating expenditures related to the implementation of the transition action plans. This encompasses expenses for research and development, phasing out plans, and social expenditure to guarantee an equitable transition. A robust sustainable procurement policy can ensure a fair transition and enhance the credibility and measurement of targets which are aimed at reducing scope 3 emissions. This should include thorough due diligence processes and the presence of a supplier code of conduct. The percentage of assets, revenues, expenditures and divestments which are aligned to various decarbonization levers must be disclosed. A quantitative assessment of the potential locked in GHG emissions from the issuer's key assets and products is also significant. The Board also have a significant role for reviewing and approving the transition plan and have the oversight for execution and monitor of the progress of the plan.

Rexel, a French electrical equipment manufacturer operates internationally in 21 countries. Addressing Scope 3 emissions, the firm engages with suppliers and consumers, setting reduction targets. As a part of its KPI for decarbonization activity, Rexel had identified the percentage reduction of scope 3 GHG emissions intensity which is related to the consumption of products sold. To achieve this KPI, Rexel issued a EUR 600 million(USD 696 million) SLB in the year 2021. The issue was aimed at a short-term target of 23% from a 2016 baseline as of end 2023 and a mid-term reduction target of 45% as of end 2030.

Non governmental organizations are involved in assessing the level of commitment of companies on the transition plan. LobbyMap of Influence Map is the world's leading system for tracking corporate climate policy engagement and industry association. Carbon Tracker Initiative assesses capex alignment, audit and accounting practices. Climate Arc is developing open source tool for reviewing several NGO transition plan reviews.

Selection of Thematic Label

Once a transition plan is prepared, the next step involves the selection of the most suitable thematic debt instrument. The potential utilization of bond standard is also significant. The different characteristics of UoP bonds and Sustainability Linked Bonds (SLBs) is a major determinant for selection based on the transition plan, sector, entity or geographic jurisdiction.

UoP bonds, a popular asset class, offer investors trust and a standardized structure. Issuers must identify sufficient green projects for bond eligibility. The most common labels used are green and sustainability bonds. Green bonds have been historically used to finance low carbon assets and its usage remains limited in hard to abate sectors. Sustainability bonds are used for projects with combination of social and environmental objectives. Green bonds and SLBs are the main labels used to finance the climate transition. Green label is applied to activities aligned with a net zero economy since these activities are at near zero emissions. For example, wind power generation. Transitional activities help sectors which follow the 1.5 °C or Paris-aligned decarbonisation pathway.

Transition bonds are viewed as a subset of green bonds which is gaining significance as a result of the implementation of national sustainable finance frameworks and technology roadmaps.

Sustainable Financing Framework

The sustainable financing framework is the main document which supports the issuance of transition linked bonds. The document provides highlights on history of GHG emissions and assurance reports on the GHG emission disclosures. Information is included with respect to pre-issuance external review and the alignment of the bond framework with the standard chosen or ICMA principles. Grupo Bimbo uses Sustainability financing framework to cover both green bonds and SLBs. The Bimbo Group Sustainable Investments Committee, comprising representatives from various teams, evaluates and selects projects eligible for the Green Finance Framework based on sustainability criteria and Bimbo's policies.

Bond Issuance

The lead underwriter plays a significant role in guiding the bond issuance processes. The lead underwriter will lead an underwriter syndicate for large deals. The syndicate consists of a group of investment banks. The syndicate receives the underwriting spread which is the difference between the price paid to the issuer and the price received from the investors when the issue goes public. The bond issuer will decide if the bond to be issued is a domestic, Eurobond or a foreign bond.

The legal documentation, such as the bond prospectus, outlines financial aspects like maturity, seniority, and currency, referencing the chosen bond framework to meet the label and standard requirements. SLBs can adopt one or multiple KPIs from the sustainability linked bond framework.

Post Issuance Reporting

Post issuance, the issuer should report on the progress made to make aware the investors of the impact of their investments on decarbonisation efforts. For this update on the GHG emissions and other transition related KPIs, transition plans are to be provided. The impact report aims to highlight the environmental and possibly social effects of projects funded trough the bond framework. It includes if spending is aligned with the plan, explanations of the proceeds' contribution to transition, and GHG emission reduction or other relevant metrics. By end 2022, Air Liquide allocated the complete EUR 500 million proceeds of its inaugural green bond in which approximately 43% was used for financing new projects and 57% for refinancing. In the energy efficiency category, two projects were financed for a total of EUR 27.2 million and the annual reduction of energy consumption amounted to 17,520MWh while the estimated CO2 emissions were 7008 tCO2eq/y.

Trends in Fuel Financing Related to Sustainability

France's La Banque Bank in the year 2021 made a commitment to end financing for all oil and gas companies and exit the oil sector by the year 2030. Credit Agricole and Nordea bank have made similar commitments in the coal sector. In year 2021, 44 of 60 banks have committed to "net zero emissions" by the year 2050. In the same year these banks have provided $145.9 billion in financing for 100 companies in the oil, gas and coal sector. During this period approximately, financing of $11.6 billion was given to Qatar Energy, $13 billion to Saudi Aramco and $10 billion to ExxonMobil. Financing to coal and mining generally represent only about 4% of the fossil fuel lending whereas 26% went to utilities which included coal power generators. In 2021, the Net Zero Banking Alliance and Glasgow Finance Alliance for Net Zero(GFANZ) was established. By end 2021, the capital commitment to GFANZ amounted to $130 trillion. The top four fossil fuel funders in the world are the big four banks of America-JP Morgan Chase, Citi, Wells Fargo and Bank of America. JP Morgan Chase is the world's largest banker of fossil fuels. The Climate Action Tracker during COP26 estimated that despite full implementation of all mitigation pledges outlined by countries' nationally determined contributions (NDCs), the outcome would still lead to catastrophic consequences with global warming increasing by 2.4 °C by the close of the century. In 2021, a Dutch court had ruled that Shell company has to slash its greenhouse gas emissions as part of its sustainability efforts. In 2021, the International Energy Agency released its initial energy scenario analysis aligned with a 1.5 °C target, determining that no additional oil or gas fields are required beyond those currently in production or undergoing development. Globally only one oil major BP has made commitments to make an absolute cut to oil and gas extraction by the year 2030 excluding its commitment of around 30% of the carbon pollution associated with its extraction via its investment in

Russian company Rosneft. It can be pointed out that only 10 of the world's 60 biggest banks have policies for financing restrictions for ultra deepwater offshore oil and gas activities. In this context it is noteworthy to mention about the Deepwater Horizon oil spill in the year 2010. Banks ought to take steps to commence the cessation of financial support for fossil fuel extraction, combustion and related infrastructure to align with the timeline synchronized with the goal of restricting global warming to 1.5 °C. Financial Institutions must also prioritize actions for discontinuing financing for coal mining and coal power along with projects in tar sands oil, Arctic oil and gas, offshore oil and gas, fracked oil and gas, and LNG. There must be concerted efforts for long term impact commitments along with urgent action on fossil fuels which is the single largest source of financed emissions.

References

32 Air Liquide, Sustainability Report. (2022). air-liquide-sustainability-report-2022.pdf (airliquide.com).

ACT. https://actinitiative.org/.

Alogoskoufis, S., Dunz, N., Emambakhsh, T. et al. (2021). *Occasional Paper Series. ECB Economy-wide climate stress test. Methodology and results*. European Central Bank.

Ambrose, J. (2019, July 12). World's biggest sovereign wealth fund to ditch fossil fuels. *The Guardian.*

"Amount of Finance Committed to Achieving 1.5°C Now at Scale Needed to Deliver the Transition," Glasgow Financial Alliance for Net Zero, 3 November 2021.

Banking on Climate Chaos. (2022). *Fossil fuel finance report*. BankingonClimateChaos.org.

Bloomberg Intelligence. (2022). ESG may surpass $41 trillion assets in 2022, but not without challenges, finds Bloomberg intelligence. .

Brower, D. (2021, May 26). ExxonMobil shareholders hand board seats to activist nominees. *Financial Times.*

Carbon Tracker. https://carbontracker.org/.

Clerc, L., Bontemps-Chanel, A.-L., Diot, S. et al. (2021). A first assessment of financial risks, op. cit.

Climate Bonds Initiative. https://www.climatebonds.net/climate-bonds-standard-v4.

EIB. (2021). *Common principles for climate mitigation finance tracking*. https://www.eib.org/attachments/documents/mdb_idfc_mitigation_common_principles_en.pdf.

EIOPA. (2022). *Discussion paper on physical climate change risks*. European Insurance and Occupational Pensions Authority.

Emambakhsh, T., Giuzio, M., Mingarelli, L. et al. (2022). Climate-related risks to financial stability. *Financial Stability Review.*

European Central Bank. (2021). *Overcoming the tragedy of the horizon: requiring banks to translate 2050 targets into milestones*. https://www.ecb.europa.eu/press/key/date/2021/html/ecb.sp211020~03fba70983.en.html

European Commission. (n.d.). FAQ list for IPSF common ground taxonomy table. ec.europa.eu.

Financing the corporate climate transition with bonds Climate Bonds Initiative.

Financing the corporate climate transition with bonds. Report prepared by Climate Bonds Initiative and the European Bank for Reconstruction and Development.

Fitch Ratings. (2022). *What to expect from the Bank of England Climate Stress Test*. Fitch Ratings. https://www.bankofengland.co.uk/stress-testing

Global Fossil Fuel Divestment Commitments Database. (n.d.). The database of fossil fuel divestment commitments made by institutions worldwide. divestmentdatabase.org.
Goodvest: y-vie responsable "nouvelle génération" – Challenges.
Green Fintech. Who are the B2C players offering sustainable financial alternatives? | by Solène Brébant | BlackFin Tech | Medium.
ICMA. (2021a). *Green bond principles, voluntary process guidelines for issuing green bonds.*
ICMA. (2021b). *Sustainability bond guidelines.*
ISSB. (2023a). *General requirements for disclosure of sustainability-related financial information.* https://www.ifrs.org/issued-standards/ifrs-sustainability-standards-navigator/ifrs-s1-general-requirements/
ISSB. (2023b). *IFRS S2 climate-related disclosures.* https://www.ifrs.org/issued-standards/ifrs-sustainability-standards-navigator/ifrs-s2-climate-related-disclosures/
Kerber, R., & Jessop, S. (2021). *Analysis: How 2021 became the year of ESG investing.* Reuters.
La Banque Postale Is Stepping Up Its Decarbonisation Strategy. La Banque Postale, 14 October 2021; "French Bank La Banque Postale Quits Oil & Gas, Sets International Precedent," Reclaim Finance, 14 October 2021.
La BCE prend de nouvelles mesures visant à intégrer le changement climatique à ses opérations de politique monétaire (europa.eu).
Lobby Map. https://lobbymap.org/.
"Members," Net-Zero Banking Alliance, accessed March 2022; "Net Zero Banking Alliance Germany," Green and Sustainable Finance Cluster Germany, accessed March 2022.
Net Zero Asset Managers Initiative (NZAM). Net-Zero Asset Owner Alliance (NZAOA), Net-Zero Banking Alliance (NZBA), Net Zero Financial Service Providers Alliance (NZFSPA), Net-Zero Insurance Alliance (NZIA), Net Zero Investment Consultants Initiative (NZICI), and the Paris Aligned Asset Owners (PAAO).
Observatory on non-state climate action, Finance for tomorrow. (2022). Global Synthesis report on climate finance. *Climate Chance*, 4–40.
Oil & Gas Policy Tracker. (2022, March). Reclaim Finance.
Orowitz, H., Kumar, R., & Hagel, L. A. (2022). *An early look at the 2022 proxy season.* Harvard Law School Forum on Corporate Governance.
Reuters. (2021a). *French lender Banque Postale commits to exit oil and gas by 2030.* Reuters.
Reuters. (2021b). *Chevron investors back proposal for more emissions cuts.* Reuters.
Roelfsema, M., et al. (2020). Taking stock of national climate policies to evaluate implementation of the Paris agreement. *Nature Communications, 11.*
SBTi. https://sciencebasedtargets.org/set-a-target.
TCFD. (2017). Recommendations of the Task Force on Climate-related Financial Disclosures.
Thanawalla, R., & Grnac, J. (2021). *The 2021 Bank of England Climate Stress Test: Motor your way through with our 4x4.* Deloitte. https://www.bankofengland Bank of England (2022). Key elements (...), op. cit.
Transition Pathway Initiative. https://www.transitionpathwayinitiative.org/sectors
United Nations Global Compact and BSR. (n.d.). *Supply chain sustainability.* https://d306pr3pise04h.cloudfront.net/docs/issues_doc%2Fsupply_chain%2FSupplyChainRep_spread.pdf.
Vermeulen, R., Schets, E., Lohuis, M. et al. (2018). An energy transition risk stress (...), op. cit.
"Watershed Decision Orders Shell to Slash Emissions to Respect Human Rights," Center for International Environmental Law, 2021.
World Energy Outlook. (2021, May). IEA, October 2021. Net Zero by 2050: A Roadmap for the Energy Sector. IEA.

Chapter 3
Exploring Impact Investment

Investors shape societal challenges, operating in a market where incentives lack equilibrium among social, environmental, and economic impacts. Impact Investing, a multi stakeholder issue, involves governments for efficient public service delivery, engages civil society in project design, and incorporates various business sectors. Impact investing offers avenues which contributes to the growth of organizations which possess sustainable business models. The new generation of investors aim to achieve social objectives along with financial returns.

Deloitte Report suggest that over the next 40 years, Generation X and the Millennial Generation would potentially inherit about an estimated US$ 41 trillion from the Baby Boomer Generation.

Impact investment is an investment approach criterion in which investments are made across asset classes. Impact investment in the real sense creates social or environmental value. Investments such as production of life saving drugs just for financial returns cannot be considered as impact investment. Increase in productivity or crop yield due to improved technology can be considered as an example of measurable environmental outcome in agriculture sector. Increase in the participation of girl students in education system in least developed countries can be viewed as a positive signal in terms of measurable social outcomes in education sector. Number of micro-insurance products sold to people with AIDS is an example of measurable social outcome in the financial services sector.

The term "impact investing" was coined in year 2007 with the aim of an ex-ante investment strategy to achieve positive impact returns along with financial returns. Global Impact Investing Network(GIIN) was established in year 2009 to strengthen the impact investing ecosystem and build the tools and infrastructure to assist the impact investing practice and measure its performance. In modern era, impact investing is considered as a strategy to be used across all asset class. Impact investing have emerged as an asset class which proactively aims to achieve positive environmental and social outcomes.

B. R. Kumar, *Green Finance*, Sustainable Finance,
https://doi.org/10.1007/978-3-032-03333-8_3

Responsible investing encompasses various approaches, such as socially responsible, sustainable, and impact investing, emphasizing the importance of stable and well-governed social, environmental, and economic systems for generating long-term sustainable returns. Socially responsible investing involves screening out investments with negative impacts, while sustainable investing actively integrates ESG criteria into decisions, prioritizing financial returns over social or environmental outcomes.

The investor in Impact investing may be interested in a tradeoff to accept a lower financial return in exchange for achievement of a social outcome. According to Monitor Institute 2009 study, the impact investment market was estimated to be US$ 500 billion by year 2020 which amounted to 1% of the total managed assets which was estimated at US$ 50 trillion. According to GIIN, the market size of allocated capital to impact investment is estimated to be $1.164 trillion by 2022. This represent approximately 3% of the responsible investing market. In 2022, the compound annual growth rate of impact assets under management was approximately 18%.

Impact Investment Ecosystem

In the first decade of impact investment, Credit Suisse raised a US$500 fund of funds which invested in agricultural opportunities in Africa. In 2010, Deutsche Bank raised a US$ 15 million "Eye Fund" for ophthalmic treatment. In 2007, J P Morgan established a Social Finance which actively co-invested in impact investment funds. UBS developed an internal position which was dedicated to develop impact investment products for its clients. In 2008, the Inter-American Development Bank invested $US 25 million in IGNIA to encourage investment in businesses which focused on low income communities in Latin American and the Caribbean.

The most active capital providers in the impact investment sector are high net worth individuals and family offices. These capital providers are characterized by greater flexibility and more autonomy than others. BSW Wealth Partners, an independent wealth adviser and multifamily office increased its assets under management from US$ 225 million to US$736 million in 10 years as means of impact investment in all its asset classes.

Foundations are well-suited for impact investing due to their dedicated efforts in tackling social-sector issues. In the United States, Programme-Related Investments (PRIs) and mission-related investments (MRIs) enable foundations to invest in line with their mission, with PRIs fulfilling charitable purposes and MRIs focusing on market returns while aligning with the foundation's goals. The KL Felicitas Foundation dedicated more than 85% of its portfolio to impact investments. In the earlier period, Pension funds, insurance companies, and other liability-constrained investors are less involved in the impact investment sector, particularly in investments that might yield below-market risk-adjusted financial returns. The African Development Bank(AfDB) had provided a US$ 100 million anchor investment into

Credit Suisse's $US 500 million Agvance Africa Fund targeted towards agribusiness sector in Africa. In early stage, pension funds, insurance companies and other liability constrained investors made less investment in impact investment sector. University endowments are not active in impact investing. In 2013, the Harvard Management Company had appointed a vice president in charge of sustainable investments related to endowments.

Many sovereign wealth funds have social or environmental objectives. The Mubadala Development Company owned by Government of Abu Dhabi was established in 2002 for socio-economic benefits for the people of Abu Dhabi. Malaysian government's investment fund Khazanah National Berhad focuses on social and developmental issues such as poverty alleviation and humanitarian support for local communities.

Impact investment funds are also integral part of impact investment. These funds differs in terms of institutional context, target sector or geography, use of subsidy and return targets. Funds such as Bridge Ventures and Bamboo Finance makes equity investments in small and mid cap stocks across different impact sectors. Banks or development institutions-based funds focus on social and economic development. For example, Prudential Social Investment fund of about US$ 300 million fund focused on housing, quality education and community development. UBS's US$100 million impact investment fund focuses on small enterprises in developing countries. Some funds have focus on specific sectors. For example, funds such as Leapfrog Investments' focus on financial services. Vital Capital focusses on integrated community building in sub Saharan Africa through investment in affordable housing, collaborative agriculture, infrastructure, healthcare and education. Nonprofit organizations such as Acumen, Calvert Foundation, LGT Venture Philanthropy and Root Capital offers a mix of grants, subsidized loans and equity investments in undercapitalized sectors, pioneer funding and seed capital. Another trend observed is the emergence of Impact investment fund of fund structures. For example, Sarona Asset Management, a boutique investment firm in Canada invests in private equity funds in high impact sectors in frontier and emerging markets.

In the realm of impact investment, the predominant landscape of intermediaries is predominantly occupied by smaller, specialized entities, while notable investment banks such as Goldman Sachs' Urban Investment Group, JP Morgan's Social Finance Group, and Morgan Stanley's Global Sustainable Finance Group have also become active in the area. In 2012, Morgan Stanley introduced its Investing with Impact platform which offers access to range of investment vehicles which are assessed for its financial return potential and social impact.

Exchanges and investment platforms also play a significant role in impact investing. Social Stock Exchange was established in London in the year 2013. The Impact Investment Exchange (IIX) based in Mauritius supports trading activities of securities issued by social enterprises in Africa and Asia. ImpactBase, the database managed by GIIN offers services related to impact investments to accredited investors. Impact investment advisers offer consulting and structuring services to asset managers and owners, aiding in the establishment of impact investing programs, construction of portfolios, and development of strategies across various asset classes.

Social Finance UK had launched the first social impact bond in year 2010. Networks such as GIIN, ANDE offer resources and services for the growth of the impact investment ecosystem. Rating and certification organizations authenticate the social and environmental performance of impact funds. B Lab, a US based certification firm authenticates rigorous standards of social and environmental performance of firms. By 2013, there were 760 Certified “B Corps” from 27 countries and 60 industries. GIIRS evaluates the social and environmental impact performance of companies and funds and assigns scores based on certain criteria across 15 categories. By 2013, there were approximately 450 GIIRS rate companies in 40 countries and 52 GIIRS rated funds. Accelerators offers early stage impact enterprises mentorship, incubation and technical assistance. Echoing Green awards competitive fellowships offer selected social entrepreneurs up to US$ 90,000 over a two-year period to aid in launching their organizations. Furthermore, fellowship recipients gain access to strategic and financial assistance from Echoing Green’s diverse community and advisory board.

Depository Institutions offers debt capital to impact enterprises. Some European lenders such as Charity Bank of England and Triodos Bank are pioneers in the impact investment sector. The Global Alliance for Banking on Values (GABV) is an association of banks adhering to sustainable banking principles.

Impact Investments Across Asset Classes

Cash assets such as certificates of deposits, savings accounts and money market accounts maintained at community banks and local financial institutions are used for investments into organizations with social or environmental objectives. For example, Triodos Bank offers liquid offerings to firms with environmental or social aims.

Short term and long-term bonds which are issued by governments or financial institutions are sources of funds for projects which focus on social or environmental issues. The International Finance Corporation (IFC) issues green bonds to finance projects aimed at reduction of greenhouse gas emissions in developing countries. In early 2013, IFC had issued AAA rated three green bond worth US$ 1 billion with an interest rate set at three year US treasury rates.

Social impact bonds (SIBs) are pay-for-success contracts where private investors fund interventions addressing social challenges, earning returns based on actual savings resulting from successful interventions. Typically structured with private foundations guaranteeing a portion of the initial investment, SIBs enable philanthropists to leverage their balance sheets for more impact, with payment contingent on intervention success. Unlike green bonds, SIBs are highly structured products with sophisticated and stable legal framework. SIBs can be classified as a unique form of fixed income with high transaction costs.

Private equity and venture capital are investment instrument used by impact investment funds. There are approximately 250 impact investment funds listed in

ImpactBase which offers instruments across asset classes, sectors and geographies. For example, LeapFrog Investments make equity investments into impact enterprises which provide financial services to low income populations. Real Estate investments in the ecosystem involve funding sustainably managed or developing properties with intentional social and environmental objectives such as such as smart growth, green buildings, urban regeneration, and affordable housing. For example Vital Capital have made investments of over US$200 million to construct 40,000 affordable houses in Angola and achieve a targeted IRR of over +20%.

In the context of infrastructure development, with support from a consortium of investors and the Kenyan government, the AfDB invested €115 million in wind power in Kenya's Lake Turkana region, delivering clean energy, lowering energy expenses for consumers, and enhancing infrastructure connectivity for landlocked areas.

Equilibrium Capital, overseeing US$ 500 million, specializes in real asset investments (such as croplands, forestry, and agricultural and food waste) and employs a "sustainable alpha" strategy, emphasizing long-term asset stewardship and comprehensive ecosystem considerations, including community and environmental factors, in investment decision-making.

Institutional Challenges

One of the institutional challenges is due to the early stage of the ecosystem. Numerous impact-driven enterprises require expansion, scalability, and the ability to consistently generate cash flow, with product development. Alongside the absence of inventive financial products, there's a necessity for an index or standard against which investors can gauge the effectiveness of their impact investments. Institutional investors encounter a challenge when deliberating on the allocation of capital to impact investments, particularly concerning the scale of transactions. Impact investments in real estate, infrastructure and fixed income typically involve larger deal sizes. Mainstream institutional investors encounter limitations when attempting to engage in impact investments within the confines of their current decision-making processes and regulatory norms. In managing portfolios, institutional investors assess factors like volatility, liquidity, match, exit timeline and investment size including in impact investments. The uncertainty surrounding the financial returns of impact investments due to their infrequency, structures and value propositions often deters institutional investors citing fiduciary duty concerns. The absence of widely accepted measurement standards complicates comparing social impact and evaluating investments. Measuring social outcomes demands long-term commitment, potentially misaligned with institutional investors' investment horizons and approaches. The success of investments in education sector necessitates long term measurement, evaluation and analysis which may not align with institutional investors' horizons.

Impact Priorities

According to GIIN Report (2021) on Institutional Asset Owners, majority of asset owners aim to make an impact across three to five key categories which focuses on climate, real estate, energy and infrastructure. Institutional asset owners have predominantly converged around climate change as a significant financial risk factor in the context of its profound negative effects on their long-term investment strategies. The institutional asset owners prioritize climate action, recognizing that portfolios geared towards mitigating climate change and transitioning to a low carbon economy are likely to yield stronger long-term financial performance. Some asset owners focus on addressing social challenges and prioritize social impact categories. The Sustainable Development Goals targeted by investors include Affordable and Clean Energy, Climate Action and Sustainable Cities and Communities.

Holistic Portfolio Construction

Over the past decade, major institutional investors like pension funds and sovereign wealth funds have adopted holistic portfolio construction which aims to integrate market analysis with financial and impact considerations on account of the dynamic nature of global markets impacted by factors such as wars, social inequality and climate crisis. The Chief Investment officer crafts the investment thesis and aligns efforts with managers to achieve performance expectations integrating an impact lens to target social or environmental outcomes across the portfolio. Teachers Pension Fund is an emerging market pension fund which focus on housing affordability as a critical issue for beneficiaries. The fund integrates environmental, social and governance (ESG) criteria into their investment strategy with the emphasis on properties with solar power and financially sound institutions. The fund's impact theory of change aims to enhance affordable housing availability, guiding investments to align financial returns with social impact goals, potentially diversifying into construction companies and engaging with banks to develop affordable housing, loan offerings, ensuring both impact and financial returns over time. The pension fund's conventional investments portfolio includes retail property and well capitalized financial institutions. The asset manager of the pension fund trustees committee evaluates investments against an environmental, social and governance risk matrix to preserve value. For example, the fund includes shopping centers in its property portfolio which install solar power to minimize unreliable electricity supply. The fund also has weighted investments in financial institutions which follow governance procedures to manage fraud and capital adequacy.

The landscape of Impactful Asset Owners includes the world's pension funds, insurers and sovereign wealth funds who are players in the global economy. IAOs have universal ownership of all asset classes across sectors. The significance of IAOs have become significant in the context of regulations related to sustainability reporting standards and the disclosure of social and environmental factors which impact long term valuations. These stringent reporting mandates serve to enhance transparency, offering insights to both investors and taxpayers who rely on IAOs to safeguard their savings and fiscal contributions.

Regulatory Environment

New regulations and reporting standards with respect to governance have opened opportunities for asset owners to invest in impact-oriented business solutions. In EU countries environmental considerations are now included within the fiduciary duty of care. Regulatory bodies are encouraging asset owners to assess and disclose climate-related risks and opportunities, driven by initiatives like the Task Force on Climate-related Financial Disclosures (TCFD). Regulations like the Sustainable Finance Disclosure Regulation (SFDR) mandate disclosure of sustainability effects on investments, particularly focusing on environmental and social characteristics. The EU's Action Plan for Financing Sustainable Growth and the EU Taxonomy Regulation further propel sustainable investment practices, emphasizing ESG considerations and carbon emissions disclosure. The EU is also developing a social taxonomy to standardize social impact classification. In March 2020, the European Commission launched an Action Plan for financing sustainable growth to propel the financial sector forward in tackling climate change and offer guidance for incorporation of sustainability into the portfolio of institutional investors. The recent launch of EU taxonomy regulation for environmentally sustainable activities are influencing investment strategies of institutional asset owners. For example, institutional asset owners are increasingly disclosing carbon emissions thereby recognizing the urgency of climate action.

The Net-Zero Asset Owner Alliance, a UN-convened group focused on climate leadership, has gained traction among global pension funds and insurers. With 37 institutional investors committed to achieving net-zero greenhouse gas emissions by 2050, the Alliance provides guidance through its 2025 Target Setting Protocol, aligned with IPCC recommendations and the Paris Agreement.

Target Goals by Institutional Asset Owners

Climate oriented targets are being set by pension funds and insurance companies. Members of the Net Zero Asset Owner Alliance have commitments to asset or portfolio wide targets of achieving net zero emissions by 2050 or decarbonization targets. Aware Super, the Australian superannuation fund with USD 69.7 billion in assets under management aims to reduce carbon emissions by at least 30% in the equity portfolio. Aware Super also advocates for an economy wide 45% reduction in emissions across their portfolio by the year 2030. United Kingdom based local pension scheme Brunel Pension Partnership with USD 41.7 billion in assets under management aims to reduce carbon intensity by 7% on yearly basis. The fund aims to achieve a minimum of 30% female representation on boards and 25% on their executive teams. The Insurance major, Swiss Re Insurance with about USD 125.7 billion in assets under management aims to achieve net zero emissions across portfolio by the year 2050. Moreover by 2025, Swiss Re have commitments to reduce the carbon intensity of corporate credit and listed equities portfolios by 35%. The insurance major also had commitments to improve financial access to basic healthcare for one million low income people. Zurich Insurance Company, a Swiss-based global insurer with assets under management totalling USD 395.3 billion, prevents the emission of five million metric tons of carbon dioxide equivalent annually.

Principles of Responsible Investment[1]

The Principles for Responsible Investment (PRI) emerged from collaboration among global institutional investors, highlighting the growing significance of environmental, social, and corporate governance factors in investment strategies. The initiative was spearheaded by the United Nations Secretary-General.

The following are six principles of Responsible Investment

- **Principle 1:** We will incorporate ESG issues into investment analysis and decision-making processes.
- **Principle 2**: We will be active owners and incorporate ESG issues into our ownership policies and practices.
- **Principle 3**: We will seek appropriate disclosure on ESG issues by the entities in which we invest.
- **Principle 4:** We will promote acceptance and implementation of the Principles within the investment industry.
- **Principle 5**: We will work together to enhance our effectiveness in implementing the Principles.
- **Principle 6:** We will each report on our activities and progress towards implementing the Principles.

The possible actions for principle 1 involve integration of ESG considerations into investment policies and support the creation of relevant tools. The other actions include evaluation of both internal and external investment managers ability to integrate ESG factors, while encouraging research and advocating ESG training for professionals. The possible actions for principle 2 include establishment and disclosure of an active ownership policy in line with principles. Other initiatives include active engagement with companies on ESG matters, exercise voting rights, promote shareholder rights and encourage investment managers to report ESG engagement

[1] https://www.unpri.org/about-us/what-are-the-principles-for-responsible-investment

reports. The possible actions for principle 3 consist of adoption of standardized reporting on ESG issues with tools such as the Global Reporting Initiative, integration of ESG issues within annual financial reports and information from companies regarding adoption of/adherence to relevant norms, standards, code of conduct or international initiatives such as the UN Global Compact. The possible actions for principle 4 include embedded principles requirement in request for proposals, align mandates and monitor. The other actions include communication of ESG expectations, reassess service provider relationships and advocate for tools and policies for fostering principles implementation. The possible actions for adoption of principle 5 include engagement in networks and platforms to share tools and resources, utilization of investor reporting for learning and collectively tackling emerging issues and fostering collaborative initiatives. The possible actions for principle 6 involve public disclosure, ESG integration in investment practices, active ownership activities, service provider requirements, beneficiary communication and impact assessment.

References

African Development Bank Group. (2013, May 22). AfDB Sponsors Fund of Funds for Agribusiness in Africa – Board Approves Equity Investment of USD 100 Million in Agvance Africa.

Beth Healy. (2013, July 30). Harvard endowment adds adviser position. *The Boston Globe*.

Freireich, J., & Fulton, K. (2009). *Investing for social and environmental impact*. Monitor Institute.

From the Margins to the Mainstream Assessment of the Impact Investment Sector and Opportunities to Engage Mainstream Investors Industry Agenda September 2013 A report by the World Economic Forum Investors Industries Prepared in collaboration with Deloitte Touche Tohmatsu.

GIIN. (2021). Institutional asset owners: Approaches to setting social and environmental goals.

Global Impact Investing Network. (2013). IRIS data brief: Focus on employment.

Hand, D., & Gilbert, S. (2023). *Holistic portfolio construction with an impact lens: A vital approach for institutional asset owners in a changing world*. Global Impact Investing Impact Network.

Hand, D., Sunderji, S., & Kommineni, U. (2021). *Institutional asset owners: Approaches to setting social and environmental goals*. The GIIN. https://thegiin.org/research/publication/institutional-asset-owners-approaches-to-setting-social-and-environmental-goals.

Hope Consulting. (2010). Money for good: Impact investing.

http://report.triodos.co.uk/en

http://www.asiaiix.com/product-offerings-and-operations

http://www.bcorporation.net/what-are-b-corps

http://www.echoinggreen.org

http://www.morganstanley.com/globalcitizen/pdf/investing-with-impact.pdf

Inter-American Development Bank. (2008, June 18). IDB partners with IGNIA venture capital fund to address needs of region's poor.

Leila Boulton. (2013, April 23). MFO thrives on impact investing focus.

Mubadala Development Company PJSC. (2013, April 11), p. 5.

To learn more, visit: http://www.thegiin.org/cgi-bin/iowa/resources/spotlight/58.html.

Chapter 4
Sustainable Debt Markets and Instruments

Characteristics of Sustainable Finance

In historical sense sustainable finance emphasized on concessionary finance which included grants and finances to support the social economy. Social economy played a pivotal role with respect to provision of nonmarket goods and services outside the mainstream markets. As an illustration, the cooperative and mutual sector plays a vital role in numerous economies worldwide, with over 1.2 billion individuals employed (equivalent to one in six of the total workforce) across more than three million organizations.[1]

Over 12% of the global population is affiliated with one of the three million cooperatives worldwide. According to the World Cooperative Monitor (2020), the top 300 cooperatives and mutuals collectively generate an impressive turnover of $2146 billion USD. This cooperative sector significantly contributes to sustainable economic growth, offering stable and high-quality employment opportunities to 280 million individuals globally. To put it in perspective, this constitutes 10% of the world's total employed population.[2] Cooperatives and mutual organizations are active in several key sectors, including work integration, agriculture, microfinance, and consumer groups.

The broader social economy within the European Union (EU) constitutes a significant component of the overall economy. It makes a substantial economic impact, contributing to 13.6 million jobs and representing 8% of the EU's gross domestic product (GDP).[3]

---

[1] https://bccm.coop/what-is-a-co-operative/co-operatives-and-mutuals-around-the-world/

[2] https://www.ica.coop/en/cooperatives/facts-and-figures

[3] 5 https://s3platform.jrc.ec.europa.eu/documents/20182/313344/SEE-Action+Plan+for+Social+Economy

B. R. Kumar, *Green Finance*, Sustainable Finance,
https://doi.org/10.1007/978-3-032-03333-8_4

Major investment banks such as J P Morgan, Barclays, UBS and Credit Suisse have introduced specialized ESG equity and debt funds, with Credit Suisse launching the Environmental Impact Equity Fund in 2020. The secondary market for ESG equity and green bonds is evolving with the establishment of various green bond indexes like the Solactive Green Bond Index, S&P Green Bond Index, and Bloomberg Barclays MSCI Green Bond Index, each with distinct criteria for tracking performance.

Sustainable Green Finance Defined

Green finance landscape lacks institutionalization and consistent terminology though numerous reporting standards and principles such as the UN Principles for Responsible Investment (PRI), the Global Reporting Initiative (GRI) and the Social Accounting Standard Board (SASB). Sustainable finance can be categorized in different ways such as grants (philanthropic finance), venture philanthropy (long term start up grants), mission and program related finance (charitable asset finance), development finance (sourced from transnational development finance institutions), ethical finance (based on moral judgement of performance linked to faith systems, social (impact) finance, green finance (focus on issues related to climate crisis and associated pollution issues).

Sustainable finance generally refers to the process of taking due account of environmental, social, and governance (ESG) considerations when making investment decisions in the financial sector, leading to increased longer-term investments into sustainable economic activities and projects.

Types of Sustainable Finance Market

There would be greater need for sustainable securities by investors. Issuers would increase their supply of sustainable securities. The sustainable finance market can be categorized as negative sustainable and positive sustainable finance. Negative sustainable (Exclusionary) finance involves investments which are evaluated by considering their material risk profile across the three ESG dimensions with the aim of preventing harm. Positive sustainable (Integrated) finance is defined by investments selected based on their potential to generate substantial and additional social or environmental impact. Negative sustainable finance category involves risk screening using non-financial metrics across ESG categories, leading to a recalibration of long-term risk profiles and strategic actions like divesting from or avoiding high-risk ESG investments, such as those with high carbon intensity. The most important risk screen in this category is high carbon intensity. The other risks in this category include internal organization structures, practices, processes and external organizational effects. The former ensure accountability, transparent governance, worker relations, diversity and community investment. Recycling optimizes resource use. The later impacts the results of organizational actions such as human rights, inequality addressing strategies and pollution reduction.

Positive sustainable finance is often referred to as Socially Responsible Investment (SRI). SRI contributes towards one or more of the 17 UN SDGs. This market is crucial for achieving the 2030 SDG targets, given a $3 trillion-$4 trillion annual finance gap. Sustainable finance strategies with a positive impact prioritize channelling new capital into high-impact companies.

Green finance invests in eco-friendly technologies, conservation, renewable energy, clean transportation, and pollution control for sustainability. The positive green finance market is dominated by debt products such as green bonds.

Climate Bonds Initiative

Climate Bonds is an international organization whose objective is to mobilize global capital for protection of environment through appropriate climate action. The Initiative focusses on investment in projects which are needed for a rapid transition to low carbon climate resilient economy. The primary objective is to reduce the cost of capital for significant climate and infrastructure ventures and to assist governments in securing greater investments from capital markets and achieve their climate and greenhouse gas (GHG) emission reduction objectives. Climate Bonds carries out market analysis and policy research and advises government and regulators. The organization also administers a global green bond Standard and Certification scheme. Certification under the Climate Bonds Standard accounts for approximately 20% of the global green bond market. This program relies on stringent scientific criteria to verify that certified bonds and issuers align with the Paris Agreement's goal of keeping global warming well below 2 °C. To attain and retain certification, rigorous third-party verification is necessary both initially and in continuous manner to ensure that assets adhere to sector specific criteria metrics.

Sustainable Debt Market Instruments

Under the sustainable debt themes, five debt instruments can be included for projects and activities. They are classified into green, social, sustainability, sustainability linked bonds (SLB) and transition. Pandemic bonds can be considered as a sub set of the social theme.

Financial instruments such as green, social and sustainability (GSS) and sustainability linked bonds (SLBs) are major intermediation tools between capital markets, and sustainability.

By end 2021, Climate Bonds have estimated records of more than 16,000 GSS plus debt instruments with a cumulative volume of USD 2.8 trillion. By end 2021,

Table 4.1 Size of the thematic markets in 2021

Types of Bonds	Green	Sustainability	Social	SLB	Transition
Total Size of bond market	USD 1.6 trillion	USD 520.5 billion	USD 38.8 billion	USD 135 billion	USD 9.6 billion
Number of Issuers	2045	425	861	225	15
Number of Instruments	9886	2323	3471	317	32
Number of Countries	80	51	44	37	12
Number of Currencies	47	38	33	16	7

Source: Climate Bonds Initiative, Sustainable Debt, Global State of the Market 2021

the annual green bond issuance amounted to USD 522.7 billion. Europe was the most prolific region for the issue of green bond in the year 2021. US was the largest country source of green debt in year 2021. In US, the volume of green debt increased by 63% to USD 81.9 billion by year 2021 compared to the previous year. In 2021, Germany's annual green bond volume increased by 49% to amount to USD 63.2 billion. Energy, building and Transport were the three largest Use of Proceeds (Uop) categories which collectively contributed 81% to the total proceeds. Hard currencies accounted for 82% of the green bond issuance in year 2021. By 2021, companies from the industrial sector accounted for 65 of the 317 SLBs. Italian motorway operator ASTM SpA is the largest issuer, with USD 3.4 billion of debt tied to a reduction in its scope 1, 2, and 3 emissions in line with a target verified by the Science-Based Targets Initiative (SBTi). Agriculture and Food is the fastest growing sector for SLB issuance by issuer count basis. In the transition segment, SNAT made the largest contribution with debt issued from EBRD and Inter-American Development Bank (IDB) constituting 19.9% of volumes.

Table 4.1 shows the size of the sustainable debt market in the year 2021.

Green Bonds

Green bonds are issued for dedicated environmental benefits and are accounted from the year 2012. The Climate bonds based green bonds with 100% of the net proceeds are earmarked for green activities, assets, projects and/or expenditures which are aligned with the Climate Bonds Taxonomy. The average growth rate of the green bond market had been 54% during the past five years. All deals related to green theme are screened based on a set of process rules stipulated in climate Bonds GBD methodology. The basic criteria is that deals must carry a variant of the green label.

Green bonds aim to provide funds for projects which have a positive environmental or climate benefits such as renewable energy plants to reduce dependence on fossil fuels, public transportation and others such as installation of optical fibres for energy efficiency.

Different Forms of Green Bonds

Green bonds in the form of corporate bonds are issued by firms to finance asset acquisitions. Project bonds are used as green bonds which are backed by single or multiple projects. Green bonds in the form of asset backed instruments are collateralized by one or more specific projects which form recourse financing. Green bonds are also issued as sovereign or agency bonds issued by financial institutions such as the World Bank. Municipal government also issue green bonds. High polluting firms issue green "transition" bonds to fund decarbonizing projects. In 2020, the British firm Cadent Gas, issued a €500 million green bond to fund projects which involve reduction of leakages from its pipelines. Similarly, in the year 2019, Enel the Italian electric firm issued a green bond index which was related to increasing the shares of renewables in its generation capacity. Green bonds channel debt capital to foster growth in start-ups, green energy, water management, meat alternatives, and carbon capture. New bonds such as blue bonds and other blended finance models have emerged which focus on ocean economy, biodiversity and marine sustainability.

Sustainability Label

This label encompasses a combination of green and social projects, activities or expenditures. For example, Sustainable Development Goal (SDG); Socially Responsible Investment (SRI) or environmental, social and governance (ESG) etc.

Social Label

Social label is associated with social projects involving housing, gender, women, health and education. Social bonds are termed as use of proceeds bonds which raise funds for new and existing projects which address specific social issue and/or seek to achieve positive social outcomes.

Sustainability Linked Bonds

Sustainability-linked bonds (SLBs) are debt instruments designed to support the transition to a net zero economy by reducing capital costs for issuers who meet predefined sustainability performance targets (SPTs) at an entity-wide level within a specified timeframe. These SPTs are based on key performance indicators (KPIs). Though KPIs related to the reduction of greenhouse gas(GHG) emissions are more dominant, KPIs can also refer to energy consumption, renewable energy installation, waste/recycling, fauna protection, water use etc. Unlike traditional green bonds, which finance specific projects, funds raised from SLBs can be used for general financing purposes. If the issuer fails to meet the performance targets, they incur a financial penalty, typically additional payments to bondholders in the form of a step-up coupon, a redemption premium, or an offset mechanism. This incentive mechanism differentiates SLBs from conventional green bonds. Systematic external verification of KPIs against the targets is incorporated into the bond documentation. The growth of the SLB market have been increasing in both advanced and emerging market economies. It has averaged in the range of $25 billion-$35 billion per quarter since Q2 2021.[4]

Table 4.2 compares sustainability linked bonds with green bonds.

Table 4.2 Comparison between sustainability linked bonds and green bonds

Features	Sustainability linked bond	Green Bond
Use of Proceeds	General Financing purpose	Green Projects
Issuer Type	Potentially any entity with a commitment to an ambitious sustainability trajectory	Entities able to generate large-scale green projects
Performance Indicator	Metrics-based KPIs at the issuer level and associated SPTs	Impact evaluation relying on metrics-based KPIs at the activity level
Penalty for missing green targets	Reputational costs and financial penalty	Reputational costs
Pre-issuance review	Second-party opinions, notably on alignment with ICMA's sustainability-linked bonds principles	Second-party opinions, notably on alignment with ICMA's green bonds principles—Certifications (Climate Bonds Standard
Post Issuance review	Systematic external verification of KPIs vs. SPTs integrated in the bond documentation	More variability regarding the availability and quality of impact reporting

Source: Network for Greening the Financial System (NGFS) (2022): "Enhancing market transparency in green and transition finance", section 2.4, pp. 37–41

[4] BIS 2022.

Transition Bonds

Transitions bonds are issued to facilitate decarbonization of an activity which supports an issuer in its transition to Paris Agreement alignment. The transition label includes a diverse set of sectors and activities and consist of both blue transition and green transition. Transition bonds basically originate from high polluting and hard-to abate industries. Transition bonds are relevant in extractive sectors such as mining, steel and cement and industrials.

Table 4.3 cites certain examples for recent transition bond issues.

Transport is the largest climate aligned theme. In year 2021, China Railway was the top climate aligned issuer by volume with USD 222 billion outstanding. Spanish electric utility company Iberdrola is focussing on transition to a low carbon economy with a robust plan incorporated into its corporate strategy. By end 2021, Iberdola had almost USD14 billion of labelled green bonds outstanding. The company have committed to reduce the intensity of its direct emissions globally to 50gCO2 per kWh generated by 2030, and to reach net-zero emissions by 2050.

Table 4.3 Examples for Transition bond issues

Issuer	Deal	Motivation	Strategic goals
Cadent Gas Ltd	USD 743.2 million; Coupon 0.625; Maturity 2030	UoP focusses on financing for the retrofit of gas pipelines for integration of hydrogen and other low carbon gases. Includes an exclusion of any gas network expansion	Cadent Gas have made commitments to reduce its emissions by 80% by the year 2050 against a 1990 baseline. The company have identified three main areas for emission reduction within its business and have committed to transform its gas distribution network for hydrogen and low carbon gases.
Seaspan Corp	USD750m Coupon: 5.5 Maturity: 2029	UoP includes financing of alternative fuel sources which include LNG, biodiesel and other viable low carbon fuel sources.	Seaspan follows Poseidon Principles' trajectory of 50% GHG reduction by 2050.
NYK Line	Amount issued: JPY10bn (USD90m) Coupon: 0.26 Maturity: 2026 Amount issued: JPY10bn (USD90m) Coupon: 0.38 Maturity: 2028	UoP includes both Green and Transition Projects. NYK has developed a long-term transition plan to use ammonia and hydrogen fuel sources, decarbonise onshore activities, and develop offshore wind capacity	NYK has SBTi-approved targets for 50% reduction in emissions intensity by 2050, and 30% by 2030

Source: Harrison C., MacGeoch M., Michetti C., Sustainable Debt Global State of the Market 2021, Climate Bonds Initiative 2022, Page 22

On the basis of three-year period 2019–2021, Chile is the only sovereign to have issued in all three GSS themes. In 2020, Chile published its Sustainable Bond Framework which identified nine social project categories which included financing support to disadvantaged groups through pension schemes; support for low income families and victims of human rights violations through subsidies and contributions. The other social project sectors include food security, education and health services. In 2019, UK became the first major economy to commit to a legally binding target to reach net zero by the year 2050. A green taxonomy is being developed in UK. In 2021, the GBP non-sovereign green bond grew by 79%. London Stock Exchange has significant green, sustainable and transition bond segments which attracts issuers across the globe. During June 2021, UK published its green bond framework which listed clean transportation, renewable energy, energy efficiency, pollution prevention and control, living and natural resources, and climate change adaptation as six eligible project categories. Non -financial corporates have issued the most Renewable Energy green bonds. Energy Efficiency has mostly been financed by financials and Asset backed Securities.

Blue Bonds

Oceans provide natural resources and employment for millions of people in fields such as fishing, maritime transport, underwater mining, renewable energies and coastal tourism. The UN Global Impact report suggest that all these productive sectors known as blue economy account for 2.5% of global GDP.

Blue bonds are a type of environmental or impact bond which focus on ocean health. Blue bonds were issued in the year 2018. The objective of the blue bond is to direct finance towards ocean-based project which contribute towards positive environmental, economic and climate benefits.

In 2023 on World Ocean day, Ørsted became the first energy company in the world to issue blue bonds. The five-year EUR 100 million blue bond was issued in private placement format. This blue bond offers 3.625% fixed rate and matures in the year 2028. The funds raised through this offering will be used by the company to target offshore biodiversity and sustainable shipping. The fund proceeds aim to protect and restore marine and coastal biodiversity. With respect to sustainable shipping, the company aims to play a vital role in developing green ocean fuels for decarbonization of ocean vessels.

Seychelles was the first country to issue blue bonds through the issuance of 10-year bond in 2018 to raise 15 million dollars to promote sustainable fishing industry and to facilitate investment in businesses which target blue economy activities. During the period 2018–2020, 12 blue bonds valued at $2.856 billion dollars were issued. In 2020, the sustainable debt issuance including green bonds amounted to $732 billion which amounted to an increase of 23% compared to the previous year.

Social Finance Strategy of Deloittee

Social finance encompasses diverse investment strategies across asset classes, offering risk-adjusted returns aligned with investor goals. Deloitte, as a thought leader and strategic partner, navigates the integration of ESG factors, pioneers blended finance, and introduces pay-for-performance approaches to attract investments to underserved markets. Their expertise aids clients in deploying capital in alignment with mission-driven objectives and financial expectations.

Deloittee strategy in social finance is based on the following pillars.

Building adaptive strategies
Designing innovative models
Measuring Impact
Building Market

This pillar covers diverse subjects including innovative finance and strategies for domestic resource mobilization, ESG and socially responsible investing, Social Impact Bonds (SIBs) and pay-for-performance, Impact Investing, Blended Finance, and alternative financing vehicles tailored for non-profit organizations.

Deloittee provides strategic advisory for investors, development finance institutions, intermediaries and innovators. Stories of successful impact includes that of B Lab's GIIRS which addresses the lack of tools hindering impact assessment for investors. Deloitte, a pioneering funder of GIIRS, is the preferred provider for reviews, offering expertise in helping organizations scale and integrate impact activities into the dynamic global impact investing market

Source: https://www2.deloitte.com/xe/en/pages/financial-services/articles/social-finance.html

Social (Impact Investment) Finance

Social finance aims to support innovative enterprises tackling social market failures in health, education, and employment positively, excluding inequality perpetuating companies. The concept of impact investment has emerged over the past 20 years. Social finance involves the management of investments with the aim of generating financial returns while simultaneously delivering measurable positive social and environmental impact.

Social Bonds

Social funds focus on social sustainable development goals such as poverty reduction, primary education, health and gender equality.

Social bonds, akin to conventional bonds in terms of structure, risk, and return, prioritize projects with clear social benefits, like affordable housing, job creation, and improved access to education and healthcare, targeting vulnerable populations for positive impact. The government related sectors consisting of multinational issuers such as the EU and national agencies such as CADES accounts for 67% of the social bond market. European policy makers are using sustainable bonds as an important tool for achieving sustainable goals. In 2015, the first social bond was issued by the Instituto de Credito in Spain. The three-year social bond raised €1 billion from different international investors and focussed on offering sub market loans to small and medium sized organizations. In 2015, a second €1 billion Spanish social bond was issued by Kutxabank to provide affordable housing in the Basque country. In 2017, the IFC introduced a Social Bond Program providing investors a chance to invest in SDG-focused bonds with AAA credit, supporting banking for women and inclusive business programs to aid underserved populations in emerging markets, particularly women and low-income communities lacking access to essential services. By the year 2020, the IFC had issued 39 social bonds which raised $3.1 billion. Social bond issuance increased by 20% to €110 billion in the first nine months of year 2023 compared to the previous year 2022. In the year 2023, UK based Motability Operations Group issued its latest social bond to raise £250 million. The Group offers financing for the acquisition of vehicles for disabled people. The proceeds of these bonds were used to fund its existing fleet of vehicles as well as new vehicles. Goldman Sachs Green report 2023 suggest that issuers typically direct 58% of proceeds towards social projects and 42% towards green initiatives. French real estate development and investment firm, Praemia Healthcare issues sustainability bonds to fund its social initiatives. In September 2023, the company issued €500 million for its healthcare facilities.

ESG investing have become a driving force in asset management. During the period 2016–2021, global assets under management (AuM) in sustainable investing grew at 19% per year. By end of year 2021, the global AuM in ESG strategies amounted to US$2.1 trillion.

Table 4.4 provides the global social bond issuance statistics.

Table 4.4 Global Social bond issuance

Year	Amount in billions of euro
2016	1.4
2017	6.2
2018	8.9
2019	13.6
2020	123.8
2021	172.4
2022	126.3
2023(Three quarters)	109.5

Source: Goldman Sachs Asset Management, Bloomberg

Innovative Instruments

Revenue-based models generate liquidity by predetermined redemptions or dividends based on growth metrics like revenue, free cash flow, or net profitability. Private equity investments structured this way offer dividends based on free cash flow until reaching an agreed multiple of the initial investment, reducing downside risk and providing flexibility. In 2015, Barclay launched a high growth and entrepreneurs fund which was backed by £100 million from the EIB. The fund focused on job creation in UK and provided early stage venture debt capital to growth stage businesses with an option to buy equity. In the year 2016, Barclays increased the fund to £200 million.

Quasi-equity blends benefit of equity and debt, sharing investment risk and reward; structured as a loan, its return depends on future revenue streams, making it a flexible option when conventional debt is costly or risky, particularly for social enterprises or charities, with payments tied to performance. For example in UK, the Hackney Community Transport (HCT), a social enterprise bus company in London raised £4.145 million in a combination of a fixed loan (5% for 5 years £2.128 million) and a quasi-equity social loan (£1.917 million). The social loan model allowed investors to share risks and returns with HCT; if growth thresholds weren't met, no returns occurred, yet exceeding thresholds provided uncapped upside returns, reflecting HCT's impact linked to its financial performance, supporting community transport for those with mobility challenges.

Acumen Fund introduced "patient capital," a form of high-risk, long-term, early-stage growth financing, structured as debt or equity, primarily targeting sectors like healthcare, water, housing, alternative energy, or agriculture, with investments ranging from $300,000 to $2.5 million over 7–10 years. The Calvert Foundation launched the Calvert Community Investment Note, allowing individual investors to customize their impact investment by region, program focus, maturity (1–15 years), and interest rate (0.5%–3.5%), raising $478 million by 2020 for deployment to US community development financial intermediaries and social enterprises.

Three types of co-mingling fund structures include pari-passu, risk-reward, and but-for, wherein investors share equal terms, mitigate risk through cornerstone investments, or take higher-risk positions for anticipated higher returns. The African Agricultural Fund combined high-risk equity from foundations (Gatsby, Rockefeller, and Gates), unsecured debt from JP Morgan, and a 50% loan guarantee from USAID, enabling investments in smallholder farmers.

The Eye Fund blended equity and subordinate debt from foundations and individual impact investors with senior debt from commercial banks and DFIs, leveraging $1.48 million to secure $13 million in senior debt at almost 13 times leverage, facilitating direct loans to global eye care organizations.

Impact Bonds

An impact bond, unlike green or social bonds, is a future liability contract structured as a partnership to enhance social, developmental, or environmental outcomes. Typically, investors provide upfront capital, service providers, deliver innovative services, outcomes payers repay with returns tied to achieved outcomes, and third-party assessors audit performance. Unlike traditional contracts, such as fee-for-service or grants, impact bonds prioritize outcomes over inputs and activities. For instance, a bond supporting young people in school focuses on grade improvements rather than after-school classes or mentoring sessions. Impact bonds encompass Social Impact Bonds (SIBs), Development Impact Bonds (DIBs), and Environmental Impact Bonds (EIBs). In 2010, UK government issued the first SIB which focusses on reducing re-offending rates in HM Peterborough Prison. In 2015, the first DIB with focus on girls' education was introduced in North India. In 2018, the first environmental impact bond was launched.

Outcome Funds

Outcome funds aggregate funds to incentivize successful outcome delivery with disbursement contingent upon achieved results based on predetermined criteria. Payments from such funds are made only upon meeting agreed-upon criteria set by funders, distinguishing them from investment funds as there's no expectation of repayment. The Bertha Centre at the University of Cape Town initiated a Green Outcomes Fund, resembling a social impact incentive at a fund level, where managers invest capital in green enterprises for predetermined social, environmental, and financial outcomes, claiming payments as milestones are achieved, funded by a mix of public and private grants. These outcome-linked loans allow funders to leverage capital, differing from SIBs and DIBs where funders cover full outcome costs, while at the fund-manager level, impact performance could influence rewards and fees.

Sustainable Bond Funds

Investment funds which invest primarily in sustainable bonds are sustainable bond funds. Asset managers channel their clients' savings into environmentally and socially responsible projects through sustainable bond funds. These funds provide returns to investors while supporting the economy's transition towards greater sustainability. Sustainable or ESG bonds are fixed income instruments whose proceeds are designated exclusively for financing or refinancing both environmental and social projects. By the end of September 2022, the net assets of sustainable UCITS bond funds were estimated at EUR 343 billion, encompassing 1067 funds. This category represented 13% of the total UCITS bond net assets.

Sustainability Linked Bonds in Developing World

It is estimated that the annual SDG financing gap in developing world is estimated to be at USD 3.9 trillion (OECD, 2022). The Sustainability Linked Bond (SLB) market have grown remarkably since its first issuance in year 2019. However, issuances from developing countries accounted for a small share of the total SLB market. Members of the OECD Development Assistance Committee (DAC) have a significant role to play in providing support to the SLB market through blended finance instruments. DAC donors play an intermediating role for focussing the interest of investors towards sustainable investment and financial innovation in capital markets. They play a pivotal role for the sustainable development ambitions of low- and middle-income countries. The share of SLBs from issuers in ODA-eligible countries as a percentage of the total issued amount had decreased from 13% to 5% during the period 2021–2022. Green, social, sustainability, and sustainability-linked (GSSS) bonds hold significant potential to address the increasing finance gap for sustainable development and climate goals, especially in developing countries. Till date, the sustainability linked bond issuance have been concentrated in developed countries and issued by corporates rather than public sector firms. According to ICMA 2020, the global bond market stands at approximately USD 128.3 trillion. There offers immense potential for private finance mobilization through debt markets. Green, social and sustainability bonds are use -of-proceeds instruments used to refinance specific projects with positive environmental or social impact. The proceeds of SLBs can be used for general purposes. The structural and financial characteristics of sustainability-linked bonds (SLBs) change based on whether issuers achieve predefined sustainability objectives.

Structural characteristics associated with SLBs.[5]

SLB issuances can be categorized along four characteristics. In coupon set up, if the issuer does not meet its predetermined sustainability targets by the target observation date, the subsequent interest payments will be increased by a predetermined penalty amount which are usually quoted in basis points. In coupon set down, if the issuer meets its predetermined sustainability targets by the target observation date, subsequent interest payments will be decreased by a predetermined amount which is quoted in basis points. The Chilean sovereign SLB issuance is characterized by coupon step up. The Uruguay sovereign SLB issuance have both step-up and

[5] Ul Haq and Doumbia (2023[12]), "Structural loopholes in sustainability-linked bonds", https://documents1.worldbank.org/curated/en/099237410062223046/pdf/IDU0e099a50307f86045a80b33201d0b7057cedf.pdf; ICMA (2023[13]), Sustainability-Linked Bond Principles Related Questions, https://www.icmagroup.org/assets/documents/Sustainable-finance/2023-updates/SLB-QA-2023-Sept-250923.pdf

step-down characteristics while Development Bank of Rwanda issue has a coupon step down only. In redemption premium, if the issuer does not meet its predetermined sustainability targets by the target observation date, the issuer will have to pay a predetermined premium on the bond's redemption price during the time period of redemption. In donation, if the issuer does not meet its predetermined sustainability targets by the target observation date, an amount equal to a predetermined of the bond's issuance will be donated to the foundation or the firm according to the issuer choice.

In early redemption, if the issuer does not meet its determined sustainability targets by the target observation date, the bond will be redeemed early at a predetermined redemption price. In case of purchase carbon emission credits, if the issuer does not meet its predetermined sustainability targets, the issued can purchase carbon offsets for an amount equal to a determined percentage of the aggregate principal amount of the bonds. In some cases, there is a penalty fee if the issuer fails to deliver the Sustainability Certificate and limited assurance report.

SLB Issuance by Chile

Inspite of greater sustainable financing need of developing countries, the SLB market is highly concentrated in developed markets. Corporate issuers account for 98% of issuances in the SLB market. In 2022, sovereigns entered the SLB market with the issuance by countries such as Chile and Uruguay. In the year 2023, Chile issued the first sovereign SLB followed by another SLB aimed at social targets. For sovereigns, the issuance of SLBs are impactful in areas such as biodiversity, climate change and social outcomes. The first sovereign to issue green bond was Poland. The first SLB issued by Chile matures in the year 2042 raised USD 2 billion and achieved diversified investor demand of USD 8.1 billion. Chile also had issued a USD 3 billion multi-currency package of SLBs composed of USD 1.15 billion 12-year SLB, a USD 1.1 billion 30-year SLB, and a EUR 750 million 11-year SLB. This first sovereign SLB was the first sovereign to incorporate social targets and issued in euros.

2023 Chile sustainability linked bond framework was greenhouse gas emissions (GHG) per year, measured in metric tonnes of CO2 equivalent. The SPT target was to achieve GHG emissions of 95 metric tonnes of carbon dioxide by the year 2030. The observation date was 31st December 2030. Chile will link the bond's financial characteristics to the achievement of the SPTs such as a coupon step up or premium payment in the scenario where an SPT which includes an intermediate SPT is not met at the target observation date. In the scenario wherein more than one SPT is not met, the premium paid will be cumulative.

SLB Issuance by Uruguay

The first sovereign SLB issued in 2022 by Uruguay have both a coupon step -up and step down mechanism. This SLB was the world's second sovereign SLB with above stated two way pricing structure. The bond matures in the year 2034 with investor demand of USD 3.96 billion. The two KPIs of Uruguay aims to link the country's cost of capital to the realization of its climate and nature based goals under the Paris Agreement.

In 2023, the Development Bank of Rwanda (BRD) introduced its first SLB with a seven-year tenor and a target size of Rwandan Franc 30 billion (equivalent to USD 24.8 million). This bond benefitted from the innovative credit enhancement mechanism from the World Bank International Development Association (IDA) funds.

During the period 2020–2023, approximately 60% and 22% of all global bond issuances were accounted by Europe, Central Asia, East Asia and Pacific region.

SLB Ecosystem

The International Capital Market Association (ICMA) is basically responsible for best practices for all types of issuers in terms of structuring features and disclosure and reporting for use-of-proceeds bonds and SLBs. The ICMA Sustainability Linked Bond Principles (ICMA SLBPs) aims to provide information which is required to increase capital allocation to such financial products. The major components of ICMA SLBP consists of selection of KPIs, calibration of SPTs, bond characteristics, reporting and verification.

Donors such as World Bank links the financing conditions to environmental targets by reducing loan interest rates if emission reduction targets are achieved. In this context during November 2023, World Bank had approved an innovative USD 350 million sustainability linked loan for Uruguay.

In terms of Issuers, corporates and public sector account for approximately 98% of the SLBs. The first city to issue an SLB for emission reduction efforts were Helsingborg in Sweden. The case of Singapore based Sembcorp Industries, the energy and urban development company is a classical example of how issuers can use financial engineering to achieve sustainability performance target. Sembcorp Industries had announced in year 2022 to sell two of its coal fired plants to an Oman based private consortium. Through this sale, Sembcorp met its decarbonization targets without actual emissions reductions as the emissions from the two coal plans were shifted from Semcorp Industries to Oman based company.

Challenges for the Development of SLB Market

One of the major challenges is the lack of coordination between local capital and stakeholder coordination. A certain level of financial sector and local capital market development is essential for issuing Sustainability Linked Bonds (SLBs) and establishing its guidelines. Currently there are no SLB standard or guidance which exist in Europe. The development of capital markets varies based on specific country conditions and contexts. A sustainable and well functioning capital market necessitates macroeconomic stability, developed financial sector and strong legal and institutional framework. Another challenge involve adaptation of ICMA Sustainability Linked Bond Principles (SLBPs) to local contexts. Technical, financial, and human resource constraints can limit issuers' capacity to collect and report data with the same level of detail in different contexts. The absence of locally adapted principles or standards can lead to issuers misusing Sustainability-Linked Bonds (SLBs), potentially resulting in greenwashing accusations that damage the SLB market's reputation. Another grey area is that the selected key performance indicators (KPIs) and sustainability performance targets (SPTs) are often immaterial, difficult to compare and insufficiently ambitious. According to Climate Bonds Initiative, approximately 84% of oil and gas companies' issuance of SLB do not encompass scope 3 emissions. The differing KPIs and SPTs of bonds hinder comparability, creating a bottleneck for SLB market growth. Additionally, the lack of standardized expectations for the format and content of SLB pre-issuance frameworks and post-issuance reporting further limits comparability. The data available to monitor KPIs and SPTs is often of poor quality and limited in availability. There are substantial variations in what issuers in different country contexts can measure. Data measurement practices are underdeveloped in key areas such as biodiversity, climate change adaptation, and social outcomes areas where SLBs could be most beneficial.

Financial incentives embedded in bond characteristics often outweigh sustainability incentives, creating potential credibility challenges for SLBs. While SLBs are designed to link financial outcomes with sustainability commitments through mechanisms like coupon step-ups, structural loopholes can weaken this relationship, especially as issuers navigate the relatively new market with minimal guidance. Macroeconomic trends exacerbate the already challenging environment for financing sustainable development, further reducing investor demand in developing countries.

References

148. http://instiglio.org/educategirlsdib/wp-content/uploads/2015/09/Educate-Girls-DIB-Sept-2015.pdf.
149. https://www.goldmansachs.com/media-relations/press-releases/current/dc-water-environmental-impact-bond-fact-sheet.pdf.

Bruni, J., & Lewis, J. (2023). *Chile opens sovereign SLBs to euros and social KPIs*. https://www.ifre.com/story/3993906/chile-opens-sovereign-slbs-to-euros-and-social-kpis-m3cqrnvxnp

"Carbon footprint arbitrage of a lifetime". https://img1.wsimg.com/blobby/go/946d6aac-e6cc-430a-8898-520cf90f5d3e/AFII_Sembcorp_061122-819d41d.pdf.

Climate Bonds Initiative. (2023). *Sustainable debt global State of the market 2022*. https://www.climatebonds.net/files/reports/cbi_sotm_2022_03e.pdf

Cripps, P., & Jenkins, M. (2022). *Investors urged to vote against Sembcorp coal plant deal*. https://www.environmental-finance.com/content/news/sembcorp-coal-plant-deal-highlights-slb-weaknesses-claims-afii.html

DCD. (2024). *Sustainability linked bonds*. Unclassified, OECD.

Dembele, F., Schwarz, R., & Horrocks, P. (2021). *Scaling up green, social, sustainability and sustainability-linked bond issuances in developing countries*. OECD Publishing. https://www.oecd.org/dac/financing-sustainable-development/blended-finance-principles/documents/scaling-up-green-social-sustainability-sustainability-linked-bond-issuances-developing-countries.pdf.

Harrison, C., MacGeoch, M., & Michetti, C. (2022). *Sustainable debt global state of the market 2021*. Climate Bonds Initiative.

http://instiglio.org/educategirlsdib/wp-content/uploads/2015/09/Educate-

https://acumen.org/about/patient-capital/

https://boardagenda.com/2020/

https://carbontracker.org/can-you-see-stranded-assets-through-the-smog/

https://connect.sustainalytics.com/ebook-how-sustainable-finance-shaping-banking

https://golab.bsg.ox.ac.uk/knowledge-bank/indigo-data-and-visualisation/impact-bond-dataset-v2/

https://golab.bsg.ox.ac.uk/the-basics/outcomesfunds/#what-is-an-outcomes-fund

https://gsgii.org/case_studies/eye-fund/

https://orsted.com/en/media/news/2023/06/20230608684811#:~:text=%C3%98rsted%20is%20proud%20to%20be,crucial%20for%20enhancing%20ocean%20health

https://www.credit-suisse.com/media/assets/asset-management/docs/ch/investment

https://www.economist.com/finance-and-economics/2020/09/19/what-is-the-point-of-green-bonds

https://www.gbm.hsbc.com/-/media/gbm/reports/insights/social-bonds.pdf

https://www.gsam.com/content/gsam/uk/en/advisers/market-insights/gsam-insights/2024/social-bonds-bounce-back

https://www.hks.harvard.edu/sites/default/files/centers/mrcbg/files/Mayer_2.19.19.transcript.pdf. An good example is the B-Corps model: https://bcorporation.net

https://www.icmagroup.org/assets/documents/Regulatory/Green-Bonds/June-2019/Mapping-SDGs-to-Green-Social-and-Sustainability-Bonds06-2019-100619.pdf

https://www.ifc.org/wps/wcm/connect/corp_ext_content/ifc_external_corporate_site/about+ifc_new/investor+relations/irproducts/socialbonds

https://www.rbcwealthmanagement.com/gb/en/research-insights/the-growth-of-impact-investing-building-wealth-with-positiveoutcomes/detail/?gclid=Cj0KCQjw5eX7BRDQARIsAMhYLP8jHs3GyRFi-Cy6Lq6cNqVCbEjALIDvJ745GkaWjl-U7T0979Kdjz0aAj43EALw_wcB

https://www.santander.com/en/stories/blue-bonds

https://www.socialfinance.org.uk/peterborough-social-impact-bond

ICMA. (2020). *Bond market size*. https://www.icmagroup.org/market-practice-and-regulatory-policy/secondary-markets/bond-market-size/

ICMA. (2023a[11]). *Sustainability-linked bond principles voluntary process guidelines*. https://www.icmagroup.org/assets/documents/Sustainable-finance/2023-updates/Sustainability-Linked-Bond-Principles-June-2023-220623.pdf; (OECD, 2023[3]), Green, Social and Sustainability Bonds in Developing Countries: The Case for I.

ICMA. (2023b). *Market integrity and greenwashing risks in sustainable finance*. https://www.icmagroup.org/assets/documents/Sustainable-finance/Market-integrity-and-greenwashing-risks-in-sustainable-finance-October-2023.pdf

Ministry of Finance. (2020). *Chile's sustainable bond framework.* https://www.hacienda.cl/english/work-areas/international-finance/publicdebt-office/sustainable-bonds/chile-s-sustainable-bond-framework

Nicholls, A. (2021). *Sustainable finance: A primer and recent development, a Asian development outlook.* Financing a Green and Inclusive Recovery. https://ec.europa.eu/info/business-economy-euro/banking-and-finance/sustainable-finance/overview-sustainable-finance_en

OECD. (2024). *Sustainability-linked bonds: How to make them work in developing countries, and how donors can help*. OECD Publishing.

"Sustainability-linked bonds and how to use them credibly", https://www.eco-business.com/news/sustainability-linked-bonds-and-how-to-use-them-credibly/; ICMA (2023[13]), Sustainability-linked Bond Principles Related Questions. https://www.icmagroup.org/assets/documents/Sustainable-finance/2023-updates/SLB-QA-2023-Sept-250923.pdf.

UK Government. (2021). *UK Government green financing framework.* https://assets.publishing.service.gov.uk/government/uploads/system/uploads/attachment_data/file/1002578/20210630_UK_Government_Green_Financing_Framework.pdf

Chapter 5
Sustainable Finance Market Trends

The sustainable finance market often referred to as green finance, is a financial ecosystem which integrates environmental, social and governance (ESG) factors into investment decision making choices. The fundamental aim of green finance is to channel funds into endeavors and enterprises which advance sustainable development, combat climate change, protect natural resources thereby making a positive contribution to society. Financial instruments such as green bonds and sustainable debt instruments are designed to support eco-friendly initiatives such as renewable energy initiatives, sustainable infrastructure projects and other conservation initiatives. These instruments have facilitated the adoption of projects with environmental benefits. A major trend observed is the integration of ESG factors into investment strategies by investors and financial institutions.

Environmental, social, and governance (ESG) risks and opportunities have transitioned into mainstream factors when evaluating sustainable and ethical investments. Consequently, investors are actively searching for opportunities that harmonize with their principles and make meaningful contributions to both societal and environmental betterment.

The notion of sustainable investing has garnered significant attention in the market as well. Approaches such as socially responsible investing (SRI) and impact investing have witnessed widespread adoption, signaling a movement toward investment strategies that foster sustainability and generate favorable societal outcomes. Businesses are facing increasing pressure to divulge their environmental, social, and governance (ESG) practices and performance. This heightened demand for transparency regarding the environmental and social effects of companies significantly shapes the investment choices of investors.

The increasing focus on corporate sustainability highlights the significance of responsible financial practices. Favorable policies and regulations are pivotal in propelling sustainable finance. Many nations and regions are adopting measures to promote sustainable finance initiatives. Governments and financial authorities are encouraging environmentally friendly investments and integrating sustainable

B. R. Kumar, *Green Finance*, Sustainable Finance,
https://doi.org/10.1007/978-3-032-03333-8_5

principles into the financial sector, nurturing an atmosphere conducive to sustainable development. The market growth is propelled by rising awareness and conscious consumerism, driving demand for sustainable investments and ethical financial products.

In response to increasing demand for sustainable investments, the financial sector has diversified its offerings. Products like green bonds, sustainability-linked loans, social impact bonds, and green mutual funds cater to diverse investor preferences and risk appetites, promoting accessibility and inclusion in sustainable finance. The increasing awareness and concern surrounding environmental and social issues, including climate change, resource depletion, and social inequality, are anticipated to drive the sustainable finance market's growth.

The sustainable finance market has expanded rapidly, gaining recognition from market participants and national authorities for its role in addressing climate change and supporting SDGs. Yet, it remains small globally, posing challenges for firms, especially in developing countries and SMEs, to access. For instance, green bonds from lower middle-income countries make up only 1.7% of global issuance. Similarly, Green Sukuk have mobilized less than US$ 15 billion, contrasting with the vast Islamic finance assets. The global sustainable fund market represents just 4% of the total fund market value.[1] SMEs, crucial for economic activity and employment, face barriers in accessing sustainable finance due to high costs. Bridging these gaps is critical for Paris Agreement and 2030 Agenda goals.

Trends in Sustainability Finance Market

The global sustainable finance market was valued at US$ 519.88 billion and is expected to grow at a compound annual growth rate (CAGR) of 22.6% during the period 2023–2030. In year 2022, the sustainable finance Asset Under Management (AUM) was valued at US$ 37.80 trillion.[2]

According to Precedence research data, the global sustainable finance market is expected to grow from US$ 4562.85 billion in year 2022 to US$ 29111.04 by the year 2032 representing a CAGR of 20.36% during the period 2023–2032.

The sustainable finance market is the major source of capital for investment in sustainable development and the Sustainable Development Goals (SDGs). According to the UNCTAD World Investment Report 2023, the value of the global sustainable finance markets amounted to $5.8 trillion in the year 2022. The fund market value amounted to $2.7 trillion in 2021 and $2.5 trillion in year 2022. The cumulative value of the sustainable bond market increased, from $2.5 trillion in

[1] Sustainable Finance Working Group (SFWG), 20 2 2 G 2 0 Sustainable Finance Report

[2] https://www.ebf.eu/ebf-media-centre/ebf-launches-a-roundtable-for-sustainability-leaders-in-banking/

2021 to $3.3 trillion in 2022.[3] The voluntary carbon markets were valued at $2 billion. In 2022, the total number of sustainability themed funds worldwide were 7012. Europe with 5300 funds accounted for 76% of the sustainable fund universe. The United States and China accounted for 9% and 4% of sustainable funds in year 2022. In 2022, the share of sustainable funds in the total European fund market grew from 16% to 20%. The value of sustainable fund assets in United States decreased from $357 billion in year 2021 to $286 billion in year 2022 and accounted for 12% of the global market. China is the world's third largest sustainable fund market with 279 sustainable funds with assets under management of approximately $50 billion by the end of year 2022. Global net investment flows to sustainable funds had declined from $557 billion in year 2021 to $159 billion in year 2022. Net investment flows to sustainable funds in Europe dropped from $472 billion in 2021 to $141 billion in 2022. According to UNCTAD estimation, sustainable funds in developing economies account for less than 3% of global sustainable fund assets.[4]

Table 5.1 shows the value of the global sustainable bond market during the period 2017–2022.

Table 5.2 shows the bond statistics by category and its value during the period 2022.

Table 5.3 shows the bond value by issuer type.

Table 5.4 gives the bond value by region wise.

Table 5.1 Global sustainable bond market

Year	Value in billions of dollars
2017	179
2018	203
2019	321
2020	702
2021	1004
2022	892

Source: UNCTAD, World Investment Report 2023

Table 5.2 Bond value by category

Category	Value in billions of dollars
Green	501
Social	169
Mixed Sustainability	144
Sustainability linked	75

Source: UNCTAD, World Investment Report 2023

[3] UNCTAD World Investment Report 2023 Chapter 3 Capital Markets and Sustainable Finance Investing in sustainable energy for all.

[4] UNCTAD World Investment Report 2023 Chapter 3 Capital Markets and Sustainable Finance Investing in sustainable energy for all.

Table 5.3 Bond value by issuer type in year 2022

Issuer	Value in billions of dollars
Corporate	289
Financial Institution	199
Government Agency	148
Supranational	106
Sovereign	94
Municipal	56

Source: UNCTAD, information from Environmental Finance

Table 5.4 Bond value by region wise

Issuer	Value in billions of dollars
Europe	402
Asia & Oceania	207
Supranational	106
North America	135
Latin America	31
Middle East & Africa	11

Source: UNCTAD, World Investment Report 2023

Key elements of basic infrastructure, including energy, buildings, transport, and water, continue to receive the majority of investment through green bonds. The NextGenerationEU Green Bond framework continued to drive growth in Europe, solidifying its position as the leader in the green bond market. In 2022, France, the Netherlands, and Germany were among the top five issuing countries in the Eurozone, with the European Union itself being the largest single issuer of green bonds.

The European Union (EU) has been actively promoting sustainable finance and implementing regulations to boost investments in sustainable projects. Since its introduction in 2018, the EU's Action plan on sustainable finance has been instrumental in mobilizing private capital for sustainable initiatives, aligning the financial sector with climate and sustainability goals, leading to increased green bond issuance and ESG integration in Europe.

Public Development Banks (PDB) are significant part of the global financial landscape. They manage 23 trillion of total assets and provide up to USD 2.7 trillion of annual investments, out of which more than 83% is from PDBs from G20 countries. Institutions such as IFC, UNCTAD, UNDP, UNEP and World Bank have been involved in the alignment tools and approaches which can be implemented to promote sustainable finance in countries.

Sustainability Investments by Institutional Investors

The rise of ESG investment has signalled to firms that investors value environmental, social, and governance performance and these concerns are now mainstream. Over $20 trillion USD, approximately a quarter of all professionally managed assets worldwide, follow ESG strategies. About 2500 signatories, representing over $80 trillion USD assets under management, have pledged to follow the UN's Principles of Responsible Investment. The global public pension fund assets dropped from $22.3 trillion in 2021 to $21.3 trillion in the year 2022. According to UNCTAD, 2023 report, the institutional investors such as PPFs and SWFs are now more active in terms of assessment and response to sustainability risks such as UNCTAD. In 2022, the world's top 100 PPFs accounted for $12.2 trillion of assets under management and the top 30 SWFs accounted for $9.2 trillions of assets under management. In the year 2022, 55 of the top PPFs reported sustainability activities either through specialized responsible investment or ESG reports.

Institutional investors, such as public pension funds (PPFs) and sovereign wealth funds (SWFs), are in a pivotal position to address sustainability challenges and finance sustainable energy investments. The long-term and capital-intensive nature of renewables investment aligns well with the maturity profiles of pension fund liabilities and sovereign demand for infrastructure investment. UNCTAD's 2022 monitoring revealed that more institutional investors are taking climate action, including investing in sustainable energy and divesting from fossil fuels. Over two-thirds of reporting funds have committed to achieving net-zero portfolios by 2050. Capital market infrastructures, such as stock and derivatives exchanges, are crucial points in the investment chain, influencing entities, issuers, index providers, and other stakeholders. In 2022, the number of exchanges with mandatory sustainability reporting and those providing sustainability disclosure training to listed companies increased.

Unethical practices' costs, like carbon emissions, are often unaccounted for by firms, burdening societies and communities. ESG investments allow governments to align strategies with market interventions, urging sovereign wealth and pension funds to prioritize firms with sustainable practices. Sovereign wealth funds (SWFs) and pension funds, with their long investment horizon, face heightened ESG risks' impact on financial returns. Many argue these risks aren't fully reflected in equity prices yet. Short-term focus may hinder investment in firms with strong ESG performance, making government intervention appealing. Sovereign wealth funds (SWFs) and pension funds wield substantial global assets, with SWFs projected to hit $15 trillion USD by 2020. Norway's Government Pension Fund Global alone manages over $1 trillion USD, including 1% of global equity shares.

While some SWFs implement negative screens against unethical firms or prioritize environmentally-friendly companies, such as Norway's Government Pension Fund Global's restrictions on fossil fuel investments, broader adoption of ESG investing among SWFs and pension funds has yet to materialize, despite evidence of societal benefits and comparable financial performance.

Many reporting funds fair better in sustainability integration, detailing their ESG considerations, governance, social dimensions, and policies on investee engagement and voting. Top performing funds outline criteria for screening for aggressive tax avoidance or gender diversity on company boards. More funds are adopting a thematic approach, integrating the SDGs into their investment decisions. Nearly 75% of reporting funds employ an impact investment strategy, focusing on thematic sectors like renewables and climate solutions or utilizing specific ESG-related instruments like green bonds.

Canada Pension Plan Investments (CPP) publishes a detailed sustainable investment report, highlighting its comprehensive sustainability integration throughout the investment life cycle, from pre-investment research to constant monitoring of investee operations. CPP's approach involves thorough risk identification and value creation via benchmarking and assessments. Similarly, Norges Bank Investment Management (NBIM) emphasizes active ownership and regular dialogues with investee companies on sustainability issues, publishing expectation documents to encourage sustainable practices.[5] The NYSCRF Climate Action Plan aims to invest $20 billion in renewable energy over 10 years and shift from fossil fuels to low-carbon options. MN plans to fully divest from coal mining companies by 2025. CDC will invest €60 billion in ecological transition by 2024 and phase out investments in companies heavily reliant on coal by 2030. KLP commits to significantly increasing renewable energy in its global mix. BPI France's Climate Action Plan focuses on accelerating ecological and energy transition, with criteria for excluding thermal coal.[6]

However, many topics related to sustainability performance are revealed by small number of funds. For instance, the use of external auditing of ESG reporting was reported by only 16% of funds. Though many reporting funds are now targeting net zero by 2050 in their policies, only a third of funds publish information about their specific targets for renewable energy investment and fossil fuel divestment.

PPFs and SWFs are increasingly interested in standardizing sustainability reporting using recognized international standards. Most reporting funds now follow at least one international standard or benchmark as a framework for their sustainability reporting. The Principles for Responsible Investment (PRI) and the Task Force on Climate-Related Financial Disclosures (TCFD) are the two most commonly used reporting frameworks, followed by those of the Global Reporting Initiative (GRI) and the Sustainability Accounting Standards Board (SASB).

Most net-zero emission commitments are made by North American and European funds, driven by strong climate regulations. In contrast, weaker environmental regulations and carbon markets in developing economies discourage climate action by investors.

---

[5] CPP Investments, 2022 Report on Sustainable Investing, and NBIM, 2022 Annual Report.

[6] UNCTAD

Table 5.5 Fossil fuel and Green investments (in billions of dollars)

Year	Green investment	Fossil fuel investment
2016	4.2	12
2017	9.4	7.5
2018	5.8	16
2019	5	13.8
2020	8.3	14.5
2021	23.6	6.9
2022	18.7	6.7

Source: UNCTAD, Global SWF, January 2023

Table 5.5 compares the fossil fuel investments and green investments made by sovereign wealth funds during the period 2016–2022. The values are given in billions of dollars.

Canadian pension funds were the largest investors in renewable energy in 2022, contributing 33% of the total investment. Gulf investors provided 29%, and Singaporean funds accounted for 26% with GIC (Singapore) being the largest single investor, followed by Mubadala (United Arab Emirates). Gulf SWFs play a crucial role in renewable energy investments, aiming to diversify economies and advance Paris Agreement goals.

Renewable energy investment is concentrated in North America and Europe, driven by opportunities, favourable regulations, and FDI efforts. In contrast, investment in developing economies, particularly the least developed, remains limited despite high need and potential. Barriers such as the absence of bankable projects, lack of supportive policies, and high-risk perceptions hinder long-term institutional investment in these regions. Overcoming these challenges is crucial to unlocking significant renewable energy investments in developing economies.

Sustainable Stock Exchanges

Stock exchanges have been integrating their sustainability related activities into their operations for the past two decades. By 2022, more than half of the world's stock exchanges have written guidance on ESG reporting. The number of stock exchanges which provided training on ESG topics to market participants increased from 61 in 2021 to 81 by 2022.

Since its inception in 2009 with five founding signatories, the UN SSE initiative has expanded its network to encompass over 119 stock exchanges and 13 derivatives exchanges globally. These exchanges collectively list more than 62,709 companies, with a combined market capitalization exceeding $127 trillion.[7]

Stock exchanges globally promote international ESG disclosure instruments. The most referenced instrument is the GRI Standards, followed by standards and

[7] UNCTAD, SSE database.

guidance from SASB and the International Integrated Reporting Council, each cited in approximately three-quarters of guidance documents. Climate-specific reporting instruments like the recommendations from the Financial Stability Board's TCFD and the Carbon Disclosure Project are referenced by over half of the guidance, with about a third mentioning the Carbon Disclosure Standards Board.

Despite the increasing number of exchanges promoting gender equality among their listed companies, women in high-level positions remain underrepresented in many markets. In 2022, women held only 23% of the 21,561 board seats at top listed companies across 22 major G20 stock exchanges. (UN SSE and IFC, 2022). Women hold 45% of board seats in the top 100 firms on Euronext Paris, making it the leading G20 exchange for boardroom gender diversity.

Investment Vehicles with Focus on Gender Aspects

Investors are adopting new investment vehicles and mechanisms that incorporate a gender lens into their decision-making. These include gender-themed bonds, gender-lens ratings or benchmarks, and gender-themed equity indices, which can be tracked by exchange-traded funds, mutual funds, and other equity or derivative products. In 2020, Investments through structured private equity, venture capital and private debt funds with focus on gender lenders amounted to $6 billion.[8] The magnitude of gender lens investing was estimated to be in excess of $12 billion in the year 2020.[9]

The 2X Challenge, an initiative launched at the 2018 G7 Summit, committed and mobilized $11 billion for investment in women, and called for the G7, development finance institutions, and private sector investors to collectively mobilize $15 billion from 2021 to 2022. Additionally, gender-lens "co-benefits" are being integrated into other thematic investment vehicles, such as green bonds and carbon credits.

According to 2018 data from US Forum for Sustainable and Responsible Investment (US SIF, 2020) asset owners managing approximately $868 billion were incorporating gender-lens issues into their investment decisions. The Euronext Gender Equality Indices, launched in November 2022, evaluate companies based on four criteria: gender balance in leadership and workforce, equal compensation and work-life balance, policies promoting gender equality, and commitment, transparency, and accountability. The Bloomberg Gender Equality Index launched in year 2016 have evaluation criteria of leadership and talent pipeline, equal pay and gender pay parity, inclusive culture, anti-sexual harassment policies and external brand. The index covers 484 companies from 45 countries and regions across 11 sectors and 54 industries. In 2017, Central banks had set up an organization -Network for

[8] Catalyst at Large, Wharton Social Impact Initiative, 2021

[9] Gendersmart, 2021.

Greening the Financial System (NGFS) for strengthening the global response to climate change and net zero transition.

Sustainable Investment in European Asset Management Industry

According to survey conducted by strategy consultants INDEFI and European Fund and Asset Management Association (EFAMA),[10] the size of the European ESG market, a total of EUR 10.7 trillion of assets had applied an ESG selection strategy by end of the year 2019, which accounted for approximately 45% of the total assets under management (AUM). Firm level ESG integration framework accounted for EUR 8.8 trillion of assets. Approximately EUR 10.2 trillion of assets were subject to ESG related engagement or voting policies which accounted for over 43% of total AUM. Asset of investment funds and mandates which apply product specific exclusions amounted to EUR 2.9 trillion by the end of year 2019. ESG integration is the most common sustainable investment practice which is used at the product level in European market. Approximately, EUR 3.8 trillion of assets are managed through ESG integration which account for 16% of the total fund and mandate assets. By 2019, EUR 2 trillion of assets were managed in sustainability themed products which explicitly target specific themes of sustainable development.

According to EFAMA survey 2021, SFDR Article 8 funds which promote environmental and social characteristics amounted to EUR 3.7 trillion accounted for 22% of the European fund market. By March 2021, equity funds accounted for half of the total universe of SFDR Article 8 funds, followed by bond funds (26%), multi asset funds (16%) and money market funds (8%). SFDR Article 9 fund net assets amounted to EUR 340 billion which accounted for approximately 2% of the European fund market. Equity funds account for 71% of all SFDR Article 9 funds by end of March 2021. Approximately a total of EUR 11 trillion of assets were accounted by assets which applied an ESG investment approach by end of Q1 2021. Assets in discretionary mandates that take an ESG investment approach amounted to EUR 5 trillion, whereas AUM in funds using some form of ESG features accounted for EUR 6 trillion.

Segment wise, equity investments dominated the sustainable finance sector in the year 2022. The focus is on purchase of stock or other ownership interests in businesses with environmental, social and governance (ESG) principles. The target companies are basically leaders in sustainability initiatives within their respective industry sectors. In the sustainable finance market, the main fixed income investments comprise green bonds, social bonds, and sustainability-linked bonds. Green

---

[10] EFAMA represents 28 Member Associations, 60 Corporate Members and 24 Associate Members. At end Q2 2020, total net assets of European investment funds reached EUR 17.1 trillion. These assets were managed by almost 34,200 UCITS (Undertakings for Collective Investments in Transferable Securities) and more than 29,100 AIFs (Alternative Investment Funds)

bonds are used to fund environmentally friendly projects such as renewable energy and infrastructure project. Social bonds cover projects which focus on social objectives such as affordable housing and healthcare, employment generation in underserved communities and initiatives to promote social welfare. Sustainability linked bonds link the bond's financial terms to the issuer's sustainability performance and offer incentives to enhance ESG metrics.

Mixed allocation strategies within the sustainable finance market entail combining equity and fixed-income investments to create a balanced portfolio. These strategies offer investors the opportunity to diversify their sustainable holdings across different asset classes, thereby managing risks and capitalizing on opportunities in both equity and fixed-income markets. These approaches are ideal for investors aiming to construct a comprehensive and sustainable investment portfolio that encompasses various sectors and themes.

Mixed sustainability bonds comprise of both green and social bonds. The cash flows from these bonds are allocated to projects which contribute to both environmental and social goals. During the first half of 2023, sustainable bond worth $526 billion were issued. In 2023, Goldman Sachs Asset Management launched two new sustainable bond funds, the Goldman Sachs Global Impact Corporate Bond Fund and the Goldman Sachs USD Green Bond Fund.

Sustainable Finance Regionwide

North America dominates the market for sustainable finance. The Asia Pacific region is witnessing huge growth in the sustainable finance market. Countries such as China, Japan, South Korea and Australia have taken steps to promote sustainable finance and green investments.

Europe is the most developed and diverse ESG market which accounts for about 82% of the global sustainable fund universe. During Covid 19 pandemic, European Commission had planned to issue EU SURE bonds of €100 billion as social bonds under the ICMA Social Bond Principles. Emerging and developing economies have strong sustainable targets. In 2020, China alone accounted for over 80% of social bond issuance The green bond issuance by Egypt witnessed five times oversubscription during September 2020. In 2018, official development finance interventions mobilized US$ 46.4 billion from the private sector. However, only 5.3% of this private finance reached the least developed and other low-income countries.

Sustainable Finance in Industry Sectors

The energy industry, whose share of total investment declined from 50% in 2014 to 35% in 2021, re-emerged in 2022 as the recipient of the highest volume of green bond financing, experiencing a 15% year-on-year increase. The sustainable finance initiatives in the transport and logistics sector aims to address environmental impacts related to emissions reduction and fuel efficiency. In this sector, the sustainable finance promotes investments in electric vehicles, sustainable aviation fuels, public transportation infrastructure, and environmentally-friendly logistics solutions. In addition, social bonds focus on projects which improve accessibility and mobility in underserved communities.

Utilities sector have prominent position in the sustainable finance market with specific focus on renewable energy generation and distribution. Sustainable finance initiatives in this sector focus on funding projects such as solar and wind power plants, hydroelectric facilities, energy storage solutions and grid modernization.

Chemical industry sector faces challenges with respect to adoption of sustainable practices and reduction of ecological footprint. Sustainable finance initiatives in this sector focus on funding of projects in sustainable chemistry, eco friendly manufacturing processes and development of biodegradable or non-toxic materials.

Green finance initiatives in the food and beverage sector focus on sustainable agriculture, food waste reduction and ethical sourcing. Sustainable finance initiatives related to food and beverage sector support projects which promote responsible land use, water conservation and social development within the food supply chain.

Governments and municipalities are active participants in the sustainable finance market as green bonds are issued to fund sustainable infrastructure projects and climate change mitigation initiatives.

Energy, buildings, and transport dominate the green debt market, primarily focusing on climate change mitigation. In the first half of 2020, these categories constituted 87% of green bond proceeds, while renewable energy and power alone comprised 70% of green loans. Conversely, other sustainability themes such as biodiversity, agriculture, forestry, and land use struggle to attract investment. In 2019, biodiversity conservation raised just US$ 6 billion, less than 4% of total green securities funding, despite a significant annual financing gap estimated at between US$ 598 billion and US$ 824 billion. Sustainable agriculture and forestry received less than 3% of green-bond funding in the same year, despite the sector's significant role in global greenhouse gas emissions, presenting a substantial opportunity for cost-effective emissions mitigation. Agriculture sector accounts for 27% of global greenhouse gas emissions.

Sustainability-themed products are crucial for financing sustainable development as defined by the SDGs. They should channel essential investments into sectors like transport infrastructure, telecommunication infrastructure, WASH (water, sanitation, and hygiene), agrifood systems, climate change mitigation, health, education, and ecosystem diversity. These sectors are vital for achieving the SDGs and represent significant investment opportunities. Institutional investors increasingly use the SDGs to shape their sustainable investment strategies, and UNCTAD monitors fund alignment with these goals to evaluate their impact. As of the end of 2022, the 2843 sustainable funds covered by the assessment had committed $537 billion, or 30% of their holdings, to the eight SDG sectors, up from 26% in 2021. The largest recipients of funding remain the four sectors of health, renewable energy, agrifood systems, and WASH, which account for 95% of the assets committed to these

SDG sectors. Health, encompassing health infrastructure, medical services, pharmaceuticals, and medical devices, remains the single largest sector for fund investment, followed by climate change mitigation, including renewable energy.[11]

Carbon Markets

Carbon markets facilitate the buying and selling of emission allowances, credits, and related financial instruments. Carbon credits, typically representing 1 ton of CO2 equivalent, allow buyers to offset their emissions. Article 6 of the Paris Agreement permits countries to use international carbon markets to meet their nationally determined contributions (NDCs). Over two-thirds of countries plan to use these markets, and many are investing in digital infrastructure. The World Bank estimates that carbon trading could halve the cost of implementing NDCs. Carbon markets are divided into compliance carbon markets (CCMs), which are jurisdiction-specific and mandatory, and voluntary carbon markets (VCMs), which cater to entities outside regulated schemes. VCMs involve various participants, including companies, governments, and individuals, and rely on verification to ensure the validity of emissions reductions. The value chain of a VCM is typically made up four elements: project initiation, project verification and credit issuance, trading and finally retirement of the credit when the emissions offsets are claimed.

Compliance carbon markets (CCMs), with an estimated value of issued credits between $700 billion and $800 billion per year, are much larger than voluntary carbon markets (VCMs) which are estimated at about $2 billion per year. Voluntary carbon markets (VCMs) uniquely enable cross-border investment to fund new emissions reduction or avoidance projects. Most VCM credits are issued for projects in developing countries and sold to buyers in developed countries, mainly in Europe and the United States. This emerging market has significant potential as a new channel for sustainable finance in climate sectors like renewable energy and reforestation.

Table 5.6 shows the voluntary carbon market size by the value of traded carbon credits. The values are given in millions of dollars.

The value of carbon credits increased by four times in 2021 compared to the previous year. Decarbonizing the energy sector is critical in combating climate change as this sector is the leading contributor to emissions. Renewal energy projects comprises about 37% of all projects which issue VCM credits.[12] Renewable energy projects encompasses subcategories of wind, solar, hydro, renewable biomass and mixed source. In the year 2022, approximately 93% of renewable energy carbon credits issued were related to three technologies of large-scale wind,

[11] UNCTAD World Investment Report 2023 Chapter 3 Capital Markets and Sustainable Finance Investing in sustainable energy for all

[12] Climate Focus,2022

Table 5.6 Voluntary carbon market size

Year	Value in millions of dollars
2012	530
2013	339
2014	298
2015	278
2016	199
2017	146
2018	296
2019	320
2020	520
2021	1985

Source: UNCTAD, Ecosystem Marketplace (2022)

hydropower and solar projects. Through various compliance mechanisms, including Voluntary Carbon Markets (VCMs), Compliance Carbon Markets (CCMs), and carbon taxes, approximately 23% of global emissions are now subject to some form of carbon pricing (UNDP, 2022).

Voluntary Carbon Markets (VCMs) should be integrated with other policy tools to attract private investment for climate mitigation in developing countries, supporting a fair transition to net-zero emissions. In 2022, the United Nations Sustainable Stock Exchange (UN SSE) initiative started a new project to examine the role of stock exchanges in carbon markets. At COP27, a Market Monitor for VCMs was released and established an SSE Advisory Group to provide guidance for exchanges involved in carbon markets. In 2022, IOSCO had initiated steps to enhance understanding and functioning of CCMs and VCMs, focusing on market integrity, cross-border trading, and resilience, with ongoing consultations and recommendations.

Regulatory Trends

As part of the UN GSFO's work, UNCTAD, in partnership with PRI and the UNEP Finance Initiative (UNEP FI), has been monitoring recent developments in sustainable finance policies and regulations across 35 economies and country groupings. In 2022, economies tracked by the GSFO's Sustainable Finance Regulation Platform introduced over 50 sustainable finance dedicated measures. As a result, the total number of all regulations and policy measures were 388 by end 2022. In addition, more than 50 measures are under development in these economies.

Table 5.7 shows the number of sustainable finance policy measures and regulations in select developed and developing economies during 2012–2022.

The most active area of policy making in sustainable finance was sustainability disclosure. In the year 2022, 14 economies covered by the GSFO database had introduced 19 measures. The Council of the European Union adopted the Corporate Sustainability Reporting Directive in 2023 which required all large companies listed

Table 5.7 Number of sustainable finance policy measures

Year	G20	Select developing countries
2012	75	28
2013	81	32
2014	95	34
2015	107	41
2016	117	48
2017	135	56
2018	155	61
2019	179	67
2020	193	82
2021	241	97
2022	276	112

Source UN Global Sustainable Finance Observatory (GSFO.org), based on UNCTAD, PRI and World Bank data

on regulated markets to report on ESG and human rights activities. Developing economies like Bangladesh, China, Egypt, India and Malaysia introduced measures which required financial institutions and companies to report on sustainability issues such as carbon emissions. The EU and Singapore implemented new regulations on sustainability disclosure for financial products such as sustainable investment funds.

Following the EU's adoption of the Corporate Sustainability Reporting Directive (CSRD) in November 2022, the European Financial Reporting Advisory Group approved the European Sustainability Reporting Standards (ESRS). The CSRD, effective December 2022 expanded sustainability disclosure requirements from about 11,000 to nearly 50,000 companies, including large EU companies, those listed on EU-regulated markets, parent EU companies, and certain non-EU companies. The ESRS, based on double materiality, will be phased in from 2024 for large companies and 2026 for SMEs, covering ESG matters with sector-specific standards to follow.

Carbon Pricing is an important policy area for sustainable finance. By end 2022, 15 out of 35 economies covered by the GSFO platform had put in place carbon trading schemes or carbon emission taxes. Similar sustainability measures are being developed in 11 countries, including Brazil, Chile, Colombia, Indonesia, Japan, Malaysia, Nigeria, Thailand, Turkey, and Vietnam. In December 2022, the European Commission, Parliament, and Council reached a provisional agreement on the "Fit for 55" package, reforming the EU Emissions Trading System with a target of 62% emissions reduction by 2030. In 2022, over 80% of disclosure measures at the national and regional levels imposed mandatory actions.

Countries use incentives such as financial, fiscal and administrative as an important policy tool to support the growth of the sustainable finance market. Governments use incentives to encourage investments in sustainable financial instruments. Green Funds Scheme of Netherlands offers a combination of tax credit and tax exemption to both institutional and individual investors who invest in green funds. Banks can offer cheaper loans to green projects as the interest rate for investors is lower than market rates. The lower interest rate is then offset by tax credit and exemption of taxes on dividends and interest payments. Through this incentive program, individual investors have invested more than €6.8 billion in green funds, funding more than 5000 projects since its implementation in year 1995. In 2022, Brazil extended tax reduction for investment in social or green bonds in projects. Hong Kong had announced a three-year Green and Sustainable Finance Grant Scheme to cover some part of the expenses for bond issuance and external review services. Malaysia had introduced its Sustainable and Responsible Investment (SRI) Sukuk and Bond Grant Scheme to support green bond issuance. This scheme offers tax exemption for sukuk bonds issued in accordance with the ASEAN, Green, Social and Sustainability Bond Standards. In the year 2022, US Government issued Clean Renewable Energy Bonds and Qualified Energy Conservation Bonds to support the issuance of taxable bonds by municipalities for clean energy conservation. Under these programs, 70% of the coupon from municipal bonds is offered as a tax credit or subsidy to bondholders, incentivizing investment in clean and renewable energy. With respect to sustainable banking, incentives are being provided to promote sustainable loans with a climate or social focus. The Chinese government provides interest rate subsidies and preferential tax treatment to banks or borrowers to encourage increased lending for green projects. Singapore offers grants to help corporations obtain green and sustainability-linked loans, while also reducing the costs of sustainable loans through streamlined procedures.

The International Organization of Securities Commissions (IOSCO) is actively working to advance sustainability reporting and assurance standards. In 2021, IOSCO supported the IFRS Foundation's ISSB to establish globally consistent sustainability disclosure standards. In 2022, IOSCO began assessing the existing sustainability assurance ecosystem and engaging with stakeholders like the International Auditing and Assurance Standards Board to develop robust standards. In early 2023, IOSCO proposed a workstream on net-zero transition plans and published a report on a global assurance framework. Capacity-building in sustainable finance remains a priority, with ongoing efforts to assist regulatory authorities in implementing sustainability reporting standards.

The International Sustainability Standards Board (ISSB), formed in 2021, develops global standards for disclosing sustainability-related risks and opportunities to meet investor needs. Supported by international policymakers, the ISSB's standards draw on frameworks like TCFD and SASB. Initial standards, S1 and S2, cover general and climate-related financial disclosures, respectively. These standards require entities to disclose material information on sustainability risks, opportunities, governance, and risk management. The ISSB also coordinates capacity-building initiatives and engages with market oversight institutions and participants to facilitate global adoption and implementation of these standards.

The GRI Standards, widely used for corporate sustainability reporting, are often referenced in stock exchange guidance. The revised Universal Standards, effective from January 2023, ensure relevance through updates by the Global Sustainability Standards Board.

In 2022, The GRI's Global Sustainability Standards Board and the ISSB entered into a memorandum of understanding to coordinate standard setting activities. UNCTAD, through its Intergovernmental Working Group of Experts on International Standards of Accounting and Reporting, is assisting countries in strengthening their regulations, institutions, and human capacity to implement the ISSB standards.

UNCTAD established regional partnerships to promote sustainability and SDG reporting, with 50 members from 26 African countries and 29 members from 14 Latin American countries. It is also working to establish two additional partnerships in Asia and the Gulf region. The sustainable finance market consisting of funds, bonds and VCMs grew to $5.8 trillion in the year 2022.

Net Zero Transition[13]

According to Mckinsey report 2022 on net zero transition, the capital spending on physical assets for energy and land use systems during the period 2021–2050 would amount to $9.2 trillion per year on average. The report further states that as the power industry develops renewable energy source and enhances transmission and distribution capabilities, the comprehensive cost per unit of electricity production will increase by 25% approximately during the period 2020–2040. The transition is expected to result in a net gain of approximately 200 million jobs and a net loss of about 185 million direct and indirect employment opportunities globally by the year 2050. This is based on the job demand estimation in both operational activities and construction of physical assets. The transition may lead to a reduction of around nine million direct jobs in fossil fuel extraction, four million in fossil-based power sectors and eight million direct jobs in renewable power, hydrogen and biofuels by the year 2050. The sectors associated with high emission products or operations which constitute roughly 20% of global GDP will face significant challenges with respect to demand, production costs and employment. NGFS Net Zero 2050 scenario estimates that coal production for energy use is projected to cease by 2050 and the oil and gas production volumes is expected to decrease by approximately by 55–70%. By 2021, over 70 countries accounted for over 80% of global CO_2 emissions. As part of United Nations' Race to Zero campaign, 90% of global GDP as well as 5000 companies have adopted net zero commitments. According to the Mckinsey report 2022, the essential economic transformation requires substantial huge investment. The estimates in the report suggest that the total capital expenditure for the transition to net zero during the period 2021–2050 is estimated to be approximately $275 trillion. This implies a notable escalation in spending, with the need for an annual average increase from the current $5.7 trillion to $9.2 trillion

[13] The net-zero transition: What it would cost, what it could bring, Jan 2022, Mckinsey Report

throughout the period, resulting in a growth of $3.5 trillion. Considering anticipated rises in spending due to income and population growth, along with existing legislated transition policies, the mandated spending increase would be somewhat reduced but still approximately $1 trillion would be required. The report further states that a front-loaded impact will be anticipated with spending surging to nearly 9% of GDP between 2026 and 2030, up from the current 7%, before subsequently decreasing. Additionally, the projected delivered cost of electricity is expected to increase by approximately 25% from 2020 to 2040 in the modelled scenario, reaching a peak before experiencing regional variations and eventual decline.

Transformation of global economy is required for reaching net zero emissions. Financing the net zero transition involves determination of the most effective strategy for financing the transition. The most important factor towards this step is the need to assess which approach can swiftly and substantially raise the necessary capital. The financing plan must also involve consideration of the historical emissions record and identification of institutions with the capacity to contribute based on this history. The stakeholders must carefully evaluate the broader ripple effects associated with different financing approaches.

There are socioeconomic consequences of a net zero transition. Raising capital such as implementing taxes on consumers have the potential to constrain expenditures in other sectors of the economy. This imbalance could be mitigated through the implementation of fiscal stimulus in other areas. However, failure to strike a balance might lead to cascading effects on corporate revenues affecting industries, job creation, and overall economic growth. Developing countries might face challenges in independently securing the necessary capital for the transition.

The nature of the financing employed can play a crucial role in influencing the pace of the net-zero transition. For instance, certain technologies like electric vehicle (EV) charging infrastructure may necessitate extensive public financing to achieve the rapid deployment required to meet net-zero targets. It is imperative to consider these factors collectively to ensure that the financing strategies chosen are not only effective in raising capital but also mindful of the nature of the financing employed which can play a crucial role with broader implication on economic dynamics, equality, and the pace of the transition to a net-zero future.

Net zero emissions is achievable through the global transformation of energy and land use systems. It is estimated that energy use accounts for 83% of the CO_2 emitted across energy and land-use systems. Power consisting of electricity and heat generation account for 30% of CO_2 emissions, and 3% of nitrous oxide (N_2O) emissions. Industrial processes such as production of steel, cement, chemicals, extraction and refining of oil, gas and coal account for 30% of CO_2 emissions, 33% of methane emissions and 8% of nitrous oxide (N_2O) emissions. Transportation sector consisting of road, aviation, rail, maritime account for 19% of CO_2 emissions and 2% of N_2O emissions. Heating and cooking accounts for 6% of CO_2 emissions. Agriculture sector consisting of direct on farm energy use and emissions from agricultural practices and fishing account for 1% of CO_2 emissions, 38% of methane emissions, and 79% of N_2O emissions. Forestry and other land use basically cover 14% of CO_2 emissions, 5% of methane emissions, and 5% of N_2O emissions. Waste consisting of solid waste disposal and treatment, incineration and waste water treatment accounts of 23 percent of methane emissions and 3% of N_2O emissions. CO_2 is generated through the combustion of fossil fuels and non-energy emissions due to industrial processes such as reduction of iron ore to produce steel.

Power and industry sectors are major energy consumers which together account for approximately 60% of CO2 emissions. Decarbonization strategies involve transitioning from fossil fuels to zero-emission electricity and low-emission energy sources like hydrogen, optimizing industrial and agricultural processes, improving energy efficiency, adopting circular economy practices, reducing consumption of emissions-intensive goods, implementing carbon capture technology, and enhancing sinks for greenhouse gases. Preserving forests and promoting restoration are crucial for bolstering greenhouse gas sinks.

A net zero transition often have frontloaded effect on demand, capital allocation, costs and job creation. Achieving decarbonization in energy and land-use systems requires system level requirements involving physical infrastructure, economic and societal changes, and governance, institutions, and commitment.

Shifts in policies, technologies, and preferences during a net-zero transition may drive increased demand for low-emissions goods and services, while decreasing demand for high-emissions counterparts, leading to ripple effects throughout value chains. Achieving global economic decarbonization and ensuring low emissions in the future necessitates substantial capital investments in creating new physical assets and transforming existing ones. The implementation of low-emissions processes, investment, and a shift towards low-emission energy sources would lead to alterations in operating and production costs. Workforce needs would undergo changes as markets reshape and organizations adopt new operational practices and processes. The physical building blocks encompasses technological innovation, scalable supply chain system and support infrastructure along with the availability of necessary natural resources. According to McKinsey report, expenditure on physical assets for energy and land-use systems in the NGFS Net Zero 2050 scenario is projected to reach approximately $9.2 trillion annually. Production costs in the steel and cement sectors, encompassing operating costs, capital charges, and depreciation, may increase by approximately 30% and 45%, respectively, from their current levels, though ongoing innovation could potentially mitigate these estimates.

The McKinsey report suggest that the NGFS Net Zero 2050 scenario indicates that the transition may lead to a rise in demand for approximately 162 million direct and indirect jobs (termed “job gains”) and a reduction in demand for about 152 million direct and indirect jobs (referred to as “job losses”) in operations and maintenance by 2050 across various sectors of the economy.

Features of Net Zero Transition

Major energy and land use systems are required to undergo transformation for net zero goals given their significant individual contributions to emissions and high interdependence; coordinated actions across sectors, geographies, and global value chains are essential, recognizing variations in countries' roles and contributions. There would be significant shifts in demand for various goods and services such as demand for coal, oil and gas production along with a complete end to manufacturing of cars with internal combustion engines and dominance of zero emissions alternatives such as battery electric and fuel cell electric vehicles. It is expected that the capital spending is expected to rise in the early shift stage. Over time, the up front capital spending for the net zero transition could also lower other operating costs for consumers. Sectors such as steel, cement and automobiles which account for approximately 20% of GDP are directly exposed to the transition. According to Mckinsey report, lower-income countries, especially those heavily dependent on fossil fuels like sub-Saharan Africa, Latin America, India, and some Asian nations, face heightened exposure, needing capital spending of over 10% of GDP—1.5 times more than regions like Europe and the United States.

This capital deployment poses challenges due to the greater exposure of their economic activity, employment and capital stock that may require transformation.

The net zero transitions is characterized by physical climate risks as well as labor market disruption due to insufficient time for adaption. A substantial risk involves large-scale asset stranding if an abrupt transition results in the premature retirement or replacement of relatively new high-emissions assets with low-emissions alternatives before their standard replacement cycles.

Countries, sectors, and companies stand to gain considerable opportunities by accessing expanding markets during the transition to a net-zero economy, with nations possessing abundant natural capital such as more hours of sunshine or investing in technological, human, and physical capital being well-positioned to thrive. Companies have the potential to benefit from three opportunity categories: firstly, by decarbonizing processes and products, enhancing cost-effectiveness or accessing new markets for lower-emissions products; secondly, by developing entirely new low-carbon products and processes to replace established high-carbon options, such as meeting the demand for electric vehicles over internal combustion engine vehicles; and thirdly, by offering new products and services to support production in the first two categories. The potential opportunities include provision of inputs like lithium and cobalt for battery manufacturing, physical assets such as solar panels, and a diverse range of technical services spanning from forest management to financing to emissions measurement.[14]

[14] The net-zero transition: What it would cost, what it could bring, Jan 2022, Mckinsey Report

Economic and Societal Factors to Support Net Zero Transformation

Effective capital reallocation and new financing structures are required for net zero transition. Net zero transition necessitates both an increase in capital spending on low emissions assets and reallocation of capital from high emission assets to low emission assets. Scaling up climate finance requires increased commitments from public and private financial institutions toward net-zero emissions, necessitating additional funding from both conventional and specialized instruments like green bonds, while partnerships between financial institutions and real-economy stakeholders can facilitate mobilizing financing.

New financial products and structures, including special-purpose vehicles, can aid companies in phasing out high-emission legacy assets while scaling up new low-emission assets. Possible solutions involve ring-fencing legacy assets to align with a net-zero pathway and implementing financing structures like long-term purchase agreements for low-emission plants, which offer lower total life-cycle costs, along with the introduction of new financial instruments for negative emissions or nature-based solutions.

Establishing and expanding voluntary carbon markets in the short term and compliance markets in the long term could contribute to financing the transition, with carbon credits serving as a significant tool to support the net-zero journey by directing capital, for instance, toward forest-rich developing countries to prevent deforestation or promote afforestation.

The Taskforce on Scaling Voluntary Carbon Markets projects a potential increase in demand for carbon credits by a factor of 15 or more by 2030 and up to 100 by 2050, with the carbon credits market anticipated to be valued at over $50 billion in 2030. Governments have to explore policies involving organizations paying for their emissions to incentivize capital spending on emissions -reduction projects, with carbon pricing potentially generating revenue to support the transition.

Public or private entities assuming low-carbon project risks can attract investor financing through guarantees, aiding capital flow to critical infrastructure with market financing challenges. Organizations aiming to expedite the retirement of obsolete assets can consider purchasing and retiring coal-fired power plants, reinvesting the proceeds in low-emission energy projects.

Established by the United Nations Framework Convention on Climate Change, the Green Climate Fund, a major blended-finance facility have $30 billion funding equally allocated for climate-change mitigation and adaptation, with 173 approved projects since 2015. Technological innovation can reduce capital costs for net zero technologies faster than expected.

Role of Financial Institutions in Climate Transition

Financial institutions through their integral function of capital allocation, client advisory services and market infrastructure services play a significant role in climate transition-based economy. The trend observed is that there have been a growing number of voluntary net zero or sustainability commitments by financial institutions. The Sustainability Finance Working Group (SFWG) has initiated efforts to enhance the transparency and credibility of voluntary commitments by financial institutions. This includes identifying key elements of a credible net-zero commitment and suggesting voluntary actions that financial institutions, international organizations, and jurisdictions can undertake to support these commitments within existing legal frameworks. SFWG suggest integration of net-zero commitments into all operations and strategies, aligning with efforts to limit global temperature rise to well below 2 °C and pursuing 1.5 °C targets. The recommendation of SFWG also include suggestion to engage clients and portfolio companies to align practices with sectoral pathways and support voluntary net zero commitments. The SFWG has created voluntary recommendations for Multilateral Development Banks (MDBs), International Organizations (IOs), financial institutions, and country authorities to boost sustainable finance instruments, particularly for developing economies and SMEs, aligning with national development objectives and priorities.

The G20 highlights governments' role in a just transition and resilient finance's role in mobilizing private finance, addressing gaps in sustainable finance. The G20 Sustainable Finance Roadmap, endorsed as voluntary by G20 Leaders in October 2021, outlines actions to integrate transition considerations in sustainable finance. It tasked the G20 SFWG to collaborate with international organizations to create high-level principles for financing a just climate transition. These principles, developed with input from various organizations and market practice analyses, are for voluntary use by jurisdictions and financial institutions, considering local contexts. The principles focus on five pillars: identifying transitional activities and investments, reporting transition activities, developing transition finance instruments, designing policy measures, and assessing and mitigating the negative social and economic impacts of transition activities. To enhance the financial sector's resilience and support investment for a just and affordable climate transition, it is essential to develop and utilize diverse financial instruments to finance the transition of the entire economy. The SFWG have identified a range of transition finance instruments to facilitate funding for the climate transition process. This includes debt instruments, equity related instruments and risk mitigation products. The debt instruments consist of Use of proceeds green/transition bonds/loans, sustainability-linked loans/bonds, fixed/term deposits, reimbursable loans, and other debt finance tools. The equity related instruments consist of transition-focused buyout funds, venture capital funds, mezzanine financing, and other equity investments, particularly for companies adopting new technologies or highly indebted companies and SMEs. The risk mitigation products consist of insurance products for hedging transition-related risks, risk mitigation tools like guarantees, credit enhancement products, and blended-finance instruments to mitigate transition risks. The other instruments include asset backed securities, real estate investment trusts, blended finance and exchange traded funds which align investment portfolios with the climate transition. The emphasis ought to be on contribution toward decarbonization and financial stability considerations.

Private Financial Institutions play a crucial role in advancing the climate transition and achieving Agenda 2030 by financing activities and investments in low-emission technologies and adaptation measures. During the period 2020–2022, over 4508 private sector financial firms primarily in developed countries have voluntarily committed to net-zero or other climate-related goals. There are many challenges faced by FIs from making credible net zero commitments. The lack of capacity to collect and verify emissions data or climate adaptation needs poses challenges for FIs to track and report the emissions of their clients with supply chains.

The absence of tools, methodologies, and technical capabilities, such as those for transition pathways or scenario analysis, can deter some FIs from making commitments. This challenge is compounded for firms operating across jurisdictions with varying national climate goals, net-zero timelines, or adaptation requirements. Moreover, FIs, like other corporations, must fulfill pre-existing legal obligations to clients and stakeholders.

Market Practices on Climate Commitments

Various market-led alliances, voluntary standard-setters, think tanks, and organizations, such as Partnership for Carbon Accounting Financials(PCAF), Science -based Targets Initiative(SBTi), Transition Pathway Initiative (TPI), Paris Agreement Capital Transition Assessment(PACTA) manager, UN Partnership programmes such as Principles for Responsible Banking; Sustainable Principles for Sustainable Insurance; Principles for Responsible Investing; Sustainable Stock Exchanges, U.N. Race to Zero and Glasgow Financial Alliance for Net-Zero(GFANZ) offer or are developing guidance and recommendations. These resources assist FIs in adopting tools and methodologies to voluntarily set and implement net-zero commitments. SFWG recommends the need to adopt monitor metrics consistently to track net zero strategy implementation for example emissions targets and climate solution scaling. There is a need to integrate net zero into governance, skills and culture. Sector specific decarbonization strategies are required to be deployed which aid client alignment with sector pathways. There is a need for collaboration for an orderly climate transition which addresses social impacts with clients, companies and governments.

Clear policies must be established and applied in relation to high emitting sectors and associated low emission technologies. Policies must be developed with respect to use of carbon credits and offsets. For example, policies related to prioritizing mitigation actions to reduce direct emissions before offsetting with carbon credits, only using carbon credits for residual emissions, neutralize residual financed emissions with permanent removals.

Challenges for Scaling Up Sustainable Finance Instruments[15]

The barriers to scaling sustainable finance instruments can be categorized as generic financial market challenges and specific sustainable finance obstacles. Generic barriers, like inadequate market infrastructure and risk management tools, hinder overall financial market development. Addressing these foundational issues is crucial for effective sustainable finance policies and project quality. In different countries, regulators, financiers, and corporations still inadequately integrate sustainability into decision-making processes due to limited technical and financial expertise. Developing nations often lack the capacity to initiate and manage demonstration projects, crucial for proving sustainable project viability. There is a need to mitigate risk perceptions and redirect capital towards sustainable investments in emerging markets. Many countries face challenges in establishing clear approaches, rules, and regulations to enhance risk management and steer investments towards sustainability. This includes gaps in regulations for alternative financing mechanisms like Islamic finance, increasing the risk of greenwashing and deterring investors from adopting sustainable finance instruments. Coordinating sustainable finance regulatory frameworks across diverse domestic agencies proves particularly challenging.

International investors demand detailed sustainability information, often missing in financial statements. Developing country corporates and SMEs struggle to provide this due to regulatory gaps and high costs, complicating capital access and increasing sustainable finance product costs. Low-income countries often have low credit ratings, hindering investment. Despite positive impacts from technical assistance and international de-risking facilities, supply remains insufficient and needs expansion. In nascent sustainable finance markets, perceived risks and low returns deter investors. Demonstration projects could mitigate these concerns, but developing countries often need international assistance to initiate them. Low investment in transitional activities in low-income countries is lagging due to a risky environment. These risks include political conflicts, climate events like droughts, geophysical threats like earthquakes, and epidemics and disease outbreaks. There is a shortage of sustainable finance instruments for firms in low-income countries and SMEs. Many of these firms struggle to find relevant instruments for their primary industries, and SMEs often lack the expertise and capital to access sustainable loans, sukuk, and bond markets.

Steps to Improve Sustainable Finance Access and Affordability

Some of the key emerging options suggested by SFWG to improve sustainable finance access and affordability include capacity building, de-risking facilities, policy incentives, and deploying digital technologies, and sustainable supply chain financing.

---

[15] Sustainable Finance Working Group (SFWG), 20 2 2 G 2 0 Sustainable Finance Report

For enhancing capacity building on sustainable finance, stakeholders, including governments, stock exchanges, asset owners, financial firms, and corporates, need expertise in sustainable finance to design and implement policies supporting SDGs and the Paris Agreement. Key areas include climate risk awareness, policymaking, alignment approaches, disclosure requirements, and sustainable finance data ecosystems. SMEs and local financial institutions face challenges accessing sustainable finance due to high costs and capacity limitations. Capacity-building efforts by IOs, MDBs, and other organizations have positively shaped sustainable finance frameworks and can be scaled up to enhance sustainability in domestic financial systems. Blended finance was a key focus of the G20 Development Working Group (DWG) for developing G20 Principles to scale up blended finance in developing countries which include Least Developed Countries (LDCs) and Small Island Developing States (SIDS). Blending practices differ across institutions, using concessional and non-concessional public finance from MDBs, DFIs, development aid programs, and donors. Blended finance attracts private capital, increasing sustainable finance availability and improving affordability and accessibility. It can also develop sustainable markets. Successful cases exist, but supply from MDBs and IFIs falls short of demand due to limited concessional financing, complex relationship management, high administrative costs, and MDBs' risk limitations. Specialized expertise, high costs, and long project durations further challenge the scaling up of blended finance and de-risking facilities.

Public policy can enhance access to sustainable finance and improve the risk-return profile of sustainable investments to attract private sector participation. The G20 Sustainable Finance Roadmap commits the SFWG to work with relevant groups and organizations to analyze public policy impacts on market signals. Policy instruments include carbon taxes, emission trading, fiscal subsidies, green procurement, and regulatory measures for transparency and risk management. These incentives can reduce investment risks, enhance returns, and attract private capital, complementing ambitious financial sector policies. Innovation is crucial for financing transformative climate technologies, especially in developing countries and smaller companies. Digital technologies can reduce data collection and reporting costs, aiding in identifying sustainable assets and tracking ESG information. They can lower costs for SMEs and firms in sectors like agriculture and tourism, improving access to sustainable finance. Technologies like mobile payments and SSCF enhance financial inclusivity and reduce funding costs for SMEs. Integrating technologies such as AI and blockchain with sustainable asset management can improve transaction efficiency and risk management, though these technologies are still nascent and not widely deployed, especially in developing countries. Using methodologies and data to rank supplier's sustainability performance, Sustainable supply chain finance integrates ESG aspects into regular supply chain finance and offers preferential financing for suppliers with good sustainability performance.

Supply Chain Sustainable Finance (SSCF) involves financial institutions (FIs), focal companies, SME suppliers, and third-party rating agencies. Fintech tools like digital platforms and blockchain facilitate SSCF operations, benefiting sectors such as manufacturing, electronics, textiles, and agriculture in global and regional economies. SSCF enhances SME access to sustainable finance, lowering their funding costs through mechanisms like low-cost loans and payment advances based on sustainability scores assessed by focal companies or third-party ratings. Regulatory frameworks, like the EU's due diligence regulations, are increasingly incorporating SSCF to address environmental and social issues across supply chains, with potential government support.

Climate Transition Initiatives by Nations and Institutions[16]

In March 2020, Japan's Ministry of Economy, Trade, and Industry (METI) introduced principles on Transition Finance. In May 2021, METI, the Ministry of Environment, and the Financial Services Agency issued the "Basic Guidelines on Climate Transition Finance" based on ICMA's Handbook, guiding market participants on transition finance issuance. Issuers must outline transition pathways and targets aligned with the Paris Agreement. Sector-specific decarbonization roadmaps for industries like iron, steel, chemistry, and more have been developed, with an automobile roadmap planned for FY2022. A subsidy scheme for third-party verification supports companies' transitions.

The EU Taxonomy for Sustainable Activities (EU Regulation (EU) 2020/852) is basically a classification system listing environmentally sustainable economic activities. It offers taxonomy to assist companies, investors, and policymakers identify sustainable activities, aiming to secure investments, prevent greenwashing, and guide climate-friendly business practices. Larger and/or listed companies must report on their sustainable activities, although use of the classification beyond reporting is voluntary. The regulation defines six environmental objectives and four conditions for qualifying as environmentally sustainable. The delegated acts outline the technical criteria for each objective. The taxonomy includes low carbon and transitional activities for climate change mitigation. Transitional activities lack feasible low-carbon alternatives but aid in moving towards a climate-neutral economy, aligned with limiting temperature rise to 1.5 °C above pre-industrial levels. They must achieve best sectoral performance in emissions, support low-carbon development, and avoid locking in carbon-intensive assets. Currently, the Taxonomy identifies 28 transitional activities across five sectors: manufacturing, energy, transport, construction and real estate, and information and communication. Criteria for these activities focus on carbon intensity, energy efficiency, and transition pathways. For example, the activity "renovation of existing buildings" would be a transitional activity if it meets the following two technical screening criteria of substantial contribution to climate change mitigation and no significant harm to any of the five other objectives of the EU. The building renovation must meet the applicable major renovation requirements or achieves a minimum 30% reduction in primary energy

[16] 2022 G20 Sustainable Finance Report, Sustainable Finance Working Group

demand. In addition to meeting the Technical Screening Criteria, transitional activities must adhere to minimum social safeguards and information disclosure requirements for both financial and non-financial undertakings. For instance, a financial product must disclose the environmental objectives it supports and describe how and to what extent its investments qualify as transitional activities under the EU Taxonomy.

Taxonomy for Transitions

The EU's green and sustainable finance Taxonomy provides a science-based classification system for investors, governments, and organizations to make informed financial decisions addressing climate and environmental emergencies. It offers robust definitions and transparent reporting to boost financing for activities significantly contributing to environmental goals while avoiding harm and meeting social safeguards. Despite its rigorous criteria, the Taxonomy acknowledges that many sectors must transit to sustainable models even if they can't achieve green performance levels. Some activities are not included due to a lack of sustainable options or low impact. These require specific financing to transition from harmful practices (e.g., inefficient power production) to more sustainable ones.

The current Taxonomy leaves many economic activities unclassified, which some might misinterpret as negative, risking reduced financing for these areas. However, the Taxonomy's initial focus was to clarify top-end green classifications, not to signal negatively about non-aligned activities. Expanding the Taxonomy framework to include other performance levels could enhance transparency, support nuanced decision-making, and aid the entire economy's environmental transition.

The Taxonomy Regulation mandates the European Commission to explore extending the Taxonomy to additional activities. The forthcoming report under Article 26 will incorporate recommendations from the Platform, offering guidance to financial markets and stakeholders on extending the framework to better support a comprehensive environmental transition.

A Sustainable Finance approach addressing environmental objectives must robustly define and incentivize funding for activities that can significantly contribute to resolving global climate and environmental crises. However, this approach should also:

- Define and incentivize opportunities to urgently transform activities that are currently exacerbating climate and environmental crises but have the potential to improve.
- Identify activities that cannot undergo transition and for which the only compatible action with environmental goals is to decommission or shut them down, while implementing robust measures to support affected people and economies.

(continued)

(continued)

- Encourage finance across all sectors to enhance environmental performance, aiming for an overall benefit, even if individual contributions are not substantially significant.

Source: Platform on Sustainable Finance, The Extended Environmental Taxonomy: Final Report on Taxonomy extension options supporting a sustainable transition, March 2022.2203 29-sustainable-finance-platform-finance-report-environmental-transition-taxonomy_en.pdf (europa.eu)

Another example for transitional finance activity can be illustrated through China's Huzhou City Transition Finance Catalog. This catalog was issued in 2022 as the first municipal level transition finance taxonomy in China. The catalog lists different financial instruments to assist the decarbonization of GHG-intensive companies and adoption of low carbon technologies. Local governmental agencies in the province collaborated to create a catalogue of 30 transitional activities with low-carbon transition performance targets in nine sectors: power, ferrous metal, non-ferrous metal, non-metal mineral products, chemical, fibre, textile, paper, and agriculture. Each sector includes specific technical transition pathways, such as installing solar panels on agricultural greenhouses, integrating fisheries for carbon sinks, returning crop straw to farmland for carbon sequestration, and managing livestock manure to reduce GHG emissions. The catalogue sets performance benchmarks and targets, measured by energy efficiency improvements and/or GHG intensity reduction. Huzhou initiated transition projects based on the catalogue, offering incentives like interest subsidies and guarantees.

The Ministry of Economy (ME) in Brazil has integrated ESG criteria into public debt management and sovereign guarantees for international loans, and simplified the approval process for green bond issuance for infrastructure investments in consultation with Brazil's Financial Innovation Lab (Lab). The Lab is a platform comprising over 1000 sustainable finance experts from various sectors, promoting sustainable finance through knowledge sharing, innovative instrument piloting, and policy dialogue. Led by Brazil's Securities and Exchange Commission (CVM), the Brazilian Association of Development Banks (ABDE), the Inter-American Development Bank (IDB), and Deutsche Gesellschaft für Internationale Zusammenarbeit (GIZ), the Lab has published 44 reports, conducted 40 webinars, and engaged in regulatory initiatives. It is a member of the International Network of Financial Centres for Sustainability (FC4S). Since 2018, Brazil has partnered with countries to advance sustainable finance through the Finanças Brasileiras Sustentáveis (FiBraS) project, funded by Germany's BMZ and implemented by GIZ, ME, and the Central Bank of Brazil (BCB), aiming to mobilize investments for green economic development and resilience against climate and social risks.

The Bank of China (BOC) had issued its first transition bond in the offshore market in the year 2021 and raised a total amount of approximately RMB 6 billion. By December 2021, the issuance proceeds were allocated to the BOC Transition

Portfolio which was split between two sectors of 92% for the public utility industry and 8% for the cement industry. Through these projects, the expected annual emission reductions were 418,915 tons and 3531 tons respectively in these sectors. The proceeds were used to support eligible projects in both China and the EU, covering acquisition, research and development, manufacturing, construction, equipment operation and maintenance, procurement, and installation of equipment and related facilities. The Bank of China (BOC) set thresholds for project eligibility based on "Avoidance of Carbon Lock-in," "Do No Significant Harm," and a list of "Explicitly Excluded Projects." For the public utility industry, projects must emit below 72.8 tons CO2/TJ of natural gas in China and below 100 grams CO2e/kWh in the EU. In the cement industry, the clinker-to-cement ratio must be below 0.64 in China, with energy consumption at or below 105 kg standard coal/ton (3.07 GJ/ton), and carbon emissions below 0.766 tons CO2e/ton in the EU.

During April 2021, the North America based BMO Financial Group entered into a deal with Canadian energy company Gibson Energy by amending an existing credit facility deal of $750 million Canadian dollar to a five-year Sustainability linked revolving credit facility. This facility featured a margin adjustment incentive mechanism linked to Gibson's commitment to reducing carbon emissions and increasing the representation of women, as well as racial and ethnic minorities, in its workforce and on its board. Part of Gibson's borrowing costs in this transaction will depend on meeting pre-determined sustainability targets. This facility included commitments to reduce Scope 1 and Scope 2 GHG emissions intensity by 15% by 2025 and to increase the representation of women in its workforce to 40–42% and racial and ethnic minorities to 21–23% by 2025. Additionally, it aimed to enhance governance by increasing the representation of women on the Board to at least 40%, with at least one Board member identified as a racial, ethnic, or Indigenous minority by 2025.

The EU, committed to climate neutrality by 2050 through its European Climate Law, faces socio-economic challenges, particularly in fossil fuel-dependent regions. To address these, the EU launched the Just Transition Mechanism (JTM), offering financial resources and technical assistance through three funding pillars: the Just Transition Fund (JTF), the Invest EU Just Transition Scheme, and a new Public Sector Loan Facility. The JTF, with a budget of €19.32 billion for 2021–2027, supports economic diversification and clean energy projects, prioritizing regions most impacted by fossil fuel phase-out. The Public Sector Loan Facility combines EU grants with loans from the European Investment Bank to mobilize €25–30 billion in public investment for just transition territories.

The primary focus of the Energy Transition Mechanism (ETM) in Southeast Asia is the retirement of legacy coal plants and ensuring a just transition for the affected regions. Funded by grants and highly concessional loans from governments and philanthropies, the pilot ETM will provide concessional finance and technical assistance. ETM funding will be channelled in two ways: investing in private sector independent power producers (IPPs) and state-owned utilities via direct support or co-financing from the Asian Development Bank (ADB), and supporting legacy coal retirement and clean energy projects through country facilities in collaboration with international financial institutions (IFIs) and local/international investors.

The pilot ETM will invest through the Carbon Reduction Fund (CRF) and the Clean Energy Fund (CEF), focusing on early coal plant retirement and renewable energy investments, respectively. Various transaction models will be explored to achieve earlier coal plant retirements. Technical assistance under ETM will cover a range of topics, including just transition, skills and livelihood development, policy and regulatory support, and carbon finance development. Commitment to safeguards and a just transition are crucial components of ETM's mission. Planned activities include regional feasibility studies, environmental and socio-economic scoping studies, and just transition assessments.

In 2021, Italy's Ministry of Economy and Finance (MEF), supported by the European Commission, initiated the "Sustainable Finance and Investments for the Transition to a Green Economy" project. This aimed to develop Italy's Sovereign Green Bond (SGB) Framework, assess the investment needed for climate neutrality by 2050, devise policies to channel private finance towards sustainable investments, and evaluate the socio-economic impacts of the low-carbon transition. Italy entered the sovereign green bond market with the "2045 BTP Green," raising €13,265.13 million through two tranches. The inaugural issue attracted around 530 investors, mostly ESG-focused, with a total demand exceeding €80 billion. The funds will support Italy's Green Transition strategy, aligned with EU Sustainable Finance Taxonomy objectives and the UN's 2030 Sustainable Development Goals. A draft Sustainable Finance Action Plan (SFAP) was also developed, proposing 15 high-level recommendations to integrate climate and environmental factors into the financial system and mobilize private finance for sustainable growth. The Bank of Italy published its first report on sustainable investments and climate-related risks, aligned with TCFD recommendations, demonstrating significant progress in integrating ESG criteria into its investment strategies. The report highlighted Italy's governance enhancements, sustainable investment strategy expansion, improved risk management incorporating climate-related factors, and superior ESG metrics and targets. The Bank's internally managed equity portfolio reduced its carbon footprint by 60% since 2018, outperforming market benchmarks in environmental and social metrics.

The UAE committed to achieving net-zero emissions by 2050 through its Net-Zero 2050 strategic initiative, aligning with the Paris Climate Agreement. Sustainability is also a key pillar of the UAE's Vision 2021, which set eleven KPIs for environmental sustainability. The UAE has a notable international presence in sustainability, highlighted by its upcoming hosting of COP28. To support these commitments, the UAE established the Sustainable Finance Working Group (SFWG) in 2019, which advances the nation's sustainability agenda by developing a national sustainable finance taxonomy and setting governance and disclosure standards for the private sector. In 2021, SFWG members publicly committed to achieving the UAE's sustainability objectives and net-zero goals.

Guided by the Sustainable Finance Framework 2021–2031, the SFWG aims to mobilize capital for sustainable investments and create innovative financial products like green bonds and loans. The Framework has three main pillars: integrating environmental sustainability into financial policies, providing sustainable financial products and incentives, and fostering skills, research, and entrepreneurship in sustainable finance.

Table 5.8 gives the policy incentive experiences of select countries and economic unions.[17]

The InsuResilience Global Partnership (IGP) for Climate and Disaster Risk Finance and Insurance Solutions is a global initiative involving multiple stakeholders. Its goal is to enhance the resilience of developing countries and safeguard the lives and livelihoods of poor and vulnerable populations against climate risks and disasters through Climate and Disaster Risk Finance and Insurance (CDRFI) solutions.

The InsuResilience Global Partnership (IGP) originated from the 2015 G7 InsuResilience Initiative and was established in 2017 by the G20 and the Vulnerable Twenty (V20) Group at the UNFCCC COP23. The Partnership collaborates within the international resilience and climate community to amplify efforts and foster collaboration for expanding Climate and Disaster Risk Finance and Insurance (CDRFI) in developing nations. By the end of 2021, IGP included over 110 members from various sectors and had implemented more than 300 CDRFI projects in over 100

Table 5.8 Policy incentive experiences

Incentives	Examples
Carbon pricing and emission trading mechanisms	EU Emissions Trading System (ETS) started in year 2005. US GHG emission cap and trade regimes started in year 2009. Korea Emission Trading Scheme started in year 2015. UK Emissions Trading Scheme started in year 2021.
Central Bank Initiatives	In November 2021, China central bank, PBOC, introduced the carbon reduction supporting facility to support three key green sectors. The European Central Bank (ECB) has accepted bonds with coupons linked to sustainability performance targets as eligible central bank collateral. The ECB has also announced its intention to gradually decarbonize its corporate bond holdings, aligning this process with the goals of the Paris Agreement. Hungarian Central Bank, Magyar Nemzeti Bank, introduced the Green Mortgage Bond Purchase programs with focus on sustainability. In 2021, Bank of Japan introduced the Funds Supplying Operations to support financing for climate change responses. By July 2022, a total amount of JPY 3643.6 billion was disbursed under the operations. Bank Indonesia introduced Green RPIM which allowed the bank to fulfil the Macroprudential Inclusive Financing Ratio (RPIM) requirement through the purchase of sustainable/green bonds. Banco Central do Brasil developed a regulatory framework on rural credit in compliance with environmental standards and created a new section on social, environmental and climate impediments.

(continued)

[17] 2022 G20 Sustainable Finance Report, Sustainable Finance Working Group

Table 5.8 (continued)

Incentives	Examples
Other Policy Instruments	Ministry of Finance and Environmental Protection, China introduced a government green procurement system in the year 2006 with guidance on the scope, working procedures and specific management methods for green procurement. Since 2016, Indonesia have started green budgeting though climate budget tagging system. In 2018, Indonesia introduced the SDG Indonesia One (SIO) platform as a financing channel for infrastructure projects with the SDGs impacts. The SIO platform uses blended finance mechanism and have partnership with International organizations, development banks and commercial banks. In 2021, the government of Japan had developed a Green Innovation Fund with value of two trillion yen for the goal of achieving carbon neutrality by the year 2050. The government of Singapore launched Green and Sustainability linked loan grant scheme (GSLS) to cover corporate expenses for independent sustainability assessment services to develop green frameworks, obtain external reviews and report on sustainability targets. The Australian government in the year 2020 launched the AUD 300 million Advancing Hydrogen Fund to support hydrogen powered projects. In 2021, Canadian government introduced the Green Homes Grant to facilitate homes to save energy and combat climate change. In 2011, South Africa introduced the National Green Fund to offer finance for investment in green initiatives.
Regulatory Measures	Additional floorspace allowance for green buildings were introduced by India. UK introduced the Ten Point Plan to establish the foundation for a Green Industrial Revolution and reduce UK emissions by 180 million tonnes during the period 2023–2032. Germany adopted Sustainable finance strategy to promote sustainability aspects into schemes of governmental agencies. This strategy consist of a comprehensive package of a total of 26 measures within financial market policies. The German Future Funds initiative aims to bolster the European Venture Capital ecosystem, addressing Germany's growth financing gap with over €10 billion from state-owned investors. Germany is founding member of the international coalition "Export Finance for Future" ("E3F") in order to develop sustainable and climate friendly export finance policies

countries, offering financial protection to over 150 million people. IGP supports sovereign-level CDRFI instruments for rapid government liquidity in disasters, as well as meso- and micro-level instruments for direct financial relief to households and businesses. Under the 2022 German G7 Presidency, efforts began to create a Global Shield against Climate Risks, aiming to consolidate and enhance CDRFI activities globally, ensuring systematic, coordinated, and sustained financial protection.

The European Bank of Reconstruction and Development (EBRD) has been actively supporting green and sustainable finance in Kazakhstan and other member countries. As a leading green bond issuer and investor, the EBRD has facilitated 34 green bond issuances in Central Asia since 2017. Their technical assistance (TA) program provides issuers with tools like Gap Analysis Checklists and Energy Performance Criteria. Additionally, the EBRD has helped create an enabling environment for green capital markets by developing policy frameworks for sustainable finance. In Kazakhstan, the EBRD has supported the creation of a local green financial system roadmap and policy recommendations for green market incentives. In 2021, the EBRD and Kazakhstan signed a five-year partnership to design a framework for decarbonizing the energy sector by 2060. The EBRD also collaborates with Kazakhstan's financial regulatory body to promote ESG and corporate climate governance, aiding in the development of guidelines to address climate-related risks.

The International Finance Corporation (IFC) has assisted regulators and financial institutions (FIs) in developing countries by enhancing their skills and knowledge through platforms like the Sustainable Banking and Finance Network (SBFN). Originally called the Sustainable Banking Network, SBFN aims to build capacity for financial regulators, ministries, and industry associations in emerging markets. It offers peer-to-peer knowledge sharing and technical support from IFC and World Bank programs. SBFN now includes 72 member institutions from 62 countries, representing 86% of banking assets in emerging markets. It issues biennial Global Progress Reports and individual Country Progress Reports to benchmark sustainable finance initiatives. SBFN's four thematic working groups focus on Measurement, Sustainable Finance Instruments, Low-income Member Countries, and Data & Disclosure, supporting members in ESG risk management and increasing capital flows to socially and environmentally positive activities. As of April 2022, 47 SBFN member countries have issued over 200 national sustainable finance frameworks, with guidelines for green finance instruments established in 24 countries.

Nepal, rich in hydropower resources, has struggled to utilize them due to insufficient investment in large projects. As a result, the country imports electricity and fossil fuels to meet its power needs. In 2019, with blended concessional finance support from Canada, IDA18 Private Sector Window, Finland, and Climate Investment Funds, Nepal secured its largest foreign direct investment for the UT-1 hydropower project. This $650 million project, financed by IFC, ADB, MIGA, AIIB, Proparco, FMO, and CDC, will develop a 216 MW run-of-the-river hydropower plant north of Kathmandu. UT-1 aims to improve electricity access, create jobs, and set new environmental and social standards for future projects.

CRAFT, sponsored by the European Investment Bank, is the first private sector investment vehicle dedicated entirely to climate adaptation and resilience in Latin America, Asia, and Africa. It provides growth capital to companies offering tech-enabled services, engineering, data, and solutions aimed at enhancing climate adaptation and resilience, primarily in developing countries. Structured as a layered fund, CRAFT includes first-loss protection through junior shares, which constitute around 10% of total commitments. These junior shares are initially provided by the Government of Luxembourg and the Nordic Development Fund. The total project cost is approximately USD 250 million.

The Mongolia Green Finance Corporation (MGFC) is a joint public-private initiative designed to address climate change mitigation challenges in Mongolia. It aims to provide green, affordable, and gender-inclusive financing for households and businesses to adopt low-carbon technologies. The MGFC also seeks to improve policy environments and build stakeholder capacity and awareness. The total project financing is estimated at USD 49.7 million, with USD 26.7 million requested from the Green Climate Fund. The Mongolian government has committed at least USD five million in equity investment, with additional interest from financial institutions. A key component involves wholesale lending to Participating Financial Institutions (PFIs) for energy-efficient, low-carbon, and affordable housing projects.

The Islamic Development Bank (IsDB) and TRINE, a crowdfunding platform, partnered to promote solar home systems (SHS) in developing countries through a crowdfunding financing mechanism. The IsDB invested in various crowdfunding campaigns using Murabaha (cost-plus financing), catalyzing investment with patient repayment terms and longer loan tenors. This structure allows the IsDB to receive repayment in one bullet payment, reducing cash flow management stress for borrowers and prioritizing smaller investors in case of default. The IsDB's involvement shortened campaign periods significantly, showcasing a catalytic effect.

Crowd investing in solar is new, with an undefined risk profile. Institutional investors like IsDB absorb potential volatility impacts, boosting smaller investor confidence. This combined investment approach benefits both investors and off-grid solar solution users. Investments transition communities can shift from fossil fuels to renewable energy, contributing to climate change mitigation and offering broader development benefits beyond achieving SDG 7. The debt financing model also ensures returns for investors.

Carbon Pricing is viewed as a cost-effective method to reduce emissions. Country and/or sector specific assessments are essential for developing an appropriate policy mix. It is important to understand the international impacts of Carbon Adjustment Mechanisms (CBAM) on emerging markets. Steps ought to be initiated to monitor the effectiveness of carbon pricing relative to non-pricing mechanism. The allocation of revenues from carbon taxes is a crucial element in policy design. There exist several challenges in allocating policy incentives to influence investment decisions. If information asymmetry is not managed properly, it can result in green and SDG washing where project stakeholders falsely claim sustainability to gain incentives. The cost effectiveness of policy incentives varies by country, thereby necessitating further analysis to determine the price equivalency of non-pricing policy instruments.[18]

[18] 2022 G20 Sustainable Finance Report, Sustainable Finance Working Group

Significance of Financial Market Infrastructure for Sustainable Finance[19]

In response to climate emergency, the market for sustainable finance is witnessing rapid growth. The sustainable finance market directly and indirectly advances the United Nations' Sustainable Development Goals (SDGs), which faces an annual financing gap of US$ 2–4 trillion. A cross border Financial Market Infrastructure (FMI) driven approach encourages greater sustainable finance issuance through reducing infrastructure, regulatory and informational barriers for issuance. FMI approach will facilitate processing ESG information flows which include ESG metrics, disclosure and assurance. According to strategy& Pwc executive report on sustainable finance market 2021, the adoption of FMI approach will mobilize around $25 trillion additional capital in global sustainable finance market by the year 2030. Around 1.3% of the current global annual CO2 equivalent emissions will be saved by the additional capital mobilised by the year 2030. The report suggests that if all expected social finance by sovereign, supranational, agency and municipal issuers are directed towards funding education, then about 430 million low and lower middle-income children could afford primary school education.

There are challenges with respect to sustainable finance market. Differences in taxonomy and criteria for ESG performance have resulted in varying asset classifications and ESG scores, each with distinct methodologies. This, at best, complicates comparability and, at worst, fuels perceptions of greenwashing. Greenwashing occurs when there is a discrepancy between the expectations of issuers and investors regarding what qualifies as 'green' or 'sustainable.' It typically arises from miscommunication and misunderstandings between issuers and investors.

Tokenising proof-of-impact data involves using blockchain to create digital representations of sustainability metrics like CO2 reductions or trees planted. These impact tokens can provide investors with immediate access to impact data, potentially integrating impact reporting into asset servicing through a blockchain system managed by financial market infrastructures (FMIs). The UNDP CedarCoin initiative, reforesting Lebanon's cedar forests, uses impact tokens to instantly share GPS-located tree planting photos with investors, streamlining post-issuance reporting. It can also aid automated data collection and real time impact data. This type of automated reporting is particularly viable for clean energy projects where megawatt hours of clean energy produced can be measured directly. Through the use of impact tokens, the impact of an investment can be tracked through supply chains, providing a more accurate view of the total impact of investments. FishCoin utilizes blockchain technology and a peer-to-peer network, enabling all parties in the seafood supply chain, including consumers and governments, to trace their fish back to the sea. Registering impact data on a blockchain ledger creates a transparent, secure

[19] Scaling the sustainable finance market, A cross-border financial market infrastructure-driven approach, Executive Report, 2021. strategy&Part of the Pwc network.

record of a sustainable asset's performance. This prevents greenwashing, promotes issuer accountability, and enhances investor trust in sustainable securities.

The advantage of FMI systems to transfer rules based information can be applied for tagging the universe of sustainable finance securities and this mechanism offers an initial screening solution to investors thereby simplifying the due diligence process for investors. These interventions can optimize issuer -investor engagement. The processing of ESG information flows can be improved primarily through distribution and corporate actions processing which will improve the transparency of the sustainable finance market.

The creation of a cross border FMI database of ESG screened public sector financial system can facilitate reference data on the borrower, form of support which will enable transition of sustainable finance related investment opportunities to secondary markets within the private sector. Cross border FMI can also create linkage between the informal and formal sustainable finance markets to crowd -in participants on supply and demand sides. FMI database can facilitate the trading and settlement of pooled, sustainable crowdfunding products on platforms and exchanges.

According to Pwc Report 2021, FMI driven approach can accelerate the growth of sustainable finance market by up to 2.5% through price and non-price channels. This translates into up to US$ 25 trillion additional capital mobilised in the sustainable finance market by year 2030. United Nations Conference on Trade and Development (UNCTAD) and Global Sustainable Investment Alliance (GSIR) had estimated the value of sustainable finance market at US$ 30 trillion in year 2018. The report states that through the cross border FMI driven approach, even with a modest annual increase of 1 percentage point in the market share of emerging and developing economies, could result in an additional US$17.7 trillion for emerging and frontier economies and US$7.4 trillion for developed economies by 2030. In April 2021, the US government has announced its target to reduce emissions by 50–52% by 2030, compared to 2005 levels.

A cross-border FMI-driven approach could accelerate financing for the UN's SDGs by up to 0.6 to 1.1 years (7–13 months). Achieving the SDGs requires US$5 to 7 trillion annually, with a current shortfall of US$2 to 4 trillion per year until 2030. Increasing the sustainable finance market share by just 1 percentage point from 2023 to 2030 could help bridge this gap, resulting in significant time savings.

Emerging and frontier economies currently face the most significant SDG financing shortfall, with the UN's Sustainable Development Solutions Network estimating a funding gap of US$1.4 trillion to US$3 trillion per year for low-income countries.

The Strategy& 2021 report find that cross-border FMI-driven approach to sustainable finance could reduce global CO_2 emissions by 0.1–1.3% annually. Environmental finance, prioritizing climate change mitigation and adaptation, will dominate the sustainable finance market until 2030, reflecting its historical emphasis over social and governance ESG categories. The study by Gibon et al. (2020) estimates the aggregated life-cycle assessment based impacts of green bonds issued by the European Investment Bank during the period 2015–2018 and finds a savings range of 29–359 tonnes CO_2 eq per million euro.

A cross-border FMI-driven approach could provide primary education to up to 430 million children. Social finance is expected to comprise about 20% of the sustainable finance market by 2030. With an annual average of US$232 billion potentially allocated to education, this could bridge the US$193 billion annual financing gap for SDG 4, ensuring inclusive and equitable quality education and promoting lifelong learning in lower and lower-middle-income countries.

References

CBI. (2019). Post-issuance reporting in the green bond market.

Climate Bonds Initiative. (2020, October). Sustainable Debt Global State of the Market H1 2020.

EBRD will help Kazakhstan achieve carbon neutrality by 2060. 31 March 2021. https://www.ebrd.com/news/2021/ebrd-will-help-kazakhstan-achieve-carbon-neutrality-by-2060.html

EBRD and Kazakhstan's financial regulator promote ESG standards. 22nd March 2022. https://www.ebrd.com/news/2022/ebrd-and-kazakhstans-financial-regulator-promote-esg-standards-.html

EFAMA INDEFI, Market Insights, Issue 3, November 2020.

EFAMA INDEFI, Market Insights, Issue 7, November 2021.

Ehlers, T., Mojon, B., & Packer, F. (2020). Green bonds and carbon emissions: Exploring the case for a rating system at the firm level. *BIS Quarterly Review*, 31–57.

Environmental Finance. (2020). Sustainable bonds insight 2020, p. 24.

FP153 – Mongolian Green Finance Corporation, Funding Proposal. https://www.greenclimate.fund/sites/default/files/document/funding-proposal-fp153.pdf.

Gibon, T., et al. (2020). Shades of green: Life cycle assessment of renewable energy projects financed through green bonds. *Environmental Research Letters, 15*, 2020.

Global and Country Progress Reports 2021&2022. https://www.sbfnetwork.org/publications/global-progress-report-2021/

Global Sustainable Investment Alliance. (2019). 2018 global sustainable investment review, March 2019, p. 8, Figure 1: Snapshot of Global Sustainable Investing Assets, 2016–2018.

HSBC. (2019, September 24). Blockchain. Gateway for sustainability linked bonds.

http://www.tanpaifang.com/tanguwen/2020/0709/72319_21.html

https://g20.org/3rd-g20-dwg-prioritize-blended-finance-to-overcome-developing-countries-sdg-funding-constraints/

https://www.boj.or.jp/en/announcements/press/koen_2021/data/ko210727a.pdf

https://www.boj.or.jp/en/mopo/measures/mkt_ope/ope_x/index.htm/

https://www.bundesfinanzministerium.de/Content/EN/Standardartikel/Press_Room/Publications/Brochures/sustainable-finance-strategy.pdf?__blob=publicationFile&v=8

https://www.canada.ca/en/natural-resources-canada/news/2022/01/canada-greener-homes-grant-winter-2022-update.html

https://www.energy.gov.au/news-media/news/government-announces-300m-advancing-hydrogen-fund

https://www.gov.br/produtividade-e-comercio-exterior/pt-br/assuntos/assuntos-economicos-internacionais/cooperacao-internacional/projeto-fibras-2013-financas-brasileiras-sustentaveis

https://www.gov.uk/government/publications/the-ten-point-plan-for-a-green-industrial-revolution/title .

https://www.gov.za/about-government/government-programmes/green-fund?msclkid=30de17a8cea611eca98a141db4777a43

https://www.mas.gov.sg/news/media-releases/2020/mas-launches-worlds-first-grant-scheme-to-support-green-and-sustainability-linked-loans
https://www.mee.gov.cn/gkml/sthjbgw/qt/200910/t20091023_180041.htm
https://www.meti.go.jp/english/press/2021/0312_002.html
IISD. (2019, April). Impact Tokens: A blockchain-based solution for impact investing.
Insights, September 2021; and McKinsey Global Energy Perspectives.
Kell, G. *Forbes*. The remarkable rise of ESG. July, 2018. https://www.forbes.com/sites/georgkell/2018/07/11/the-remarkable-rise-of-esg/#2535cd7b1695
McKinsey & Company. Agriculture and Climate Change, April 2020.nt from mainstream capital markets.
MSCI. (2020, April 14). Green bonds: Growing bigger and broader.
Open Insights by Nordea. (2020, October 29). The sustainable loan market: A snapshot of recent developments.
Paulson Institute, The Nature Conservancy and Cornell Atkinson Center for Sustainability, Financing Nature: Closing the Global Biodiversity Financing Gap, 15 September 2020.
Principles for Responsible Investment. What is responsible What is responsible investment? www.unpri.org/pri/an-introduction-to-responsible-investment/what-is-responsible-investment.
SBFN Task force for low income member countries https://www.sbfnetwork.org/working-groups/task-force-for-low-income-member-countries/.
sustainability-and-central-bank-policy-green-aspects-of-the-magyar-nemzeti-bank-s-monetary-policy-toolkit.pdf (mnb.hu)
Sustainable Finance Working Group (SFWG), 2022 G 2 0 Sustainable Finance Report.
Final report, Taskforce on Scaling Voluntary Carbon Markets, January 2021.
The net-zero transition: What it would cost, what it could bring, Jan 2022, Mckinsey Report.
The White House. (2021, April 23). FACT SHEET: President Biden's Leaders summit on climate.
UN Food and Agriculture Organization (FAO). (2020). "Energy use," FAOSTAT; EMIT database, McKinsey Sustainability.
UNDP. (2019, February 7). Adopting a cedar tree brings diaspora money home.
UNEP Finance Initiative. (2018, November). Rethinking impact to finance the SDGs: A position paper and call to action prepared by the Positive Impact Initiative, p. 3.
United Nations Association UK. (2019, June 19). Filling the financing gap.
United Nations Conference on Trade and Development. (2020). World investment report 2020: International production beyond the pandemic, p. 187.
United Nations Department of Economic and Social Affairs – Sustainable Development.
US climate envoy supports 'indispensable' GCF role during climate forum," Green Climate Fund, April 21, 2021.
World development indicators Data Bank, World Bank. Emissions data for 2018 from emissions database for global atmospheric research.
World Economic Forum. (2018, September 20). 5 ways blockchain can transform the world of impact investing.

Chapter 6
Policies, Regulations and Standards in Sustainable Finance

The seven central pillars of the current architecture of the sustainable finance policy and regulation advocated by United Nations Conference on Trade and Development (UNCTAD) are national strategy, national framework and guidelines, taxonomy, product standards, sustainability disclosure, sector specific regulations and carbon pricing. The policy making activities are centered around these themes in 35 economies which are monitored by UNCTAD.[1] The objective is to develop national sustainable finance taxonomies and standards and sustainability disclosure requirements.

As part of the UN GSFO's efforts, UNCTAD, in collaboration with the PRI and the UNEP Finance Initiative (UNEP FI), has been monitoring the latest developments in sustainable finance policies and regulations across 35 economies and country groupings. These include the G20 member states (including the EU) and Switzerland, as well as 13 developing economies: Bangladesh, Chile, Colombia, Egypt, Hong Kong, Kenya, Malaysia, Nigeria, the Philippines, Singapore, Thailand, the United Arab Emirates, and Vietnam. Additionally, the Association of Southeast Asian Nations (ASEAN) is also included. Approximately 70% of all measures addresses sustainable finance disclosure and sector specific regulations involving asset management, sustainable banking and insurance. Significant part of new policies being developed are in the area of taxonomy and carbon measures.

With respect to sustainable finance regulation, EU, China and United States have taken two different approaches. EU have adopted a regulatory approach which focus on establishment of a comprehensive regulatory framework for sustainable finance. The policy measures and frameworks adopted by EU is used as a reference for sustainable policy making in other regions of world. The EU taxonomy related to the principles of "sustainable contribution "and "do no significant harm" is used as model by ASEAN, South Africa for the development of their respective taxonomy.

[1] Policies, Regulations and Standards, Chapter III Capital markets and sustainable finance, World Investment Report 2023 Investing in sustainable energy for all, UNCTAD.

B. R. Kumar, *Green Finance*, Sustainable Finance,
https://doi.org/10.1007/978-3-032-03333-8_6

China and United States focusses on a hybrid approach by giving significance to both regulation and integration of both climate and sustainable development dimensions into industrial policies. For example, in the year 2022, the US had passed a law titled "inflation reduction act" with the emphasis on green investment.

Sustainability Reporting Standards Initiatives

The development of sustainability reporting standards is supported by several key international initiatives, including the Task Force on Climate-related Financial Disclosures (TCFD), the Task Force on Nature-related Financial Disclosures (TNFD), the Sustainability Accounting Standards Board (SASB), the Global Reporting Initiative (GRI), and the International Financial Reporting Standards (IFRS).

Task Force on Climate Related Financial Disclosures (TCFD)

The TCFD seeks to enhance climate-related disclosures to facilitate informed investment and credit decisions, thereby improving understanding of carbon-related assets and climate risks.

Task Force on Nature Related Financial Disclosures (TNFD)

The TNFD is developing a framework for managing nature-related risks and opportunities, aiming to shift toward nature-positive outcomes. It aligns with the Kunming-Montreal Global Biodiversity Framework, encouraging firms to adopt TNFD recommendations.

Sustainability Accounting Standards Board (SASB)

SASB, now part of the Value Reporting Foundation (VRF) through its merger with the International Integrated Reporting Council, provides industry-specific standards for sustainability disclosures. The VRF will offer guidance on integrating SASB and IIRC standards.

Global Reporting Initiative (GRI)

GRI standards assist corporations report on environmental, social, and economic impacts.

International Financial Reporting Standards (IFRS)

IFRS is developing consistent sustainability standards through the International Sustainability Standards Board (ISSB), aiming to improve transparency and comparability in sustainability reporting to build public trust and aid investors.

Financial Implications of Climate Change[2]

Organizations frequently misjudge climate change risks, perceiving them as distant and not immediately relevant. This misconception overlooks the unpredictable and far-reaching economic and social consequences of ongoing global warming. To address the concerns related to climate change, in the year 2015, 200 countries agreed to reduce greenhouse gas emissions and facilitate the transition to a low carbon economy. This transition will see the movement away from fossil fuel energy and other physical assets. The declining costs and enhanced deployment of clean and energy efficient technologies would have financial implications for companies which depend on extraction, production of fossil fuels and which uses coal, oil and natural gas. The phenomena of transition to a lower carbon economy and climate related risks would affect majority of economic sectors and industries. The transition to a lower-carbon economy poses considerable risks but also offers substantial opportunities for organizations committed to climate change mitigation and adaptation strategies. The expected transition to a lower carbon economy is estimated to require around $1 trillion of annual investments.[3] A study estimated that value at risk due to climate change would be in the range of $4.2–$43 trillion of global manageable assets by the end of century. Climate risks will affect a broad range of assets which creates challenges for investors. There is the need for long term strategic planning and efficient capital allocation. The transition to lower carbon economy will lead to disruptive changes across economic sectors and industries with implications for global financial system in terms of avoiding financial dislocations and sudden losses in asset values.

[2] https://www.fsb-tcfd.org/about/

[3] International Energy Agency, World Energy Outlook Special Briefing for COP21, 2015.

Taskforce on Financial Disclosure

The G20 Finance Ministers and Central Bank Governors tasked the Financial Stability Board with reviewing the financial sector's response to climate-related issues. The review emphasized the need for better information to support informed investment, lending, and insurance decisions, aiding investors in assessing company resilience and ensuring a smoother transition to a lower-carbon economy.

The Financial Stability Board (FSB) has created the TCFD to provide recommendations on information which companies must disclose to assist investors, lenders and insurance underwriters for assessing and pricing risks related to climate change. In 2017, the TCFD introduced recommendations for climate-related financial disclosures to assist companies in delivering improved information, thereby enhancing market transparency and enabling more informed capital allocation decisions. The recommendations are structured around thematic areas of governance, strategy, risk management and metrics and targets.

After the TCFD recommendations were published, the Financial Stability Board (FSB) asked the Task Force to encourage adoption of the framework by offering additional guidance, supporting educational initiatives, monitoring climate-related financial disclosure practices for alignment with the recommendations, and preparing annual status reports through 2023. With the submission of the Task Force's 2023 Status Report, and at the request of the FSB, the TCFD has now been disbanded.

The 32 -member Task Force was selected by the Financial Stability Board and were global in nature. The members represented a diverse range of organizations, including major banks, insurance companies, asset managers, pension funds, large non-financial firms, accounting and consulting firms, and credit rating agencies. The members were entrusted to develop a singular accessible framework for climate related financial disclosure.

The taskforce developed four widely adoptable recommendations on climate related financial disclosures applicable to organizations across sectors and jurisdictions. The recommendations are applicable to financial institutions such as banks, insurance companies, investment firms and asset management companies.

The new trend observed is that financial market participants are increasingly seeking clear, consistent, and reliable climate-related risk information. This demand, driven by investors and creditors, has intensified since the 2007–2008 financial crisis, highlighting the need for greater transparency on corporate governance and climate risk management. In most G20 jurisdictions, companies must disclose material risks in their financial reports, including climate-related ones. However, the lack of a standardized framework leads to inconsistent and fragmented climate risk disclosures, making it difficult for stakeholders to compare information and assess financial impacts. This inconsistency hinders informed economic decisions and challenges regulators in evaluating system-wide climate risk exposure. The FSB tasked the Task Force with creating climate-related disclosures to improve investment, lending, and insurance decisions, enhance understanding of carbon-related risks, and support systemic risk assessment in the financial sector.

Climate Related Risks, Opportunities and Financial Impacts

Climate Related Risks

Climate related risks can be categorized into two major categories- the risks related to the transition to a lower carbon economy (Transition Risks) and the risks related to the physical impacts of climate change (Physical Risks).

Transition Risks

The transition to a lower carbon economy may entail transition risks due to extensive changes in terms of policy, legal, technology and market factors which are essential for mitigating and adapting requirements related to climate change. Policy risks arises due to policy actions that seek to promote adaptation to climate change. For example, policy actions such as implementation of carbon pricing mechanism to reduce GHG emissions, adoption of energy efficiency solutions, greater water efficiency measures and sustainable land use practices. The risks in terms of the financial impact of policy changes depend on the nature and timing of the policy change. Litigation or legal risk is another transition risk. There has been an increase in climate related litigation in recent years. Climate related litigation claims are being filed by municipalities, states, insurers, public interest organizations due to failure of companies to mitigate impacts of climate change, failure to adapt climate change and insufficient disclosure related to material financial risks. Technology risks arises due to the impact of technological innovations or changes which are essential for transition to lower carbon, energy efficient economic system. The new technology would displace old systems. For instance, advancements in technologies like renewable energy, battery storage, energy efficiency, and carbon capture will impact organizations' competitiveness, production and distribution costs, and ultimately, the demand for their products and services. Market risks arises due to shifts in supply and demand for specific commodities, products and services on account of climate related changes. Climate change is a potential source of reputational risk in the context that shifting customer and community perceptions may reflect positively or negatively on an organization's role in the transition to a lower carbon economy.

Physical climate risks include acute event-driven risks (like severe weather) and chronic risks (such as long-term temperature increases). These can damage assets, disrupt supply chains, and impact financial performance.

Climate Related Opportunities

The taskforce had suggested several areas of climate related opportunities. Efforts to mitigate and adapt to climate change offer opportunities for organizations in areas like resource efficiency, low-emission energy adoption, new products and services, market expansion, and resilience building. These opportunities result in cost savings, innovation, and improved competitive positioning. Resource efficiency, for instance, reduces operating costs through improved energy, water, and waste management. Transitioning to low-emission energy sources offers potential savings and market growth. Developing low-emission products and entering new markets enhance diversification and readiness for a lower-carbon economy. Building resilience helps organizations manage risks and seize opportunities, particularly in sectors with long-term assets and supply networks. Climate change affects all economic sectors. However, the level and type of exposure and the impact of climate related risks differs by sector, industry, geography and organization.

Potential Financial Impacts

Transition and physical risks can impact demand and revenues. Organizations should explore opportunities to enhance or develop new revenue streams, especially considering potential carbon pricing effects. A company's response to climate-related risks and opportunities may depend on its cost structure and flexibility. Lower-cost suppliers might be more resilient and adaptable, which can attract investors. Transparency in capital expenditure plans and flexibility to adjust them can improve access to capital and financing terms, enhancing investment potential. Changes in policies, technology and market dynamics on account of climate change might affect the value of assets and liabilities of organizations. Organizations must analyse the potential climate related impact on the assets and liabilities of long-term assets through scenario analysis. For policy risk such as increased pricing of GHG emissions, the financial impact could increase operating costs such as higher compliance costs and increased insurance premiums. For technology risks of substitution of existing products, the potential financial impact would be write-offs and early retirement of existing assets. For market risk of changing customer behaviour, the potential financial impact would be reduced demand for goods and services as a result of shift in consumer preferences. For reputation risk of shifts in consumer preferences, the financial impact would be reduced revenue from decreased demand for goods/services. For climate related opportunity in resource efficiency in terms of use of more efficient modes of transport, the potential financial impact would be reduced operating costs. For energy source in terms of use of supportive policy incentives, the potential financial impact would be reduced exposure to future fossil fuel price increases. For product and services opportunities such as development of climate adaptation and insurance risk solutions, the financial impact would be increased revenues through new solutions to adaptation needs such as insurance risk transfer products and services. Access to new markets can lead to increased revenues. Participation in renewable energy programs and adoption of energy efficiency measures may have financial implications of increased market valuation through resilience planning for infrastructure, land etc.

Recommendations

The recommendations by the Task Force were structured around four thematic areas of governance, strategy, risk management and metrics and targets.

Governance

Disclose the organization's governance around climate related risks and opportunities.

Recommended Disclosures

- Describe the board's oversight of climate related risks and opportunities
- Describe management's role in assessing and managing climate related risks and opportunities.

Strategy

Disclose the actual and potential impacts of climate related risks and opportunities on the organization's businesses, strategy and financial planning where such information is material.

Recommended Disclosures

- Describe the climate related risks and opportunities which the organization has identified over the short, medium and long term.
- Describe the impact of climate related risks and opportunities on the firm's businesses, strategy and financial planning.
- Describe the resilience of the firm's strategy taking into consideration different climate related scenarios which includes a 2 degree Celsius or lower scenario.

Risk Management

Disclose how the organization identifies and manages climate related risks.

Recommended Disclosures

- Describe the organization's processes for identifying and assessing climate related risks.
- Describe the organization's processes for managing climate related risks.
- Describe how processes for identifying, assessing and managing climate related risks are integrated into the organization's overall risk management.

(*continued*)

(continued)

Metrics and Targets

Disclose the metrics and targets used to assess and manage relevant climate related risks and opportunities when such information is material.

Recommended Disclosures

- Disclose the metrics used by the organization to assess climate related risks and opportunities in line with its strategy and risk management process
- Disclose Scope 1, Scope 2 and if appropriate Scope 3 greenhouse gas (GHG) emissions, and related risks.
- Describe the targets used by the organization to manage climate related risks and opportunities and performance against targets.

Source: Recommendations of the task Force on Climate related Financial Disclosures, TCFD Report 2017.

Supplemental guidance prepared for the financial sector comprised of four industry sectors such as banks, insurance companies, asset management companies and asset owners which include public and private pension plans, endowments and foundations. The Task Force also developed supplemental guidance for non-financial industries which account for the largest proportion of GHG emissions, energy and water usage. These industries were categorized into the sectors-Energy; Materials and Building; Transportation; and Agriculture, Food and Forest Products. The Task Force prioritized non-financial sectors with high climate-related financial risks, focusing on GHG emissions, energy, and water usage, as these factors most broadly indicate physical and transition risks.

The Task Force required all organizations, especially those with public debt or equity, asset managers, and asset owners, to implement its recommendations for more informed investment decisions. The Task Force recommended organizations disclose climate-related financial information in annual public filings, aligning with national requirements, to help investors understand governance and risk management in their decisions. The Task Force recommended that organizations disclose strategy and metrics information in annual filings if its material. Firms in the non-financial sector with annual revenues exceeding one billion U.S. dollars should consider disclosing information in other reports if it is not deemed material and thus not included in financial filings.

The Task Force advises asset managers and owners to adopt its recommendations using their existing reporting formats, considering materiality based on their mandates and investment performance for clients and beneficiaries. In its recommendation, the Task Force suggest asset managers and owners to use existing reporting formats for climate related disclosures to ensure materiality and that internal governance processes align with those used for financial reporting.

Guidance for All Sectors

Governance

In terms of disclosure for board's oversight for climate related risks and opportunities, organizations should consider discussing how the board or board committees are informed about climate-related issues, their role in guiding strategy and risk management, and how they oversee progress toward climate-related goals and targets. Task Force recommends that organizations should describe management's role in addressing climate-related issues, including assigned responsibilities, reporting to the board, organizational structure, processes for informing management, and how management monitors these issues through specific positions or committees.

Strategy

Organizations should describe relevant short-, medium-, and long-term time horizons for climate-related issues, identify specific issues that could materially impact finances over these periods, and outline their process for determining these risks and opportunities. Organizations should discuss how climate-related issues impact their business, strategy, and financial planning, including effects on products, supply chains, adaptation activities, R&D, and operations. They should also explain how these issues influence financial planning, costs, revenues, capital allocation, and access to capital, using relevant scenarios. Organizations should describe their strategies' resilience to climate-related risks, including transition to a lower-carbon economy and increased physical risks, outlining potential impacts, strategy adjustments, and relevant scenarios.

Risk Management

The Task force recommended that organizations should detail their processes for identifying and assessing climate-related risks, including how these risks compare to others. They should consider regulatory requirements and other factors, describe how they assess the size and scope of these risks, and define or reference the risk classification frameworks used. Organizations should outline their processes for managing climate-related risks, including decisions to mitigate, transfer, accept, or control these risks. They should also describe how they prioritize risks and determine materiality.

Metrics and Targets

Organizations should report key metrics for managing climate-related risks and opportunities, including water, energy, land use, and waste. They should also disclose their Scope 1, 2, and possibly Scope 3 GHG emissions, using GHG Protocol methodologies. Metrics should cover historical periods for trend analysis and include descriptions of calculation methods. Additionally, organizations should outline their climate-related targets, such as GHG emissions and energy usage, including target types, time frames, base years, and key performance indicators.

Recommendations for Scenario Analysis

Scenario analysis assist organizations address highly uncertain, medium-to-long-term outcomes and potential disruptive effects related to issues like climate change and GHG emissions. Scenario analysis helps organizations explore different future scenarios, including significant climate impacts, enhancing strategic and financial planning. It aids in identifying key indicators, adjusting strategies based on evolving conditions, and allows investors to assess and compare the robustness of strategies and financial plans across organizations.

Climate change impacts vary by sector, so all organizations should use scenario analysis in strategic planning and risk management. Those heavily affected by transition risks (e.g., fossil fuel industries) or physical risks (e.g., agriculture, infrastructure) should conduct more detailed analyses. Transition risk scenarios, like the 2 °C pathway from the Paris Agreement, help assess policy and market changes. Physical risk scenarios are crucial for organizations with fixed assets or operations in climate-sensitive areas, highlighting extreme weather risks and changes over time. While models often extend beyond 2050, institutions typically focus on risks relevant to their asset lifetimes and operations.

Scenario analysis should involve multiple scenarios to cover a range of future outcomes, both positive and negative. The Task Force recommends using a 2 °C or lower scenario alongside two or three additional relevant scenarios, such as those based on Nationally Determined Contributions (NDCs) or physical climate risks. Organizations in early stages should disclose how resilient their strategies are to various scenarios. Those more exposed to climate-related issues should also share key assumptions and pathways used in their scenarios to clarify the analysis process and limitations, helping stakeholders understand the robustness of their strategies and financial plans.

Non-financial organizations exposed to climate-related risks should consider disclosing key aspects of their scenario analysis. This includes the scenarios used, such as a 2 °C or lower scenario, and critical input parameters, assumptions, and analytical choices. Key factors include assumptions about technology responses, regional differences, and sensitivities to these assumptions. Organizations should also disclose the time frames used, covering short-, medium-, and long-term milestones. Additionally, they should provide information on the resiliency of their strategy, including potential impacts on their value chain, capital allocation, R&D focus, and possible financial implications.

Task Force on Climate Related Financial Disclosures Status Update

The Task Force on Climate related Financial Disclosures 2023 status report reviews current climate-related financial disclosure practices in alignment with the Task Force's recommendations. Using AI, the Task Force analysed reports from over 1350 large companies globally over 3 years and surveyed the top 50 asset managers and owners. The findings reveal a growing trend in TCFD-aligned disclosures, with 58% of companies meeting at least five of the 11 recommended disclosures in 2022, up from 18% in 2020. However, only 4% fully aligned with all recommendations. Disclosure rates for climate risks, board oversight, and targets have significantly increased, and many jurisdictions now require climate disclosures in financial filings. Over 40% of the largest asset managers and 30% of the largest asset owners had described their targets on GHG emissions associated with their assets under management in public reports.[4] Around 20% of the largest asset managers and 14% of the largest asset owners mentioned the weighted average carbon intensity of their funds, products or investment strategies in public reports. The Task Force survey suggest that investors and other stakeholders are interested in companies' disclosures regarding their assessments and evaluations of assets for potential impairment, contingencies, and useful lives, as these provide insight into the impact of climate-related issues on the companies' financial position and performance.

According to a 2022 TCFD survey, asset managers and asset owners viewed that the biggest challenge to climate reporting is insufficient information from investee companies.

Companies in Asia Pacific and Europe had higher levels of reporting on climate related metrics than those in North America. Insurance firms had high levels of disclosures in Latin America and Europe, however had lowest levels in Asia Pacific, Middle East and Africa. Across all regions, technology and media companies had significantly lower levels of disclosure compared to companies in other industries.

The Task Force analysed responses from approximately 5000 companies to a 2022 CDP questionnaire on climate-related issues. Over 4000 companies noted that the most common type of financial impact estimated for climate related risks was increased operating costs and increased revenues on account of increased demand with respect to climate related opportunities.

[4] Task Force on Climate related Financial Disclosures 2023 status report.

Government and Regulatory Updates

In year 2023, the Australian Government Treasury published for consultation proposed climate related financial disclosure requirements in line with TCFD recommendations and ISSB standards. The requirements would apply to large listed and unlisted firms as well as financial institutions and would be phased in over a three-year period starting 2024–2025. In October 2022, the Canadian Securities Administrators (CSA) reviewed its proposed TCFD-aligned disclosure requirements, considering U.S. SEC proposals and the ISSB's draft standards. In March 2023, the Office of the Superintendent of Financial Institutions issued guidance on climate-related risk management for financial institutions, including expectations on climate-related financial disclosures. This guidance includes an annex detailing mandatory disclosure requirements that align with the Task Force's 11 recommended disclosures.

In December 2022, the EU Parliament and Council approved the Corporate Sustainability Reporting Directive (CSRD), replacing a previous directive. The CSRD took effect on January 5, 2023. Companies covered by the previous directive must report under the CSRD starting in fiscal year 2024. Other large companies begin in 2025, small and medium-sized public companies in 2026, and non-EU companies in 2028. Reporting will follow sustainability standards developed by EFRAG, aligned with TCFD recommendations. In August 2023, the Hong Kong Monetary Authority (HKMA) issued high-level principles to guide authorized institutions in planning for a net-zero transition. These principles are based on international recommendations, including the Task Force's Guidance on Metrics, Targets, and Transition Plans.

In January 2023, the Japan Financial Services Agency introduced new rules requiring listed companies to disclose sustainability information, including climate-related data, aligned with TCFD recommendations. Governance and risk management disclosures are mandatory, while strategy and metrics are based on materiality. These rules apply to fiscal years ending on or after March 31, 2023.

In November 2022, New Zealand's Ministry of Business, Innovation and Employment and Ministry for the Environment published a consultation on adding an assurance requirement to the climate-related disclosure law. The law, passed in October 2021, mandates climate-related disclosures for large publicly listed companies, insurers, banks, and investment managers, based on TCFD recommendations.

In July 2023, Singapore's Accounting and Corporate Regulatory Authority and Singapore Exchange Regulation launched a public consultation on climate-related reporting aligned with ISSB standards and TCFD recommendations. The proposal suggests expanding existing disclosure requirements, currently for select industries, to include all listed issuers and large non-listed companies. In November 2022, Switzerland's Federal Council finalized an ordinance requiring large public companies, banks, and insurance firms to report climate-related information starting January 1, 2024. The disclosures must align with the TCFD recommendations and its 2021 implementation guidance. In January 2023, the Thai Securities and

Exchange Commission issued guidelines for asset managers on managing and disclosing climate-related risks following TCFD recommendations. In February 2023, the Bank of Thailand also mandated that all financial institutions disclose climate-related information annually according to TCFD guidelines, starting in 2024.

International and Regional Standards

In November 2022, EFRAG drafted the European Sustainability Reporting Standards (ESRS), which were integrated into the CSRD in December 2022 and aligned with TCFD and ISSB standards. The European Commission adopted the ESRS in July 2023. Also, New Zealand's External Reporting Board finalized its TCFD-aligned climate-related disclosure standards, effective January 1, 2023. In June 2023, the ISSB finalized its general sustainability disclosure standards (IFRS S1) and climate-related disclosure standards (IFRS S2), with IFRS S2 incorporating all 11 TCFD recommended disclosures. In July 2023, ISSB released a comparison of IFRS S2 and TCFD recommendations. Additionally, the International Public Sector Accounting Standards Body announced plans to develop a public sector sustainability reporting standard for climate-related disclosures, based on IFRS S2 and TCFD recommendations.

Updates on Sustainability Initiatives from Stock Exchanges

In December 2022, the Swiss Stock Exchange released an investor relations handbook to facilitate listed companies comply with Swiss regulations on climate related disclosures in line with the TCFD recommendations. In March 2023, the Prague Stock Exchange released sustainability reporting guidelines to assist companies in Czech Republic to understand their obligations under the CSRD and ESRS. In April 2023, the Hong Kong Stock Exchange proposed revising its ESG reporting framework to mandate climate-related disclosures aligned with TCFD and ISSB standards, effective January 1, 2024.

Industry Initiatives

In October 2022, the Japan TCFD Consortium published the third edition of its guidance on climate related financial disclosures. In November 2022, the U.K. Transition Plan Taskforce (TPT) released draft guidelines on climate transition plans for companies, with consultation ending in February 2023. These guidelines, building on the Task Force's transition planning guidance, included a disclosure framework and implementation advice. The final framework was published in

October 2023. In November 2022, the Glasgow Financial Alliance for Net Zero (GFANZ) released a report offering voluntary guidance to financial institutions on creating net-zero transition plans. During November 2022, the World Business Council for Sustainable Development (WBCSD) introduced a climate scenario tool with climate related transition risk scenarios designed specifically for companies in the Food, Agriculture and Forest Products industry. In January 2023, the centre for Sustainable Finance and the Cambridge Leadership published an independent review which analyses the insurance industry's role in mitigating climate change.

In January 2023, the Science Based Targets initiative (SBTi) released guidance for the financial sector outlining recommended pathways for institutions adopting either the SBTi-FI framework, the TCFD framework, or both. In March 2023, the U.K. Climate Financial Risk Forum released an updated guide for U.K. companies on disclosing climate-related risks according to TCFD recommendations. The guide features example disclosures and tailored suggestions for asset managers, banks, and insurers.

Task Force on Nature-Related Financial Disclosures (TNFD)

TFND is a market led, science based, and government backed initiative which provides organizations with tools to solve nature related issues. TFND is supported by national governments, businesses and financial institutions worldwide. The Taskforce consists of 40 individual taskforce members representing financial institutions, corporates and market service providers with over $20 trillion in assets. The TNFD disclosure are structured around four pillars which are consistent with the Task Force on Climate related Financial Disclosures (TCFD) and the International Sustainability Standards Board (ISSB). These disclosures are aligned with the goals and targets of the Kunming-Montreal Global Biodiversity Framework. Building on the approach developed by the TCFD and incorporated into the ISSB's IFRS -S1 general requirements, the TFND has organised its recommended disclosures around the four pillars of governance, strategy, risk and impact management, metrics and targets. There are 14 recommended disclosures. All the eleven TCFD recommended disclosures are included to support integrated climate and nature reporting. The recommendations by TNFD are fully aligned with the Global Biodiversity framework Target 15 requirement to disclose dependencies, impacts and risks. The recommendations emphasis on the importance of nature and its biodiversity for business and finance. TNFD recommendations aim to assist business and financial institutions integrate nature related issues into decision making, risk management and disclosures.

International Organization of Securities Commissions

International Organization of Securities Commissions (IOSCO) is an international body which regulates more than 95% of the world's securities markets in more than 130 jurisdictions. IOSCO develop, implement and promote adherence to internationally recognized standards for financial markets regulations. IOSCO works with other international organizations on global regulatory reform agenda. The objectives and principles of securities regulation are endorsed by both the G20 and the FSB. IOSCO is working on the development of advanced sustainability reporting along with the focus on areas such as assurance and transition planning. IOSCO is addressing the need for global level comparable and reliable standards for sustainability disclosure. IOSCO have engaged with International Auditing and Assurance Standards Board and the International Ethics Standards Board for Accountants for promoting global consistency for sustainability assurance standards. During the year 2022, these groups have initiated plans for project development related to assurance and ethics standards related to sustainability reporting. In 2023, IOSCO had proposed the establishment of a workstream on plans for transition to net zero emissions. The Financial Stability Board's Standing Committee on Supervisory and Regulatory Cooperation have initiated work plans in 2023 to understand the implications of net zero emissions from the perspective of financial stability. As a part of its key priorities related to capacity building in sustainable finance, IOSCO in collaboration with IFRS foundation have launched a program for assisting regulatory authorities in implementing future sustainability reporting standards.

International Sustainability Standards Board

In November 2021, the Trustees of the IFRS Foundation formed the International Sustainability Standard Board (ISSB) to develop standards which would result in high quality comprehensive global baseline of sustainability disclosures which are based on the needs of investors and financial markets. This initiative is supported by members of the G7, G20, Financial Stability Board, IOSCO, African Finance Ministers and Central Bank Governors from more than 40 jurisdictions. The ISSB standards are based on a range of voluntary investor focused standards and frameworks which include the TCFD recommendations, the CDSB framework, the SASB Standards and the Integrated Reporting Framework. The initial standards detailed out in ISSB Standard S1 focus on general requirements for sustainability related financial disclosures while specific requirements for climate related financial disclosures are outlined in ISSB Standard S2.

The Standards outline guidance sources like the industry-based SASB Standards for S1 and the TCFD structure for S2 to assist companies in identifying their risks, opportunities, and metrics. Companies must disclose their governance and risk management of sustainability and climate-related risks and opportunities, along with the strategies, metrics, and targets used for managing them. Jurisdictions may enhance the ISSB's global baseline standards to meet local reporting objectives, provided that these local provisions do not obscure the globally required information. This aligns with the concept of establishing a global baseline for sustainability-related financial disclosures.

The four key objectives set out by ISSB are the following:

(a) Develop standards for a global baseline of sustainability disclosures
(b) Understand the information requirement of investors
(c) To facilitate companies to provide comprehensive sustainability information to global capital markets
(d) To facilitate interoperability with disclosures which are jurisdiction-specific and/or aimed at broader stakeholder groups.

ISSB builds upon the foundation laid by several market driven investor-centric reporting initiatives such as the Climate Disclosure Standards Board (CDSB), the Task Force for Climate related Financial Disclosures (TCFD), the Value Reporting Foundation's Integrated Reporting Framework, and industry specific SASB Standards. Moreover, ISSB incorporates the Stakeholder Capitalism Metrics developed by the World Economic Forum. ISSB has incorporated the SASB's industry-based approach to sustainability disclosure into its standard-setting process. Over 300 mandatory reporting schemes and more than 200 voluntary reporting schemes are currently in use.[5]

IFRS S1

IFRS S1 deals with the overall disclosure requirements for sustainability related financial information. IFRS S2 highlights disclosure requirements for climate related financial information. IFRS S1 is effective for annual reporting periods which begin on or after 1st January 2024.

The objective of IFRS S1 is to mandate that entities disclose information about sustainability-related risks and opportunities, aiding users of financial reports in resource allocation decisions. IFRS S1 requires disclosure of all sustainability-related risks and opportunities that could impact the entity's cash flows, access to finance, or cost of capital over various timeframes. It also prescribes how entities should prepare and report these disclosures, ensuring the information is useful for decision-making regarding resource provision to the entity.

IFRS 1 stipulates companies and entities to disclose information about an entity's sustainability related risks and opportunities with particular focus on the following:

[5] C. van der Lugt, P.P. van de Wijs and D. Petrovics, Carrots & Sticks: Sustainability Reporting Policy: Global Trends in Disclosure as the ESG Agenda Goes Mainstream, Amsterdam and Stellenbosch, Global Reporting Initiative and the University of Stellenbosch Business School, 2020.

1. The governance processes, controls and procedures which the entity uses to monitor, manage and oversee sustainability related risks and opportunities.
2. The firm's strategy to manage sustainability related risks and opportunities.
3. The processes which the entity uses to identify, assess and monitor sustainability related risks and opportunities.
4. The firm's performance and its targets related to sustainability related risks and opportunities.

In summary, the objective of IFRS S1 is to mandate that companies disclose material information about sustainability-related risks and opportunities, aiding investors in resource allocation decisions. This includes details on a company's governance, strategy, risk management, and metrics and targets for sustainability-related risks and opportunities.

IFRS S1 mandates companies to disclose comprehensive information on several key aspects related to sustainability risks and opportunities: IFRS S1 also outlines how these disclosures relate to a company's financial statements, specifying that sustainability-related financial disclosures should be included as part of the general-purpose financial reports.

1. Governance: Details on the processes, controls, and procedures used to monitor, manage, and oversee sustainability-related risks and opportunities.
2. Strategy: The company's approach to managing these risks and opportunities, including their potential impact on prospects, business model, and value chain.
3. Risk Management: Processes for identifying, assessing, prioritizing, and monitoring sustainability-related risks and opportunities.
4. Metrics and Targets: Information used to measure and monitor performance concerning sustainability risks and opportunities, including progress towards company-set and mandated targets.

These disclosures aim to provide investors with material information to make informed decisions about resource allocation to the company. As sources of guidance, a company applying IFRS1 can use IFRS Sustainability disclosure standards, SASB standards, the CDSB Framework Application Guidance and materials of investor focused standard setters. IFRS1 also mandates usage of the GRI Standards and the European Sustainability Reporting Standards (ESRS). A Memorandum of Understanding was signed between the IFRS Foundation and the Global Reporting Initiative (GRI) to coordinate work programmes and standard setting activities. The ISSB and the European Commission have taken steps to maximize interoperability of their standards.

IFRS 2

IFRS S2 deals with specific disclosure requirements for climate related risks and opportunities and supplements the general requirement in IFRS 1. IFRS S2 applies to climate related physical risks and transition risks and also climate related opportunities for organizations. Investors are likely to benefit from applying IFRS S1 and IFRS S2 by avoiding costs related to manual data handling. These standards enhance the consistency, comparability, and verifiability of sustainability-related financial disclosures. Companies are likely to benefit from improved data quality, positively affecting governance, strategy, access to capital, cost of capital, reputation, and engagement. Applying IFRS S1 and IFRS S2 can streamline sustainability reporting, confirmed by academic and market research and voluntary standard-setters.

Objective of IFRS S2

A company which apply IFRS S1 applies IFRS S2 in order to provide material information about its climate related risks and opportunities. The objective of IFRS S2 is to mandate that companies disclose material information about their climate-related risks and opportunities, providing investors with the insights needed to make informed decisions about allocating resources to the company. IFRS S2 mandates companies to disclose material information about the governance processes, controls and procedures which are used to monitor, manage and oversee climate related risks and opportunities. IFRS S2 requires companies to disclose material information about the company's strategy for managing climate related risks and opportunities which also include expected financial effects of climate related risks and opportunities on the company's financial performance over short, medium- and long-term duration. IFRS S2 also mandates firms to use climate related scenario analysis to report disclosures about resilience to climate change. IFRS S2 mandates companies to disclose material information about their processes for identifying, assessing, prioritizing, and monitoring climate-related risks and opportunities. This includes detailing whether and how these processes are integrated into and inform the company's overall risk management framework.

Metrics and Targets Mandated by IFRS S2

IFRS S2 requires companies to disclose metrics and targets to facilitate stakeholders such as investors to understand company's performance related to its material climate related risks and opportunities. Companies are required to provide industry specific metrics. These include disclosure of a company's absolute greenhouse gas (GHG) emissions which are expressed as metric tonnes of carbon dioxide equivalent (CO_2e) and calculated using the GHG Protocol Corporate Standard. The disclosure is classified as Scope 1, Scope 2 and Scope 3 GHG emissions. Scope 1 emissions include all emissions which a company makes directly. Scope 2 emissions include indirect emissions from the generation of purchased energy which are consumed by the company, Scope 3 emissions include all other indirect emissions that occur in the company's value chain. According to IFRS S2 stipulation, asset managers, commercial banks and insurers have to disclose GHG emissions which are financed through their loans and other investments.

In certain situations, a company may provide qualitative rather than quantitative information on sustainability-related risks and opportunities affecting its financials. This applies if effects are not separately identifiable, measurement uncertainty is too high, or if the company lacks the skills, capabilities, and resources to provide quantitative data.

The ISSB offers several reliefs for applying IFRS S1 and IFRS S2 which includes (a) Delayed reporting of sustainability disclosures in the first-year (b) No comparative information required in the first-year (c) Only climate related disclosures needed in first year (d) Exemption from Scope 3 GHG emissions disclosure in the first-year (e) Flexibility in applying the GHG Protocol Corporate Standard (f) Non-reassessment of value chain scope for Scope 3 GHG emissions unless significant changes occur.

The ISSB's application guidance for IFRS S1 include guidance on sustainability related risks, materiality, connected information, interim reporting and comparative information. The IFRS S2 guidance offers guidance on scenario analysis, GHG emissions, financed emissions, cross industry metrics and climate related targets. The guidance also helps companies to determine their Scope 3 GHG emissions and offers a framework for climate related scenario analysis to assess climate resilience. It also helps firms in evaluating and reporting their sustainability related financial impacts and compliance with IFRS standards.

The ISSB believes IFRS S1 and IFRS S2 can greatly enhance investors' data processes. Currently, sustainability reporting is fragmented with multiple frameworks, diverse topics, varied timing, and inconsistent, unstructured reports. This fragmentation leads to high costs for acquiring sustainability data. Implementing these standards aims to streamline and improve the efficiency and consistency of sustainability data management for investors.

IFRS S1 and IFRS S2 are expected to impact ESG data and rating providers positively. Enhanced data collection and aggregation could lead to greater comparability, completeness, and verifiability of sustainability information. This may result in increased rating consistency, cost savings in verification, improved modelling, and continued innovation among ESG data providers.

The ISSB gives importance for the viewpoint that disclosing sustainability-related risks and opportunities helps investors gauge a company's resource dependencies and assess its impacts on those resources. For instance, companies heavily reliant on natural resources (like oil, water, and forests) face risks from changes in availability, quality, and pricing. Operations in regions prone to extreme weather can suffer disruptions, impacting production, assets, and revenue. Activities causing negative impacts on local communities may lead to stricter regulations or reputational harm.

IFRS S1 and IFRS S2 mandate disclosures of metrics and targets to help investors assess a company's sustainability performance. These standards specify quantitative disclosure requirements, subject to materiality assessments and industry-specific needs. This ensures relevance and accuracy in disclosing information critical for investor decision-making. The benefits of adoption also include improved market transparency, improved risk adjusted cost of capital and investment uncertainties.

Companies may incur costs related to recruiting additional staff or acquiring expertise, changing data collection and analysis processes, establishing or modifying internal systems, and producing or modifying reported information. The ISSB through applying IFRS S1 and IFRS S2 have build on well established sustainability frameworks and standards. IFRS 1 and IFRS 2 have incorporated the TCFD Recommendations.

The ISSB has enhanced the interoperability of IFRS1 and IFRS2 with the European Sustainability Reporting Standards (ESRS) and other major jurisdictional requirements. ISSB offers sources of guidance with reference to the GHG Protocol Corporate Standard for the measurement of greenhouse gas (GHG) emissions and on how to measure Scope 3 GHG emissions including the process to estimate the emissions.

The ISSB has introduced temporary and permanent relief measures to ease the initial application of IFRS S1 and IFRS S2. These include allowing companies to report only on climate-related risks and opportunities in the first year, deferring the simultaneous reporting requirement of financial and sustainability disclosures, and exempting disclosure of Scope 3 GHG emissions in the first year.

The ISSB has addressed the needs of emerging economies and smaller companies, many in global value chains, by reducing costs through targeted relief measures and scaling requirements for those with fewer resources. This includes small companies, newcomers to sustainability reporting, and those in less developed markets. For example, IFRS S2 considers a company's available skills, capabilities, and resources in determining its approach to scenario analysis. The ISSB has established a Partnership Framework for capacity building to support companies, investors, and other capital market stakeholders in preparing to use IFRS S1 and IFRS S2.

Sustainability related risks and opportunities are drivers in sustainability related disclosures. The sustainability related risks and opportunities arises due to companies' dependency on resources and relationships and its impact on resources and relationships. For example, the business model of a company which depends on natural resource such as water will be impacted by the changes in the quality, availability and pricing of such resources.

When a company's activities negatively affect resources, it can face reputational damage, fines, penalties, or increased government regulation. Additionally, if a company's business partners and suppliers encounter sustainability-related risks and opportunities, the company itself may also be impacted by these related consequences.

The TCFD survey conducted in year 2022 reveal that 90% of investors and other users utilize climate-related disclosures in their financial decision-making, and 66% of investors incorporate these disclosures into their asset pricing strategies.[6] The

[6] Task Force on Climate-related Financial Disclosures, 2022 TCFD Status Report, New York and Basel, 2022, p. 5.

Sustainability survey conducted by the World Federation of Exchanges (WFE) found that investor demand for sustainability related disclosure among WFE member exchanges and affiliated increased to 96% in 2022 compared to 70% in 2018.[7] The TCFD survey 2022 noted that larger companies with US$12 billion in market capitalization or above are more likely to disclose sustainability information along the lines of the TCFD recommendations. Companies in developed economies have made sustainability disclosures. Out of the 2750 companies which have applied for the SASB Standards, majority are located in North America, the Asia Pacific region and Europe. According to 2022 KPMG study, 64%,49% and 44% of the content of sustainability disclosures covered environmental risk, social risk and governance risk respectively.[8]

Sustainability disclosure rates vary by industry, influenced by perceived risk exposures and their significance. Climate-related disclosures are most common in the energy, mining, technology, and automobile industries. Biodiversity-related disclosures are frequently seen in the mining, forest and paper, food and beverages, energy, utilities, and chemical industries.[9]

Many reporting frameworks and standards are used by companies and investors to report sustainability disclosures. The survey conducted by Carrots & Sticks (2020) find that there are about 266 voluntary and 348 mandatory sustainability reporting schemes in 60 countries.[10] The study by Reporting Exchange found that about 215 voluntary and over 980 mandatory sustainability reporting schemes worldwide cover schemes related to environmental, social, governance and economic disclosures in different industries.[11] The sources of these reporting schemes were from public law and regulation, stock exchanges or industry bodies, standards and guidelines for non-financial reporting and index questionnaires. Voluntary frameworks and standards developed by non-governmental or market led groups are used by different companies. GRI Standards, the Integrated Reporting Framework, the SASB Standards and the TCFD Recommendations are the most commonly used voluntary frameworks. The 2022 KPMG survey found that among the top 100 companies in each of 58 countries, 68% uses the GRI Standards, 34% uses the TCFD Recommendations and 33% uses the SASB Standards. The benchmarking study conducted by the International Federation of Accountants (IFAC) and the Association of International Certified Professional Accountants (AICPA) in year 2020 found that the GRI Standards were used by 999 companies, the TCFD Recommendations by 851 companies and the SASB standards by 662 companies.[12]

---

[7] World Federation of Exchanges, Exchanges Keep Up Efforts to Support a Sustainable Recovery, London, 2022.

[8] KPMG, Big Shifts, Small Steps: Survey of Sustainability Reporting 2022, London, 2022.

[9] KPMG, *Big Shifts, Small Steps*.

[10] Van der Lugt, van de Wijs and Petrovics, *Carrots & Sticks*.

[11] ESG Book, *The Reporting Exchange—Global Source for Sustainability Reporting* [database], London, 2023.

[12] International Federation of Accountants and Association of International Certified Professional Accountants, *The State of Play in Sustainability Assurance*, New York and Durham, NC, 2023.

The survey by the Center for Audit Quality (CAQ) in year 2020 found that 410 companies used the SASB standards, 329 companies used the GRI standards and 302 companies used the TCFD recommendations.[13] The UN Sustainability Stock Exchange (SSE) Initiative has identified 34 exchanges with 19,929 listed companies that mandate sustainability disclosure as part of their listing rules. Additionally, 70 exchanges with 48,182 listed companies issue voluntary sustainability reporting guidance. The KPMG survey 2022 found that approximately 23% of the top 100 companies in each of 58 countries use stock exchange guidance to disclose sustainability information.[14]

The variety of frameworks and requirements for sustainability disclosures complicates maintaining quality, affecting internal controls, assurance processes, and investor engagement. There are highlighted deficiencies in fundamental disclosure areas. There exist deficiencies in fundamental disclosure areas, particularly regarding the relevance of sustainability factors to a company's business model.

The trend suggests that there has been growing demand for sustainability information. The KPMG survey of sustainability reporting find that 80% of large companies globally had undertaken sustainability reporting in 2020 compared to 20% in year 2002. However disclosures vary by company in terms of sustainability reporting frameworks, standards, sustainability topics and jurisdictional differences in sustainability reporting requirements.[15] The study[16] analysed the health and safety disclosure mechanism of 50 large publicly traded companies from the Fortune 500 and identifies over 20 different ways in which these companies vary in their reporting which include differences in terminology and units of measurement. The survey on global sustainability disclosures of 1350 companies in 21 jurisdictions by IFAC and AICPA found wide variation in sustainability reporting practices.[17] This study finds that approximately 86% of companies had applied different sustainability reporting standards and frameworks and large variation was observed with respect to standard and framework adoption practices within jurisdictions. When a company opts to apply different frameworks or standards for its sustainability reporting, it faces increased complexity, which imposes substantial costs on both the company and its employees. This uncertainty about which frameworks and standards to use to meet investors' needs, coupled with the significant costs of applying various frameworks and standards, can lead to either a lack of disclosure of relevant sustainability information or no clear disclosures. The ISSB aims to prioritise to develop a digital taxonomy and digital reporting of sustainability related information. PwC report[18] suggest that leading practices for disclosure management application

[13] Center for Audit Quality, *S&P 500 ESG Reporting*, Washington, DC, 2022.

[14] Sustainable Stock Exchanges Initiative, 2023, https://sseinitiative.org/

[15] Effects Analysis | IFRS S1 *General Requirements for Disclosure of Sustainability-related Financial Information* and IFRS S2 *Climate-related Disclosures* | June 2023.

[16] S. Kotsantonis and G. Serafeim, 'Four Things No One Will Tell You About ESG Data', *Journal of Applied Corporate Finance*, vol. 31, no. 2, 2019, pp. 50–58.

[17] International Federation of Accountants and Association of International Certified Professional Accountants, *The State of Play in Sustainability Assurance.*

[18] PwC, *Disclosure Management: Streamlining the Last Mile*, London, PwC, 2012.

implementations led to 30% reductions in cost and enhanced reporting control environment and improved information quality.

IFRS S1 and IFRS2 is expected to decrease disclosure processing costs and enhance the reliance and scrutiny of reported sustainable information for investors. Increased investor monitoring of disclosures prompts more management actions, enhancing sustainability performance and achieving sustainability goals. IFRS S1 and IFRS S2 aims to standardize reporting, reducing benchmarking costs and aiding companies in setting relevant sustainability targets. The study by Johnson (2020) find that disclosing work safety violations prompted nearby facilities to significantly enhance their safety measures, resulting in fewer occupational injuries.[19] The study by Tomar (2023) find that facilities have used peer GHG emissions disclosures to evaluate their own performance, leading to reductions in GHG emissions.[20]

Companies while preparing sustainability related disclosures based on application of IFRS S1 and IFRS S2 will require to consistently quantify and keep track of their sustainability performance. For instance, after the 2006 Carbon Disclosure Project questionnaire completion, Walmart discovered that the refrigerants used in its grocery stores accounted for major source of GHG emissions than its truck fleet. About 92% of emissions in its value chain were outside the company's direct control. These findings enabled Walmart to focus on reducing refrigerant and supply chain emissions.[21] Companies using SASB standards had fewer sustainability incidents, lower GHG emissions, toxic releases and work related injuries.[22] Mandated mine safety disclosures in financial reports result in fewer mining related violations and injuries.[23] The ISSB anticipates high initial sustainability disclosure costs due to data collection setup, but expects compliance costs to decrease over time as companies become more experienced in applying the Standards.

Global reporting standards are vital for the information flow in capital markets. They enhance corporate reporting transparency and help bridge the information gap between companies and their stakeholders. Academic research on voluntary and mandatory sustainability reporting have discussed the impact of disclosures on performance. Improved sustainability disclosures might result in the lower cost of capital and lower cost of debt. The study P Bolton and Kacperczyk (2022) find that carbon disclosure has a material effect on companies' cost of capital and stock

---

[19] M.S. Johnson, 'Regulation by Shaming: Deterrence Effects of Publicizing Violations of Workplace Safety and Health Laws', *American Economic Review*, vol. 110, no. 6, 2020.

[20] S. Tomar, 'Greenhouse Gas Disclosure and Emissions Benchmarking', SMU Cox School of Business Research Paper no. 19–17, European Corporate Governance Institute—Finance Working Paper no. 818/2022, 1 January 2023.

[21] N. Topping, 'How Does Sustainability Disclosure Drive Behavior Change?', *Journal of Applied Corporate Finance*, vol. 24, no. 2, 2012.

[22] Bochkay, K., Choi, S. and Hales, J., '"Mere Puffery" or Credible Disclosure? The Real Effects of Adopting Voluntary ESG Disclosure Standards', 2022, SSRN: https://ssrn.com/abstract=4167391 or https://doi.org/10.2139/ssrn.4167391

[23] Christensen, H.B., et al., 'The Real Effects of Mandated Information on Social Responsibility in Financial Reports: Evidence from Mine-safety Records', *Journal of Accounting and Economics*, vol. 64, no. 2–3, 2017, pp. 284–304.

returns.[24] A survey by Sustainability Institute by Environmental Resources Management (ERM) in year 2022 found US institutional investors spend an average of $993,000 annually on climate-related data, including $473,000 on external sustainability ratings and consultants, $226,000 on asset-related climate data collection, and $294,000 on internal climate-related investment analysis.[25] The survey also found that an average of US$533,000 are spend by companies on climate related disclosure on annual basis. The US SEC's quantitative estimate of the climate disclosure burden aligns with ERM's estimate, amounting to $530,000 in annual issuer costs after the first year of implementation.

Some studies found that after adopting SASB Standards, US publicly traded companies improved their material sustainability disclosures. Additionally, companies applying these standards saw significant improvements in sustainability performance, such as reduced GHG emissions, lower pollution levels, and fewer workplace injuries.[26] The study based on a sample of 17,680 companies across 65 countries find that ESG disclosure have beneficial informational and real effects.[27] CPD Global Supply Chain Report in 2020 found that Scope 3 GHG emissions are on average 11.2 times higher than Scope 1 and Scope 2 GHG emissions.[28]

In 2023 the report by the International Federation of Accountants (IFAC) and the Association of International Certified Professional Accountants (AICPA) reviewed sustainability information assurance based on the data in year 2021 and noted a rise from 51% in 2019 to 64% of companies in the year 2021 with some form of assurance. Certain jurisdictions like China, Hong Kong, India, Japan, Singapore, Spain, South Africa, Turkey, and the UK saw increases in sustainability assurance. ISSB analysis shows that over 70% of companies in the S&P Global 1200 Index representing 69 markets had reported sustainability related information using the SASB standards.[29]

[24] P. Bolton and M.T. Kacperczyk, 'Carbon Disclosure and the Cost of Capital', 2021, and 'Global Pricing of Carbon-Transition Risk', *Journal of Finance*, forthcoming, August 2022.

[25] Sustainability Institute by ERM, *Costs and Benefits of Climate-Related Disclosure Activities by Corporate Issuers and Institutional Investors*, https://www.sustainability.com/thinking/costs-and-benefits-of-climate-related-disclosure-activities-by-corporate-issuers-and-institutional-investors/

[26] K. Bochkay, J. Hales and G. Serafeim, 'Disclosure Standards and Communication Norms: Evidence of Voluntary Disclosure Standards as a Coordinating Device for Capital Markets', Miami, Florida, University of Miami Business School Research Paper no. 3928979, 2021; K. Bochkay, S. Choi and J. Hales, '"Mere Puffery" or Credible Disclosure? The Real Effects of Adopting Voluntary ESG Disclosure Standards', 2022; E. Rouen, K. Sachdeva and A. Yoon, 'The Evolution of ESG Reports and the Role of Voluntary Standards', 2022; and M. Goettsche et al., 'Materiality Indications as a Double-Edged Sword: Real Effects of Sustainability Disclosure Standards', 2023.

[27] P. Krueger et al., 'The Effects of Mandatory ESG Disclosure Around the World', European Corporate Governance Institute—Finance Working Paper no. 754, Brussels, 2021, pp. 21–44.

[28] Carbon Disclosure Project, *Transparency to Transformation: A Chain Reaction*, London, Carbon Disclosure Project, 2021, https://www.cdp.net/en/research/global-reports/transparency-to-transformation

[29] Effects Analysis | IFRS S1 *General Requirements for Disclosure of Sustainability-related Financial Information* and IFRS S2 *Climate-related Disclosures* | June 2023.

Global Reporting Initiatives (GRI)

Table 6.1 shows the timeline of GRI history.

GRI was established in Boston in the year 1997 following the public protest over the environmental damage caused by the oil spillage related to Exxon Valdez episode. GRI had its origin in the non-profit groups such as CERES and the Tellus Institute which was supported by the UN Environment Programme. The basic aim of GRI was to ensure that companies adhere to responsible environmental conduct principles which included social, economic and governance issues. The year 2022 marked the 25th anniversary of establishment of GRI. GRI have offices in Brazil, China, India, USA, South Africa, Colombia and Singapore. In 2016, GRI set up the first global standards for sustainability reporting termed GRI standards. In 2019, the new Standards on Tax were introduced. In 2020, Standards on Waste were introduced. The Universal Standards was updated in year 2021 and Sector Standards were introduced in year 2021.

The GRI Standards are one of the global best practice for reporting publicly on a range of economic, environmental and social impacts. The GRI Standards is a modular system of interconnected standards. Three series of standards are involved in the reporting processes. The GRI Universal Standards apply to all organizations. The GRI Sector Standards apply to specific sectors and GRI Topic Standard list disclosures which are relevant to a specific topic.

The total GRI Standards downloads during the period 2021–2023 were 2,454,898. In the year 2022, approximately 78% of the G250 largest companies used the GRI Standards for their sustainability reporting. In 2023, Global Sustainability Standards Board (GSSB) approved two critical standards GRI Biodiversity and GRI Mining

Table 6.1 Timeline of GRI history

Year	
1997	GRI founded in Boston USA
2000	First version of GRI guidelines launched
2002	Second version of GRI guidelines launched
2003	Membership program launched
2006	Third version of GRI guidelines launched
2008	Certified Training Partner Program launched
2012	Rio+ 20 UN Conference on Sustainable Development held
2013	Fourth version of GRI guidelines launched
2015	SDG framework developed
2016	GRI Sustainability Reporting Standards launched
2017	Guidance for corporate reporting on SDGs in collaboration with UN Global Impact
2019	Sector program launched
2020	Waste standard launched; GRI Academy established
2021	Revised Universal Standard published. Launch of first GRI sector standard in Oil and Gas
2022	Sector standards for coal, agriculture, aqua culture and fishing established. 25th anniversary of GRI establishment

Source: https://www.globalreporting.org/about-gri/mission-history/

sector. GRI Biodiversity highlights the importance of site-specific impacts and highlights factors which contribute directly to biodiversity loss. The mining sector highlight disaggregation of information at the mine site level, particularly for operations where significant impacts occur.

Table 6.2 gives the topics for the Ongoing GRI Standards projects.

The major goal for Topic Standards Project for Labor is to develop labour related standards to facilitate organizations to disclose their significant impacts on workers and explain how they manage these impacts. This project adopts a human right based and due diligence approach which reflect a greater understanding of firm's responsibilities with respect to human rights and labour relations. The GSSB's Standards Division represented by the Labor Technical Committee is involved in the revision of eight different labor topic standards within two sets of complementary topics. The Standard Project for economic impact revises GRI's economic impact disclosures in order to align with socio economic developments and the UN's SDGs. The Sector Standard Project for Financial Services aims to develop new sector standards for the banking, insurance and capital markets sectors. In 2023, GRI launched a new project to develop a Climate Change Topic Standard to enable organizations to disclose their most significant climate change related impacts.

Carrots & Sticks is the world's most comprehensive database for ESG and sustainability policies which includes 2461 policies from 131 countries and 75 international organizations. The database highlights GRI's pivotal role with its standards referenced in policies across 80 countries. GRI joined the UNFPA-led Coalition for Reproductive Justice in Business in 2023 to advance workplace sexual and reproductive health rights.

GRI leads the Governmental Advisory Group to discuss policy developments. In the year 2023, the Governmental Advisory Group facilitated three key discussions between GRI and various governments on European corporate sustainability reporting developments, due diligence policymaking, and GRI's standard-setting activities. In 2023, GRI worked with European Financial Reporting Advisory Group to develop sector specific European Sustainability Reporting Standards (ESRS) along with the implementation guidance. With over 500 members across 35 industries in 83 countries, the GRI Community is a global network of organizations with the purpose to advance sustainability reporting. By 2023, GRI Networks were based in

Table 6.2 Topic standards

Topic standards	Sector standards
GRI Topic Standard Project for Biodiversity	GRI Sector Standard Project for Mining
GRI Topic Standards Project for Labor	GRI Sector Standards Project for Financial Services
GRI Topic Standard Project for Climate Change	GRI Sector Standard Project for Textiles and Apparel
GRI Topic Standard Project for Economic Impacts	

Source: GRI Annual Report 2023

Africa, ASEAN, Latin America, North America and South Asia. Other regions including Europe are supported by the GRI's head office in Amsterdam. Each Network is guided by advisory groups that include high-level representatives from the region. GRI Networks participate in and initiate various programs, engaging in advocacy efforts that are sometimes funded by donors.

In 2023, the GRI Africa Network advanced sustainability reporting in African capital markets, collaborating with ASEA and various stock exchanges. They developed ESG guidance for countries like Kenya, and Ghana, and engaged in capacity-building and educational sessions to promote responsible investment, enhancing ESG standards and reporting quality across the continent.

The Discovering GRI Program focusses on SMEs and about 300 companies had participated in the program during the years 2022 and 2023. GRI South Asia Network have significant collaborative initiatives with regulatory bodies across the South Asia region particularly with seven key regulators such as Securities and Exchange Board of India (SEBI), Bombay Stock Exchange (BSE), Bangladesh Securities and Exchange Commission (BSEC), Dhaka Stock Exchange (DSE), Chittagong Stock Exchange (CSE), Securities and Exchange Commission (SEC) of Sri Lanka, and Colombo Stock Exchange (CSE). The document titled "Linking the GRI Standards and the SEBI BRSR Framework" maps the GRI Standards against SEBI's regulatory requirements for the Business Responsibility and Sustainability Report (BRSR). In 2023, GRI established the Sustainability Innovation Lab (SIL) in Singapore to develop best practices.

The GRI's Global Sustainability Standards Board and the ISSB have entered into a memorandum of understanding in the year 2022 to coordinate work programmes and standard setting activities. GRI also have collaboration with associations such as European Financial Reporting Advisory Group and the Technical Expert Group.

GRI Standards

GRI 1: Foundation 2021

The GRI Sustainability Reporting Standards aim to enhance transparency by enabling organizations to disclose their significant impacts on the economy, environment, and people, including human rights. This public disclosure promotes sustainable development and increases organizational accountability. The GRI Standards are based on guidelines set up in intergovernmental instruments such as the organization for Economic Cooperation and Development (OECD) guidelines for multinational enterprises and the United Nations guiding principles on Business and Human Rights.

GRI 2: General Disclosures 2021

This contains disclosures which the firms use to provide information about its reporting practices and organizational details such as its activities, governance and policies. GRI 2: General Disclosures 2021 contains disclosures for organizations to provide information about their reporting practices; activities and workers; governance; strategy, policies, and practices; and stakeholder engagement.

Disclosure 2-1 Organizational Details

The organization shall report its legal name, nature of ownership and legal form, location of its headquarters and countries of operations.

Disclosure 2-2 Entities Included in the Organization's Sustainability Reporting

The organization shall list all its entities which are included in its sustainability reporting. If the organization has audited consolidated financial statements or financial information filed on public record, it should specify the differences between the entities included in its financial reporting and those included in its sustainability reporting. If the firm has multiple entities, the approach for consolidating the information must be stated. The approach must specify the adjustments related to minority interests, mergers or acquisitions and divestments of entities or divisions. It also has to be stated if and how the approach differs across the disclosures in the standard and across material topics.

Disclosure 2-3 Reporting Period, Frequency and Contact Point

The organization shall specify the reporting period for and the frequency of its sustainability reporting. The organization shall report the publication date of the report and specify the contact points for questions related to the report or reported information.

Disclosure 2-4 Restatements of Information

The organization should provide a restatement of information in scenarios where the previously reported information needs to be revised. Restatements of information from previous reporting periods can correct errors, or account for changes in measurement methodology or business nature. These restatements ensure consistency and enable comparability between reporting periods.

Disclosure 2-5 External Assurance

The organization must describe its policy and practice for seeking external assurance which also describes how the highest governance body and senior executives are involved. If the organization's sustainability reporting has been externally assured, then it must provide a link or reference to the external assurance report(s) or assurance statement(s). The organization must describe what was assured and on what basis, including the assurance standards used, the level of assurance obtained, and any limitations of the assurance process. The relationship between the organization and the assurance provider must be outlined.

Disclosure 2-6 Activities, Value Chain and Other Business Relationships

In the report, the organization must report the activities of the organization, products, services and markets, supply chain etc.

Disclosure 2-7 Employees

The organization must report the total number of employees and breakdown in terms of gender and region.

Disclosure 2-8

The organization must report the total number of workers who are not employees and whose work are controlled by the organization.

The disclosures 2-9 to 2-21 provide information about the organization's governance structure, composition, knowledge, roles and remuneration. The organization shall describe its governance structure and list the committees of the highest governance body involved in the decision making. The organization shall describe the nomination and selection processes for the highest governance body and its committees. The company must describe how the highest governance body delegates responsibility for managing the company's impacts on the economy, environment and people.

With respect to strategies, policies and practices, the disclosure stipulates a statement from the highest governance body regarding the relevance of sustainable development to the organization and its strategy for contributing to sustainable development. With respect to stakeholder engagement, the disclosures provide information about the organization's stakeholder engagement practices, which includes how it engages in collective bargaining with employees.

Key Concepts in GRI Standards

Impact refers to an organization's economic, environmental, and social effects, including human rights, contributing to sustainable development. For example, an organization's impact on economy refers to its competition practices, its procurement practices and its taxes and payments to governments. An organization's impacts on the environment and people include effects on living organisms, natural resources, human rights, and stakeholders, influencing sustainable development interrelatedly. An organization using GRI Standards prioritizes reporting on its most significant impacts on the economy, environment, and people, including human rights. These are termed material topics. Examples of material topics are anti -corruption, occupational health and safety, or water and effluents.

Sustainability reporting, using GRI Standards, allows organizations to disclose their significant impacts on the economy, environment, and people, including human rights. These impacts are essential for sustainable development and important to stakeholders. They can have both positive and negative operational and reputational consequences, which may affect financial performance. Over time, most impacts will become financially material, highlighting their relevance to financial performance and long-term success. Therefore, sustainability reporting is vital for identifying financial risks and opportunities, supporting financial valuation, and making materiality judgments. It is also an important public interest activity, independent of immediate financial considerations.

Due diligence in GRI Standards involves identifying, preventing, mitigating, and addressing an organization's negative impacts on the economy, environment, and people, prioritizing severity and likelihood, especially for human rights impacts. Stakeholders are individuals or groups whose interests are impacted by an organization's activities. Typical stakeholders include business partners, civil society organizations, consumers, customers, employees, governments, local communities, NGOs, shareholders, investors, suppliers, trade unions, and vulnerable groups.

Reporting Based on GRI Standards

Requirement 1: Apply the reporting principles
Requirement 2: Report the disclosures in GRI 2: General Disclosures 2021
Requirement 3: Determine material topics
Requirement 4: Report the disclosures in GRI 3: Material Topics 2021
Requirement 5: Report disclosures from the GRI Topic Standards for each material topic
Requirement 6: Provide reasons for omission for disclosures and requirements that the organization cannot comply with
Requirement 7: Publish a GRI content index
Requirement 8: Provide a statement of use
Requirement 9: Notify GRI

Source: Consolidated set of GRI Standards.

To enhance the credibility of sustainability reporting, organizations can use internal controls, seek external assurance, and consult stakeholder or expert panels. These methods, while not mandatory under GRI Standards, strengthen reporting integrity. Internal controls ensure objective achievement, external assurance verifies report quality and credibility, and stakeholder panels provide diverse perspectives on reporting practices.

GRI 3: Material Topics 2021

GRI 3 offers step by step guidance on how to determine material topics and contains disclosures which an organization uses to report information. The process to determine material topics consists of three steps of understanding the organization's context; identifying the actual and potential impacts and assessing the significance of these impacts. The organization should consider the following factors to understand the sustainability context of its activities and business:

- Economic, environmental, human rights, and other societal challenges at local, regional, and global levels that relate to its sectors and the geographic locations of its activities and business relationships. This includes issues such as climate change, lack of law enforcement, poverty, political conflict, and water stress.
- The organization's responsibility to comply with authoritative intergovernmental instruments.

The first step in the due diligence process is identification of actual and potential negative impacts of the organization. For each material topic, the organization must describe the actual and potential negative and positive impacts on the economy, environment and people including impacts on human rights. The negative impacts on account of its activities or result of its business relationships must be reported. An organization contributes to a negative impact if its actions lead, facilitate, or incentivize harmful activities by others, such as causing excessive overtime. An organization may be directly linked to a negative impact through its business relationships, even if it doesn't cause or contribute to it. For example, using products which involve child labor.

The organization can categorize impacts into topics based on general categories related to business activities, stakeholder groups, types of business relationships, or economic and environmental resources. For example, if the organization's activities lead to water pollution, negatively affecting both ecosystems and local communities' access to safe drinking water, these impacts can be grouped under the topic of 'water and effluents,' as both are related to water usage.

Sector Standards[30]

Oil and Gas Sector

The Sector standards provide information for organizations about their likely material topics. The Topic Standards contain disclosures for the organization to report information about its impacts in relation to particular topics. The GRI Sector Standards provide information for organizations about their likely material topics. For example, an organization in the oil and gas sector must use GRI 11: Oil and Gas Sector 2021 when identifying its material topics. One of the key topics in this Sector Standard is land and resource rights. Oil and gas projects often require land for operations, access routes, and distribution, leading to significant impacts. These can include the involuntary resettlement of local communities, resulting in both physical displacement and economic displacement through lost access to resources.

A low-carbon economy relies on affordable, reliable, and sustainable energy. To limit global warming to 1.5 °C above pre-industrial levels, achieving net-zero GHG emissions by 2050 is essential, as this level poses significantly lower risks to natural and human systems compared to 2 °C.

The activities of the oil and gas sector cause significant negative impacts on the environment and people, including their human rights. These impacts include loss of biodiversity, soil, water, and air pollution, conflict and social disruption, and threats to human health. Vulnerable groups, such as indigenous peoples and women, may be disproportionately affected. Additionally, oil and gas operations may continue to generate negative impacts even after their closure. Negative impacts can be exacerbated by poor governance of natural resources. The substantial revenues from the oil and gas sector can lead to corruption and resource mismanagement. Additionally, economies reliant on oil and gas are vulnerable to fluctuations in commodity prices and production levels.

The International Energy Agency (IEA) estimates that, under current policies, demand for oil will stabilize around 2030, while demand for gas will begin to decrease in some regions by 2040. In a scenario where the energy transition accelerates to achieve net-zero GHG emissions by 2050, oil demand could drop by almost 75% between 2020 and 2050, and gas demand could peak before 2030.

A decrease in demand for oil and gas will lead to lower utilization of existing production facilities and reduced development of reserves. Depending on the pace of this decline, some fields and facilities may need to be re-evaluated or prematurely written off, becoming stranded assets. This will have financial implications for oil and gas organizations and significant impacts on workers, governments, and other stakeholders. The transition could affect employment, government revenues, and economic development in regions where the sector operates. Workers may face challenges with employability, reskilling, and finding new job opportunities. Additionally, the closure of operations without proper decommissioning and

[30] www.globalreporting.org, Consolidated set of the GRI Standards.

rehabilitation could impose economic burdens on governments and local communities, especially in countries where oil and gas production are a major revenue source.

Oil and gas activities can significantly pressure the environment, causing direct, indirect, and cumulative impacts on biodiversity. These include contamination of air, soil, and water, soil erosion, sedimentation, animal mortality, habitat fragmentation, and the introduction of invasive species and pathogens.

Oil and gas activities can significantly contribute to local communities, countries, and regions through investment and income. While these revenues are crucial in resource-rich areas, mismanagement can lead to economic instability and distortions. Economies dependent on the sector are vulnerable to price and production fluctuations. However, the sector also has positive impacts, including tax revenues, infrastructure investment, local employment, and procurement. Skills development through education and training enhances job access, while local procurement supports supplier development and boosts local businesses.

Lack of transparency in payments to governments can lead to inefficient public fund management, illicit financial flows, and corruption. In the oil and gas sector, where financial transactions and payments such as licensing fees, taxes, and royalties are complex, transparency is crucial. Clear disclosure can highlight the sector's economic impact, facilitate public debate, and guide government decisions. It also sheds light on contract terms, enhances government accountability, and improves revenue management. Conversely, insufficient transparency can obscure revenue misallocation and foster corruption.

The International Energy Agency (IEA) estimates that based on current policies, demand for oil will level off around 2030 while, in some regions, demand for gas will begin decreasing by 2040.[31] In a scenario that sees the energy transition accelerate to achieve net-zero GHG emissions by 2050, demand for oil could drop by almost 75% between 2020 and 2050 and demand for gas could peak before 2030.[32]

Coal Sector

GRI12 standards can be used by any organization in the coal sector. These standards apply to firms involved in exploration, mining and processing of thermal and metallurgical coal. The standards also apply to firms involved in the supply of equipment and services to coal mines such as drilling, exploration, seismic information services and mine construction, transportation and storage of coal such as slurry pipelines. The burning of coal is the largest single source of carbon dioxide (CO_2) emissions. The consumption of coal for electricity generation has been steadily

[31] International Energy Agency (IEA), *The Oil and Gas Industry in Energy Transitions: World Energy Outlook special report*, 2020.

[32] International Energy Agency (IEA), *Net-zero by 2050: A Roadmap for the Global Energy Sector*, 2021.

declining due to decarbonization efforts and the decreasing cost of renewable energy, shifting the focus toward less GHG-intensive energy sources.

Most countries aim to limit global temperature rise to well below 2 °C, targeting 1.5 °C, per the Paris Agreement. Current NDCs project a 2.7 °C increase by 2100, causing severe climate impacts.

Despite global decarbonization efforts, coal may remain a key energy source in developing countries due to its revenue and energy independence benefits. While coal activities promote local economic development, employment, and infrastructure, they can also lead to economic instability, conflict, environmental damage, and human rights issues. Inadequate governance and mismanagement of resources often exacerbate these negative impacts.

The coal sector contributes positively by providing revenues through taxes and royalties, local procurement, and employment, stimulating local businesses and infrastructure development. The benefits to local communities depend on their development levels, capacity for qualified workers, and coal organizations' training commitments. However, coal activities can also generate negative impacts, including economic disparity, pressure on housing and services, and environmental legacy costs. The transition to a low-carbon economy poses risks to coal-dependent regions, necessitating collaboration for a just transition and sustainable economic opportunities.

Agriculture Products, Farming, Fishing and Plantations

GRI 13 applies to sectors such as Agriculture Products, Farming, Fishing and Plantations, Crop and animal production, Fishing and aquaculture.

Agriculture, aquaculture, and fishing are crucial for feeding a growing population but significantly impact sustainable development due to intensive resource use, rural operations, and large labor demands. The agriculture, aquaculture, and fishing sectors are the second largest source of employment worldwide. Over 2.5 billion rural people rely on agriculture, aquaculture, and fishing for jobs, but high informality in these sectors challenges human rights. With 80% of the world's poor in rural areas, ensuring sufficient income for these workers is crucial. Agriculture, aquaculture, and fishing have a substantial environmental footprint. Agriculture accounts for an estimated 70% of freshwater withdrawals globally and is a substantial source of greenhouse gas emissions which accounted for 22% of the total global emissions. Fishing accounts for at least 1.2% of global oil consumption.[33]

Economic inclusion addresses an organization's impact on local communities' access to economic opportunities and the potential of suppliers. It focuses on

[33] European Commission, DG Maritime Affairs and Fisheries—Energy Efficiency, https://stecf.jrc.ec.europa.eu/web/ee/home?p_p_auth=ippYeq6n&p_p_id=49&p_p_lifecycle=1&p_p_state=normal&p_p_mode=view&_49_struts_action=%2Fmy_sites%2Fview&_49_groupId=12762&_49_privateLayout=false

including farmers and fishers, who are key suppliers. There are 500 million smallholder farmers in agriculture, producing up to 80% of agricultural products in some regions, and small fishing vessels make up over 80% of the global fishing fleet.

Mining Sector

GRI 14 covers the mining sector. These standards apply to firms in mining sector such as exploration, extraction including quarrying and primary processing of all types of minerals, metallic and non-metallic. The standards also apply to firms which support activities for mining such as transport and storage, supply of specialized products and services to mining organizations. Mining sector is both a supplier of materials and significant user of natural resources, materials and products. Mining organizations are using circularity measures throughout the value chain. Circular economic measures contribute towards improved resource efficiency through the reduction of the requirement for raw materials, minimize waste generation and repurpose waste for productive purposes. Mining organizations can repurpose tailings and waste rock for uses such as backfill, landscaping, and construction materials. Reusing and recycling metals can significantly contribute to the circular economy, as many metals can be melted and reused infinitely.

Mining activities can provide significant economic benefits to local communities and countries through investment, employment, and infrastructure development. Properly managed, mining can transform national economies, reduce poverty, and improve well-being. Local impacts include job creation, procurement spending, and capacity building, while national benefits come from taxes and royalties. The scale and duration of operations, governance quality, and local employment practices influence these impacts. Globally, mining supports essential infrastructure and the low-carbon transition. However, benefits depend on local development levels, workforce qualifications, and organizational commitment to training. Poor practices can exacerbate economic disparities and gender inequalities.

GRI 101: Biodiversity 2024 contains disclosures for organizations to report information about their biodiversity-related impacts, and how they manage these impacts. Biodiversity refers to the variety of organisms and ecosystems, including genetic diversity within species and distinct ecosystem features. Organizations must describe its policies or commitments to halt and reverse biodiversity loss and how these are informed by the 2050 Goals and 2030 Targets in the Kunming-Montreal Global Biodiversity Framework. The Global Biodiversity Framework envisions a 2050 world in harmony with nature, valuing, conserving, and restoring biodiversity for essential benefits.

GRI 201: Economic Performance 2016 contains disclosures for organizations to report information about their economic performance-related impacts, and how they manage these impacts. Organizations should use audited financial statements or management accounts for economic disclosures, following International Financial Reporting System (IFRS), International Public Sector Accounting Standards

(IPSAS), or internationally recognized financial reporting standards. Information on direct economic value generated and distributed (EV&D) on an accruals basis which include the basic components for the organization's global operation must be provided. Firms must report information on the risks and opportunities posed by climate change that have the potential to generate substantive changes in operations, revenue or expenditure. Climate change poses risks and opportunities for organizations. Regulatory measures on emissions can increase costs but also create markets for new technologies and energy-efficient products.

GRI 202: Market Presence 2016 contains disclosures for organizations to report information about their market presence-related impacts and how they manage these impacts. The standard addresses the topic of an organization's market presence which includes its contribution to economic development in the local areas or communities where it operates.

GRI 203: Indirect Economic Impacts 2016 contains disclosures for organizations to report information about their indirect economic impacts, and how they manage these impacts. This Standard focuses on indirect economic impacts, such as changes in productive potential affecting communities and development prospects, from an organization's financial transactions. The requirements include reporting of information on the extent of development of significant infrastructure investments and services, current or expected impacts on communities and local economies which include positive and negative impacts.

GRI 204: Procurement Practices 2016 contains disclosures for organizations to report information about their procurement practice-related impacts, and how they manage these impacts.

GRI 205: Anti-corruption 2016 contains disclosures for organizations to report information about their corruption related impacts, and how they manage these impacts.

This Standard address anti-corruption, covering practices like bribery, fraud, extortion, and money laundering. Corruption negatively impacts poverty, the environment, and human rights, and undermines democracy and the rule of law. Organizations are expected to adhere to integrity, governance, and responsible practices to meet marketplace and stakeholder expectations.

GRI 206: Anti-competitive Behavior 2016 contains disclosures for organizations to report information about their anticompetitive behaviour-related impacts, and how they manage these impacts. Anti-competitive behaviour involves collusion to limit market competition, including price-fixing and market restrictions. Anti-trust practices erect barriers to prevent competition, such as cartels and unfair practices.

GRI 207: Tax 2019 includes disclosures for organizations to report their tax-related impacts and management strategies. These disclosures allow organizations to share information on their tax management, revenue, and business activities on a country-by-country basis. Taxes are essential sources of government revenue and are crucial for fiscal policy and macroeconomic stability in countries. The United Nations recognizes their vital role in achieving the Sustainable Development Goals.

GRI 302: Energy *2016* contains disclosures for organizations to report information about their energy-related impacts, and how they manage these impacts. An organization can use energy in forms like fuel, electricity, heating, cooling, or steam. This energy can be self-generated or purchased externally and may originate from renewable sources (such as wind, hydro, or solar) or non-renewable sources (such as coal, petroleum, or natural gas).

GRI 303: Water and Effluents 2018 contains disclosures for organizations to report information about their water related impacts, and how they manage these impacts. Freshwater access is a human right. The UN's Sustainable Development Goal 6 targets sustainable water management, including universal access and improved water quality.

GRI 305: Emissions 2016 contains disclosures for organizations to report information about their emissions-related impacts, and how they manage these impacts. The organization must report: (a) gross direct (Scope 1) GHG emissions in CO_2 equivalent, (b) gases included, (c) biogenic CO_2 emissions, (d) base year details and changes, (e) sources for emission factors and GWP rates, and (f) consolidation approach for emissions.

The reporting organization shall report information related to gross location-based energy indirect (Scope 2) and Gross other indirect (Scope 3) GHG emissions in metric tons of CO_2 equivalent.

GRI 306: Waste 2020 requires organizations to report on waste impacts, management, and prevention efforts in their activities and value chain.

GRI 401: Employment 2016 provides disclosures for organizations to report on employment-related impacts and how they manage these impacts.

Interoperability of Associations

The IFRS Sustainability Disclosure Standards and the GRI Standards are two interconnected reporting approaches with each offering distinct but complementary perspectives. Together they form a comprehensive corporate reporting system for disclosing sustainability information and provides assurance to reporting companies. The EU and the United States have plans to develop their own sustainability reporting requirements and cooperates with ISSB to achieve interoperability. UNCTAD through its Intergovernmental Working Group of Experts on International Standards of Accounting and Reporting supports countries to reinforce their regulations and institutions and implement the ISSB standards. UNCTAD, through its Intergovernmental Working Group, supports countries in implementing ISSB standards by enhancing regulations, institutions, and human capacity. They gather best practices, address developing countries' challenges, and promote sustainability reporting through regional partnerships in Africa, Latin America, Asia, and the Gulf, facilitating the exchange of good practices and technical assistance.

Challenges

The sustainable finance market faces challenges with respect to market's limited size and growth which affect the energy transition. The commitments made by investors with respect to net zero and market exposures in developing countries are not adequate. Moreover, SMEs are excluded from sustainability standards. More awareness and training are significant to meet CO_2 reduction targets particularly in developing countries.

Regulation and Global Initiatives in Europe

New standards with wide ranging implications are being set with the expansion of EU financial services regulations. The EU Taxonomy Regulation has legally defined "environmentally sustainable" activities, impacting both corporate reporting and financial services regulation. There are six broad categories in the regulation distinguishing between green and brown economic activities. New ESG disclosure requirements will apply to institutional investors (including insurance companies and pension funds), asset managers, and managers of collective investment funds or personal pension products. These requirements will have significant impact on all companies. Financial advisers and product distributors must now include ESG factors in their suitability assessments. Banks and insurers are being compelled by supervisors to integrate climate-related risks into their risk frameworks and stress testing, with further regulation anticipated. The renewed sustainable finance strategy adopted by European Commission recommends that climate and environmental risks must be fully managed and integrated into financial institutions and social risks must be also considered.

Two new categories of low-carbon benchmarks have been established, ESG disclosures are now required for all benchmarks, and the guidelines for disclosures by EU credit rating agencies have been strengthened. Legislation under consideration include a green bond standard and a EU Ecolabel investment products. The Commission's five-year Gender Equality Strategy includes a proposal for mandatory measures aimed at enhancing gender balance on corporate boards. The European Commission's High-Level Expert Group (HLEG) advocates the importance of improving the contribution of the financial sector to sustainable and inclusive growth and speeding up the shift to a sustainable economy.

In May 2018, the Commission released a package of legislative proposals that have all been adopted. These include the Taxonomy Regulation for defining environmentally sustainable activities, Sustainable Finance Disclosure Regulation (SFDR) for mandatory ESG disclosures by investors and advisers, new low-carbon benchmark categories, and amendments to MiFID II and IDD to integrate ESG factors into suitability tests. The SFDR mandates that financial market participants and advisers disclose how they incorporate sustainability risks and adverse impacts into their processes and financial products.

Financial products with sustainable investment objectives must disclose the methodologies for assessing, measuring, and monitoring their environmental or social characteristics and impacts. Products using indices must explain how these indices align with their objectives and differ from broad market indices. Products must provide clear explanations on considering principal adverse sustainability impacts or justify their exclusion. Additionally, remuneration policies must be tied to sustainability risks and targets, and all related policies and documents must be reviewed and updated for both pre-contractual and periodic disclosures.

In July 2018, the International Association of Insurance Supervisors (IAIS) and Sustainable Finance Forum (SIF) released a paper on climate change risks to the insurance sector, focusing on enterprise risk management, governance, investment, and disclosures. In April 2020, the Basel Committee's report highlighted that BCBS members are addressing climate-related financial risks through regulatory and supervisory initiatives, with future efforts on analytical reports and supervisory practices. In May 2020, the NGFS published a guide for integrating climate change into prudential supervision, offering a snapshot of global practices and five non-binding recommendations to harmonize regulatory responses to climate and environmental risks.

The first EU legislative package mandates firms to integrate ESG factors into product governance and suitability assessments. The Commission is developing new product labels and standards for green bonds and eco-products. The Green Bond Standard (GBS) includes alignment with the EU Taxonomy, publication of a Green Bond Framework, mandatory reporting on proceeds and environmental impact, and external verification. The Commission is also considering an eco-label to promote green investments and consulting on an EU Green Bond Standard and potentially a similar standard for social bonds. The Joint Research Centre proposed criteria for an EU ecolabel for retail financial products, aiming to balance inclusion and exclusion of products.

The EU Taxonomy Regulation and its associated technical screening criteria have developed an EU-wide classification system for economic activities that are environmentally sustainable. The regulation was applied in 2022 concerning climate change mitigation and adaptation objectives. The aim of the taxonomy is to provide information for investors and direct investment towards projects that enable the EU to meet its climate and energy targets.

The Sustainable Finance Disclosure Regulation (SFDR) establishes mandatory and standardized disclosure requirements to assist investors in understanding, comparing, and monitoring the sustainability characteristics and goals of investment firms and financial products. The SFRD is supplemented by the Regulatory Technical Standards and have significant impact on the asset management industry. The SFDR requires asset managers to classify funds offered in Europe as ESG (Article 8 or 9) or non-ESG (Article 6). Article 8 funds promote environmental or social characteristics, while Article 9 funds have a sustainable investment objective. Sustainable investments within Article 8 and 9 must not harm environmental or social objectives, and investee companies must follow good governance practices.

SFDR also mandates asset managers to disclose how they integrate sustainability risks into their investment processes and the principal adverse impacts (PAI factors) of their investment decisions on sustainability factors, especially climate change. Principal adverse impacts refer to the potential negative effects of investment decisions on environmental, social, and governance (ESG) matters. Asset managers must describe their policies for assessing good governance practices, including management structure, employee relations, staff remuneration, and tax compliance.

The EU Corporate Sustainability Reporting Directive (CSRD) is new legislation designed to expand non-financial reporting requirements, aiding the transition to a fully sustainable and inclusive financial system. It mandates companies to publicly disclose information on their sustainability impacts, risks, and opportunities in their management reports, using sustainability reporting standards developed by the European Financial Reporting Advisory Group (EFRAG). This aims to provide users with relevant, comparable, and reliable information to facilitate sustainable decision-making.

Companies already subject to the Non-Financial Reporting Directive (NFRD) will be required to disclose sustainability information starting January 1, 2024. Other large listed and non-listed companies must comply by January 1, 2025. The CSRD will expand non-financial reporting requirements from 11,600 companies under the NFRD to 49,000 companies, covering 75% of the total EU turnover. Many asset managers are expected to be included, along with subsidiaries that have significant turnover in Europe.

Regulatory policies for Sustainable Finance in Europe[34]

The European Commission's sustainable finance strategy proposes over 50 legislative and non-legislative initiatives to be implemented. The EU Commission's "Fit for 55" package promotes new climate targets for the EU. The EU Taxonomy Regulation imposes product level disclosure obligations for financial market participants with respect to the extent to which their financial products are Taxonomy aligned or not. Taxonomy eligibility disclosures must be made by EU listed issuers, EU banks, EU insurers. These organizations must have at least 500 employees, balance sheet of EUR 20 million and net turnover of EUR 40 million which is measured on single or consolidated group basis. Taxonomy eligibility is covered by the technical screening criteria in the delegated acts published under the Taxonomy Regulation. Taxonomy alignment requires an assessment against actual technical screening criteria and social/labour safeguards. Taxonomy technical screening criteria (TSC) are set out for climate change mitigation and climate change adaptation. Different TSCs are prescribed for different economic activities and industries. TSCs will prescribe the criteria for determining if particular economic activities contribute substantially to the environmental objectives of climate change adaptation,

[34] Sustainable Finance in Europe: Regulatory State of Play: Key impacts for banks and capital markets March 2023, Association for Financial Markets in Europe, www.afme.eu

climate change mitigation, sustainable use and protection of water and marine resources, transition to a circular economy, pollution prevention and control and protection and restoration of biodiversity and ecosystems.

The Platform on Sustainable Finance (PSF) is entrusted with the responsibility to advise European Commission regarding the scope of the Taxonomy Regulation to cover economic activities that significantly harm environmental sustainability. To support net zero transition, PSF proposes a traffic light system consisting of three levels-Significant Contribution (green); Intermediate Contribution (amber) and Significant Harm (red). PSF has also suggested that the minimum safeguards alignment should be assessed by reference to topics such as human rights, bribery and corruption, taxation and fair competition.

European Commission adopted a delegated act which sets out the content, methodology and presentation of the KPIs that financial and non-financial undertakings are required to disclose under Article 8 of the Taxonomy Regulation. The non-financial undertakings must report on the Taxonomy eligibility and alignment of their business activities based on proportion of their turnover, capital expenditure and operating expenditure related to taxonomy aligned business activities. The metrics for financial undertakings is more complex. The main metric for banks is the green asset ratio in terms of balance sheet exposures consisting of loans and advances, treasury holdings but excludes trading portfolio. Secondary KPIs are applied to other business activities such as brokerage and asset management. The metric for asset managers is the AUM green ratio which is weighted average of investments in Taxonomy aligned economic activities in comparison to total AUM. Insurers apply different KPIs for investment activities which are weighted average of investments which are directed at funding or associated with taxonomy aligned economic activities.

Disclosure and reporting are key mechanisms for financial services firms to achieve sustainability objectives. In EU, these mechanisms are offered by the EU's Corporate Sustainability Reporting Directive (CSRD) and Sustainable Finance Disclosure Regulation (SFDR). The EU's Sustainable Finance Disclosure Regulation (SFDR), introduced in March 2021, established sustainability-related disclosure requirements for financial market participants, including financial advisers. The SFDR mandates that asset managers provide specific sustainability disclosures across their entire product range.

This package of legislation intends to curb greenwashing efforts in terms of sustainability by financial institutions. The EU SFDR (Level) stipulates that financial market participants such as fund managers, firms conducting investment management activities such as pension schemes and insurance, financial advisors must publicly disclose how sustainability risks are integrated into their investment management/advisory services and in their remuneration policies and procedures. The financial market participants must classify products based on green goals and comply with corresponding disclosure and eligibility requirements. The product categories are:

- Article 6 products: These do not promise environmental or social benefits but must consider sustainability risks or explain their irrelevance. These requires all fund managers to disclose how they integrate sustainability risks and the impacts of these risks on the returns of the financial products they offer.
- Article 8 products: These promote environmental or social characteristics through design, strategy, and marketing, considering ESG factors in investment decisions. They require good governance in investee companies. These requires funds which promote sustainability characteristics to detail in pre-contractual disclosures about how they will support environmental or social characteristics, or both, and ensure that the companies in which they invest adhere to good governance practices.
- Article 9 products: These target "sustainable investments," aiming to achieve environmental or social good, with good governance, and must pass the "do no significant harm" (DNSH) test. It requires funds with a sustainability objective to outline in pre-contractual disclosures how they will achieve that objective and if a reference benchmark index has been designated. Article 8 and 9 products have specific disclosure and reporting obligations to inform investors about ESG commitments.

The EFAMA survey results suggest that SFDR Article 8 and Article 9 funds amounted to EUR 3.7 trillion and EUR 340 billion respectively, at the end of March 2021.[35] At firm level, the asset managers in Europe were managing EUR 11 trillion of assets using an ESG investment approach by end of Q1 2021 which included assets invested in funds and discretionary mandate. As of the end of Q1 2021, SFDR Article 8 funds held net assets totalling EUR 3.7 trillion, representing 22% of the European fund market. The primary domiciles for these funds were Luxembourg (35%), France (16%), the Netherlands (13%), Sweden (13%), and Ireland (9%), collectively accounting for 85% of the total net assets.[36] By the end of March 2021, equity funds made up 47% of SFDR Article 8 funds, bond funds accounted for 26%, multi-asset funds 16%, and money market funds 8%. Equity funds had a higher market share among SFDR Article 8 funds compared to the overall net assets of UCITS and AIFs.[37] At the end of Q1 2021, SFDR Article 9 funds held net assets of EUR 340 billion, comprising about 2% of the European fund market. Luxembourg accounted for over half of these assets, followed by France (16%) and the Netherlands (9%). Equity funds dominated SFDR Article 9 funds, making up 71%, significantly higher than their 30% share across all UCITS and AIFs. Bond funds and multi-asset funds represented 22% and 7% of Article 9 funds, respectively. By end of 2021 Quarter 1, asset managers in Europe had applied an ESG investment approach to a total of EUR 11 trillion of assets. During the period assets in discretionary mandates following an ESG investment approach totalled EUR 5 trillion, while assets under management in funds incorporating ESG features reached EUR 6 trillion.

---

[35] EFAMA Market Insights, Issue #7, November 2021.

[36] EFAMA Market Insights, Issue #7, November 2021.

[37] EFAMA Market Insights, Issue #7, November 2021.

Limitations of SFDR[38]

EFAMA supports the SFDR's goals of reducing information asymmetry, harmonizing ESG disclosures, enhancing comparability, and fostering a level playing field in the internal market. However, the regulation's incomplete implementation, due to the absence of necessary Level 2 measures and legal uncertainties, has led to inconsistent application and potential market fragmentation. The lack of standardized templates and unclear fund categorization under SFDR Articles 6, 8, and 9 creates challenges for asset managers and risks investor trust. Additionally, national divergences in guidelines further hinder comparability, cross-border distribution, and the development of a unified sustainable investment market in the EU. The EU's SFDR aims to standardize sustainability disclosures, reduce information asymmetry, and drive capital towards sustainable investments. In 2022, the European Commission initiated steps for the overview and assessment of relevant regulatory practices related to greenwashing cases and risks related to greenwashing.

Trends on Regulatory Initiatives

On November 22, 2021, the ECB released a report assessing banks' progress in meeting climate and environmental risk management expectations. Key findings include that no bank fully meets ECB standards, progress is slow, and supervisory reviews will continue. The ECB will integrate climate risk into SREP methodology, affecting Pillar 2 capital requirements. Upcoming steps include investigating climate risk disclosures, a full review of banks' climate risk management, and publishing results in early 2022. This "Walking the Talk" report, published in November 2021 details the thematic review results.

The Swiss government is considering a sustainable finance law or amendments to current laws. A June 2020 report led to the State Secretariat for International Finance (SIF) evaluating EU sustainable finance developments. Key objectives are maintaining product exportability, establishing Switzerland as a sustainable finance hub, and preventing greenwashing. FINMA's November 2021 guidance introduced transparency and reporting rules for Swiss funds. The Federal Council published a position paper in December 2022, outlining steps to combat greenwashing and instructed a working group to propose implementation methods. The Swiss Ordinance on Climate Disclosures, adopted in November 2022, mandates TCFD reporting for public companies, banks, and insurance companies with at least 500 employees, total assets exceeding CHF 20 million, or a turnover above CHF 40 million.

In 2021, the Green Technical Advisory Group (GTAG) was formed to advise the UK Government on how to adapt the EU Taxonomy for UK. The UK's strategy

[38] EFAMA Market Insights, Issue #7, November 2021.

titled "Greening Finance: A Roadmap to Sustainable Investing" outlines the legislative and regulatory changes to facilitate environmentally positive investment decisions. This roadmap proposes three phases for greening the UK's financial system through information to investors and consumers; actions on the information and shifting the financial flows. As a part of the first phase of the roadmap, UK government focusses on three key initiatives—Sustainability Disclosure Requirements (SDRs), The UK Green Taxonomy and setting out the Government's expectations of investor stewardship. SDRs require asset managers and owners of investment products to substantiate how ESG related matters will be accounted for in governance, investment policies and strategies. The SDRs will require disclosure against minimum safeguards to promote sustainable investments. The UK's Green Taxonomy will set out the criteria for economic activities which are "environmentally sustainable and taxonomy aligned. A set of Technical Screening Criteria (TSC) is in place to examine if or not an activity is Taxonomy aligned. For investor stewardship, UK Stewardship code for organizations is being developed for information generated by SDR during allocation of capital. The UK government had conducted an independent review of how best to meet the UK's legally binding climate target of net zero by 2050.

In 2021, the UK government announced mandatory TCFD reporting across the economy by 2025. The FCA implemented rules for mandatory TCFD disclosures for premium and standard listed commercial companies and UK asset managers, life insurers, and pension providers. The FCA's Primary Markets Bulletin 36 outlines disclosure expectations and supervisory strategy. The DWP introduced similar obligations for pension schemes. The FCA's policy statement 21/24 extends reporting to asset managers and insurers, requiring annual TCFD compliance reports at entity and product levels. Exemptions include firms with under £5 billion in assets and overseas firms under temporary permissions. UK Transition Plan Task Force (TPT) was established to develop a gold standard for climate transition plans. The Taskforce was given a two-year mandate to strengthen its disclosures working with FCA. In UK, Bank of England have taken steps for climate stress test. The 2021 Climate Biennial Exploratory Scenario (CBES) reveals UK banks and insurers need to improve climate risk management. While the transition to net zero is manageable without threatening solvency, delays could increase climate-related losses significantly. The "no additional action" scenario presents the worst outcomes, with persistent economic costs and adverse impacts on vulnerable households and sectors.

In France, The AMF's Position-Recommendation 2020-03 on non-financial disclosures, known as the AMF ESG Doctrine, applies to asset managers and distributors of French AIFs, UCITS, and foreign UCITS marketed in France. It categorizes funds based on their ESG engagement level, requiring specific documentation and marketing standards. Funds must meet minimum criteria to be classified as "significantly" or "non-significantly" engaging, with non-compliant funds restricted in their ESG communications. The January 2022 update added requirements for Total Return Swaps. The Doctrine complements SFDR, with potential revisions for alignment with EU standards expected.

In August 2021, BaFin of Germany proposed a Sustainability Guideline for German retail funds using "ESG" labels, requiring 75% sustainable investments.

Though the guideline was not finalized, BaFin applies it administratively, likely requiring adherence to these standards amid geopolitical uncertainties.

Austrian Financial Market Authority have published guide for managing sustainability risks. The guide focusses on integrating climate and ESG risks into risk management for FMA-supervised entities, preparing them for SFDR and Taxonomy Regulation applications.

Glasgow Financial Alliance for Net Zero (GFANZ)

The Glasgow Financial Alliance for Net Zero (GFANZ) is a global coalition aiming to decarbonize the economy and support the Paris Agreement's 1.5 °C target by developing actionable tools and methodologies. The Glasgow Financial Alliance for Net Zero (GFANZ) has released a report detailing the essential elements of credible and actionable climate transition plans for companies. GFANZ members, which include financial institutions, will use these criteria to guide capital allocation and engagement with companies on their net-zero transitions. The report notes that access to financial products and services may increasingly depend on a company's climate targets, strategies, and progress. Companies with robust transition plans could benefit from tailored low-carbon financial products, while those lacking credible plans might face higher costs or restricted access to financial services.

Frameworks, Standards and Labels

EU Green Bond Standards

During 2021, the European Commission proposed a regulation for European green bonds (EuGB) as part of its sustainable finance agenda. This framework sets common rules for issuers of green bonds, requiring proceeds to be allocated to environmentally sustainable projects per the EU Taxonomy Regulation. It includes templates for disclosures and mandates pre- and post-issuance reviews by registered external reviewers. The framework applies to both public and private sector issuers and aims to ensure proceeds fund eligible green assets or projects.

UK Green Bond Reforms

During the year 2022, the FCA published a Feedback Statement on ESG integration in UK capital markets, focusing on Green, Social, and Sustainable (GSS) debt instruments. It encourages issuers to adopt industry standards and ensure accurate advertisements. The FCA may review standards for bond frameworks and regulatory oversight for verifiers and second party opinion providers in the future.

Securitization

In 2021, the European Commission conducted a consultation on the EU securitisation framework, with a focus on sustainability disclosures. In May 2022, the ESAs proposed draft RTS for STS securitisations, aiming to enhance disclosure of principal adverse impacts on ESG factors. The EBA's March 2022 report supports integrating these disclosures into all securitisations, suggesting future mandatory PAI disclosures.

Ecolabels

Since 1992, the EU Ecolabel has certified the environmental quality of goods. It will now extend to retail investment products, including UCITS, AIFs, and insurance-based products, leveraging EU Taxonomy criteria. To qualify, products must meet strict criteria on Taxonomy-aligned investments, exclusions, engagement, and impact, with regular updates and reapplications required.

Green Retail Lending and Mortgages

The EU strategy focusses on the creation of a framework for green retail loans and mortgages which ought to be linked to EU Taxonomy Regulation. There are also initiatives to review Mortgage Credit Directive for promoting the adoption of energy efficiency mortgages.

Sustainability Related Rating

The European Commission is considering ESMA guidelines or amending the CRA Regulation to address ESG ratings. ESMA proposed a legal framework for robust, reliable ESG ratings to prevent greenwashing. This includes defining ESG ratings, requiring registration and oversight, imposing stringent product requirements, and ensuring transparency. Dutch and French regulators also advocate for mandatory regulation of ESG data providers. In 2022, the FCA's Feedback Statement 22/4 highlighted issues with ESG ratings providers, such as transparency, conflicts of interest, and interpretability. It called for regulatory oversight and alignment with IOSCO's recommendations. During 2021, IOSCO released a consultation report proposing reforms for ESG ratings and data providers. Recommendations include increased regulatory attention on ESG products, improved transparency, defined methodologies, conflict management, and due diligence by users. The aim is to enhance the quality and reliability of ESG ratings and data.

Multiannual Financial Framework (MFF)

The EU's Multiannual Financial Framework (MFF) for 2021–2027 focuses on aligning expenditures with ESG priorities. Key areas include "Cohesion, Resilience and Values" for sustainable development and "Natural Resources and Environment" for climate action and rural development. The MFF also includes a €1 billion boost to the InvestEU fund to support sustainable projects.

Public/Private Finance Initiatives

The European Green Deal Investment Plan aims to raise at least €1 trillion from 2021 to 2030 for a climate-friendly economy. Half of this funding will come from the EU budget, with the rest from other sources. The InvestEU program will mobilize investment, offer technical advice, and connect investors with sustainable projects aligned with EU priorities.

Corporate Sustainability Due Diligence

During 2022, the European Commission proposed a Directive on Corporate Sustainability Due Diligence, imposing due diligence obligations on large EU and non-EU companies to address human rights and environmental impacts throughout their value chains. It targets companies based on size and sector, with specific thresholds.

German Supply Chain Due Diligence Act

The German Supply Chain Due Diligence Act requires companies with at least 1000 employees to implement human rights and environmental protections in their supply chains. Obligations include risk management, preventive measures, a complaint system, and documentation. Enforcement includes financial penalties and potential civil liability.

Shareholder Rights Directive II

SRD II enhances transparency for institutional investors and asset managers by requiring them to publicly disclose engagement policies and how these align with investment strategies. It promotes shareholder engagement, aligns with EU sustainability goals, and overlaps with ESG reforms. ESMA has called for evidence on its implementation aspects.

Principles for Responsible Investment (PRI)

The Principles for Responsible Investment (PRI) is an international organization dedicated to promoting the integration of ESG factors into investment decision-making. Established in April 2006 with support from the United Nations, the PRI had nearly 4000 participating financial institutions, managing assets with over EUR 106 trillion by the end of 2021. These institutions participate by becoming signatories to the PRI's six key principles and regularly reporting on their progress.

Principle 1: We will incorporate ESG issues into investment analysis and decision-making processes.

Principle 2: We will be active owners and incorporate ESG issues into our ownership policies and practices.

Principle 3: We will seek appropriate disclosure on ESG issues by the entities in which we invest. Principle 4: We will promote acceptance and implementation of the principles within the investment industry.

Principle 5: We will work together to enhance our effectiveness in implementing the principles.

Principle 6: We will each report on our activities and progress towards implementing the principles.

Guidelines for Central Banks[39]

Central banks should lead by disclosing climate-related risks, which encourages broader transparency, meets public demand, and shows commitment to managing and reducing greenhouse gas emissions. Central banks should disclose their strategies and objectives for managing climate-related risks, including board discussions and decision-making processes, to ensure comprehensive integration of climate materiality. Central banks should disclose their governance structures related to

[39] NGFS Technical document, December 2021. Central Banks and Supervisors, Network for Greening the Financial System.

climate risks and opportunities across various functions, including monetary policy, asset management, sustainable investment, financial stability, and internal operations. This includes details on how these structures ensure adherence to sustainability principles and manage climate-related risks effectively. Central banks have to establish a comprehensive framework which spans all functions and integrates climate related risks and opportunities in the relevant areas.[40] The implications of the legal mandates of climate related disclosure must be made by the central banks. The mandates of majority of central banks focusses on price stability and in areas of employment and /or financial stability. Mandates could compel central banks to actively employ policy tools to facilitate the transition to a net-zero economy. Network for Greening the Financial System (NGFS) recommends that central banks are required to disclose how governance structures for their specific areas and functions encompass climate related risks and opportunities. Central banks should disclose their governance structures for adapting credit facilities and investment portfolios to climate-related risks, including responsible bodies, decision-making processes, and checks and balances. They should also clarify the implications for various accounts and portfolios, and outline how they manage climate-related risks to financial stability. Central banks can also disclose governance structure related to internal physical operations. Many central banks have published climate related disclosure covering governance.

During September 2021, the Central Bank of Brazil introduced its first report on social, environmental and climate related risks and opportunities. The report details the central bank's purpose, structure and engagement and explains how social, environmental and climate related risks are integrated into its strategic risk evaluation. The Central bank of Netherlands, De Nederlandsche Bank in its report discusses how climate priorities are integrated and the details about the internal bodies which are responsible for shaping policies. In its annual report Bank Negara Malaysia highlights the bank's approach for managing climate related risks and climate related collaborative initiatives with international organizations. The Bank of England in its disclosure report gives highlights on the committees and steering groups which govern the central bank's initiatives on climate change. The Bank of Russia has a section in its website dedicated to sustainable development including governance aspects. The Monetary Authority of Singapore have established a distinct management forum to coordinate green finance and sustainability efforts. The monetary authority is focussing on providing support for the development of a green finance hub as part of Singapore's green economic growth strategy. The Bank of Finland uses its blog to detail responsible investment groups and procedures. The Banque de France's report outlines responsible investment governance and its integration with overall strategy. Norges Bank describes its climate risk governance in annual and responsible investment reports. Sveriges Riksbank's sustainability

---

[40] NGFS Technical document, December 2021. Central Banks and Supervisors, Network for Greening the Financial System.

strategy includes regular carbon footprint disclosures and a sustainability perspective in managing foreign exchange reserves.

With reference to climate related risks, Central banks can provide description of the material physical and transition risks to credit facilities, investment portfolios and internal operations. Strategies ought to be designed for identifying and assessing the inward and outward impacts of physical and transition risk. Central banks should disclose whether they use quantitative or qualitative methods to identify climate-related risks, including their impact on credit facilities and investments. Disclosures should cover financial materiality, evaluate risks in combination, and include direct and indirect impacts, assumptions, and relevant methodologies like scenario analysis and stress testing. Central banks are encouraged to enhance transparency by disclosing their data usage, including sources, incorporation into risk analysis, and any limitations. They should also specify the proportion of issuers in their portfolios covered by the data used in analyses and provide details on external data providers' methodologies, considering any contractual restrictions.

Central banks are encouraged to disclose how they integrate climate-related risks into their risk management frameworks. This includes specifying whether they use a top-down approach, treating climate-related risks as a standalone risk, or a bottom-up approach, viewing them as amplifiers of other risks. They should also clarify whether risk metrics capture both climate-related and non-climate-related risks or if separate frameworks exist for each. Additionally, they should explain how they handle discrepancies between the management of climate-related and non-climate-related risks.

Central banks are encouraged to disclose the impact of physical and transition risks on credit facilities and investment portfolios using both backward- and forward-looking methodologies, acknowledging potential limitations. They should detail their processes for developing, validating, and using models to analyse these risks, including key assumptions and metrics like financed greenhouse gas emissions, scenario analysis, stress testing, and reverse stress testing. Central banks should also assess the ability of counterparty banks and issuers to handle natural disasters and higher temperatures and report on the impact of these risks on internal operations, with a focus on greenhouse gas emissions.

Central banks are required to assess and disclose the impact of direct and indirect material physical risks on their credit facilities, investment portfolios and internal operations. Central banks can use forward looking methodologies to assess the impact of physical risks.

The Bank of England employs a scorecard method to assess the current and anticipated physical risk exposures of specific assets. These assets are ranked within their respective asset classes based on percentile rankings. This approach provides the central bank with a measure of relative physical risk exposure across its sovereign and corporate holdings. For sovereign holdings, the assessment uses a variety of indicators—such as flood risk, heat stress, hurricanes, sea-level rise, water stress, and wildfires—to evaluate each country's risk exposure. This evaluation is expressed as a proportion of the country's gross domestic product, population, and agricultural land use. The Banque de France uses a forward-looking methodology from an external data provider to manage its funds and pension fund portfolios.

The European Central Bank has released a paper on its climate stress test for the entire economy. The assessment of expected losses from physical risks combines the direct impact on firms' exposure to extreme weather events with indirect impacts, such as anticipated regional damage, measured as a percentage of gross domestic product.

Central banks should assess and disclose the impact of transition risks on credit facilities and investment portfolios and explain their modelling approaches. The Paris Agreement serves as a benchmark for resilience. Financed greenhouse gas emissions, a backward-looking metric, help evaluate exposure to transition risk, affecting banks and issuers with high emissions. Financed greenhouse gas emissions can be calculated using the weighted average carbon intensity. Central banks are required to disclose the emissions of counterparty banks and issuers represented in a central bank's credit facilities and investment portfolios. Company emissions are often categorized into three scopes:

- Scope 1 emissions: Direct emissions from sources controlled or owned by the company.
- Scope 2 emissions: Indirect emissions related to the company's purchase of electricity, steam, heat, or cooling.
- Scope 3 emissions: Indirect emissions not included in Scope 2, occurring in a company's supply chain or as a result of using the company's products and services.

Examples of forward-looking metrics for assessing transition risk include:

1. Binary measurements of alignment: Assessing the proportion of portfolio assets issued by companies with targets aligned with climate goals, such as the Paris Agreement.
2. Benchmark divergence metrics: Evaluating individual companies' alignment with climate goals by comparing forecast performance to climate scenarios.
3. Implied temperature rise metrics: Estimating the global temperature increase if an issuer's activities represented the global economy.

Some central banks have published estimates of the implied temperature rise associated with their portfolios. For example, Banque de France have set and achieved a target of aligning the equity component of its own funds' investment portfolio with a goal of below 2 °C by 2019. By the end of 2022, it aims to apply the same target to the equity component of the pension liabilities investment portfolio, which had an implied temperature rise of 2–3 °C in 2020. Bank of England had reported an implied temperature rise of 3.0 °C for 2021 for its Corporate Bond Purchase Scheme portfolio. The Bank of England also adopted a binary target measurement approach, comparing corporates' decarbonisation plans with an emissions reduction pathway consistent with the UK achieving net-zero emissions by 2050.

Forward Looking Assessment Methods

Scenario Analysis

Central banks can leverage scenario analysis to identify, assess, and disclose financial risks related to climate change and the transition to a net-zero economy. By using diverse data sources and narratives, they can explore various plausible scenarios that consider spatial, political, social, regulatory, and environmental factors across countries and regions. The results, combined with non-climate-related analyses, enable comprehensive climate-related risk assessments of credit facilities and investment portfolios. Central banks can utilize scenario analysis to pinpoint sovereigns, sectors, industries, or individual issuers with significant climate-related risk exposure, thereby assessing potential balance sheet risks. By conducting detailed scenario analyses on a representative sample of issuers based on their activities, location, and climate risk exposure, central banks can extrapolate the findings to evaluate the broader impact on their portfolios.

Stress testing

Stress testing for climate-related risks on central banks' balance sheets is a new approach that helps identify vulnerabilities and enhance risk awareness. It uses increasingly accessible granular data, though challenges include longer time horizons and unreliable future data. Central banks may disclose test details and scenarios to promote transparency and comparability.

Reverse stress testing

Reverse stress testing can complement scenario analysis and stress testing for central banks. When using climate-related reverse stress tests, central banks should disclose their design and execution processes, including the critical loss level, time horizon, and key scenario features. Unlike commercial banks, where the critical loss level relates to default scenarios, for central banks it signifies a scenario where they cannot effectively implement monetary policy. Disclosure should include evaluations of scenario plausibility and the impact of scenarios on balance sheets.

Source: NGFS REPORT, NGFS Technical document, December 2021. Central Banks and Supervisors, Network for Greening the Financial System.

Green Finance Policies of Banks in Select Countries

Green Finance Policies in Indonesia[41]

Bank Indonesia had launched green finance policies in year 2010. In 2012, it became one of the founders of the national Sustainable Banking Network (SBN). In the same year, Bank Indonesia published the green lending model guidelines. In 2013, the banking supervision responsibilities were handed over to the Financial Services Authority of Indonesia (OJK). OJK formulated a national green taxonomy to develop 11 environmentally friendly business activities. These activities included (1) renewable energy; (2) energy efficiency; (3) pollution prevention and control; (4) sustainable management of living natural resources and land use; (5) conservation of terrestrial and aquatic biodiversity; (6) environmentally friendly transportation; (7) sustainable water and wastewater management; (8) climate change adaptation; (9) products that can reduce the use of resources and produce less pollution (eco-efficient); (10) environmentally friendly buildings that meet national, regional or international recognised standards or certifications; and (11) other environmental friendly business activities. These activities are eligible for green bond issuance in accordance with Indonesian regulation standards.

Institutional Framework on Climate Change in Costa Rica[42]

The Central Bank of Costa Rica (BCCR) has recognized that climate change poses significant risks to its ability to achieve strategic objectives, such as maintaining inflation within target ranges and ensuring a stable, efficient, and competitive financial system. Acknowledging that many factors influencing these risks are beyond its control, the BCCR has implemented three major initiatives. First, it established the Group for Strategic Analysis of Climate Change (GAECC) in 2019, bringing together representatives from various departments to address climate-related impacts on the bank's objectives and liaise with external stakeholders. Second, BCCR joined the Network for Greening the Financial System (NGFS) to share best practices and support the transition to a sustainable global economy. Third, it developed a roadmap linked to its Strategic Plan 2020–23 to integrate climate change into monetary and financial policies. This roadmap focuses on data collection, scenario analysis, climate risk management, and greening international reserves. For greening international reserves, BCCR follows twofold investment strategy of investments in assets with prime green ratings and in green funds directly.

[41] Irving Fisher Committee on Central Bank Statistics, IFC Report No 14, Sustainable finance data for central banks, 2021 survey.; POJK No 51/POJK.03/2017.

[42] Irving Fisher Committee on Central Bank Statistics, IFC Report No 14, Sustainable finance data for central banks, 2021 survey.

European Central Bank (ECB) Initiatives[43]

The European Central Bank (ECB) has developed a comprehensive top-down climate stress test to analyse the resilience of non-financial corporations (NFCs) and euro area (EA) banks to climate risks under different assumptions regarding future climate policies. This stress testing framework is based on three pillar components (a) climate specific scenarios which would forecast climate and macroeconomic conditions over the period of 30 years (b) extensive dataset with backward and forward looking climate and financial information for European firms and monetary financial institutions in the euro area (c) innovative set of climate specific models to capture the direct and indirect transmission channels of climate risk drivers which affect firms and banks. The ECB framework for advanced climate stress testing incorporates granular firm level data which allows for detailed estimation of climate risk distribution and accounting for variations in firm size and asset location. The data set integrates four key streams (a) banks' NFC counterparty balance sheets (b) firms' transition risk with emissions data (c) physical risk from future extreme weather events (d) banks' loan exposures and corporate bond holdings, enabling comprehensive climate risk assessment. The data set is based on four comprehensive streams of regulatory and private data sources such as Orbis, Eikon, Bloomberg and Ibach. The mapping of data covers the financial and climate risk data for about 2.3 million European firms and 1600 EA banks which covers over 80% of total loan exposures.

Measurement of Carbon Foot Print of Bank Loans in Finland

In 2021, Bank of Finland launched an experimental project to compile carbon footprint indicators for banks' loans to non-financial corporations. The estimation of the carbon footprint of banks' loans to NFCs serves two purposes: (i) measuring and monitoring transition risks based on counterparty risk, requiring consideration of Scope 1, 2, and 3 emissions, especially for sectors with indirect CO_2 exposure like trade and services. It can also lead to assessment of the contribution of the Finnish banking sector to pursue the national net zero emissions goal by the year 2035. The total emissions in Finland amounted to 53.1 million tons of CO_2 in year 2019 and requires to be reduced by 60% by the year 2035 to achieve net zero emission targets by year 2035. The data compilation process involved five steps: defining the target NFC population using the statistical business register, merging corporate ETS data with firm-level loan data, estimating missing emissions data using industry totals, acquiring loan and balance sheet data for carbon footprint indicators, and using National Accounts and ETS data to estimate recent air emission accounts.

[43] Irving Fisher Committee on Central Bank Statistics, IFC Report No 14, Sustainable finance data for central banks, 2021 survey.

Sustainable Finance Data Initiatives in Colombia

Colombia faces significant climate-related risks, primarily from riverine floods, which have caused substantial economic damage, with minimal insurance coverage. Climate change is expected to increase the frequency and severity of these events, potentially causing annual losses of USD 23–25 billion by 2030. The Financial Superintendence of Colombia (SFC), with World Bank assistance, developed a climate risk assessment framework focusing on physical and transition risks. This includes stress testing banks' vulnerability to floods, using spatial data and various flood scenarios. The analysis aimed to estimate the impact of climate risks on banks' loan portfolios, bond holdings, profitability, and solvency.

IFC Blue Finance Guidelines

International Finance Corporation (IFC), the arm of World Bank Group is the largest global development institution serving the private sector in emerging markets. IFC have presence in over 100 countries. In the year 2021, IFC committed $31.5 billion to private companies and financial institutions in developing countries.

Blue finance is an emerging sector within climate finance that has garnered significant attention from investors, financial institutions, and issuers worldwide. It offers substantial opportunities by contributing to economic growth, better livelihoods, and healthier marine ecosystems. The ocean economy is projected to double to $3 trillion by 2030, creating 40 million jobs compared to 2010. Innovative financing solutions are crucial for preserving oceans and coasts and increasing clean water resources, with blue finance playing a key role in achieving these objectives. Blue Bonds and Blue loans are new innovative financing instruments used for funding ocean friendly projects involved in clean water resources protection. In recent times, there have been exponential growth of sustainable finance and introduction of different instruments based on sustainability targets. Important integrating principles such as Green Bond Principles (GBP) and Green Loan Principles (GLP) were introduced by International Capital Markets Association (ICMA) and Loan Market Association (LMA).

The Sustainable Blue Economy Finance Principles were launched in March 2018, focusing on the sustainable use and conservation of oceans and marine resources, beyond just tackling plastic pollution. These principles align with Environmental and Risk Management practices like the IFC Performance Standards. With increasing interest in expanding Blue Finance, the IFC has adapted the Green Bond and Green Loan Principles, along with the ICMA Handbook for Impact Reporting, to guide the implementation of Blue Finance within green bonds and loans. The guideline document offers eligible uses of proceeds for private investment aligned with the Green Bond and Loan Principles which support UN Sustainable Development Goals 6 and 14 on water and marine conservation. The framework also covers Sustainable Development Goals 2, 12, 13 and 15 related to pollution in rivers and coastal areas. A project can be classified as a blue project if it is consistent with project categories of Green Bond and Green Loan principles and must contribute to either Sustainable Development Goal 6 or 14. A project can be labelled "blue" only if it does not pose significant risks to other key Sustainable Development Goals, including those related to hunger, clean energy, climate action, and responsible consumption.

The project must adhere to internationally recognized sustainability standards, such as the IFC Performance Standards and World Bank Environmental, Health, and Safety guidelines. Additionally, industry-specific and product-specific standards may be required for blue investments, exceeding national requirements.

On the basis of Green bond principles and green loan principles, blue financing is provided for activities such as sustainable water management and ocean protection. Blue finance is eligible for activities (blue finance areas) such as water supply, water sanitation, Ocean friendly and Water friendly products (blue products), Ocean friendly chemicals and plastic related sectors, sustainable shipping and port logistics, fisheries, aquaculture and seafood value chain, marine ecosystem restoration and sustainable tourism services and offshore renewable energy production.

Blue finance is available for investments in the research, design, development and implementation of efficient and clear water supply. Financing or refinancing opportunities are offered for water efficiency technologies such as drip irrigation, water recycling solutions etc. Blue finance is offered for investments in the conservation, enhancement, and restoration of marine and coastal ecosystems, including the development of innovative governance structures that facilitate both private and public sector investments. Blue finance is applicable for investments in the development of ecosystems' insurance products which covers coral reefs, mangroves and wetlands. Offshore wind farms in the Blue Finance Guidance must include no-fishing zones, artificial reefs, and conduct year-long Environmental Impact Assessments with ongoing environmental monitoring.

Summary Status of Regulations in Select Jurisdictions

CVM Resolution, Brazil

In December 2021, the Brazilian Securities Commission (CVM) introduced ESG information disclosure criteria on its Resolution No. 59 (RCVM 59) which is amendment of CVM Rule No. 480. The resolution was enacted and became effective in year 2023. Listed firms must disclose ESG information or explain their absence and include the following.

- Whether the firm report on a materiality matrix and key ESG indicators, and which indicators are deemed material.
- The firm's consideration of UN Sustainable Development Goals (SDGs) and which SDGs are relevant to their business.

- Adherence to TCFD recommendations or other recognized climate-related financial disclosure standards.
- Details on greenhouse gas emission inventories, including the scope of reported emissions, if applicable.

Climate Related Disclosure, USA

In 2022, the Securities Exchange Commission (SEC) has proposed rule changes requiring registrants to include climate-related disclosures in their registration statements and periodic reports. These disclosures must cover climate-related risks that could materially impact their business, financial condition, and operations, including greenhouse gas (GHG) emissions. Companies must report their governance of climate risks, how these risks affect their strategy and financial statements, and the impact of climate-related events. The rules also mandate disclosures of Scope 1, Scope 2, and, if material, Scope 3 GHG emissions. The proposal includes a phase-in period and safe harbours for smaller companies and those disclosing Scope 3 emissions. This move aims to provide investors with consistent, comparable information, supporting informed investment decisions and reflecting the growing demand for transparent climate risk reporting. The rules, aligning with frameworks like the TCFD and GHG Protocol, will be open for comment following publication in the Federal Register.

Climate Related Disclosure, Canada

The Canadian Securities Administrators (CSA) is evaluating international climate-related disclosure rules to inform its proposed regulations published in October 2021. The CSA aims to align with global standards, particularly the Task Force on Climate-Related Financial Disclosures (TCFD), while addressing Canadian market needs and issuer realities. Recent developments include proposed rules by the U.S. SEC and the ISSB on sustainability disclosures. The CSA is analysing differences between these proposals and reviewing stakeholder feedback to develop disclosure requirements that enhance consistency, comparability, and market efficiency in Canadian capital markets.

Corporate Disclosure of Environmental Information, China

The "Measures for the Administration of Disclosure of Environmental Information by Enterprises" set guidelines for lawful environmental information disclosure in China. These rules, guided by laws like the Environmental Protection Law, standardize disclosure practices and enhance supervision. Enterprises must disclose accurate, timely, and complete environmental information, including pollution data and GHG emissions. The Ministry of Ecology and Environment oversees the process, with local departments managing regional compliance. Key polluters, listed companies, and bond-issuing firms have specific disclosure requirements. The rules also address violations, with penalties ranging from fines to criticism. The system aims to ensure transparent, standardized environmental reporting and effective supervision.

Business Responsibility and Sustainability Reporting by Listed Entities, India

Securities Exchange Board of India (SEBI) through its Circular No. CIR/CFD/CMD/10/2015 initially established the Business Responsibility Report (BRR) format for ESG (Environment, Social, and Governance) disclosures by listed entities. However, a regulatory amendment effective May 5, 2021, introduced the Business Responsibility and Sustainability Report (BRSR) to replace the BRR. The BRSR, accompanied by a guidance note, mandates disclosures based on the nine principles of the National Guidelines on Responsible Business Conduct (NGBRCs). It requires listed entities to report on essential indicators compulsorily and encourages reporting on leadership indicators voluntarily. The BRSR aims to enhance transparency with standardized, quantitative ESG disclosures to facilitate comparability across companies, sectors, and time periods, thereby aiding investors in making informed decisions. It also encourages companies to address social and environmental impacts beyond financial performance. Starting from the financial year 2022–2023, the top 1000 listed companies by market capitalization must file the BRSR, while for FY 2021–2022, its submission is optional. In FY 2021–22, more than 175 companies reported on the BRSR framework on a voluntary basis.[44]Companies already using international reporting frameworks, like GRI, SASB, or TCFD, can cross-reference their reports with the BRSR. Stock exchanges are required to notify listed entities and publish these updates on their websites. In 2023, SEBI has announced a consultation paper which seeks public comments on the regulatory framework of ESG Disclosures by listed entities, ESG ratings in the securities market and ESG investing by mutual funds.

Japan Corporate Climate Disclosures

Japan Financial Services Agency (JFSA) stipulates companies listed on the prime market segment of the Tokyo Stock Exchange to make disclosure based on the recommendations of the Task Force on TCFD or an equivalent framework based on the

[44] SEBI | Consultation Paper on ESG Disclosures, Ratings and Investing.

revision of the Corporate Governance Code. The Disclosure Working Group under the Financial System Council will discuss how listed companies must disclose their sustainability related initiatives based on framework by IFRS foundation. In collaboration with Japan Exchange Group (JPX), JFSA aim to establish an information platform to consolidate information on green bonds and policies with respect to ESG. JFSA plans to develop a code of conduct for ESG rating organization and data providers regarding issues related to comparability of evaluation methodologies and governance. JFSA in collaboration with the Bank of Japan, will conduct a pilot exercise of scenario analysis using NGFS scenarios as common scenarios for three megabanks and three major non-life insurance group.

ESG Corporate Disclosure Rules, South Korea

The Korea Exchange plans to issue guidelines on ESG (Environmental, Social, and Governance) disclosure to encourage voluntary sustainable management reporting by listed companies. By 2030, it will require all KOSPI-listed companies to make such disclosures mandatory. Additionally, the implementation of the Korea stewardship code, introduced in 2016, will be reviewed for potential revisions to strengthen fiduciary duties related to ESG. To enhance accountability, proxy advisory services will be required to disclose more information about their operations, and the authorities will gradually increase their supervision over these services.

Corporate Sustainability Reporting Directive (CSRD), European Union

EU law mandates that all large companies and listed companies (excluding listed micro-enterprises) must disclose information on the risks and opportunities related to social and environmental issues, as well as the impact of their activities on people and the environment. This disclosure helps investors, civil society organizations, consumers, and other stakeholders assess the sustainability performance of companies in alignment with the European Green Deal. The European Green Deal aims to address climate change and environmental degradation by transforming the EU into a modern, resource-efficient, and competitive economy. Its objectives include achieving net-zero greenhouse gas emissions by 2050, decoupling economic growth from resource use. The Green Deal is also a key part of Europe's recovery from the COVID-19 pandemic, with one-third of the €1.8 trillion from the Next Generation EU Recovery Plan and the EU's seven-year budget dedicated to financing it. The European Commission has proposed measures to align climate, energy, transport, and taxation policies to reduce net greenhouse gas emissions by at least 55% by 2030, compared to 1990 levels.

The Corporate Sustainability Reporting Directive (CSRD), which took effect on January 5, 2023, updates and strengthens the rules for reporting social and environmental information by companies. It expands the reporting requirements to include a broader range of large companies, listed SMEs, and some non-EU companies generating over EUR 150 million in the EU market. The new rules aim to provide investors and stakeholders with the necessary information to assess companies' impacts on people and the environment, as well as financial risks and opportunities related to sustainability. The first companies will begin applying these rules in the 2024 financial year, with reports due in 2025. Reporting must follow the European Sustainability Reporting Standards (ESRS), developed by EFRAG, and includes requirements for assurance and digital taxonomy of the reported information.

Climate Related Financial Disclosures Regulations 2022, United Kingdom

The Companies (Strategic Report) (Climate-related Financial Disclosure) Regulations 2022, effective from April 6, 2022, amend sections of the Companies Act 2006 to require certain companies to include a non-financial and sustainability information statement in their strategic reports. This statement must include detailed climate-related financial disclosures, such as governance arrangements, risk management, impacts on business strategy, and performance targets related to climate risks and opportunities. High turnover companies and those listed on the Alternative Investment Market are subject to these requirements, with provisions allowing directors to omit disclosures if deemed unnecessary, provided a clear explanation is given.

JSE Climate Change Disclosure Guidance, South Africa

The JSE Sustainability Disclosure Guidance aligns with global sustainability and climate change disclosure initiatives, such as the GRI Standards, TCFD recommendations, and the IIRC's IR Framework, while also addressing the South African context. It aims to help companies navigate various reporting standards rather than replace existing global frameworks. The JSE has a history of promoting strong governance and sustainability, evident through initiatives like its progressive listing requirements, the 2004 SRI Index, and its role in global organizations like the SSE and WFE. Despite its established sustainability links, this is the JSE's first detailed guidance for listed companies on sustainability/ESG reporting.

Singapore Listing Rules, Singapore

Listing Rule 711A mandates that every issuer prepares an annual sustainability report, which must describe the issuer's sustainability practices in accordance with the primary components outlined in Listing Rule 711B on a 'comply or explain' basis. The report should include key elements such as material ESG factors, climate-related disclosures, policies, practices, performance, targets, and a Board statement on sustainability governance. Issuers must use globally recognized frameworks, like the TCFD recommendations, for their reporting to ensure transparency and comparability.

The Board holds ultimate responsibility for the issuer's sustainability reporting, ensuring that ESG factors are monitored and managed effectively. The sustainability report should provide a balanced view of the issuer's risks and opportunities, aiming to give stakeholders a comprehensive understanding of the issuer's performance and future prospects.

The report must also consider stakeholder engagement and the broader value chain, reflecting the issuer's interactions with its physical environment, social community, and governance practices. Climate-related disclosures are particularly emphasized, especially for industries most affected by climate change, with mandatory reporting required for certain sectors starting from specific dates. This approach aims to provide investors with a fuller picture of the issuer's financial and sustainability performance.

Climate and Sustainability Related Disclosure Standards, Australia

The Australian Government is mandating climate-related financial disclosures to enhance transparency and provide investors with better information about entities' exposure to climate risks and opportunities. These mandatory disclosures will align Australia with international standards and are expected to improve the country's attractiveness to international capital. The disclosures will be incorporated into the Corporations Act 2001 and related legislation, with detailed standards maintained by the Australian Accounting Standards Board (AASB) and the Australian Auditing and Assurance Standards Board (AUASB). Large entities, including companies, financial institutions, and superannuation funds, will be required to disclose climate-related information. The mandate will be phased in over 4 years, starting from 1 July 2024, with different requirements based on the size and emissions of the entities. Exemptions apply to small and medium businesses and certain not-for-profits.

The disclosures will include assessments of climate resilience, emissions reporting (Scope 1, 2, and later 3), and industry-specific metrics. Assurance requirements will be phased in, starting with Scope 1 and 2 emissions. The Government endorses the adoption of the ISSB's IFRS S2 Climate-related Disclosures standard, ensuring Australia's framework is globally aligned while meeting local needs.

Sustainability Guidance by Stock Exchanges

Stock exchanges are increasingly crucial in guiding markets through Environmental, Social, and Governance (ESG) disclosure standards. By the end of 2022, 67 exchanges provided written guidance on sustainability reporting, a significant rise from 13 in 2015. The trend towards mandatory ESG disclosure continues, with 34 markets having sustainability reporting rules, up from 30 in the previous year, keeping SDG 12.6 on track for 2030.

International ESG disclosure instruments, such as the GRI Standards and recommendations from the TCFD, are widely referenced in exchanges' guidance. The establishment of the International Sustainability Standards Board (ISSB) under the IFRS Foundation is streamlining these standards. As ESG disclosure becomes more standardized, stock exchanges are expanding education and training programs to help companies comply with these evolving requirements. To support these efforts, the UN SSE launched the SSE Academy in 2021, enhancing exchanges' capacity to train on ESG topics.

Sustainable Stock Exchange Initiatives

The Sustainable Stock Exchange initiative is a UN Partnership Programme organized by UNCTAD, the UN Global Compact, UNEP FI, and the PRI. Its mission is to create a global platform for exchanges to collaborate with investors, companies, regulators, policymakers, and international organizations to improve ESG (environmental, social, and corporate governance) performance and promote sustainable investment, including financing the UN Sustainable Development Goals. The SSE pursues this mission through a comprehensive approach that includes evidence-based policy analysis, facilitating multi-stakeholder consensus-building, and offering technical assistance and advisory services.

The United Nations Conference on Trade and Development (UNCTAD) Division on Investment and Enterprise is a leading global authority on investment and enterprise for sustainable development. Drawing on decades of successful experience, its experts offer international research, policy analysis, inter-governmental consensus-building, and technical assistance to over 150 countries. The Division's flagship publication is the annual World Investment Report, and its primary global event is the biennial World Investment Forum.

The United Nations Environment Programme Finance Initiative (UNEP-FI) is a distinctive global partnership between the United Nations Environment Programme (UNEP) and the financial sector. UNEP FI collaborates with over 200 financial institutions that are Signatories to the UNEP FI Statements, along with various partner organizations, to strengthen the connections between sustainability and financial performance. Through peer networks, research, and training, UNEP FI aims to identify, promote, and implement best practices in environmental and sustainability matters across all levels of financial institutions.

The UN Global Compact is a strategic policy initiative for businesses dedicated to aligning their operations and strategies with ten universally accepted principles in human rights, labor, environment, and anti-corruption. By embracing these principles, businesses—key drivers of globalization—can help ensure that markets, commerce, technology, and finance advance in ways that benefit economies and societies globally.

The United Nations-supported Principles for Responsible Investment Initiative is a global network of investors committed to implementing six principles that integrate ESG issues into investment decision-making and ownership practices. These voluntary principles help investors align their goals with broader societal objectives.

Table 6.3 highlights the stock exchange sustainability activities.

Table 6.4 shows the statistics of instruments referred in stock exchange guidance documents.

In September 2015, the SSE introduced its Model Guidance for stock exchanges, addressing a significant gap where fewer than 10% of exchanges offered ESG reporting guidance. This lack of guidance resulted in incomplete corporate information, complicating investors' efforts to assess companies' material issues. The SSE's goal is for all exchanges to offer sustainability reporting guidance. The Model Guidance serves as a template for exchanges to create their own customized guidance, supported by additional tools available on the SSE webpage.73 of the 122 stock exchanges tracked by the SSE have published ESG reporting guidance for their listed companies.

Table 6.3 Stock exchange sustainability activities

SSE members	134
Exchanges training on ESG topics	92
Exchanges with SME listing platform	77
Exchanges providing written guidance on ESG reporting	73
Exchanges with sustainability reports	61
Exchanges with ESG bond segments	53
Exchanges whose markets are covered by an ESG index	49
Exchanges with mandatory ESG listing requirements	38

Source: https://sseinitiative.org/

Table 6.4 Instruments referenced in stock exchange guidance documents

Documents	Percent referenced in stock exchange
Global Reporting Initiative (GRI)	96%
Sustainability Accounting Standards Board (SASB)	82%
International Integrated Reporting Council (IIRC)	75%
Carbon Disclosure Project (CDP)	71%
Task Force on Climate related Financial Disclosure (TCFD)	67%
Climate Disclosure Standards Board (CDSB)	34%

Source: https://sseinitiative.org/esg-guidance-database

22% of board seats on G20 listed companies are held by women. In 2015, Stock exchanges from around the world joined UN Women, UN Global Compact and the Sustainable Stock Exchanges (SSE) Initiative to ring their opening or closing bells in support of gender equality and to highlight the pivotal role of the private sector in empowering women in the workplace, marketplace and community. The UN SSE and IFC have identified three key roles for stock exchanges in advancing gender equality: promoting gender-focused products and services, improving market performance on gender equality, and leading by example. This updated guidance, developed in collaboration with UN Women and input from 71 experts across 34 countries, builds on the 2017 SSE guidance to offer expanded and strategic recommendations.

International Integrated Reporting Council (IIRC)

The International Integrated Reporting Council (IIRC) was established in 2010 as a global coalition of businesses, investors, policy-makers, the accounting profession and civil society. IIRC is a part of IFRS foundation. The International Integrated Reporting Framework and Integrated Thinking Principles, used in 75 countries, aim to improve communication about value creation, preservation, and erosion. They promote efficient capital allocation, financial stability, and sustainable development by enhancing corporate reporting and accountability. The framework connects financial statements with sustainability disclosures, supporting integrated thinking and decision-making. Managed by the IFRS Foundation, a global non-profit, the framework is maintained by the International Accounting Standards Board (IASB) and the International Sustainability Standards Board (ISSB) to ensure high-quality, globally accepted accounting and sustainability standards. In 2021, the IIRC merged with the SASB Foundation into the Value Reporting Foundation (VRF).

Carbon Disclosure Project

Carbon Disclosure Project (CDP) is a not for profit charity which runs the global disclosure system for investors, companies, cities, states and regions to manage their environmental impacts. CDP was originally founded as the 'Carbon Disclosure Project' in 2000, began by asking companies to disclose their climate impact. Over time, CDP have expanded environmental disclosure efforts to include deforestation and water security, and extended support to cities, states, and regions. CPD collects information on climate risks and low carbon opportunities from the world's largest companies which are supported by more than 700 capital market signatories representing over US$142 trillion in assets and 330+ major purchasers with over US$6.4 trillion in procurement spend. The focus areas are climate, water, forests and plastics.

References

01.pdf (fsa.go.jp).
Bank of England. (2021). The Bank of England's climate-related financial disclosure.
Bank of Russia. (2021). Sustainable Development, webpage, Bank of Russia.
Banque de France. (2021).
Basel Committee on Banking Supervision (BCBS). (2021a). Climate-related risk drivers and their transmission channels, April.
Basel Committee on Banking Supervision (BCBS). (2021b). Climate-related financial risks—Measurement methodologies, April.
Better Tax Control Frameworks, 2016.
Canadian securities regulators consider impact of international developments on proposed climate-related disclosure rule—Canadian Securities Administrators (securities-administrators.ca)
Climate and Sustainability related disclosure standards, Australia.
CVM Resolution 59.
Delbecque, B., Jotanovic, V., Tilley, T., & Yang, H.. Asset Management in Europe, An overview of asset management industry, 14th Edition, Dec 2022, European Fund and Asset Management Association (EFAMA).
Effects Analysis | IFRS S1 General Requirements for Disclosure of Sustainability-related Financial Information and IFRS S2 Climate-related Disclosures | June 2023.
Ehlers, T., Mojon, B., & Packer, F. (2020). Green bonds and carbon emissions: Exploring the case for a rating system at the firm level. *BIS Quarterly Review*, September.
Environmental Protection Agency Victoria (EPA Victoria). Resource Efficiency Case Studies: Lower your Impact.
European Commission, Small-scale fisheries. https://ec.europa.eu/fisheries/cfp/small-scale-fisheries_en. International Fund for Agricultural Development, United Nations Environment Programme, Smallholders, food security, and the environment, 2014.
FSB, Proposal for a Disclosure Task Force on Climate-Related Risks, November 9, 2015.
Guidelines Blue Finance, Guidance for financing the Blue Economy, building on the Green Bond Principles and the Green Loan Principles, International Finance Corporation, Jan 2022. https://www.ifc.org/en/insights-reports/2022/guidelines-for-blue-finance
https://commission.europa.eu/strategy-and-policy/priorities-2019-2024/european-green-deal_en
https://ec.europa.eu/info/law/better-regulation/have-your-say/initiatives/12067-Strengthening-the-consideration-of-sustainability-risks-and-factors-for-financial-products-Directive-EU-2017-593-24. https://ec.europa.eu/info/consultations/finance-2020-eu-green-bond-standard_en25
https://ec.europa.eu/info/policies/justice-and-fundamental-rights/gender-equality/gender-equality-strategy_en
https://integratedreporting.ifrs.org/the-iirc-2/governance-archive/
https://rulebook.sgx.com/rulebook/practice-note-76-sustainability-reporting-guide
https://sseinitiative.org/gender-equality
https://tnfd.global/
https://tnfd.global/publication/recommendations-of-the-taskforce-on-nature-related-financial-disclosures/
https://treasury.gov.au/sites/default/files/2024-01/c2024-466491-policy-state.pdf
https://www.cdp.net/en/info/about-us
https://www.fsb-tcfd.org/about/
https://www.ifrs.org/groups/international-sustainability-standards-board/
https://www.ifrs.org/issued-standards/ifrs-sustainability-standards-navigator/ifrs-s1-general-requirements.html/content/dam/ifrs/publications/html-standards-issb/english/2023/issued/issbs1/#about
https://www.iosco.org/
https://www.jse.co.za/our-business/sustainability/jses-sustainability-and-climate-disclosure-guidance

https://www.legislation.gov.uk/uksi/2022/31/contents/made
https://www.sebi.gov.in/reports-and-statistics/reports/feb-2023/consultation-paper-on-esg-disclosures-ratings-and-investing_68193.html
https://www.sebi.gov.in/sebi_data/commondocs/may-2021/Business%20responsibility%20and%20sustainability%20reporting%20by%20listed%20entitiesAnnexure1_p.PDF
https://www.sec.gov/newsroom/press-releases/2024-31
https://www.securities-administrators.ca/news/canadian-securities-regulators-issue-statements-on-proposed-sustainability-disclosure-standards-and-ongoing-climate-consultation/
International Council on Mining and Metals (ICMM), Financial concepts for mine closure, 2019.
International Energy Agency (IEA), Phasing out unabated coal, 2021.
International Labour Organization (ILO), Tripartite Declaration of Principles concerning Multinational Enterprises and Social Policy, 2017.
KPMG, Delivering Sustainable Finance, September 2020, The new reality publication series, kpmg.com/regulatory challenges.
Measures for the Administration of Disclosure of Environmental Information by Enterprises in Accordance with Law (mee.gov.cn).
Natural Resource Governance Institute (NRGI), The Resource Curse, 2015.
NGFS Technical document, December 2021.Central Banks and Supervisors, Network for Greening the Financial System.
Organisation for Economic Co-operation and Development (OECD), OECD Guidelines for Multinational Enterprises, 2011.
Organisation for Economic Co-operation and Development (OECD), OECD Due Diligence Guidance for Responsible Business Conduct, 2018.
Organisation for Economic Co-operation and Development (OECD), Co-operative Tax Compliance: Building.
Peter Seley, Emerging Trends in Climate Change Litigation. Law 360, March 7, 2016.
Policies, Regulations and Standards, Chapter III Capital markets and sustainable finance, World Investment Report 2023 Investing in sustainable energy for all, UNCTAD.
Responsible Investment Report 2020, Banque de France, March.
Task Force on Climate related Financial Disclosures 2023 status report.
TCFD Report 2017.
The Companies (Strategic Report) (Climate-related Financial Disclosure) Regulations 2022 (legislation.gov.uk).
The JFSA Strategic Priorities July 2021–June 2022, Financial Services Agency, August 31, 2021.
UNEP and Copenhagen Centre for Energy Efficiency, Best Practices and Case Studies for Industrial Energy Efficiency Improvement, February 16, 2016.
United Nations Interagency Framework Team for Preventive Action, Extractive Industries and Conflict, 2012.
World Bank Group, Growing the Rural Nonfarm Economy to Alleviate Poverty, 2017.
World Wildlife Foundation (WWF), Small-scale fisheries, https://www.wwfmmi.org/medtrends/shifting_blue_economies/small_scale_fisheries/

Chapter 7
Sustainable Finance Investments in Different Regions of World

Climate Taxonomy

Taxonomies have become a key tool for implementing government climate policies by classifying activities based on their role in achieving net-zero emissions by 2050. According to Climate Bond, by 2023, more than 40 countries and regions have a taxonomy or are in the process of developing one. Globally, most green taxonomies exclude fossil fuel activities, while mixed taxonomies, which include transitional components, allow limited fossil gas power generation with strict emission and time constraints. Thailand's Taxonomy, the first science-based transitional taxonomy, was adopted in May 2023 and uses a traffic light system to classify activities based on their alignment with the Paris Agreement. While fossil gas is temporarily used to support renewable energy in countries like the US, China, and Germany, they aim for a medium-term reduction in hydrocarbon consumption. Recent studies highlight significant fugitive emissions from fossil gas, prompting stricter policies and life-cycle emissions assessments.

Green Taxonomy

A classification framework that focuses exclusively on activities aligned with the net-zero goal, such as solar power and electric vehicles, is considered green. These taxonomies typically include only climate change mitigation and adaptation activities, even if other environmental objectives are listed, as long as only those two activities are included.

B. R. Kumar, *Green Finance*, Sustainable Finance,
https://doi.org/10.1007/978-3-032-03333-8_7

Sustainable Taxonomy

A taxonomy that encompasses a broader range of activities beyond green taxonomies, typically including those related to sustainable development, environmental, and social well-being goals.

Transitional Activities

These are activities lacking rapid decarbonization solutions but can gradually reduce emissions or are temporarily necessary. They must have a credible, science-based decarbonization plan by 2050 or a defined phase-out timeframe to ensure they are eventually eliminated from the economy.

Transitional Taxonomy

A taxonomy that distinctly separates transitional activities from green activities, often using a system like traffic lights, enabling each to have a distinct label. Environmental performance can be ranked based on different categories. Climate supporting is fully aligned with environmental goals. Activities not yet meeting environmental standards, but committed to improvement are termed transitioning. They are subdivided into green transition, interim transition and watchlist. Green transition represents sectoral pathway which are aligned with net zero. Interim transition refers to advancement toward alignment with sectoral pathways. CICERO categorizes bonds into three "green shades," where Medium Green represents projects that contribute to long-term sustainable transitions (e.g., plug-in hybrid buses), while Light Green refers to projects that offer environmental benefits but are not aligned with long-term sustainability goals (e.g., energy efficiency in fossil fuel infrastructures). Watchlist category refers to activities which need monitoring for potential non-compliance.

Sustainable debt encompasses financial instruments within two main categories: use-of-proceeds debt and sustainability-linked debt. Use-of-proceeds debt refers to proceeds from bonds or loans in this category are exclusively allocated to finance or refinance specific environmental and social projects. Examples include green bonds, social bonds, and transition bonds. Sustainability-linked debt ties the financial terms of bonds or loans to predefined sustainability performance targets (SPTs) using key performance indicators (KPIs). Unlike use-of-proceeds debt, these funds can be used for general corporate purposes and include sustainability-linked loans (SLLs) and sustainability-linked bonds (SLBs).

Transition finance frameworks reveal two distinct types of financial products and instruments. First are use-of-proceeds green bonds, loans, and equity dedicated to specific transition activities. Second are general-purpose corporate bonds, loans, or thematic equities issued by entities undergoing a transition toward improved environmental performance.

Sustainable Finance Market in USA

North America primarily the United States and Canada are prominent players in the sustainable finance market. The global sustainable finance market in North American region amounted to $1476 billion in year 2023. The trend shows that companies in United States are adopting sustainable strategies and the focus is on ESG investments. Green bond issuance is showing increasing trend and institutional investors are increasingly integrating ESG factors into their decision-making processes. According to Precedence Research, the North American region accounted for approximately 29% of the total sustainable finance market in the year 2023.[1]

The State of California have been pursuing green economy initiatives over years. In 2006, California established a rebate program for solar homes and small businesses with the goal for a million homes to be powered by solar power. California state also had a very generous state level electric vehicle tax credit program which lowered the cost of electric vehicle purchases. As a result of this incentive, sales for EV went up by more than 20% in the State of California. In 2020, New York implemented regulatory streamlining to accelerate the permitting process for large-scale renewable energy projects. Before this legislation, it typically took five to 10 years for a renewable project to reach full scale. Now, most projects are approved within 2 years.

US markets dominate the global finance arena in different aspects. US institutions own one of the largest component of global debt and equity ownership. By the end of 2012, North American asset managers supervised over 54.7% of the assets managed by the largest 500 asset managers in the world.[2] Institutional investors hold a significant portion of public companies, with 73% of the largest 1000 U.S.-listed companies owned by these investors, most of which are managed within the United States.[3] Most of the largest 100 global public companies are domiciled in the US. US stock exchanges are largest in terms of overall market capitalization. USA has the largest annual GDP in the world.

Growing awareness of sustainability issues in the U.S., particularly among millennials, is driving increased sustainable investing, a stronger focus on sustainability risks by major financial institutions, the development of sustainability risk frameworks by insurance companies and regulators, and the acceleration of

[1] https://www.precedenceresearch.com/sustainable-finance-market

[2] https://www.towerswatson.com/en-US/Insights/IC-Types/Survey-Research-Results/2014/11/The-worlds-500-largest-asset-managers-year-end-2013

[3] https://www.conference-board.org/retrievefile.cfm?filename=TCB_DN-V5N22-131.pdf&type=subsite

low-carbon energy transitions through federal and state policies. Financial and social innovations are also contributing to significant changes in various investment sectors.

Growing awareness of sustainability issues in the U.S., particularly among millennials, is attracting increased sustainable investing, a stronger focus on sustainability risks by major financial institutions, the development of sustainability risk frameworks by insurance companies and regulators, and the acceleration of low-carbon energy transitions through federal and state policies. Financial and social innovations are also contributing to significant changes in various investment sectors.

The following trends are contributing towards a sustainable financial system in USA. (1) Sustainable investment, banking and lending practices in the US. (2) New trends in the US insurance industry and credit risk (3) Revisions in federal and state policy (4) Financial market innovation (5) Social Innovation and culture.[4]

The focus on ESG has been on rise in Mutual funds industry in USA. ESG based mutual fund strategies have been showing an increasing trend. Since 2015, firms such as Black Rock, Bank of America have strong focus on sustainability aspects. Some of US asset owners have initiated efforts such as PRI's new climate change pilot framework for Action. Pension funds such as the New York State Common Retirement Fund have initiated steps directed towards low carbon goals. In November 2015, Goldman Sachs made clean energy investment commitments of US$150 billion by the year 2025. Bank of America had committed US$125 billion in low carbon business through lending, investing and related efforts during the post 2015 period. By 2015, BlackRock managed more than US$200 billion of assets across environmental, social and governance and impact investment portfolios.

High net worth (HNW) and ultra-high net worth (UHNW) individuals are the fastest-growing segments of public equity ownership, with the wealthiest 1% owning 33% of all U.S. stocks. This concentration of wealth results in U.S. investors holding a higher share of public equity than global counterparts. Within this group, some investors are increasingly focused on climate change and impact investing, driving greater interest in ESG initiatives. Negative screening accounts for the largest component of global ESG investment strategy as well the dominant ESG investment strategy in the United States. Mainstream banking institutions are actively involved in ESG initiatives. Bank of America and Morgan Stanley are introducing innovative products in the field of ESG. Bank of America have increased its lending activities in terms of low carbon business commitments. Bank of America have enhanced its second environmental business initiatives in 2015 from US$50 billion to US$125 billion in low carbon business by the year 2025. This ten-year investment commitments were focussed towards sectors such as renewable energy, transportation, water conservation and land use. Since the year 2007, Bank of America have financed more than US$39 billion for low carbon activities. In 2015, the US

[4] The State of Sustainable Finance in the United States, Design of a Sustainable Financial System, UNEP. Feb 2016.

Department of Labor had ruled that US pension funds can include ESG factors in their investment decision. Investors have been measuring and reporting their portfolios' carbon footprints for about a decade. Today, US investors like Green Century, Calvert, Pax World, and those joining the Montréal Carbon Pledge and Portfolio Decarbonization Coalition are part of this growing trend.

CalPERS leads in creating Investment Beliefs to ensure future generations enjoy the same financial and societal benefits as today. Clean Trillion initiative projects US$44 trillion of clean energy spending over the next 35 years. Ceres is a non-profit organization mobilizing business and investor leadership on climate change, water scarcity and other sustainability challenges. Ceres directs the Investor Network on Climate Risk (INCR), a network of over 100 institutional investors with collective assets totalling more than $12 trillion. The Clean Trillion initiative is a campaign launched by Ceres. The term "Clean Trillion" refers to estimated $1 trillion per year which is required to be invested globally in clean energy and low carbon technologies in order to limit global temperature rise to below 2 degrees Celsius, as outlined in the Paris Agreement.

Table 7.1 shows the scorecard of the Green Social and Sustainability (GSS) debt market in year 2020.

During the period 2016–2020, the US GSS market grew by an average of 72% a year. There were 48 green bonds issued from the US during the above period. During the period, the cumulative total for green bond amounted to US$241.4 billion, while social bond and sustainability bond issues amounted to US$14 billion and US$21 billion respectively.

By Q1 2021, the North American GSS debt market amounted to US$311 billion and approximately 5935 instruments were issued under the GSS labels since the year 2011. US have been the second largest source of GSS debt market and the largest single country. During the Leaders' Summit on Climate in year 2021, the US had pledged to cut emissions to 50–52% below 2005 levels by year 2030.

Table 7.1 Statistics of (GSS) debt markets

	USA with Fannie Mae	USA ex Fannie Mae	Canada	China	European Union (27 states)
Amount of GSS debt issued USD	USD276bn	USD182bn	USD35bn	USD211bn	USD689bn
No of issuers	403	402	36	660	398
No of repeat issuers	171	170	21	159	195
Number of Instruments	5840	1640	95	1061	1635
Average Instrument size	USD47m	USD111 m	USD366m	USD199m	USD421m

Source: North American State of the Market Report 2021, Climate Bonds Initiative

US Sustainable Finance Policy Initiatives

There have been key drivers in US legislation to promote sustainable activities. The Inflation Reduction Act (IRA) is projected to reduce greenhouse gas emissions. The Inflation Reduction Act of 2022 marks a historic $369 billion investment in modernizing the American energy system. According to a preliminary assessment by the U.S. Department of Energy (DOE), this legislation, combined with other enacted policies and previous actions, is expected to reduce economy-wide greenhouse gas (GHG) emissions by 40% below 2005 levels by 2030. This law significantly advances the U.S. toward its overall 2030 climate goals, potentially achieving a 50–52% reduction in GHG emissions below 2005 levels by 2030. Achievements of these targets depends upon the continued efforts from federal government, states, local government and private sector.

Achieving these targets will require continued efforts from the executive branch, states, local governments, and the private sector. Continued actions might include implementing the recently enacted CHIPS Act and updating standards to enhance energy efficiency and reduce pollution across the transportation, power, building, and industrial sectors.

The Bipartisan Infrastructure Law stipulates $7.5 billion investment to facilitate the establishment of a national network of 500,000 new electric vehicle chargers. The Bipartisan Infrastructure Law also commits more than $50 billion to the Environmental Protection Agency (EPA) for developing US drinking water, waste water and storm water infrastructure. Data reveals that over $800 billion in private investments have been announced in the US since the passage of this legislation. After the passage of IRA, the US investment in manufacturing for the battery sector had tripled and amounted to $27 billion in year 2023 compared to $9 billion in year 2022. The Department of Energy (DOE) and Environmental Protection Agency (EPA) are two agencies who play a critical role in sustainable activities. The DOE is in charge for loan guarantee program for clean energy projects. The EPA have the authority to enforce regulations such as fuel economy standards and various provisions of the Clean Air Act. According to DOE estimates, the clean energy provisions of the Inflation Reduction Act and Bipartisan Infrastructure Law could reduce emissions by approximately 1000 million metric tons by year 2030. The specific provision in the two laws are expected to lower energy costs for consumers, mitigate climate change, improve health and energy security. The hydrogen tax credit would drive hydrogen production and subsequent use in subsectors such as ammonia, petroleum refining, biofuels, steel and heavy-duty transportation. The Inflation Reduction Act includes tax incentives for efficient homes and buildings, rebate programs for home efficiency and electrification, and funding to support state and local building-code adoption. These measures are crucial for reducing direct emissions from the building sector. The Bipartisan Infrastructure Law allocates $3.5 billion to the Weatherization Assistance Program and supports various energy efficiency initiatives, including the Energy Efficiency and Conservation Block Grant Program and grants for public schools. These programs promote building electrification with efficient, low-carbon equipment like electric heat pumps for heating, cooling, and hot water. Tax credits for clean cars, trucks, vans, SUVs, commercial vehicles, and heavy-duty vehicles will encourage drivers and fleets to adopt advanced technologies, cutting operating costs and reducing emissions. Electric US Postal Service trucks will facilitate reduction of pollution from mail deliveries. For the objective of decarbonization of all modes of transportation, the Inflation Reduction Act creates tax credits to facilitate the use of clean fuels such as biodiesel, renewable diesel, advanced biofuel and sustainable aviation fuel.[5]

Water infrastructure is critical for reliable, affordable and safe water. The Bipartisan Infrastructure law offers historic investment to replace pipes, upgrade water treatment facilities for a resilient future for America's water systems. The Bipartisan Infrastructure Law facilitate investment of more than $50 billion through EPA's highly successful water infrastructure programs. Over $20 billion is provisioned for safe drinking water and $15 billion is dedicated to projects for replacing lead pipes. Over $12 billion is projected for initiatives for clean water for communities and $1.8 billion to protect regional waters and $135 million for additional water improvements.[6]

US government have established a National Climate Task Force of representatives for drafting USA's Nationally Determined Contribution (NDC) to develop the national climate strategy. The NDC focus for a 50% reduction in emissions by 2030 and supports targets for a zero-carbon electricity sector by 2035 and a net-zero economy by 2050. The US International Climate Finance Plan aims to double climate mitigation and adaptation financing in developing countries and encourage blended finance mechanism. The initiative also focusses on closure of international fossil fuel funding. The U.S. joined the G7's "30x30" initiative to protect 30% of Earth's land and sea by 2030, leveraging nature-based solutions like restoring carbon sinks to achieve decarbonization and combat climate change. The May 2021 Executive Order on Climate-Related Financial Risk tasked the National Climate Advisor and the Director of the National Economic Council with developing a government-wide strategy to identify and report on climate-related financial risks affecting government programs, assets, and liabilities. In 2021, the Treasury joined the global Coalition of Finance Ministers for Climate Action and prioritized co-chairing the G20 Sustainable Finance Working Group. This group aims to enhance international sustainability disclosures and coordinate efforts to identify sustainable, climate-aligned investments, including developing taxonomies. The new Treasury Climate Hub will coordinate climate-related activities, focusing on using Treasury's tools, including public investment and fiscal policy measures, to address climate challenges.

The "American Jobs Plan," introduced in March 2021, targets mitigation, adaptation, and resilience across key sectors like electricity, water, transportation, and housing. If passed, the $2.7 trillion plan would be the most comprehensive

---

[5] DOE Fact Sheet (DOE/OP-0018), U.S. Department of Energy Office of Policy, August 2022.

[6] https://www.epa.gov/system/files/documents/2021-11/e-ow-bid-fact-sheet-final.508.pdf

infrastructure investment since the 1960s. The "Made in America Tax Plan" aims to eliminate fossil fuel subsidies and reintroduce payments from polluters, ensuring that responsible industries help cover environmental remediation costs.

The Fed joined the Network for Greening the Financial System (NGFS), collaborating with 80 peers to integrate climate risk management into regulation. Additionally, it formed Supervision and Financial Stability Climate Committees to assess climate risks in the U.S. financial system and evaluate the preparedness of financial institutions. The Securities and Exchange Commission (SEC) established a task force for identification of ESG related misconduct.

The proposed Climate Risk Disclosure Act of 2021 stipulates public companies to report on climate related risks. Economy wide emission reduction targets are in place in half of the 50 states of USA. California State introduced a new Climate Corporate Accountability Act which stipulates large corporations to disclose science-based emissions reduction target starting in year 2025. New York's Department of Financial Services (DFS) published a proposed guidance on how climate related financial risks are to be managed by state insurers.

In September 2021, the US joined the Global Methane Pledge and introduced the US Methane Emissions Reduction Action Plan. The plan aims to reduce methane emissions by 30% from 2020 levels by 2030 without limiting hydrocarbon production. It focuses on reducing fugitive emissions, preventing gas leaks, and improving operational efficiency.

US Insurance Industry and Climate Risks

The U.S. insurance sector, employing around 2 million people, plays a crucial role in the financial industry by providing risk protection and generating returns for investors. Insurers profit when premiums exceed claims and expenses. They manage diverse portfolios, applying actuarial science to forecast risks and achieve returns. However, climate change poses increasing challenges, particularly for nonlife insurers facing greater variability in claims and risks. Both life and nonlife insurers manage surplus portfolios to meet investor demands but face liquidity concerns and regulatory constraints. Interest rates and market risks further impact their ability to meet coverage obligations and achieve necessary returns. Few US states insurance regulators require insurers selling policies to state their approaches to mitigate climate change risks inherent in their businesses. According to National Association of Insurance Commissioners (NAIC), insurance regulators in California, Minnesota, New York and Washington disclose climate related risks. Insurers are not obligated to cover risks they can't profitably predict, leading many U.S. insurers to exit markets severely affected by climate change. This trend, especially in the property and casualty sector, has increased the financial burden on government programs like the National Flood Insurance Program. The lack of adequate private insurance also raises costs for governments, businesses, and individuals in post-disaster rebuilding. This insurance gap is expected to widen as climate change risks, like sea level rise, become increasingly uninsurable. For example, Hurricane Sandy resulted in $68 billion in total losses, with over $29 billion in insured losses. Today, many U.S. coastal properties face significant threats from acute climate events like hurricanes and extreme weather, as well as chronic impacts such as sea-level rise and shifting precipitation patterns. CorelLogic report in year 2014 estimated that 6.5 million US homes with a total reconstruction value of $1.5 trillion are at risk from climate change events.

The 2014 CERES Insurer Climate Risk Disclosure Survey Report and Scorecard analysed responses from 330 insurance companies, covering 87% of the U.S. market, on their climate risk strategies. The findings revealed that most insurers are ill-equipped to address climate change risks. Only 3% demonstrated leading practices in this area, and less than 1% had integrated climate change or carbon asset risks into their portfolio management. The CERES report found that life, annuity, and health insurers are not prepared yet to assess climate change risks, despite its expected impact on human health. Few property and casualty insurers have adjusted their policies based on climate change modelling. Across the industry, few insurers have publicly addressed climate change in their risk management strategies or urged investment in mitigation and adaptation. The report concludes that most insurers have not proactively analysed climate change as a fundamental risk to their business and the communities they serve, with few demonstrating leadership in climate change modelling, risk governance, management, and stakeholder engagement.

The Principles for Sustainable Insurance (PSI) launched by the United Nations Environment Programme Finance Initiative in 2021 aims to promote insurance industry as a trusted fiduciary which enables the establishment of a sustainable society. PSI have collaborated with Climate Bonds Initiative to assess the insurance industry portfolios for climate risk and promote green bond initiatives. NAIC along with American Academy of Actuaries, Society of Actuaries, Canadian Institute of Actuaries and the Casualty Actuary Society aims to launch an Actuaries Climate Risk Index (ACRI). This index is expected to assess the frequency and intensity of extreme climate events over past decades and assist actuaries to improve their climate risk modelling.

CalPERS has led in developing Investment Beliefs that balance current beneficiary payments with a fiduciary duty to future generations. This approach is increasingly adopted by global asset owners, reflecting the evolving concept of fiduciary duty, as highlighted in UNEP FI's "Fiduciary Duty in the 21st Century" report. CalSTRS, the California based pension fund representing retired state teachers, have established initiatives for energy efficiency as well as green investments.

The State of California have adopted various green investment schemes. In 2014, US$8.6 million was invested across 129 specific projects under the State Water Efficiency and Enhancement Program. Under the Energy and Solar Generation program, an amount of $403 million was invested across 2000 sites during the period 2013–2015. Over US$1.8 billion was spend as part of Energy Efficiency and Solar Generation program.

The NY Green Bank is a state-sponsored financial entity that partners with the private sector to boost investments in New York's clean energy markets, fostering a more efficient, sustainable energy system. It aims to improve energy affordability, build a resilient power grid, and align energy innovation with market demand. By leveraging private capital and reducing reliance on government support, NY Green Bank accelerates clean energy deployment, spurring economic development and environmental benefits. In July 2015, the Public Service Commission approved $150 million in state funding, helping the NY Green Bank move toward its $1 billion funding goal.

Sustainable Finance Innovations in US Markets

Yieldcos are exchange-traded companies designed to finance renewable energy projects. First established in 2013, they serve as low-risk investments similar to fossil-fuel-based Master Limited Partnerships (MLPs). Created by parent energy companies, yieldcos buy completed renewable energy projects and use the cash flow to pay dividends with tax benefits to shareholders. The revenue from selling projects to yieldcos is then reinvested in new energy projects. During 2015, two large solar panel producers First Solar and Sunpower launched a joint yieldco which raised US$400 million. In 2023, Bloomberg New Energy Finance have reported that in US and Europe, about 15 yieldcos have raised $12 billion in the public markets over the last 30 months and their market values have risen 84% to $28 billion over the same period.

The Aligned Intermediary

The Aligned Intermediary (AI) is an investment advisory group which assists sovereign funds, pension funds and foundations in targeting private capital into climate infrastructure projects which include clean energy, water infrastructure and waste -to-value initiatives. Till date twelve long term investors have pledged over $1.6 billion for transactions selected by AI.

Conservation finance refers to mechanisms that channel financial investments into ecosystems—either directly or through intermediaries with the aim to preserve the ecosystem's value for the long term. The US Forest Service Conservation Finance Program aims to develop innovative finance models that engage private capital by creating investment opportunities which align environmental, social and financial outcomes. According to the Global Canopy Programme, conservation finance receives about US$52 billion annually in terms of financing. Conservation finance instruments include specific set of asset classes such as green commodities, private equity impact investing, property tax financed municipal bonds, forest conservation bonds, biodiversity offsets, wetland and conservation mitigation banking etc.

Market Trends of US Sustainable Finance Market[7]

The largest source of Green, Social and Sustainable (GSS) bonds market is the US with bonds worth USD 275.9 billion being issued till date. However, the GSS debt comprises only 0.6% of the USD 46 trillion bond market. By 2021, the green bond segment accounted for approximately 87.5% of the US GSS debt labelled bond segment. In 2011, the first green bond was issued in the US when Yuba Community College District issued a USD 15 million note to finance solar PV. By 2021, Fannie Mae had issued about 4200 deals with value of USD 94 billion. The first US sustainability bond was issued by Starbucks in the year 2016. Social theme bond was first issued by New York Housing Finance Authority in 2018 and now accounts for 5% of the GSS market.

The U.S. GSS market is predominantly defined by numerous small transactions involving Fannie Mae securities and municipal bonds, which are primarily purchased by domestic retail or individual investors. In terms of both number of bonds and volume, USA is the largest source of green debt globally. The U.S. green bond market is largely dominated by agency MBS, classified under the ABS issuer type, and U.S. municipal bonds, categorized under either local government or government-backed entities. Agency MBS, primarily issued by Fannie Mae, are used to finance green mortgage loans. U.S. municipal bonds, primarily issued by local governments which comprises 76% of issuance, finance public projects across various green categories. The market began with the first green municipal bond in 2011 and agency MBS in 2012. The leading issuer in the American financial corporate sector is Digital Realty Trust, a Real Estate Investment Trust (REIT), with $5.4 billion issued to date. USD accounts for almost 95% of total US green bond issuance.

The largest nonfinancial corporate deal was Apple Inc.'s 2016 issuance of $1.5 billion to fund various projects in renewable energy, buildings, energy efficiency, water efficiency, and waste management. The biggest green bond in the American market remains Bank of America's $2.3 billion issuance in 2018. The second-largest deal was from New York MTA, which raised $2 billion in 2017. The Transport Authority has issued $11.3 billion across 18 deals, eight of which were benchmark size, all certified under the Climate Bonds Standard's Low-carbon Transport Criteria. Other municipalities issuing benchmark-sized instruments include Los Angeles County MTA ($1.4 billion), Central Puget Sound Transit Authority ($943 million), and San Francisco BART ($625 million), all financing transport projects. Since 2016, the 5–10-year maturity bucket has consistently dominated issuance, making up at least 40% annually, driven largely by Fannie Mae's contributions.

Many U.S. municipal bonds are issued in series with varying maturities, often extending beyond 20 years. For instance, District of Columbia Water issued a $350 million bond in 2014, maturing in 2114, making it the longest-dated green bond to date. AES Corporation follows with a $450 million bond due in 2079.

[7] North America State of Market Report, 2021, Climate Bond Initiative.

Financial corporates, like Bank of America, Citigroup, JP Morgan, and Morgan Stanley, typically prefer shorter maturities, with most green bonds maturing within 10 years, including $8.5 billion of their $8.6 billion total issuance falling into the 5–10-year range. In 2019 and 2020, Verizon issued green bonds valued at USD one billion each.

Since the U.S. market's inception, Buildings have led as the top Use of Proceeds (UoP) category, reaching $109 billion by the end of Q1 2021. Renewable Energy follows with $58 billion, and Water with $42 billion.

U.S. issuers typically obtain a Second Party Opinion (SPO), aligning with the broader market trend. Since the inception of the market in US, non-financial corporates represented 16.8% of the total green issuance volume. Thirty-six issuers have issued 107 green instruments with total value of US$40.4 billion. Renewable Energy and Low-carbon Buildings account for the majority of projects and assets financed via green bonds by non-financial corporates.

The New York State Finance Housing Authority was the first U.S. issuer to focus on social themes with a 35-year, $84 million affordable housing bond in June 2018. By the end of 2018, five social bonds totalling $816 million had been issued, with an additional $1.3 billion issued in 2019. Approximately 68% of the US social bond volume was accounted by the private sector.

The U.S. social bond market features a barbell maturity structure: nearly half (48%) of the volume has maturities of 5 years or less, while a third (30%) extends to 20 years or more. The shortest maturity bucket includes 147 bonds with an average size of $59 million, while the 20-year-plus category contains 60 bonds with an average size of $69 million.

Alphabet emerged as the largest issuer with a $5.8 billion, three-tranche deal. The proceeds supported projects across nine categories, including energy efficiency, circular economy, affordable housing, racial equity, and small business support. Meanwhile, Starbucks issued four sustainability bonds totalling $3 billion between 2016 and 2019.

In 2020, Pfizer became the first pharmaceutical company to issue a thematic bond, raising $1.3 billion through a 10-year sustainability bond. The proceeds supported environmental sustainability and the health of vulnerable populations, with the issuer obtaining a Second Party Opinion (SPO).

Adaptation and Resilience (A&R) investments enhance the resilience of assets and systems to climate-related stresses by improving their ability to persist, adapt, or transform. These investments, which include both hard infrastructure and 'soft' areas like technology and services, aim to reduce risk, avoid maladaptation, and support development and benefits.

The European Bank for Reconstruction and Development (EBRD) issued the first labelled 'Climate Resilience Bond' in January 2020. This green bond was entirely focused on supporting climate-resilient infrastructure, businesses, and agriculture. Michigan's green bonds have funded projects for environmental protection, site clean-up, water quality improvement, pollution prevention, waterfront revitalization, state park upgrades, and enhanced local recreation opportunities.

Sustainable Finance in Canada

Canada Taxonomy

In May 2021, the Sustainable Finance Action Council (SFAC) was tasked with creation of a green and transition investment taxonomy. By September 2022, SFAC released the "Taxonomy Roadmap Report: Mobilizing Finance for Sustainable Growth by Defining Green and Transition Investments," outlining strategies to support sustainable finance in Canada. Most of Canada's main trading partners, except the US, have developed taxonomies to guide investment towards sectors that align with climate objectives, preventing the lock-in of outdated technologies, especially in the energy sector, which contributes 75% of global greenhouse gas emissions. Canada's Taxonomy Roadmap Report proposed creating a dual-label system for green and transition activities and financial instruments.

Green activities include projects with low or zero Scope 1, 2, and 3 emissions, such as green hydrogen production, zero-emission vehicle manufacturing, and electricity transmission infrastructure, which are expected to grow during the global low-carbon transition.

Transition activities cover high-emission projects with no viable net-zero alternatives after 2050 (e.g., steel production with electric arc furnaces) and activities with high downstream emissions, like oil and gas energy generation, that must be phased out as green alternatives develop. Activities related to solid fossil fuels are ineligible.

During the period 2018–2020, the Canadian GSS market grew by an average of 70% year on year. In 2021, the green finance issue amounted to US$30 billion while the social finance issue amounted to US$1.5 billion while the sustainability issues totaled US$3.3 billion. The total sustainable bond market in Canada was estimated to be US$49 billion by year 2021. The sustainable bond issuance in Canada reached a record of US$20 billion in 2021 which was almost double the $9.75 billion issued in year 2020. The local governments account for approximately 25% of cumulative issuance volume. The Province of Ontario is the largest issuer followed by Province of Quebec and the cities of Ottawa, Toronto, and Vancouver.

Canada has committed to a 40–45% reduction during the Leaders' Summit on Climate during April 2021. In 2020, the Canadian government had introduced legislative proposal "the Net Zero Emissions Accountability Act "to supplement the implementation of Canada's existing net zero by the year 2050. Canada is also introducing its own taxonomy for low carbon transition. The new legislation introduced interim emission reduction checkpoints at five-year intervals. Canadian market is characterized by larger deals compared to US with average size of US$366 million. Canadian GSS bonds had been issued in six currencies. The Canadian green bond market was established in year 2014.

Market Analysis of Canada[8]

By 2021 first quarter, the Canadian GSS bonds and loans amounted to USD 34.8 billion. Canada occupied 11th place in global ranking. In 2020, the Canadian GSS bond market peaked with bond issuance of value USD 9.4 billion. In 2018, Canadian Imperial Bank issued the first social bond. The deals in Canadian market are larger compared to the US market with an average size of USD 366 million. Canadian GSS bonds have been issued in six currencies. In 2021 first quarter, the green bonds and loans originating from Canada amounted to USD 30 billion. The GSS debt accounts for 0.8% of the Canadian debt market. Among the financial corporates, CPPIB, the Canadian asset manager had raised USD 4.6 billion through seven deals. Issuers such as Brookfield Asset Management, Copower Manulife Financial, RE Royalties, RioCan Real Estate Investment Trust and TD Bank had raised GSS bonds valued at USD 4.1 billion. The largest issue of GSS debt was issued by the Province of Ontario, valued at USD 6.2 billion. In terms of local government participation, two cities (Ottawa, Toronto) and two provinces (Province of Ontario, Province of Quebec) have issued multiple green bonds. Ontario is the leading issuer of Canadian dollar green bonds. In 2021, the province issued its largest green bond to date, valued at CAN$2.75 billion. This program has been crucial in funding Ontario's mass transit expansion. With CAN$148 billion in planned infrastructure investments over the next decade, including CAN$61 billion for transit infrastructure, Ontario aims to sustain the program and have plans to issue multiple green bonds annually.

Non-financial corporates such as Brookfield Renewable Partners and Algonquin Power had made issues worth USD 1.7 billion and USD 825 million respectively. In 2020, Brookfield Asset Management issued a bond with the longest original term, a 60-year tenor, raising USD 400 million to fund various renewable energy projects. Most projects and assets financed via green bonds by non-financial corporates are in the renewable energy sector. This sector which contributes the largest proportion to electricity generated in Canada accounts for 71% of the total issue. Low-carbon buildings represent the second-largest use-of-proceeds theme in the Canadian green bond market, accounting for 11% of total issuance. One-third of total issuance supported renewable energy projects, with 59 of 79 deals allocating funds to this category, including 18 deals fully financing renewable energy assets like solar, wind, and hydro. Low-carbon transport followed, accounting for 23% of issuance, while buildings and water projects represented 18% and 11%, respectively. Most deals issued by Canadian organizations carry third party review such as SPO. Fifty-five deals out of 79 deals with total value of USD 24.9 billion were issued with this type of third-party review. In 2022, Ontario Power Generation had issued a $300 million nuclear green bond to refurbish the Darlington nuclear power generating facility.

Social and sustainability bonds are emerging in Canada, with 15 bonds worth USD 4.8 billion issued by Q1 2021. Four social bonds, all CAD-denominated, were

[8] North America State of Market Report, 2021, Climate Bond Initiative.

issued by Canadian entities, funding projects like social housing, female empowerment, and essential services.

In Q1 2022, the Government of Canada issued the largest sovereign green bond valued at CAN$5 billion sovereign green bond, which attracted strong demand with a final order book of CAN$11 billion from 98 institutional investors. First-time issuers like OMERS and PSP joined the green bond market alongside repeat issuers such as CPPIB, OTPP, and CDPQ, with Canadian public pension plans collectively issuing US$9 billion in green debt. Provincial and municipal governments contributed at least US$2.3 billion, while first-time corporate issuers like iA Financial and Tamarack Valley Energy, along with repeat issuers, also participated in the growing market.

Climate Aligned Bond Trends

The North American State of the Market 2020 Climate Bonds Initiative reports that there was a total of 65 organizations from North American region which had cumulative climate aligned outstanding bonds of value USD 119.7 billion. Union Pacific Corp, Hydro Quebec and American Water Capital were the top three issuers of climate aligned bonds. Transport and energy companies are the dominant climate aligned bond issuers in North America.

US dollars is the dominant currency accounting for 77% of the issues. In the North American climate-aligned market, medium-sized deals are most common. Transactions in the USD 250 million to 500 million range make up 32% of the total amount issued, while deals between USD 500 million and 1 billion account for 27%. Climate-aligned issuers can refinance maturing liabilities through the labelled bond market, gaining extra visibility and additional benefits from these specialized financial instruments.

There are a number of resources and tools which North American issuers use to provide green bond disclosure. The US EPA's GHG Equivalencies Calculator was utilized by American Municipal Power, Bank Windhoek, and the North American Development Bank to estimate GHG emissions reductions. AMP also used the EPA's Landfill Gas Energy Benefits Calculator. The American Carbon Registry's Green Finance Impact Program helps issuers, especially municipalities, standardize impact estimations. In Canada, Quebec used APTA's GHG emissions quantification guide for transit projects. Globally, public sector entities developed sector-specific methodological guides, such as British Columbia's, referenced by TransLink.

Highlights of Climate Transition in North American Market[9]

Most of the world's primary energy requirements are met by fossil fuels such as coal, gas and oil. USA is the largest oil producer as well as the largest natural gas producer in the world. In 2019 it was estimated that 82% of the primary energy production in the US came from fossil fuels such as natural gas and oil compared to 86% in the 1990s. The transport sector accounted for the largest share of energy related GHG emissions in US. As of 2020, fossil fuels accounted for 60.3% of electricity generation, with gas contributing 40.3% and coal 19.3%, the main sources of emissions.

President Biden's tax plan proposes replacing fossil fuel subsidies with clean energy incentives, including a 10-year extension of production and investment tax credits for renewable energy and storage. It introduces a new tax incentive for long-distance transmission lines and a blender's tax credit for sustainable aviation fuel to decarbonize the US transport sector. The US Senate passed the American Energy Innovation Act (AEIA) to explore investments in energy R&D such as geothermal, marine and hydrokinetic power and grid scale storage. The Solar Investment Tax Credit offers a 26% tax credit for solar systems on residential and commercial properties. The Renewable Portfolio Standards (RPS) is a key policy tool that requires utilities to ensure a specific percentage of the electricity they sell comes from renewable sources. The Alternative Fuel Vehicle Tax Credit can be claimed for recovering the cost of purchasing a new Alternative Fuel Vehicle or converting a vehicle to operate on an alternative fuel. Approximately 45 states offer incentives to support the growth of EVs or alternate fuels in US.

In 2019, Canada's energy was still reliant on fossil fuels with 75% accounted by fossil fuels and 25% accounted from non-fossil fuels. The non-fossil fuels were based on oil and gas. The main epicentre of oil and gas industry in Canada is Alberta. Transport sector accounts for the highest proportion of emissions in Canada. Transition financing is gaining significance in Canada. By end of quarter 2021, the value of labelled transition bonds and sustainability linked bonds in Canada amounted to USD 15 billion and USD 20 billion respectively. Green bonds along with transition bonds and SLBs can facilitate the shift from fossil fuels to renewable energy. At global level, companies such as Ørsted, EDF, Enel, and Iberdrola have used green bonds to fund their transition. These bonds have contributed significantly to meeting interim 2030 emissions reduction targets, achieving up to 43% of their goals. Many North American companies have green energy assets on their balance sheet which are financed through green bonds. For example, Algonquin Power have issued two green bonds valued at USD 900 million to finance solar and wind power.

Established in year 2018, the Canadian Task Force on Just Transition aims to manage job losses from coal phase-out. While the transition could yield CAD 4.7 billion in economic benefits and CAD 3.4 billion in avoided climate damage, the

[9] North America State of Market Report, 2021, Climate Bond Initiative.

Coal Association of Canada estimates 42,000 job losses. The Task Force suggested ten recommendations for transition of energy sector. The 2019 federal budget addressed some of these concerns. An amount of USD 26 million was envisioned over five-year period to fund Worker Transition Centres in Western and Eastern Canada, supporting re-skilling and economic diversification in coal-dependent regions. A dedicated infrastructure fund of value USD 113 million was established to support priority projects and economic diversification of communities affected by the transition.

Brookfield Renewable Partners is one of the top five Canadian green bond issuers with bonds worth USD$1.7 billion. The company is within the framework of climate aligned universe with 90% of revenues attributed to green activities. The company, Ontario Power Generation also belong to the fully climate aligned universe with multiple green bond issues.

In the US market, multiple green bond issuer MidAmerican Energy have issued green bonds worth USD 1.4 billion since the year 2017. Electric Utility company DTE Electric have issued multiple green bonds and have targets to reduce carbon emissions by 80% by year 2040 compared to 2005 levels. In 2020, General Motors had committed USD 20 billion to develop EVs over the next five-year period. General Motors was the first US based automaker to pledge to phase out all ICE vehicle production by 2035. Ford had introduced its all electric F-150 Lightning Pro, the first-ever all-electric F- Series truck purpose built for commercial customers. In September 2020, the Climate Action 100+ initiative, a coalition of over 500 institutional investors managing a combined total of USD 47 trillion in assets under management, encouraged the 161 highest-emitting companies globally to disclose their strategies for achieving net-zero emissions by 2050. Air Canada, the national airline of Canada, has recently committed to achieving net-zero emissions by setting absolute midterm greenhouse gas (GHG) reduction targets for both its air and ground operations by 2030, using 2019 as a baseline. Additionally, the company has pledged to invest USD 50 million in Sustainable Aviation Fuel (SAF), carbon reduction, and carbon removal initiatives.

Shareholders are increasingly becoming active for adoption of climate goals for high carbon emitters. In May 2021, Exxon Mobil appointed two new climate-focused Board members, following a resolution from climate activist hedge fund Engine No. 1. The company had also faced pressure from major shareholder BlackRock, urging Exxon to align its strategies with limiting global warming to below two degrees by 2050. Shareholders of Chevron also voted in favour of a resolution proposal to cut Scope 3 emissions.

By the end of 2020, the securitization market in North America was well-developed, with USD 12.7 trillion in debt outstanding across various asset classes. This included commercial mortgage-backed securities (CMBS), residential mortgage-backed securities (RMBS), and asset-backed securities (ABS). These securitizations are classified as green when the underlying cash flows are related to low carbon assets or where the stated use -of-proceeds are low carbon assets.

Examples of financial assets suitable for inclusion in green collateral pools include mortgages on certified buildings under LEED, Energy Star or other building standards; mortgage financing for energy efficiency upgrades; loans for energy efficiency improvements; loans or leases for equipment in EV charging stations etc.

US is the main source of securitised green debt. By the first quarter of year 2021, the cumulative volume of securitized green debt amounted to USD 115.5 billion and over 4250 deals. Green securitization has been largely dominated by mortgage-backed securities (MBS) issued by Fannie Mae. By the end of Q1 2021, Fannie Mae had completed 4158 deals totalling USD 92 billion, making it the largest issuer of green debt globally. The European Investment Bank (EIB) was ranked second with USD 43.5 billion. The underlying assets for Fannie Mae's green MBS consist of loans secured by properties that have green building certification or have undergone energy efficiency improvements. Toyota has the second largest presence in US green securitisation with combined value of USD 4.6 billion. Renovate America is the leading finance provider of the California based Property Assessed Clean Energy (PACE). Renovate America has issued 14 deals valued at USD 3 billion and had issued labelled green ABS as securitisation of PACE loans. The proceeds from these green ABS will be used to refinance home improvement projects which include renewable energy, energy efficiency and water enhancements through the HERO program. Solar Mosaic has issued nine deals totalling USD 2.3 billion, secured by loans for homeowners to finance solar energy systems, offered through a network of installers.

By 2020, the US mortgage backed securities market stood at $11.2 trillion while Climate bonds had issued green mortgage backed securities worth USD 93 billion. Transportation is the largest source of US GHG emissions accounting for 29% of GHG emissions.

In the U.S., plug-in hybrid electric vehicles (PHEVs) and zero-emission vehicles (ZEVs) make up only 2% of the new car market and 1% of all vehicles on the road. Lack of charging stations, long charging times, and high purchase costs are the main barriers of low market share of EVS. President Biden's USD 2 trillion infrastructure plan allocates up to USD 174 billion to address these challenges.

Nearly 95% of Americans own cars, with auto loans used for 85% of new and 53% of used car purchases. As the shift towards zero-emission vehicles (ZEVs) continues, the availability of green auto receivables for securitization is expected to increase, driving growth in the green securitization market in the medium term.

Solar ABS is the second largest source of green securitisation in the US with USD 9.9 billion spread over 44 deals issued by 2021. Solar asset-backed securities (ABS) are secured by cash flows from solar assets, typically backed by lease payments, power purchase agreements, or loans for solar panel installation, mainly for residential rooftops. While residential solar dominates, commercial solar has significant growth potential. Policies, including federal, state, and local initiatives, have driven solar energy adoption in the U.S. The federal solar investment tax credit (ITC), extended in 2020, has fuelled a 10,000% industry growth since 2006. California's solar mandate for new homes also supports this trend, offering further opportunities for securitization in the expanding solar market.

The U.S. Property Assessed Clean Energy (PACE) model finances energy improvements on properties, repaid through property tax bills. Active in 36 states and D.C., with programs in 24 states, it offers residential options in California, Florida, and Missouri. PACE loans are securitized, transferring credit risk to ABS investors and enabling new loans.

GSS debt is inadequate for addressing the scale of the climate crisis. By the end of Q1 2021, the US GSS debt constituted only 0.6% of the USD 46.2 trillion local bond market, while Canadian GSS debt accounted for only 0.9% of USD 3.7 trillion. Sovereign GSS bonds from the U.S. and Canada will bolster carbon neutrality goals and enhance the global GSS bond market's liquidity, driving green market development. A broader range of GSS bond issuers will attract high-profile investors, like San Francisco City and County Employees Retirement System and CalSTRS, who prioritize responsible investing. Expanding GSS issuance across all economic sectors, especially heavy emitters, would enable more diversified portfolios and help protect revenues from climate risks. Clear transition pathways will enable diverse issuers to participate in the GSS market. Guidance on sector-specific transitions and bond issuance is crucial for decarbonizing industries like cement and steel. Benchmarked and labelled deals can drive policy change and scale capital flow. North American issuers have significant potential for GSS market growth by refinancing or expanding with labelled bonds.

Sustainable Finance in Europe

In the year 2023, the global sustainable finance market in Europe amounted to $2145.7 billion. Europe have strong regulatory frameworks such as the EU Green Deal and Sustainable Finance Action Plan to promote sustainable finance. Europe is a leader in responsible investing. These initiatives boost investment in green technologies and sustainable projects, driven by strong investor demand for transparency and ESG criteria, supporting green bonds and sustainable investments. In year 2023, Europe accounted for 39% of the global sustainable finance market. In 2020 EU Green deal devised an investment plan which aims to deploy investments of at least EUR one trillion in sustainable projects over the next 10 years. European institutions invest in developing innovative sustainable finance products and frameworks such as sustainability linked loans and green bonds. The growth of sustainable finance is driven by green banks, development finance organizations, and European leaders, with increasing public awareness of ESG issues fueling demand for sustainable products. Several European countries, including Denmark, the Netherlands, the United Kingdom, Finland, and Sweden, are leading the way in sustainability and ESG initiatives. The digital transformation of financial services is improving access to sustainable investments via online platforms and fintech solutions. Green bonds raised USD 195.9 billion, bringing the total value of GSS+ bonds to USD 4.7 trillion during the first quarter of year 2024. Europe was the market leader with USD

149.5 billion.[10] The Buildings Breakthrough initiative, launched at COP 28, aims for near-zero emissions in buildings by 2030, with 28 countries committed, targeting net-zero by 2050.

Two thirds of the world's hard assets are accounted by buildings. Nearly EUR 9 trillion is held on European bank balance sheets. Hence funding the transition of buildings to net zero will be sourced from a diverse range of financing options. Private capital especially green bonds along with public funding through grants, loans and tax incentives are critical for funding the transition of buildings. By 2023, 21.5% of USD 4.2 trillion in green bonds funded building related projects which is critical for achieving 2050 goals. EU aims to achieve an emissions reduction of 55% by 2030 compared to the year 1990. Europe has some of the oldest building stock, with 65% built before 1980. Over 97% of buildings require renovation to meet 2050 net-zero targets, making building decarbonization as urgent as other hard-to-abate industries. Green bonds and loans are funding the construction and renovation of buildings in the EU, supported by property owners and investors like mortgage banks and REITs. However, stronger policy interventions and robust Minimum Energy Performance Standards (MEPS) are needed, with science-based emission reduction targets set for 2030 and 2040. The "Fit for 55" policy scenarios emphasize increased heat pump use, particularly in buildings. The IEA estimates that widespread adoption could reduce global CO_2 emissions by 500 million tonnes by 2030. Europe's 20 million heat pumps have already saved 54 million tonnes of GHG emissions, nearly matching Greece's annual emissions. The EU has around 131 million buildings, but only 1% undergo energy renovation each year. The slow renovation rate demands maximizing energy efficiency with low lifecycle carbon impact. The EU aims to double renovation rates by 2030 through the Energy Performance of Buildings Directive, phasing out fossil-fuel subsidies by 2040. Denmark banned the installation of new fossil fuel boilers in 2013. From the year 2018 onwards, Netherlands had restricted connections to the fossil gas grid for new buildings. In the year 2022, over 150 billion of investment was made for energy efficiency and electrification of buildings in Europe. According to European Commission estimates, an extra EUR 275 billion is required to bridge the investment gap each year to achieve the EU's 2030 objectives.

The Energy Performance of Buildings Directive (EPBD) sets harmonized sustainable building standards across the EU. Under the 2024 agreement, new buildings must meet zero-emission standards by 2030, while driving energy-efficient renovations of existing buildings. The directive establishes Minimum Energy Performance Standards (MEPS) to improve building efficiency and reduce emissions.

A study by the Greens/European Free Alliance estimates buildings will need the most additional investment (€142 billion annually) out of €360 billion required annually for the transition. Investors now have tools to assess the climate impact of

---

[10] Sustainable Finance Market Report 2024–2032, Global Market Insights. https://www.theglobaltreasurer.com/2024/06/26/record-growth-in-green-bonds-signals-a-new-era-in-sustainable-finance/

real estate portfolios, aided by SFDR disclosure requirements. Greening assets protects against transition risks, as sustainable buildings maintain value better in downturns, making energy efficiency a key hedge against market volatility for real estate investors.

The Renovation Wave, part of the Fit for 55 strategy, aims to double building renovation rates by 2030, targeting 35 million buildings. This initiative is expected to attract investment, create new skills, and generate up to 160,000 green jobs in construction. During COP 28, the EU commission announced aims to double the annual rate of global energy efficiency improvements from 2% to 4% by the year 2030 under the Global Pledge on Renewables and Energy Efficiency.

Creating a common EU-wide definition for green loans or mortgages would mandate banks to track the sustainability of their property portfolios. Building on the EMF/ECBC's green mortgage definition and the Energy Efficient Mortgage Label could support future legislation. The European Banking Authority's December 2023 Opinion emphasizes that a standardized definition would level the playing field and enhance consumer protection. It suggests aligning with the EU Taxonomy's criteria while allowing innovation in green products. Climate Bonds supports engaging market participants and leveraging existing practices to aid the legislative process. European Banking Authority's report suggest that banks raising funds through green bond issuance tend to have a higher share of green loans in their overall lending irrespective of the bank's business model.

Banks need access to NZEB (Nearly Zero Energy Building) definitions for each Member State where they lend for new construction. The revised EPBD allows Member States to set their own NZEB methodologies. Sovereign green bond issuance signals government commitment to climate targets and can create borrowing space for comprehensive green grants, subsidies, and tax measures.

EU Taxonomy

The EU Taxonomy Regulation is a major core legislative proposal on sustainable finance. It is a common classification system for sustainable activities. The Delegated Act on Article 8 of the Taxonomy Regulation outlines disclosure requirements, including Key Performance Indicators (KPIs) and reporting templates for companies and banks to disclose the sustainability of their activities. Starting January 2022, both banks and companies subject to the Non-Financial Reporting Directive (NFRD) must report on the EU Taxonomy eligibility of their activities under Article 8.

The EU's green and sustainable finance Taxonomy offers a science-based classification system for investors and organizations to make informed financial decisions in response to climate and environmental challenges. It aims to provide clear definitions and transparent reporting to boost funding for activities that significantly contribute to environmental goals, do no significant harm, and meet social safeguards. The EU Taxonomy directs sustainable finance to meet climate goals by regulating disclosures for large corporations, financial institutions, and guiding member states' policy decisions.

The EU Platform on Sustainable Finance ('the Platform') is a permanent expert group of the European Commission. The EU taxonomy, focused on climate change mitigation and adaptation, includes transitional activities like aluminium and steel production but lacks separate labels for them. Initially excluding fossil gas, it was later added under a transitional category after lobbying. This decision faced investor opposition, questioning the taxonomy's credibility. In March 2021, the Platform released its Transition Finance Report, highlighting that the current Taxonomy does not provide a binary system for financing. By focusing on capital and operational expenditures, companies can show their commitment to transition and secure green financing, even without green revenues. The Platform advocates for an expanded Taxonomy with more categories and performance levels to enhance market clarity on environmental performance and impact. The proposed extended Taxonomy will add two performance levels to the existing framework, using the DNSH threshold. This allows debt and equity instruments to fund improvements into these new categories, such as intermediate transition bonds. This approach, using the same governance and transparency as green bonds, is especially useful for industries like steel, where incremental upgrades are common. The latest industry roadmap for carbon-neutral steelmaking in Europe and an EC analysis indicate that no single technology can achieve the 80–95% GHG reduction targets for the sector by 2050.[11] Achieving these goals will require an estimated €52 billion in investment.

During the period 2000–2018, 90% of global deforestation resulted from agricultural expansion for crops and livestock. Tackling deforestation is critical to combat climate change and biodiversity loss. With over 30% of food traded globally, traceability is difficult. However downstream firms help mitigate deforestation risks in supply chain. European Union Regulation on Deforestation Free (EUDR) aims to tackle this sector. The EUDR introduces a robust due diligence system for operators and traders of commodities like cattle, cocoa, coffee, palm oil, rubber, soy, and wood within the EU, expanding the scope of the EU Timber Regulation (EUTR). It adds new commodities, requires a due diligence statement, geographic tracking of commodity origins, stronger customs cooperation, minimum inspection standards, and country-risk assessments. Unlike the EUTR, which targets deforestation from illegal timber logging, the EUDR addresses any commodity linked to deforestation, whether legally produced or not, both within the EU and globally.

In 2023, Climate Bonds released a guidance note for investors and corporations to help them navigate EUDR requirements and initiated a public consultation on investment criteria for deforestation and conversion-free (DCF) commodities. These criteria guide debt issuers (companies and banks) on ensuring DCF supply chains, enabling certification as deforestation-free and assuring investors and customers that the certified entity produces DCF commodities.

Scaling investment in the sector's transition requires redirecting finance from high to low-carbon activities and boosting agri-food investments with credible

---

[11] Platform on Sustainable Finance, The Extended Environmental Taxonomy, Final Report on Taxonomy extension options supporting a sustainable transition, March 2022.

standards. Transition plans are essential for companies to assess climate-related risks and opportunities, and to strategize financing and transformation for a sustainable future. Financial institutions use these plans to identify viable investments, while policymakers and government bodies can leverage them to allocate subsidies and incentives for transition efforts.

Chemical production in Germany, the EU's largest chemical producer, contributes 5% of the country's total emissions. Approximately 53% of the EU27's chemical production will require reinvestment by the year 2030, with over EUR one trillion needed for transition of EU chemicals industry by the year 2050. Global chemicals production is projected to grow to EUR 6.6 trillion by 2030, up from EUR 3.47 trillion in 2017, and could quadruple by 2050. The EU, currently the second-largest producer after China, held 15.6% of global production in 2017, but this share is expected to drop to 10.7% by 2030. The chemicals, cement and steel sectors account for 70% of industrial CO_2 emissions globally. Chemicals and petrochemicals account for 40% of the EU's industrial fossil gas demand. During Jan 2023, the European Commission published its transition pathway for the European chemicals industry. The European chemicals industry faces a critical juncture, requiring strategic long-term investments as many assets will expire by 2030 or earlier. Scope 3 emissions for the chemicals sector amount for approximately 64% of total emissions. At the EU level, the EU Taxonomy identifies environmentally sustainable or green economic activities by setting thresholds and technical screening criteria for its six objectives, primarily focused on emission intensity. Carbon pricing mechanisms, like carbon taxes and the EU Emissions Trading System (ETS), can drive the transition of the chemicals industry toward sustainability.

The primary performance indicator for banks to report their alignment with the EU Taxonomy is the Green Asset Ratio (GAR). Beginning in January 2024, banks will be required to disclose the aggregate GAR for covered on-balance sheet assets, including a breakdown by environmental objective and counterparty type. Additional KPIs, such as GAR for new activities (flow), financial guarantees, assets under management, and, starting in 2026, fees and commission income from taxonomy-aligned activities, must also be reported. Some banks will further need to disclose KPIs related to their trading book.

These mechanisms incentivize the use of low-emission technologies, which are typically costlier than fossil-based production and require substantial upfront capital investment. Carbon pricing generates revenue that can be used to subsidize capital expenditures, helping to adopt energy-efficient technologies and support the transition to a low-carbon economy. These mechanisms are effective as costs can be passed to consumers. Research shows a 100% increase in chemicals' carbon prices results in minimal consumer price impacts (0.7–3.2% for soft drinks).

In 2021, the OECD projected that a carbon price of EUR 120 per tCO_2 would be needed by 2030 for the chemical sector to achieve carbon neutrality by 2050. However, only 3% of industries in 44 OECD and G20 countries currently meet this price, as measured by the Carbon Pricing Score (CPS). The EU has emphasized plastics recycling, especially in packaging, to enhance chemical circularity. Packaging accounts for 40% of plastic use and over 60% of plastic waste in the EU, as well as 36% of municipal solid waste, with its usage growing faster than GDP.

The EU's 2018 Circular Economy Package includes four legislative proposals on waste management and revises existing directives, such as the Waste Framework Directive (WFD), the Landfill Directive, and the Packaging and Packaging Waste Directive (PPWD). Denmark's Action Plan for Circular Economy aims to eliminate 80% of plastic waste incineration by 2030. Currently, Denmark has the highest per capita waste in the EU and imports plastic waste for incineration. To address overcapacity, seven incinerators will be closed, and municipalities will be required to process all recyclable waste. The EU exports up to 28.7% of OECD plastic waste and 70.3% of non-OECD plastic waste, making it a major player in global plastic waste trade.

The EU Hydrogen Strategy targets a 40GW electrolyser capacity and 10 million tons of green hydrogen production yearly by 2030. The EU chemicals industry currently consumes 10 million tons of hydrogen per year. Germany has introduced a subsidy scheme to ensure hydrogen access for energy-intensive industries like chemicals, offering price guarantees for transition technologies. Support through Contracts for Difference (CCfDs) for steel, ammonia, and cement, ranging from EUR 10 billion to EUR 43 billion, would be reduced by climate policies, limiting public financing to EUR 10 billion.

During COP27, over 550 financial institutions, including many European banks, committed to aligning their financing activities with net-zero goals as part of the GFANZ initiative. European banks have joined efforts like the Net Zero Banking Alliance (NZBA) and the Collective Commitment to Climate Action by UNEP FI. Banks must design financial products and solutions for firms based on their transition plans. These financing products are complementary to the financing based on KPI targets or thresholds set at activity level.

All activities within the same sector should follow a consistent, credible sectoral benchmark transition pathway. The EU Commission should specify sectoral roadmaps, including KPIs, intermediary targets, and milestones, potentially with national or regional adaptations. These clear benchmarks would guide companies in defining their transition plans. Consistent guidelines at EU and international levels will help companies align with EU environmental objectives and support the assessment of their efforts. Given the maturity of climate objectives, it is recommended that the EU Commission prioritize climate-focused transition pathways first.

Sustainable Finance Market in China

China's hydrocarbon policy is primarily driven by economic goals rather than environmental considerations. However, China leads the world in producing technologies that reduce reliance on coal, oil, and gas. The country not only exports these technologies globally but also implements them domestically. China no longer recognizes coal and oil as clean fuels, removing "clean coal" from its taxonomy in 2021. Although fossil gas is not classified as eligible for electricity generation, it is often listed as a clean fuel. Official documents, however, do not classify fossil gas as green.

China's XIV Five-Year Plan, adopted in 2021, sets clear goals to reduce energy and carbon intensity and increase the share of non-fossil fuels. By 2025, non-fossil energy consumption is targeted at 20%, with energy consumption per unit of GDP decreasing by 13.5%. By 2030, CO_2 emissions per unit of GDP should drop by over 65% from 2005 levels, with non-fossil energy comprising 25%. China's coal reliance remains high, but the Five-Year Plan projects coal consumption to peak around 2026–2027, then decline. Renewable energy capacity overtook fossil fuels in 2023, signalling a transition toward a green economy. In 2022, oil made up 18% of China's energy mix, mainly used in transportation. While oil receives less policy attention than coal, it is impacted by the rapid growth of electric vehicles (EVs). Forecasts predict China's gasoline demand will peak by 2024–2025, with EV sales comprising 28% of all cars sold by 2023. By the year 2035, China aims to have half of all cars to be fuelled by electricity, hydrogen or a mix of electricity and fuel. Fossil gas accounts for 9% of China's energy mix with approximately 46% used in industrial processes. Natural gas is seen as a much cleaner source of energy compared to coal. In 2017, China launched a program to convert its existing coal capacities to gas. The hydrocarbon policy of China aims to strengthen energy independence, maintain economic growth and meet decarbonization targets.

Sustainable Finance in Germany

Germany has clear guidelines for decarbonization and aims to phase out fossil fuels by 2045. However natural gas is viewed as an interim fuel in the period of transition away from oil, nuclear power and coal towards renewable sources. Germany's energy mix, traditionally dominated by fossil fuels, has shifted significantly under the Energiewende policy. By 2022, renewables and fossil fuels each made up about 44% and 46% of the energy sector, respectively. The 2019 Climate Change Act commits Germany to climate neutrality by 2045 and a 65% emissions reduction by 2030. The updated Long-Term Strategy aims for 80% of electricity from renewables by 2030 and a coal phase-out. Gas use will be reduced and partially replaced by green hydrogen. With reduced reliance on Russian hydrocarbons, Germany is expanding LNG infrastructure, but new LNG terminals must be hydrogen-ready. Germany's hydrocarbon strategy includes a gradual phase-out of fossil fuels, with new gas plants convertible to hydrogen and increased renewable energy capacity.

China Taxonomy

The China Green Bond Endorsed Project Catalogue (China Taxonomy) focuses on aligned technologies rather than specific activities with criteria. First published in 2015 and updated in 2021, it now excludes standalone fossil fuel energy generation, including clean coal and liquefied natural gas. However, some fossil fuel-related activities remain eligible, such as gas turbine manufacturing, hydrogen-natural gas mixtures, and gas-powered generation in remote areas. These projects align with China's decarbonization strategy, where natural gas serves as a transitional fuel to replace oil and coal due to its cleaner emissions profile.

ASEAN Taxonomy

The ASEAN Taxonomy, still in development, introduced its first compliance criteria in March 2023, with three tiers of stringency. Tier 1, for developed countries, aligns with international standards, setting a threshold of 100 gCO_2/kWh. Tiers 2 and 3, for less developed countries, have much weaker thresholds, allowing up to 510 gCO_2/kWh, including fossil gas-based electricity generation. Though the taxonomy encourages gradual development toward higher tiers, it lacks a binding timeline for decarbonization. Criticism arises over its leniency toward fossil fuels, limiting alignment with the Paris Agreement's goals, potentially locking countries into lower tiers. In 2021, ASEAN taxonomy introduced "traffic light concept" of red (significant harm), amber (making a substantial contribution to transition) and green activities. Amber activities can be interpreted in terms of three activities (1) Activities which follow a decarbonization pathway which is aligned with the trajectory required by the Paris Agreement (2) activities which face significant challenges on account of decarbonization (3) interim solutions to reduce emissions carried out for a limited period of time. Both ASEAN and Malaysia taxonomy have adopted the principle of do-no-harm (DNSH) to other environmental objectives as well as the concept of remedial measures to transition.

In the Malayan taxonomy, corporate-wide finance qualifies if the borrower commits to transition efforts, like implementing policies or action plans. Core business transformation is essential for transition finance. A granular activity-level classification, similar to the EU taxonomy, is included in the ASEAN Plus Standard and Malayan taxonomy for six key sectors.

Russian Taxonomy

The Russian Green Taxonomy aligns with scientific principles and EU thresholds but allows gas generation to meet a 100 g CO_2e/kWh threshold based on direct emissions, ignoring methane leakages. This weakens its credibility. Russia's Transitional Taxonomy focuses on energy efficiency rather than decarbonization, allowing fossil fuel operations with minimal improvements, lacking net-zero alignment.

Thailand Taxonomy

Thailand's Taxonomy, the first to fully apply a science-based transition, uses a traffic light system: green indicates net-zero compatibility by 2050, amber for transitional activities reducing emissions, and red for activities incompatible with the taxonomy, like oil, coal, and new gas generation. Gas-to-hydrogen conversion is allowed in the green category.

Sustainable Finance in Japan

During May 2021 period, The Basic Guidelines on Climate Transition Finance was published by the Japan Financial Services Agency, Ministry of Economy, Trade and Industry and Ministry of the Environment of Japan.

In June 2021, Japan revised its Corporate Governance Code (CGC), requiring companies to disclose sustainability policies and enhance climate-related reporting per TCFD recommendations by April 2022. The Financial System Council reconvened to discuss corporate sustainability disclosure, while the Japan Exchange Group launched an ESG Bond Information Platform in July 2022.

In 2021, Japan established the Taskforce on Transition Finance, issuing guidelines and creating transition roadmaps for various industries. METI introduced subsidies for third-party evaluations and financing support programs. Additionally, the FSA promoted social bonds by publishing guidelines and indicators. Japan also launched the Asia Energy Transition Initiative to support ASEAN countries.

In July 2022, Japan's Ministry of the Environment published updated Green Bond, Sustainability-Linked Bond, and Loan Guidelines, aligned with international standards, providing evaluation criteria and eligible green projects. The Bank of Japan established a Climate Coordination Hub and announced its Strategy on Climate Change in July 2021, aiming to support private sector climate efforts and stabilize the macroeconomy.

The Japanese government's policy measures such as "the grand design and action plan for new capitalism 2023 revision and "the basic policies for economic and fiscal management and reform 2023 "focusses on green transformation investments and loans in Japan and Asia along with the promotion of impact investment. During 2020, Japan had made a national commitment to achieve net zero by the year 2050. In February 2023, the Japanese government established the basic policy on Green Transformation (GX). Green Transformation (GX) aims to shift the economy and society from fossil fuel dependency to clean energy structures, driving growth through emissions mitigation. The Green Growth Strategy for achieving carbon neutrality by 2050 outlines the government's commitment to rapidly reaching net-zero emissions. It targets industries, particularly hard-to-abate sectors crucial for economic growth, emphasizing the substantial efforts needed for decarbonization in these areas. During February 2023, the Japanese government approved the GX Plan and related legislation. The GX Plan provides a 10-year roadmap for cutting Japan's emissions by 46% by 2030 and promotes transition finance. It identifies investment opportunities in renewable energy, energy efficiency, and circular economy measures. The plan also outlines an emissions trading system (ETS) starting in 2026 and a carbon levy on fossil fuel imports.

The GX Plan consists of four key initiatives:

1. Integrated regulatory and support measures to attract government funding and private investment.
2. Introduction of new financing methods, including transition financing and public-private partnerships.
3. An international strategy promoting regional cooperation through the Asia Zero Emissions Community.
4. Growth-oriented carbon pricing, including GX transition bonds, aimed at securing USD 1 trillion in public-private GX investment by 2033.

These initiatives focus on fostering investment, enhancing international collaboration, and promoting sustainable development to achieve long-term emission reductions and economic growth. These initiatives span energy, transport, industry, and finance, offering clear targets and guidelines for action and investment. Japan's government demonstrates global leadership by committing to issue USD 144 billion in sovereign GX bonds, providing strong policy support to incentivize private sector investment.

With the aim to invest over 150 trillion yen in public and private GX investments over the next ten-year period, the government aims to provide an initial 20 trillion yen for the issuance of new sovereign bonds to finance GX initiatives. The Japanese government will promote early investments by introduction of a carbon levy on fossil fuel importers beginning in fiscal 2028 along with auctions for emission allowances starting in fiscal 2033 as part of its Growth Oriented Carbon Pricing Strategy. The Sustainability Standards Board of Japan (SSBJ) was established in year 2022. To improve sustainability disclosure, the SSBJ is developing standards tailored to Japan's investors and companies. The Financial Services Agency (FSA) plans to integrate these standards into statutory disclosure and will address assurance services, including providers, standards, scope, and frameworks, considering both domestic and international trends. During January 2022, JPX's Sustainable Finance Platform Development Working Group released an interim report to enhance the ESG market. JPX announced the creation of an "ESG Bond Information Platform" to centralize bond issuance data, issuers' ESG strategies, external evaluations, and impact reports. The platform was launched in July 2022.

The FSA aims to summarize the endorsement status of data providers by June 2024. Scope 3 emissions, covering supply chains, require coordinated efforts. Corporate ESG data should support investments, with the FSA using tools like XBRL to enhance data availability. JPX's "Green Digital Track Bond" utilizes security tokens to track renewable energy output, with future data expected to be available on the ESG Bond Information Platform. In December 2022, Japan's FSA and other ministries co-hosted an Advisory Council to improve climate change data utilization. In June 2023, they published discussion summaries and a list of government-developed climate data. The council continues discussions on scenario analysis, risk assessment, and data-driven business decisions. The PRI requires investors to integrate ESG factors into the decision making without breaching fiduciary duties. The PRI signatories have more than doubled in 5 years. By April 2023, 324 investors had joined the Japanese Stewardship Code. The Government's "Doubling Asset-based Income Plan" aims to enhance investment returns through ongoing stakeholder dialogue, incorporating sustainability considerations. The government have announced plans to fundamentally reform Japan's asset management industry with respect to sustainability.

In 2022, Japan's FSA issued "Seven Expectations for Asset Management Companies Managing ESG Investment Trusts" and revised the Comprehensive Supervisory Guidelines for Financial Instruments Business Operators. Effective March 2023, these revisions cover ESG-related investment trusts and disclosure practices. Despite a temporary decline in ESG fund sales, the FSA anticipates long-term market growth as investment policies becomes clearer to market. In Japan, the total ESG investment through mutual funds is relatively low compared to Europe and the U.S. Additionally, passive investing in ESG funds, which track market indices, constitutes about 10% of assets under management in Japan, significantly lower than in Europe. To ensure transparency and objectivity in ESG evaluations, the FSA established the Technical Committee for ESG Evaluation and Data Providers, which issued a report in July 2022. Based on this, the FSA formulated a voluntary Code of Conduct in December 2022, requiring providers to endorse and disclose their adherence, focusing on evaluation quality, engagement, and independence.

In Japan, GX League companies must procure carbon credits by mid-2026 for any shortfall in emissions reductions from 2023–2025 targets. Growth-oriented carbon pricing will begin in 2026, with emission allowances required from 2033, boosting carbon credit demand. The financial sector is expected to facilitate carbon credit trading, establish markets, and support credit generation efforts. Tokyo Stock Exchange aimed to launch a carbon credit market by the year 2030. The FSA had revised carbon credit regulations in year 2022 to encourage early financial institution participation. Japan's high ratio of indirect finance means financial institutions play a crucial role with companies. Thus, these institutions are expected to significantly contribute to sustainable finance. Japanese government will issue a new sovereign bond for financing GX investment over the next 10 years. During March 2023, Japan Fair Trade Commission issued a guideline for competition policy to be recognized as complementing environmental policies. FSA have plans to establish a consortium called the Asian GX Consortium consisting of public sector as well as private sector to provide financial or non-financial support for formulation of projects. During May 2023, GFANZ Japan Chapter had been established as the first regional office of GFANZ. By April 2023, 51 institutions had signed "Japan Impact driven financing initiative" which were adopted by private investors and financial institutions. Small and medium sized enterprises (SMEs) in Japan account for more than 90% of the number of enterprises in Japan and for 10–20% of scope 1 emissions.

Regional financial institutions must lead in understanding decarbonization and its measures, working closely with national and local governments, economic organizations, and initiatives. They are expected to promote government-supported projects, offer consulting on emissions measurement and energy conservation, and collaborate with regional companies. To address local issues in the Green Transformation (GX), such as business creation, funding needs, and energy strategies, these institutions must strengthen partnerships with governments, commerce societies, manufacturers, and energy companies. Cooperation among all stakeholders is essential to identify challenges and advance concrete solutions for sustainable regional development. Promoting Green Transformation (GX) in local areas requires collaboration among stakeholders to address challenges like business creation, funding, and energy strategies. Financing GX investment demands diverse schemes such as project finance and blended finance due to high initial costs and delayed returns. Government cooperation is essential to support local GX plans.

Japan Climate Transition bond had achieved certification under its rigorous climate bonds standard related to transition finance. Climate transition INT-bearing government bond was expected to be issued by February 2024. Notably, 55% of the bond's Use of Proceeds (UoP) is allocated to research and development, with 18% specifically dedicated to exploring hydrogen use in steel production and decarbonizing thermal processes. The remaining 44.5% of the bond's Use of Proceeds (UoP) is allocated to supporting decarbonization efforts. This includes subsidies for low-carbon transport and batteries, improving home insulation, and promoting the adoption of clean energy vehicles.

The largest portion of subsidies is allocated to silicon carbide power semiconductors, supporting renewable energy, clean transport, energy storage batteries, electricity transmission and distribution, as well as strengthening supply chains for critical materials used in battery manufacturing. The value of the green innovation fund amounted to 756.4 billion yen.

In 2017, Japan launched the Basic Hydrogen Strategy to become the first country to develop a strategy to anchor the deployment of hydrogen and ammonia as alternate fuels. The initiative span energy, transport, industry and finance. The Basic Hydrogen Strategy's thresholds start after 2030, yet Japan's major emission reductions are needed before then. This creates uncertainty about deploying low-carbon hydrogen and ammonia in time to meet climate goals. Ambitions for ammonia combustion by 2050 are insufficient for 1.5 °C alignment, raising concerns about stranded investments and high emissions.

The aim of GX is to make Japan a leader in low carbon technology. A 2023 report by Berkeley Lab states that Japan could meet 70% of its power needs by 2035 through a combination of renewable energy, battery storage, interregional transmission, and energy efficiency improvements.

The cumulative green bond issuance in Japan amounted to USD 37.3 billion in the year 2021 which placed Japan in 11th position in terms of global country rankings. The 2021 green bond issuance in Japan amounted to USD 11.40 billion. In 2021, financial corporations dominated green bond issuance, accounting for 45% of the market with USD 7.1 billion. Non-financial corporations and government-backed entities followed, contributing 30% (USD 4.8 billion) and 22% (USD 3.4 billion), respectively.[12] In 2021 the largest deal of value USD 0.35 was made by NTT Finance. Japan Finance Organization for Municipalities made the second largest green deal valued at USD280 million. During the period 2014–2021, buildings dominated the Use of Proceeds (UoP) at 41% with energy accounting for 32%. Japan Housing Finance Agency had made the largest allocation for buildings valued at USD 5.29 billion followed by NTT Finance Corporation valued at USD 2.1 billion. In energy sector, Mitsubishi UFJ Financial Group was the largest allocator with USD 2.1 billion. Six of the top ten energy issuers were financial corporations while non-financial issuers included Mitsubishi Heavy Industries, Renesas Electronics and TEPCO. Japanese issuers tend to prefer shorter tenors, with 49% of deals maturing between 5 and 10 years, while long tenors over 20 years make up only 5% of the total. Among green bonds with tenors of 10 years or more, government-backed agencies account for 56%, local governments for 38%, financial corporations for 20%, and non-financial corporations for 27%.

By 2021, Japanese thematic labelled bond market ranked 11th in terms of its global peers and accounted only 2.1% of the total volume of thematic labelled bond market. In 2020, the property and construction company Hulic Co Ltd. issued Japan's first sustainability linked bond (SLB). This 10-year JPY 10 billion (USD 95 million) deal was Japan's first publicly offered Sustainability-Linked Bond (SLB) aligned with the SLB Principles set by the International Capital Market Association (ICMA). NYK Line became Japan's first company to issue a transition bond in a two tranche deal worth USD 190 million.

Sustainable Finance in the Middle East

According to Strategy &Part of the PWc network study, green investments in six key industries across GCC could result in approximately $2 trillion in cumulative GDP contributions with generation of over one million jobs. Major players such as Amazon, Delta Air Lines, Microsoft and Unilever have made commitments to become fully carbon neutral during a time span period of 10 to 20 days. BlackRock have announced that it would exit any investment with a clear sustainability risk.

Green finance can assist GCC countries counter a 40% decline in FDI over the past decade, driven by reduced investor interest in hydrocarbon-based industries. GCC countries, with high solar exposure and strong wind resources, can generate renewable energy at one-third the global average cost, producing twice the solar output of Europe. GCC governments can restructure supply chains, secure imports and enhance sustainability in the agriculture and food sector. GCC countries currently recycle only 10% of plastic and metal waste. Raising recycling rates to 40%

[12] Noriko Shimizu, Maiko Morishita, Naoki Mori, Green Finance State of Market 2022, Climate Bonds Initiative, Institute for Global Environmental Strategies.

could create 50,000 jobs and support a $6 billion market. Green hydrogen offers significant opportunities for GCC countries, with potential access to a $300 billion annual market by 2050 and the creation of 400,000 jobs. With the right investments, GCC nations can leverage their abundant renewables, land, seawater, and low domestic demand to maximize export potential.

The GCC region can address its critical water scarcity challenge by developing the world's first low-carbon urban water utility. This utility could focus on treating wastewater through a full-resource-recovery approach, reducing reliance on energy-intensive desalination. Utilizing energy-efficient technologies like reverse osmosis and renewable sources such as solar and wind, the utility would minimize wastewater discharge and cut energy consumption. By embracing sustainable water management practices, the GCC can reduce its environmental footprint while addressing one of its most pressing resource challenges. This initiative positions the region as a global leader in innovative, low-carbon water solutions. Green bonds have immense growth potential in GCC region as the green bonds constitute just 0.3% of the global market in year 2021.

According to Bloomberg's Capital Markets League Tables data, green and sustainability debt issuance in MENA market reached $18.64 billion in year 2021 compared to $4.5 billion in year 2020. ESG debt financing was done by Riyad Bank, National Bank of Kuwait, Qatar National Bank, First Abu Dhabi Bank, Emirates NBD and Saudi National Bank in year 2021. In the year 2020, the major landmark deals included Egypt's debut $3 billion green loan, Masdar Abu Dhabi Future Energy's $100 million revolving green loan and Etihad Airway's $1.2 billion sustainability linked loan. In 2021, syndicated green loans amounted to $6.95 billion while green loans amounted to $1.6 billion. The green loans consisted of Masdar ($100 million), Saudi Electricity ($500 million), Egypt ($1.5 billion), and Red Sea Development ($3.8 billion), while green bonds include FAB's six multi-currency issuances totalling $605 million.

According to UN Framework Convention on Climate Change (UNFCCC) Needs based Climate Finance Project estimates, Arab countries required climate finance investments in the range of US$436 billion to US$478 billion by the year 2030. However, the climate finance flows to the region are estimated to be only US$5.1 -US$7.4 billion a year. The Intergovernmental Panel on Climate Change (IPCC) indicates that countries in this region will face the greatest impacts of climate change and have the highest need for adaptation investment. Loans remain the dominant form of climate finance flows in the region.

According to the International Monetary Fund (IMF), since 2000, climate disasters have caused an average of US$2 billion in direct material damages annually across the Middle East and Central Asia. The IMF also projects that a 1 °C rise in temperature could lead to an immediate 2% drop in per capita economic growth in five of the hottest countries in the MENA region: Bahrain, Djibouti, Mauritania, Qatar, and the United Arab Emirates. The World Bank estimates that climate-related water scarcity could reduce Middle Eastern nations' GDP by 6% to 14% by 2050, affecting agriculture, health, and incomes. To address these impacts, countries may need to invest up to 3.3% of their GDP annually over the next decade for climate adaptation.

UAE became the first country in the Gulf region to aim to achieve net-zero GHG emissions by year 2050. The UAE's Energy Strategy 2050 aims to invest AED 600 billion to meet energy demand while ensuring sustainable economic growth. It targets increasing clean energy's share in the energy mix from 25% to 50% and reducing power generation's carbon footprint by 70%, saving AED 700 billion by 2050.

The green bond issuance in MENA region witnessed 122% increase in year 2021 compared to year 2020. The major green bond issuers were Riyad Bank, National Bank of Kuwait, Qatar National Bank, Majid Al Futtaim Properties and Banque Centrale Populaire. Shari'a compliant green sukuk was first introduced in year 2019 by Islamic Development Bank with issue valued at US$1.18 billion bond which was directed towards renewable energy and clean transportation. This issue was the world's first AAA green sukuk. During June 2020, Islamic Development Bank had issued US$1.5 billion Sustainability sukuk. In the year 2021, Islamic Development Bank raised US$2.5 billion through sustainability sukuk.

According to a report, sustainable finance in GCC region increased from US$600 million in aggregate in year 2021 to approximately US$8.5 billion in year 2022.[13] This resulted from 15 deals in year 2022 compared to six deals in year 2021 according to Bloomberg's capital markets league data. In 2021, all deals were accounted by UAE. In 2022, Saudi Arabia was the lead issuer accounting for more than half of the total volume while the rest were accounted by UAE. In October 2022, Saudi Arabia's sovereign wealth fund, the Public Investment Fund listed its debut $3 billion green bond on the London Stock Exchange. The issue was eight times oversubscribed. During November 2022, Dubai Islamic Bank, the UAE's biggest Sharia-compliant lender by assets, raised $750 million through the sale of its debut sustainable sukuk.

During June 2015, the Emirates Green Development Council (EGDC) was established in UAE to coordinate and oversee the implementation of effective collaboration between federal and local authorities in UAE.

The UAE Green Agenda's Green Finance and Investment Support Scheme (1.2.3) aims to stimulate the country's financial sector towards investment in green projects and innovating green finance products and services. By 2015, the total amount of green investment exceeded USD 22 billion in UAE. One of the key themes of COP28 was climate finance, which focuses on financial investments and funding for projects and initiatives aimed at mitigating and adapting to climate change. The UAE was the first Middle Eastern country to ratify the Paris Agreement and has reinforced its commitment to climate-focused investments through various national and emirate-level initiatives. These include the UAE Green Agenda 2030, the UAE Guiding Principles on Sustainable Finance (2017), and the Abu Dhabi

[13] The National News, January 4, 2023, "GCC Green Bond and Sukuk Issuances Hit a Record in 2022.", retrieved from https://www.thenationalnews.com/business/markets/2023/01/04/gcc-green-bond-and-sukuk-issuances-hit-a-record-in-2022/

Sustainable Finance Declaration (2019) etc. Sustainable Finance Framework was launched in year 2021.

The UAE government has committed an initial investment of $163 billion as part of its national strategy to achieve Net Zero by 2050. By the end of 2022, six major UAE banks—FAB, ADCB, ENBD, DIB, Mashreq, and ADIB—had allocated over $51 billion in green financing for projects such as renewable energy, waste management, and green technology. Abu Dhabi Future Energy Company (Masdar) had raised $750 million in its debut sale of green bonds during July 2023. Since 2006, Masdar had developed and invested in renewable energy projects in 40 countries. Masdar City in Abu Dhabi, a leader in sustainable urban development for 15 years, led to the creation of the Masdar Green Real Estate Investment Trust (REIT) in 2020. Initially valued at over $250 million, the REIT has grown to nearly $750 million and is one of the few globally made up of LEED Platinum and Gold-rated buildings. According to Central bank in UAE, the non-bank institutions contribute approximately 30% of the country's financing for ESG initiatives. In 2022, the ESG financing in the UAE exceeded $6 billion. Dubai Financial Market became the world's first Sharia compliant capital market in year 2007 and had updated its Sharia standards to cater to investor interest in sustainability. By September 2020, the total green sukuk issuances amounted to $10 billion which were accounted by 12 distinct issuers from Indonesia, Malaysia, Saudi Arabia, the United Arab Emirates and one multilateral development bank.

As part of the Saudi Green Initiative, Saudi Arabia has committed $180 billion to achieve Net Zero emissions by 2060. The Public Investment Fund (PIF) is investing $40 billion annually in green projects through 2025 to support non-oil economic growth and diversification.

The Abu Dhabi Fund for Development, Etihad Credit Insurance, Masdar, and AMEA Power committed $4.5 billion to clean energy projects in Africa. More recently, at the Saudi-Arab-African Economic Conference, the Arab Coordination Group, led by Saudi Arabia and GCC financial institutions, announced a $50 billion plan to develop climate-resilient infrastructure in Africa.

In 2022, the Middle East's biggest mall operator, Majid Al Futtaim Holding and Dubai's largest listed developer, Aldar Properties have secured substantial funding through green sukuk issuance. In May 2019, Majid Al Futtaim issued the MENA region's first corporate green sukuk, raising $600 million, followed by an additional $600 million green bond in October 2019. By 2020, all proceeds had been fully allocated to projects supporting the green buildings sector, marking a global benchmark in corporate green sukuk. In October 2020, Etihad Airways issued a $600 million Transition Sukuk, the aviation sector's first sustainability-linked bond, tied to carbon reduction targets, including Net Zero emissions by 2050. In 2021, Etihad raised an additional USD 1.2 billion in sustainability linked loans.

The UAE's first ever dirham denominated green sukuk was issued by the First Abu Dhabi Bank (FAB). During Jan 2021, FAB issued the largest ever Swiss Francs (CHF) denominated green bond by an international issuer valued at CHF 260 million bond and the first by a MENA issuer. Emirates NBD, bank of Dubai raised Gulf region's first sustainability linked loan of value $1.75 billion in year 2022. Abu Dhabi's sovereign wealth fund Mubadala had set up a standalone ESG unit.

The critical elements for the transition to clean energy and the commitment to net zero are based on the development of voluntary carbon markets and trading mechanisms in the Middle East. The UAE's Securities and Commodities Authority is collaborating with the Ministry of Climate Change and Environment to establish a carbon-trading mechanism. In 2022, the Abu Dhabi Global Market announced plans for a fully integrated carbon-trading exchange. Saudi Arabia's PIF and the Saudi Tadawul Group had launched a voluntary carbon credits exchange.

Abu Dhabi Global Markets (ADGM) published a consultation paper in November 2022 on mandatory ESG reporting for ADGM-incorporated companies. In 2022, Bahrain's state oil company, Oil and Gas Holding Company (Nogaholding) refinanced a $2.2 billion sustainability linked corporate finance facility.

In 2018, the Dubai Financial Services Authority released its Green Bond Best Practice Guidelines to provide issuers and market practitioners with details about listing of green bonds. In January 2020, Abu Dhabi launched the Green Bond Accelerator in collaboration with Abu Dhabi Global Market and Abu Dhabi Securities Exchange to position the Emirate as a regional hub for green bonds and sukuk, promoting sustainable projects. During 2021, the Dubai Sustainable Finance Working Group launched its Sustainable Issuance Guide which highlights the major steps for issuing ESG bonds, sukuk, equities and other financial products.

In 2021, Saudi Arabia launched the Saudi Green Initiatives (SGI) combining environmental protection, energy transition, and sustainability initiatives to reduce emissions, boost afforestation, restore land, and protect ecosystems. SGI targets to plant 10 billion trees across 74 million hectares of land in Saudi Arabia. Public Investment Fund (PIF) of the Kingdom of Saudi Arabia is instrumental to implement the Kingdom of Saudi Arabia's green agenda of achieving net zero carbon emissions by the year 2060 and achieve its Nationally Determined Contribution of reducing carbon dioxide emissions by 278 million tons annually by year 2030.

The PIF is dedicated to achieving 70% of Saudi Arabia's renewable energy target by 2030. Additionally, it is one of six founding members of the One Planet Sovereign Wealth Fund initiative, which seeks to accelerate the transition to a low greenhouse gas economy among sovereign wealth funds and asset managers.

In 2021, Red Sea Global (RSG) the world's most ambitious regenerative tourism project developer, secured a SAR 14.12 billion (USD 3.76 billion) loan and credit facility from four Saudi banks. The financing, arranged by Banque Saudi Fransi, Riyad Bank, Saudi British Bank, and Saudi National Bank, is the first Riyal-denominated credit facility with Green Financing accreditation, recognizing RSG's commitment to social and environmental sustainability. Upon completion in 2030, The Red Sea Project will comprise 50 resorts, offering up to 8000 hotel rooms and more than 1000 residential properties across 22 islands and six inland sites.

In 2024, the Ministry of Finance launched Saudi Arabia's Green Financing Framework as part of the Financial Sector Development Program to promote sustainability and net zero emissions via the Circular Carbon Economy.

Investor demand for transparent ESG reporting has surged, but inconsistent sustainability metrics hinder assessments of green bonds and sukuk. The proliferation of varied reporting frameworks across countries and organizations creates complexity and confusion, making it challenging for investors to evaluate the impact of green financial instruments effectively.

Sustainable Finance in ASEAN

Physical climate risks are already affecting the cost of capital, with the Vulnerable 20 nations incurring an additional $62 billion in interest payments between 2008 and 2018. Transition risks are also becoming significant for countries heavily dependent on fossil fuel exports.[14] By 2030, global climate finance will need to increase six-fold, surpassing $4 trillion. Closing the net-zero investment gap will demand significant mobilization of private capital.[15]

The development of sustainable finance roadmap through mandate by central banks have a direct impact on financial sector and offers opportunities in terms of tax incentives, green guarantees, green finance subsidies and sovereign guarantees. Initiatives such as carbon pricing, green public investment management, environmental tax reform and fossil fuel subsidy phaseout have indirect impact on financial sector which are transmitted through real economy.

Sustainable Finance Roadmap

Developing a roadmap requires strong coordination and commitment from various stakeholders, including policymakers, industry regulators, and other key players. For instance, Thailand's roadmap was shaped by a sustainable finance working group which included the Ministry of Finance, the Securities and Exchange Commission, the Bank of Thailand, the Stock Exchange, and the Office of Insurance Commission.

Tax incentives can promote green, social, sustainability, sustainability-linked, and other thematic (GSS+) bond issuances. For example, tax credit bonds allow investors to receive a tax credit instead of interest payments from the issuer, a structure commonly used for U.S. municipal bonds. Other examples include stamp duty exemptions for investors and accelerated depreciation for net-zero projects.

---

[14] B. Buhr, U. Volz, C. Donovan, G. Kling, Y.C. Lo, V. Murinde, and N. Pullin. 2018. *Climate Change and the Cost of Capital in Developing Countries*. UN Environment. https://eprints.soas.ac.uk/26038

[15] Climate Policy Initiative. 2021. *Global Landscape of Climate Finance 2021*. https://www.climatepolicyinitiative.org/publication/globallandscape-of-climate-finance-2021/

In Malaysia, tax exemptions are available for the issuance of GSS+ bonds and sukuk. With the growing popularity of sustainability-linked instruments, the Sustainable and Responsible Investment (SRI) Sukuk and Bond Grant Scheme has been expanded to include sukuk issued under the Securities Commission's SRI-linked Sukuk Framework and bonds issued under the ASEAN Sustainability-linked Bond Standards. This initiative supports companies in raising funds to transition to low-carbon activities.

Green investments carry higher risks, leading to higher capital costs. Government guarantees reduce risk, boost investor confidence, lower costs, and increase green financial flows and project viability. A green guarantee scheme should use international standards like the EU's or Climate Bonds Taxonomy to attract global investors. Eligibility criteria, such as valid transition plans, minimum credit ratings, and project size, ensure investment viability. Sector-specific guarantees, like South Africa's, promote renewable energy, while government coordination with development banks enhances complementarity. Issuing green bonds often costs more than regular bonds due to extra due diligence, second-party opinions, and use of proceeds reports. Subsidies like interest rate cuts, stamp duty exemptions, and covering verification costs can remove this barrier, especially for smaller issuers, encouraging green bond issuance over traditional ones. For instance, Malaysia's SRI Sukuk and Bond Grant Scheme reimburses up to 90% of external review costs, with a maximum of RM300,000 per issuance. The Green and Sustainability linked loan grant scheme covers the cost of verification, assessment and up to 60% of the cost of framework development in Singapore.

Several ASEAN+3 countries have issued GSS+ bonds and could expand market diversity by using different labels. Sovereign issuance can fund strategic infrastructure, like power grid expansion, essential for private sector transition investments. Investors see sovereign GSS+ bonds as key to financing ASEAN power grid connectivity and related incentives or subsidies. ASEAN's GSS+ market is highly diversified, with a strong presence of social and sustainable bonds, as well as green sukuk, primarily issued by sovereign entities. Additionally, loans, particularly sustainability-linked and green loans, surpass bond volumes in the market.

Challenges for Sustainable Finance Investments in ASEAN Market

The lack of a sustainable project pipeline and limited issuance of sustainable bonds in ASEAN region can be attributed to the lack of capacity to manage and report sustainable investments to some extent. Studies have shown that Asian asset owners invest only 10% of portfolios in ESG strategies.[16] Developing sustainable

[16] Willis Towers Watson. 2021. Asian Asset Owners: Raising Their ESG Game. ESG Beliefs and Practices Survey 2021: Asia. https://www.wtwco.com/en-hk/insights/2021/10/asian-asset-owners-raising-their-esg-game

investment pipelines requires costly feasibility studies, with limited tools available. These upfront expenses are often unsuitable for commercial financing. Issuing smaller green bonds is costlier than loans, with additional expenses like green certification and second-party opinions, making it less viable for smaller deals.

ASEAN's sustainable investment faces structural barriers, including MSMEs' limited access to capital markets, insufficient long-term debt financing, inconsistent cross-border policies, and currency risks for international investors. Policies should support green loans for MSMEs and address these challenges by offering hedging tools and aligning regional regulations to attract sustainable investment.

High fossil fuel capacity in ASEAN countries like Indonesia, the Philippines, and Vietnam limits demand for renewables, as current and planned capacity exceeds future electricity needs. Green investments often have longer payback periods (3–5 years), but available credit options typically have shorter maturities, creating a mismatch in financing needs.

In ASEAN region, only Brunei Darussalam, Cambodia, Lao People's Democratic Republic, Malaysia, Singapore and Vietnam have a 2050 net zero target.

Sustainable Finance Trends in ASEAN Market

In 2020, the ASEAN GSS debt market was valued at USD 12.1 billion which were accounted by Six ASEAN countries of Singapore, Malaysia, Vietnam, Indonesia, Thailand and the Philippines. In 2021, the ASEAN sustainable debt market consisting of green, social and sustainability (GSS) bonds and loans were valued at USD 24 billion. Cumulatively the ASEAN GSS market stood at USD 54.5 billion during the period 2016–2021. Singapore was the regional leader with GSS debt issuance valued at USD 13.6 billion in year 2021 compared to USD 4.9 billion in year 2020. By end of 2021, cumulative green volumes in ASEAN stood at USD 39.4 billion which accounted for 72% of the region's GSS market, followed by sustainability debt valued at USD 14.4 billion which accounted for the remaining 27%. The social theme had a cumulative volume of USD 0.6 billion.

In 2021, Singapore was the biggest issuer of green finance. In the same year, The National Environment Agency (NEA) issued its first green bond worth SGD 1.65 billion (USD 1.23 billion), with 10- and 30-year terms. The funds are allocated to sustainable waste management projects, including the Tuas Nexus Integrated Waste Management facility. Additionally, significant green loans were issued, mainly targeting the buildings sector. In 2021, Thailand's major green bonds focused on transport and energy sectors. BCPG Public Company Limited issued renewable energy green bonds totalling USD 365 million. Other notable deals in renewable energy included B. Grimm Power Public Company Limited (USD 93 million), SPCG PCL (USD 44 million), and Energy Absolute PCL (USD 50 million in green loans). In the transport sector, the largest issuer was Bangkok Mass Transit System PCL with a USD 309 million green bond in November, followed by Toyota Leasing (Thailand) Co., Ltd. with a USD 64.1 million green bond in April. Additionally, a USD 22 million green loan was granted to Asian Capital Real Estate for eco-friendly residential development in Phuket. In 2021, under its green sukuk programme, Indonesia issued its fifth sovereign sukuk (Islamic bond) valued at USD 750 million. The government of Indonesia had also issued a green retail sukuk worth USD 350 million to finance projects in energy, waste and water themes. PT Bank BTPN offered a green loan facility of IDR 1.06 trillion to PT Kepland Investama for building projects with a three-year tenor. In 2021, Philippines witnessed two green bond issuances in energy sector. ACEN Finance, the wholly owned subsidiary of AC Energy Corporation had issued a USD denominated USD 400 million green bond with a fixed perpetual coupon of 4%. Energy Development Corporation (EDC) issued PHP 5 billion worth of green bonds. In 2021, solar energy sector accounted for all the three green deals from Malaysia.re NIKOLA issued a green sukuk facility valued at up to RM390 million (USD 95 million). MFP Solar Sdn Bhd secured a MYR100 million (USD 24.3 million) green term loan to fund several rooftop solar photovoltaic (PV) projects. Additionally, UiTM Holdings issued green financing deals, including a green sukuk and loan, totalling MYR100 million (USD 24.5 million). In 2021, most of Vietnam's green debt came from the transport and energy sectors. Dau Tieng Tay Ninh Energy, a solar farm project by B. Grimm in Vietnam, secured USD 160.5 million in syndicated green loans, including a USD 32.5 million loan from the Asian Development Bank (ADB) and LEAP, and a USD 128 million loan from Thai commercial banks. Other notable green loans included Lien Lap Wind Power Joint Stock Co. (USD 173 million), Thuan Binh Wind Power JSC (USD 57 million), and VinFast (Vingroup) (USD 400 million).

Singapore demonstrated market maturity with green bonds and loans issued in various currencies. Vietnamese, Indonesian, and Philippine issuers preferred USD for green debt, while Thailand and Malaysia used domestic currencies. From 2016 to 2021, all Malaysian green debt was in MYR, and 98% of Thailand's in THB. The ASEAN green bond market is dominated by shorter tenors, with 49% of issuances from 2016–2021 having terms of 5 years or less. Another 28% had terms of 5–10 years. Longer-term deals made up 23%, with 10–20-year deals at 14%, over-20-year deals at 7%, and perpetual bonds at 2%.

Among ASEAN-6 countries, Singapore and Indonesia had the most diverse range of green deal sizes, from under USD 100 million to over USD 1 billion. The Philippines focused mainly on medium-sized deals (USD 100–500 million), with some smaller and larger deals. No green instrument from Thailand, Vietnam, or Malaysia exceeded USD 500 million. In 2021, two social bonds valued at USD 0.13 billion issued in ASEAN had originated from Thailand. Thaifoods Group issued its first social bond worth THB 1 billion (USD 30.5 million) with a 5-year maturity. The proceeds will fund projects focused on job creation and economic advancement in local communities. This marks the first social bond issue by a non-financial corporate issuer under ASEAN social bond standards. In September 2021, Indonesia issued Southeast Asia's first sovereign SDG bond, raising USD

584 million for social and environmental projects supporting the SDGs. In March 2021, Rizal Commercial Banking Corporation (RCBC), one of the largest banks in the Philippines, raised PHP 17.9 billion (USD 368.28 million) through ASEAN sustainability peso bonds with tenors of 2.5 and 5.2 years.

Vietnam's Vinpearl JSC issued the world's first Exchangeable Sustainable Bond (ESB), a USD 425 million bond maturing in 2026 with a 3.25% annual coupon rate, exchangeable for shares of Vingroup JSC. In April 2021, Malaysia launched the first sovereign USD-denominated sustainability sukuk, an oversubscribed USD 800 million 10-year deal for green and social projects aligned with UN SDGs.

In 2021, ASEAN witnessed its first transition bond as the Chinese Construction Bank issued a USD 2 billion deal in Singapore to support carbon-intensive industries. By the end of 2021, Singapore led ASEAN in Sustainability-Linked Loans (SLLs) and Sustainability-Linked Bonds (SLBs), with 94 of 129 deals totalling USD 33.6 billion, representing 84.5% of the market. Thailand followed with 19 deals totalling USD 2.3 billion.

During March 2021, Trafigura Group Pte Ltd. of Singapore had sustainability linked deal of USD 5.5 billion which included the closing of its new 365-day European multicurrency syndicated revolving credit facility worth of USD 1.85 billion. In 2021, Sembcorp Industries issued a SGD 675 million sustainability-linked bond at a 2.6% coupon, with a 0.25% rate increase if emission reduction targets are unmet by 2025.

Thai Union Group, a leading seafood processor, issued Thailand's first sustainability-linked bond (THB 5bn, USD 150.7 m) in July 2021 with a 2.47% coupon rate. The bond's interest is tied to achieving sustainability performance targets, including Dow Jones Sustainability Index inclusion, 4% annual carbon emission reduction, and improved tuna supply chain monitoring.

In 2021, Japfa Comfeed Indonesia issued a USD 350 million sustainability-linked bond at 5.375%, maturing in 2026. The bond targets reducing water pollution, with a 25-basis point penalty for non-compliance. In 2021, Yinson Holdings issued Malaysia's first sustainability-linked sukuk (MYR 1billion, USD 236.3 million), supporting its climate transition strategy to achieve carbon neutrality by 2030 and net zero by 2050. By the end of 2021, 67% of ASEAN's cumulative SLL and SLB volume was USD-denominated, 20% in SGD, and 3% each in AUD, CNY, and JPY.

In 2022, the overall number of issuers dropped to 64 compared to 103 in year 2021. Singapore was the market leader accounting for 63% of the ASEAN issuance in green, SLL and SLB segments. In the green segment, the largest deal was done by Perennial Shenton Property Pte valued at USD 2.1 billion. In the social segment, the Government Savings Bank of Thailand was the largest issuer with deal of USD 295 million. In the sustainability segment, Thailand Government had the largest issue valued at USD 2.7 billion. In the SLB segment, Ascott REIT MTN Pte Ltd. had the largest issue valued at USD 259 million. Cumulatively SembCorp Financial Services Pte Ltd. had undertaken deals valued at USD 497 million. In SLL segment, Olam International Ltd. was the largest issuer with deals valued at USD 4.9 billion. Olam International cumulative deal value was estimated at USD 9.9 billion.

Green Debt

The green debt issuance in 2022 accounted for 25% of the cumulative green volume issued since 2016. The green debt issuance in 2022 amounted to USD 12.8 billion. Only 20% of the 2022 green volume was issued in foreign currencies. Energy projects are the most heavily financed category in many countries, accounting for over 50% of allocated funds in Malaysia, Thailand, Vietnam, and the Philippines.

Social and Sustainability Debt Issue

In social and sustainability debt segment, Thailand is the market leader with USD 9.1 billion with cumulative value followed by Philippines (USD 6.4 billion) and Malaysia (US 4.4 billion). In 2022, only 10 social bonds were issued from five issuers totalling USD 905 million. Sustainability Linked Loans (SLLs) is the largest thematic finance segment in ASEAN region.

ASEAN Initiatives for Sustainable Development

In 2021, ASEAN launched a Taxonomy for Sustainable Finance, developed by key sectoral bodies to establish a common framework for sustainable finance, complementing national initiatives. Version 1 promotes inclusivity, addressing diverse ASEAN economies' needs.

In March 2021, ASEAN central banks endorsed Sustainable Banking Principles, providing guidance for sustainable banking. A collaborative report offered non-binding recommendations on managing climate risks and supporting a low-carbon transition, with several banks already implementing actions.

The ACGF Green Recovery Program, launched in 2021, builds on the ASEAN Catalytic Green Finance Facility (ACGF) to stimulate green investment and support government green stimulus packages. With an estimated USD 500 million commitment from the ASEAN Infrastructure Fund (AIF) for nine projects, and a total portfolio of USD 3 billion, including ADB co-financing, the program will provide technical assistance and concessional loans to around 20 green infrastructure projects. These projects are expected to reduce 119 million tonnes of CO_2 emissions, create 340,000 green jobs, and address ASEAN's annual green investment needs, estimated at USD 210 billion.

Launched in 2002 by ASEAN+3, the Asian Bonds Markets Initiative (ABMI) aims to develop local currency bond markets for financial stability. In 2021, the ADB provided technical assistance to Thaifoods Group's social bond, supporting asset identification, sustainable finance framework development, and external review under the ASEAN+3 Multicurrency Bond Issuance Framework, with full CGIF guarantee.

Launched in 2021 during UNFCCC COP 26, the Energy Transition Mechanism (ETM) aims to accelerate ASEAN's shift from coal to clean energy. It focuses on early retirement of coal plants and scaling renewable energy solutions, utilizing low-cost financing through public, private, and philanthropic resources, with two multibillion-dollar funds supporting these efforts.

In 2021, ASEAN countries announced new net-zero commitments to enhance regional capital mobilization for decarbonization. Key targets include Thailand's carbon neutrality by 2050, Indonesia's aim for net-zero by 2060, Vietnam's commitment to net-zero by 2050, and Malaysia's goal for carbon neutrality by 2050 while halting new coal-fired plants. In March 2023, ASEAN released Version 2 of its regional taxonomy, introducing technical screening criteria as part of the second phase, the Plus Standard. The ACMF released the ASEAN SLBS and ASEAN Sustainable and Responsible Funds Standard (SRFS) in year 2022.

Country Trends

Malaysia

The green debt issuers in Malaysian market are focussing on the social dimension-based projects related to affordable infrastructure and employment. In 2014, the Malaysian government introduced the Green Technology Tax Incentive to support industry adoption of eco-friendly solutions. The Green Investment Tax Allowance offers incentives to companies developing eligible green technology projects, either for business use or self-consumption, as listed under the MyHIJAU Directory. The incentive also applies to those purchasing qualifying green technology products.

In 2017, the world's first green Sukuk issuance was made by Malaysian Tadau Energy. Malaysian issuers have collectively issued 13 green Sukuk and bonds to finance various projects, including large-scale solar farms, green buildings, and a mini-hydropower plant. In 2018, Malaysia launched its Green SRI Sukuk Grant Scheme. By December 2020, green bond issuance from Malaysian firms amounted to USD 1.36 billion.

By 2021, Malaysia's GSS+ market grew for three consecutive years, with sustainability labels comprising 51% of the market. Green debt made up 29%, while sustainability-linked instruments accounted for 20%. The SRI Sukuk Grant Scheme supports green bond issuance through tax exemptions, incentivizing projects. In April 2021, Bank Negara Malaysia released the Climate Change and Principle-based Taxonomy to standardize climate-related classifications and enhance risk assessments. In 2022, Malaysia, released the revised sustainability reporting guide and expanded the SRI Sukuk and Bond Grant scheme for performance linked instruments. The Securities Commission Malaysia (SC) and Bank Negara Malaysia (BNM), through the Joint Committee on Climate Change (JC3), are developing a taxonomy to enhance climate resilience in finance. In 2022, Malaysia introduced SRI Taxonomy. In green segment, the sukuk based issuer, Permodalan Nasional Berhad was the largest issuer with deals valued at USD 383 million. In S&S segment, the largest bond issues were CIMB Bank and Cagamas with deals valued at USD 1180 million. By November 2020, 17 SRI Sukuk were introduced in Malaysia valued at MYR 5.38 billion. Two incentive schemes -The Green Investment Tax Allowances (GITA) and Green Income Tax Exemption (GITE) was introduced in year 2014 for strengthening the development of green technology. The Green Technology Financing Scheme (GTFS) was launched in year 2021 with a total target financing approval of MYR 3.5 billion to support the development of green technology in Malaysia. In 2010, about 13 green projects were granted soft loans amounting to MYR 164.3 million under GTFS scheme. By 2017, 319 green projects were allocated MYR 3.638 billion under the GTFS. Approximately 5000 green jobs were created and 3784 million tons of carbon dioxide has been saved each year. The Asian Development Bank offers technical assistance to develop green cities and energy sector in Malaysia. Malaysia accounts for approximately 48% of the global sukuk market. Presently, Malaysia is among the countries with the highest CO_2 emissions per capita in ASEAN with 7.27 tons of emissions. Malaysia's first solar vehicle charging station was launched in year 2018. In terms of innovation, Malaysia had significant achievements. The current BRT system is an all-electric bus service which can serve up to 1000 passengers per hour. Green Building Index (GBI) was introduced in the year 2009 to guide green building certification based on the criteria of energy efficiency, indoor environment quality and innovation. Low carbon cities framework introduced in year 2011 by the Ministry of Energy, Green Technology and Water guides local authorities, residents and businesses in transitioning cities to low carbon through environment, infrastructure, transportation and buildings.

Introduced in 2016, Malaysia Carbon Reduction and Environment Sustainability Tool (MyCREST) quantifies carbon emissions and sustainability in the built environment. It offers four rating tools for new and existing buildings, including healthcare facilities. Launched in 2014 by the Securities Commission Malaysia, the SRI Sukuk Framework facilitates financing sustainable projects, extending the sukuk framework with additional guidelines for issuance, disclosure, and reporting.

In 2022, Malaysia's Securities Commission introduced the SRI Taxonomy, focusing on four environmental and three social objectives, guiding sustainable investment in the capital market.

Thailand

In 2021, Thailand's sustainable finance landscape was led by sustainability-labelled bonds, making up 49% of GSS+ instruments. Green bonds followed at 24%, sustainability-linked instruments at 21%, and social bonds at 5%. The SEC's 2021–2023 Strategic Plan aims to enhance sustainable finance through new regulations and five strategic initiatives for growth. Thailand Working Group on Sustainable Finance is involved in developing a taxonomy for sustainable finance. Thailand's sustainable finance highlights include sustainable banking guidelines, sustainable funds guidelines, taxonomy development, and capacity-building initiatives led by its central bank, industry, and international organizations. Thailand waives approval and filing fees for GSS+ issuances, along with an application fee waiver from the Thai Bond Market Association (ThaiBMA). In green segment, BTS Group Holdings was the largest issuer with total amount of USD 1000 million. In S&S segment, Thailand Government have issued bonds worth USD 7742 million. Indorama Ventures PCL was the largest issuer in SLB/SLL category with deals valued at USD 802 million. In 2022 and 2023, Thailand's EXIM Bank issued SME-focused green bonds with a 3-year maturity, raising nearly $100 million to support clean energy projects in the bio-circular-green economy. The bonds, with low interest rates and semi-regular payback, were oversubscribed by 2.5 times.

Singapore

Singapore is the ASEAN region's green finance hub. Singapore is the largest and most diverse thematic debt market in ASEAN region. There were 127 issuers from Singapore accounting for USD 81 billion. Green debt and SLLs comprised approximately 96% of the issuance amount. Singapore introduced the Sustainable Bond Grant Scheme in year 2017 for promoting the issuance of GSS bonds and followed by the world's first Green and Sustainability Linked Loan Grant Scheme in year 2021.

By the end of 2021, Singapore's GSS+ market saw significant growth in sustainability-linked instruments, which constituted 57% of cumulative GSS+ debt, followed by 40% in green debt and 3% in sustainability bonds. The Green Finance Industry Taskforce, initiated by the Monetary Authority of Singapore, proposed a taxonomy for green activities. Additionally, the Singapore Green Plan 2030 outlines five key pillars for sustainable development, aiming to position Singapore as ASEAN's green finance hub. The government announced plans for green bond issuances to finance public projects, with SGD 19 billion (USD 13.7 billion) in eligible projects identified. In December 2021, SGX enhanced its sustainability reporting regime for listed entities. In 2022, Singapore launched ESG Impact Hub and ESGenome Disclosure Portal. The new listing requirement in Singapore Stock Exchange required firms to provide climate reporting on a "comply or explain basis. In the GSS+ market, Singapore accounts for 63% of the cumulative volume and is the clear leader in the region. In January 2021, Singapore's Green Finance Industry Taskforce (GFIT), convened by MAS, proposed a taxonomy using a traffic light system to guide ASEAN financial institutions in identifying green or transitioning activities. Singapore has established an international advisory panel on sustainable finance and launched GFANZ APAC Network central office and the China-Singapore bilateral green finance taskforce. Singapore have launched Point Carbon Zero Programme in collaboration with Google Cloud.

In green loan segment, Fraser Property Ltd. and Perennial Shenton Property Pte Ltd. were the largest issuers with loan value of USD 2723 million and USD 2091 million respectively. In the green bond segment, Singapore government and Singapore Housing & Development Board were the largest issuers with bond values of USD 1753 million and USD 1638 million respectively. In the S&S segment, United Overseas Bank was the largest issuer with value at USD 1500 million. In the SLL segment, Olam International Ltd. was the largest issuer with loan value of USD 9925 million.

The Monetary Authority of Singapore will set supervisory expectations and provide guidance on financial institutions' transition planning, helping them manage climate-related risks and support the real economy's transition.

Indonesia

By the end of 2021, Indonesia's GSS+ market was primarily green-themed, with green debt at 65% of volume, followed by 15% in sustainability bonds and sustainability-linked instruments each. The Financial Service Authority launched the Sustainable Finance Roadmap Phase II to develop a market ecosystem, enhance sustainability reporting, and finalize a green taxonomy. In 2022, Indonesia introduced carbon tax, launched Energy Transition Mechanism (ETM) Country Platform and launched Just Energy Transition Partnership (JETP) at G20 Summit. The Financial Services Authority of Indonesia (OJK) is involved in developing a taxonomy for sustainability issues. The Indonesian financial regulator introduced its own green taxonomy based on Sustainable Finance Roadmap Phase II. Indonesia's regulator and local bourse offers fee incentives for green bond issuances and listing. In the green segment, the Indonesian government was the largest sukuk issuer with deals valued at USD 5485 million. In the SLB/SLL segment, PT Bank Rakyat Indonesia was the largest issuer with loan value of USD 1000 million.

Indonesia's 47-megawatt Rajamandala hydropower project received a $200 million political risk guarantee, facilitating a 19-year loan, but lacks specific green guarantee facilities. Indonesia's green sukuk is a sharia-compliant bond used to fund green projects, ranging from mitigation to resilience. It has spurred Indonesia's green bond market, with over half of its investors coming from outside ASEAN and support from regional partnerships, including the Monetary Authority of Singapore.

Philippines

The first green bond from ASEAN was issued in February 2016 by AP Renewables, Inc., a wholly owned subsidiary of Aboitiz Renewables, in the Philippines. By 2020, Philippine based firms had issued over USD 2.6 billion worth of green bonds.

As of 2021, the Philippines' GSS+ market was dominated by UoP debt, comprising 93% of volumes: 52% green and 41% sustainability debt, with sustainability-linked instruments at 7%. The Philippine Sustainable Finance Guiding Principles and Roadmap were launched to promote sustainable development and harmonize green policies, while the Bangko Sentral ng Pilipinas aims to strengthen its sustainable finance framework. In 2022, Philippines released Sustainable Central Banking Strategy. There were no green loans or SLBs from the Philippines till now. In the green bond segment, Ayala Corporation was the largest issuer with issuance amounting to USD 1170 million. In S&S segment, Philippines government was the largest issuer with deal valued at USD 2307 million. The Philippines Public Private Partnership (PPP) Centre supported by ADB's Urban Climate Change Resilience Trust Fund (UCCRTF) have intensified technical assistance for developing climate-resilient projects particularly outside Metro Manila. The National Economic and Development Authority (NEDA) developed the Philippine Action Plan for Sustainable Consumption and Production (PAP4SCP) with assistance from the Asian Development Bank. By 2020, four domestic banks—the Bank of the Philippine Islands (BPI), Rizal Commercial Banking Corporation (RCBC), China Bank and BDO Unibank, have issued green bonds in three currencies namely US Dollar, Philippines Peso and Swiss Franc. The SEC Philippines have been entrusted with the responsibility for development of the Sustainability Reporting Guidelines for publicly listed companies. The Green Financing Program initiated by the Development Bank of the Philippines provides financing and technical assistance for LGUs for its green strategic sector projects. The People's Survival Fund (PSF), led by the Climate Change Commission, provides annual funding for local governments and organizations to implement climate adaptation projects for vulnerable communities. The CCC is the National Designated.

Authority (NDA) in the Philippines for the Green Climate Fund (GCF). Most sustainable water projects in the Philippines are funded through bilateral agencies, multilateral banks, and the national budget, including the Metro Manila Flood Control Management Project.

Vietnam

In 2021, Vietnam's bond market exceeded USD 70 billion, predominantly from government debt. The Environmental Protection Law 2020 introduced new definitions and incentives for green bonds. In 2022, Vietnam launched the Just Energy Transition Partnership (JETP) with initial investment of USD 15.5 billion to support the green transition process. The Vietnamese government plans to develop national green classification standards to identify sustainable economic activities focused on environmental and social initiatives. In the green segment, Vingroup JSC was the largest issuer with deal size valued at USD 900 million.

Sustainable Finance in Latin American Region

Sustainable Finance in Mexico

The Financial Stability Committee established in year 2020 as part of the Financial Stability Council is the lead agency in Mexico for sustainable finance. There are five working groups associated with the Committee. According to the UN 2019 report,[17] 39% of global CO_2 emissions stem from buildings. Mexico aims to reduce GHG emissions by 22%–36% by 2030 through sustainable construction. The General Climate Change Law established by Mexico in year 2012 aims to reduce GHG emissions by 50% by the year 2050. Over 50,000 new houses are expected to be built annually in Mexico City until 2030, creating an USD 18 billion investment opportunity in green buildings. According to the National Institute of Statistics and Geography (INEGI), the building sector accounted for approximately 7% of GDP in year 2019. The World Green Building Council estimates that approximately 24 cities and states in Latin America aims to improve energy efficiency through public-private initiatives such as Building Efficiency Accelerator program. Studies[18] have estimated that approximately USD 901 billion is required for developing green buildings for Latin America's future sustainable cities. The National Institute of Ecology and Climate Change (INECC) of Mexico statistics suggest that emissions from the residential and commercial building sector accounts for 3.9% of GHGs and black carbon emissions account for 24% of energy emissions.

According to Mexico's Federal Mortgage Society (SHF), housing offers significant energy-saving potential due to options like efficient materials, ecotechnologies, and better design. These measures are cost-effective, with reduced electricity bills covering upfront costs over time, leading to lower operating expenses and environmental benefits. According to Sustentabilidad para Mexico (SUMe), building Torre Mayor in Mexico City have reduced operational costs and enhanced value when it became LEED Gold certified in retrofit. Approximately only 10.6% of green proceeds raised by Mexican issuers go to low carbon buildings.

Mexico City issued two green bonds in year 2016 and 2018. Approximately USD 54 million issued during the second green bond issuance were allocated to finance low carbon building sector projects. In 2017, Mexico City issued a sustainability bond. Vinte issued Mexico's first company SDG bond, raising 400 million pesos to finance sustainable infrastructure, including energy-efficient social housing and water adaptation projects like rainwater collection. In September 2020, Mexico issued a 750-million-euro Sustainability Bond, supporting the UN's Sustainable Development Goals and funding projects aligned with the 2030 Agenda. BBVA became the first financial corporation in Mexico to issue a green bond and raised USD 186 million through the issue. Over half of the proceeds funded low-carbon

[17] UN Environment Programme, 2019 Global Status Report for Buildings and Construction Sector.

[18] IFC, Climate Investment Opportunities in Emerging Markets, 2018.

buildings, while the rest supported sustainable buildings, infrastructure, public services, transport, and renewable energy projects.

CADU Real Estate will issue Latin America's first Certified Climate Bond under the Low Carbon Buildings Criteria, using proceeds to develop sustainable housing through the EcoCasa program. This program aims to reduce GHG emissions by at least 20% and up to 40% against the existing baseline. By September 2020, the green and sustainable bond market accounted for USD 2.98 billion of cumulative issuance of bond market in Mexico.

In 2016, NAFIN issued Latin America's first green bond by a national development bank, funding renewable energy projects. In 2017, ROTOPLAS issued a MXN 2 billion sustainability bond for clean water infrastructure, sanitation, and recycling, later expanding it to MXN 4 billion by 2020 for water efficiency. In 2018, FIRA, a local development bank, issued Mexico's first green bond for sustainable agriculture, certified under the Protected Agriculture Criteria. Supported by the Inter-American Development Bank, FIRA issued two more green bonds in 2019 and 2020, plus a social bond, financing projects with social and environmental benefits in agriculture.

In Mexico, alternative financial instruments like CKDs, CERPIS, and FIBRAS are used for low-carbon buildings, offering opportunities for green product issuance if linked to sustainable assets or projects. CKDs (Certificates of Capital Development) are equity funds in Mexico used to finance projects like real estate, infrastructure, and renewable energy. As of September 2018, 22 CKDs were focused on buildings, supporting CO_2 mitigation. CERPIS (Investment Project Certificates) finance projects or invest in companies, while FIBRAS are real estate investment trusts and include eligible sustainable assets. FIBRA focuses on energy and infrastructure, with potential for green investments.

Mexico's Green Finance Advisory Board (CCFV) promotes financing for environmentally impactful projects. Some FIBRAS, like FIBRA UNO, FIBRA Prologis, and FIBRA DANHOS, already fund green/sustainable buildings with LEED certifications. These properties focus on reducing energy, water consumption, GHG emissions, and waste, minimizing their environmental footprint during operation. Mexico is the second country in the Latin American region and is among the global top 10 countries with most LEED certified buildings. Through innovation and financial tools, green housing initiatives support informal sector housing demand in growing cities, with increased EcoCasa certification boosting supply in Mexico. Private sector interest in Mexico is strong, with major real estate companies pursuing low-carbon building projects, supported by thematic bonds for energy efficiency and climate-smart initiatives. CONUEE, Mexico's technical body for sustainable energy, promotes energy efficiency by developing building evaluation systems similar to the U.S. "Energy Star," in collaboration with INECC. SUMe, Mexico's official World Green Building Council representative, partners with USGBC to promote market transformation and capacity building through educational programs. IBALCA, a team of experts in sustainable project consulting, provides comprehensive support throughout project lifecycles, particularly in construction, ensuring compliance with rigorous international quality and efficiency standards.

Sustainable Finance in Brazil

In 2020, Brazil was ranked as the 7th largest greenhouse gas (GHG) emitter globally accounting for 3% of the global total of 50 $GtCO_2e$. Land use changes and agriculture contribute to 75% of Brazil's emissions, primarily from livestock, with increasing crop emissions linked to deforestation.

In the year 2021, Climate Bonds launched the Agri-food Systems Transition Programme (ASTP) to mobilize global capital for transitioning agri-food systems toward net-zero, deforestation-free production. It focuses on building a shared understanding of 1.5-degree climate pathways and issuing financial instruments like transition and green bonds for credible agri-food transitions.

Syngenta the global Agri Tech company which supplies pesticides and fertilizers have adopted sustainable agricultural practices. The Syngenta Foundation for Sustainable Agriculture (SFSA) supports small-scale farmers through focus on improving seed access, offering insurance and agricultural services. Syngenta also targets scope 1, 2, and 3 emissions and promotes transparency through its Good Growth Plan (GGP) and KPIs. Under the GGP, Syngenta have set four targets. (a) Innovating for sustainable agriculture with two new technologies annually. (b) Achieving carbon-neutral agriculture by improving biodiversity and soil health, and reducing carbon intensity by 50% by 2030. (c) Ensuring safety by training farm workers and promoting fair labour. (d) Building partnerships for sustainability. Syngenta's carbon targets are validated by the Science Based Targets initiative (SBTi), though further ambition toward a 1.5 °C scenario is encouraged. Syngenta's ESG strategy includes a delivery plan to achieve its 2030 carbon reduction target. It focuses on improving manufacturing efficiency, energy-saving programs, renewable energy, and supplier collaboration, aligned with its Health, Safety, and Environment Policy Framework.

Amaggi, a major Brazilian corporation, is a key player in the agri-food value chain, specializing in grain production, commodity trading, and logistics. It operates globally and invests in renewable energy through hydropower and solar plants. Amaggi aims for a deforestation-free grain supply by 2025 and net-zero emissions by 2050. Amaggi had partnered with ReNature, a consultancy firm specialized in regenerative transition for developing a regenerative agriculture programme called Amaggi Regenera in the year 2022.

Green Financial Instruments in Brazil

The major agricultural finance instruments in Brazil include the Agribusiness Letter of Credit (LCA), Rural Product Notes (CPR), Agribusiness Receivable Certificate (CRA) and Investment Fund in Agro-industrial Production Chains (FIAGRO). These instruments have potential sustainability characteristics. LCAs is key funding source for rural credit in Brazil which rose from under 1% in 2014 to about 15% by

2020 valued at BRL 43 billion. This instrument has 35% income tax exemption in order to support rural credit financing. CPR is the credit instrument which rural producers and cooperatives use to secure resources for production costs. By 2021, registered CPR transactions were valued at BRL 86 billion.

The Green Rural Product Certificate (Green CPR), funding reforestation and resource protection, innovates traditional CPRs but faces challenges due to stringent environmental verification requirement. CRAs, backed by receivables, are fixed-income securities issued by securitization companies, allowing firms to anticipate receivables and diversify the credit market. FIAGROs introduced in year 2021 are investment funds for agri-food assets such as credit rights, real estate, securities and shares. Brazil have immense potential for sustainable finance growth in sectors related to land use and Agri food. The 2020 Climate Bonds report suggest that there is an estimated USD 163 billion green investment potential for agricultural sector by 2030 in Brazil. The Land Use category of the Climate Bonds Taxonomy contributes about 60% of Brazil's green bonds, while agriculture-related sectors like energy and industry make up 30%. During September 2023, the Sovereign Sustainability Bond Framework was published. Brazil's sub-sovereign market is restricted due to government-required guarantees for municipal and state debt issuance. The International Chamber of Commerce (ICC) pioneered definitions and guidelines for sustainable trade finance, defining it as trade that supports the UN Sustainable Development Goals (SDGs).

Brazil's agri-food sector, a major Foreign Direct Investment recipient, faces structural challenges, including farmgate investment risk assessment bottlenecks and inadequate infrastructure. Despite these, over 1500 start-ups focus on innovation and resilience, supported by institutions like EMBRAPA, which provides research for scaling up agricultural advancements and addressing value chain challenges. Brazil must address increasing global pressure for traceable, deforestation-free supply chains to maintain market access, driven by the EU's new regulation requiring proof of deforestation-free products.

Brazil's agriculture, responsible for 9.8% of global sector emissions in 2022, primarily emits methane from cattle. Addressing this is key to Brazil's net-zero transition. Brazil's agriculture sector, accountable for deforestation and increased GHG emissions, now accounts for 25% of the economy. Sustainable finance plays an important role towards the decarbonization of the agricultural sector. Brazil's sustainable debt market reached USD 33.3 billion, making it the third-largest issuer of green, social, sustainability, and transition debt in Latin America after Chile and Mexico.

Brazil's GSS+ debt market is dominated by green bonds (45%) and sustainability-linked bonds (32%). Agriculture, Forestry, and Bioenergy dominate green bond proceeds from corporate issuers. Recent regulatory advances have promoted aggregating smaller projects into asset-backed securities (ABS), further driving their entry into the sustainable debt market. Green, social, sustainability, and transition bonds support climate and social initiatives through specified use of proceeds (UoP). Green bonds fund climate-friendly projects, while transition bonds, targeting hard-to-abate sectors like steel or cement, are a green subset. Social bonds focus on education and marginalized communities. Sustainability-linked bonds (SLBs) set performance targets linked to coupon adjustments, rather than specific UoP. As of end of H1 2023, Brazil is the leading source of green bonds in the LAC region with a cumulative volume of USD 15.1 billion. The sustainability linked bond market in Brazil is valued at USD 10.9 billion. Brazil is the only Latin American Country (LAC) to issue transition labelled bonds valued at USD 170 million. In the green theme, renewable energy and land use are the leading use of proceeds (UoP) which accounts for 56% and 20% of funding respectively. The market is predominantly driven by the private sector, with non-financial corporate issuers providing 76.6%, followed by financial corporates (13.8%), development banks (7.8%), and government-backed entities (1.8%).

Brazil leads the LAC region in sustainability-linked bonds (SLBs) with a cumulative volume of USD 12 billion, making up 36% of its GSS+ market.

Sustainability bonds account for 16.2% of Brazil's labelled market, totalling USD 5.4 billion. Non-financial corporates lead issuance, with renewable energy as the top use of proceeds category. In 2023, the social label constitutes only 2% of Brazil's GSS+ bonds, with a cumulative volume of USD 699 million. Banco do Brasil's USD 500 million social bond, issued at the end of 2022, is the largest to date, funding healthcare, employment generation, microfinance, affordable infrastructure, and socioeconomic empowerment. Financial institutions are the sole issuers, with microfinance and employment & training each receiving 21% of the proceeds. Transition bonds make up 2% of Brazil's GSS+ debt. In 2020, utility company Eneva S.A. issued two deals with a cumulative volume of USD 670.4 million.

The Land Use category in Brazil, which includes agriculture, livestock, and forestry, accounts for 19% of the country's Green and Sustainability-Linked Bonds (GSS+ UoP) volumes, second only to Energy at 57%. Bioenergy, part of Renewable Energy, is significant in this context, as several companies in the Bioenergy sector have issued Sustainability-Linked Bonds (SLBs). Feedstocks for bioenergy are a major source of Land Use. Additionally, 17.5% of the cumulative UoP allocated for Renewable Energy in green and sustainability bonds is earmarked for bioenergy. Forestry is the largest Land Use segment in Brazil's GSS+ bonds, with USD 5.6 billion in cumulative volume. Most bonds had 5–10-year tenors, and 82% were issued in USD. Bullet UoP bonds dominated, accounting for 92.1%. Tanac issued a USD 37.3 million sustainability bond, the only one with green UoP designated for forestry. Tanac is one of the world's leading producers of vegetable extracts. Agriculture is the second-largest category in Brazil's Land Use UoP, with a cumulative volume of USD 2.3 billion. Green UoP primarily funded efficient machinery, equipment, and intelligent systems for crop production. Most deals were sustainability bonds (76%), while green bonds accounted for 7% and SLBs for 17%.

Climate Bonds certified three ABS deals under its Agriculture Criteria, totalling BRL 218.3 million (USD 40.8 million). In 2021, Gaia Securitizadora issued two Agribusiness Receivables Certificates (CRA) for supply chain verifier Produzindo Certo and Ag-tech company Solinftec. In 2020, Ecoagro Securitizadora issued a CRA to finance organic farm operator Rizoma Agricultura. In 2022, Banco Bradesco

SA issued a USD 500 million sustainability bond of five-year maturity and with Use of Proceeds allocated to various sectors which included food security under Land Use. True Securitizadora structured a 5-year, BRL 50 million (USD 9.3 million) sustainability CRA for Oakberry Açaí in 2022, funding sustainable agriculture and social projects supporting Amazon riverside communities.

Green UoP primarily funded corn and sugarcane ethanol plants, while SLB KPIs focused on circular economy and CSR. Most Bioenergy projects had tenors of 5–10 years, with bonds (79.9%) being the main financing source. USD dominated (49%), followed by BRL (28%) and EUR (24%). In March 2022, Raízen issued its first SLB with KPIs focused on increasing Bonsucro certification and women's leadership participation. Two tranches totalling BRL 1.2 billion (USD 256 million) were issued.

In 2021, 49% of Brazil's GHG emissions came from land use changes and 25% from agriculture and livestock, primarily due to deforestation in illegal areas of the Cerrado and Amazon. The financial market pressures agriculture entities to adopt deforestation-free plans and climate targets. Investors aim to finance only companies committed to reducing emissions and supporting biodiversity. In June 2023, the EU introduced regulations requiring key agricultural exports from Brazil to be deforestation-free, aiming to reduce global deforestation and forest degradation.

Brazil initiated national taxonomy discussions in 2022, launching an action plan in September 2023. The final version is expected in 2024, mandating standardization for financial instruments to support sustainable development. The Ministry of Agriculture, Livestock, and Food Supply (MAPA) issued guidelines for sustainable development in Brazilian agriculture, supported by initiatives like the Plano Safra, which received BRL 364 billion (USD 70.7 billion) in 2023. Additionally, the ABC Plan promotes low-carbon practices and subsidized loans to reduce GHG emissions and adapt to climate change. The ABC+ Plan was introduced as an extension of the ABC Plan and will continue until 2030. Its goal is to create a more resilient agricultural production system through technological advancements and integrated landscape management.

Securitization in Brazil, including Real Estate Receivables Certificates (CRI) and Agribusiness Receivables Certificates (CRA), accounts for 3.5% of the GSS+ market. The thematic ABS market has grown, focusing on low-carbon agriculture and bioenergy. To scale GSS+ instruments, lenders should adopt international taxonomies and promote green development among borrowers. Securitization in Brazil, encompassing Real Estate Receivables Certificates (CRI) and Agribusiness Receivables Certificates (CRA), constitutes 3.5% of the GSS+ market. Thematic ABS for low-carbon agriculture and bioenergy is gaining traction. To enhance GSS+ instruments, lenders must adopt international taxonomies and encourage borrowers to prioritize green development and effective tagging.

The Climate Bonds Certification Scheme is an international, science-based labelling system for debt instruments and assets. It offers certification for sustainability-linked bonds, aligning with the Paris Agreement's climate goals. The scheme ensures rigorous, independent verification, fostering investor confidence, and has certified over USD 270 billion in debt instruments as of mid-2023.

Agribusiness contributes about 25% to Brazil's GDP and is crucial for domestic and international food security. However, agriculture and land use account for nearly 75% of the country's greenhouse gas emissions. To ensure sustainable production, Brazil must decarbonize the sector, with green finance playing a key role in this effort. Government guarantees, like partial-risk or liquidity guarantees, de-risk GSS+ debt, boost investor confidence, lower capital costs, and attract long-term institutional investors, expanding the green bond market. Slow approval processes hinder renewable energy projects. Streamlining approvals for taxonomy-aligned projects boosts the GSS+ deal pipeline and enhances investor confidence, offering a low-cost solution.

Brazil's USD 2 billion sovereign sustainability bond will boost its green finance market. By mid-2023, nine Latin American countries, including Chile, Mexico, and Peru, had issued GSS+ debt. Such sovereign deals signal government commitment to environmental and social transformation, accelerating market infrastructure and attracting private sector investment.

Local banks should prioritize lending based on credible green taxonomies, encouraging borrowers to adopt sustainable practices. Aggregating green loans could lower funding costs, creating a cycle of affordable, sustainable finance.

Sustainability-linked bonds (SLBs) are key in Brazil's debt market, especially for hard-to-abate sectors like agriculture. Issuers must ensure robust transition plans, material KPIs, and ambitious targets.

Green Finance Market in China

During the period 2015–2020, the capital required for green transition in China is estimated to be approximately RMB 2 to 4 trillion per year. It is estimated that trillions of RMB is required to achieve China's Carbon Neutrality target by 2060. In 2016, seven regulators of People's Bank of China (PBOC) had promulgated the Guidelines for establishing the Green Financial System. China is the largest ABS market in Asia. In a few years' time, China's green bond market became the second largest market in the world. In 2015, PBOC adopted Green Bond project catalogue for green projects in six environmental themes.

China was the largest source of green issuance in year 2019. In 2019, Chinese issuers raised RMB386.2bn ($55.8bn) in green bonds domestically and internationally, a 33% increase from 2018, driven by regulatory support. The Industrial and Commercial Bank of China (ICBC) was the largest green bond issuer in 2019. The Climate Bonds Standard certifies bonds aligning with a zero-carbon 2050 goal, using science-based criteria. Leading Chinese issuers adopt it for green bonds. China Three Gorges issued its first offshore green bond in 2017, raising EUR650 million for European wind projects and achieving Climate Bonds certification. China Development Bank followed with China's first quasi-sovereign Certified Climate Bond, supporting Belt and Road Initiative projects. ICBC London issued a record USD 1.58 billion green bond on LSE in 2018. China Construction Bank Luxembourg issued a EUR500 million Certified Climate Bond in 2018 under renewable and low-carbon criteria. Bank of China's Tokyo branch issued a USD379 million green bond, marking its third Certified Climate Bond. Industrial Bank listed Hong Kong's first dual-currency Certified Climate Bond in 2018, while Jiangsu Financial Leasing issued RMB1billion for China's first domestic Certified Climate Bond in 2019. By 2019, provincial and sub-provincial governments across China had issued over 500 green finance policies, including more than 300 targeted measures to advance green finance locally.

It is estimated that China would require RMB 3 trillion to RMB 4 trillion in green investment annually. Green bonds are an ideal financing tool to support the required investment. By July 2020, six provinces and nine regions were recognized as green finance pilot zones.

In China, despite the continued growth in low carbon energy sources like hydropower, these sources account of only 15.3% of total energy consumption with coal remaining the primary energy source. On the basis of 2015 data, it has been estimated that the cost of China's ecosystem destruction and pollution is around 2.1% of the GDP. The 13th Fiscal Year Plan released in year 2016 by the National Energy Administration (NEA) and the National Development and Reform Commission stated that the new installed capacity of energy sources such as wind energy, solar energy, hydropower, geothermal energy, biomass energy and other renewable sources must exceed 200 mkW by year 2020. In 2017, the Ministry of Transport and the NDRC had envisaged investment in rail, public transport, bicycle infrastructure and electric vehicles amounting to over USD 480 billion.

By the end of year 2021, the cumulative green bond issuance in China amounted to USD 200 billion (RMB 1.3 trillion). In 2021, the total labelled issuance in the domestic and international markets increased by approximately 2.4 times compared to year 2020 to reach USD 109.5 billion. In 2021, over 60% of overall Use-of - Proceeds (UoP) were accounted by the renewable energy sector. In year 2021, China was the market leader for green bond issuance globally. The Investment Association of China estimate that RMB 70 trillion infrastructure investment is required to achieve carbon neutrality goal of China in year 2030. In 2021, the growth in green bond volumes of USD 44.4 billion were from non-financial and financial corporates. The most active issuers in the green bond market during the period 2016–2021 were Bank of China, Wuhan Metro Group and Modern Land. State Owned Enterprises accounted for 97% of onshore green bonds by the number of deals in year 2021. China Development Bank had the largest three green bond issues among the state-owned enterprises in year 2021. In 2021, private companies such as Jiangsu Shenghong Technology and Shanying International Holdings issued onshore green bonds. In 2021, 122 issuers participated in the onshore green bond market. During the year 2021, Industrial and Commercial Bank of China (ICBC) was the only issuer who participated in both onshore and offshore green bond markets. New issuers included Shenzhen Metro Group, Kunming Rail Transit Group, and Capital Airports Holding Company. New issuers in the utilities sector included Huaneng Power International, Fujian and Huadian Furui Energy Development. In 2021, local governments began issuing offshore green bonds, with Shenzhen

Municipality leading the way by launching a dual-tranche RMB-denominated green deal in Hong Kong. The proceeds are designated for clean transportation, water treatment, and sponge city projects, supporting the city's green finance framework. Approximately 71% of the offshore green bonds were denominated in USD followed by EUR and CNH. Approximately over 85% of the Use of Proceeds (UoP) of Chinese green bonds issued in 2021 was allotted for Renewable Energy, Low Carbon Transport, and Low Carbon Building. In 2021, the volume of Certified Climate Bonds increased by nearly four times to USD 16.9 billion. Most of the deals in 2021 were short-term bonds issued by nonfinancial corporates and had tenor of 3 years.

A Carbon Neutrality Bond (CNB) is an innovative label introduced by the NAFMII, a self-regulated organization supervised by the PBOC, in March 2021. Unlike other green bonds in China, CNBs specifically focus on carbon reduction and mandate detailed carbon reduction disclosures according to established guidelines. In 2021, CNBs represented over 40% of all labelled green bonds issued in China. During November 2021, NAFMII introduced a pilot programme to allow overseas issuers to issue social and sustainability bonds in China known as panda bonds. In November 2021, Far East Horizon, a financial leasing company issued the first sustainability bond in China. China Huaneng, Datang International Power, Yangtze Power, GD Power Development, Shaanxi Coal and Chemical Group, Liuzhou Steel Group, and Hongshi Group issued China's first set of Sustainability Linked Bonds (SLBs) in year 2021.

Sustainable Debt Market in China -Recent Market Trends

The green debt market in China was estimated to be over USD 151 billion in 2022 and USD 131.3 billion in year 2023. In terms of green bond issuance, China has issued a total of USD 616.2 billion worth of green bonds in domestic and overseas markets. China continues to maintain its position as the world's largest green bond issuance market. Green debts with Use of Proceeds (UoP) financing energy and transport projects dominated the volume of debts.

The largest cumulative issuer of green bonds is USA with approximately USD 454.4 billion of self labelled green debt issued to date. China maintained its position was the second largest source of cumulative volume of debt issued to date with value of USD 372 billion. Approximately 94% of aligned green debt in China had a maturity of 5 years or less.

In 2023, the largest aligned deals with the Use of Proceeds (UoP) for Renewable Energy and Low-Carbon Transport came from Shanghai Pudong Development Bank, Bank of China, and Industrial & Commercial Bank of China. These top three deals, financing wind, solar, energy storage, and low-carbon public transport infrastructure, were valued at USD 4.4 billion, USD 4.3 billion, and USD 4.2 billion, respectively.

BYD Auto Finance Co., a leading automobile corporation, issued two of 2023's largest onshore green ABS deals, with 100% of the Use of Proceeds (UoP) designated for electric vehicle (EV) development, totalling USD 2.2 billion. Beijing remained as the leading region nationally for green bond issuance in 2023.

The Hong Kong Stock Exchange (HKEx) remained the largest venue for offshore Chinese green bonds at 43% of listings. China's 14th Five-Year Plan, announced in 2020, targets a peak in fossil fuel consumption by 2025, with projected annual reductions in carbon emissions starting afterward. China aims to expand low-carbon energy, with renewables occupying 25% of its energy sector by 2025.

China has consistently exceeded its renewable energy targets, installing 300%, 42%, and 66% more capacity than planned in the 11th, 12th, and 13th Five-Year Plans, positioning it to meet its 2030 goal of 1200 GW of solar and wind capacity.

In 2023, Climate Bonds recorded significant deals, including CGN Wind Energy's green and blue bonds totalling USD 700 million for solar, energy storage, and offshore wind projects. China Three Gorges issued USD 1.46 billion in bonds for hydropower, while China Southern Power Grid issued USD 96.6 million for grid expansion. Green ABS volume rose 45.5% YOY, with 70.6% for EV financing. Additionally, China Three Gorges' green loan funded 411 MW of overseas wind and solar installations in Egypt and Jordan.

In 2023, the issuance volume of social and sustainability (S&S) bonds from China rebounded to USD 13.7 billion, up from USD 11.5 billion in 2022. In December 2023, Fujian Zhangzhou City Investment Group issued China's largest sustainability bond at USD 537 million for pollution management, green buildings, and healthcare. Hainan Province's USD 411.2 million bond supported education, healthcare, and social resilience projects. In 2023, offshore S&S bonds accounted for 28.2% of total Chinese issuance volumes.

Resilience financing addresses climate risks through risk-reduction measures and flexible management, focusing on physical assets, water management, and sustainable land use. "Sponge cities" adopt nature-based solutions like rain gardens and permeable paving to support the natural water cycle and manage rainwater effectively.

A sponge city is an urban development model that uses infrastructure and natural ecosystems to absorb, store, and slow rainwater runoff, enhancing resilience to extreme weather. In 2015, China set a goal for 70% of rainfall to be absorbed on-site, with 20% of urban areas achieving this by 2020 and 80% expected by 2030. By 2023, China had implemented pilot sponge city projects in 30 cities. Challenges include high investment costs, estimated at CNY100 million –150 million per square kilometre. To address funding gaps, China issued USD 2.51billion in social and sustainability bonds for resilience, including USD 400 million in 2023. Most of Chinese SLB debt had relatively short tenors and some Chinese SLB issuers have deployed perpetual structures issued without a fixed maturity date.

Sunny Optical Technology, a lens manufacturer, issued the largest Sustainability-Linked Bond (SLB) at USD 400 million, linked to greenhouse gas (GHG) reduction targets for scope 1 and 2 emissions. In 2023, Chinese Chemicals and Technology

Table 7.2 Timelines for China's key green bond policies

Year	Event
2015	NDRC issues guidelines for green bond market in China
2016	Guidelines from seven ministries and pilot programs by Shanghai and Shenzhen stock exchanges aimed at the development of green corporate bonds market issued
2017	The China Securities Regulatory Commission's Guiding Opinions on Supporting the Development of Green Bonds introduced to encourage the issuance of corporate bonds National Association of Financial Market Institutional Investors Guidelines on Green Note of non-financial enterprises green bond policy guidelines issued PBOC and CSRC guidelines on evaluation and certification of green bonds introduced
2020	NDRC, CSRC Green Bond endorsed project catalogue 2020 edition introduced
2021	PBoC: Guidelines on Environmental Disclosure for Financial Institutions published PBoC: monetary policy tool to support carbon emission reduction projects introduced IPSF: the first EU-China Common Ground Taxonomy (CGT) Instruction Report published

Source: China green securitisation report—State of the market 2020 Climate Bonds Initiative/ China Green Bond Market Report 2021 Climate Bonds Initiative

sectors debuted SLBs. Huaxin Cement issued a CNY900 million dual-tranche SLB in July 2022, targeting GHG scope 1 and 2 emission reductions by 2024. Listed on the Shanghai Stock Exchange, it marked China's first low-carbon transition bond in the cement sector.

Table 7.2 gives the timeline for green bond policies implemented in China.

Policy Developments on Green Securitization

The Overall Plan for the Structural Reform for Ecological Civilization issued by CPC and SC in 2015 encourages the Securitisation of green credit assets. Article 7 of the 2016 Guidelines for Establishing the Green Financial System promoted green credit asset securitization, expanding participation, standardizing asset selection, improving liquidity, and enhancing information disclosure. The 2017 CSRC Guidelines for Supporting Green Bond Development, Article 14 specified that the requirements for green corporate bonds also apply to the issuance of green asset-backed securities (ABS). NAFMII's 2017 Guidelines encouraged issuers to introduce structural innovations in green notes, including green asset-backed notes (ABN) supported by income from green projects. In May 2016, the CSRC supported green project financing through asset securitization, allowing subsidies for renewable energy, clean energy, and green projects to count as cash flow. In August 2018, the Shanghai Stock Exchange's Q&A on Green ABS established the definition, eligibility criteria, verification, and disclosure for green asset-backed securitization. An ABS qualifies as "green" if 70% of cash flows or funds raised come from green assets/projects, or if the asset owner's main business is predominantly green.

Securitization transforms illiquid financial assets, like mortgages or lease receivables, into tradable instruments known as asset-backed securities (ABS). This process allows lenders to sell pools of loans or leases to institutional investors, generating new lending capacity. It isolates risk through a special purpose vehicle (SPV), protecting investors from the originator's financial issues. A securitization is considered green if its cash flows are linked to low-carbon assets or if proceeds fund such investments. Financial institutions can leverage rising demand for climate-related investments, with collateral typically including mortgages on certified buildings, loans for electric vehicles, solar and wind assets, energy efficiency, and green SMEs.

There are different benefits of green securitization. Securitizing loans to small-scale projects allows access to bond markets, raising capital through asset-backed securities. Labelling the securitization as "green" taps into demand for environmentally friendly investments. Asset-backed securities can offer lower capital costs than bank financing, especially in high-interest environments, benefiting projects with high capital expenditures.

Pension and insurance companies, with long-term liabilities, are key investors in long-dated asset-backed securities (ABS). Securitization can align short-tenor SME loans with investor demand for long-term deals, benefiting green financing. Green financing in China is largely driven by green credit and accounts for over 90%. Securitizing green credit assets helps banks free up their balance sheets for further lending.

The credit asset securitisation scheme is regulated by China Banking and Insurance Regulatory Commission (CBIRC) and the People's Bank of China (PBoC). Under this scheme, banks and non-bank financial institutions licensed by the CBIRC may entrust loan receivables comprising "credit assets" to a CBIRC-licensed trust and investment company as trustee.

Chinese regulators have developed green finance definitions for Asset backed securities. NAFMII a self-regulatory organization issued green bond guidelines aligned with PBoC's definitions, while China Securities Regulatory Commission (CSRC) expanded green bond issuance rules for listed companies. CBIRC emphasized green financial products, including green bonds and asset securitization, promoting sustainable development in China's banking and insurance sectors.

China's regulators and market infrastructure institutions have adapted steps for green washing trends. In February 2024, the three major exchanges introduced a mandatory sustainability reporting scheme for listed companies, modelled largely on the ISSB framework. Meanwhile, in the bond market, the Shanghai and Shenzhen Stock Exchanges refined their guidelines for issuing green corporate bonds in 2023, aligning them with recent standards. China's Green Bond Standards Committee (GSC), a self-regulatory body for green bonds, has progressively introduced rules for market participants. These include a requirement for eligible external review providers to conduct annual self-inspections of their green bond evaluation and certification activities.

International Green Securitization Market

Most green ABS issuances have occurred in the U.S., led by companies like SolarCity, Renovate America, and Hannon Armstrong. Fannie Mae, a major player in green mortgage-backed securities, remains the largest green bond issuer with $85 billion in green ABS issued by the end of 2020. SolarCity, the largest U.S. residential solar panel installer, issues ABS backed by cash flows from power-purchase agreements for electricity generated by rooftop installations. Renovate America, a PACE financing provider, issues green ABS to refinance home improvement projects, such as renewable energy, energy efficiency, and water conservation through the HERO program.

In the European market, green securitization is led by RMBS, accounting for 60% of issuance. ABS and CLO follow with 18% each, while CMBS and SME contribute 6%. Dutch lender Obvion issued Europe's first 100% green RMBS, targeting energy-efficient homes and refinancing with the Storm RMBS program.

Chinese Green Securitization Market

In 2016, the first Chinese green ABS was issued. By 2020, there were 85 ABS deals valued at RMB 115 billion. The proportion of green ABS had increased from 1.7% of the total green bond issuance in 2016 to 11% by 2020. Green ABS allocations have diversified, covering climate themes like renewable energy, low-carbon buildings, and water management. Securities now include revenues from wind turbines, renewable energy equipment leasing, green commercial building mortgage receivables, and account receivables, reflecting the growth of China's green ABS market. The total amount of ABS from State Owned Enterprises amounted to RMB 86 billion by December 2020. The largest ever green ABS deal in China was issued as 3 tranches deal by China Development Bank in the year 2018.

In 2019, two green Asset-Backed Securities (ABS) with the longest tenor of 18 years were issued. One of these was a RMB 3.0 billion transaction from Beijing Rail Transit Daxing Line Investment, collateralized by ticket revenue receivables. The other was a 20-year Commercial Mortgage-Backed Security (CMBS). Majority of green ABS issued in Chinese market received a high-grade credit rating.

More than a third of Chinese green ABS deals are structured in two or three tranches, with senior tranches offering lower risks and interest rates, attracting conservative investors. In contrast, subordinated tranches absorb first losses, carry higher risk, and offer higher interest rates to compensate investors. During the period 2016–2020, China Zheshang Bank was the largest lead underwriter with RMB9.0 billion in underwriting deals. China continues to the market leader in terms of additions of new wind and PV capacity. In 2018, China added a combined 66 GW of wind and solar energy.

The first green ABS backed by public transport revenue receivables was a 12-tranche, RMB 2.0 billion deal issued by Wuxi Communications Industry Group Co., Ltd. in 2016. From 2018 onwards, electric vehicle (EV) auto leasing also became a primary collateral type for transport sector securitizations, alongside ticket revenue receivables.

China has only issued two green Mortgage-Backed Securities (MBS), but non-green Residential Mortgage-Backed Securities (RMBS) have grown rapidly since 2014, becoming the largest asset class in the domestic interbank bond market. With a compound annual growth rate of 204%, issuance volumes reached USD 83 billion and USD 73 billion in 2018 and 2019 respectively.

In solar or wind lease agreements, the leasing company owns and maintains the equipment, while ABS deals are backed by lease payments, power purchase agreements, or related loans. In November 2017, SPIC Ronghe Financial Leasing, a subsidiary of the State Power Investment Corporation (SPIC), issued a RMB 2.48 billion green ABN deal. The deal consists of four senior and one subordinated tranche, collateralized by lease payments from 18 lessees in wind, solar, and hydro sectors. Proceeds will fund renewable energy assets, including 13 wind farms and four solar farms across China.

In securitized public transport receivables, the originator is typically the transport service provider, with notable deals from Guangzhou Metro, Wuhan Metro, and Hangzhou Public Transport Company. Guangzhou Metro issued a six-tranche ABS deal totalling RMB 3 billion, secured by ticket revenue receivables from 24 stations on metro line 2 (2019–2023). The green proceeds include RMB 1.5 billion for six rail transit projects, while the remaining RMB 1.5 billion will repay bank loans and supplement working capital.

China had five ABS deals secured by Feed-in Tariffs (FITs), which incentivize renewable energy investment through long-term contracts. FITs provide cost-based compensation and price certainty for producers, promoting the development of various renewable technologies. Eligible generators, including homeowners and businesses, receive payments for the renewable electricity supplied to the grid.

China State Power (Ningxia) issued a RMB 560 million deal backed by feed-in tariffs from four solar farms and 11 wind farms, with expected subsidies of RMB 626 million. Eighty-two percent of proceeds will repay previous loans, while the remainder supports working capital and operational expenses. An external review confirms its "green issuer" status, with 87.5% of revenue from wind and 12.2% from solar.

EV leasing companies have securitized leasing claims, generating stable cash flows from customer payments for vehicles owned by the leasing company, enhancing financing channels. During the year 2018 and 2019, there were four ABS deals which were backed by EV auto leasing in the Transport sector. Two of these deals were issued by Shenzhen Byd International Financial Leasing Co., Ltd., the parent company of Byd International Financial Leasing which is China's biggest electric car manufacturer. BYD issued China's first EV-leasing-backed ABS in 2018, totalling RMB 366 million and backed by 24 leasing claims from 17 lessees, mainly affiliated with DIDI. Proceeds financed direct leasing and sales-and-leaseback operations.

China's steel industry, responsible for 15% of national and 60% of global steel emissions, is focusing on low-carbon methods like energy efficiency, scrap steel use, hydrogen injection, and carbon capture. Although policies support decarbonization, funding—estimated at CNY1.6 trillion—is needed, achievable through sustainable debt markets.

Chinese Green Policy

China have developed a comprehensive framework for green finance. China's Green Credit Guidelines by China Banking Regulatory Commission outline how banks should address environmental issues at the board level, integrate them into lending, and track green credit metrics. The guidelines for establishing the green financial system were jointly issued by seven ministries in year 2016. China's green finance policy framework has been extended to all financial markets including insurance and capital markets. The Revised Code of Corporate Governance for listed companies in China was released by the China Securities Regulatory Commission. This code stipulates companies to take action based on green development and gives emphasis on integration of ecological and environmental protection into development strategies and corporate governance processes.

In 2017, China's State Council approved the creation of green finance reform and innovation pilot zones. China's 2018 Green Investment Guidelines encourage fund managers to prioritize environmental sustainability, raise awareness of environmental risks, and define green investment practices for sustainable growth. The 2019 Green Industry Guidance Catalogue (GIGC) classifies green industries, guiding investment, finance, and tax policies to boost green investment across six major sectors.

Green Finance Pilot Zones in China

In 2017, China launched green finance reform pilot zones in five provinces, later expanding to Gansu. These zones test local green finance policies tailored to regional resources and economic traits, enabling successful models to be replicated nationwide. The focus includes energy, transport, water conservation, waste treatment, and green buildings. The Climate Bonds Taxonomy identifies eligible green projects in eight sectors to unify global green definitions, aiding a cohesive green bond market. China's Green Industry and Bond Catalogues define green projects differently, considering national policies. Clear green labelling could boost private investment, support low-carbon development, and meet global demand.

To support green investment, various databases have been developed across China's green finance pilot regions. Examples include Sichuan's "Green Rong Rong" and the CBEEX Green Asset Trading Platform, which lists 839 projects in areas like clean energy and pollution control. The China Public Private Partnerships Centre also maintains a comprehensive green project library, featuring nearly 10,000 projects across 19 categories, including affordable housing, transport, and energy. These databases incorporate standards like the Green Bond Principles and Climate Bonds Standard, helping align green initiatives with recognized green finance guidelines. Zhejiang Province, with a strong economy and diverse industries, selected Huzhou and Quzhou as green finance pilot zones. The Master Plan focuses on industry upgrade and green transformation, with Quzhou targeting traditional industries and Huzhou leading green innovation.

Guangdong, China's top GDP province, leverages its manufacturing strength and Guangzhou's achievements in green finance include launching a green finance service platform, creating a green enterprise-finance connection platform, and implementing policies for regional green development in Huadu District city. Guangzhou's Huadu District, a green finance pilot zone, focuses on low-carbon financial innovations, supporting strategic industries like new energy vehicles.

Guizhou's Green Finance Master Plan supports underdeveloped regions with green credit for farmers, eco-friendly agriculture, and diversified financing for industries like big data and green transport. In 2019, Guizhou introduced standards to identify key green projects eligible for tax incentives and policy support. Jiangxi's Green Finance Master Plan aims to build a green finance system in the Ganjiang New Area, supporting eco-agriculture, green industries, and green services. By 2019, Jiangxi's green project database included 696 projects worth RMB 748.2 billion with 171 projects in Ganjiang. Gansu's Green Finance Master Plan targets sustainable development in the Lanzhou New Area, focusing on eco-friendly upgrades for industrial parks, smart logistics, and low-carbon projects. Established in 2019, the area began implementing green finance policies in 2020 with a new Integrated Green Finance Service Platform Project.

Transition Finance Market in China

China's power sector must decarbonize to achieve its 2030 and 2060 targets. In 2022, thermal power generated 4.85 billion tons of CO_2, about 40% of total emissions. Coal capacity declined by 3%, dropping below 60% of total output. To meet China's 2030 and 2060 climate goals, renewable energy must replace fossil fuels in stages. Coal plants will shift from baseload to flexible support, with phased retirements and retrofits. Coal capacity is expected to peak in 2025 and then decline. Transition finance will aid resource allocation and risk management. Market stakeholders seek credible transition finance with clear decarbonization plans to ensure transparency, ambition, and avoid greenwashing, supporting KPIs for performance-linked instruments.

Transition plans are integral to climate initiatives like Climate Bonds, CA100+, CPI, GFANZ, and ICMA, with countries such as Australia, the EU, UK, and USA emphasizing their importance. The UK's TPT aligns with ISSB and IFRS S2 standards, signalling broad consensus on advancing transition plans across financial and nonfinancial sectors to enhance the transition finance market. The 2022 Climate Bonds survey shows Chinese green bond investors prioritize renewable energy and seek more holdings, emphasizing strong green credentials and credit quality. China Huaneng Group, a major state-owned power producer, has issued RMB 83.8 billion (USD12.4 billion) in green bonds and RMB13.5 billion (USD2 billion) in SLBs, primarily targeting renewable energy. Although it aligns with China's 2030–2060 goals, Huaneng lacks specific emissions targets. Its low-carbon transition plan includes CO_2 capture, clean energy expansion, and coal plant efficiency improvements.

Green Finance in India

India is the third largest greenhouse gas emitter. India accounts for only 3.2% of cumulative emissions. Major population centres such as Mumbai and Kolkata face significant risks from storm surges, increasingly severe tropical cyclones, and rising sea levels.

India have committed to achieve net zero emissions by the year 2070 at COP26. Indian government have also committed to increase its non-fossil energy capacity to 500 GW and reduce the carbon intensity of its economy by less than 45% by the year 2030. In April 2021, the Reserve Bank of India (RBI) joined the Network for Greening Financial System (NGFS). NGFS is a group of central banks and supervisors with focus on the development of environment and climate risk management in the financial sector.

Indian insurance industry with a gross written premium of over USD 100 billion focusses on ESG training and capacity building to address gaps in climate risk assessment and uninsured losses. The General Insurance Council has become a member of the UN's Principles for Sustainable Insurance (PSI) initiative, aiming to enhance awareness and promote sustainable insurance practices in India.

The largest borrowers in emission intensive sectors are Reliance Industries Ltd. from the Oil and gas refining sector and Tata Steel Ltd. from the Iron and steel sector.

Table 7.3 discusses the key sustainable policies adopted in Indian context.

Reserve Bank of India was the first regulator in India to issue advisory related to CSR, sustainable development and non-financial reporting. The RBI guidelines were drawn from Global Reporting Initiative (GRI) on ESG disclosures, International Finance Corporation (IFC) Equator Principles on environmental and social performance standards for project finance and on the Kyoto Protocol on carbon markets. India became a signatory to the Paris Agreement and the Sustainable Development Goals in 2015. The G20 established a Green Finance Study Group (GFSG)

Table 7.3 Key Sustainable Policy Milestones in India

Year	Highlight
2007	RBI publishes guidance on CSR, sustainable development and non financial reporting
2012	Ministry of Corporate Affairs publishes National Voluntary Guidelines (NVG) on ESG responsibilities of business. SEBI adopts NVG report
2015	RBI revises priority sector lending
2016	Indian Banks Association publishes the NGV guidelines for responsible financing
2018	RBI acknowledges climate related financial risk
2019	RBI bulletin publishes analysis of green finance landscape in India. RBI joins NGFS
2021	Ministry of Finance forms taskforce on sustainable finance. SEBI issues new guidelines on business requirements and sustainability reporting

comprising ministries of finance and central banks with the aim to identify mainstream green finance.

In January 2021, the Indian Ministry of Finance's Department of Economic Affairs established a Task Force on Sustainable Finance to define a sustainable finance framework, develop a roadmap, propose a taxonomy for sustainable activities, and create a risk assessment framework for the financial sector. Members include the Reserve Bank of India (RBI), Securities Exchange Board of India (SEBI), Pension Fund Regulatory and Development Authority (PFRDA) and Insurance Regulatory and Development Authority of India (IRDAI). The Task Force operates through four working groups focused on taxonomy, disclosure regulations, a roadmap, and best practices. The RBI chairs the Regulations Working Group, addressing disclosures, risk, resilience, and regulatory recommendations. Additionally, the RBI set up a Sustainable Finance Group in May 2021 to spearhead its climate risk and sustainable finance initiatives. In its July 2021 Financial Stability Report, the RBI recognized climate risks as rising threats to financial stability globally. It emphasized monitoring financial risks, stress testing resilience, and engaging with international coalitions like NGFS. India's sustainable finance policy emphasizes aligning with best practices, transparency, and standardization. The Ministry of Finance's roadmap includes taxonomy, disclosure, regulation, and ecosystem development to foster market growth.

Sustainable Debt Market in India

India's green bond market with focus on social impact and sustainability linked bonds (SLBs) is gaining prominence. While offshore investors dominated, the domestic market saw sizable deals. Utility-scale energy projects remain the primary focus, but funding for diverse uses like solar rooftops, waste management, agriculture, real estate, and EVs is growing. The thematic investing space is increasingly active, paving the way for larger issuers. India's Ministry of Finance has established a Sustainable Finance Task Force to develop sustainable activity taxonomy, recommend reporting policies, devise financial regulations, and promote market growth.

This initiative is expected to strengthen the sustainable finance market, providing significant policy support and driving momentum in the medium to long term.

Indian GSS debt issuance was valued at USD 7.5 billion in year 2021. The cumulative volume of deal value during the two-year period 2020–2022 amounted to USD 19.5 billion. The first social bond in India was issued in the year 2018. In 2021, SLBs valued at USD 1.2 billion was introduced in the Indian market. India is the 19th largest GSS market globally and sixth in the APAC region. India is one among the eight countries in the region to have bond issuance under all the three GSS themes. Approximately 75% of the cumulative labelled bond volume in India is contributed by the private sector. More than 85% of India's bond issuances include some form of external review. Climate Bonds Certification is the most popular choice by volume, closely followed by second-party opinions (SPO). KPMG is the largest approved verifier for Climate Bonds Certification in India with USD 4.5 billion worth of deals verified since the year 2016. The largest certified deal in year 2021 was from Renew Power related to wind and solar projects valued at USD 585 million.

In 2021, Shriram Transport Finance issued a social bond, and Axis Bank Ltd./ Gift City launched a sustainability bond, both supported by second-party opinions (SPOs) from Sustainalytics. US dollars are the preferred currency for raising GSS debt in the Indian market accounting for 87% of the cumulative amount issued. The largest deals of 2021 were green bonds issued by Adani Green, totalling USD 1.35 billion and USD 750 million, and Greenko Investment, which raised USD 940 million. The Indian Railway Finance Corp's USD 500 million Certified Green Bond signifies a significant step toward funding sustainable transport solutions.

Indian issuers are increasingly using sustainability-linked bonds (SLBs) to raise capital, with three deals totalling USD 1.2 billion by the end of 2021. Notable issuances include JSW Steel's USD 500 million bond targeting a 23% reduction in CO_2 emissions intensity by 2030, UltraTech Cement's USD 400 million bond linked to a 22.2% GHG reduction, and Adani Electricity Mumbai's USD 300 million bond aiming for 60% renewable energy by 2027. These bonds are backed by second-party opinions (SPOs).

India's utility-scale renewable energy sector drives the success of green finance, supported initially by international DFIs like the World Bank and now largely funded by domestic banks. Accessible financing has reduced costs in renewable energy auctions and encouraged refinancing through green bond issuances. The Reserve Bank of India classifies renewable energy under priority sector lending for loans up to USD 4.1 million.

India's renewable energy sector is attracting bids from emerging Independent Power Producers (IPPs) like ReNew Power and Azure Power, alongside established corporate giants like Reliance Industries and JSW. Public sector entities such as Coal India and GAIL are also advancing significant renewable investments, strengthening the green finance issuer pipeline.

India's rooftop solar segment contributes around 7GW to the nation's generation capacity, driven initially by policies like net metering, which allowed users to export surplus solar energy to the grid. However, restrictions from distribution companies

(DISCOMs) curtailed growth, falling far short of the 40GW 2022 target. Falling battery costs are expected to boost power backup solutions, with standalone battery systems becoming cost-competitive with diesel generators by 2025. Additionally, renewable energy developers are tapping into open-access agreements, enabling customers to choose power suppliers. This trend may drive future bond issuances as investor interest in renewables continues to grow.

Continuum Energy issued a green bond backed by open access contracts, with installations serving corporates through grid transmission. By the end of 2021, approximately 18GW of rooftop and utility-scale renewable installations were involved in open access, providing energy to corporate clients. Corporates investing in on-site and open access solar projects can refinance through green bonds, a market expected to grow. With rising installations driven by cost savings and potential virtual power purchase agreements (PPAs), large corporates like Hindalco and ACC Ltd. are increasing investment, expanding the pool of green bond issuers. Electric vehicle (EV) sales in India surged by 168% in 2021, with 329,190 units sold. December 2021 marked a record high of 50,866 units sold, driven by supportive government policies like the FAME scheme, state-level EV policies, and incentives for EV purchases, manufacturing, and charging infrastructure. EVs, particularly electric two- and three-wheelers, now dominate the market, with over 90% share.

Traditional auto manufacturers like Tata Motors, Hyundai, Mahindra, and Hero dominate India's passenger car market but are now entering the two-wheeler EV sector, previously led by start-ups. Investment in EV production and charging infrastructure is growing, with USD 6.5 billion invested in 2021, primarily from DFIs, venture capitalists, and high-net-worth individuals.

India's waste management sector is growing due to factors like population density, industrial activity, and updated regulations. The Swachh Bharat Mission and a focus on sustainability support this growth, pushing for a circular economy. Innovations in recycling, such as PET bottle recycling, complement established industries in paper and metal recycling. India's waste management industry has significant growth potential, with only 30% of recyclable waste currently recycled. Poor infrastructure for segregation, collection, and recycling contributes to inefficiency. Strong policies for waste collection, disposal, and recycling, including extended producer responsibility initiatives, are needed to address these challenges.

Agriculture is the primary income source for 60% of India's population. Climate-smart agriculture (CSA) promotes sustainable farming, enhancing production, resilience, and climate adaptation while reducing greenhouse gas emissions. CSA supports income generation, food security, and contributes to achieving SDG 3 (Zero Hunger) and SDG 13 (Climate Action).

Samunnati Financial Intermediation issued the first green bond in 2021 with agriculture as a use-of-proceeds category, raising USD 4.6 million. The deal, arranged by Symbiotics, followed Climate Bonds Initiative standards. Other transactions include bonds supporting agtech companies. Despite small issuance, Climate Bonds is engaging more issuers with green bond intentions. Agtech applies technology to agriculture, with stronger communication with farmers as a key enabler. Affordable data and mobile tools like WhatsApp can share cultivation advice and market updates. ITC's e-Choupal is a pioneering platform that increased farmers' incomes by 50%. Some agtech firms are profitable, most are young firms. According to the Indian Green Building Council, the green building space in the country stands at 7.97 billion square feet and ranks second only to US in terms of coverage area. Green bonds for green buildings in India remain limited, primarily issued by corporates or financial institutions for loans or owned commercial spaces. Interest is growing among housing finance companies, top developers, and REITs. Deals are linked to achieving certifications like LEED or IGBC, with concessional rates encouraging participation. Green building fund disbursements are tied to certifications like LEED and IGBC and incentivized by preferential rates. Borrowers access concessional loans through intermediary banks for construction and mortgage financing.

India's impact investing ecosystem, excluding philanthropy, has mobilized USD 11 billion for over 550 social enterprises, benefiting 490 million underserved individuals. Climate-focused investments target renewable energy, waste management, precision agriculture, and EVs. With a well-defined ecosystem, this sector is poised for growth, potentially leading to significant green bond issuances.

Deforestation and forest degradation account for approximately 15% of the world's greenhouse gas emissions. India faces land loss from desertification, extreme weather, and floods, alongside regulatory uncertainty and rising costs of sustainable materials. Companies report brand damage from forest-risk commodities and climate-related threats to water security and social stability, highlighting the urgency of addressing these environmental and societal challenges. Supply chain resilience, reducing food loss, demand for certified materials, climate adaptation, enhanced brand value, and market access drive sustainable growth and competitiveness.

References

2020 estimates in the Renovation Wave strategy EUR-Lex—52020DC0662—EN—EUR-Lex (europa.eu).

ACC Ltd. (2022). https://www.acclimited.com/sustainable/climateand-energy

ADB. (2019). *ASEAN Infrastructure Fund: Financing Infrastructure for Growth and Development.* https://www.adb.org/publications/aseaninfrastructure-fund-brochure

Administrative Measures for the Recognition of Green Enterprises and Green Projects in the Guangdong Guangzhou Green Finance Reform and Innovation Pilot Zone (Trial).

Agriculture Sustainable Finance State of the Market 2023, Brazil briefing paper, Climate Bonds Initiative.

Amaggi ESG Report. (2022). Available at: https://www.amaggi.com.br/wp-content/uploads/2023/07/ESG_Amaggi_2022_EN.pdf

An EU framework for financing the transition, February 2023, European Banking Federation.

Anouti, Y., Elborai, S., Kombargi, R., & Hage, R. (2020). The dawn of green hydrogen: Maintaining the GCC's edge in a decarbonized world. *Strategy&*. https://www.strategyand.pwc.com/m1/en/reports/2020/the-dawnof-green-hydrogen.html

ASEAN, ASEAN Taxonomy for Sustainable Finance (ASEAN Taxonomy Board), November 2021.

ASEAN Sustainable Finance State of the Market 2021 Climate Bonds Initiative.
Bank of Thailand. Sustainable Finance Initiatives for Thailand. https://www.bot.or.th/content/dam/bot/financial-innovation/sustainablefinance/green/Sustainable_Finance_Initiatives_for_Thailand.pdf
Berkeley Lab. (2023). *The 2035 Japan Report*. https://etapublications.lbl.gov/sites/default/files/lbnl_2035_japan_report_english_publish.pdf
Board of Governors of the Federal Reserve System. (2021). https://www.federalreserve.gov/newsevents/speech/brainard20210323a.htm
BPIE. (2017). 97% of buildings in the EU need to be upgraded. BPIE -Buildings Performance Institute Europe.
Brazilian Central Bank Data. (2022). Available at: https://dadosabertos.bcb.gov.br/
BRIEFING NOTE JAPAN'S CLIMATE TRANSITION BOND.
Buildings Performance Institute Europe (BPIE), 2020. A guidebook to European building policy. https://www.bpie.eu/wp-content/uploads/2020/08/BPIE_Guide-on-Building-Policy_Final.pdf
Burge, L. Accelerating the fossil gas transition to net zero, Climate Bonds Initiative 2022. https://www.climatebonds.net/files/page/files/cbi_gaspolicy_2022_01d.pdf
Burge, L. (2023). *101 Sustainable Finance Policies for 1.5°C*. Climate Bonds Initiative. https://www.climatebonds.net/resources/reports/101-sustainable-finance-policies-15%C2%B0c-0
Business Lin. (2021). https://www.thehindubusinessline.com/companies/electric-2-and-3-wheelers-see-highest-ever-monthlysales-in-oct/article37288269.ece
Camarate, J., Elborai, S., Vincent, A., & Yammine, A. *Middle East green finance, A US$2 trillion opportunity*. Strategy & Part of the Pwc network.
Capital Markets Malaysia. (2018). *Incentives—SRI Sukuk and Bond Grant Scheme*. https://www.msfi.com.my/incentives-sri-sukuk-and-bondgrant-scheme/
CBRE. (2023). Energy efficient assets deliver stronger investment returns report. Energy Efficient Assets Deliver Stronger Investment Returns, Reports CBRE.
Center for Climate and Energy Solutions. (2021). https://www.c2es.org/document/greenhouse-gas-emissions-targets
China Green Bond Market Report 2021, Climate Bonds Initiative, May 2022. www.climatebonds.net
China Green Bonds Investor Survey 2021 Scaling a credible transition finance market in China: Opportunities for Electric Utilities, Scaling a Credible Transition Finance Market in China Climate Bonds Initiative, Report 2022.
China green securitisation report—State of the market 2020. Climate Bonds Initiative. www.climatebonds.net
China Sustainable Debt State of the Market 2023 Climate Bonds Initiative.
China's Green Bond Issuance and Investment Opportunity Report Climate Bonds Initiative. *Statistical Communique of the People's Republic of China on the 2019 National Economic and Social Development*. National Bureau of Statistics of China. 2020.
Chinese Government Work Report. (2024). 政府工作报告--2024年全国两会--人民网 (people.com.cn).
Climate Bonds. (2021). *Sovereign Green, Social, and Sustainability Bond Survey*. https://www.climatebonds.net/resources/reports/sovereign-green-social-and-sustainability-bond-survey
Climate Bonds Initiative. (2020). *Assurance statement*. https://www.climatebonds.net/files/files/Ecoagro-Rizoma-pre-issuance-statement-PUBLIC.pdf
Climate Bonds Initiative. (2021). *Green CRA Tech receives certification from the Climate Bonds Initiative as the first collective Green CRA issuance in the world*. https://www.climatebonds.net/files/releases/media_release_gaia_june2021_english_vf_lb.docx_1_0.pdf
Climate Bonds Initiative. April 2022.
Climate Bonds Initiative. (2023a). *Brazil Sustainable Securitisation State of the market Q3 2022*. https://www.climatebonds.net/files/reports/cbi_bra_sec_2022.pdf
Climate Bonds Initiative. (2023b). *Agri-Food Transition*. https://www.climatebonds.net/transition-finance/agri-food-transitions

Climate Bonds Initiative, Climate Resilience Principles. https://www.climatebonds.net/files/page/files/climate-resilience-principlesclimate-bonds-initiative-20190917-.pdf

Climate Bonds Initiative data. https://policy.asiapacificenergy.org/sites/default/files/National%20Green%20Technology%20Policy%202009.pdf

Climate Policy Initiative. (2019). *Developing a Guarantee Instrument to Catalyze Renewable Energy Investments in Indonesia*. https://www.climatepolicyinitiative.org/publication/developing-a-guarantee-instrument-to-catalyze-renewable-energy-investments-in-indonesia/

Commission on Submission of Green Credit Statistics Form. China Banking Regulatory Commission. 2014.05.14. http://www.cbirc.gov.cn/cn/view/pages/ItemDetail

CTFC. (2020). https://www.cftc.gov/sites/default/files/2020-09/9-9-20%20Report%20of%20the%20Subcommittee%20 on%20Climate-Related%20Market%20Risk%20-%20Managing%20 climate%20Risk%20in%20the%20U.S.%20Financial%20System%20 for%20posting.pdf

DOE Fact Sheet (DOE/OP-0018), U.S. Department of Energy Office of Policy, August 2022.

DZ BANK AG Deutsche Zentral-Genossenschaftsbank, Frankfurt am Main ("DZ BANK") 10 November 2023, Sustainable Finance Bulletin.

EU climate Advisory Board. (2024). EU climate Advisory Board: focus on immediate implementation and continued action to achieve EU climate goals (europa.eu).

EU Commission. (2020). Renovation Wave. Renovation Wave: doubling the renovation rate to cut emissions, boost recovery and reduce energy poverty (europa.eu).

EU Commission. (2023). EPBD provisional agreement New rules to boost energy performance of buildings (europa.eu).

Eurofer. (2019). Low carbon roadmap—Pathways to a CO_2-neutral European steel industry.

European Commission. (2021). Towards competitive and clean European steel. Commission Staff Working Document SWD (2021) 353 final Brussels, 5.5.2021.

European Commission. (2022a). International Agreement to support Viet Nam's ambitious climate and energy goals, December 2022.

European Commission. (2022b). *Green Deal: EU agrees law to fight global deforestation and forest degradation driven by EU production and consumption*. https://ec.europa.eu/commission/presscorner/detail/en/ip_22_7444.

European Heat Pump Association (EHPA). (2023). Heat pump sales falling, risking €7 billion in investments. European Heat Pump Association (ehpa.org).

European Mortgage Federation. (2023). Hypostat EMF Hypostat 2023: United in Diversity—Multidimensional Patterns in European Housing and Mortgage Markets in 2022—ECBC.

FAB prices first Green Bond deal by a MENA issuer in Swiss Francs (CHF). January 28, 2021. First Abu Dhabi Bank. Retrieved from https://www.bankfab.com/en-ae/about-fab/group/in-the-media/20210128-fab-prices-first-green-bond-deal

FAO. (2020). *In brief to the state of agricultural commodity markets 2020. Agricultural markets and sustainable development: Global value chains, smallholder farmers and digital innovations*. FAO. https://doi.org/10.4060/cb0677en

Far East Horizon. (18 November 2021). *Voluntary Announcement the Company Completed the Issuance of the First Sustainability Bonds in China*. https://en.fehorizon.com/column/83/

Financial Express. (2022). https://www.financialexpress.com/auto/industry/tvs-motor-to-roll-out-full-portfolio-of-evs-over-period-ofeight-quarters/2429116

Financing low-carbon buildings in Mexico in the green bond market Climate Bonds Initiative, November 2020.

Fiscal Policy and Sustainable finance enhancing the role of the financial sector in achieving the sustainable development goals, June 2024 Asian Development Bank Report.

Fit for 55 targets a minimum 55% reduction in emissions by 2030 compared to 1990 levels. EU Commission. Fit for 55—The EU's plan for a green transition—Consilium (europa.eu).

Global Traceability, EUDR—EU Deforestation-free Regulation What is the new deforestation-free regulation and what does it mean for businesses? https://www.global-traceability.com/eudr-eu-deforestation-free-regulation/

Government of Canada. (2020). https://www.canada.ca/en/services/environment/weather/climatechange/climate-plan/net-zeroemissions-2050.html

Government of Canada. (2021). https://www.canada.ca/en/environment-climate-change/news/2021/02/government-of-canadadelivers-on-commitment-to-appoint-an-independent-net-zeroadvisory-body.html

Green Finance for Low-Carbon Cities. Paulson Institute. June 2016. https://www.bbhub.io/dotorg/sites/2/2016/06/Green-Finance-for-Low-Carbon-Cities.pdf

Green Finance Service Platform of Guangzhou Carbon Emission Exchange. http://finance.cnemission.com/

Green, sustainable debt issuance in MENA hit $18bln in 2021. Zawya, Jan. 6, 2022. https://www.zawya.com/en/markets/green-sustainable-debt-issuance-in-menahit-18bln-in-2021-lzfpdlbn

Guidance on Establishing a Green Finance System. (2016).

Guiding Opinions on the Credit Work for Energy Conservation and Emission Reduction. China Banking Regulatory Commission. http://www.cbirc.gov.cn/cn/view/pages/ItemDetail.html?docId=2511&itemId=928&generaltype=0 Notice of the China Banking Regulatory

http://about.bankofamerica.com/en-us/global-impact/environmental-sustainability.html#fbid=Glpv3EjduRk

http://greenbank.ny.gov/News/In-the-News. https://www.jpmorgan.com/insights/esg/governance-strategies/current-state-of-us-climate-policy#section-header#0

http://socialinvesting.about.com/od/Sustainable-Investing/fl/BlackRock-Fidelity-and-Vanguard-Exposed-on-Climate-Change.htm

http://www.mee.gov.cn/gkml/hbb/gwy/201611/t20161124_368163.htm

http://www.szse.cn/lawrules/rule/listed/bond/t20160422_565143.htm

https://a9w7k6q9.stackpathcdn.com/wpcms/wp-content/uploads/2023/04/Chinas-climate-and-energy-policy-after-the-Two-Sessions.pdf

https://acen.com.ph/2021/09/acen-subsidiary-successfullyissues-us400-million-in-fixed-for-life-green-bonds/

https://cefic.org/a-pillar-of-the-european-economy/facts-and-figures-of-the-european-chemical-industry/our-contribution-to-eu-industry/

https://cgc.ifi.u-tokyo.ac.jp/research/chemistry-industry/planet-positive-chemicals.pdf

https://communicateonline.me/category/industry-insights/post-details/riding-the-rising-green-wave-of-sustainable-finance-across-the-gulf

https://en.ndrc.gov.cn/policies/202110/t20211024_1300725.html

https://en.ndrc.gov.cn/policies/202110/t20211027_1301020.html

https://indonesia.un.org/en/151089-indonesia-launchessoutheast-asias-first-sdg-bond-bring-agenda-2030-back-track

https://links.sgx.com/FileOpen/20210316_Japfa%20Ltd_SLB%20Press%20Release.ashx?App=Announcement&FileID=652264

https://media.ford.com/content/fordmedia/fna/us/en/news/2021/05/24/all-electric-f-150-lightning-pro.html

https://mei.nus.edu.sg/publication/insight-286-climate-finance-in-the-mena-region/

https://mp.weixin.qq.com/s/cxEhkFI7fLh0Vd_1SJNDeg

https://ourworldindata.org/energy-mix

https://spa.gov.sa/en/N2075164

https://static.agora-energiewende.de/fileadmin/projekte/2020/2020_10_Clean_Industry_Package/A-EW_194_Clean-Industry-Package-EU_WEB.pdf

https://thainews.prd.go.th/en/news/detail/TCATG230607114605705

https://vir.com.vn/vinpearl-issues-425-million-exchangeablesustainable-bond-88160.html#:~:text=Vinpearl%20JSC%20has%20successfully%20issued,3.25%20per%20cent%20per%20annum

https://web.archive.org/web/20161006040920/http://www.bmwi.de/English/Redaktion/Pdf/energyconcept%2Cproperty%3Dpdf%2Cbereich%3Dbmwi%2Csprache%3Den%2Crw b%3Dtrue.pdf. https://www.bmuv.de/fileadmin/Daten_BMU/Download_PDF/Gesetze/ksg_final_en_bf.pdf

https://www.adb.org/news/300-million-green-climate-fund-adbfirst-green-recovery-program-southeast-asia

https://www.adb.org/news/adb-energy-absolute-sign-green-loanrenewable-energy-and-electric-vehicle-charging-network

https://www.adb.org/news/adb-president-meets-primeminister-malaysia-reaffirms-support

https://www.adb.org/news/first-social-bond-issuednonfinancial-corporate-issuer-under-asean-social-bondstandards#:~:text=MANILA%2C%20PHILIPPINES%20(17%20 November%20 2021,Southeast%20Asian%20Nations%20(ASEAN)%20social

https://www.amaggi.com.br/wp-content/uploads/2023/06/AmaggiRegenera_PT-azul.pdf

https://www.bgrimmpower.com/en/investor-relations/newsroom/news-clippings/2356289/bgrim-wins-green-certificationfor-loan

https://www.bp.com/content/dam/bp/business-sites/en/global/corporate/pdfs/energy-economics/statistical-review/bp-stats-review-2022-full-report.pdf

https://www.business-standard.com/article/markets/indiaesg-assets-up-4-7-times-in-two-years-to-rs-12-300-crore-showsdata-121121900670_1.html

https://www.businesstimes.com.sg/banking-finance/chinaconstruction-bank-issues-three-esg-themed-bonds-one-to-list-on-sgx

https://www.businesstimes.com.sg/companies-markets/japfaunit-prices-us350m-sustainability-linked-bond-at-5375

https://www.businesstimes.com.sg/companies-markets/sembcorpsecures-first-sustainability-linked-bond-investment-from-ifc. https://www.thaiunion.com/en/newsroom/press-release/1397/thai-union-launches-thailands-first-sustainability-linked-bond

https://www.bworldonline.com/bankingfinance/2022/01/19/424319/rcbc-sets-offer-of-sustainable-bonds/

https://www.bworldonline.com/corporate/2021/06/25/378248/edc-lists-p5b-worth-of-asean-green-bonds/

https://www.canada.ca/en/department-finance/news/2021/05/canada-launches-sustainable-finance-action-council.html

https://www.cas.go.jp/jp/seisaku/atarashii_sihonsyugi/pdf/ap2023.pdf

https://www.cas.go.jp/jp/seisaku/gx_jikkou_kaigi/pdf/kihon.pdf

https://www.climatebonds.net/files/reports/brazil_agri_roadmap_english.pdf

https://www.climatebonds.net/files/reports/cbi_indonesia_giio_en.pdf

https://www.climatebonds.net/resources/reports/greeninfrastructure-investment-opportunities-thailand. https://www.climatebonds.net/files/reports/cbi_indonesia_giio_en.pdf

https://www.cnbc.com/2020/03/04/gm-to-spend-20-billion-onnew-electric-autonomous-vehicles

https://www.devex.com/organizations/aligned-intermediary-ai-109150

https://www.energymonitor.ai/tech/hydrogen/a-half-decadeafter-its-first-plan-japans-hydrogen-goals-remain-distant/

https://www.euractiv.com/section/energy-environment/news/investors-worth-e50-trillion-call-on-eu-to-exclude-gas-from-green-finance-taxonomy/

https://www.europarl.europa.eu/RegData/etudes/BRIE/2018/614766/EPRS_BRI(2018)614766_EN.pdf

https://www.fsa.go.jp/en/news/2022/20220527/20220527_3.pdf

https://www.greentechmalaysia.my/malaysias-co2-emissions-among-highest-in-asean-low-carbon-mobility-solutionsneeded/

https://www.hoganlovells.com/~/media/hogan-lovells/pdf/2018/v3_global_china.pdf?la=en

https://www.iea.org/countries/canada

https://www.iea.org/reports/energy-technology-perspectives-2020

https://www.ifc.org/wps/wcm/connect/98ed795e-559a-496c-b76d-b89ddb8c2716/SBN_Brief+20210511.pdf?MOD=AJPERES&CVID=nBpj8ZX
https://www.islamicfinancenews.com/renikola-solar-to-issuegreen-sukuk.html
https://www.lexingtonlaw.com/blog/news/american-auto-loansurvey.html
https://www.meed.com/what-sustainable-finance-and-carbon-markets-mean-for-the-gcc
https://www.mgtc.gov.my/what-we-do/green-incentives/green-investment-tax-incentives-gita-gite/
https://www.mof.gov.my/portal/en/news/press-release/worlds-first-sovereign-u-s-dollar-sustainability-sukuk-issuance-by-thegovernment-of-malaysia
https://www.newsdirectory3.com/ban-muang-spcg-is-pleasedwith-the-success-of-the-sale-of-green-bond-debentures-investors over-subscribed-3-times/
https://www.nytimes.com/2021/03/31/business/biden-electricvehicles-infrastructure.html
https://www.oecd.org/tax/tax-policy/effective-carbon-rates-2021-highlights-brochure.pdf
https://www.pif.gov.sa/en/our-financials/green-finance-framework/
https://www.prnewswire.com/news-releases/major-us-airlinescommit-to-net-zero-carbon-emissions-by-2050-301259109.html
https://www.redseaglobal.com/en/-/media-center/rsg-secures-sar-14-billion-loan-and-first-ever-green-finance-credit-facility
https://www.reuters.com/business/energy/chinas-installed-non-fossil-fuel-electricity-capacity-exceeds-50-total-2023-06-12/
https://www.sc.com.my/resources/media/media-release/expansion-of-sri-sukuk-and-bond-grant-scheme-to-facilitate-sustainable-finance
https://www.sciencedirect.com/science/article/pii/S0098135422001338
https://www.sembcorp.com/en/media/741988/issuance-of-series-002-sustainability-linked-notes-by-sembcorp-financial-services.pdf
https://www.trafigura.com/press-releases/trafigura-closes-therefinancing-and-extension-of-its-usd5-5bn-eu-syndicated-revolvingcredit-facilities-its-first-sustainability-linked-loan-structure/
https://www.unep.org/explore-topics/chemicals-waste/what-we-do/policy-and-governance/global-chemicals-outlook
https://www.worldbank.org/en/programs/pricing-carbon
https://www.wri.org/insights/7-things-know-aboutdecarbonization-american-energy-innovation-act
https://www2.deloitte.com/xe/en/pages/energy-and-resources/articles/the-potential-of-hydrogen-for-the-chemical-industry.html
IEA. (2022). *Coal in Net Zero Transitions*. https://www.iea.org/reports/coal-in-net-zero-transitions
India Sustainable Debt State of the Market Climate Bonds Initiative, 2021.
Input paper for G20 Sustainable Finance Working Group, CDP, Disclosure Insight Action.
Institutional Investor Group on Climate Change (IIGCC). (2023). New climate solutions guidance helps investors identify, measure and engage (iigcc.org).
International Energy Agency, Net Zero by 2050. https://iea.blob.core.windows.net/assets/deebef5d-0c34-4539-9d0c-10b13d840027/NetZeroby2050-ARoadmapfortheGlobalEnergySector_CORR.pdf
Investment Opportunities Agri-food sector in Brazil Climate Bonds Initiative, 2023.
IPCC, Climate Change 2022: Impacts, Adaptation, and Vulnerability: Contribution of Working Group II to the Sixth Assessment Report of the Intergovernmental Panel on Climate Change (Cambridge University Press, 2022), https://www.ipcc.ch/report/ar6/wg2/
Islamic Development Bank. *Islamic Development Bank Issues Largest Sustainability Sukuk Ever*, 25 March 2021. https://www.isdb.org/news/islamic-development-bank-issues-largest-sustainability-sukuk-ever
Islamic Development Bank Issues Largest Sustainability Sukuk Ever. Islamic Development Bank. March 25, 2021. Retrieved from https://www.isdb.org/news/islamic-development-bank-issues-largest-sustainability-sukuk-ever
Japan Cabinet (2023) METI (2023). *GX Basic Policy for Realization, Roadmap for the next 10 years Reference Materials'*. https://www.cas.jp/jp/seisaku/gx_jikkou_kaigi/dai5/siryou2.pdf

Jeffries, E. (2021). *Hard reality: Why Canada's pensions are blazing a trail in green bond issuance*. Capital Monitor. https://capitalmonitor.ai/institution/asset-owners/canadas-pensions-are-world-leaders-in-greenbond-issuance/

Juan Manuel Viver Gargallo. (2023). European Union chemical sector transition policy brief. Climate Bonds Initiative.

Kombargi, R., Anouti, Y., Elborai, S., & Hage, R. (2018). The outlook for renewable energy in the GCC: Mostly sunny with a chance of rain. *Strategy&*. https://www.strategyand.pwc.com/m1/en/reports/2018/theoutlook-for-renewable-energy-in-the-gcc.html

LEED stands for Leadership in Energy and Environmental Design.

Legislative Train. (2022). A European Green Deal. 06 2022 | A European Green Deal | Renovation wave initiative in the buildings sector (europa.eu).

Malaysia GIIO Report Climate Bonds Initiative 2023.

Malaysian Green Technology and Climate Change Centre. Green Investment Tax Allowance (GITA) & Green Income Tax Exemption (GITE).

Malaysian Green Technology Corporation. Green Technology Financing Facility (GTFS & GTFS 2.0). 2018. https://www.myhijau.my/wp-content/uploads/2019/04/Slide-Presentation-GTFSv2-Business-Clinic-2019-compressed.pdf

MAS, Green Finance Industry Taskforce.

METI. (2021). *Green Growth Strategy Through Achieving Carbon Neutrality in 2050*. https://www.meti.go.jp/english/policy/energy_environment/global_warming/ggs2050/pdf/ggs_full_en1013.pdf

MexiCO2, ¡Primer bono verde bancario: BBVA Bancomer!

Ministry of Agriculture, Livestock and Food Supply. (2020). *Brazilian Sustainable Agriculture Strategies*. https://www.gov.br/mre/pt-br/delbraspar/seminario-brasil-portugal/agritalks-brazilian-sustainable-agriculture-strategies.pdf

Ministry of Agriculture, Livestock and Food Supply. (2021). Plan for adaptation and low carbon emission in Agriculture. https://www.gov.br/agricultura/pt-br/assuntos/sustentabilidade/agricultura-de-baixa-emissao-de-carbono/publicacoes/abc-english.pdf

MOFA. (2021). *Leaders' Summit on Climate Remarks by H.E. Mr. Suga Yoshihide, Prime Minister of Japan*. https://www.mofa.go.jp/files/100181623.pdf

Monetary Authority of Singapore. (2023). MAS to Set Expectations on Credible Transition Planning by Financial Institutions. News release. 8 June. https://www.mas.gov.sg/news/media-releases/2023/mas-to-set-expectations-on-credible-transition-planning-by-financialinstitutions

Morishita, M., Bonelli, R., & Hemingway, R. Japan: Policies to grow credible transition finance. Climate Bonds Initiative, October 2023. www.climatebonds.net

NAFMII. (2023). *Green bond assessment and certification business Self-examination report reference text*. nafmii.org.cn/xhdt/202303/P020230324635519378092.pdf

NASDAQ. (2021). https://www.nasdaq.com/articles/biden-tax-planreplaces-fossil-fuel-subsidies-with-incentives-for-clean-energy-u.s.-0

New York Department of Financial Services. (2021). https://www.dfs.ny.gov/system/files/documents/2021/03/proposed_ins_climate_guidance_2021_public_comment_1.pdf

NINT. (2022). *Assessment report*. https://www.solinftec.com/wp-content/uploads/2022/11/Pre--Issuance-CBI-Report-CRA-3-Solinftec-20221017-v2.pdf

No.39 [2015] Notice on Financial Corporate Bonds. http://www.gov.cn/xinwen/2015-12/22/content_5026636.html

North American State of the Market Report 2020 Climate Bonds Initiative.

Notice of the Shanghai Stock Exchange on Rolling out the Pilot Program concerning the Green Corporate Bonds". Shanghai Stock Exchange. 2016.03.16. http://www.sse.com.cn/lawandrules/sserules/listing/bond/c/c_20160316_4058800.shtml

Notice of the Shenzhen Stock Exchange on Rolling out the Pilot Program concerning the Green Corporate Bonds". Shenzhen Stock Exchange. 2016.04.22.

Obras, Asi crece la Vivienda verde en Mexico.

OECD-FAO, 7 July 2023, Business handbook on deforestation and due diligence in agricultural supply chains. https://www.oecd.org/publications/oecd-fao-business-handbook-on-deforestation-and-due-diligence-in-agricultural-supply-chains-c0d4bca7-en.htm

Origin IP Solutions. (2022). https://www.origiin.com/2021/09/15/leading-electric-vehicle-companies-in-india/

PBoC. (2016). http://finance.china.com.cn/money/bank/yhyw/20160317/3631992.shtml

Philippines Green Infrastructure Investment Opportunities (GIIO) Report Climate Bonds Initiative 2020.

Platform on Sustainable Finance, The Extended Environmental Taxonomy, Final Report on Taxonomy extension options supporting a sustainable transition, March 2022.

Policy levers to decarbonise buildings in Europe, Climate Bonds Initiative.

Prime Minister Justin Trudeau of Canada. (2020). https://pm.gc.ca/en/news/news--releases/2020/12/11/prime-minister-announcescanadas-strengthened-climate-plan-protect

Pulido, M., & Hemingway, R. (2023). EU regulation on deforestation-free products. Climate Bonds Initiative.

Pulido, M. A., & Hemingway, R. (2024). EU Regulation on Deforestation-Free Products: A potential game changer for commodity driven deforestation, Climate Bonds Initiative.

RaceToZero. (2021). *Finance Sector Deforestation Action (FSDA)*. https://racetozero.unfccc.int/system/nature-and-tackling-deforestation/

Report on Gross Economic-Ecological Product Accounting Research in China 2018. Ministry of Ecology and Environment. http://www.nea.gov.cn/2016-12/19/c_135916140.htm9

Retrieved from https://www.isdb.org/sites/default/files/media/documents/2021-08/The%20Road%20to%20the%20SDGs%20English%2002.pdf

Rotoplas, Rotoplas emite exitosamente su segunda reapertura de Bono Sustentable https://www.climatebonds

Royal Institute of Chartered Surveyors. (2020). Energy Efficiency of the building stock in the EU Energy efficiency of the building stock in the EU (rics.org).

Sandler, R. *Microsoft, Unilever Join Amazon's Climate Pledge*. Forbes, December 9, 2020. https://www.forbes.com/sites/rachelsandler/2020/12/09/microsoft-unilever-join-amazons-climatepledge/? sh=129bb3bd271c

SC Malaysia, Sustainable and Responsible Investment Roadmap for the Malaysian Capital Market, November 2019.

Securities Commission Malaysia. (2022). Expansion of SRI Sukuk and Bond Grant Scheme to Facilitate Sustainable Finance.

SEEG/Observatório do Clima. (2022). *Análise das emissões de gases de efeito estufa e suas implicações para as metas climáticas do Brasil*. https://www.oc.eco.br/wp-content/uploads/2023/03/SEEG-10-anos-v4.pdf

Sorkin, A. R. BlackRock CEO Larry Fink: Climate Change Will Reshape Finance. *New York Times*, January 14, 2020. https://www.nytimes.com/2020/01/14/business/dealbook/larryfink--blackrock-climate-change.html

Sovereign Green, Social, and Sustainability Survey 2021.

State of Green Finance in the UAE The first national survey on contributions of financial institutions to Green Economy.

The State of Sustainable Finance in the United States, Design of a Sustainable Financial System, UNEP. Feb 2016.

Sustainable Finance Indonesia, Indonesia Green Taxonomy Edition 1.0 – 2022, January 2022.

The Economic Times. (2021). https://energy.economictimes.indiatimes.com/news/renewable/statutory-approval-processinitiated-for-solar-projects-at-four-sites-hindalco/83797702

The Edge markets. (2021). *Malaysia's sustainability sukuk oversubscribed by 6.4 times, allocation well spread globally*. https://www.theedgemarkets.com/article/malaysias-sustainability-sukukoversubscribed-64-times-allocation-wellspread-globally

The Expert panel on sustainable finance, FSA, The Third Report-Enhancing sustainable finance.

The Hindu. (2022). https://www.thehindu.com/real-estate/creatinga-sustainable-future-with-green-buildings/article38077205.ece

The International Institute of Green Finance of the Central University of Finance and Economics. (2022). China Green Bond Market Annual Report 2021.

The Investment Association of China and Rocky Mountain Institute. (2020). *Zero-carbon investing: Opportunities from China's carbon neutrality goal.* https://www.rmi-china.com/static/upfile/news/nfiles/202011081345186465.pdf

The National Law Review. (2021). https://www.natlawreview.com/article/california-leads-nation-introduction-ambitious-climatedisclosure-bill-state

The role of fossil fuels in taxonomies: Canada case study white paper. Climate Bonds Initiative. IBC, BAC. October 2023.

The role of fossil fuels in taxonomies: Canada case study -Climate Bonds Initiative. https://eur-lex.europa.eu/legal-content/EN/TXT/?uri=uriserv:OJ.L_.2022.188.01.0001.01.ENG

The Securities & Commodities Authority Master Plan for Sustainable Capital Markets. Securities & Commodities Authority. Retrieved from https://www.sca.gov.ae/Content/Userfiles/Assets/Documents/29e6ef1d.pdf

The White House. (2021a). https://www.whitehouse.gov/briefingroom/presidential--actions/2021/01/27/executive-order-on-tacklingthe-climate-crisis-at-home-and-abroad/

The White House. (2021b). https://www.whitehouse.gov/briefing-room/statements--releases/2021/04/22/fact-sheetpresident-biden-sets-2030-greenhouse-gas-pollution-reductiontarget-aimed-at-creating-good-paying-union-jobs-and-securing-u-sleadership-on-clean-energy-technologies/

Thompson, S., & Caridia, A. (2022). *Canada's inaugural green bond.* RBC Capital Markets. https://www.rbccm.com/en/insights/story.page?dcr=templatedata/article/insights/data/2022/03/canadas_inaugural_green_bond

Times of India. (2021). https://timesofindia.indiatimes.com/auto/news/how-govts-rs-18100-crore-pli-may-transform-electric-vehiclesin-india/articleshow/82631723.cms

UAE Green Bond and Sukuk Program Development, Situation Analysis Report, 2022.www.moccae.gov.ae

UN Framework Convention on Climate Change (UNFCCC), *Technical Assessment of Climate Finance in the Arab States.* 2022. https://unfccc.int/sites/default/files/resource/UNFCCC_NBF_TA_AS_final.pdf

UNFCCC, "Technical Assessment of Climate Finance.

United Nations Development Programme. Indonesia's Green Sukuk Initiative. INS-UNDP-Indonesia-Sustainable-Develop.

US Department of the Treasury. (2021). https://home.treasury.gov/news/press-releases/jy0134

Vaze, P., Kumar, N., Colenbrander, S., Burge, L., & Sharma, N. (2022). *Identifying, managing and disclosing climate-related financial risks in India: Options for the RBI of India. ODI Report.* ODI. https://odi.org/en/about/our-work/strengthening-climate-risk-assessment-in-indias-financial-sector

Vazquez, Fibras verdes, con posibilidad de emerger via Bolsa, Real Estate Market Magazine, 2017.

Warren, E. (2021). https://www.warren.senate.gov/newsroom/press-releases/warren-casten-colleagues-reintroduce-billrequiring-public-companies-to-disclose-climate-related-risks

Welch, C., Canada's transition and green taxonomy for sustainable finance, Sustainable finance market snapshot, Institute for sustainable finance.

White House. (2021). https://www.whitehouse.gov/briefingroom/statements-releases/2021/04/22/executive-summary-u-sinternational-climate-finance-plan/

World Bank. (2017). *Beyond Scarcity: Water Security in the Middle East and North Africa.* https://openknowledge.worldbank.org/handle/10986/27659

World Economic Forum and McKinsey. (2021). http://www3.weforum.org/docs/WEF_Consultation_Nature_and_Net_Zero_2021.pdf

World Energy Outlook 2023 Executive Summary. https://www.iea.org/reports/world-energy-outlook-2023/executive-summary

www.amazon.com/Sustainable-Investment-Invest-Changing-Finance/dp/0470888490/ref=sr_1_3?ie=UTF8&s=books& qid=1299539960&sr=1-3

www.dot.ca.gov/hq/MassTrans/lctop.html

www.pionline.com/article/20151022/ONLINE/151029940/department-of-labor-opens-the-door-for-esg-considerations

www.thinkadvisor.com/2015/06/29/sustainable-investing-no-longer-a-backwater?utm_content=buffer48f10&utm_medium=social&utm_source=twitter.com&utm_campaign=buffer

Zawya.com. Green, Sustainable Debt Issuance in MENA Hit US$18bln in 2021, 6 January 2022. https://www.zawya.com/en/markets/green-sustainable-debt-issuance-in-mena-hit-18bln-in-2021-lzfpdlbn

Zhengwei, L. (2020). A research on the green securitisation.

Chapter 8
Sustainable Finance in Different Industry Sectors

Sustainable Finance in Chemical Industry

Diverse sectors in chemical industry such as cosmetics, fertilizers, pharmaceuticals and plastics are used to manufacture some 70,000 products. The chemical sector is one of the world's largest industrial consumers of energy and accounts for 6% of all greenhouse gas (GHG) emissions. Most chemicals produced today depend on fossil fuels, either as an energy source or as a feedstock. The chemicals industry will play a crucial role in helping the world achieve the goals of the 2015 Paris Agreement on climate change and reach global net-zero targets. The chemicals industry is the second largest emitter of CO_2, after the steel industry. According to the One Earth Climate Model (OECM) developed by the University of Technology Sydney (UTS), to align with the Paris Agreement goals, the chemicals sector would have a remaining carbon budget of 19.6 gigatons for energy-related emissions between 2020 and 2050. Research funded by PwC Germany and conducted by UTS's Institute for Sustainable Futures indicates that the chemicals industry's global emissions can be significantly reduced through rapid investment in and development of low- and zero-carbon production. The study focused on the seven major base chemicals—methanol, ammonia, benzene, toluene, xylene (BTX aromatics), ethylene, and propylene (light olefins) which accounted for 74% of the industry's energy use (excluding electrical energy) and on G20 markets, responsible for 97% of all energy-related emissions in the chemicals sector.[1]

The chemical sector is also a major source of localized pollution affecting air, land, and water. In the United States, chemical production is responsible for nearly 30% of all air emissions reported in the latest Toxic Release Inventory (TRI)

[1] Volker Fitzner, Jürgen Peterseim, Sven Teske and Maartje Feenstra, Sustainable Chemical Pathways, https://www.pwc.com/gx/en/issues/esg/the-energy-transition/net-zero-chemicals-industry-transformation.html

B. R. Kumar, *Green Finance*, Sustainable Finance,
https://doi.org/10.1007/978-3-032-03333-8_8

National Analysis by the US Environmental Protection Agency (EPA). The World Health Organization estimates that different forms of chemical exposure cause more than 1.5 million deaths a year. According to the International Energy Agency (IEA), chemical sector is the largest consumer of energy within the industrial domain and ranks as the third-highest industrial sub-sector in terms of direct CO_2 emissions. Among primary chemicals, ammonia and methanol production are the leading contributors to direct CO_2 emissions.

The chemical industry has witnessed significant growth propelled by growing global population. Global development has driven a rising demand for agricultural fertilizers, essential automotive components, and a variety of consumer products and household items such as detergents, plastic bottles, packaging, and adhesives.

Reliance on the seven key base chemicals is increasing, with production expected to rise nearly 70% from 2020 to 2050. This growth conflicts with the Paris Agreement's 1.5 °C warming scenario. To align, the industry must adopt circularity practices, reduce plastic use, and extend product lifespans. Despite efficiency gains, energy demand will grow by 81%, with an 85% reduction in emissions needed. Defossilizing the chemicals industry requires investment in three key infrastructure pillars. It involves building new facilities and retrofitting existing ones to produce renewable chemicals. The second pillar involves offering heat for conversion processes through direct electrification. The third pillar involves securing renewable feedback stock supplies which include biogenic sources such as lignin, synthetic renewable carbon and renewable hydrogen.

For net zero transformation in chemical industry, cumulative investment in the range of US$440 billion to US$1 trillion is required through 2040 and investment in the range of US$1.5 trillion to US$3.3 trillion is required through 2050.[2] Ammonia defossilisation require a total cumulative investment of US$200 billion to US$970 billion. According to European Chemical Industry council data, the global capital spending in the year 2022 amounted to US$290 billion. The pathway for methanol defossilisation requires a total cumulative investment of US$150 billion to US$440 billion.

The Chemical sector have a significant role in nearly all manufacturing supply chains. Hence the sector plays a key role for reducing emissions particularly in Scope 3 value chain emissions. Substantial investment is required for achieving net zero and innovative sustainable investments is pivotal for credible transition plans. It is estimated that more than 95% of manufactured products rely on chemicals. Approximately half of the total fossil fuel related emissions is contributed by emissions from the chemical sector's use of heat, steam and energy for compression and cooling. The rest of the fuel related emissions is associated with the use of fossil fuels as inputs in chemical reactions due to production of plastics or fertilizers. Overall the chemical sector ranks third among industry subsectors in terms of direct carbon dioxide emissions. In the context of net zero commitments such as the Paris

[2] Volker Fitzner, Jürgen Peterseim, Sven Teske and Maartje Feenstra, Sustainable Chemical Pathways, https://www.pwc.com/gx/en/issues/esg/the-energy-transition/net-zero-chemicals-industry-transformation.html

Agreement and the EU Green Deal, the chemical industry is facing challenges for decarbonization. Growing supply chain complexity leads to high energy costs and rising carbon emissions and companies have to streamline ecologically wasteful processes and achieve sustainability targets. The trend observed is that due to sustainability concerns, firms are making real investments through venture capital initiatives, joint ventures and acquisitions. Opportunities to provide environmentally friendly offerings such as digital manufacturing and carbon recycling are showing promising trends.

The global annual plastic production has increased more than 200-fold since 1950. Seventy years ago, 2 million tons of plastics were produced. Now more than 400 million tonnes of plastics are produced each year. Only 1% of all the plastic ever made have entered a true circular loop. The rest have ended in landfill, been incinerated or leaked into environment. The plastic waste results into an annual economic loss of USD 120 billion.[3]

PPG a manufacturer and distributor of paints, coatings and specialty materials have introduced different sustainable products such as paints from recycled materials. PPG focus on circular product design and aims to target 50% of sales from sustainably advantaged products by 2030. PPG's sustainability initiatives aim to promote circular economy through introduction of technology to capture and reuse industrial paint overspray, coatings made from recycled materials etc. The company has entered into a joint venture with Entrotech, the provider of innovative paint and film products to develop sustainable technologies.

Sandvik, the product and services provider for mining, metal cutting and machining focusses on subscription-based business model to assist manufacturers to meet their sustainable goals through digital manufacturing offerings. The decentralized operating model ensures that products and services are aligned with customer needs. The company aims to achieve target of $600 million in digitalized offerings revenue by the year 2025. The company focusses on acquiring firms with digital manufacturing technology to focus on this sustainability goals. LanzaTech, a company specializing in carbon recycling, out-licenses its gas fermentation technology to enable customers to capture and monetize their waste carbon. LanzaTech monetizes carbon-rich gases by converting them into products like fuels and chemicals, leveraging technology acquisitions, strategic partnerships, and its core carbon-recycling capabilities. Ecolab, a global leader in water, hygiene, and infection prevention, established a global intelligence center that uses data from connected devices to provide insights and enhance customer relationships. Integrated within the sales organization, this centre drive innovation, measures value through eROI, and boosts customer satisfaction and retention through digital solutions. LyondellBasell, a global leader in plastics, chemicals, and refining, utilizes digital ledgers to accurately calculate and trace recycled content in finished products, ensuring transparency and auditability. LyondellBasell's new CLCS business positions the company as a service provider, enabling circular economies in supply chains through a digital

[3] https://www.lombardodier.com/home/rethink-sustainability/eradicating-plastic-waste.html

product passport and sustainability-focused leadership. Chemical major BASF have partnered with other global chemical companies to develop steam reforming process to reduce carbon emissions.

Nexus Circular, an advanced recycling company, partners with the nonprofit Live Thrive to collect hard-to-recycle plastics. Using proprietary technology, Nexus converts these plastics into high-quality feedstocks for petrochemical companies like Shell, creating a sustainable solution for challenging waste materials. Avantium developed technology to convert plant sugars into chemical building blocks, partnering with Henkel to produce adhesives, fueling growth and enabling commercial production.

Chemical products are fundamental to almost all manufactured goods and must be included in manufacturers' Scope 3 emissions. The Greenhouse Gas Protocol, the leading emission classification system for corporate reporting, categorizes emissions into three scopes: direct emissions (Scope 1), indirect emissions from purchased energy (Scope 2), and emissions related to the value chain outside a company's own operations (Scope 3).

Globally 70 chemical companies have set targets for Corporate net zero pledges by year 2050. The UN Race to Zero Data Explorer offers a concise platform to explore the net zero targets of 500 firms globally.

Sustainable Finance Trends in Chemical Sector

Decarbonizing the chemical sector poses significant technical and financial challenges due to the need for innovative solutions and high implementation costs. Increased financing is crucial to support the transition, yet Green, Social, Sustainability, and Sustainability-linked (GSSS) bonds have had limited impact in this area. Similar challenges are seen in hard-to-abate sectors like mining and logistics. Chemical companies face obstacles such as high R&D costs, large capital expenditures, and complex production shifts. For small and medium-sized enterprises, which make up 96% of the EU's chemical industry, these challenges represent a substantial burden.

Debt issuances in chemical sector are concentrated around green bonds and to a lesser extent sustainability linked bonds. Use of proceeds (UoP) vary across the sector's labelled debt bond issuances. Energy and waste related projects are most attractive for financing.[4]

The Climate Bonds Initiative (CBI) estimates that over EUR 1 trillion in investments will be necessary for the chemical sector's green transition by 2050, requiring companies to increase capital expenditures by 50% beyond business-as-usual levels. Given the substantial capital expenditures and significant investment in research and development, green bonds have primarily been issued by larger companies.

[4] Sustainable Insight | 1 July 2024, fitchratings.com

Issuances of labelled bonds in the chemical sector remain modest, with regional and national differences in categorization and regulations contributing to this trend. Strong regulatory frameworks could play a critical role in promoting issuances. South Korea stands out, with POSCO Future M of South Korea issued the sector's largest green bond in 2021, valued at USD 1.2 billion. Government subsidies for green bond interest and updated regulations, approved in 2023, are expected to drive further issuance. In Europe, BASF issued two green bonds, each valued at EUR 1 billion in 2020 and 2022, funding projects focused on R&D, emissions reduction, plastic recycling, and EV battery materials development.

The EU has recognized the transformation of the chemical industry as a crucial step in achieving carbon neutrality by 2050. In 2023, it launched the Chemical Transition Pathway to facilitate the sector's move toward sustainability. More than half of the labelled bonds issued by chemical companies are green bonds, with the primary use of proceeds directed toward renewable energy, followed by eco-efficient products that support the circular economy.[5]

Leading chemical manufacturers, including LyondellBasell and Dow Chemical, have issued green bonds to support their decarbonization efforts. LyondellBasell allocated proceeds from a USD 500 million green bond to enhance plastic recycling, advancing its circular economy goals. In its February 2024 offering, Dow Chemical committed funds to circular economy projects, energy efficiency, and renewable energy initiatives. Air Products and Chemical, the largest chemical issuer of green bonds at over USD 3.8 billion, is focused on the hydrogen economy. It became the first U.S. chemical company to include green and blue hydrogen in its eligible expenses and plans to invest USD 15 billion in energy transition projects by 2027, including carbon capture technologies.

SLBs are the second largest labelled bond category issued by chemical entities. Mexico is the leading issuer of SLBs in the chemical industry. Orbia is among the top three issuers of SLB in Latin America in the year 2021. Orbia has set an ambitious 44% reduction target in sulphur oxide from the year 2018. Many issuers have opted for carbon absolute based targets. However, 40% of the issuers have set intensity-based targets. Braskem Idesa issued the largest SLB in the global chemical sector valued at USD 1.2 billion. Braskem Idesa have pledged 15% reduction in scope 1 and 2 emissions on an absolute basis by the year 2028. The company focuses on increased reliance on renewable feedstock-based chemicals, investment in carbon offsets and research and development for carbon capture and sequestration technology.

Along with sustainability linked bonds, sustainability linked loans are also gaining traction. In 2019, the specialty chemical company Kemira set three sustainability KPIs for its five-year, €400 million revolving credit facility: improving emission efficiency, generating 50% of its revenue from products that enhance customer resource efficiency, and maintaining the highest rating from the external rater EcoVadis. Other industrial firms that have adopted sustainability-linked loans (SLLs) include DSM, Indorama Ventures, Solvay, and Stora Enso.

[5] Sustainable Insight | 1 July 2024, fitchratings.com

The objective of decarbonization of the chemical industry can be achieved through large scale investment into sustainable technologies. Climate aligned finance will play a critical role in decarbonization efforts. Basic chemicals such as ammonia, ethylene, propylene, methanol and aromatics such as benzene, toluene and xylene dominate the chemical industry by production, volume, investment, energy consumption and carbon emissions. The high GHG intensity of chemical production is on account of the use of fossil resources such as coal, crude oil and natural gas as both a fuel and feedstock. In order to achieve decarbonization objective of net zero targets and cap the global average temperature rise at 1.5 degree, several chemical companies have targets for reducing GHG emissions or achieving carbon neutrality by the year 2050. The Climate Bond Initiative have developed first of its kind criteria for climate aligned bonds for decarbonization measures in basic chemical industry sector. Green bonds are financial instruments used to fund or refinance projects and expenditures aimed at combating climate change. These bonds can be certified by organizations like the Climate Bonds Initiative, which apply strict standards to verify that the projects or expenditures meet the criteria required to be classified as green bonds. Investor demand for climate bonds is robust and expected to grow as more quality products enter the market. However, concerns about the credibility of green labelling are rising. To address this, standards, assurance, and certification are crucial for enhancing confidence and transparency, driving further market growth. The Climate Bonds Standard and Certification Scheme serves as a screening tool to ensure the climate integrity of certified bonds. Proposals are underway to extend certification to entities with climate integrity. Sector-specific eligibility criteria, developed through multi-stakeholder engagement and public consultation, are key to this certification process. Certification requirements address climate change mitigation and resilience. The following can be certified under the basic chemicals criteria[6]

- Use of Proceed (UoP) bonds financing decarbonisation measures (e.g. retrofits)
- Use of Proceed (UoP) bonds financing basic chemicals production facilities (e.g. assets and activities)
- Assets not linked to any specific financing instrument (basic chemicals production facilities)
- Entities (basic chemicals production companies)
- Sustainability Linked Bonds (SLBs) issued by those entities.

Most of the investments in the chemical industry come from the private sector. The investment portfolios are managed primarily by the International Finance Corporation (IFC) and other multilateral financing institutions. It is estimated that decarbonization of the chemical and petrochemical industry will require $75 billion for new chemical plants and energy supply.[7]

---

[6] Climate Bonds Initiative—Basic Chemicals Criteria Document.

[7] Saygin D and D Glelen, Zero Emission Pathway for the Global Chemical and Petrochemical Sector, Energies, 14(3), pp. 1–28, June 23, 2021.

In Europe, the European Union allotted more than 750 billion euros as stimulus package for investments in sustainable technologies. German companies have plans to invest 2–3 billion euros for achieving climate targets by 2030. In immediate future, BASF have announced plans to invest one billion euros by year 2025 to achieve climate target. In 2020, BASF issued a green bond valued at one billion euros with a term of 7 years. In 2019, Kaneka Corp, the Japanese chemical manufacturer issued green bond to finance the construction and R&D costs of new biodegradable polymer production facilities. Arkema, the French Chemical company issued its first green bond to finance a new production facility to produce bio-based polyamide. In 2019, LG Chem issued bonds to fund production of electric vehicle batteries, construction of green building and expansion of water treatment operations. According to Bloomberg data, the chemical industry has issued loans worth $14 billion for carbon reduction targets during the period 2018–2020.

Chemical companies are focussing on sustainability issues across oil and gas value chain. Specifically, chemical companies are investing in sustainability initiatives such as advanced recycling and hydrogen production. McKinsey[8] survey shows that 90% of the top global companies have commitments to achieve net zero emissions, near zero emissions or carbon neutrality by the year 2050. Mckinsey research indicates that chemical companies with exposure to sustainability-driven markets tend to have higher valuations. Pure-play companies in sustainability-aligned markets, like those involving EVs, circular packaging, and natural ingredients, achieve an enterprise-value-to-revenue ratio of around eight, compared to just two for companies in sustainability-neutral markets. This suggests that investors value products that support sustainable end markets. Lithium-based chemicals, despite sustainability concerns, receive higher valuations due to their role in the EV transition, while pine-based chemicals, produced sustainably, are undervalued as they serve markets with limited sustainability-driven growth. However, as carbon reduction gains focus, the value of pine-based chemistries may increase.

Despite the growing focus on ESG and sustainability, there is still uncertainty about the connection between ESG ratings, TSR performance, and valuations. Many chemical companies have diverse portfolios, with some segments benefiting from sustainability-driven demand, while others operate in markets that are neutral or facing challenges. The chemical industry's shift toward sustainability presents chemical companies with the opportunity to proactively pursue top-line growth by tapping into emerging green demand and value pools.

Chemical companies can capitalize on the industry shift toward sustainability by targeting end markets that are driving green trends, such as EVs and energy efficiency. They should focus on selling existing materials to these markets, "greenifying" products for premium pricing where applicable, and investing in green substitutes, new functionalities, and sustainable feedstocks. Aligning with sustainability-driven demand can lead to top-line growth and shareholder value.

---

[8] Haripreet Batra, Craig Poeppelman, and Jeremy Wallach (2022), Sustainability value in chemicals: Market tailwinds versus ESG scores, https://www.mckinsey.com/industries/chemicals/our-insights/sustainability-value-in-chemicals-market-tailwinds-versus-esg-scores#/

Companies must leverage their strengths and carefully select markets where green solutions command premiums, positioning themselves as leaders in the evolving landscape focused on ESG and sustainability targets.

Voluntary initiatives are underway to improve transparency in the chemical sector. Since 2009, the Strategic Approach to International Chemicals Management has been a global policy framework enhancing chemical information transparency across international supply chains in industries such as textiles, toys, electronics, and building materials. The Together for Sustainability initiative aims to promote sustainability and transparency among its member organizations, which collectively have an annual turnover exceeding EUR 800 billion, and throughout their supply chains.

Hydrogen is essential for the chemical industry's decarbonization, serving as both a clean energy source and a low-carbon feedstock. Transitioning to green hydrogen from renewable energy or blue hydrogen with carbon capture can significantly cut CO_2 emissions in chemical manufacturing. According to the International Renewable Energy Agency (IRENA), lower-emissions hydrogen could contribute to 6–15% of emissions reductions and up to 12% of global primary energy consumption by 2050. However, high production costs of clean hydrogen pose a significant challenge. In recent years, hydrogen has begun to be used more as a renewable energy carrier, overcoming barriers related to transportation and scaling. Ammonia, a well-supported international commodity, can be used directly as feedstock or fuel and is projected to see a surge in demand, reaching 690 million tons annually by 2050, with the majority used in chemicals and energy sectors, and the rest as a hydrogen carrier.

Economies of scale, technological advancements, and operational efficiencies are crucial for cost-effective hydrogen trade between low-cost production and high-demand regions. Over 30 countries, including major economies, have reignited interest in hydrogen, launching the COP28 Declaration to promote blue and green hydrogen production for a green economy transition. The US government have initiated a number of schemes to promote green hydrogen projects. Bipartisan Infrastructure law have allocated US dollars one billion to research and development for clean hydrogen technologies. The Inflation Reduction Act (IRA) provides tax credits and incentives to enhance the economic viability of low emission hydrogen. The US Department of Energy had proposed a US dollars 750 million investment to support 52 projects in 24 states to reduce clean hydrogen costs and strengthen the position of US in the growing hydrogen market. In 2020, European Commission launched "Strategy on Clean Hydrogen" to focus on scaling up clean hydrogen production and achieve climate targets under the EU Green deal.

The European Commission's Strategy on Clean Hydrogen, launched in 2020 alongside the Strategy on Energy System Integration, focuses on scaling up clean hydrogen production and use to meet climate targets under the EU Green Deal. The EU established the European Clean Hydrogen Alliance to foster private sector investment by bringing together industry, governments and civil society.

The EU strategy aims to decarbonize hydrogen production through renewable energy-powered electrolysis. It proposes a phased approach, starting with 6GW of renewable hydrogen electrolysers by 2024 and targeting 10 million tonnes of renewable hydrogen production by 2030. Companies in Europe have announced the highest annual production volume of clean hydrogen by the year 2030. In Austria, national funding of EUR 3 billion was allocated until the year 2030 to support demand for hydrogen in chemicals and other hard to abate sectors. Estonian government have offered government subsidies of EUR 49.1 million to support investments aimed at developing green hydrogen value chain with focus on transportation and chemical sectors. Since the year 2020, Estonia had allocated over EUR 120 million to support hydrogen technology and supply chain development. Estonia have plans to establish hydrogen refuelling stations every 100–200 km along the Trans-European Transport Network.

A key regulatory element of the EU Green Deal with major implications for businesses outside the EU is the upcoming Carbon Border Adjustment Mechanism (CBAM). CBAM will apply a levy on the carbon emissions embedded in certain imports, including iron, steel, cement, fertilizers, hydrogen, aluminium, and electricity. This mechanism aims to prevent carbon leakage and ensure that imported goods adhere to the EU's climate standards. EU Green Chemistry Subsidy program offers financial support for research, development and innovation projects in the field of green chemistry.

Recent research by Accenture show that over next five-year period, sustainability focused products and services are projected to drive nearly one third of the chemical industry's growth, potentially unlocking a USD 200 billion opportunity for chemical companies. There will be increasing demand for sustainability enabling products such as materials used in wind turbines, and solar panels, as well as for products produced through sustainable methods which include bio-based materials and materials produced from recycled content. The Accenture research suggest that market for sustainability products valued at approximately USD 200 billion in year 2022 was projected to reach USD 500 billion by the year 2027. Sustainability related products such as insulation materials and plastics for electrical vehicles will account for two thirds of the chemical industry growth and requires minimal investment. The remaining one third of growth will come from new markets such as carbon-capture materials.

During the past 5 years, the chemical industry had made investments in the range of USD60 billion- USD 90 billion in new plants which focusses on sustainability related products, excluding start-ups and GHG reduction initiatives. These investments were basically for recycled bio-based chemicals, recycled polymers and bio-based intermediaries.

Sustainability-related chemicals, such as those with low carbon footprints or made from bio-based feedstocks, will require new production methods, assets, and equipment. To succeed, chemical companies should prioritize acquiring intellectual property (IP) and proprietary knowledge in these areas, particularly in production and information technology.

Sustainable Finance in Banking Sector

Currently the size of the global bond market has been estimated at $90 trillion of which $694 billion are categorized as climate aligned bonds. Among these, value of green bonds which constitute approximately 17% are valued at $118 billion. The G20, Financial Stability Board, and Paris Agreement, along with nationally determined contributions, have bolstered the financial sector's role in advancing sustainable development and addressing climate change. The global platform NAZCA (Non-State Actor Zone for Climate Action) was established by 479 global investors, companies and other organizations to emphasis their commitment towards climate initiatives. However still only a minuscule percentage of bank lending is explicitly classified as green category. Less than 1% of global bonds are labelled as green, and under 1% of institutional investors' holdings are categorized as green infrastructure assets.[9]

Financial markets have significant influence in driving the transition to a low-carbon economy through investments in climate-friendly projects. Beyond lending standards, financial institutions must consider environmental and social risks. Sustainable investments, particularly in energy, clean technology, and infrastructure, are significant. Studies show a positive link between sustainability-focused investments and financial performance.

Building on the efforts of the G20 Green Finance Study Group, the IFC Climate Policy team has introduced a new approach to evaluate and monitor green finance, specifically within the banking sector. This approach aims to assess the current state of green lending and offer recommendations for better alignment across the industry. This initial bottom-up approach maps green financial flows by defining "green" at the project level based on the intended use of investments. It estimates each project's green share using available company or sector information, aggregates data by industry and country, and compares results with policy targets to identify gaps and action points.

A 2016 report by Bloomberg New Energy Finance and Ceres estimates that achieving the Paris Agreement goals will require $12.1 trillion over the next 25 years. This amount is $5.2 trillion more than current projections, translating to an additional $208 billion per year. International Finance Corporation (IFC) report in 2016 estimated that nationally determined contributions of 21 emerging market countries represented a $23 trillion investment opportunity during the period 2016–2030.

If a project's use of funds is clearly green, such as for renewable energy, the entire loan is considered green. This approach includes green projects from companies in sectors that are not entirely green, like energy, which may also involve fossil-fuel investments.

[9] G20 Green Finance Synthesis Report. G20 Green Finance Study Group, 2016. http://unepinquiry.org/wp-content/uploads/2016/09/Synthesis_Report_Full_EN.pdf

The United States receives the largest share of global green loans at 35%, followed by the United Kingdom at 8%, Australia and France at 6% each, and Japan at 5%. Among emerging markets, China, and India each account for about 4% of the total global green loan value. In 2014, the Green Bond Principles, formulated by international banks, investors, issuers, and the International Capital Market Association, offered voluntary guidelines for issuing credible green bonds. They ensure transparency on environmental impacts and standardize disclosure processes to aid in the evaluation and facilitation of green bond transactions. Green bond principles focus on use of proceed which is exclusively green; process for project evaluation and selection; management of proceeds and reporting. Certification is recommended through third parties.

The Investor Platform for Climate Actions highlights 19 initiatives promoting low-carbon and green investments, involving over 400 investors from 40 countries and totalling $25 trillion in assets. The financial sector is recognizing its role in transitioning to a low carbon economy with net zero banking gaining importance. The market for sustainable finance is estimated to be USD 23 trillion by the year 2031. Net-zero banking is a bank's commitment to achieving a net-zero carbon footprint by balancing the greenhouse gases (GHGs) it removes from the atmosphere with those it emits. The banking industry's commitment to net-zero goals reflects the rise of sustainable practices. In 2023, the UN formed the Net-Zero Banking Alliance (NZBA), with 138 top banks from 44 countries, representing 41% of banking assets. The sector, managing over USD 9.5 trillion, aims to align with the Paris Agreement by achieving net-zero emissions by 2050. Banks are integrating environmental and sustainable components of ESG into their frameworks, with governance evolving accordingly, signalling a shift toward responsible banking focused on financed emissions and environmental impact.

A study[10] published in January 2023 found that out of USD 2.5 trillion in loans and bond underwriting provided by 60 major banks to 377 leading energy companies, only USD 178 billion, or 7%, was allocated to clean energy projects. According to non-profit organization, the Rainforest Action Network, the five banking giants in the FTSE had lent USD 35.7 billion to fossil fuel companies in year 2022 compared to USD 51.6 billion in year 2021. Banks such as HSBC and BNP Paribas have committed that it would no longer directly finance new oil and gas fields. In 2023, UAE banking sector pledged to mobilize over $270 billion in green financing by the year 2030. Another major bank in UAE, FAB have delivered $27 billion in energy projects, waste water infrastructure and green buildings. In 2023, the bank has made green financing commitments valued for $135 billion.

A recent McKinsey survey[11] reveals a significant and increasing interest among American consumers in climate-related financial products. To seize climate-related opportunities, financial institutions should identify product-market fit by addressing

---

[10] https://www.sierraclub.org/sites/www.sierraclub.org/files/2023-02/Background%20briefing%20renewables%20data.pdf

[11] https://www.mckinsey.com/capabilities/sustainability/our-insights/green-growth-unlocking-sustainability-opportunities-for-retail-banks#/

real customer needs; quickly test consumer interest versus behaviour; outline steps to build, launch, and scale climate products. The Alliance for Green Commercial Banks is a global initiative uniting financial institutions, industry associations, research institutions, and technology providers to create green commercial banks in emerging markets and finance climate-focused infrastructure and business solutions.

According to Institute of International Finance, the world requires investment of $8 trillion every year to achieve net zero emissions. However, the amount spends in 2023 was only $2 trillion. Commercial banks play a major role in supporting green development. By end 2023, China's green loans amounted to $4.24 trillion which represented an increase of 36.5% and were lend mostly by commercial banks.

Agricultural Bank of China (ABC) ABC integrates green and low-carbon criteria into its credit guidelines and decision-making, supporting over 2000 green finance projects in areas like green transportation, clean energy, and low-carbon transitions.

International Financial Corporation's (IFC) Initiatives

Climate action is a key strategic priority for IFC and the World Bank. IFC have resolved to increase its climate related investments to represent an average of 35% of its own account long term commitment volume during the period 2021–2025. In addition, IFC collaborates with financial institutions to support projects which advance both climate mitigation and adaptation efforts. To achieve the objectives of the Paris Agreement, IFC has committed to align 85% of its new investment projects starting July, 1 2023 and 100% of these investments starting July 1, 2025. By July 2023, IFC has committed $15.2 billion from its own account to climate related projects and leveraged an additional $5.8 billion through 210 plus emerging market financial institution partners. These investments help partners avoid 22.7 million tons of GHG emissions annually. Additionally, IFC's advisory services assist global financial institutions in developing climate finance portfolios, leading to the avoidance of millions of tons of GHG emissions each year. The climate mitigation and adaptation need in emerging markets and developing countries are substantial, with estimates ranging from $1.7 trillion to $3.4 trillion annually by 2030. Approximately 80–90% of climate finance required in emerging markets will be sourced from private sector. Financial institutions are increasingly building climate finance into their long-term strategies and portfolios. Financial markets are integrating climate transition risks and opportunities into investment decision making. IFC have been active in climate finance since 1980s and have been focussing on five strategic areas of clean energy, climate-smart cities, climate-smart agribusiness, green buildings and green finance. In the year 2023, IFC's Financial Institution Group's (FIG) climate finance projects amounted to 51 projects with value of $4.5 billion. This consisted of $1.2 billion for green buildings, $850 million for climate bonds, $600 million for climate trade and $500 million for climate-smart vehicles.

FIG's investments have supported partners in avoiding GHG emissions of 30 million tCO_2e/year. In 2012, IFC issued its first green bond valued at $1 billion. By end of fiscal 2023, IFC had issued more than $12.5 billion in 198 green bonds in 21 currencies. IFC's advisory services support global financial institutions to develop climate finance portfolios which facilitate in the prevention of millions of tons of GHG emissions every year. The Upstream Global Blue Bonds Initiative was launched by IFC in year 2020 to address the depletion of the blue economy and clean water resources through innovative financing. By the fiscal year 2022–2023, IFC financed over $1.5 billion in bonds and loans across Asia, Latin America and the Caribbean, Europe and Central Asia. Blue Finance Guidelines was developed in year 2022 which provide definitions, eligibility criteria and guidance frameworks for ocean friendly and clean water projects. IFC also collaborated with ICMA and other development financial institutions to develop the Practitioners Guide to Blue Bonds. FIG offered a $400 million, 4-year loan to Société Générale's subsidiary ALD to support e-mobility across seven emerging markets. This largest e-mobility project in IFC history focusses to deploy 15,000 green vehicles, potentially reducing annual carbon emissions by 22,180 tons by 2026. FIG offers investment and advisory services to projects involved in rooftop/distributed solar system. This encompasses investment projects with banks, non-bank financial institutions, and debt funds for commercial and industrial solar, as well as financing for off-grid solar and appliances through companies like M-KOPA. FIG's Global Climate team utilizes donor resources to assist clients with advisory services for rooftop solar installations. In South Africa, FIG committed $241 million to expand ABSA's certified green building finance portfolio, the largest project supported by IFC's Market Accelerator for Green Construction Program. This investment aims to reduce over 12,000 tons of emissions annually, support affordable housing, and help meet South Africa's 2025 GHG reduction targets.

European banks play a critical role in providing support and financial solutions for environmentally sustainable projects. Banking regulators are required to associate with banks to adopt current best practices for the management of environmental issues.

Banks are increasingly financing sustainable activities, but attracting private capital for a sustainable economy remains challenging. Regulatory requirements, risk assessment difficulties, and higher premiums make long-term finance less viable. Targeted regulatory changes and policy incentives are needed to support green projects. Clear, stable regulations and public policies are crucial, along with incentives and technical assistance from the public sector to foster long-term sustainability finance. Incorporating climate-related criteria into banks' risk models is crucial for managing loan defaults and financial stability. Methodologies are developing to measure and mitigate these risks uniformly. Banks are increasing their involvement in sustainable finance, but attracting private capital remains challenging. Debate continues about banks' role, given the mismatch between their short-to-medium-term horizons and the long-term nature of sustainable investments. Issues include short-term green bonds, small project sizes, and risk assessments, which complicate bridging supply and demand for long-term funding. Regulatory instability forces banks to build balance sheets conservatively to comply with current requirements and avoid capital lock-in. For green financing, projects must be economically and financially viable. While short-term finance needs are natural, long-term finance challenges—due to regulations and risk assessments—require targeted policy decisions to incentivize sustainable investments.

The banking sector is committed to supporting the EU's climate goals and the COP 21 objectives by advancing a two-degree economy. Banks aim to reduce their environmental impact and support clients in adopting sustainable practices. They are increasing investment in renewable energy and offering a range of green products and services to enhance sustainability across various customer segments.

Key recommendations suggested by European banking federation include aligning EU sustainable finance with political goals, developing a common taxonomy and disclosure framework, and implementing an ECC risk categorization system. They also propose fostering public-private cooperation, introducing green incentives, integrating environmental risk in banking, and adjusting regulatory frameworks to encourage sustainable financing and risk mitigation.[12]

Environmental Initiatives by Banks

Banks offer financial solutions for environmentally sound projects and companies. Banks are expanding renewable energy financing, reducing carbon exposure and offers sustainable products to support environmental protection across all customer segments. The trend observed in corporate banking sector is that business loans are offered for projects related to photovoltaic panels, biomass plants, hydropower plants and energy efficiency measures. The banking sector also focusses on sustainability initiatives related to agricultural protection covering crop damage. In retail market segment, banks disburse loans for environmental purposes. This includes loans for energy efficient renovation of property, purchase of ecological equipment and installation of solar and photovoltaic panels. In the retail market sector, banks are associated with the European Mortgages Federation-European Covered Bond Council (EMF-ECBC) initiative on green mortgages. The Green bonds and investment funds market is primarily driven by large institutional investors, targeting high-credit-quality issuers, medium maturities, and substantial public transactions.

The role of digital technology is becoming increasingly relevant in the sustainable ecosystem. The relationship between FinTech and green finance is still emerging but shows promise as digitalization transforms banking. Innovations like debit/credit cards tracking climate impact and AI-driven solutions are gaining traction. FinTech start-ups are spurring innovation, fostering partnerships with traditional banks, and accelerating sustainable development in a regulated environment. In order to promote environmental sustainability, Green Digital Finance Alliance platform was created to address the potential for Fintech powered business innovations in lending, investment and insurance. Many private equity (PE) firms in Europe

---

[12] Towards a green finance framework, European Banking Federation, www.ebf.eu

have incorporated ESG criteria into their investment processes. Non-financial KPIs such as carbon foot print are being reported by portfolio companies. Private Equity firms also invest in green infrastructure such as waste management, biomass plants, hydro or solar power plants. Some banks have set up impact funds which invest in social organizations in Europe. Banks have also initiated steps to issue green revolving credit facilities wherein margins are linked to the sustainability performance of the borrower. Banks is also aiming for the introduction of assessment criteria related to climate risks for energy industry clients. Climate change impacts credit risk assessment. For banks, integrating environmental and climate-related criteria into credit ratings, Probability of Defaults (PDs), and Loss Given Defaults (LGDs) helps differentiate between sustainable and unsustainable businesses. Many banks now conduct environmental due diligence audits, using Climate Risk Management Models to assess and mitigate risks at various business levels, ensuring informed and responsible lending practices. Natural Capital Finance Alliance offers examples for integrating environmental factors into pricing.

In collaboration with institutions like the IFC and EBRD, many banks have adopted the Environmental and Social Management System (ESMS) within their internal processes. ESMS integrates environmental and social risk management into credit assessments, aligning lending policies with international standards. It applies to both new and existing financing and involves identifying, evaluating, and mitigating risks. This system can result in lower pricing for green products and services. Since 2017, Greek banks require clients to provide an "Environmental Risk Assessment" to support the evaluation of environmental and social risks, including corrective action plans if needed.

The regulatory framework should address systemic risks, such as poor governance and environmental risk management, as well as risks from non-sustainable assets. Environmental and Climate Change (ECC) risk management should be part of the Internal Capital Adequacy Assessment Process (ICAAP) and risk assessments for credit, market, and operations. Basel III's Pillar 1 requires banks to monitor environmental risks related to collateral and assigns higher capital requirements for long-term, environmentally sustainable loans. Pillar 2's Supervisory Review (SREP) adds sustainability assessments for business models and governance, with potential for forward-looking stress tests to evaluate financial stability impacts of sustainable lending.

In the short term, ECC scenarios and stress testing offer viable prudential and competitive solutions, focusing on soft measures like know-how investments and data collection without requiring additional capital requirements. Pillar 2 "brown" exposure add-ons should be avoided, as banks rely on external ECC data. Pillar 3 encourages standardized disclosure of systemic environmental risks, ensuring transparency across the financial sector.[13]

---

[13] Towards a green finance framework, European Banking Federation, www.ebf.eu

Initiatives to Stimulate Development of Green Finance in Banking Sector

Bank credit dominates EU financing, but only a small portion is classified as green due to unclear definitions. Harmonized definitions and metrics are needed for green finance activities, enabling banks and investors to efficiently allocate resources and integrate climate risks across the financial system. In the context of emerging green asset classes such as ESG funds and green securities, a common taxonomy and minimum standards are required to prevent greenwashing which refers to the overstating of the environmentally or socially conscious attribute of a firm's offering. Clear frameworks with controls and sanctions along with multi stakeholder development are essential to ensure accurate green claims and prevent misleading environmental marketing as science evolves. For informed market analysis and product development, comparable disclosures on environmental and climate risks are required. A common EU taxonomy and disclosure framework is essential for improvement of performance indicators and sustainability related to the lending process. The European commission ought to take steps to leverage the TCFD's recommendations with mandatory quantitative disclosures phased in once common definitions and metrics. Over 100 global firms which included financial services have committed support for TCFD's recommendations.

The green bond market is gaining traction in the financial system. However still it represents around 1% of the bond market. The traceability of the green bond market is rather complex in nature. There is public reporting for 74% of green bonds which are issued before 1 April, 2016 according to study by Climate Bond Initiative on green bond post issuance reporting.[14] A common EU standard could support the growth of the Green Bond market without imposing overly strict requirements. Initial development could focus on green covered bonds and project bonds, using a common taxonomy and third-party assessments to mitigate greenwashing and promote market expansion. European banking federation recommends that banks could reduce financing costs by developing standard contracts for green projects, with public institutions facilitating efforts. Joint work on risk data dissemination would enhance performance analysis, benefiting smaller projects.

Public-private cooperation is crucial for sustainable development financing. Aligning public policies with private sector needs and sharing unmarketable risks between public entities and private institutions can facilitate investment. A coherent EU-wide framework and collaboration between financial and public entities will support risk mitigation and accelerate sustainable financing. Phasing out inappropriate subsidies to fossil intensive industries will influence the risk and pricing of financial assets. Direct subsidies in the form of tax benefits or subsidized funding may be offered for sustainable projects. National monetary authorities should develop targeted policies, including green reserve management, green finance

[14] https://www.climatebonds.net/resources/reports/post-issuance-reporting-green-bond-market-trendsbest-practice-june-2017

guidelines, and accepting high-quality green assets as collateral to support sustainable financing. To promote and accelerate green finance, the global green council have introduced Green Lending Principles and a Directory of the Global and European Green Finance Policy Initiatives. The directory provides policymakers and market participants guidance on green and climate change initiatives.

The European Investment Project Portal (EIPP) promotes EU investment projects to global investors, aiming to accelerate project development and boost employment and economic growth through the European Fund for Strategic Investments (EFSI). To encourage green bond issuance, Singapore's Monetary Authority (MAS) introduced the Green Bond Grant scheme, allowing qualifying issuances to offset 100% of external review costs, capped at $100,000 per issuance. OECD export credit agencies will not provide loans to heavily indebted poor countries without World Bank or IMF appraisal, hindering green growth and favouring carbon-intensive alternatives. The EBF supports revising sustainable lending guidelines to allow more commercial loans for climate-related and infrastructure projects.

UN Principles for Responsible Banking are the world's foremost sustainable banking framework with over 330 signatory banks representing over half of the global banking industry. Since 2018, the world has consumed more than half a trillion tonnes of materials as much as was consumed in the entire twentieth century according to Circle Economy 2024 estimates. The environmental damages are estimated at USD 5 trillion to USD 7 trillion.[15] The transition to circular economies could generate USD 4.5 trillion in annual economic output by 2030.[16]

Financial institutions, particularly banks, are vital in promoting circular business models by offering financial products that help businesses conserve resources and reduce waste. They can support SMEs in innovating sustainable technologies and create synergies across value chains. Engaging clients through awareness, data collection, and tailored services is essential for facilitating this transition. Additionally, banks can assess the impact of circular solutions on greenhouse gas emissions, aligning their efforts with climate transition goals like those outlined by the Glasgow Financial Alliance for Net Zero (GFANZ).

The Carbon Footprint of Bank Loans (CFBL) developed by the IMF's Climate Change Indicators dashboard serves a tool for policymakers to measure the carbon intensity of bank loan portfolios. The CFBL is currently available for 41 countries in emerging markets and developing economies.

At COP26 in November, the Glasgow Financial Alliance for Net Zero (GFANZ), a coalition of around 450 banks, insurance companies, and asset managers from 45 countries, announced a commitment of $130 trillion in assets to drive the global economy toward net zero emissions.

---

[15] Dasgupta, P., 2021. The Economics of Biodiversity: The Dasgupta Review. [Online] Available at: https://assets.publishing.service.gov.uk/government/uploads/system/uploads/attachment_data/file/962785/The_Economics_of_Biodiversity_The_Dasgupta_ Review_Full_Report.pdf

[16] Accenture Strategy, 2015. Waste to Wealth. [Online] Available at: newsroom. Accenture. https://newsroom.accenture.com/news/2015/the-circular-economy-could-unlock-4-5-trillion-of-economic-growth-finds-new-book-byaccenture.htm

Green Finance in Insurance Sector

Insurance can play a vital role in sustainable finance by integrating environmental, social, and governance (ESG) factors into underwriting, investments, and client engagement. Insurers assess ESG risks to their portfolios and liabilities, affecting business strategy, competitive positioning, and reputation. ESG regulation is increasing, requiring insurers to prioritize sustainability across their operations. Insurers can contribute to sustainability by offering green products, incentivizing responsible behaviour, and collaborating with partners. Transparency in ESG reporting and benchmarking is essential for progress. Ultimately, embracing ESG enhances insurers' growth, talent retention, and positive impact on the environment while aligning with global sustainability goals.

The insurance sector is crucial in transitioning to a sustainable economy by managing and pricing ESG risks, especially climate change. It integrates ESG issues into risk management, supports emission reduction efforts, and contributes to sustainable development through inclusive insurance for low-income populations. Global initiatives like UNEP support this effort. Insurance mechanisms can enhance societal resilience by offering financial compensation for disaster losses, aiding faster recovery. Insurers also assess and communicate environmental risks, encouraging risk reduction through lower premiums. Additionally, price signalling and resilience requirements incentivize firms and authorities to adopt risk-reduction measures, benefiting both insurers and insured parties.

The Alliance Global Insurance Report 2023 estimates that insurers worldwide have collected USD 6.93 trillion in premiums and registered growth of 7.5% during the year 2023. The industry trend shows alignment with global standards such as SASB and GRI and adoption of TCFD recommendations. However there exists concerns for certain risks to be uninsurable if the climate crisis aggravates as more than half of the world's GDP is moderately or heavily dependent on nature. A 2019 survey carried out by 1170 insurers within 15 jurisdictions suggest that 73% of assessed insurers expect that climate change would affect their business.

According to MunichRe, natural catastrophes globally have resulted in US$210 billion in damages during the year 2020. The World Economic Forum (WEF) 2020 report have identified extreme weather as the top global risks. It was estimated that more than half of the world's GDP in terms of economic value is moderately or highly dependent on nature. Boston Consulting Group report in 2020 suggest that the risk of assets becoming stranded due to the transition to a low carbon economy could impact the financial performance of insurance companies.

ESG in Insurance Value Chain

ESG driven competitive advantage offers opportunities across value chain for insurance industry. In the context of value chain of discovery in insurance sector, accessibility of products for marginalized populations offers opportunities. In terms of value chain of products and pricing, consumers can be motivated to support ESG related activities such as incentivizing customers to install solar panels on their residential roofs. ESG factors can also be considered for underwriting and claims & servicing.

Policy Advisor is a digital aggregator offering accessible quotes and impartial insurance advice, providing affordable, equitable solutions for underserved customer groups across multiple insurers. In product and pricing category, Insurance giant, Aviva have stopped insuring standalone operational fossil fuel power generation in London market by 2019 and replaced the product with renewable energy insurance for world's largest solar and wind farms. In the area of quoting & advice, Aegon's qualitative to quantitative pilot program offers an instant quote app for improving customer acceptance rates and reduce processing times by over 95%. In underwriting business, French insurance giant AXA had integrated ESG data in its underwriting methodologies and stopped property and construction covers for coal mines and plants, oil sands, extraction sites and drilling in the Artic region. AXA have made several commitments related to sustainable finance. Sedgwick's repair solutions division has minimized the environmental impact of on-site repairs by adopting alternative restoration methods and offering sustainable claims guidance. For capital and risk control purposes, Allianz have strategically integrated sustainability into its investment and asset management solutions. In 2022, Allianz invested Euro 132 billion of proprietary assets and Euro 360 billion of third-party assets under management. Foresters partnered with Dacadoo to incorporate wellness and behavioral science into the post-purchase experience, aiming to inspire and reward healthy lifestyles and wellness-focused goals. UK based Legal & General insurer has been proactive in addressing climate risks. Netherlands based NN Group have been involved in impact investing with focus on areas such as renewable energy and microfinance. Prudential Finance focusses on impact investment in areas such as affordable housing and social entrepreneurship. Swiss Re has integrated ESG benchmarks into its investment process. Zurich focusses on impact investment through green bond investment.

Studies have shown that sustainability reporting guidelines and standards are being increasingly used by insurance industry. More than 30 insurance companies with approximately US$6 trillion are using SASB, ESG and industry specific sustainability standards. The TCFD 2020 Status report evaluated the reporting practices of 141 insurance companies with assets in the range of USD 1billion -USD 1.1 trillion and points out that insurers have improved their disclosures across all 11 recommendations.

Sustainable insurance can be viewed as a strategic approach which integrates environmental, social and governance (ESG) elements into every aspect of the insurance value chain. The concept of sustainable insurance gives emphasis on responsible engagement with stakeholders and proactive management of ESG related risks and opportunities. The aim of sustainable insurance is to mitigate risk, foster innovation and promote environmental, social and economic sustainability. The UNEP FI Principles for Sustainable Insurance (PSI) adopted during the 2012 UN Conference on Sustainable Development is a global framework for the insurance industry for addressing environmental, social and governance risks and opportunities. The PSI Initiative is the largest initiative between UN and the global insurance industry with over 300 members from different regions of the world. The PSI Initiative pioneers efforts such as the V20 Sustainable Insurance Facility, net-zero and nature-positive insurance, ESG guidelines, and supports the implementation of TCFD and TNFD frameworks. The UNEP FI Principles for Sustainable Insurance are part of the insurance industry criteria of the Dow Jones Sustainability Indices and FTSE4Good.

UNEP FI

United Nations Environmental Program Finance Initiative (UNEP FI) founded in 1992 was the first organization to engage finance sector on sustainability and advocated the Principles for Responsible Investment. UNEP FI have a network of more than 500 banks and insurers with assets exceeding US$170 trillion. Around 110 insurance companies have joined the PSI and report progress related to implementation of principles for sustainable insurance. By the year 2020, insurance participants have underwritten more than 25% of the global industry premiums with approximately $US 14 trillion in AUM. In the year 2020, UNEPFI had issued the first global guide to manage ESG issues in risk assessment and insurance underwriting with focus on non-life insurance. In collaboration with 22 leading insurers and reinsurers, the PSI launched the "TCFD Insurance Pilot Projects" to create standardized analytical approaches for identifying, assessing, and disclosing climate change-related risks and opportunities within insurance portfolios.

UNEP FI Principles for Sustainable Insurance[17]

Principle 1 deals with decision making environmental, social and governance issues relevant to insurance business. Company strategy should address ESG issues at the board and management levels, integrating them into recruitment, risk management, and operations. ESG factors must be incorporated into underwriting, product development, claims management, and investment decisions. Sales and marketing should promote ESG awareness, while products and services should reduce risks and promote positive ESG impacts.

Principle 2 advocates working together with clients and business partners to raise awareness of environmental, governance and social issues, manage risk and develop solutions. Principle 2 focusses on engaging with clients and suppliers on managing ESG issues, providing tools and setting clear expectations. Incorporate ESG criteria

[17] https://www.unepfi.org/insurance/insurance/the-principles/

in supplier selection and encourage transparent ESG reporting. Promote ESG principles within the insurance industry and support their inclusion in professional education and ethical standards for insurers, reinsurers, and intermediaries.

Principle 3 highlight the commitment of the industry to work together with government regulators and other key stakeholders to promote widespread action on environmental, governance and social issues. This Principle support policies and regulations that enhance ESG risk management and innovation. Engage with governments, NGOs, businesses, academia, and the media to promote sustainable development, improve ESG understanding, foster research, and raise public awareness on ESG issues and risk management within the insurance industry.

Principle 4 states that the industry will demonstrate accountability and transparency in regularly disclosing publicly the progress in implementing the Principles. Regularly assess, monitor, and publicly disclose the company's ESG progress. Engage in relevant reporting frameworks and dialogue with stakeholders to emphasize the value of ESG disclosure. There are 169 signatories and 112 supporting institutions for the PSI.

Insurance product manufacturers should integrate sustainability factors into the product approval and oversight process, clearly defining target markets for customers seeking sustainability-focused insurance products at a detailed level. To ensure strong investor protection, insurance intermediaries and undertakings distributing sustainable insurance-based investment products must identify conflicts of interest related to sustainability. They should implement measures to prevent mis-selling, ensuring that integrating sustainability factors doesn't harm customer interests during the advisory and distribution processes.

Regulatory Aspects in Green Insurance

The TCFD (Task Force on Climate-related Financial Disclosures) has gained broad recognition as the gold standard among insurance companies and regulators. The number of insurers supporting the TCFD framework has grown significantly, from 8 in 2017 to 77 in 2021.[18]

ClimateWise, established in 2007, is a global insurance industry network with 33 leading organizations. It helps members address climate change challenges and opportunities by aligning their expertise. Since 2019, its principles have followed TCFD recommendations, requiring members to report annually on climate-related actions, enabling progress benchmarking.

[18] Sustainable finance market update series, Sustainable finance across insurance providers, FC4S. ORG. July 2021

Green Insurance

Green Insurance can be designed to solve environmental issues and promote sustainability by means of offering coverage for environmentally friendly projects and investments in green technology. Approximately $1.2 trillion in annual premiums were generated worldwide as a response to climate change.[19] Insurance providers offer green insurance policies which cover renewable energy sources, energy efficient homes and green automobiles. Many green insurance packages in Europe cover renewable energy projects, energy efficient infrastructure and environmentally friendly transportation. Developing countries are also offering innovative insurance products targeted towards green initiatives. Government of India have implemented a scheme which offers insurance protection for financial investments in the sector. Indian insurance providers have also collaborated with renewable energy developers to create special insurance coverage for projects. Insurance providers in Africa have introduced green insurance policies for covering climate related risks such as droughts and floods. For example, a Kenyan insurer offers a plan which safeguard farmers against crop failures which are caused by drought. There are many examples of successful green insurance schemes in developing countries. African Risk Capacity is a green insurance scheme in different African countries which support sustainable projects such as Climate Risk Management and Agricultural Drought Insurance. Blue Marble Micro Insurance scheme adopted in India, Philippines and Kenya offers microinsurance products for small scale farmers and fishermen. MicroEnsure offered in multiple developing countries offer climate and health insurance for low income communities. Adoption of sustainable practices have been initiated in numerous industries such as forestry and agriculture and often facilitated by green insurance coverage.

Sustainable or Green Insurance Products[20]

Personal Lines of Insurance Products

Green Property Rebuilding

After a covered loss, this coverage pays for environmentally friendly materials and energy-efficient equipment during repairs. Policyholders with green practices may receive premium discounts.

---

[19] Kaminker C, Stewart F (2012) The role of institutional investors in financing clean energy. OECD Working Papers. Available from: https://www.oecd-ilibrary.org/finance-and-investment/the-roleof-institutional-investors-in-financing-clean-energy_5k9312v21l6f-en

[20] Rita Zona, Kevin Roll and Zora Law, Sustainable /Green Insurance Products, Casualty Actuarial Society *E-Forum*, Winter 2014.

Property Renewable Energy Reimbursement

This coverage protects homeowners with alternative-energy systems, compensating for lost income from energy sales, replacement electricity costs, and fees for inspections or reconnections after a power outage.

Property Loss Mitigation Device Discount

Homeowners in catastrophe-prone areas can receive premium credits for installing mitigation devices, like storm shutters, or using storm-resistant construction techniques to protect their homes.

Pay as You Drive/Low Mileage Discount

Pay-as-you-drive insurance incentivizes reduced driving, lowering pollution, and offers personalized rates based on driving habits and mileage.

Fuel Efficient/Low Emission Vehicle Discount

Many insurers provide discounts for hybrid or electric passenger vehicles.

Commercial Lines

Upgrade to Green Commercial Fleets

In this product category, an option is offered to upgrade the company's fleet to hybrid vehicles for new vehicle replacement as part of an endorsement to the policy.

Insurance for Renewable Energy Projects

These insurance products offer coverage for companies in the renewable industry sector to manage risks and protect assets.

Insurance for Renewable Energy Property, Equipment and Loss of Use

This policy offers replacement cost coverage for renewable energy equipment, including current, under-construction, or new assets, with efficient upgrades. Green roofs are also covered.

Green Building Coverage Against Adverse Publicity

This reputation coverage protects green buildings from adverse publicity, providing funds for crisis management specialists to guide personnel and restore the company's reputation.

Perishable Food Reduction Products

These products promote the use of technology to reduce produce loss and improve quality during distribution from growers to retailers. Devices monitor temperature and condition, estimating remaining shelf life.

Global Weather Insurance

This product fills gaps in traditional property damage insurance, covering unpredictable weather. Event promoters can hedge against specific weather conditions like rain or wind exceeding defined thresholds.

Political Risk Insurance for Carbon-Trading

This product provides financial protection to project sponsors, investors, and lenders against risks like government interference, embargoes, license cancellation, war, and political violence impacting carbon credit projects.

Specialty Lines

Insurance for Pollution/Environmental Liability

This coverage addresses various risks across industries, including general liability, pollution liability, and environmental responsibilities. It applies to hazards affecting both large corporations and small subcontractors.

Directors & Officers Insurance

Litigation against companies contributing to climate change is rising, including for inaction on adaptation strategies. Some insurers now offer directors and officers policies with global warming litigation protection.

Architects & Engineering Professional Liability Insurance Discount for Building

Commissioning

Some insurers link sustainable practices, like energy efficiency, to lower risk. Building commissioning ensures systems work effectively, reducing liability claims. Architects and engineers using it may receive insurance premium credits.

Professional Liability Insurance for Raters and Home Energy Survey Professionals

Many specialist professionals in energy-efficiency lack suitable insurance. Qualified raters and home energy surveyors can obtain liability and property coverage to protect against accidents and lawsuits.

Offering sustainable insurance products provides insurers direct benefits like competitive advantages, increased market share through discounts on hybrid vehicles, entry into niche sectors like renewable energy, attracting lower-risk environmentally conscious customers, and building a green, socially responsible brand.

It is estimated that £1 trillion in UK infrastructure investment is required to reach net zero by the year 2050. Private capital is essential to achieve this goal. In this context, the role of insurance and pension funds is significant. Green Finance Institute has proposed solutions blending project finance techniques. The Institute works closely with the Investment Delivery Forum of British insurers, Department of Energy Security and Net Zero, the UK Infrastructure Bank and the Office for Zero Emissions Vehicle to demonstrate the insurance sector's ability to invest £100 billion of capital in the green infrastructure transition over the next decade.

The Green Transition Funds (GTFs) aim to attract private capital, especially from insurance and pension funds, for critical infrastructure by issuing bonds. Loans to infrastructure developers, secured by assets, serve as bond repayment sources. Initially, a government guarantee, or environmental tax allocation, supports the loans. As performance data improves, public backing becomes unnecessary, creating stable, large-scale green investment opportunities for insurers and pension funds.

Applying the Green Transition Fund (GTF) to the EV charging network could replace public grants with guaranteed loans, saving taxpayers about £13 billion on a £20 billion national infrastructure project. This approach promotes competition, accelerates deployment, and aligns with public policy goals, delivering a sustainable investment opportunity for insurance and pension funds.

Role of Insurance in Preservation of Biodiversity

The insurance industry can play a key role in climate restoration and biodiversity preservation. Coral reef and beach insurance are significant protection measures as reefs provide $36 billion annually in tourism value. These mechanisms can reduce 97% of wave energy and lower storm related property damage. California has issued Forest Restoration Resilient Bonds to finance ecological forestry projects. The savings from reduced fire risk and watershed protection are used to redeem the bond. The Insurance Bureau of Canada have initiatives which suggest that cities at high flooding risk purchase parametric or indemnity insurance for public infrastructure, with a trust fund supporting flood resilience projects. Mangrove forests are vital for coastal protection, reducing flood risk, erosion, and storing carbon. They safeguard over 18 million people and prevent $82 billion in annual flood damage. AXA's 2020 Report outlines insurance products tailored for mangroves, offering quick payouts through parametric covers and later assessed payouts via indemnity cover.

Insurance Linked Securities

Insurance-Linked Securities (ILS) are financial instruments that allow insurance companies to transfer the risks associated with the insurance policies they have underwritten to the capital markets. Catastrophe bonds (CAT bonds) are the most common type of Insurance Linked Securities (ILS) which transfer catastrophe risk to the capital markets. In 2006, the first parametric CAT Bond known as "Cat Mex", was issued by Mexico valued at US$160 million. In the event of a catastrophe which triggers a pay-out, the debtor's obligation to pay interest and return the principal is either deferred or waived. Sponsors of CAT bonds who are the parties seeking catastrophe insurance pay premiums to the bond issuer in exchange for receiving a pay-out if a disaster occurs. CAT bonds are typically short to medium term, high yield instruments with low liquidity and are primarily issued by insurance and reinsurance companies. A CAT bond transaction is typically organized by an issuance group that handles the structuring, underwriting, and marketing of the instruments, along with a risk modelling firm that evaluates the downside risk for investors. The proceeds from the bond sales are placed in a collateral account, where the funds are invested in low-risk securities. By April 2021, outstanding ILS bonds amounted to US$48 billion.

Since 2007, the Caribbean Catastrophe Risk Insurance Facility (CCRIF), the world's first multi-country risk pool, has provided parametric insurance for tropical cyclones, earthquakes, excess rainfall, and the fisheries sector to 23 countries and one electric utility. In 2014, the World Bank introduced its Capital at Risk Notes program, offering risk transfer solutions through the issuance of CAT bonds, with streamlined structuring to reduce clients' transaction costs.

In 2018, Southeast Asian nations created the Southeast Asia Disaster Risk and Insurance Facility, the first regional catastrophe risk facility by ASEAN members. In 2019, Quintana Roo, The Nature Conservancy, and Swiss Re launched parametric insurance to quickly protect coral reefs and beaches along Mexico's Yucatán peninsula.

Derivative Instruments for Sustainable Finance

Derivatives can play a significant role for mobilizing sustainable finance. Agricultural, energy, metals markets, and financial entities use various OTC and exchange-traded climate-related derivatives, including weather derivatives, electricity futures, ESG futures, and carbon derivatives. The Chicago Mercantile Exchange (CME) offers standardized weather futures contracts based on weather indexes for nine U.S. cities, Amsterdam, London, and Tokyo, providing a hedging tool for volumetric risks from adverse weather conditions. In December 2020, CME launched water futures based on the Nasdaq Veles California Water Index, allowing users in the California water market to hedge price risks. The InsuResilience Solutions Fund (ISF), funded by KfW Development Bank, supports climate risk insurance solutions by funding studies and providing advisory services in several countries, including Colombia and Bangladesh.

Insurance Products for Green Assets and Activities

Insurance products for green activities can be categorized into insurance products with preferential insurance premiums based on environmentally related characteristics and insurance products for clean technology and emission reduction activities. The Insurance Information Institute outlines green insurance in three areas: (1)

Motor vehicle insurance, offering discounts for hybrid or alternative energy cars and "Pay-As-You-Drive" options. (2) Business insurance, covering green rebuilding after losses. (3) Home and building insurance, with eco-friendly materials and discounts for LEED-certified properties.

During the G20 Climate Summit in Venice the Net Zero Insurance Alliance (NZIA) was established by eight global reinsurance firms with commitments to underwrite portfolios to net zero greenhouse gas (GHG) emissions by year 2050. Previous initiatives included Asset Manages Initiative, Asset Owner Alliance and Banking Alliance which reflected AuM of approximately US$86.6 trillion. The IAIS issued the Insurance Core Principles (ICPs), a globally accepted framework of principles, statements, standards, and guidance. It aims to promote high, consistent supervisory standards across member jurisdictions, ensuring effective oversight and regulation of the insurance industry worldwide.

Regulatory Framework for Green Insurance

Insurance regulatory frameworks vary by country but ensure policyholder protection and industry stability. Recently, regulators have integrated ESG considerations, requiring insurers to disclose policies and incorporate ESG factors into risk management. To promote ESG policies, insurance regulators are enforcing disclosure requirements. Insurers must report on ESG risks, progress, and how these factors are integrated into investment decisions, aligning with frameworks like the EU's Solvency II and UN's Principles for Responsible Investment (PRI). Regulators are urging insurers to align investment activities with ESG policies, promoting sustainable investments while avoiding those that conflict with ESG objectives, integrating ethics into core strategies. In 2012, the UN Environment Finance Initiative established a framework for the insurance industry to adhere to ESG norms in order to promote sustainable insurance practices.

Regulatory Developments Related to Sustainable Insurance

In 2016, UNDP's Sustainable Insurance Forum (SIF) was established with support from International Association of Insurance Supervisors (IAIS). SIF is a global network of 38 insurance supervisors and regulators which oversees about 92% of the global insurance market. The IAIS has issued the Insurance Core Principles (ICPs), a globally accepted framework comprising Principles, Statements, Standards and Guidance to encourage the maintenance of consistently high supervisory standards in their member jurisdictions. In 2023, SIF established the Capital and Supervisory Frameworks Working Group (CSWG) to examine the incorporation of climate related risks in insurance capital and supervisory frameworks related to Pillars 1 and 2.

In 2021, the Financial Supervisory Commission of China has mandated insurers to assess the impact of climate change in the 2020 Own Risk and Solvency

Assessment (ORSA) supervisory report to identify risk identification of climate change, major risk exposure status, risk assessment methods and response strategy. In the same year, French Prudential Supervision and Resolution Authority published a first assessment of financial risks due to financial risks on account of climate change. In 2018, Instituto per la Vigilanza Sulle Assicurazioni of Italy emphasized the importance of E&S factors in the activities of insurance undertakings. During the period 2020–2021, thematic reviews on natural disaster risk management for non-life insurers were done by Financial Services Agency of Japan and covered key areas such as retention and reinsurance strategies, group reinsurance policies, claim management, protection gaps among SMEs for water related disasters and risk exposure to large natural disasters.

In 2021, Financial Services Agency and Tokyo Stock Exchange published a draft version of the corporate governance code which required companies listed in the prime market including insurance companies to disclose information based on TCFD recommendations based on a "comply or explain" basis.

In 2018, the Netherlands Bank through the Good Practice and Q&A document formulated principles on how insurers should integrate climate risks in the ORSA. In 2022, the Netherlands Bank mandated climate related and environmental risks to become a standard part of proper assessment for Board members of insurers, banks and pension funds. The Monetary Authority of Singapore conducts industry wide stress tests for selected direct insurers which account for 80% of the market. The Monetary Authority of Singapore also introduced proposed guidelines on environmental risk management which outlined guidelines for insurers to incorporate environmental considerations for their strategies and business plans. In 2022, Swiss Financial Market Authority proposed that large insurance firms and groups must disclose their climate related financial risks which are aligned with the recommendations of the Task Force on Climate related Financial Disclosures (TCFD). Prudential regulation authority of UK conducts biennial industry wide insurance stress tests for the UK's largest regulated life and general insurers who account for 70% of the market. In 2017, the National Association of Insurance Commissioners of USA published guidance manual which required insurers to explain how they identify, assess, monitor, prioritize and report all material and relevant risks. In 2020, California Department of Insurance launched the first ever database of green insurance products, featuring over 400 options. These products offer businesses green rebuild coverage, lower premiums for energy-efficient and low-emission buildings and vehicles, and protections for low-income communities and natural ecosystems. New York State Department of Financial Services was the first regulator in the US to establish climate related expectations which urged insurers to incorporate climate risks into their governance framework and risk management practices and business strategies.

According to PwC study[21], climate change will drive demand for property insurance due to increased investments in eco-friendly buildings and growing urban households. Higher premiums are expected in high-risk areas, with some properties

[21] The PwC Point of View "How Climate Change Affects Insurance: A 2050 Perspective" focuses on the socio-economic impacts on insurance products and underwriting.

becoming uninsurable. Rising construction costs, circular economy approaches, and greater government involvement will create new insurance opportunities.

The 2050 trends for energy sector suggest that there would be substantial increase in stranded assets due to transition risks. Product design and climate change liabilities will emerge as a major issue for insurance sector. There would be significant growth opportunities for insurers in terms of new energy suppliers and new markets such as energy storage. For the global food supply sector, agricultural insurance will become more responsive to extreme weather events. Incentives in insurance premiums for sustainable preventive mechanism will be another trend for the global food supply system. In the area of IT & digital systems, the insurance service landscape will become a highly sophisticated digital enabled market place. IT insurance would account for a larger share of the market.

ESG Practices in Insurance Industry

To reduce their environmental impact, insurance companies are minimizing reliance on non-renewable energy by shifting to renewable sources and promoting paperless operations to lower their carbon footprint. Insurance companies, as major investors, are increasingly integrating ESG factors into their decisions, divesting from fossil fuel companies and redirecting investments towards renewable energy to mitigate environmental impact. Insurance companies are integrating environmental risks into underwriting, applying higher premiums to disaster-prone areas. This helps manage risk and encourages environmentally responsible behaviour. Insurance firms promote environmental sustainability by offering products that incentivize eco-friendly practices, like discounts for hybrid or electric vehicles, encouraging policyholders to adopt sustainable actions. Insurance companies are increasing scrutiny of climate-related risks, like hurricanes and floods, and are adjusting underwriting policies and premiums to reflect the higher risk of these events.

Insurance firms are proactively encouraging homeowners to reduce their carbon footprint by offering discounts for eco-friendly measures like solar panel installations and improved insulation. In response to rising climate risks, insurance companies are introducing specialized coverage for events like hurricanes and wildfires, which were previously included in general policies. Many insurance companies are adopting environmental policies to reduce exposure to carbon assets, aligning with the Paris Agreement's climate goals. Insurance companies are reducing investments in carbon-sensitive assets, including those in fossil fuel production and industries with high carbon emissions, to minimize environmental impact.

Emerging pricing trends aim to develop meaningful ESG scores for risk assessment and pricing, especially for carbon-sensitive businesses facing challenges like natural catastrophes and litigation. Different insurance lines encounter unique ESG-related issues, such as property underwriters worrying about physical damage and liability underwriters concerned about lawsuits. Insurers are modernizing by automating underwriting processes and incorporating real-time data for personalized pricing. ESG scoring evaluates a company's long-term risk exposure, guiding underwriters in pricing decisions and promoting environmentally friendly practices through incentives. Enhanced data integration improves risk assessment, allowing underwriters to better evaluate and price risks associated with various businesses.

Dynamic pricing enables insurance adjustments based on changing macroeconomic conditions, consumer preferences, and regulatory requirements. It incorporates ESG factors, allowing for discounts when companies adopt sustainable practices to better match risk profiles.

Insurance reserving is a complex, data-driven process for estimating and establishing reserves to cover future claim payments. It involves analyzing historical claims data and assessing loss development patterns, especially for climate-related incidents like storms and floods. Given the increasing frequency of these events, insurers must adopt robust reserving practices to ensure financial stability and compliance. This specialized aspect of reserving focuses on accurately estimating costs associated with climate events. Actuaries analyze past claims to identify loss development patterns, although volatility in climate events can complicate future cost estimates. Understanding environmental factors will help refine these reserving practices.

Insurance companies face several environmental risk drivers that impact their operations. **Catastrophe risk** has increased due to rising climate-related claims, leading to higher reinsurance costs that reduce profitability and necessitate more capital reserves. **Underwriting risk** arises from unpredictable weather patterns, complicating future claim estimations and prompting insurers to maintain larger capital buffers. Additionally, **investment and market risk** are heightened by investments in non-green assets, which pose significant risks due to unfavorable regulations and market sensitivities. **Operational risk** is a concern for insurers vulnerable to natural disasters, as disruptions can necessitate additional capital. Finally, **credit risk** emerges when reinsurers fail to account for climate risks, potentially leading to financial contagion and requiring upward adjustments in capital reserves.

Sustainable or Green Investment Funds

Achieving net-zero emissions by 2050 will necessitate additional global investments ranging from 0.6% to 1% of annual global GDP over the next two decades, totalling a cumulative $12 trillion to $20 trillion.[22] Investments in sustainable funds can drive capital toward emissions-reducing initiatives. By leveraging proxy voting and shareholder engagement, these funds can influence companies to adopt more sustainable business models and strategies. During the period 2015–2021, the assets under management of global ESG funds increased from euro 0.5 trillion to euro 1.3 trillion. During the period 2015–2020, the number of sustainable investment

[22] IEA 2021; IMF 2021.

funds doubled to reach 3987 with assets under management of over $1.7 trillion. In 2019, net investment flows to these funds amounted to $159 billion. By 2020, the sustainable fund universe consisted of 3435 mutual funds and 552 ETFs, with assets under management (AUM) of $1.56 trillion and $174 billion, respectively. Around two-thirds of sustainable funds, by both number and assets, are equity funds, while the remainder are fixed income and mixed allocation funds. On average, these funds deployed 27% of their assets across eight key SDG sectors such as health, renewable energy and infrastructure. Nearly half of the sustainable funds were launched during the period 2015–2020. Majority of sustainable funds are domiciled in Europe (73%) followed by North America (18%) and regions including developing countries account for less than 10% of domiciled funds.[23]

The total global assets under management in sustainable investment funds amounted to $35.3 trillion in year 2020 registering an increase of 15% compared to year 2018 according to Global Sustainable Investment Alliance report. This represented 36% of all professionally managed assets across the U.S., Canada, Japan, Australasia, and Europe, according to the Global Sustainable Investment Alliance (GSIA). ESG has emerged as a widely accepted investment approach, with over $300 billion invested into sustainable funds as of 2023.[24] In 2020, the total assets under management of sustainable investment funds amounted to $3.6 trillion of which climate-oriented funds accounted for $130 billion.

According to Morningstar, 60% of sustainable funds rank within the top two quartiles of their respective categories based on performance over a five-year period.[25] Over the past 3 years, the MSCI World ESG Leaders Index delivered an average annual return of 8.51%, compared to the MSCI World Index's 7.83% annual return.[26] Over the past decade, companies in the top quintiles of MSCI ESG Ratings within the MSCI ACWI Index have consistently outperformed those in the lowest quintile.[27]

According to the Morgan Stanley Institute for Sustainable Investing's "Sustainable Reality" report, sustainable funds outperformed traditional funds in 2023, achieving median returns of 12.6% compared to 8.6%. This report was based on the performance analysis of approximately 97,000 funds globally during the period Jan 1, 2023 -December 31, 2023. Assets under management rose 15% from 2022 to $3.4 trillion, with sustainable funds now representing 7.2% of global AUM. This study by Morgan Stanley based on Morning star data find that an investment of a hypothetical $100 into a sustainable fund during the year 2018 would

[23] The rise of the sustainable fund market and its role in financing sustainable development, United Nations Conference on Trade and Development, https://unctad.org/system/files/official-document/diae2021d1_en.pdf

[24] Morningstar ESG Investing Trends 2023.

[25] Morningstar, "ESG Funds Recover, but Still Trail Conventional Peers by a Small Margin" Feb. 5, 2024.

[26] Bloomberg.

[27] MSCI, "MSCI ESG Ratings in Global Equity Markets: A Long-Term Performance Review" March 2024. Data from Dec. 31, 2012—Dec. 29, 2023

have been increased by 35% if it had achieved the median return for each of the past 5 years. For traditional funds, the investment would have increased by 25%.

In 2023, 87% of sustainable fund assets under management (AUM) are in Europe, with 10% in the Americas and 3% in other regions. Notably, 42% of sustainable AUM is in funds with a global investment focus. European sustainable funds experienced inflows of $146 billion (5.8%), while North American funds faced $13 billion in outflows (4.4%), primarily due to procedural changes. However, funds investing in the Americas recorded inflows of 6.2%.[28]

A sustainable investment fund pursues both financial returns and sustainability objectives. It employs strategies like negative screening (excluding certain sectors), positive screening (selecting firms meeting sustainability criteria), or impact investing. Funds may focus on specific themes like climate change or broader environmental, social, and governance (ESG) issues. Sustainable investment funds make up only a small portion of the overall investment fund universe. A fund's title and objective description typically indicate whether its focus includes sustainability, environmental concerns, or climate change. IMF study[29] have analysed a sample of over 36,500 active funds at the end of 2020 and classified 4000 of them as sustainable funds. Out of these 4000 funds, 1000 focused on environmental themes and just over 200 had specific focus on climate related themes. According to the IMF study, as of the end of 2020, the shares of equity, fixed-income and allocation funds within the subsample of thematic climate funds were 56%, 21% and 17% respectively. The share of passive funds was higher for funds with a climate focus (about 22%) compared with conventional funds and other sustainable funds (about 13%). The fees of sustainable funds were also slightly higher than those of their conventional peers.

Sustainable and climate-focused investment funds have grown faster than conventional funds in recent years. From 2010–2019, net flows into sustainable funds were similar to conventional funds but surged in 2020 to 5% of assets. Climate-labelled funds saw significant growth, rising 48% in net flows during 2020, surpassing conventional funds since 2017. During this period, net flows into climate-labelled funds increased significantly, consistently exceeding those of conventional funds since 2017. In 2020, these flows surged by an impressive 48% of assets under management over the course of the year.

Conventional funds have increasingly integrated sustainability aspects into their investment processes. The number of asset managers and owners signed onto the Principles for Responsible Investment more than doubled from 1400 in 2015 to over 3000 by 2020. Investment fund labels and sustainable finance classifications are essential for directing capital toward sustainable and climate-focused funds, guiding firm behaviour and helping investors assess transition pathways.

---

[28] Sustainability Reality Report, Morgan Stanley Institute for Sustainable Investing /2024

[29] International Monetary Fund I October 2021, Global Financial Stability Report-Chapter 3 Investment Funds: Fostering the transition to a green economy.

Sustainability funds employ diverse strategies, including exclusionary screening, investee engagement, best-in-class selection, ESG performance integration, thematic investment, or a combination of these. Their sustainability performance can vary significantly. Major fund providers like BlackRock, Amundi, and Robeco have introduced funds specifically focused on the Sustainable Development Goals (SDGs), with some using the SDGs as a framework to assess their portfolio's impact.

A study by the Forum for Sustainable and Responsible Investment in year 2020 suggest that investment companies managed approximately $3.1 trillion in assets with ESG criteria which included both mutual funds and index funds. In 2019, sustainable funds outperformed conventional funds with 66% of them ranking in the top half of their categories and 35% in the top quartile.

The focus of green mutual funds is on companies and projects which promote sustainability initiatives and aim to reduce carbon footprints. Green sector funds invest primarily in specific sectors such as renewable energy, clean technology, sustainable agriculture, green transportation, water and waste management. Socially Responsible Investing (SRI) funds focus on companies which adhere to ethical business practices, prioritize employee welfare and demonstrate commitment towards community development. These funds avoid investments in industries which are harmful to society such as tobacco, firearms and fossil fuels.

Thematic ESG Mutual Funds

Thematic ESG investing has surged in popularity, as investors seek financial returns while supporting sustainability. Thematic-ESG mutual funds target specific sectors, such as clean energy, water conservation, or sustainable agriculture, integrating ESG factors. These funds allow investors to align their portfolios with personal values while tapping into growth opportunities in these sectors. Water Funds are water focused mutual funds which focus on investments in companies dealing with water treatment, infrastructure development and water related technologies. Some of the important water funds include Invesco Water Resources ETF, Invesco S&P Global Water ETF, First Trust Water ETF, Calvert Global Water A(CFWAX) etc. Alternative Energy Funds focus on firms involved in renewable energy generation, energy storage and other clean energy technologies. These funds facilitate the transition to a low carbon economy and focus on the growth potential of the renewable energy sector. Some of the major alternative energy funds include iShares Global Clean Energy ETF(ICLN), Invesco Wilderhill Clean Energy ETF(PBW), First Trust NASDAQ Cln Edge, VanEck Vectors Low Carbon Energy ETF and Invesco Global Clean Energy ETF etc. Clean Tech Funds invest in companies which offer innovative solutions to environmental challenges in sectors such as renewable energy, waste management and sustainable transportation. Clean Energy mutual fund focuses on renewable energy companies and invests in solar, wind and battery technology firms. Some prominent clean tech funds include First Trust Global Wind Energy ETF, First Trust NASDAQ Cln Edge, Tortoise Global Water ESG, iShares

Global Clean Energy ETF (ICLN) and First Trust Global Wind Energy ETF(FAN). Rare Resources Funds focus on companies which are engaged in the extraction, production and recycling of rare resources while giving emphasis on ESG factors related to responsible mining and resource conservation. Important rare resources funds include VanEck Vectors Rare/Strategic Metals ETF, Global X Lithium & Battery Tech ETF (LIT), VanEck Vectors Uranium + Nuclear Energy ETF, iShares Global Clean Energy (ICLN) and First Trust NASDAQ Cln Edge (GRID). Energy Transition Funds invest in companies which are involved in renewable energy and clean technologies. Some of the major energy transition funds include First Trust NASDAQ Cln Edge (GRID), iShares Global Clean Energy ETF(ICLN), Invesco Wilderhill Clean Energy ETF(PBW), First Trust NASDAQ Cln Edge and Invesco Global Clean Energy ETF. Sustainable Housing Fund focusses on companies in the sustainable living sector and invests in businesses which produces energy efficient materials for reducing carbon footprint of residential and commercial buildings.

Fidelity's Thematic Sustainable Investing Funds

Fidelity sustainable funds prioritize ESG factors into their fundamental research and investment disciplines based on environmental, social and governance themes.

Fidelity® Healthy Future Fund (FAPHX) NEW invests in health and wellness companies. Fidelity® Climate Action Fund (FCAEX) invests in companies which mitigates the effects of climate change. Fidelity® Water Sustainability Fund (FLOWX) invests in companies which offers easily accessible water. Fidelity® Environmental Bond Fund (FFEBX) invests in the debt of companies and projects which aims to reduce environmental risk. Fidelity® Women's Leadership Fund (FWOMX) invests in firms which advance women's leadership and development. Fidelity® Environment & Alternative Energy Fund (FSLEX), focusses on alternative and renewable energy, energy efficiency, pollution control, water infrastructure, waste and recycling technologies, or other environmental support services.

Fidelity® Clean Energy ETF (FRNW) is an ETF that invests in companies involved in producing, distributing, or supplying technology and equipment for energy production from solar, wind, hydrogen, and other renewable resources. Fidelity® Women's Leadership ETF† (FDWM) is an actively managed ETF which advances women's leadership.

Source: https://www.fidelity.com/mutual-funds/investing-ideas/sustainable-investing

There are ESG mutual funds which focus on ESG integration, green sectors, SRI and impact investing. BlackRock iShares ESG MSCI USA ETF (ESGU) track the performance of an index composed of US companies with high ESG ratings relative to their sector peers. Parnassus Core Equity Fund (PRBLX) is an actively managed fund which invests in US companies which demonstrate strong ESG performance. Prominent green sector funds include Invesco Solar ETF(TAN) and First Trust Global Wind Energy ETF (FAN). TAN ETF targets global solar energy industry and tracks the performance of the MAC global solar energy index. FAN ETF focusses on global wind energy index comprising firms involved in the wind energy business which includes turbine manufacturers and wind farm operators.

Two examples for Socially Responsible Investing (SRI) Funds are Calvert Equity Fund (CSIEX) and Pax Ellevate Global Women's Leadership Fund (PXWEX). CSIEX is an actively managed fund which invests in high ESG intensity US companies. PXWEX invests in global companies which promote gender equality and empowerment of women for leadership roles. Impact investing funds such as TIAA-CREF Social Choice Bond Fund (TSBRX) invests in fixed income securities in sectors such as affordable housing, renewable energy and community development projects. Community Capital Management CRA Qualified Investment Fund (CRANX) is a fixed income fund which invests primarily in US government backed securities which focus on community development initiatives.

The Parnassus Core Equity Fund (PRBLX) with assets under management of $30.1 billion is the market leader among green mutual funds in terms of assets under management. With a focused portfolio of 40 stocks led by Microsoft and Alphabet, the fund is both a core large cap fund as well as a green mutual fund. Putnam Sustainable Leaders Fund (PNOPX) with assets under management of $6.6 billion with stocks such as Microsoft, Apple and Amazon invest in firms which have shown leadership in key sustainability issues. Fidelity US Sustainability Index Fund (FITLX) with assets under management of $4.2 billion is a sustainability focused mutual fund with diversified portfolio of 285 stocks. The Schwab Ariel ESG ETF invests primarily in exchange-traded equity securities of U.S. companies that have been evaluated based on specific environmental, social, and governance (ESG) criteria. Morningstar Direct tracks nearly 600 ESG-focused mutual funds and exchange-traded funds. The MSCI KLD 400 Social Index fund launched in year 1990 tracks 400 US companies with outstanding ESG ratings and consists of mix of small cap, mid cap and large cap companies.

According to Forbes Advisor, the best ESG ETFs of year 2024 were Vanguard ESG U.S. Stock ETF (ESGV), Pimco Enhanced Short Maturity Active ESG ETF (EMNT), Nuveen ESG Dividend ETF (NUDV), iShares MSCI Global Sustainable Developmental Goals ETF (SDG). The best mutual funds in 2024 consisted of Fidelity US Sustainability Index Fund, Fidelity International Sustainability Index Fund, Calvert US Mid Cap Core Responsible Index Fund and BlackRock Sustainable CoreAlpha Bond Fund. CIBC, the leading diversified North American financial institution pays 5% of the management fees earned by CIBC after payment of trailer fees, as applicable on Series A, F and ETF series of the CIBC sustainable investment strategies to organizations which support climate transition activities.

Some examples for broad based ESG Equity funds include American Century Sustainable Equity Fund, Brown Advisory Sustainable Growth Fund, Walden Midcap Fund Calvert International Equity Fund, Mirova Global Sustainable Equity Fund and Vanguard FTSE Social Index Fund. Examples for broad based ESG fixed income funds include DFA Social Fixed Income Fund, Domini Impact Bond Fund, RBC BlueBay High Yield Bond Fund. Examples for environmentally focussed funds include Calvert Global Water Fund, River bridge Eco Leaders Fund and AllianzGI Water Fund.

The first SRI mutual fund, Pax World Fund was launched in year 1971. Some of the pioneering firms in Socially Responsible Investing (SRI) in the U.S. include notable fund companies such as Impax Asset Management which had acquired Pax World Funds, Calvert Research and Management, Parnassus Investments, Domini Impact Investments, Green Century Capital Management, and Praxis Mutual Funds. Additionally, boutique asset managers like Trillium Asset Management and Boston Trust Walden have also played a key role in advancing SRI.

Morningstar has created tools to help investors and advisors build sustainable portfolios. Beyond the traditional Morningstar Rating, which provides peer comparisons on financial performance, it offers resources like the Morningstar Sustainability Rating, ESG Commitment Level, and the Sustainable-Investing Framework, all designed to support sustainable investment decisions. Sustainable investing aims to achieve competitive financial returns while promoting positive environmental, social, and corporate governance (ESG) outcomes. The Morningstar Sustainable-Investing Framework highlights that sustainable investing is diverse, incorporating various investor motivations and management strategies. Refinitiv Lipper Fund ESG scores evaluate 19,000 portfolios, representing $15.7 trillion in assets. These scores assess performance, commitment, and effectiveness across 10 areas, including carbon emissions and human rights, spanning the environmental, social, and governance (ESG) pillars.

Policy makers must initiate steps to strengthen global climate information systems including data, disclosures and sustainable finance classifications to prevent greenwashing. Climate oriented investments ought to be complemented with carbon tax and steps must be taken to ensure an orderly transition by implementing climate policy, scenario analysis and stress testing to mitigate financial stability risks.

Pension Funds and Sustainable Investments

By the end of 2020, global asset owners, including pension funds, sovereign wealth funds, insurers, endowments, and foundations, controlled approximately USD 154 trillion. These entities typically operate with long-term or even indefinite time horizons, with over 70% of their assets managed through the global asset management industry.

A study by the Thinking Ahead Institute (2020) identifies pension funds as the largest asset-owning group, holding 37% of total assets, or USD 57 trillion. The United States dominates the pension market with approximately USD 32.5 trillion, followed by Japan at USD 3.6 trillion and the UK at USD 3.5 trillion.

Governments have pledged over USD 4 trillion toward environmental initiatives, exceeding historical spending on major projects. Global pension assets, growing faster than the economy, rose 15% in 2019 and 11% in 2020. Shifts favour global, alternative investments, supporting large-scale ESG efforts. There are many reasons for pension funds attraction towards ESG investments. Pension funds incorporate ESG for better risk management and opportunity identification, aligning with fiduciary duty. Strong ESG stock performance, partly due to fossil fuel declines, has attracted investors, positioning ESG stocks for sustained long-term growth. Companies focusing on long-term, stakeholder-driven approaches often outperform peers. Reputational concerns and legal risks drive pension funds' focus on ESG. The Rest pension fund case involving legal issues in Australia highlights climate change as a critical financial risk, prompting proactive ESG actions. Rising regulatory pressure drives pension funds to integrate ESG, with 95% of ESG regulations developed since 2000. However, global ESG policy remains fragmented and coordinated action is often challenging.

The UN sponsored Net-Zero Asset Owner Alliance have commitments to transit its investment portfolios to net zero greenhouse gas emissions by 2050. Sixteen of the current 35 Net Zero Alliance members are pension funds from US, UK, Sweden, Denmark, France and Australia.

Pension funds have a significant role to play in green growth initiatives. Green projects with focus on sustainable energy sources and clean technology which include multiple technologies require different types of financing vehicles. Pension funds are interested in lower risk investments which offer a steady, inflation adjusted income stream. In this context, green bonds are gaining traction as an asset class for institutional investors like pension funds. To boost pension funds' green investments, returns must be competitive. Attracting funds beyond the SRI niche requires financial viability alongside environmental benefits.

Achieving a low-carbon economy requires redirecting capital from fossil fuels to clean technology and infrastructure, supported by policies that incentivize green investments. Green growth aims to foster economic development while minimizing environmental harm, enhancing resource productivity, and creating sustainable economic opportunities.

Increasing investments in low-carbon energy by 17% by 2050 could generate an estimated USD 112 trillion in fuel savings. Climate change adaptation and mitigation from now until 2030 will require substantial financing, with actual needs varying based on mitigation goals, adaptation efforts, and the implementation of effective price signals or regulations.

The UN estimates an annual USD 1.6 trillion investment is needed for a global energy shift that meets emissions targets and harmonizes energy use across nations. Additionally, the IEA projects USD 9.3 trillion in power sector decarbonization by 2050, with fossil fuel and nuclear infrastructure replacement costs estimated at USD 15–20 trillion. Pension funds, with USD 28 trillion in OECD assets and annual contributions of 850 billion can significantly finance green growth, especially if emerging markets are included.

Pension funds need long-term, inflation-protected, stable-yield assets with low portfolio correlation, often due to conservative investment rules. To attract these funds to green projects, tailored financing instruments meeting these conservative criteria are essential. Pension funds favour lower-risk, inflation-adjusted investments like deployable renewables, aligning with conservative regulations. Pension funds invest minimally in infrastructure and private equity, typically under 1% in most countries, focusing instead on traditional assets like equities and bonds due to familiarity and comfort. To boost green investments, governments should encourage greater pension fund allocation to infrastructure and private equity instruments.

The Japanese Government Pension Investment Fund, the world's largest pension fund exemplifies how universal owners can positively impact the financial system by creating ESG indices, promoting corporate transparency, and requiring ESG integration from asset managers. New Zealand based pension fund-Super Fund have US$40 billion under management. Super Fund had signed the Paris Pledge for Action in year 2015 as part of its commitment to emission reduction target. The Super Fund have embedded climate change into its investment strategies and ownership practices.

The Institutional Investors Group on Climate Change (IIGCC) is a European investor forum with 72 members including pension funds representing €6 trillion in assets. The Investor Network on Climate Risk (INCR), a U.S.-based group with nearly 100 members and over $9.5 trillion in assets, includes major institutions like CalPERS, CalSTRS, US State Retirement boards, Deutsche Asset Management BlackRock and Prudential Asset Management. INCR, part of Ceres, addresses climate risks and opportunities, offering specialized working groups on ESG integration in fixed income investments. The P8 Group, comprising 12 top global pension funds manages $3 trillion, includes members from the U.S., Europe, Asia, and Australia, like the UK's Universities Superannuation Scheme and CalPERS. Focused on climate and sustainable growth in developing nations, this group also focus on favourable investment regulations and financial conditions.

The largest pension fund of Denmark, ATP Pension Fund has long invested in renewable energy infrastructure, including solar, wind, and biofuels, committing DK 600 million to renewables and over DK 2 billion in clean energy equities. In 2009, ATP earmarked €1 billion to a new climate change fund for investing in emerging economies.

The California State Teachers' Retirement System (CalSTRS) was the first North American pension fund to incorporate ESG risk analysis into its investment policies. CalSTRS Global Equity investments have a sustainable manager portfolio and is one of the CalSTRS best performing equity portfolios. CalSTRS Private Equity Clean Technology and Energy Program is a diversified portfolio of venture and buyout investments across the clean technology and clean energy.

CalSTRS' Real Estate unit launched a Sustainable Returns Program to enhance risk-adjusted returns by integrating sustainability in portfolio planning and investment decisions, with resource-use benchmarks. The Fixed Income Green Program screens ESG risks and opportunities, adopting a Green & Sustainable Benchmark and supporting green bonds.

The Californian Public Employees' Retirement System (CalPERS), the largest pension fund in the United States have made commitments which amount to USD 500 million to external managers in its Global Equity asset class which restrict companies with a negative environmental footprint. CalPERS has committed over $1.5 billion to its Private Equity Environmental Technology Program and actively promotes environmental risk reporting in its interactions with federal regulators and portfolio companies. CalPERS have invested $500 million in a strategy targeting global public companies focused on environmental improvement and climate change mitigation, modelled after HSBC's Climate Change Benchmark Index, with companies deriving significant revenue from low-carbon energy and related sectors. CalPERS Board invests in stock portfolios which uses environmental screens. CalPERS' Environmental Investment Initiatives aim for positive financial returns while promoting energy savings, sustainable growth, and sound environmental practices. Key programs include the AIM Environmental Technology Program, which invests in efficient, less-polluting technologies, and a Corporate Governance Environmental Strategy focused on enhancing transparency and disclosure of corporate environmental impacts.

Green bonds are crafted to attract capital from institutional investors with sustainable and responsible investment (SRI) mandates, including the Danish pension fund ATP, the UN Joint Staff Pension Fund, and the Norwegian Global Fund, while also serving as a tool for governments to fund climate change mitigation efforts.

The Caisse des Dépôts, a French public investment group, has partnered with three other European public financial institutions—Cassa Depositi e Prestiti, KfW Bankengruppe, and the European Investment Bank—to create the "Long-term Investors Club." This alliance collaborates with financial institutions from Europe, Asia, and the Gulf, collectively managing assets of USD 3 trillion. The club focuses on long-term investment, pooling resources from institutions with minimal short- to medium-term liabilities, like public financial entities, sovereign funds, and select pension and insurance funds. Their goal is to address significant long-term challenges, such as securing the estimated USD 2 trillion needed for infrastructure investment in transport, energy, water, and telecom sectors by 2020–2030.

Nikko Asset Management has introduced two World Bank Green Funds, allowing up to 100% of assets to be invested in World Bank Green Bonds. Most of Nikko's clients are in the Japanese retail market. Additionally, Nikko is preparing to launch a World Bank Green Bonds fund aimed at institutional investors, including pension funds in Europe and the Middle East.

Australia, the UK, and the US hold over half of the world's private retirement assets, largely managed by a few dominant fund management and consulting firms. In the US, the top ten consulting firms manage 80% of institutional, tax-exempt assets, while in the UK and Australia, a few firms also hold substantial market shares. Consequently, these firms have considerable influence over the integration of sustainability practices within private retirement systems. Investment consultants play a crucial role in embedding sustainability in retirement plans by advising on funding, asset allocation, and training sponsors on investment trends. However, limited incentives and regulatory cost controls have hindered broader adoption of sustainable practices, posing a structural challenge to long-term system sustainability. By 2020, US pension funds managed US$6.2 trillion of total assets which incorporated ESG principles.

Countries with strong institutional ownership, like the US, UK, Canada, and the Netherlands, lead in ESG investing. Nations with less institutional ownership, such as France, Germany, Japan, and Sweden, also contribute but to a lesser extent.

The world's largest pension fund Government Pension Investment Fund (GPIF) of Japan with US$1.4 trillion in assets have incorporated sustainable investment practices.

Sustainable Finance in Energy Sector

Globally the average annual investment in energy is estimated to be around US$413 billion. It is estimated that developing countries require an estimated annual investment in electricity of US$165 billion through the year 2010 which would increase by about 3% per year through 2030. Civil society advocates are pushing IFIs to adopt strict environmental and social policies, shifting energy financing from fossil fuels to renewables to prevent environmental harm and promote equitable benefits. Many IFI-supported energy projects face opposition from civil society, citing high costs and insufficient local benefits. Advocacy has led to stricter environmental and social standards, as seen with the Baku-Tbilisi-Ceyhan and Chad-Cameroon pipelines. Some projects, like the Camisea pipeline and China's Three Gorges Dam, lost funding due to these concerns, while others, such as Turkey's Ilisu dam, were delayed or cancelled.

During the period 1992–2004, the World Bank Group had financed approximately US$28 billion towards fossil fuel projects. These projects have resulted in 43.3 billion tons of lifetime carbon emissions. According to the UNCTAD's World Investment Report 2021, there is an SDG financing gap of about US$2.5 trillion dollars per year. By 2020, green bond issuance had exceeded US$1 trillion. Most of the sources of funds in this category were issued by the banking sector and were deployed for renewable energy projects at the global level.

According to Bloomberg NEF (2021), the annual investment in energy sector is estimated to be between $3.1 trillion and $5.8 trillion on average over the next three decades. In developing world, Asia requires investment of $26 trillion between 2016 and 2030 for adequate response to climate change.

According to the International Energy Agency's 2018 World Energy Investment report, global energy investment in 2017 reached USD 1.8 trillion, marking a 2% decline from the previous year. Of this total, over USD 750 billion was allocated to the electricity sector, while USD 715 billion was invested in oil and gas supply worldwide.

New financing methods like green bonds and green banks support clean energy by offering favourable credit, aggregating small projects, and providing long-term capital post-construction. Fossil fuels still dominate energy investment, posing challenges in shifting funding toward renewable energy (RE). Due to Basel capital requirements, banks view renewable energy projects as high-risk and avoid financing them. Furthermore, banks rely on short- to medium-term deposits, while renewable energy projects need long-term funding, causing a maturity mismatch. Alternative financing channels are essential to bridge this gap. Insurance firms and pension funds hold long term financial resources for green infrastructure investment. Institutional investors are the largest suppliers of capital to listed firms and manages $100 trillion assets in OECD countries.

By 2017, 40 countries had a carbon pricing system in place. Community-based funds like the Hometown Investment Trust (HIT) Fund support local green projects by connecting investors to nearby solar and wind initiatives. In Japan, Hometown Investment Trusts (HITs) fund wind and solar power projects by enabling individuals to invest small amounts (USD 100–5000) in green energy. Internet marketing plays a key role by promoting these projects online, allowing broad participation. Local banks also leverage HIT fund information for green investments.

Hometown Investment Trust (HIT) funds, originating in Japan, have expanded to Cambodia, Vietnam, and Peru, with interest from Thailand, Malaysia, and Mongolia. In many developing countries, limited venture capital and bank-dominated financial systems make HIT funds and internet-based financing vital for supporting high-risk sectors. The Hokkaido Green Fund, a community-based green finance initiative in Japan, was founded in 2000 to fund wind power projects. With only 20% bank funding, it relies on individual investors for 80% of funding. Community wind power firms sell electricity at a 5% premium to support environmental goals, with over 19 projects launched. Local governments in Japan have also supported solar projects by seeding community funds to attract private investment.

Clean Energy Initiatives in USA[30]

In 2023, the U.S. added a record 42GW of new renewable capacity in solar sector. In power sector, renewables accounted for 23% of total US power generation in year 2023. In the same year, zero carbon power comprising renewables generation plus nuclear power accounted for all time high of 41.1% of all output. In 2023, hydrogen project pipelines totalling 10.4 million metric tons per year were announced. In 2023, 437 MW of hydrogen producing electrolysers were shipped to USA. The US is the global leader on carbon capture and storage (CCS) with 23 million metric tons per annum (Mtpa) of operational capacity. By 2023, 17 natural gas utility companies have regulatory approval to sell renewable natural gas to customers using a special tariff mechanism. In the year 2023, US had emitted 6229 million metric tons of carbon dioxide equivalent of greenhouse gases as per BNEF estimates. In 2023, the US invested $303.3 billion in energy transition financing for clean energy technologies which included renewables, electric vehicles and power grid investment. About 1.46 million electric vehicles were sold in US in year 2023. The total US

[30] ©BloombergNEF L.P. 2024. Developed in partnership with the Business Council for Sustainable Energy.

renewable energy capacity stands at 425 GW. The sustainable debt issuance in the US amounted to $147 billion in year 2023.

The Asian Development Bank supports green finance projects, including solar parks, waste-to-energy, green bonds, and ASEAN initiatives. In Central Asia, including Kazakhstan, Turkmenistan, Uzbekistan, Kyrgyz Republic, and Tajikistan, green finance projects funded by the Green Climate Fund, Global Environment Facility, Clean Development Mechanism, and domestic investors focus on energy transformation, hydropower, agriculture, water management, and hydro-meteorological systems like flood warning. Approximately USD 37 billion was invested in the region as of 2020. Some of the major projects financed by the Asian Development Bank under the green finance schemes are initiatives such as 100 MW(e) Cambodia Solar Park Project of 2019 (USD 26.7 million total investment), Waste to Energy Project of Greater Male (USD 151.13 million total investment), investments in Green, Sustainability and Social Bonds issued by Georgia (USD 20 million), Thailand (more than USD 1.67 billion) etc.

For achieving net zero emissions by the year 2050, clean energy investment requirements are estimated to about US$4 trillion by the year 2030. China is the world's largest emitter of greenhouse gases and is actively involved in the development of sustainable energy utilities. The Chinese government has promulgated and introduced policies such as the Renewable Energy law of China, China's Energy Development in a new Era and the 14th Five-year plan for Renewable Energy Development in order to promote sustainable energy utilities. China had announced its "carbon peak" and "carbon neutrality" (dual carbon) targets in the year 2020. As per the National Bureau of Statistics, the renewable energy generation accounted for approximately 32% of the electricity consumption in China. The dual carbon targets aim to achieve the proportion of non-fossil energy consumption in the total energy consumption to be around 25% by the year 2030. By 2030, the entire installed capacity of wind and solar energy is expected to surpass more than 1.2 billion kilowatts in China.

Financial instruments are essential to overcoming barriers to sustainable energy investments by promoting efficiency, reducing fossil fuel reliance, and mitigating climate change. The IDB employs tools like concessional loans, green bonds, and Energy Savings Insurance (ESI) to drive private investment, strengthen institutions, and enhance regulatory frameworks.

The ESI program, operational from 2016 to 2022, addressed investment risks through standard contracts, energy savings insurance, savings validation by independent entities, and project financing via partner financial institutions. It fosters confidence by ensuring energy savings or generation commitments. Implemented in countries like Argentina, Brazil, Chile, and Colombia, the ESI combines loans with risk mitigation measures to develop bankable projects. Variants, like Mexico's Clean Technology Fund-backed guarantee, cater to specific needs. These initiatives demonstrate a collaborative approach involving regional banks and IDB assistance, enabling renewable energy adoption and energy efficiency across sectors.

Promoting renewable energy and sustainable infrastructure requires financial and non-financial mechanisms to overcome barriers for solar, wind, biogas, geothermal, and biomass projects. The Inter-American Development Bank (IDB) focuses on innovative tools like concessional funds and risk mitigation strategies to advance energy efficiency and renewable solutions. In transport, Latin America's sector accounts for 34% of GHG emissions. Investments in hybrid and electric mobility reduce emissions, improve air quality, and lower health risks in urban areas. Financial interventions include risk mitigation for investors, concession contract analysis, and capacity-building for sustainable transport. Energy storage, vital for renewable expansion and electrification, relies on falling battery costs. The IDB promotes hybrid solar/wind systems and storage solutions, addressing regulatory and scaling challenges.

In 2023, Deutsche Bank had raised USD 670 million for a loan facility for Plus Power to construct three fully merchant, utility scale battery energy storage projects in Texas with 700 MW in capacity. Société Générale acted as the lead arranger and hedge provider for a $1.2 billion green loan to ReNew Power, a major renewable energy developer in India. The loan will fund the construction of 900 MW of wind, 400 MW of solar, and a 100 MWh battery storage system and marked one of India's first utility-scale projects combining wind, solar, and battery technologies for continuous power supply.

In 2021, Standard Chartered financed a 145 MW floating solar power plant on the Cirata reservoir in West Java with a $112 million, 16-year project finance facility. It was Indonesia's first floating solar project and largest in Southeast Asia. The project was expected to power 50,000 homes, cut 214,000 tons of CO_2 annually, and create 800 jobs.

In March 2023, Mizuho Bank invested $5 million in MCi Carbon, an Australian clean-tech firm using Carbon Capture and Utilization (CCU) to transform industrial CO_2 emissions into valuable materials. This aligns with Mizuho's plan to invest ¥50 billion in early-stage sustainability technologies over the next decade.

In September 2023, H2 Green Steel secured €1.5 billion in equity for Europe's first green steel plant, raising over €1.8 billion since 2021. Its hydrogen-powered Boden facility aims to cut CO_2 emissions by 95%, producing the world's greenest steel. Morgan Stanley advised and supports its $750 billion low-carbon pledge.

Achieving net-zero greenhouse gas emissions by 2050 will demand annual global energy sector investments of $5 trillion to over $7 trillion. However, current yearly investments fall short, totalling less than $2 trillion.

Global investment in low-carbon energy technologies is accelerating, driven by rapidly falling costs. However, achieving net-zero emissions by 2050 will require a significant scale-up, with annual clean energy investments needing to surpass $4 trillion by 2030—more than triple current levels.

The GCC countries experience some of the highest levels of solar exposure globally. A Strategy& analysis indicates that solar power plants in the region can achieve between 1750 and 1930 hours of full-load operation annually. The cost of producing solar, wind and green hydrogen in the GCC region is about one-third that of the global average. The global supply and demand analysis suggest that exporting countries can potentially capture a market of approximately 200 million tons of green hydrogen by 2050 which is worth $300 billion yearly. Transport sector also holds immense potential as GCC governments can facilitate development of smart charging infrastructure for electric vehicles. Smart charging infrastructure can accelerate EV adoption.

Sustainable Energy Initiatives

The Sustainable Energy Initiative (SEI) by the European Bank for Reconstruction and Development. (EBRD) aims to enhance energy efficiency and foster the use of small-scale renewable energy through its Sustainable Energy Financing Facilities (SEFFs). SEFFs provide credit lines to local financial institutions, which on-lend funds to small and medium enterprises, corporate and residential borrowers, and renewable energy developers. These loans support energy-saving measures, equipment upgrades, and renewable energy installations, with financing typically ranging from a few thousand to several million euros. Each SEFF includes a Project Implementation Team of local and international experts offering training, marketing, technical advice, and support for environmental standards. They assist borrowers in identifying energy-saving opportunities, improving project designs, and adopting high-performance technologies. The EBRD also focuses on climate change adaptation, integrating climate risk assessments into investments. This includes addressing risks such as resource scarcity, extreme weather, and aging infrastructure, particularly in vulnerable regions. The bank supports clients in creating resilience strategies and investing in technologies that mitigate long-term risks.

SEI projects span diverse sectors, including agribusiness, construction, and manufacturing. They emphasize resource efficiency, such as on-site energy generation, waste recovery, and process optimization. By fostering energy efficiency and climate resilience, SEI helps businesses reduce costs, enhance competitiveness, and adapt to evolving environmental conditions.

Energy Finance

To achieve net zero emissions by the year 2050, the annual clean energy investment worldwide is required to be tripled to around $4 trillion by the year 2030. UNEP leverages partnerships and innovative finance tools to drive investment in low-carbon development and sustainable energy. It engages governments, private sectors, and financial institutions to mobilize funding, reduce risks, and accelerate climate resilience, renewable energy adoption, and sustainable resource management, supporting nations in achieving their low-carbon development goals.

UNEP's Energy Finance Work focuses on promoting clean energy through innovative financing, technical assistance, capacity building, and knowledge sharing. By leveraging tools like credit guarantees and interest rate subsidies, UNEP de-risks investments and fosters adoption of sustainable energy technologies. It supports project development, conducts feasibility studies, and builds local capacity through training and partnerships. UNEP also raises awareness of clean energy's fiscal and environmental benefits via communication platforms and outreach strategies. Active in over 50 countries, UNEP has mobilized over $6 billion in clean energy investments, showcasing the financial viability and energy-saving potential of sustainable technologies worldwide.

Finance plays a pivotal role in combating climate change, requiring an estimated $200 trillion to achieve net-zero emissions by 2050. Banks are central to this transition, influencing capital allocation and driving decarbonization. They fund renewable energy projects, offer green loans, and implement sustainability-linked financing to incentivize emissions reduction. Voluntary frameworks, such as Green Loan Principles, guide these efforts, though concerns persist over the "green" credibility of some projects.

Banks are also shifting strategies, reducing fossil fuel financing, and fostering corporate transitions through sustainability-linked loans and partnerships. Emerging areas like trade finance, leveraged finance, and blended finance further contribute to climate goals, though challenges in adoption and transparency remain. Initiatives like the Just Energy Transition Partnerships highlight blended finance's growing role, leveraging public and private funds for clean energy in developing countries.

As climate pressures intensify, banks are increasingly held accountable for their impact, with regulators and stakeholders demanding robust transition strategies and expanded efforts in clean energy financing. Banks' evolving engagement reflects their critical role in advancing global decarbonization and sustainability goals.

India's sustainable energy market, valued at nearly $4 billion, offers significant financing potential, including $3 billion for industrial renewable energy and $1 billion for energy access. Focusing on rooftop solar in commercial and industrial segments, channelling impact capital through tailored financial instruments can accelerate investments, provided standardized impact measures are ensured.

Sustainable Energy Bonds (SEBs) are Non-Convertible Debentures (NCDs) designed for impact investors to finance sustainable energy projects while tracking investment impact. SEBs can be structured as domestic or foreign issuances. Domestic issuances allow direct investor participation without an SPV, eliminating currency risks, while foreign issuances involve SPVs pooling impact investors internationally.

SEBs offer impact investors financial returns while enabling enhanced measurement of investment impact in sustainable energy. A pilot SEB issuance of $5 million for the rooftop solar sector could contribute 6.2 MW of renewable energy capacity, create approximately 100 jobs, and reduce CO_2 emissions by 9638 tonnes annually. cKers Finance projects that SEBs have the potential to mobilize $3 billion for decentralized renewable energy and energy efficiency in industrial segments, along with $1 billion for the energy access sector.

Green Finance in Materials and Building Sector

The Paris Agreement, adopted on December 12, 2015, replaced the Kyoto Protocol. Under this accord, 196 parties committed to limiting global temperature increases to well below 2 °C, striving to cap the rise at 1.5 °C above pre-industrial levels.

Real estate represents the major asset class which accounts for two -thirds of global real assets. This built environment accounts for 37% of energy related emissions and generates approximately 100 billion tonnes of construction, renovation and demolition waste every year. IFC estimates that buildings contribute 40% of CO_2 emissions, over 50% of electricity use, 35% of waste production, and serve as workplaces for 75% of the global workforce. Steel and cement production, essential yet carbon-intensive materials, contribute 20% of building emissions, generating over 4.9 billion tonnes of CO_2 annually due to raw materials and energy demands according to International Energy Agency statistics. By 2050, the United Nations projects that over 80% of the global population will reside in cities, doubling the demand for building materials. Real estate asset class accounts for 10% of global GDP and is at risk from both physical and transition risks. Climate change effects could potentially impact residential assets by USD 16 trillion and commercial assets by USD 5 trillion.[31]

Construction value chains account for about 40% of energy and industrial-related CO_2 emissions globally. Building operations account for 80% of lifecycle energy use, offering Facility Managers and IFM providers a key opportunity to drive sustainability through efficient asset management.

Green real estate investment secures financing for environmentally friendly properties, emphasizing energy efficiency, water conservation, and sustainable materials to reduce environmental impact. Approximately 50% of the buildings which would exist in year 2060 have not yet been constructed in emerging markets. IFC have estimated that approximately $3.5 trillion would be required to decarbonise the building sector of which $1.5 trillion alone is required in emerging markets. In growing markets, it is cheaper and easier to decarbonize the new construction than to renovate old buildings. Green building materials emphasize sustainability by reducing emissions across their lifecycle. Innovations like hydrogen-powered processes and carbon capture aid production, but supply chain emissions from raw materials remain challenging to manage and mitigate.

Sustainable building certifications—also known as green building rating tools—are used to assess and recognise buildings which meet certain sustainability requirements or standards. Green building rating tools assess and verify a building's sustainability across its lifecycle, rating performance in climate action, resource efficiency, resilience, biodiversity, health, and social impacts. There exist a number of green building standards, such as LEED (Leadership in Energy and Environmental Design) and BREEAM (Building Research Establishment Environmental

[31] Muldoon-Smith & Greenhalgh, 2019. Suspect foundations: Developing an understanding of climate-related stranded assets in the global real estate sector

Assessment Method), Green Star and Singapore's Building and Construction Authority (BCA) Green Mark.

The World Green Building Council (WorldGBC) is a leading global network driving sustainable, decarbonized built environments. Its Europe Regional Network (ERN) includes over 20 national Green Building Councils, 8 regional partners, and nearly 5000 members from both EU and non-EU countries. Green Building Councils in 10 European countries have published National Decarbonisation Roadmaps to guide the transition of the sector. The World Green Building Council (WorldGBC) run certification schemes are an established, de facto gold standard in the real estate market.

Estimates[32] suggest that buildings in Europe are liable for 40% of energy consumption and 36% of GHG emissions due to usage, construction, renovation and demolition. In France, building operations contribute approximately 45% of the final energy consumed and account for 20% of total GHG emissions.[33]

Europe's gas and oil crisis has sharply increased housing costs, disproportionately impacting vulnerable households. Heating consumes two-thirds of household energy, with one-third relying on natural gas. In 2020, 8% of the EU population struggled to heat their homes, and gas inflation rose by 40% in 2022 before moderating to 25%.

The Singapore Green Building Masterplan have ambitious targets to green about 80% of Singapore's buildings and push boundaries on the best in class energy efficiency performance of buildings. Under the Singapore Green Building Product (SGBP) certification scheme, steel and ready-mixed concrete products are now evaluated based on GWP reported in accepted EPDs for certification.

Progress in low-emission materials is slow due to challenges like high-temperature processes in cement and fossil fuel reliance in steel. Innovations like room-temperature electrolysis and hydrogen-based steelmaking show promise but require significant investment, infrastructure, and renewable energy. Climate tech funding, addressing 34% of global emissions, supports scaling these transformative technologies.

Characteristics of Green Buildings

Green buildings typically have features such as energy efficient lighting and appliances, water saving fixtures and recycled materials. Green buildings have lower operating costs and higher occupancy rates. Green buildings command higher rental rates and resale prices compared to conventional buildings. Green buildings often have higher upfront costs than conventional building on account of use of more expensive materials and technologies. Green Building Councils (GBCs) catalyses sustainable finance at local, regional and global level. The European Union's

[32] European Commission, 2020.

[33] Ministère de la transition écologique, 2022.

Taxonomy Working Group have developed the sustainability criteria for the built environment and supports the implementation of the EU Taxonomy.

Innovations in Green Building Finance

Financial intermediaries can drive the green transition by offering green mortgages, construction loans, and sustainability-linked financing for eco-friendly buildings, alongside transition finance for emissions-intensive sectors. Regulatory incentives and product innovation enable access to capital markets through green bond issuances, promoting sustainable practices and supporting the shift toward greener economies.

A green mortgage loan offers favourable terms for financing energy-efficient construction or renovations, repayable through property sale, promoting sustainable building practices and eco-friendly homes. Blockchain technology offers a secure, transparent platform, revolutionizing green building project financing by efficiently tracking and managing investments to promote sustainability and accountability. Globally, governments offer support for green building finance through initiatives such as tax incentives, grants and subsidies. Taxonomies and certifications are major elements which are central to the performance of transition based financial intermediaries. International Finance Corporation (IFC)'s EDGE is a certification based free tool employed across 100 different countries and facilitated over 80 billion of investment worldwide. Green building rating tools are used to align with performance improvement thresholds in taxonomies. Malaysia's Green Building Index (GBI), where an asset attaining greater than 30% improvement in its Building Energy Index (BEI) target may be eligible for a transition loan under the Singapore-Asia Taxonomy.

Materiality

Single materiality focuses on how ESG issues impact investment performance, assessing risks like rising sea levels, emissions regulations, or supply chain practices, and opportunities from pollution-reduction technologies. Double materiality extends single materiality by assessing a firm's impact on ESG issues, considering its effects on people, society, and the environment alongside financial risks and opportunities. The distinction between single and double materiality is vital for green buildings, as they aim to reduce environmental and social impacts beyond financial risks or opportunities. LEED's system goals reflect a holistic approach to materiality, prioritizing climate action, health, resources, and biodiversity. Rooted in double materiality, green building emphasizes benefits to developers, society, and the environment. Understanding materiality helps professionals engage in ESG discussions and advocate effectively for sustainable building practices.

Green Legislations Related to Buildings in Europe

As of 2024, EU firms have to report on their environmental and social impacts under the Corporate Sustainability Reporting Directive (CSRD) or the Sustainable Financial Disclosure Regulations (SFDR) for real estate investors. The Climate Related Financial Disclosures had already come into effect for UK companies. The Energy Performance of Buildings Directive (EPBD), a key non-financial legislation, is under review to align with the EU Green Deal and Fit for 55 packages. Proposed revisions include: (a) Minimum Energy Performance Standards (MEPS): Extend to existing buildings, mandating improved energy ratings. (b) Zero Emission Buildings (ZEB): Require all new buildings to meet ZEB standards by 2030 (2027 for public buildings). (c) Whole Life Carbon (WLC) Reporting: Mandate Global Warming Potential disclosure for new buildings from 2030, with earlier reporting for large buildings by 2027. The EU aims to harmonize Energy Performance Certificates (EPCs) by 2025, rescaling them for a zero-emission building stock by 2050, with new mandatory indicators for energy use. Building Renovation Passports, detailing renovation plans, must be introduced by 2025. Leading countries like Denmark and Sweden are advancing embodied carbon reporting and GHG limits for new buildings, paving the way for whole life carbon regulations.

Sustainable Built Environment Strategy

A strong decarbonization strategy is key to sustainability, focusing on green materials, waste reduction, and strategic design flexibility. A UK high-speed rail project aims to halve embodied emissions by 2030 through green materials, recycled content, and energy-efficient construction. Research suggests flexibility enhances sustainability, value, and project longevity. Effective planning involves understanding supply chains, balancing economic and environmental factors, and securing leadership buy-in, especially from finance directors. Continuous improvement, accountability, and new technologies like AI-powered digital twins are crucial for optimizing sustainability and accelerating green material development, ensuring projects meet both environmental and cost goals throughout their lifecycle.

Assessing green materials is vital for decarbonization, involving certification, feasibility evaluation, and comparison of costs and benefits. Project owners must consider quality, availability, embodied emissions, and cost implications, including initial investment, maintenance, and long-term sustainability. Tools like Pathways to Paris help compare costs and emissions, providing a comprehensive life cycle view for better decision-making. Pathways to Paris is a collaborative project between WWF Germany and PwC Germany, funded by the German Federal Ministry for Economic Affairs and Climate Action to create a range of comparative, territory-specific scenarios of cost versus emissions for steel and cement, aligned with the Paris Agreement's goal to limit global warming to below 2 degrees Celsius. This comparative approach examines the entire material life cycle, considering emissions from extraction, production, transportation, construction, and disposal.

Under science-based targets, companies should decarbonize first, offsetting only unavoidable emissions. Leaders should assess trade-offs, identify green material abatement costs, plan long-term sourcing, and leverage data to select low-impact materials, aligning with sustainability goals and future regulations to reduce costs and maximize environmental benefits in building projects.

A sustainable procurement strategy involves selecting suppliers committed to sustainability, fostering innovation, and promoting green materials. This includes setting performance indicators and incorporating design and circular economy principles, like recycled aggregates in concrete. Collaborative partnerships, such as those in the automotive sector, drive innovation and long-term green material adoption. Challenges in supply availability and supplier mindset shifts must be addressed. Leaders should seek joint innovation opportunities, cost-effective sourcing, and integrate sustainability metrics into supplier evaluations. Long-term alliances and shared goals can drive efficiency and enhance environmental performance, advancing the transition to sustainable procurement practices across industries.

The delivery phase focuses on quality control, monitoring green materials, and adaptability. Key actions include collaborating with partners, embracing digitization, prioritizing training, and communicating results for successful sustainable procurement. Sustainability continues after project completion through documenting lessons, fostering a learning culture, investing in R&D, scaling operations, and acting early to drive industry-wide transformation.

WorldGBC's Advancing Net Zero program aims for full decarbonization of the building and construction sector by 2050. Collaborating with 34 Green Building Councils and 170 signatories, including major financial institutions, it supports zero-carbon building initiatives across 20,000 assets, addressing 7.3 million tonnes of CO_2 emissions. The Net Zero carbon buildings commitment aims that by 2030, the existing buildings reduce energy use, eliminate emissions from energy and refrigerants and phase out fossil fuels. Setting energy and emissions pathways faces challenges due to assumptions and stakeholder divergence. Tools like Carbon Risk Real Estate Monitor (CRREM) help mitigate transition risks and prevent stranded properties. Building sustainability depends on its context. In Europe, renovation, space efficiency, and urban planning are key to reducing embodied carbon and preventing unsustainable real estate expansion. Building products, often carbon-intensive, significantly impact sustainability. Using a lifecycle approach, lean construction, and low-carbon materials helps minimize upfront carbon, supported by tools like Life Cycle Assessment (LCA) and Life Cycle Costing (LCC). In Europe, building operations account for 42% of energy consumption. Enhancing energy efficiency, electrifying energy use, and decarbonizing electricity and heat are crucial for reducing emissions. New buildings should be decarbonized from the start, meeting ZEB standards to avoid future retrofitting. Improving existing buildings and using efficient materials reduces energy waste. In 2017, there were 2500 net zero buildings worldwide which were recognized through green building certification or adhered according to official standard. By June 30th 2022, over 9.7 million square meters of floor space had been EDGE Advanced certified in 55 countries.

World Bank estimation shows that improvement in material efficiency for the construction of new buildings and structures could cut embodied construction emissions in half by the year 2050. Computer driven designs could handle the increased complexity of design and prevent construction errors. The replacement of carbon intensive refrigerants and heating materials can significantly reduce emissions from the operations of buildings. For instance, in Eastern Europe, older supermarkets have high leakage rates in fridges and freezers. Another option would be to substitute cement and steel for less carbon intensive materials. For example, timber can be used as an alternative to steel in buildings under 12–18 stories in both residential and commercial settings. Using timber in place of steel and cement is considered one of the most effective ways to reduce greenhouse gas emissions through biomass utilization. Reflective painting and film coating can enhance thermal efficiency in buildings. Studies have shown that reflective roofs could save more than $20,000 per year in electricity bills relative to a conventional building in one floor warehouses in Bogota, Colombia. Utility savings due to tinted windows could reach up to $2000 per year in three floor retail buildings in Jakarta, Indonesia. Keppel Industries managed to enable energy savings of up to 40% through use of solar panels, innovative thermal energy storage technologies and smart optimization systems through development and operation of district cooling systems for industrial and commercial parks in Singapore and China. Through the adoption of district cooling systems, the Energy Centre for the Olympic Park in London were able to reduce emissions by more than 20% and resulted in energy savings consumption.

With buildings typically having long operational lifespans, retrofitting can deliver comparable or even greater energy savings than constructing new green buildings. Standard retrofits often cut energy use by up to 25%, while deep retrofits can achieve savings exceeding 50%. ABN AMRO and ING have financed retrofits to access the green bond market, meet stricter emission regulations, and reduce exposure to carbon-intensive assets. In countries like Germany, governments offer tax incentives to enhance building energy efficiency through measures such as heating system upgrades, new windows, and improved insulation. Innovative construction technologies such as 3D printed process can minimize construction waste and achieve higher energy efficiency. For example, the developer 14Trees in Kenya built an IFC EDGE Advanced 3D printed sustainable home, the first of its kind in Africa. The International Energy Agency's Super-Efficient Equipment and Appliance Deployment Initiative supports over 20 governments in implementing energy-efficient policies and promoting smart devices and systems.

Kimco Realty, North America's largest operator of open-air shopping centers, used $365 million from a 2020 green bond to acquire green residential and commercial buildings and fund energy-efficiency upgrades in 123 existing properties. This transaction helped the company achieve a reduction of 7200 tons of carbon dioxide equivalent in greenhouse gas emissions.

Green equity funds invest in green buildings and decarbonization of cement and steel, promoting sustainable construction in emerging markets. While nascent, they suit middle-income economies with strong policies; development finance supports low-income countries.

The first exchange traded fund for green buildings was launched in year 2021. This passive fund tracks the MSCI Global Green Building Index which focuses on the global construction value chain. Since 2013, approximately 4% of $88 billion were invested by venture capital funds in green technologies targeted towards green buildings and materials.

High-income economies can support construction decarbonization in emerging markets through carbon markets, blended finance, and carbon transition bonds, encouraging gradual greening of carbon-intensive industries like steel and cement. In 2022, JFE Holdings, Japan's largest steelmaking company had issued a $230 million transition bond for investments in research and development of innovative technologies such as carbon recycling blast furnaces and hydrogen-based steel making.

Sustainable Construction and Financing in Emerging Markets

Emerging markets account for two thirds of construction related global emissions with about three fifths of these emissions from China on account of its dominant share of both brown buildings and global production of materials.

Green Buildings in Emerging Markets

Energy-efficient measures in buildings deliver significant benefits: The Menarco Tower in Manila achieved 41% energy savings through efficient cooling systems, appliances, and lighting with occupancy sensors. In Gujarat state in India, a district cooling system has been installed in the Gujarat Finance Tech City which reduces power demand and CO_2 emissions. Residential green developers like Signature Global (India) and Capital House (Vietnam) report faster sales and stronger cash flows. In South Africa, International Housing Solutions reports that renters save a month's rent annually on utilities and green homes have higher occupancy rates and profits as compared to conventional properties. In 2015, Colombia introduced Latin America's first mandatory green building code, spurring $9 billion in private investment. Policies like tax incentives boosted green construction, mortgages, and bank confidence. In 2016, Bancolombia pioneered green building finance in Latin America with $400 million in green bonds. By 2021, five Colombian banks, including Davivienda and BBVA, offered green mortgages, supported by CAMACOL's 2017 educational push for EDGE certification. By 2021, 20% of Colombian construction was green-certified. CAMACOL promotes zero-carbon goals, while banks expand green financing, like BBVA's EDGE Advanced preferential loans.

Source: Building Green, Sustainable Construction in Emerging Markets, October 2023, International Finance Corporation.

Innovative technologies contribute towards reduction of emissions in cement and steel production. For example, replacement of carbon intensive clinker with alternative natural materials and industrial by-products can reduce process emissions. Sococim, a subsidiary of French cement maker replaced clinker lines with alternative fuel biomass and recycled tyres. Ghana's Rider Steel's new Kumasi plant uses steel scrap and energy-efficient technology, reducing carbon emissions by 332,000 tons annually, supported by IFC's $12 million loan. Anhui Conch Cement initiated carbon capture in Wuhu, China (2017). India's Dalmia Cement leads globally, developing a plant capturing 500,000 tons CO_2 annually.

Carbon capture, utilization, and storage (CCUS) can halve CO_2 emissions but needs subsidies until 2035. Innovations like green hydrogen, renewable biomass, and higher scrap usage promise carbon-neutral steelmaking, though economic viability depends on fiscal support. Pure oxygen and renewable electricity further reduce emissions in steel and cement industries. Implementing these technologies could counteract projected emissions growth in construction value chains, necessitating a global investment of $3.5 trillion during the period 2022–2035. According to IFC calculation,[34] investment needs for building green will amount to $1.5 trillion in emerging markets in the next decade. Investment needs reflect the cost difference between electrifying brown buildings and using low-emission energy in new builds, comparing no mitigation and energy efficiency scenarios.

Several emerging market countries have begun implementing green building policies. In 2015, Colombia became the first Latin American country to adopt a mandatory green building code followed by policies to incentivize voluntary certification. The average incremental capital expenditure for green buildings is estimated to be in the range of 1–10% based on data from IFC EDGE certified projects. Utility costs savings for green buildings compared to traditional buildings could result in short payback periods in the range of 2–3 years for some residential projects. Tata Realty & Infrastructure Ltd., India had estimated incremental costs of 2% for its green residential projects. Indian Housing developer, Joyville Shapoorji Housing Pvt. Ltd., has managed to keep incremental costs to under 1% attributed to passive design features which had resulted in energy savings of up to 45%. According to Indian housing financing company, Aavas Financiers Ltd., green homes cost 2% more to build than traditional ones, but homeowners recover costs within 2–3 years through significant savings. Incremental upfront costs and payback periods can vary based on the type of buildings, countries, climate zones and resource efficiency.

The IFC EDGE data also suggest that incremental costs are highest for retail buildings (5%) and lowest for hospitals with shortest payback of 2.5 years. Residential homes had the longest payback period at up to 5 years. Payback periods and incremental costs vary widely by country due to factors like design, regulations, labour, technology, and climate. Projects in Kenya and Vietnam had longest payback periods with over 6 years whereas projects in Indonesia, Jordan and Peru had lowest payback period of less than 2 years. In terms of incremental costs, both

[34] Building Green, Sustainable Construction in Emerging Markets, IFC Report October 2023.

Malaysia and Peru had the highest incremental costs of over 10%. These variations arise from differences in design, building codes, regulations, labour and service costs, availability of technology and materials, and climatic conditions. According to Dodge Data and Analysis (2021), green buildings have an average of 10–17% lower operating costs and 9% higher asset values compared to comparable conventional buildings.

The investment needs for building green in China is estimated to be $1.33 trillion. Table 8.1 shows the investment needs for green building in other emerging markets.

Gross investment refers to fixed capital investment. Decarbonizing emerging market construction needs increased green private debt finance, which reached $23 billion in 2021. Emerging markets receive only a small share of domestic and foreign green finance for decarbonizing construction. It was estimated that only 10% of global debt and foreign green debt finance for construction decarbonization was issued in emerging markets. China accounts for 6% of global private green debt financing, with other emerging economies accounting for 4%. Most financing targets green buildings, while only 9% supports decarbonizing construction materials globally. Development finance institutions can play an important role in promoting financing toward construction value chains decarbonization in emerging markets. Latin America and the Caribbean region account for more than 50% of private green debt issuance for construction decarbonization in emerging markets outside China.

About 56% of the global emissions from buildings' operation originates in emerging markets. China contributes approximately 45% of global building operation-related emissions, while 55% originates from other emerging regions, notably Europe, Central Asia, the Middle East, North Africa, and South Asia. Emerging Markets account for about 90 and 70% of Global Cement and Steel Production. China is the largest contributor, accounting for about 40% of the world's construction-related emissions. Other emerging markets contribute about 30% of emissions.

Sustainability linked finance requires well developed regulatory, prudential and sustainability frameworks and domestic financial markets. In 2021, India's largest cement producer, UltraTech, issued a $400 million sustainability-linked bond. The

Table 8.1 Investment needs in other emerging markets

Region	Amount
Sub Saharan Africa	$12.4 billion
East Asia Pacific	$12.9 billion
MENA	$14.9 billion
Europe & Central Asia	$17.6 billion
South Asia	$25.4 billion
Latin America & the Caribbean	$76.7 billion
Total	$160 billion

Source: Building Green, Sustainable Construction in Emerging Markets, IFC Report October 2023, Global Trade Analysis Project (GTAP) at Purdue University

bond's interest rate is tied to meeting a 22% carbon emissions reduction target by 2030; failure to meet the target results in a 75-basis point increase in the interest rate. Sustainability-linked finance for green construction reached a record high of approximately $27 billion globally, with about 70% allocated to decarbonizing construction materials.

In 2016, Bancolombia, Colombia's largest commercial bank, issued a $400 million green bond in three tranches to build a pipeline of green construction projects and offered green mortgages in local currency with a discount rate of 65 basis points.

Concessional finance from development institutions supports green building and materials sectors with below-market-rate tools like grants, subsidized loans, equity, and guarantees. Subsidized loans offer low-interest rates, while concessional equity provides upfront funding without repayment obligations, aiding capital-intensive industries like steel and cement. Guarantees and risk-sharing facilities mitigate loan risks and uncertainties, unlocking private capital and addressing currency risks in emerging markets. Blended finance leverages concessional funds to attract private investment, improving project viability and delivering greater impact per dollar. By combining public and private resources, these mechanisms address liquidity constraints, reduce emissions, and advance innovative, climate-aligned construction projects. Green banks, mainly in high-income countries, fund small-scale green building projects through specialized loans and guarantees. Development finance institutions drive green construction by mobilizing private capital, acting as anchor investors, offering concessional financing, and utilizing supranational climate funds.

By 2022, 36 carbon pricing initiatives covered 6% of global emissions across 28 nations and 8 subnational systems, with emerging markets like Botswana and Indonesia introducing carbon taxes. Alternative carbon-pricing mechanisms are growing in prominence.

From 2014 to 2019, IFC invested and mobilized $4.4 billion for green buildings, with loan disbursements growing from $226,000 in 2015 to $495 million in 2019. Since 2018, IFC's $15.4 million Market Accelerator for Green Construction (MAGC) program, co-funded by the UK's BEIS, promotes greener construction in developing markets via technical assistance, blended finance, capacity building, IFC's EDGE certification, and performance reporting. The program spans Latin America, Africa, Asia, and the Middle East. In 2017, IFC supported South Africa's green home market with $21 million in a $300 million affordable housing fund managed by HIS. This included $10 million in concessional equity from Global Environmental Fund donor funds, coupled with technical assistance and blended finance to boost the sector's development.

Cement and Steel Decarbonization Initiatives in Emerging Markets

International Finance Corporation invests in cement and steel industries in emerging markets, promoting energy and resource efficiency, waste recycling, and decarbonization through advanced technologies and sustainability standards.

Ciments de l'Afrique is investing in advanced cement technologies across Ghana, Mali, and Senegal, reducing CO_2 emissions by 332,000 tons annually. IFC provided €165 million financing for CIMAF. The IDA19 Private Sector Window Blended Finance Facility also provides up to €7.5 million to support the project in Mali. NCCL, Kenya's largest cement producer reduced fuel consumption and carbon emissions through energy-saving measures and waste heat recovery. IFC supported NCCL with loans and equity totalling \$195.5 million. Rider Steel is building a greenfield plant in Ghana with a 240,000-ton capacity, using steel scrap and energy-efficient induction furnaces to reduce CO_2 by 332,000 tons annually. IFC provided \$12 million in 2020. Two of the largest steelmakers Baowu Group and ArcelorMittal have committed to become carbon neutral by year 2050.

Green hydrogen offers potential for significant carbon abatement in cement production by 2050 but remains uncommercially viable without fiscal support. While some companies in developed countries have piloted hydrogen for cement kilns, high costs and challenges hinder adoption in emerging markets. Some companies in emerging markets, like Compañía Siderúrgica Huachipato in Chile, are piloting green hydrogen technology. CEMEX plans to expand its hydrogen use globally, including in its Dominican Republic plant, leveraging Chile's low-cost solar and wind resources.

Tata Steel has launched a 5-ton-per-day carbon capture plant in Jamshedpur, extracting CO_2 from blast furnace gas for reuse, with plans for wider implementation. Brazil offers significant green steel investment opportunities with abundant renewable energy, iron ore reserves, and operational carbon storage facilities. It is also developing green hydrogen plants. Additionally, Brazil's cement sector requires investment to shift from hand-mixed to bulk cement. Other emerging markets like Türkiye and South Africa present similar opportunities.

Sustainable Finance in Transportation and Logistics Industry

The auto industry is the major factor of biodiversity loss and desertification. Globally the industry uses about 30% of the leather hide produced in Brazil which is the primary reason of rainforest depletion in the Amazon. The global freight transport totalled approximately 140 trillion net ton kilometres and its activities generated an estimated 5.2 million GHG emissions which accounted for approximately 10% of total global emissions. The total freight demand is estimated to reach 329,000 trillion tkm by the year 2060 primarily due to growth in demand driven by economic growth in developing countries. The global freight transport is dominated by maritime shipping which accounts for over 70% of total ntkm. Road freight by heavy and medium trucks account for 15% while rail transport account for 8% of the total freight transport. Diesel-powered road transport remains the most carbon-intensive freight mode, generating four to five times more GHG emissions per tonne-kilometer (tkm) than rail. Diesel small vehicles for last-mile deliveries produce even higher emissions. Maritime shipping, especially with large vessels, has the lowest emissions, followed by electric rail services on low-carbon electricity. Diesel rail, inland waterways, and pipelines have higher emissions than maritime shipping but still significantly outperform road transport.

Sustainable transport can save up to $70 trillion by 2050 when accounting for full transport costs, including fuel, operations, congestion, and vehicles. Additionally, the OECD estimates that $6.9 trillion annually in infrastructure investments, including transport, is needed through 2030 to achieve climate and development goals. Achieving sustainable transport globally requires annual investments of approximately $2 trillion, comparable to current "business as usual" spending of $1.4–$2.1 trillion. Transport is the largest recipient of public climate investment, with $94 billion allocated in 2017–2018, primarily from domestic, bilateral, and multilateral development finance institutions.[35] Private investment in transport PPPs in developing countries grew 400% from 2000 to 2012, according to the World Bank. Transport projects remain the largest recipient of PPP investment, surpassing energy, with $25.8 billion allocated across 78 projects by the year 2021. Key actions for decarbonizing transport include discouraging carbon-based fuel use, enhancing truck efficiency, shifting to rail/waterways, electrifying trucks, investing in infrastructure, and adopting green fuels with carbon taxation.

Green Financing in Automobile Market

The financing for clean transport has grown nine-fold from $6 billion in year 2015 to $53 billion in year 2019. Toyota Motor Corp, the world's largest automaker by sales announced plans to issue 100 billion-yen ($740.5 million) worth of green or sustainable bonds. The funds raised through green bonds would be used for R&D, capital investment in battery electric vehicles and fuel cell electric vehicles. As a part of sustainable finance framework, General Motors issued green bonds to attract investments for promotion of clean transportation ecosystem. As part of electric vehicle initiatives, other OEMs such as Ford, Honda and Daimler have issued green bonds to focus on their electric vehicle initiatives. The transport infrastructure spending in the OECD countries grew on an average 7% during the period 2010–2017. In 2019, global green bond issuance surpassed $200 billion, with nearly 25% allocated to transport sector investments, following energy and buildings. The estimated annual financing gap for transport infrastructure is approximately USD 440 billion for meeting the United Nations (UN) sustainable development goals by the year 2030. The Multilateral Development Bank (MDB) Working Group on Sustainable Transport reported approximately USD 22 billion in new funding for sustainable transport in 2017 and nearly USD 19 billion in 2018. In 2019, transport accounted for 20% of green bond proceeds, emerging as the third largest sector after energy and buildings in terms of green bond issuance.

[35] United Nations Sustainable Transport Conference Beijing, Fact Sheet, 14–16 October 2021.

Globally, achieving low-carbon transport pathways will require investments of USD 2.7 trillion annually from 2016 to 2030, amounting to a total of USD 40.5 trillion, with 60–70% of these investments focused on emerging economies. The regional investment gaps for transport infrastructure by 2040 are estimated at USD 0.8 trillion for Africa, USD 1.6 trillion for Asia, and USD 6.0 trillion for the Americas. As of December 2020, G20 countries allocated over half of their tracked stimulus spending (USD 276 billion out of USD 506 billion) to transport projects, but only about one-third (USD 103 billion) was directed toward green transport improvements. China allocated 5.6% of its GDP to transport, significantly higher than Denmark, France, Germany, Mexico, Russia, and the UK, which each spent approximately 0.7% to 0.9%. In terms of electric vehicles, China is an early adopter propelled by combination of government policy and environmental awareness. Volvo cars had raised funds to finance passenger EVs with a plan to move 50% entirely EV cars and 50% hybrid vehicles by the year 2025. BNP Paribas acted as the green structuring advisor to Volvo Cars. China was the largest issuer for green transport financing in year 2019.

According to the International Energy Agency estimates, EVs operations saved approximately the consumption of 600,000 barrels of oil products per day. Electricity generation to power the global electric vehicle fleet produced 51 Mt. CO_2-equivalent emissions, roughly half the emissions that an equivalent fleet of internal combustion engine (ICE) vehicles would have generated. The cost of EV engines is still about 30% higher than ICE vehicles. According to the International Energy Agency, a record 10 million electric cars were sold globally in 2022, up from 6.9 million in 2021. China, Europe, and the US account for maximum market share of electric cars. By 2027, EVs are expected to surpass new car sales of drive systems in Europe. The global sales of internal combustion engine vehicles are predicted to be below 1% by 2040. The green financing for transport sector in China increased from $10.1 billion in year 2018 to $11.2 billion in year 2019.

Green financing tools such as green bonds facilitate auto manufacturers to plan investments in clean transportation and electric vehicles. Daimler issued 10-year green bond valued at €1 billion for implementing low carbon business strategy model. Volvo Cars established a green financing framework to raise €500 million 7-year green bond to facilitate investment in EV. The EU rules specify that newly built vehicles emit no more than 95 g of CO_2/km and auto manufacturers could face penalties of up to $39 billion under the new emission rules.

The global expenditure for electric cars had increased by 50% in year 2022 compared to year 2021. In December 2022, Barclays facilitated a $300 million securitisation for Swedish electric freight company Einride, enabling fleet expansion, R&D investment, and sustainable freight mobility growth. BBVA acted as mandated lead arranger for EUR 801 million syndicated loan arrangement for Envision AESC for EUR 1.1 billion battery Gigafactory project in Northern France.

To get aligned with net zero emissions by 2050 scenario, CO_2 emissions from the transport sector must fall by more than 3% per year by 2030. Vehicle manufacturers focus on four key areas of steel, batteries, cast iron and aluminium to reduce their carbon footprint.

Steel accounts for approximately 20% of global steel consumption in the transport sector. The automotive industry has significantly driven the demand for green steel, prompting the steel industry to initiate extensive conversion plans.

The transportation sector accounts for approximately 25% of CO_2 emissions globally. A significant shift is required for transition to low carbon economy which includes electrification of vehicles, low carbon mass transport systems and greener replacement for aviation and shipping fuels. According to OECD estimates, approximately $3 trillion of investment is required for global land transport infrastructure needs by the year 2050 with governments leveraging public private partnerships to address funding gaps and share costs.

In UK, transport sector is the largest contributor to Green House Gases accounting for 24% of domestic emissions in year 2019. The Green Finance Institute launched the Coalition for Decarbonisation of Road Transport in 2021 to overcome financial barriers and support zero-carbon road transport and infrastructure.

Utilization Linked Finance

With respect to transition to a net zero economy, electric car markets have experienced exponential growth. The new electric car sales growth has increased from 5% of market share in year 2020 to 14% by year 2022. There exists a disparity in the speed of installation which would lead to gaps in infrastructure particularly in rural and seasonal areas.

Utilisation Linked Finance (ULF) promotes EV charging infrastructure by linking payments to charge point usage, mitigating short-term demand risks. It supports a UK-wide network, boosts installer confidence, and ensures equitable access, addressing socio-economic disparities. Complementing this, the Battery Investment Facility (BIF) drives UK battery sector growth through blended finance, scaling innovations efficiently.

The automotive sector in the UK accounts for over £79 billion a year and employs over 800,000 in the automotive industry. Transitioning the automotive sector to net zero with battery electric vehicles presents a $2.7 billion investment opportunity. The government designed the Battery Investment Facility (BIF), a blended finance facility to attract initial public investment via a co-investment model. The BIF will focus on key components of the battery supply chain, essential for ensuring the long-term sustainability of current and future large-scale battery manufacturing plants in the UK.

The transportation sector accounts for 23% of global energy related greenhouse gas (GHG) emissions. Electric Vehicles will lower GHG emissions and reduce air pollution in urban areas. IFC's Green Banking Academy (GBAC) provides online training and advisory services to help financial institutions in Europe and Central Asia build, measure, and report green investment portfolios.

The global sales of electric cars were 3 million in year 2020. According to IFC estimation, the total global inventory of electric cars was 10 million. Financial institutions offer specialized loan products for consumers to purchase new or used electric cars. Electric buses accounted for approximately 4.6% of the total bus sales in year 2020. Smaller vehicles such as electric bikes, small electric scooters, electric motorcycles are important in low income areas on account of affordability. Electric two and three wheelers account for the biggest share of electric vehicles with a total fleet of 190 million vehicles. In 2021, IKEA had initiated plans to ensure that by the year 2025, 100% of its last mile deliveries will be made by electric vehicles.

On account of research advancement, battery technology for EVs is changing rapidly. Cheaper options in development would reduce costs and increase battery life span. The increased demand for battery materials will be offset by recycling used batteries thereby creating a circular economy. Majority of EV batteries are currently made in China.

T&E study suggest that €39 billion a year in public investment is required to maintain green transport in Europe. The study suggests that €271 billion every year in private spending on green tech in Europe up to 2030 and the investment required would increase to €507 billion a year by 2040. e-fuels for planes and ships are still in the early stage of their development. During the period 2006–2021, emissions from car manufacturing in the European Union had declined by more than 45%. The auto industry accounts for approximately 15% of the total carbon dioxide emissions in the EU.

Business models grounded in the principles of the circular economy play a pivotal role in addressing sustainability challenges. Currently, only 5% of lithium-ion batteries are recycled worldwide. The World Economic Forum estimates that by 2030, recycling could reduce the annual demand for raw materials by approximately 7%. Global investments in walking, cycling, and EV charging infrastructure offer the highest employment potential, surpassing sectors like building retrofits and renewable energy. Developing regions in Africa, Asia, Eastern Europe, and Latin America could see over 50 million jobs in public transport and vehicle electrification by 2030.

Sustainable Transport Investment in Europe

It is estimated that Europe requires over €310 billion annually by 2030 for manufacturing of clean technologies for transport sector. Approximately 87% of the investment is expected to come from investors which include manufacturers, banks and institutional investors. By 2030, €86 billion is needed to develop e-fuels for planes and ships. For electric vehicles and zero emission trucks, approximately €250 billion investment is required by the year 2030. In the year 2021, the funding for expansion of highways in the EU amounted to €61 billion. The European Commission estimates that approximately €870 billion in annual investments are required to meet the EU's 2050 targets. During the period 2025–2040, €86.7 billion will be needed for Sustainable Aviation Fuels (SAF), including €6.8 billion by 2030. Hydrogen-powered planes are expected to emerge from 2035, requiring an additional €1 billion for fuel by 2040. According to T&E report[36] studies show that by the year 2030, nearly 4% of European shipping could use green e-fuels, however only a sixth of announced production capacity had secured investment. Current funded projects account for just 0.24% of projected marine energy needs.

Decarbonizing Europe's shipping fuels will require €559 billion by 2040, with annual investments of €21 billion by 2030, €37 billion from 2031 to 2035, and €50 billion thereafter until 2040. The overall investment required for light vehicle infrastructure would be €300 billion by 2040. By the year 2030, approximately €15.8 billion would be required to be spent on installing public chargers and an additional €68.7 billion is required to be invested in private chargers across Europe.

The European regulation has set a target of 100% zero emission new car sales by the year 2035. For achieving decarbonization by the year 2050, the EU requires to substitute its old polluting car fleet which accounts for 56% of transport CO_2 emissions.

Meeting the Green Deal objectives for the transport sector in European cities by 2050 will require an additional €1.5 trillion. This includes €500 billion in investments, yielding approximately €300 billion in revenues, and €1.3 trillion in user costs.[37]

The T&E study also proposes that around €1 trillion is required by the year 2040 to produce enough batteries for supporting the transition to a fully electric, zero emission fleet by the year 2050. The study also suggests that an overall investment of €783 billion would be required by the year 2040 for decarbonising the heavy-duty fleet completely by the year 2050. The total investment needed for clean technologies for the purpose of decarbonization of aviation, shipping and e-mobility sectors is expected to be in the range of €507 billion—€7.6 trillion billion per year by 2040 according to the T&E report.

Sustainable Transport Investments by Different Countries

China extended subsidies and tax breaks for 2 million EVs annually until 2022 and invested $1.45 billion in 600,000 EV charging points. The EU's recovery fund supports cycling initiatives, while Germany allocated €2.5 billion for public transport and €50 billion for EVs and decarbonization. Finland committed $1.7 billion to public transport and active mobility, and France launched $8.72 billion programs for EV adoption, R&D, and charging infrastructure. Ireland allocated USD 136 million for active travel and public transport. Italy approved tax incentives for EVs, cycling, and infrastructure, and increased subsidies for new EVs. New Zealand committed USD 720 million to improve rail and ferry services. South Korea's Green New Deal, worth USD 61 billion, aims for 1.33 million electric vehicles. Spain

[36] T&E report, Nov 2024, Financing transport decarbonisation, Study on investments for sustainable transport in the EU.

[37] https://www.eiturbanmobility.eu/publi/study-on-the-costs-and-benefits-of-the-urban-mobility-transition/

invested USD 1.12 billion in public transport and zero-emission vehicle replacement. The UK approved GBP 5 billion for buses, cycling, and walking infrastructure. The USA proposed USD 174 billion to build EV charging networks and electrify transit and school buses. City recovery plans with sustainable transport investments include Bogotá, Colombia, expanding its cycleways by 35 km, building on a 550-km network. Mexico City will invest USD 1 billion to create 1 million jobs, improve public transport integration, and promote shared vehicles. Seoul plans to increase goods delivery via robots and expand its bicycle expressway network to reach a 15% cycling mode share by 2030. Milan, Italy, launched an integrated strategy for sustainable transport. India's commitment to the EV30@30 initiative, aiming for a 30% electric vehicle sales share by 2030, represents a cumulative investment opportunity of up to $266 billion. India's EV finance market have the potential to reach US$50 billion in advances by the year 2030.[38] The Government of India supports the Dedicated Freight Corridor Corporation to build high-capacity freight corridors, shifting traffic from road to rail. A new truck-on-train service saves diesel and reduces GHG emissions, cutting transport time from 24–36 hours to 10 hours.

Inefficient regulation in the freight sector leads to empty running and underloading, especially in countries with restrictive rules. In India, around 30–50% of trucks return empty due to regional operators and state trucking licenses that limit operations. This inefficiency is compounded by practices protecting inefficient operators. However, the rise of online platforms for buying and selling vehicle capacity, supported by mobile phone availability, has significantly improved operational efficiency. These platforms, widely used in high-income countries, are rapidly expanding in nations like India, China, Indonesia, and Nigeria, promoting greater flexibility and efficiency in freight management. Freight Tigers, India's largest online freight platform had captured approximately 2–3% of all road freight transactions of $130 billion market within 6 years of establishment. In Spain, Santander provides financing for hybrid and electric vehicles as well as the installation of charging stations. Banks can also issue green bonds, as demonstrated by the management of ALD Automotive's highly oversubscribed green bond. The primary barrier to used EV adoption is affordability, as subsidies and incentives have predominantly targeted new EV purchases, limiting accessibility for used EV buyers. The Brazilian Green Logistics Program is an initiative of freight and logistics companies which focusses on promotion of sustainable practices in logistics and transportation throughout Brazil.

Pricing Measures

Governments can influence supply chain structures by providing infrastructure, warehousing, and pricing measures that impact transport costs and modal choices. Pricing mechanisms, such as road-use charges and fuel taxes, are effective for

[38] https://rmi-india.org/insight/mobilising-finance-for-evs-in-india/

reducing emissions by incentivizing actions like improving fuel efficiency, shifting to low-emission modes, and adopting green technologies. Differential pricing, like exempting zero-emission trucks from taxes, encourages the use of cleaner technologies. In Switzerland, diesel-heavy trucks face high road taxes, while zero-emission trucks, like battery electric or fuel cell models, are exempt, encouraging companies to pilot new technologies. Additionally, governments can adjust subsidies and taxes on fossil fuels to promote greener logistics. For example, Indonesia's 2015 reduction of diesel and gasoline subsidies. Phasing out fossil fuel subsidies can incentivize reduced consumption, impacting freight logistics. However, it may cause social and economic challenges, particularly for smaller companies. Mexico's fuel pricing and taxation reform, which shifted from subsidies to net positive taxes, successfully mitigated these impacts through gradual price increases and market liberalization. Carbon pricing mechanisms, including emissions trading systems (ETS) and carbon taxes, incentivize GHG emission reductions. ETS sets emission caps and allows trading of credits, while carbon taxes are levied on fossil fuel sales, including transport. Over 60 countries and regions have implemented carbon pricing, with about a third affecting transport. Globally, carbon prices range from less than \$1 to \$120 per ton CO_2 equivalent (tCO_2e). Fuel and carbon taxes can play an important role in funding and financing transport climate actions. To reduce fossil fuel consumption in maritime shipping, governments should eliminate subsidies and introduce carbon pricing. Currently, bunker fuels benefit from tax exemptions, which act as indirect subsidies. The European Commission has proposed a minimum tax for intra-EU maritime and air transport. Governments can further support the transition to green fuels by fostering demand or incentivizing supply through mandates or carbon pricing. The International Maritime Organization (IMO) is considering technical measures, like green fuel mandates, and economic measures, such as carbon pricing, to accelerate the adoption of green fuels and reduce carbon intensity over time. Aviation which accounts for 3% of global logistics GHG emissions is a challenging sector to decarbonize. As in the case of shipping, it would require shifting from traditional fuel to SAF.

Sustainable Finance in Agriculture, Food and Forest Sector

Agri-food systems drive biodiversity loss and emissions, threatening food security. Sustainable practices and scaled long-term investments are essential to mitigate climate risks and unlock green financial opportunities. Currently, food and agriculture systems contribute to nearly one-third of global emissions, with 39% linked to agricultural production, 32% to land use, and the remainder to supply chain activities.[39] However only 3% of climate finance attributable to banking and capital markets

[39] Crippa, M., E. Solazzo, D. Guizzardi et al., "Food systems are responsible for a third of global anthropogenic GHG emissions", Nature Food, vol. 2, 2021, pp. 198–209, https://www.nature.com/articles/s43016-021-00225-9#citeas./ United Nations Environment Programme (UNEP), Emissions Gap Report 2022: The Closing Window—Climate crisis calls for rapid transformation of societies, 2022.

target the Agriculture, Forestry and Other Land Use (AFOLU) sector. Unless transformative measures are adopted, emissions attributed to the food system are projected to increase between 60 and 90% during the period 2010–2050.[40] Approximately $300–$350 billion per year is required to transform the food system.

Preserving forests is among the most effective strategies for combating climate change, preventing biodiversity loss, and delivering essential ecosystem services that underpin a robust economic and financial system. It is estimated that approximately 11% of global greenhouse gas emissions are due to deforestation. In monetary terms approximately, 55% of global GDP depends directly on nature. In the year 2022 alone, tropical primary forest loss totalled 4.1 million hectares mostly driven by agricultural expansion. Agricultural expansion drives almost 90% of global deforestation according to the Food and Agriculture Organization (FAO) of the United Nations. The AFOLU sector, on average, accounted for 13% to 21% of total global anthropogenic greenhouse gas (GHG) emissions between 2010 and 2019, while the rate of deforestation accounts for 45% of total AFOLU emissions.

It is estimated that over 800 million people are hungry and many more suffer from malnutrition.[41] At the same time two billion people are overweight or obese.[42] Food production basically drives climate change, water scarcity and biodiversity loss. Agri-food systems present unique opportunities for climate action, including promoting sustainable agriculture, building climate-resilient food systems, and conserving and restoring natural resources and ecosystem services. The agri-food systems offer employment to 1.23 billion people in the world and approximately half of the world's population live in households which are dependent on agri-food systems.

A widely recognized green finance taxonomy can curb greenwashing in agri-food, leveraging PPPs, fintech, innovation, and regulatory frameworks to attract nature-friendly investments and scale sustainable financing. Policymakers must foster collaboration, policy coherence, and long-term strategies to scale green financing, involving diverse stakeholders, green funds, and global partnerships to support sustainable agrifood growth. Changes in the agriculture sector's climate sensitive activities will severely impact global food and nutrition security. Agriculture had significant importance during the 26th Conference of the Parties (COP26) held in Glasgow during November 2020. International development agencies are promoting Climate-Smart Agriculture (CSA) to balance food security and climate change, aiming for increased productivity, resilience, and reduced emissions. Financing CSA supports sustainable growth, food security, carbon sequestration, and

[40] Riahi, K., D.P. van Vuuren, E. Kriegler, J. Edmonds et al., "The Shared Socioeconomic Pathways and their energy, land use, and greenhouse gas emissions implications: An overview", Global Environmental Change, vol. 42, 2017, pp. 153–168, https://www.sciencedirect.com/science/article/pii/S0959378016300681?via%3Dihub

[41] http://www.fao.org/news/story/en/item/1037253/icode/

[42] http://www.who.int/news-room/fact-sheets/detail/ obesity-and-overweigh

co-benefits like gender equality and youth employment, helping agriculture contribute to climate solutions and SDGs.

Food system contributes to approximately one quarter of greenhouse gas emissions and three quarters of biodiversity loss. The global food system is estimated to generate environmental, health and poverty costs estimated at approximately USD $12 trillion a year. It is estimated that USD 49 billion is required every year for forest and landscape restoration on account of deforestation and forest degradation. However, research shows that only 13–17% of the total annual funding needs are used for restoration and conservation. The International Fund for Agricultural Development (IFAD) estimates that USD 400 billion is required until 2030 for rural development and improvement of food systems. Decarbonizing the diverse, fragmented agri-food sector requires tailored approaches, balancing climate goals, biodiversity, resilience, and equity, with investment needs ranging from USD 212 billion to USD 1.3 trillion according to three recent studies (FOLU,2019; UNEP,2022; Thornton et al., 2023).

The agri-food systems had received 4.3% of the total global climate finance at the project level with an average of USD 28.5 billion during the period 2019–2020.[43] An annual average investment of USD 2.3 billion in venture capital investments were made for companies which focussed on climate change solutions. According to a world bank study conducted in 2023, public subsidies for agriculture and fisheries are estimated at approximately USD 670 billion annually which facilitates harmful practices. Private capital investment in food systems is estimated at USD 630 billion per year.[44] Essential components of the agri-food system which are essential for climate mitigation such as food loss/waste, low carbon diets collectively receive less than 1% of tracked investment. Over a third of climate agri-food investments (USD 10.4 billion) go to East Asia and the Pacific, led by China. Sub-Saharan Africa (USD 4.4 billion) and the US/Canada (USD 2.9 billion). South Asia and Latin America, receive minimal funding. During the period 2019–2020, debt accounted for the largest share of the project level finance to agri-food systems (44%) followed by grants and equity.

During the period 2019–2020, approximately 85% of climate finance for agri-food systems amounting to USD 24.2 billion came from public sources led by development finance institutions. Private sources contributed USD 3.3 billion in renewable energy. Additionally, USD 2.3 billion was tracked in private venture capital investments for agri-food tech companies. During the above period, adaptation finance accounted for 26% of project level climate finance for agri food systems.

The United Nations Framework Convention on Climate Change (UNFCCC) supports agri-food systems through mechanisms like Global Environment Facility (GEF), Green Climate Fund (GCF) and the new Loss and Damage (L&D) fund. The

[43] CPI [Daniela Chiriac, Harsha Vishnumolakala, Paul Rosane], 2023. Landscape of Climate Finance for Agrifood Systems. Climate Policy Initiative.

[44] Elwin, P., Amadi, E., Mitchell, E., Hunter, P., 2023. *Financial Markets Roadmap for Transforming the Global Food System, Planet Tracker.* Available at: https://planet-tracker.org/wp-content/uploads/2023/03/Financial-Markets-Roadmap-for-transforming-the-Global-Food-System.pdf

Green Climate Fund (GCF), Global Environment Facility (GEF), and Adaptation Fund (AF) support climate projects in developing countries. GCF focuses on low-emission, climate-resilient agriculture, GEF targets biodiversity and climate adaptation in agriculture, and AF enhances resilience in agricultural systems and rural livelihoods against climate change impacts.

On the foundation of the Koronivia Joint Work on Agriculture (KJWA) from COP23, the Sharm el-Sheikh joint work (2022–2026) focuses on implementing climate action in agriculture and food security, emphasizing finance, adaptation and the Paris Agreement's 1.5 °C warming limit.

During the period 2000–2021, climate-related development finance for agri-food systems totalled USD 183 billion, with contributions reaching USD 19 billion in 2021 alone.[45] During the period 2000–2021, bilateral transactions accounted for approximately 68% of the total climate related development finance flows to agri-food systems, while multilateral transactions accounted for 30% of total flows. In the year 2021, the major contributors in bilateral resources were Germany, France, EU institutions and Japan accounting for 66% of the total bilateral flows. Among the multilateral funding sources, World Bank is the major contributor having provided USD 24 billion to the agrifood system since the year 2013.

The estimated annual global need for climate change adaptation is at least USD 105 billion, while sustainable food systems and land use require USD 300–350 billion annually to meet the 2030 Agenda. The GCF sectoral guide outlines three investment pathways for agriculture: promoting resilient agriculture, providing climate-informed advisory services, and reconfiguring food systems to improve resilience, reduce food loss, and encourage sustainable diets, with a focus on supporting vulnerable groups and integrating climate solutions.

In 2023, Climate Bonds recorded USD 871.9 billion in green, social, and sustainability bonds, including USD160 billion for agriculture or fishery projects and USD 3.6 billion fully aligned sustainability-linked bonds in the agri-food sector. During the period 2017–2018, approximately USD 11 billion was invested in agriculture, forestry, land use and natural resources management.

Transitioning to sustainable agri-food systems demands significant investment, leveraging innovations like precision farming, bio-inputs (biofertilizers and biocontrol), improved rice production management, cold chain technologies, alternative proteins, and low-emission technologies to reduce emissions and attract critical financing.

In the year 2021, the Climate Bonds Initiative introduced its Agri Foods Transition Programme.

The 'Agri-Food DCF (Deforestation and Conversion Free) Criteria' ensure deforestation-free sourcing, aligning with and exceeding EU Deforestation-free Regulation (EUDR), supporting global sustainability, compliance, and competitive advantage in agricultural supply chains. With the emphasis on climate change

[45] Galbiati, G.M., Yoshida, M., Benni, N. & Bernoux, M. 2023. *Climate-related development finance to agrifood systems—Global and regional trends between 2000 and 2021*. Rome, FAO. https://doi.org/10.4060/cc9010en

mitigation, there had been an increasing demand for funding green infrastructure such as green warehouses and cold chains.

The Tropical Forest Alliance (TFA) is a global partnership of over 120 businesses, governments, and civil society organizations committed to reducing tropical deforestation linked to key commodities like soy, beef, palm oil, and paper by year 2020. TFA focusses on sustainable supply chains for development goals. Kunming-Montreal Global Biodiversity Framework have made commitments to place 30% of the world's land and 30% of oceans under protection and to mobilise 200 billion US dollars a year for biodiversity-related measures in all countries by 2030.

Sustainable Finance in the Agriculture and Food Sector

Public Private Partnership for Integrated Agriculture Development (PPP-IAD) is a joint initiative between the World Economic Forum (WEF) and over sixty organizations and almost half a million farmers in India. PPP-IAD have made over USD 50 million in investments for accessibility to markets, water resource management and energy requirements. The project aimed to provide grassroot support to over 2.5 million farmers by year 2020. Local commercial banks played a key role in supporting the development of market-driven business models, which ultimately led to the establishment of commodity-based farmer producer organizations (FPOs).[46] The Yield Uganda Investing Fund supports small and medium-sized agribusinesses by providing long-term financing, focusing on both financial returns and social impact, while considering ESG factors.[47]

The Green Climate Fund, established in 2010, mobilizes private funding through public investments, approving USD 5.42 billion in funding and leveraging additional co-financing for sustainable projects. Only USD 8.1 billion of total tracked climate funding for agriculture, forestry and land use could be accessed by small scale farmers. This constituted only 40% of the total funds pledged across the three sectors. Small scale farmers benefit from an additional 1.72 billion in climate financing through renewable energy generation, sustainable rural transportation and water management.

Climate risk mitigation in agrifood requires long-term investments, but high perceived risks and long loan tenors limit bank financing, leaving small farmers underserved. Cooperative Rabobank, the second largest bank in Netherlands is a global leader in food and agriculture financing. The bank offers sustainability-oriented banking across all major food chains in 40 countries. The trade and commodity

[46] WEF. 2016. *New Vision for Agriculture Transformation Leaders Workshop 2015. Summary Report.* Cologny, Switzerland. http://www.eaglesoncassava.com/wp-content/uploads/2016/03/WEF_NVA_TLW15_Report.pdf

[47] Habte-Selassie, D. 2019. Uganda Yield Fund: early lessons from IFAD's first private sector investment fund. IFAD Blogs, 20 May 2019. Rome. https://www.ifad.org/en/web/latest/blog/asset/41168206

finance division of the bank serves international clients which include 17 out of the top 20 global diary firms. The Rabo Research Food and Agribusiness segment offers bank's clients with tailored research and news on the latest market developments. Rabo Loss and Waste Hub facilitate bank's clients convert food waste/loss into revenues. The Kickstart Initiatives of banks such as Kickstart Stability, Kickstart Nutrition, Kickstart Food Programme focusses on sustainable food supply by partnering with private businesses and international organizations such as FAO and UNEP.[48] These organizations have launched a USD 1 billion fund (AgriFund3) to accelerate forest conservation and sustainable agriculture. Olam International secured a USD 500 million revolving credit facility, set to grow to USD 1.35 billion, with loans tied to sustainability goals. Meeting targets related to thriving communities, prosperous farmers, and environmental impact can lower interest rates by 10–15 basis points.[49]

The Bank Gospodarstwa Krajowego (BGK) in Poland, utilizing resources from the European Agricultural Fund for Rural Development (EAFRD), developed financial instruments such as loans, guarantees, and other schemes, offering farmers and the agrifood sector improved financing opportunities, including low interest rates and favourable lending conditions. The SLWRMP project of Mozambique aims to reduce poverty by improving agricultural productivity through better water and land management. The total cost of the project was estimated at USD 21.5 million consisting of USD 4.9 million from the African Development Fund, USD 15.9 million from the CIF and USD 0.5 million from the Government of Mozambique.[50] The private sector window of the Global Agriculture and Food Security Programme (GAFSP) had piloted a project in Honduras to support smallholder farmers to access finance. In China, Henan Province had secured a USD 300 million world bank loan for greening agriculture. Tropical Landscape Finance facility (TLFF) of Indonesia is a partnership between UNEP, World Agroforestry Centre, ADM Capital and BNP which stimulate green growth and job opportunities by supporting projects in sustainable agriculture and renewable energy sector.

There are potential for different financial products for green finance in the agrifood sector. Green loans in the form of bilateral or syndicated loans can be used for sustainable farming. Green asset finance is a subset of asset financing which support sustainable agricultural and forestry development. Other allied financial products such as blue finance, landscape finance, livelihoods finance offer financing for fisheries, landscapes and livelihoods. Commercial banks and developmental financial institutions in different countries offers green financing to the agrifood sector. Agricultural Bank of China (ABC) provides financial solutions to the agri-food industry in China. In 2018, ABC's total green credit balance amounted to USD 14.73 billion.

---

[48] https://www.rabobank.com/en/images/annualreport-2018.pdf

[49] https://www.olamgroup.com/news/all-news/press-release/asias-firstsustainability-linked-club-loan-facility-us500million.html

[50] https://climateinvestmentfunds.org/cif_enc/sites/cif_enc/files/knowledge-documents/afdb_booklet_slwrmp_v17_web.pdf

Supply chain finance tools enable suppliers to access funds quickly, facilitating sustainable solutions. Financial institutions support these tools through infrastructure, policy frameworks, technology, and awareness-building. Multinational banks, development banks, fintech companies, and lenders offer supply chain finance tools, including sustainable payables finance, trade loans, carbon payments, and offtake agreements. The IFC's Global Trade Supplier Finance program offers short-term financing to suppliers in emerging markets, linking favourable rates to sustainability measures, with partnerships like Barry Callebaut in Mexico.

Financial institutions like investment banks and venture capital firms provide equity capital to scale sustainable technologies, supporting Monitoring, Reporting and Verification (MRV) methods in developed countries and addressing resource gaps in emerging market. FAO's AgrInvest initiative partners with United Green to mobilize $20 million for sustainable growth in Ethiopia's dairy sector, using FAO tools to assess impacts. The cooperative of European investors, Pymwymic's Healthy Food Systems Impact Fund II, launched in 2021, plans to invest €60 million by 2030 in innovative technologies transforming food systems.

Transition risks hinder global food system transformation. Insurers can offer solutions like crop yield insurance, weather-based policies, and trade credit insurance, supporting sustainable practices and mitigating disruptions. The United States Agency for International Development (USAID) and Fundación REDDOM, with partners like Swiss Re, are developing index insurance in the Dominican Republic to boost climate resilience for farmers, focusing on severe weather impacts. Tata AIG, an Indian general insurance company, collaborates with the InsuResilience Solution Fund to offer weather insurance, enhancing the financial and socioeconomic resilience of smallholder farmers in rural, poverty-stricken areas across India.

Farmers and SMEs in the food system face financial constraints for expansion and transformation. Financial institutions can support them with tools like climate-risk loans, green bonds, and sustainability-linked bonds. The British multinational food service company Compass Group issued two sustainable bonds under a framework aligned with international standards to fund decarbonization, responsible sourcing, food waste reduction, and healthy eating initiatives within its supply chain. In 2019, HSBC partnered with Mercon Coffee Group to launch a green revolving credit facility tied to ESG goals, supporting Mercon's LIFT sustainability program.

The market size of blended finance investment in agriculture have received aggregate financing of $13.4 billion. IDH's Farmfit Fund incentivizes investment in smallholder farmers using tools like loans and guarantees. In Zambia, a $4 million loan supports CHC Commodities' climate-smart initiatives. The Agri3 Fund blends public and private capital to unlock $1 billion for sustainable agriculture, offering credit enhancements to support farmers' transition to climate-smart practices. Tyson Foods and partners received a USDA grant to accelerate climate-smart practices in agriculture, investing $152 million over 5 years to support underserved producers.

Innovations in Agriculture Related Climate Finance

Innovation drives efficient climate-smart agriculture financing, with green and climate bonds aiding technological investments. Stakeholder engagement and private sector involvement are crucial for aligning climate plans with sustainable development goals. Climate-smart agriculture (CSA) activities by smallholder farmers in West African countries are classical example of blended finance fund. The West African Initiative for Climate-Smart Agriculture aims to improve food security and incomes for 90,000 smallholder households across 185,000 hectares, reducing CO_2 emissions by 2 million tonnes annually. Managed by the ECOWAS Bank and RAAF, the USD 80 million fund offers equity, loans, and guarantees to promote CSA practices.[51] Climate smart agriculture financing can be accessed through new digital platforms such as Blockchain Climate Risk Crop Insurance where farmers can adopt climate smart farming methods and face challenges related to climate change.

Most investment funds focused on climate-smart agriculture collaborate with a Technical Assistance Facility (TAF), typically grant-funded (USD 3–10 million). TAFs provide technical expertise for sustainable agriculture investments, leveraging in-house experts or external consultants, and are managed by experienced service providers to support specific investment projects. Dedicated Technical Assistance Facilities (TAFs) have proven effective in de-risking and enhancing sustainable agriculture investments. Examples include the TAF of the Land Degradation Neutrality Fund, supporting land restoration projects, and the AGRI3 Fund's TAF, which focuses on sustainable agriculture and strengthening smallholders' livelihoods.

There is a need for integrated finance system which aligns climate, nature and development goals. Payment for ecosystem services (PES) programs offer a solution by monetizing benefits which include climate change mitigation, adaptation and biodiversity promotion. PES initiatives such as China's Grain for Green, US based Conservation Reserve programs have made direct payments to landowners in return for taking steps to improve ecosystem management measures. The CompensACTION initiative launched in the year 2022 aims to provide finance through PES to small holder farmers in low- and middle-income countries.

Carbon credit markets, valued at USD 2 billion, are driven by voluntary markets and projected to grow 100-fold by 2050. Forest and land use credits dominate, but direct emission cuts via reforestation or agriculture are underdeveloped.

---

[51] Global Innovation Lab for Climate Finance. 2020. The West African Initiative for Climate Smart Agriculture.San Francisco, USA. https://www.climatefinancelab.org/project/africaclimate-smart-agriculture

Challenges for Green Finance in Agrifood Industry

Agriculture, forestry, and food account for barely 3% of all climate bonds issued. Green finance in the agrifood sector faces challenges like undefined financing scopes, lack of tailored financial products, fragmented resources, and risky traditional agriculture finance. Private sector participation remains limited, with most investments focused on energy, leaving agriculture reliant on public funding. Concerns about overestimated reductions in carbon credit markets highlight the need for robust verification frameworks and government-supported emissions trading schemes.

Green Finance Initiatives in Different Regions for Agri Food and Forest Industry

A study by Green Finance Institute in 2021 find that a £3.7 billion financing gap for sustainable soils management and a £19.4 billion gap for protecting and restoring biodiversity exist to the end of the year 2030 in UK. The UK has made a legally binding commitment to net zero emissions by the year 2050. The UK government have made commitments for a farming transition. With respect to farming practices, the UK government initiatives aim to encourage about 80% of landowners and farmers to adopt nature positive farming on at least 10–15% of their land by the year 2030. Another focus area is for the creation or restoration of 30,000 miles of hedgerows by the year 2037 and 45,000 miles by the year 2050. With respect to Soil health, at least 40% of England's soils would be managed sustainably by 2028 which would be increased to 60% by the year 2030. The UK Government has a target of 70% of agricultural land, and 70% of farm holdings, to be covered by the various new farming schemes by 2028. In the UK, voluntary carbon markets are the biggest of the payment for ecosystem services (PES) markets. In 2011, UK's Woodland Carbon Code (WCC) was launched to support the PES markets. By 2022, the WCC hosted over 1800 projects on its registry which covered 67,000 hectares of land.

The German government is one of the biggest donors to biodiversity conservation worldwide. Germany have committed 1.5 billion euros annually starting from 2025 for international biodiversity conservation. For the MAR Insurance Programme, the insurance premium has until now been covered by the InsuResilience Solutions Fund (ISF), which is backed by the German government (BMZ). Colombia is the market leader for habitat banking which is a biodiversity credit system gaining prominence around the world.

China is advancing sustainable agriculture with COFCO's $30 million deforestation-free soybean deal, reflecting growing demand for eco-friendly commodities, aligning with global efforts to combat deforestation, and integrating sustainability into agri-food supply chains to meet net-zero goals. The Asia Pacific region requires an annual targeted investment of $431 billion for emission control. Agriculture emissions in the region accounted for 10.6% of the region's total emissions with 2.3 gigatons of carbon dioxide equivalent ($GtCO_2e$). The key drivers of agriculture emissions were accounted from the livestock sector and methane emissions from rice cultivation. Improved rice cultivation practices, enhanced livestock management and sustainable farming techniques would lead to emission reduction. The emissions from land use change and forestry are substantial in many economies. Deforestation for palm oil, timber and agriculture are major sources of emissions in Southeast Asian countries such as Indonesia. Bhutan's extensive forest cover helped achieve net zero targets. Several economies such as China, India, Indonesia, Malaysia and Philippines have ambitious reforestation targets to mitigate climate change and protect biodiversity. Within the developing Asia, 44 economies which account for 98% of the region's emissions have ratified the Paris Agreement and have submitted their nationally determined contributions (NDCs). In Asia and Pacific alone, an estimated $2 trillion is required annually during the period 2022–2030 to meet targets as outlined under NDCs.

Precision agriculture leverages information and technology to implement site-specific management practices, optimizing responses to climate, weather and location specific data. Nature based solutions (NBS) such as climate smart agriculture, biodiverse habitat restoration, water resource management, clean cookstove projects and green infrastructure initiatives have the potential to achieve net zero emissions by the year 2050. According to UNEP 2023 statistics, in order to meet biodiversity and land degradation targets, the required investment in NBS is estimated to be $200 billion annually and is expected to quadruple by the year 2050. According to a study by Landholm et al. (2022), nature-based solutions (NBSs) hold significant carbon market potential, particularly in agriculture (43%), followed by avoided deforestation (32%), afforestation/reforestation ((11%), improved forest management (7%), and wetland restoration/conservation (7%) by 2030.[52] The United States, China, India, Brazil, and Indonesia are the top five economies with the highest potential in agricultural carbon markets. In terms of avoided deforestation, the greatest potential lies in Latin America and Asia, particularly in Brazil, Indonesia, Colombia, Peru, and Malaysia.

Climate finance for land use in Brazil has nearly doubled, increasing from an average of $8.6 billion per year between 2015 and 2020 to $17.1 billion annually between 2021 and 2023. Domestic finance constitutes 97% of the tracked resources for climate finance in Brazil. Private sources account for approximately 72% of domestic finance valued at US$11.9 billion. The native forest sector in Brazil depends mostly on resources from the federal public budget which are supplemented by flows from international sources. International flows had mobilized US$551 million per year in climate finance for land use in Brazil. Land use includes agricultural activities such as agricultural production in the primary sector and agro

[52] Landholm, D., F. Bravo, I. Palmegiani, S. Minoli, C. Streck, and S. Mikolajczyk. 2022. Unlocking Nature Based Solutions Through Carbon Markets: Global Analysis of Available Supply Potential. Climate Focus.

industry in the secondary sector, conservation, restoration and reforestation activities related to forests and multisectoral involving policies and projects aimed at reducing vulnerability related to climate change. Agricultural risk management instruments had mobilized US$2.6 billion per year in Brazil. Thematic bonds raised an average of US$2.5 billion per year which were directed towards sectors such as bioenergy and biofuels, forest sectors and planted forests. The crop sector was the main recipient of climate finance and received an average of US$12.4 billion per year. The forest sector received US$1.6 billion per year. The Rural Insurance Premium Subsidy Program (PSR), managed by the Ministry of Agriculture and Livestock (MAPA) in Brazil supports the purchase of rural insurance to help producers recover financially from adverse climate events. The Crop Guarantee Fund supports family farming in semi-arid regions by providing conditional benefits to producers affected by drought or excessive rainfall. The government contributes an average of $40 million annually to ensure resources for beneficiaries. The Amazon Fund is Brazil's primary climate fund, channelling international resources for land use through the BNDES to support various projects. In 2023 through the fund, five projects were approved which mobilized US$26 million from the fund.

Role of Financial Institutions for Mitigating Deforestation Risk

Financial institutions are sometimes aware that the capital they provide is used by companies for deforestation. However, in the absence of relevant policies or legal compliance issues, they often proceed with approving such deals. Emissions from land-use change and agriculture, accounting for about a quarter of global emissions, were largely overlooked in climate risk reporting until recently. This is changing rapidly with the introduction of carbon accounting standards and net-zero target-setting guidelines for the forestry, agriculture, and land-use sectors. Rising regulations, like the EU's new requirements for deforestation-free products, are introducing financial risks across commodity value chains. While these regulations currently exclude financial institutions, a review is planned in 2 years.

Several new initiatives have been launched to address deforestation, promote sustainable food systems, and restore nature. Key initiatives include the FOLUR Impact Program, the IFACC project, the Good Food Finance Network, Finance Sector Deforestation Action, Finance for Biodiversity, the Investors Policy Dialogue on Deforestation, and Nature Action 100.

In 2021, leading financial institutions launched the Finance Sector Deforestation Action (FSDA) at COP26 in Glasgow. By July 2023, 37 institutions managing nearly $9 trillion of assets had joined the initiative. By July 2023, the Finance for Biodiversity Pledge launched in year 2020 had the support of 140 financial institutions which managed nearly $20 trillion in assets. Established in 2020, the Investors Policy Dialogue on Deforestation (IPDD) engages with public agencies and industry associations to address deforestation. By December 2022, it included 70 financial institutions from 19 countries, managing around $10 trillion in assets.

There are collaborative finance sector initiatives for controlling deforestation efforts. The Finance Sector Deforestation Action Initiative (FSDA) brought together over thirty financial institutions to engage in investment portfolios, and take actions to create an enabling environment to eradicate commodity driven deforestation. Forest Finance Risk Consortium (FFRC) is the consortium involving financial institutions, land-use experts, and disclosure professionals to develop tools for assessing and disclosing deforestation and land-use change risks, offering guidance and strategic support.

Green Finance in Technology Sector

Green finance and fintech hold significant relevance for policymakers, especially in emerging and developing countries, as they work towards implementing the Paris Agreement and achieving the SDGs. Fintech is contributing to sustainable finance through the development of innovative financing mechanisms. Fintech's intersection with sustainable finance fosters solutions for environmental and social challenges. By enabling green bonds and impact investing, fintech simplifies access to eco-friendly projects and aligns investments with sustainability goals. These platforms connect investors with transparent opportunities, driving measurable environmental, social, and financial outcomes through innovative financing mechanisms. FinTech innovations are advancing environmental goals by offering tools to track and reduce carbon footprints. For example, blockchain technology enables transparent and tamper-proof records of carbon emissions, simplifying the measurement and verification of businesses' and investments' environmental impacts.

Environmental issues such as climate change and resource management are significant areas of concern for technology firms. Crypto mining consumes more energy than those consumed by different countries such as Argentina. E-waste implies used hardware which is hard to recycle. The fintech industry is highly electricity reliant.

Several fintech companies have emerged as leaders in the field of sustainable finance. SmartDev is a prominent player in the fintech sector. Trine is a Swedish crowdfunding platform which connects investors with solar energy projects in developing countries. Through its platform, Trine has facilitated investments in clean energy projects in developing countries. Aspiration, an American fintech company offers socially conscious banking and investment products. The rise of decentralized finance (DeFi) and blockchain technology offers new opportunities for sustainable finance.

Fintech firms are increasingly introducing solutions focused on environmental sustainability, including green loans, green bonds, and investment platforms dedicated to supporting eco-friendly initiatives. According to a research report by Global Market Estimates, the global green fintech market is expected to expand at a CAGR of 22.4% between 2024 and 2029.

Financial services firms are developing loan products to incentivize business sustainability. Green loans offer advantages such as lower interest rates for investing in energy-efficient technologies and sustainable practices. Prominent initiatives include HSBC's Green Hub, Lloyds' Clean Growth Financing Initiative, and Barclays' Green Loan program. Digital payments and electronic signatures are transforming banking by reducing its environmental impact. By eliminating the need for checks and paper statements, these solutions promote a more sustainable and eco-friendly approach to financial transactions. Mobile payment solutions now help offset carbon emissions by funding renewable energy and reforestation projects, gaining traction for promoting environmental sustainability.

Payment processors are adopting carbon-neutral strategies, with companies like Switch2Zero driving efforts to support renewable energy and energy-efficient technologies. Innovative payment solutions are advancing sustainability in finance. Contactless payments streamline public transportation, reducing cash and paper use. Digital wallets minimize plastic waste by replacing physical cards and fostering eco-friendly transactions. Open banking, enabled by regulations like PSD2, improves transparency and efficiency in financial services. Additionally, AI-driven tools provide detailed analyses of sustainable investments, helping investors align decisions with environmental and social goals. Together, these innovations enhance sustainability, efficiency, and customer empowerment in the financial ecosystem. The integration of technologies like Internet of things (IoT), Artificial Intelligence (AI), Machine Learning (ML), big data, data analytics, and blockchain into fintech is poised to amplify technology-driven transformation in the financial sector. P2P funding can harness savings and investment capital, link it to investment opportunities, and help expand distributed energy generation. The Green Assets Wallet (GAW) is a global platform that supports sustainable financing through capital markets, providing investors with reliable data on environmental performance. Hosting data from over 100 issuers, mainly in Europe, GAW connects investors to credible investment opportunities, using a blockchain-based platform to ensure transparency, validation, and efficient reporting, particularly for debt instruments like Green Bonds.

The World Bank has identified diverse blockchain applications in the financial sector, including money transfers, financial infrastructure, agriculture, governance, healthcare records, and humanitarian aid tracking and delivery.

6th Grain leverages mobile fintech, geospatial data, and integrated mobile data collection to promote sustainable Arabic gum farming in the African Sahel, empowering smallholders with access to credit, insurance, and markets. Similarly, MistEO uses automated technology and weather analytics to deliver crop insights, parametric insurance, and a climate decision intelligence platform, helping farmers mitigate financial risks and adapt to climate challenges. Intensel leverages AI, satellite imagery, and cloud platforms to assess climate risks, translating hazards into financial value-at-risk, enabling informed resilience planning and capital allocation. Innovative technologies like blockchain, IoT, and AI enhance sustainability reporting by improving transparency, auditability, automating processes, and standardizing vast data, boosting compliance and adoption in sustainable finance. U-Reg uses

AI to standardize ESG reporting, bridging global frameworks, while Ahya enhances carbon accounting for emissions management. Trustwise leverages blockchain for transparent emission trading. Blockchain enables end-to-end digitization of carbon markets, improving data auditability and trust. Platforms like Carbon base and ZERO13 streamline reporting, trading, and connectivity for carbon credits and ESG assets.

Insurers, as major institutional investors, can leverage FinTech tools and data analytics to enhance risk management and impact underwriting, especially in developing countries. By offering affordable, mobile-based insurance solutions like microinsurance, insurers can increase resilience to climate change and support financial inclusion.

Green FinTech companies have a significant role in advancing sustainable initiatives. The creation of digital platforms facilitates both green lending and sustainable investment. For environmentally friendly projects, these platforms facilitate bringing together of borrowers and lenders. Green lending platforms simplify loan applications, assess green project feasibility, and connect investors with sustainable ventures like renewable energy, energy-efficient buildings, and sustainable agriculture. Green lending platforms help investors to allocate their funds towards renewable energy projects, climate focused funds, green bonds and socially responsible investment portfolios. FinTech has streamlined sustainable investing through robo-advisors, using algorithmic intelligence to align investments with environmental goals, automate portfolio management, and expand accessibility to investors. These platforms use data analytics, AI, and machine learning to measure sustainability metrics like carbon emissions, water usage, and social outcomes, offering real-time insights to investors. Block chain-based solutions can streamline processes like impact reporting for sustainability initiatives. Blockchain as a decentralized and transparent digital ledger can create tokenized assets for sustainable projects, enhance supply chain transparency and facilitate trading of carbon credits.

Digital technologies like satellite monitoring and advanced data analytics are enhancing sustainability in finance. For example, Vacuumlabs offers carbon-tracking tech that combines credit card purchase data with carbon tracking to guide customers toward sustainable consumption.

Fintech tools like AI and blockchain support humanitarian efforts. The UN used blockchain to distribute funds to Syrian refugees in 2020. The company Hiveonline employs blockchain to assist rural African microeconomies with online payments, crop forecasting, voucher distribution, and business management, even in areas with limited internet access. A pilot blockchain project in Indonesia tracks skipjack and yellowfin tuna provenance, ensuring compliance at origin and replacing unreliable, corruption-prone paper records.[53] In 2018, Maersk and IBM partnered to create a joint venture using blockchain technology to enhance global trade efficiency, security, and reduce costs and inefficiencies.

[53] DiCaprio, A and Beck, S (2017) Blockchain Pilots Making Waves in Developing Asia. Asia Pathways, July 20. Asian Development Bank Institute, Tokyo. https://www.asiapathways-adbi.org/2017/07/blockchain-pilots-making-waves-in-developing-asia

ANT Financial's "Ant Forest" encourages users in China to reduce their carbon footprint by tracking savings, earning green energy, and offering carbon offset rewards through tree planting.

The United Nations Development Programme (UNDP) Taskforce on Digital Financing of the Sustainable Development Goals estimate that banks have invested over US$ one trillion in developing, integrating and acquiring emerging technologies. KPMG estimates that FinTech venture capital investments amounted to US$165 billion in year 2019 and US$105 billion in year 2020.

The COP28 UAE TechSprint, a global initiative co-developed by the Bank for International Settlements (BIS), the COP28 Presidency, the Central Bank of the UAE (CBUAE), and the Emirates Institute of Finance (EIF), aims to accelerate innovative solutions in sustainable finance and climate change mitigation. The event had participation from innovators across 31 countries, resulting in a record number of creative applications leveraging AI, blockchain, and IoT technologies to advance green and sustainable finance.

According to Cleantech group, the number of companies in the blockchain ecosystem grew from 35 to over 150 in 2018 compared to previous year. By May 2018, European companies raised $723 million, compared to $251 million in Asia and $140 million in North America. Over half of blockchain energy companies and pilot projects are in Europe, with many founded in 2016–2017, indicating their early-stage development, followed by North America and Asia. By 2017, over 90 blockchain energy projects were active, including L03 Energy's Brooklyn Microgrid, PowerLedger's decentralized platform, and Energy Web Foundation's blockchain development. Statkraft in Norway demonstrated blockchain's feasibility for energy exchanges and predicted that blockchain would enable rapid, low-cost transactions in renewable energy markets within 5 years. In Europe, over 40 energy-trading firms have collaborated on the Enerchain project, using blockchain for peer-to-peer trading in the wholesale energy market. Over 40 organizations including International Emissions Trading Association (IETA), the Energy Web Foundation and Power Ledger, launched the Climate Chain Coalition (CCC) to support DLT and blockchain solutions for climate change.

Green Finance in Consumer Sector

Sustainable consumption manifests consumer behaviour which involves purchase of goods and services which are designed, manufactured and sold in environmentally or socially responsible ways. It is estimated that the current consumption rate of global resources has reached 1.7 times the earth's capacity with respect to what ecosystems can support. The typical US household's greenhouse gas emissions is accounted by consumer goods (40%), transportation sector (28%) and home energy (32%). According to research by McKinsey & Co in year 2020, there was a 71% increase in online search for sustainable goods. The McKinsey 2023 study find that two fifths of US consumers are interested in climate linked financial products and two third of consumers would allocate more than 40% of their savings to a "green" retail banking product. The 2021 Global Sustainability Study reveals that 85% of consumers in surveyed countries have increasingly chosen greener, more sustainable products in the past 5 years. A recent IOSCO report released in 2022 reveals that more retail investors are considering sustainability in their financial decisions, with younger people showing a stronger preference for sustainable investments. Sustainable finance products enable consumers to align their values on social, environmental, and governance issues with their financial choices, supporting causes like climate change mitigation or social initiatives. According to IBM's 2022 survey of 16,000 global consumers, approximately 49 % had paid a premium of average 59% or more for products branded as sustainable or socially responsible. Principle 4 of the Financial Literacy and Awareness (FCP Principles) highlights the importance of financial education in protecting consumers and maintaining confidence in the financial sector. Reports by IOSCO (2022) and OECD (2023) stress educating retail investors on sustainability-related information, aligning products with preferences, and understanding ESG certifications. They also emphasize training financial advisors to combat greenwashing and recommend national strategies and surveys to enhance financial literacy.

Organizations such as the International Consumer Protection and Enforcement Network and the Competition and Markets Authority focus on green washing. Initiatives such as Fashion for Good's innovation platform offers a platform for fashion companies to connect with innovators to create disruptive solution to sustainability challenges within the value chains of the textiles industry. The major core sustainability themes in the consumer industry are Scope 1, 2 and 3 GHG emissions, sustainable supply chains, reduction in plastic usage, waste mitigation and management, ESG education. Carbon Disclosure Project (CDP) work with large purchasing organizations such as Microsoft, Diageo and Sainsbury as part of their supply chain programmes to encourage companies to disclose their GHG emissions. Companies such as Arla are implementing sustainability incentives for their farmers. In UK, industry wide collaboration on supply chain innovation is observed across many consumer industry sub sectors. WRAP and WWF are working with eight UK Grocers to agree a common set of rules to measure and report their supply chain emissions. AIM-PROGRESS is a forum of leading consumer goods manufacturers and suppliers to share knowledge on building sustainable supply chains. The Sustainable Food Trust strives to transform global food and farming systems by collaborating with governments, organizations, and companies to create a unified framework for sustainability across farms worldwide.

US consumer spending exceeds $14 trillion annually, with a significant portion directed toward consumer-packaged goods (CPG). As a multi-trillion-dollar sector employing millions, CPG plays a vital role in advancing a sustainable and inclusive economy.

Consumer companies must demonstrate proactive efforts to reduce the overall plastic usage across their value chains. For instance, despite serving as the main sponsor of COP27, Coca-Cola faced ongoing criticism for its status as the world's largest plastic polluter. In January 2023, the UK government banned the sale of several single use plastic items used in takeaway businesses, food vendors and hospitality industry. Defra, the UK department for environment, food and rural affairs seeks to enhance accountability for packaging producers, aligning with the "polluter pays" principle. A circular economy focuses on eliminating waste, circulating materials, and regenerating nature. Organizations like the Ellen MacArthur Foundation, WRAP, and the Cradle to Cradle Products Innovation Institute promote this transition by emphasizing the separation, disassembly, and reuse of durable and consumable components.

Stakeholders are increasingly focussing on industry specific waste. The fashion industry faces criticism for its reliance on synthetic fibres, waste from fast fashion impacting low-GDP countries. IKEA buys products from more than 1300 suppliers in 50 countries and focus on collaborative product designs to minimize use of materials. IKEA have specified in its code of conduct for suppliers that waste should be avoided or recycled to be used in other products. Many consumer industry companies such as PZ Cussons, Compass Group and Burberry have set ambitious KPIs for sustainability. In 2022, PZ Cussons had £325 million sustainability linked revolving credit facility with three sustainability KPIs of reduction of Scope 1 & 2 GHG emissions, reduction of virgin plastic packaging and achieving B Corp certification across all business units. Compass Group issued €500 million and £250 million sustainable bonds for sustainable management of natural resources, land use, pollution prevention and control, clean transportation and food security. In 2022, Burberry issued £300 million sustainability linked loan for emission reduction of its extended supply chain by 46% in year 2030 and becoming net zero by the year 2040.

In 2021, Tesco introduced the UK retail sector's first sustainability-linked supply chain finance program. This initiative offers suppliers preferential financing rates contingent on their efforts to disclose greenhouse gas (GHG) emissions, set reduction targets, and achieve measurable emission reductions. Coca-Cola Europacific Partners (CCEP) introduced a program offering financial incentives tied to various sustainability KPIs. Green Asset Finance supports businesses in acquiring sustainable assets, such as electric or hydrogen vehicles, clean energy solutions like solar panels, batteries, and heat pumps, promoting environmental sustainability. Voluntary carbon credit market standards and settlement platforms like Carbonplace ensure projects are additional, permanent, community-driven, and governed sustainably.

Research suggest that there is an observable shift in consumer attitudes with consumers having inclination to pay a premium for sustainability certified products. Research shows that 90% of Gen Z are willing to pay a higher price for sustainable merchandise. Certifications such as B Corp, Fair Trade and Cradle to Cradle facilitate firms to focus on higher sustainability adoption levels. The case of IKEA proves that cost savings and risk mitigation bring financial benefits. It is estimated that on average 80% of a consumer goods company's emissions come from its supply chain. Bedding company Sol Organix ensures that their suppliers are ethical and sustainable through efficient management of its supply chain process.

The linear economy model is increasingly unsustainable and costly, especially in consumer goods sectors like food and cosmetics, where trillions of dollars in value are wasted. Recent research suggests that adopting a circular economy could enable companies in the EU to generate up to €500 billion in additional annual revenue by 2030. GoodWell, the dental company create products using new materials like bioplastics to ensure that their products are biodegradable with low carbon intensity. Market disruptors like Beyond Meat and Veja are redefining consumer expectations with sustainable products, driving a shift in industry dynamics. International Food and beverage companies such as Mars, Bacardi and Compass Group are raising sustainable finance to enhance ESG initiatives. Approximately 73% of the world's largest companies in the F&B sector have a sustainable development target.

Innovative Sustainable Financial Solutions for Consumers[54]

Sustainable deposit products allow consumers' savings to fund eco-friendly projects like renewable energy or sustainable agriculture, offering benefits like tax-free interest and green lending initiatives. Westpac Bank offers a Landcare Term Deposit, supporting sustainable agriculture, while France's Livret de Développement Durable et Solidaire (LDD) offers tax-free savings for eco-friendly building projects. Financial institutions use the amounts collected in the LDDs to sanction loans which can improve the energetic insolation of buildings.

Ethical or green credit cards offer benefits like donations to sustainable causes, rewards for eco-friendly purchases, and tree planting with every swipe. Some issuers provide apps to track carbon neutrality progress or allow cardholders to redeem rewards for planting more trees, promoting environmentally conscious spending. Sustainable insurance products consider social and environmental factors, promoting eco-friendly transport, energy efficiency, and catering to specific customer needs or underserved populations. NN Group NV, one of the largest insurers in the Netherlands, offers an insurance product that covers smartphone screen repairs instead of replacements, as repairs are the more environmentally friendly option, even though they cost the insurer more than replacing the phone. Green mortgages offer discounted interest rates or cashback incentives to consumers purchasing energy-efficient homes or making eco-friendly improvements. In Netherlands, banks offer loans with interest rates up to 25% lower, based on energy-saving measures, with loan amounts ranging from EUR 25000 to EUR 100000. Green bonds finance projects with positive environmental impacts, such as renewable energy and clean transportation. HSBC issues green bonds to support businesses promoting a low-carbon, climate-resilient, and sustainable economy.

Atmos, the American fintech company gives importance for sustainability focused rewards. The Atmos debt card obtained from recycled plastics facilitate cardholders to earn 1–5% cashback on categories such as bikes, electric mobility, sustainable clothing and apparel, purchases from climate wise farms and ranches.

[54] OECD (2023), Financial Consumers and Sustainable Finance: Policy Implications and Approaches, OECD Business and Finance Policy Papers, https://doi.org/10.1787/bf84ff64-en

Atmos allocates 100% of its loans to clean energy projects. Aspiration, the American bank offers a cashback account and debit card, Aspiration Spend & Save that allows account holders to track the impact of their expenses. For Conscience Coalition purchases, the basic and paid tiers offer 3–5% and 10% cashback. The Conscious Coalition is made up of socially and environmentally conscious firms which are selected by Aspiration. The paid account provides a feature to automatically mitigate the negative environmental impact of driving. Aspiration monitors gas station purchases by referencing local gas prices and data from the U.S. Environmental Protection Agency (EPA) to calculate CO_2e emissions. It then purchases carbon offsets on behalf of the consumer to neutralize their carbon footprint.

Mastercard have associated with Doconomy, a Swedish fintech firm to develop the carbon calculator to offer consumers data of the estimated carbon emissions generated by their purchases across different spending heads. The independently verified Åland Index, adopted by over 90 financial institutions across 40 plus countries, calculates the CO_2e footprint of transactions. It enhances understanding by providing relatable equivalents, like the number of trees needed to absorb the CO_2e, along with tips for reducing future emissions. Mastercard's Donation-as -a- service consulting solution assist financial institutions to implement successful donation initiatives for environmental reasons. These solutions offer the option to support forest restoration projects through the Mastercard Donate ecosystem. This can be integrated into third-party websites for fundraising campaigns, added as a donation option at checkout, or implemented as a point-of-sale roundup feature in physical stores. ESG Quant is a Mastercard diagnostic tool for small and medium-sized businesses, helping them evaluate their ESG readiness based on actions to improve performance and mitigate financial and regulatory risks related to ESG issues. Financial institutions can incentivize spending at sustainable retailers by offering card-linked deals, higher cashback, or reward points. Retailers are spotlighted based on third-party certifications, such as Green Seal for environmental impact or B Corps for social impact. Gasoline powered vehicles pose big challenges to sustainability and the environment. These vehicles contributed approximately 30% to the total US CO_2 emissions in 2022.

Citi has sponsored Citi Bike, a partnership between the New York City Department of Transportation and Lyft. The deployment of over 30,000 Citi Bikes and 2000 docking stations in 2023 helped 1.4 million people reduce transportation-related emissions by decreasing reliance on personal cars and other environmentally harmful transport methods.

Mastercard supports urban mobility by partnering with transit authorities worldwide to implement open, contactless payment systems, such as in the Philippines' public transport. These systems enhance convenience, efficiency, and sustainability. Additionally, credit cards now offer higher rewards for electric vehicle charging, encouraging drivers to adopt cleaner transportation options. Financial institutions offer green mortgage. A "green mortgage" applies to financing resource-efficient new builds or eco-friendly home upgrades, like heat pumps or solar panels. Fannie Mae and Freddie Mac, covering 70% of the U.S. mortgage market, offer green financing options through their affiliated lenders to support sustainable housing improvements. Government-subsidized loans enable financial institutions to provide competitive "green loans" with reduced interest rates, lower down payments, and extended terms. Sustainability-linked loans adjust interest rates based on a business's performance against predefined environmental metrics.

Majid Al Futtaim, a Dubai-based family business house raised \$500 million through green financing and introduced an innovative sustainability-linked loan with a 'penalty-only' structure. Mashreq bank in UAE have made investments worth \$1.3 billion in water related projects. The bank has set an ambitious target of investing \$30 billion in sustainable financing by the year 2030.

Risks Related to Sustainable Products

The specific risks related to sustainable finance products are greenwashing, social washing and impact washing. Greenwashing refers to the misleading marketing of financial products as more environmentally friendly or sustainable than they are. It involves inaccurate or unverifiable environmental claims to gain a competitive advantage. This practice distorts consumer decision-making and poses a significant concern for policymakers, as it undermines trust in sustainable finance products. The UK Advertising Standards Agency (ASA) recently instructed a financial service provider to remove advertisement accused of greenwashing for promoting sustainability while investing in fossil fuels. ASA emphasized that false environmental claims can mislead consumers, influencing financial decisions like opening bank accounts or taking loans. "Social washing" occurs when companies falsely promote social responsibility efforts to improve their reputation or seek economic returns, misleading consumers and investors about their actual commitments to social issues. This poses a risk similar to "greenwashing" by distorting information on the "S" factor in ESG decisions. "Impact washing" occurs when investment products falsely claim to have a measurable social or environmental impact, misleading consumers. This happens when the impact is unverifiable, overstated, or misaligned with investors' goals. A 2020 review found that over half of European retail funds making environmental impact claims were vague, unsubstantiated, or inaccurate.

References

Aegon, Exploring a more inclusive approach to insurance coverage, June 14, 2021.

Agri3 Fund. (n.d.). *AGRI3 Fund aims to mobilise additional public and private capital at scale, to contribute to sustainable agricultural value chains and avert deforestation*. AGRI3 Fund. https://agri3.com/

Ahead of the wave, Financing the transition to a decarbonized built environment, Building Life, Europe Regional Network, World Green Building Council.

Allianz. Responsible investments and insurance. Accessed 14 Jan 2023.

Anouti, Y., Elborai, S., Kombargi, R., & Hage, R. (2020). The dawn of green hydrogen: Maintaining the GCC's edge in a decarbonized world. *Strategy &*. https://www.strategyand.pwc.com/m1/en/reports/2020/the-dawnof-green-hydrogen.html

ArcelorMittal. (2020). *ArcelorMittal sets 2050 group carbon emissions target of net zero*. ArcelorMittal. Available at: https://corporate.arcelormittal.com/media/press-releases/arcelormittal-sets-2050-group-carbon-emissions-target-of-net-zero

Asia Pacific Climate Report. (2024). *Catalyzing finance and policy solutions*. Asian Development Bank. https://doi.org/10.22617/SGP240498-2

AXA. Universal registration document 2021: AXA sustainability. Accessed 20 Nov 2022.

Besnainou, J. (2018). *Blockchain in Energy & Industry Raises $1 billion—and Heads into Challenging Times*. Cleantech Group. https://www.cleantech.com/blockchain-in-energy-industry-raises-1-billion-and-heads-into-challenging-times/

Bettenhausen, C. C&EN, World Chemical Outlook 2021. C&EN. www.cen.acs.org/business

BIAC, Green Finance, Key Business Considerations for Financing a Sustainable and Low-Carbon Economy, page 6, June 2016.

Blended Finance and Agriculture, Convergence. (2021). https://www.convergence.finance/resource/blended-financeand-agriculture/view

Bryan, B. A., Gao, L., Ye, Y., et al. (2022). Bryan, B.A., Gao, L., Ye, Y., Sun, X., Connor, J.D., Crossman, N.D., Stafford-Smith, M., Wu, J., He, C., Yu, D., Liu, Z., Li, A., Huang, Q., Ren, H., Deng, X., Zheng, H., Niu, J., Han, G. & Hou, X., 2018. China's response to a national land-system sustainability emergency. *Nature, 559*, 193–204. Available at: https://doi.org/10.1038/s41586-018-0280-2

Building Green, Sustainable Construction in Emerging Markets, IFC Report October 2023.

Bullock, R., Lawrence, M., & Moody, J. *Mobility and transport connectivity series, unlocking green logistics for development*. World Bank Group. http://www.worldbank.org/transport

Capotă, L.-D., Giuzio, M., Kapadia, S., & Salakhova, D. (2022). Are ethical and green investment funds more resilient? (ECB Working Paper Series No 2747 / November 2022).

CEMEX. (2021). *Vertua® Low Carbon Concrete and UK's first CarbonNeutral® concrete solution*. Available at: https://www.cemex.co.uk/vertua-low-carbon-concrete

CEMEX. (2022). *Green Financing Framework*. Available at: https://www.cemex.com/documents/20143/53544776/cemex-green-financing-framework.pdf/2412d811-1541-08cd-d1c3-7258c10fd5f4?t=1656297024704

Chiavari, J., Souza, P., Motta, M., Florias, R., & Minsky, E. (2024). *Landscape of climate finance for land use in Brazil 2021–2023*. Climate Policy Initiative.

Circle Economy. (2024). *A shared vision for the circular economy*. [Online] Available at: circle--economy.com/resources/a-shared-mdbs-vision-for-the-circular-economy

Climate Bonds Initiative—Basic Chemicals Criteria Document.

Climate Chain Coalition. (2018). https://www.climatechaincoalition.io/ and https://www.climatechaincoalition.io/charter

Climate Investment Opportunities in Emerging Markets—An IFC Analysis. International Finance Corporation. Nov. 2016.

Climatefinance lab.org, Sustainable Energy bonds, India Innovation Lab.

Compass Group, Sustainable Financing Framework. (2022). https://www.compass-group.com/content/dam/compassgroup/corporate/Investors/debtinvestors/Sustainable_Financing_Framework_Final.pdf

CPI [Daniela Chiriac, Harsha Vishnumolakala, Paul Rosane]. (2023). *Landscape of Climate Finance for Agrifood Systems. Climate Policy Initiative.*

CRREM. (2023). Carbon Risk Real Estate Monitor.

Das, P. K., & Cungu, A. (2023). *Green finance as a critical lever for delivering sustainable agrifood systems—A global landscape study*. FAO. https://doi.org/10.4060/cc7402en

Davis, B., Mane, E., Gurbuzer, L. Y., Caivano, G., Piedrahita, N., Schneider, K., Azhar, N., et al. (2023). *Estimating global and country-level employment in agrifood systems* (FAO Statistics Working Paper Series, No. 23-34). FAO. https://doi.org/10.4060/cc4337en

De Jager, N. *EU Green Deal and cross-border carbon charges.* KPMG International. https://kpmg.com/xx/en/home/insights/2023/05/chemicals-enter-a-new-era-of-green-investment.html

Deforestation -free finance: A guide on tools and frameworks for financial institutions, World Business Council for Sustainable Development Financing a farming transition: Key enablers and recommendations, Green Finance Institute.

Della Croce, R., Kaminker, C., & Stewart, F. (2011). *The role of pension funds in financing green growth initiatives* (OECD Working Papers on Finance, Insurance and Private Pensions, No. 10). OECD Publishing. https://doi.org/10.1787/5kg58j1lwdjd-en

Deloitte. (2022). *Chemical industry outlook.* https://www2.deloitte.com/us/en/pages/energy-and-resources/articles/chemical-industry-outlook.html

Desalegn, G. Insuring a greener future: How green insurance drives investment in sustainable projects in developing countries? *Green Finance, 5*(2): 195–210. https://doi.org/10.3934/GF.2023008

Dodge Data & Analytics. (2021). *World Green Building Trends 2021.* At: https://www.construction.com/toolkit/reports/World-Green-Building-trends-2021

Elser, B. (2023). *Sustainability and the chemical industry: Where's the money?* https://www.gpca.org.ae/2023/12/26/sustainability-and-the-chemical-industry-wheres-the-money/

Environmental, social and governance (ESG) in insurance industry, Series 1: Environment, Report Grant Thornton, 2024.

European Commission. (2017). *Joint Research Centre, Boulamanti, A., Moya, J., Energy efficiency and GHG emissions—Prospective scenarios for the chemical and petrochemical industry.* Publications Office. https://data.europa.eu/doi/10.2760/20486

European Environment Agency (EEA). (2020). Final energy consumption by fuel type and sector.

European Parliament. (2021). Draft Report on the implementation of the Energy Performance of Buildings Directive (2021/2077(INI)).

Eurostat. (2022a). Energy consumption in households, Greenhouse gas emissions from energy use in buildings in the EU.

Eurostat. (2022b). HICP—monthly data (annual rate of change).

Executive Summary to WORLD BANK, vice presidency for sustainable development, an investment framework for clean energy and development: A progress report, at iv, v (2006). Available at http://www.worldbank.org/energy (follow "an investment framework for Clean Energy and Development: A Progress Report").

Fabian, N., et al. (2023). Private retirement systems and sustainability. In B. Hammond, R. Maurer, & O. S. Mitchell (Eds.), *Pension Funds and Sustainable Investment.* Oxford University Press. © Nathan Fabian et al. https://doi.org/10.1093/oso/9780192889195.003.0009

FAO AgrInvest: Enabling sustainable private investment in agri-food systems and specific value chains. (n.d.). United Nations. https://sdgs.un.org/partnerships/fao-agrinvest-enabling-sustainable-private-investment-agri-food-systems-and-specific

Finra—University of Chicago. (2022). *Consumer insights: Money & investing.* https://www.finrafoundation.org/sites/finrafoundation/files/Consumer-Insights-Money-and-Investing.pdf

G20 Green Finance Synthesis Report. G20 Green Finance Study Group, Sept. 05, 2016. http://unepinquiry.org/wp-content/uploads/2016/09/Synthesis_Report_Full_EN.pdf

Galbiati, G. M., Yoshida, M., Benni, N., & Bernoux, M. (2023). *Climate-related development finance to agrifood systems—Global and regional trends between 2000 and 2021.* FAO. https://doi.org/10.4060/cc9010en

Green Bond Principles (GBP). International Capital Market Association (ICMA). 2016. Web. Sept. 16, 2016.

Green finance case studies in the transport sector. https://www.unepfi.org/industries/banking/green-finance-case-studies-in-the-transport-sector/

Green Returns: Unleashing the Power of Finance for Sustainable Food Systems, World Economic Forum, White paper July 2023.

Green Transportation: The Banking Opportunity. https://ecagbac.org/green-transportation-the-banking-opportunity/

Greening Institutional Investors: Input Paper. UNEP FI, PRI, Sept. 05, 2016. http://unepinquiry.org/wp-content/uploads/2016/09/3_Greening_Institutional_Investment.pdf

Healthy Food Systems Impact Fund II, Pymwymic. (n.d.). https://pymwymic.com/healthy-food-systems/

Henderson, R., Serafeim, G., Lerner, J., & Jinjo, N. (2019). Should a pension fund try to change the world? Inside GPIF's Embrace of ESG. Harvard Business School case 319-067.

Herbertson, K., & Hunter, D. (2007). Emerging standards for sustainable finance of energy sector. *Sustainable Development Law & Policy, 4–9*(Spring), 70–71.

How to be profitable and sustainable in the chemicals industry. EY Parthenon.

http://beta.worldbank.org/climatechange/news/nikko-asset-management-set-launch-green-fund-world-bank-bonds

http://www.worldbank.org/en/news/feature/2015/06/18/institutional-investors-the-unfulfilled-100-trillion-promise. Accessed 13 Nov 2018.

https://aseancpa.org/2023/08/24/adopting-green-technology-in-sustainable-financce-for-asean/

https://blog.railwaymen.org/the-role-of-fintech-in-sustainable-and-green-finance

https://cib.bnpparibas/accelerating-green-financing-in-the-automobile-market/

https://economictimes.indiatimes.com/industry/renewables/green-technology-and-the-future-of-the-automotive-industry/articleshow/101687852.cms?utm_source=contentofinterest&utm_medium=text&utm_campaign=cppst

https://gfmag.com/sustainable-finance/cop28-emirati-banks-top-pledges/

https://money.usnews.com/investing/articles/best-green-mutual-funds-to-buy-now

https://smartdev.com/sustainable-finance-the-role-of-fintech-in-promoting-environmental-and-social-goals/

https://worldgbc.org/sustainable-finance/

https://www.bmwk.de/Redaktion/EN/Pressemitteilungen/2019/20191016-altmaier-tax-breaks-for-retrofitting-buildings-benefit-both-climate-change-mitigation-and-local-craft-workers-and-jobs.html

https://www.capacero.cl/cap_acero/noticias/ejecutivos-de-cap-presentan-a-ministerio-de-energia-proyecto-de/2021-11-03/115628.html

https://www.carboncollective.co/sustainable-investing/green-mutual-fund#:~:tex

https://www.cemex.com/-/cemex-successfully-deploys-hydrogen-based-ground-breaking-technology

https://www.cfainstitute.org/en/professional-insights-stories/how-banks-and-green-finance-are-helping-address-climate-change?s_cid=pMax-cfa_msq-Global-global-FY25-generic-x-b2c-7013Z0000035OtRQAU-googleads-acquisition-x-x-x-x&gad_source=1&gclid=EAIaIQobChMI6cjP-OC6iAMVn2VBAh0J3jtjEAMYAiAAEgK7I_D_BwE&gclsrc=aw.ds

https://www.cfainstitute.org/insights/articles/how-banks-and-green-finance-are-helping-address-climate-change

https://www.cibc.com/en/personal-banking/investments/mutual-funds/sustainable-investment-strategies.html

https://www.climatebonds.net/2024/03/Financing the agri-food sector's transition to net zero, Progress towards Innovative Pathways and Financial Strategies for Sustainable Agriculture

https://www.climatebonds.net/2024/05/transition-action-agri-food

https://www.constructing-sustainable-future.com/en/interviews/how-does-finance-support-the-development-of-sustainable-construction/

https://www.downtoearth.org.in/energy/green-bond-issuance-by-automakers-reflects-global-energy-conundrum-89650

https://www.ebrd.com/what-we-do/sectors-and-topics/sustainable-resources/seffs.html

https://www.elliottdavis.com/insights/esg-strategies-for-the-consumer-goods-industry-today

https://www.ey.com/en_gl/insights/financial-services/emeia/how-the-insurance-sector-can-drive-sustainable-finance

https://www.ey.com/en_pt/insights/automotive/how-to-make-automotive-companies-sustainable

https://www.fidelitycharitable.org/content/dam/fc-public/docs/programs/socially-responsible-investment-funds.pdf
https://www.finextra.com/blogposting/26473/sustainable-finance-navigating-the-emerging-world-of-green-fintech
https://www.forbes.com/advisor/investing/best-esg-funds/
https://www.ft.com/partnercontent/london-stock-exchange-group/the-rise-and-rise-of-sustainable-investment.html
https://www.grantthornton.co.uk/insights/why-f-and-b-firms-should-consider-sustainable-finance/
https://www.greenfinanceinstitute.com/casestudies/battery-investment-facility/
https://www.greenfinanceinstitute.com/insights/insurance-and-pensions-fund-investors-can-unlock-capital-to-accelerate-the-green-transition/
https://www.greenfinanceinstitute.com/products-solutions/charging-infrastructure/
https://www.greenfinanceinstitute.com/programmes/cdrt/
https://www.greenfinanceplatform.org/finance/insurance
https://www.greenfinanceplatform.org/sectors/forestry
https://www.greenfinanceplatform.org/sectors/transport
https://www.ifc.org/content/dam/ifc/doc/2024/climate-finance-factsheet-ifc-financial-institutions-group.pdf
https://www.ifc.org/en/insights-reports/2023/building-green-in-emerging-markets (IFC Report).
https://www.ifc.org/en/what-we-do/sector-expertise/financial-institutions/climate-finance
https://www.ifc.org/wps/wcm/connect/news_ext_content/ifc_external_corporate_site/news+and+events/news/green-buildings-in-india-are-reducing-emissions?deliveryName=DM170723
https://www.knowesg.com/featured-article/thematic-esg-mutual-funds-a-comprehensive-guide-for-sustainable-investing
https://www.mastercardservices.com/en/advisors/sustainability-financial-inclusion-consulting/insights/question-equity-consumer-finance
https://www.mckinsey.com/industries/consumer-packaged-goods/our-insights/consumers-care-about-sustainability-and-back-it-up-with-their-wallets#/
https://www.ml.com/solutions/impact-investing.html#footnote-4
https://www.morganstanley.com/ideas/sustainable-funds-performance-2023-full-year
https://www.morningstar.com/funds/earth-day-2023-6-top-rated-funds-sustainable-investing-pioneers-consider
https://www.natwest.com/corporates/insights/sustainability/consumer-industries.html
https://www.pwc.com/gx/en/issues/esg/the-energy-transition/sustainable-energy-infrastructure/blueprint-for-sourcing-green-building-materials.html
https://www.pwc.com/m1/en/sustainability/financing-the-green-transition.html
https://www.schwab.com/socially-responsible-investing
https://www.sgbc.sg/carbon-resources/
https://www.supermoney.com/encyclopedia/green-mutual-fund
https://www.swecogroup.com/topical/industry/transforming-transport-how-the-automotive-industry-is-going-green/
https://www.transportenvironment.org/articles/eur39bn-a-year-in-public-investment-would-ensure-green-transport-is-made-in-europe-study
https://www.transportenvironment.org/articles/what-investments-are-needed-for-sustainable-transport-in-the-eu
https://www.tropicalforestalliance.org/en/collectiveaction-agenda/finance/investors-policydialogue-on-deforestation-ipdd-initiative/
https://www.unep.org/topics/energy/energy-finance/about-energy-finance
https://www.unepfi.org/banking/bankingprinciples/
https://www.unepfi.org/industries/banking/energy-and-industry-green-finance-case-studies/
https://www.unepfi.org/insurance/insurance/projects/guidance-on-the-integration-of-esg-risks-into-insurance-underwriting/

https://www.wbcsd.org/actions/true-value-of-food/

https://www.weforum.org/agenda/2024/06/how-the-commercial-banking-sector-can-fuel-a-nature-positive-future/

IDH Farmfit Fund provides US $4 million loan to CHC Commodities Limited. IDH, 2022. https://www.idhsustainabletrade.com/news/idh-farmfit-fund-provides-us-4-million-loan-to-chc-commodities-limited/

IFAD (International Fund for Agricultural Development). (2020). *ABC fund: Agri-business capital*. https://www.ifad.org/documents/38714170

IFC (International Finance Corporation). (2021). *Ctrl Alt Del. A Green Reboot for Emerging Markets Key Sectors for Post-Covid Sustainable Growth*. Available at: https://www.ifc.org/wps/wcm/connect/topics_ext_content/ifc_external_corporate_site/climate+business/resources/a+green+reboot+for+emerging+markets

Impact Report: Are banks prepared for Climate Change? Boston Common Asset Management, 2015. https://bostoncommonasset.com/Membership/Apps/ICCMSViewReport_Input_App.ashx?IX_OB=None&IX_mId=18&IX_RD=Y&ObjectId=731308

Insurance -Canada, Aviva launches specialized insurance for renewable energy, November 26, 2019.

Intergovernmental Panel on Climate Change (IPCC). (2022). Climate Change 2022: Mitigation of Climate Change.

International Monetary Fund | October 2021, Global Financial Stability Report-Chapter 3 Investment Funds: Fostering the transition to a green economy.

International Organisation of Securities Commissions. (2022). *Retail investor education in the context of sustainable finance markets and products*. https://www.iosco.org/library/pubdocs/pdf/IOSCOPD711.pdf

Kane, E. *Many global chemicals companies trail on carbon transition goals*. Bloomberg Professional Services. www.bloomberg.com/professional/blog/many-global-chemicals-companies-trail-on-carbon-transition-goals

Kemira. (2019). *Kemira signs revolving credit facility linked to sustainability targets*. https://www.kemira.com/company/media/newsroom/releases/kemira-signs-revolving-credit-facility-linked-to-sustainability-targets/

Klein, A., Widge, V., Bergedieck, L., Maheshwari, A., & Avendano Ugaz, F. *Green Finance: A Bottom-up Approach to Track Existing Flows (Vol. 2): Full Report (English)*. World Bank Group. http://documents.worldbank.org/curated/en/788041573021878350/Full-Report

Kombargi, R., Anouti, Y., Elborai, S., & Hage, R. (2018). The outlook for renewable energy in the GCC: Mostly sunny with a chance of rain. *Strategy&*. https://www.strategyand.pwc.com/m1/en/reports/2018/theoutlook-for-renewable-energy-in-the-gcc.html

Kuntal Sur. https://www.pwc.in/blogs/net-zero-banking-creating-a-long-term-and-sustainable-financial-services-economy.html

Maheshwari, A., Avendano, F., & Stein, P. *Measuring Progress on Green Finance—Findings from a Survey*. International Finance Corporation, Sept. 05, 2016.

Manns, A., Mauro, A., Jensen, E., Reynolds, J., & Popell, F. *How financial institutions can enable sustainable consumption*. https://www.mastercardservices.com/en/advisors/sustainability-financial-inclusion-consulting/insights/how-financialinstitutions-can

Mapping the Gap: The Road from Paris. Bloomberg New Energy Finance, Ceres, Ken Locklin. 2016. Feb. 18, 2017.

Market Trends, October 2020. https://cib.bnpparibas/electric-dreams/

McKinsey & Co. (2021). *A blueprint for scaling voluntary carbon markets to meet the climate challenge*. Available at: https://www.mckinsey.com/capabilities/sustainability/our-insights/a-blueprint-for-scaling-voluntary-carbon-markets-to-meet-the-climate-challenge

Middle East Green Finance, A US$ 2 trillion opportunity, strategy& | Middle East green finance.

Naqvi, B., Mirza, N., Rizvi, S. K. A., Porada-Rochoń, M., & Itani, R. (2021). Is there a green fund premium? Evidence from twenty-seven emerging markets. *Global Finance Journal, 50*, 100656. https://doi.org/10.1016/j.gfj.2021.100656

Nassiry, D. (2018). *The role of Fintech in unlocking green finance: Policy insights for developing countries* (ADBI Working Paper 883). Asian Development Bank Institute. Available: https://www.adb.org/publications/role-fintech-unlocking-green-finance

Nikulina, L. (2023). Global Pensions and ESG. In P. B. Hammond, R. Maurer, & O. S. Mitchell (Eds.), *Pension funds and sustainable investment*. Oxford University Press. © Luba Nikulina. https://doi.org/10.1093/oso/9780192889195.003.0007

OECD. (2020). *Tracking Economic Instruments and Finance for Biodiversity*. Available at: https://www.oecd.org/environment/resources/tracking-economic-instruments-and-finance-for-biodiversity-2020.pdf

OECD. (2023). *Financial consumers and sustainable finance: Policy implications and approaches* (OECD Business and Finance Policy Papers). https://doi.org/10.1787/bf84ff64-en

PolicyAdvisor. About Us-PolicyAdvisor. Accessed 20 Nov 2022.

Pyke, C. Finance fundamentals: A green building take on materiality, https://www.usgbc.org/articles/finance-fundamentals-green-building-take-materiality, Aug 2022.

Rahut, D., Narmandakh, D., He, X., Yao, Y., & Tian, S. (2023). *Opportunities and challenges during low-carbon transition: A perspective from Asia's Agriculture Sector*. ADB.

Rajesh, K. J. C., & Majid, M. A. (2020). Renewable energy for sustainable development in India: Current status, future prospects, challenges, employment, and investment opportunities. *Energy, Sustainability and Society, 10*. https://doi.org/10.1186/s13705-019-0232-1

Ramboll. (2022). Whole life carbon models for the EU27 to bring down embodied carbon emissions from new buildings Review of existing national legislative measures.

Rodriguez, M., & Martinez, E. Decarbonizing the basic chemicals industry using sustainable finance, CEP March 2024. aiche.org/cep

Sachs, J. D., Woo, W. T., Yoshino, N., & Taghizadeh-Hesary, F. (2019). *Why is green finance important?* (ADBI Working Paper 917). Asian Development Bank Institute. Available: https://www.adb.org/publications/why-green-finance-important

Scaling climate action: Unleashing innovative technologies in sustainable finance, December 2023, Bank for International Settlements.

Sector Insights, Chemicals, Sustainable Insight/ 1 July 2024., fitchratings.com

See NN Group—Responsible investment (nn-group.com). See https://prudential.scene7.com/is/content/prudential/Impact_Management_Policies_Disclosure_Statement?$scene7DefaultPreset$

Simon Kucher & Partners. (2021). *Global Sustainability Study 2021*. https://www.simonkucher.com/sites/default/files/studies/Simon-Kucher_Global_Sustainability_Study_2021.pdf

Solarplaza. (2018). *A comprehensive guide for companies involved in blockchain and energy*. https://www.blockchain2business.eu/request-blockchain-company-guide/

Statkraft. (2018). *Renewable energy generators and industrial consumers connected via blockchain*. https://www.statkraft.com/media/news/2018/blockchain-test-trade

Sussman, F. G. (2008) Adapting to climate change: A Business approach.

Sustainable Energy bonds, Instrument Analysis, 2017, Climatefinance lab.org

Sustainable energy economy network et al., how the world bank's energy framework sells climate and poor people short: A civil society response to the world bank's investment framework for clean energy and development 6 (2006). Available at http://www.seen.org/PDFs/Energy_Framework_CSO.pdf

Sustainable finance market update series, Sustainable finance across insurance providers, FC4S.ORG. July 2021.

T&E Report-November 2024. Financing transport decarbonisation, Study on investments for sustainable transport in the EU.

The insurance industry's path to ESG impact, Deloitte. Financial Services, May 2023.

The role of green buildings in sustainable finance. https://www.ocbc.com/business-banking/articles/the-role-of-green-buildings-in-sustainable-finance.page, August 2024.

Thinking Ahead Institute. (2020). *Global Pension Assets Study 2020.* Thinking Ahead Institute, Willis Towers Watson. https://www.thinkingaheadinstitute.org/research-papers/global-pension-assets-study-2020
Towards a green finance framework, European Banking Federation. www.ebf.eu
Transforming Transport: How the automotive industry is growing green.
Transport and Climate Change Global Status Report (2nd ed.), LOCAT.
UN Environment Program. (2021).
UNEP (UN Environment Program), and Global Alliance for Building and Construction. (2021). *Global Status Report for Buildings and Construction.* https://globalabc.org/resources/publications/2021-global-status-report-buildings-and-construction
United Nations Environment Programme, UNEP, 2021.
Wollenberg, E., Tennigkeit, T., Dinesh, D., Baumert, S., Röhrig, F., Kirfel-Rühle, L., & Zeppenfeldt, L. (2022). *Compensating farmers for ecosystem services: Lessons and an agenda for innovation* (CompensACTION Policy Brief 25 p). Available at: https://cgspace.cgiar.org/handle/10568/125381
World Bank. (2011). *Climate-Smart Agriculture: Increased Productivity and Food Security, Enhanced Resilience and Reduced Carbon Emissions for Sustainable Development.* https://www.openknowledge.worldbank.org/handle/10986/27395
World Bank. (2022). *State and Trends of Carbon Pricing 2022.* World Bank. Available at: http://hdl.handle.net/10986/37455
World Bank Group, Energy. http://www.worldbank.org/energy
WorldGBC. (2022). Circularity Accelerator.
www.ceres.org
www.igcc.org.au
www.incr.com
Yang, Y. X. O., Chew, B. C., Loo, H. S., et al. (2017). Green commercial building insurance in Malaysia. *AIP Conference Proceedings, 1818*, 020071. https://doi.org/10.1063/1.4976935
Yoshino, N., & Kaji, S. (Eds.). (2013). *Hometown investment trust funds*. Springer.
Yoshino, N., Taghizadeh-Hesary, F., & Nakahigashi, M. (2018). Modelling the social funding and spill-over tax for addressing the green energy financing gap. *Economic Modelling*. https://doi.org/10.1016/j.econmod.2018.11.018

Part II
Sectoral and Institutional Case Studies in Sustainable Finance

Chapter 9
Sustainable Finance Investments by Multilateral Development Banks

Multilateral Development Banks (MDBs) comprising of World Bank Group and others such as African Development Bank (AfDB), Asian Development Bank (ADB), Asian Infrastructure Investment Bank (AIIB), the European Bank for Reconstruction and Development (EBRD), the Inter-American Development Bank (IADB) outlined their joint commitment of $50 billion annually for climate finance initiatives for low income and middle-income economies by year 2025. In the year 2023, MDBs had funded $59 billion of climate finance for public recipients and $15.7 billion for private recipients in low- and middle-income economies. In 2023, the multilateral development Banks committed a total of $ 74.686 billion to low- and middle-income economies, and $ 50.283 billion to high-income economies.

Approximately 94% of the funding was utilized for climate change mitigation finance and 6% for climate change adaptation finance. The mitigation sector of energy receives most of the resources allotted to low developed countries. Buildings, public installations and end use energy efficiency are sectors which receive highest amount of climate finance.

Table 9.1 highlights the climate finance commitments made by MDBs in the year 2023.

Table 9.2 shows the climate finance commitments made by MDBs on the basis of mitigation activities in year 2023.

Table 9.3 shows the climate finance commitments made by MDBs on the basis of adaptation activities in year 2023.

Table 9.4 gives the climate finance commitments made by MDBs region wise in year 2023.

B. R. Kumar, *Green Finance*, Sustainable Finance,
https://doi.org/10.1007/978-3-032-03333-8_9

Table 9.1 MDB climate finance commitments

MDB	Low & middle-income economies	High income economies
African Development Bank	$5838 million	$11 million
Asian Development Bank	$10,745 million	$ one million
European Investment Bank	$3963 million	$42,108 million
Inter-American Development Bank Group	$5870 million	$1677 million
Asian Infrastructure Investment Bank	$3230 million	$204 million
Islamic Development Bank	$2048 million	$50 million
Council of Europe Development Bank	$ten million	$954 million
New Development Bank	$1107 million	
European Bank for Reconstruction and Development	$4604 million	$2860 million
World Bank Group	$37,284 million	$2417 million

Source: 2023 Joint Report on Multilateral Development Banks' Climate Finance. www.eib.org/mdbs-climate-finance

Table 9.2 Climate finance commitments in terms of mitigation activity

Sector	Amount in million dollars
Energy	28,142
Mining and metal production for climate action	79
Manufacturing	4851
Agriculture, forestry, land use and fisheries	2741
Water supply and waste water	2945
Solid waste management	884
Transport	23,294
Buildings, public installations and end use energy efficiency	17,748
ICT and digital technologies	529
R&D and Innovations	2018
Cross sectoral activities	14,018

Source: 2023 Joint Report on Multilateral Development Banks' Climate Finance. www.eib.org/mdbs-climate-finance

Sustainable Finance Initiatives by World Bank

World Bank help countries achieve sustainable development. It is the world's largest source of development finance and expertise for developing countries. The World Bank have over 75 plus years of expertise in financing development projects. The World Bank have offered $260 billion in loans outstanding to 78 countries. The World Bank Group consists of International Bank for Reconstruction and Development (IBRD), International Development Association (IDA), International

Table 9.3 Climate finance commitments in terms of adaptation activity

Sector	Amount in million dollars
Water and wastewater system	4945
Other agricultural and ecological resources	1231
Institutional capacity support or technical assistance	1884
Information and communications technology	246
Industry, manufacturing and trade	141
Financial services	1184
Energy, transport and other built environment and infrastructure	47,254
Cross cutting sectors	6367
Crop and food production	2179
Coastal and riverine infrastructure	2289

Source: 2023 Joint Report on Multilateral Development Banks' Climate Finance. www.eib.org/mdbs-climate-finance

Table 9.4 Total MDB Climate finance by region

Sector	Amount in million dollars
East Asia and the Pacific	11,120
Europe: EU	46,307
Europe: Non-EU	9133
Central Asia	2388
Latin America and the Caribbean	15,859
Middle East and North Africa	5294
South Asia	12,927
Sub-Saharian Africa	17,241
Multi regional	4700

Source: 2023 Joint Report on Multilateral Development Banks' Climate Finance. www.eib.org/mdbs-climate-finance

Finance Corporation (IFC), Multilateral Investment Guarantee Agency (MIGA) and International Centre for the Settlement of Investment Disputes (ICSID). IBRD provides loans to governments of middle-income countries. IDA provides loans and grants to governments of lower-income countries. IBRD is the issuer of World bank bonds. IDA raises funds from donors and IDA bonds. All bonds issued by World Bank support sustainable development. These bonds offer investors the opportunity to invest in financial products with a high credit rating while supporting projects with positive impact. For climate finance initiatives, World Bank Group have allocated $42.6 billion in the fiscal year 2024. All IBRD projects are screened for climate risk and impact. In fiscal 2024, 94% of IBRD projects had climate financing. World Bank had been issuing debt since the year 1947 and had triple rating since 1959. World Bank offers funds only for sovereign guaranteed projects. The

Sustainable Development Bond Framework developed by the World Bank describes the process for selecting, evaluating and reporting on eligible sustainable development projects.

Sustainable development bonds issued by World Bank have supported 690 projects. World Bank have committed $38.8 billion in lending. World Bank have offered 6.7 million people with enhanced access to transportation services. The funding has benefited 8.9 million individuals through job-focused programs. The funding by World Bank have provided four million people with new or improved electricity accesses. About 487,502 farmers were offered improved agricultural technology and over 200,000 were offered with new or improved irrigation or drainage services. Through green bond issuance, about 202 km of rail tracks, public transport or pedestrian walkways were constructed. World Bank through green projects have treated 23 million m3 of wastewater annually and have resulted in 44 m3 of annual water savings.

The first green bond in the world was issued by World Bank in the year 2008. World Bank through International Bank for Reconstruction and Development (IBRD) have raised over $ 1 trillion from private investors and had funded middle income countries for more than 75 countries. In 2023, World Bank raised over $43 billion in sustainable development bonds in different structures and maturities. Since then World Bank had issued almost $290 billion in labelled bonds including $18 billion in green bonds. IBRD is the largest issuer of sustainable development bonds and uses the funds raised from capital markets to support development activities in member countries. IBRD engages with bond investors on development priorities such as biodiversity, education, climate change, road safety and water. In 2022, IBRD issued the first of its kind outcome bond for wildlife conservation. In 2023, IBRD issued five-year emission reduction outcome bond which provided additional financing from private investors to a water purifier project in Vietnam. Instead of regular coupon income, bond investors would receive a return linked to the carbon credits generated by the project. This innovative instrument facilitates raising upfront financing for a climate focussed project by means of securitizing future carbon credit sales revenue and passing project performance risk onto bond investors. This purifier project aims to provide clean water to two million children in Vietnam and reduce greenhouse gas emissions by almost six million tons of CO2 over 10 years.

IDA plays a critical role in the World Bank Group's mission of reducing poverty and fostering sustainable economic development. In 2018, IDA made its capital market debut with a $1.5 billion US dollar bond. IDA has expanded its market presence by issuing bonds across different maturities and currencies which include the euro, British pound, Swedish krona and Norwegian krone to support its funding program. The triple A rating of IDA facilitate the issuance of sustainable development bonds. In fiscal 2023, IDA issued approximately $2 billion in bonds.

World Bank offers technical assistance to countries to develop greeners and more sustainable capital markets and financial systems. The bank facilitates market-based solutions and mobilize private sector toward environmental and social priorities. The bank assisted Colombian government for their first sovereign green bond issue and developed a national green taxonomy to identify projects and activities. World Bank also offered technical assistance for post issuance impact reports for Egypt and Indonesia as well as for state owned enterprise PT Indonesia Infrastructure Finance. In 2023, World Bank provided technical assistance to government of India for establishing a sovereign green bond program and raise the equivalent of $ 2 billion in Indian rupees in domestic capital markets through two green bonds. The funds raised through the issues would be utilized to finance renewable energy and the electrification of transport systems in the country. The World Bank leverages its capital market expertise by analysing climate finance options through its Country Climate and Development Reports. In the year 2023, these analyses were conducted for Malawi, South Africa and the Sahel countries. In the year 2023, World Bank assisted countries such as Armenia and Georgia to automatically fix the interest rates at the disbursement of recent IBRD loans to fund a green and inclusive recovery. World Bank also facilitate countries to secure access to concessional climate financing by structuring blended financing packages for investments.

The IBRD has supported various initiatives with innovative funding approaches: concessional loans from climate funds were used to finance renewable energy investments in South Africa and enhance climate resilience in the Republic of Congo. In Tanzania, a record-breaking $500 million development policy loan was structured by combining funds from IDA's highly concessional Short Maturity Loan product with a regular IDA Scale-Up Window loan. Additionally, the new Investment Project Financing with Delayed Drawdown Option was introduced to provide shock-responsive financing, as demonstrated by the pilot project offering liquidity support to Romania's Bank Deposit Guarantee Fund.

World Bank pioneered and created the model for the present day labelled bond market consisting of green, blue, social and sustainable bonds. The investors in the labelled bond market consists of fund managers, pension funds and insurance companies, family offices, banks, financial institutions, religious institutions and individual investors. The Global Impact Investing Network (GIIN) estimates the size of the impact investing market to be more than US$ 1 trillion. World Bank had set the blueprint for sustainability across the capital markets. World Bank have raised over US$ 13 billion through 158 green bond transactions in 21 currencies. The bank has issued US$8 billion sustainability development bond for health and COVID-19 response in member countries. World Bank had created the green sukuk and blue bond products and facilitated emerging market sustainable finance transactions.

World Bank facilitate building of sustainable financial markets. World Bank offers technical assistance for regulators and policy makers. World Bank assist financial regulators understand the financial impact of sustainability challenges such as climate change, environmental degradation, loss of biodiversity, pandemics and social issues. World Bank promote sustainable capital markets by developing regulations, guidelines, and green taxonomies. It also supports labelled bond issuance and enhance local certifier capacity. The bank also strengthens issuers' ESG risk reporting and empower institutional investors with ESG and impact investing frameworks.

World Bank also offers technical assistance to issuers of financial solutions. The pre-issuance services include developing frameworks, action plans, and eligible project categories; share international best practices, facilitate certifications, and advise on reporting commitments and communication aligned with national priorities. The post issuance services include offering guidance on using standardized impact reporting templates, defining baselines and indicators, aligning timelines with green bond frameworks and preparation of auditor terms for assurance.

World Bank offers technical assistance for certifiers or second opinion providers. The bank deliver training to domestic environmental, climate related and sustainability related research institutions. World Bank offers insights on climate risks, financial scenarios and external reviews.

World Bank promote sustainable investment by providing technical assistance for institutional investors. World Bank offer training on ESG and responsible investment strategies and recommend ESG integration in governance, process, stewardship and reporting.

Green sukuk (Islamic bond) has the potential to channel US$ 2 trillion Islamic finance market toward funding of green and sustainable investment projects. In 2017, Tadau Energy Sdn Bhd had issued the world's first green sukuk to raise US$ 59 million to finance a 50 MW solar power plant in Malaysia. Republic of Indonesia issued a sovereign green bond valued at US$1.25 billion in year 2018. World Bank identified and leveraged Malaysia's Islamic finance expertise to merge sukuk and green bonds, conducted feasibility assessments, raised awareness among stakeholders, built local certifier capacity, supported issuers and contributed to ASEAN Green and Sustainable Bond Standards development.

In 2017, Fiji issued the first emerging market sovereign green bond in the world. The bond raised US$ 50 million to fund climate change adaptation and mitigation projects. As COP 23 President, Fiji used the bond to bring global awareness to challenges of small island nations to the impacts of climate change. World Bank supported Fiji in structuring this green bond by establishing a policy framework, identifying projects and developing post issuance impact reports. In the same year Indonesia Financial Services Authority (FSA) issued green bond regulations. In 2018, PT Sarana Multi Infrastruktur (PT SMI), a state-owned enterprise issued the first corporate green bond in Indonesia. World Bank conducted workshops on sustainability, engaged stakeholders, and supported Indonesia in green bond regulations and the world's first sovereign green sukuk. World Bank facilitated PT SMI's domestic green bond, developed frameworks, identified projects, guided reporting and reviews, and prepared post-issuance impact reports, advancing green finance initiatives.

Seychelles issued the first blue bond in the world. World Bank structured a blue bond with a custom ten-year maturity schedule which aligned with project funding requirements and Seychelles' liability profile. For this project, World Bank provided partial credit guarantee of US$ five million into the blue bond, which lowered Seychelles' borrowing cost at least 2% per year. World Bank arranged US$ five million in concessional financing from the Global Environmental Facility (GEF) which further lowered Seychelles' net borrowing cost by over 3% per year. World

Bank also facilitated in securing a donation from Rockefeller Foundation to cover most of the transaction costs. World Bank also engaged with investment banks to find a top tier placement agent and a trustee for the blue bond issuance.

The bank assists nations to increase their fiscal resilience against disasters by improving their access to the reinsurance and capital markets. The Treasury department works with government to execute risk transfer transactions before a catastrophic event occurs. In March 2023, World Bank completed a combined catastrophe bond and swap transaction, securing $630 million in insurance coverage for Chile against extreme earthquake events over three years. This included $350 million in catastrophe bonds and $280 million in catastrophe swaps. Marking IBRD's 19th catastrophe bond issuance, it was Chile's second catastrophe risk transfer transaction and the first-ever World Bank bond and catastrophe bond listed on the Hong Kong Exchanges and Clearing Limited. As of June 2023, World Bank have facilitated the transfer of $5.8 billion in disaster risk to international markets. This includes $1.3 billion in outstanding IBRD-issued catastrophe bonds and swaps covering earthquake and hurricane risks in Chile, Jamaica, and Mexico.

The World Bank Treasury's Reserve Advisory and Management Partnership offers support for public asset management institutions through advisory services, executive training and asset management services. The World Bank serves 72 central banks, public pension funds, sovereign wealth funds and international financial institutions. The World Bank manages around $82 billion for trust funds and external clients. The bank issued its inaugural impact report for its dedicated sustainable fixed income strategy which focuses on asset management mandates for trust funds managed by the bank.

IBRD had provided $160 million financing for enhancing quality of tertiary education facilities in Colombia. The project aims to expand access for disadvantaged students through loans, scholarships, and institutional support. It targets over 1.2 million disadvantaged students, provides 46,080 loans, and benefits 322,000 learners through direct interventions. Special loan allocations support victims of violence, indigenous groups, and remote-area students. IBRD had financed $200 million for Greater Cairo Air Pollution Management Project. This project aims to cut emissions from key sectors and enhance resilience to air pollution, with a focus on improving healthcare waste management in response to COVID-19. Key expected outcomes include a 10% increase in women's employment in the solid waste sector, a 23% reduction in public bus GHG emissions, and a 30% reduction in municipal solid waste emissions. IBRD had financed $100 million for the Guatemala Nutrition and Health Project. The project enhanced nutrition, healthcare and pandemic response targeting 680,000 people and trained 50,000 staff and build two hospitals. In 2023, IBRD offered $125 million to facilitate innovation in biopharmaceutical products and medical devices in India. The project aims to boost India's biotech innovation by funding early stage development, training 6295 people, advancing 50 health products, licensing 23 technologies and providing support to 14 publications. In 2023, IBRD had also provided $300 million financing for the Angola based Climate Resilience and Water Security based RECLIMA project. This project expands water infrastructure, enhancing access and resilience. It benefits 860,000 people, mobilizes 12.4 million m^3 of groundwater, and adds 110,000 household water connections. In 2023, IBRD also offered $50 million to enable digital governance project in Serbia. The project enhances online government services, expanding digital access to two million people, increasing available services from 4 to 30, and improving user satisfaction by 50%. IBRD financed project worth $150 million to improve energy efficiency of public buildings in Turkey. The project enhances energy efficiency in central government buildings, including schools and hospitals, through renovations and technical support. It aims to save 315 GWh annually, cut CO_2 emissions by 225,000 tons, upgrade 620 buildings, and reduce energy costs by $18 million per year.

Sustainable Bond Issues by World Bank in 2024

During 2024, World Bank had priced an Australian dollar 2 billion 5-year bond due January 10, 2029. This transaction had attracted over 50 orders totalling more than AUD 2.4 billion from investors. In the same year IBRD had priced two sustainable development bonds to enhance World Bank's mission to eradicate extreme poverty. These bonds consisted of a USD 3 billion, 2-year bond maturing in April 2026, and a USD 3 billion, 7-year bond maturing in April 2031. World Bank had priced a Canadian dollar 1.4 billion five-year sustainable development bond which matures in January 2029. In 2024, World Bank had priced a 5-year British pound sterling denominated sustainable development bond which raised GBP of 1.5 billion from investors. World Bank had priced a EUR 3 billion 10-year sustainable development bond which attracted over 100 orders totalling Euro 4.7 billion from European and global investors. World Bank had priced a dual tranche transaction consisting of USD 2 billion and USD 0.7 billion tranches which were linked to the Secured Overnight Financing Rate (SOFR). This transaction had attracted over 110 orders which totalled USD 4.7 billion from investors.

During April 2024, the World Bank (IBRD) issued three catastrophe bonds, providing the Government of Mexico with USD 420 million in insurance coverage against earthquakes and named Atlantic storms for a four-year period. These cat bonds replace and expand Mexico's previous catastrophe bonds for these natural disasters by an additional USD 60 million. During March 2022, the World Bank (IBRD) issued Wildlife Conservation Bond, a principal protected outcome bond which focusses on private capital for conservation outcomes. For this bond, investors deferred regular coupon payments to support conservation efforts in two South African parks, benefiting local communities environmentally and socially. In return, they receive their principal, a small guaranteed return, and a potential conservation success payment at maturity, linked to rhino population growth and funded by the Global Environment Facility. Nuveen led the investment, joined by institutional and private investors from Credit Suisse and Citi Private Bank. During 2024, the IBRD issued a plastic waste reduction linked bond which is a principal protected outcome bond which focusses on projects with positive climate goals. For these projects investors forego regular coupon payments to provide up front financing which aim to reduce and recycle plastic waste in vulnerable communities in Ghana and Indonesia. The main investors for the project include Velliv Pension, Skandia, Mackenzie Investments, T. Rowe Price and Muzinich & Co. During August 2024, the World Bank had issued the Amazon Reforestation Bond, a principal protected outcome bond which channels additional private capital for carbon removal and reforestation. Investors forego coupons to fund a $36 million reforestation project in the Amazon, which focusses on carbon reduction to enhance biodiversity, and support socio-economic development. Along with return of principal and small guaranteed return, investors receive variable coupons linked to the value of carbon removal units to be generated by the projects. Microsoft would purchase these CRUs from Mombak, the Brazilian company which implement these projects. Nuveen, T. Rowe Price, Mackenzie Investments, Rathbone Investment, Velliv Pension were the lead investors. World Bank advises member countries on green finance and green bond issuance through a guide for a national taxonomy. Green bonds carry the same financial terms and risk as other World Bank bonds. World Bank Treasury focusses on long term partnership with private sector to drive growth in green and sustainability bonds. World Bank projects were able to reduce 27.3 million tCO2 GHG emissions and about 27.5 million people had benefitted from green bond projects. The green bond projects meant for clean transportation resulted in 202 kilometres of rail tracks, public transport and pedestrian walkways. In 2023, about 4876 megawatt of renewable energy capacity were added and 38.9 million MWh of annual energy savings were achieved in year 2023.

Green Finance Investments by International Finance Corporation (IFC)

The Climate Finance team of IFC facilitate clients to identify climate friendly investment opportunities and offer business development support and customized product training for loan officers. IFC supports the development of green banking by developing tools to identify, quantify and evaluate climate friendly product lines such green bonds, blue bonds and sustainability bonds. IFC is also involved in financing renewable energy, distributed energy and storage solutions, financing for green buildings and green mortgages financing in climate smart agriculture. IFC is associated with learning platforms for commercial banks such as Green Banking Academy and the Alliance for Green Commercial Banks.

IFC was a pioneer in issuing green bonds with the launch of a Green Bond Program in year 2021 to facilitate investment for private sector projects which support renewable energy and energy efficiency. By 2020, IFC had issued 172 bonds in 20 currencies which amounted to $10.4 billion. During the period 2015–2020, IFC had assisted 19 banks to issue $2.4 billion of green bonds. In 2018, IFC had launched the world's largest targeted green bond fund, the Amundi Planet Emerging Green

One (EGO) which focusses on emerging markets. The fund valued at $1.42 billion is expected to deploy $ 2 billion into emerging markets green bonds over its lifetime. Amundi Fund known as the Build -Back-Better Emerging Markets Sustainable Transaction (BEST) strategy was launched in partnership with the IFC at COP26 in 2021. This fund aims to attract up to $2 billion in private investment into emerging market sustainable bonds.

IFC had issued HSBC Real Economy Green Investment Opportunity (REGIO) Fund the first global green bond fund which targets "real economy" issuers in emerging markets. The fund is expected to leverage around $500 million to $700 million in multilateral and private sector capital to support climate smart investments in developing countries. The REGIO fund would mainly buy bonds issued by non-financial or real economy companies such as manufacturing, agribusiness and infrastructure firms. The investment framework of this fund is closely aligned with the SDGs and the goals of the Paris Climate Agreement.

For the growth of green bonds as a new asset class from emerging markets, IFC works closely with the Sustainable Banking Network (SBN) and support its Green Bond Working Group. SBN members receive IFC technical guidance to develop green bond guidelines based on best international standards and practices. IFC also manage and administer the Green Bond Technical Assistance Program which aims to accelerate the growth of green bonds in emerging markets.

There exist $24.7 trillion investment opportunity in emerging markets for green buildings. IFC's Market Accelerator for Green Construction (MAGC) program focusses on energy saving and water saving technologies. Under this program, green building projects are required to have EDGE certifications. The off grid solar sector had grown into a $1.75 billion annual market under the aegis of IFC. In the year 2009, the World Bank Group had launched Lighting Africa, followed by Lighting Asia and Lighting Global to provide off grid solar energy for about 789 million people living without access to energy. The global off grid lighting sector serves about 420 million users and is projected to serve 823 million users by the year 2030. The sector is expected to witness an investment of US$ 1.7- $ 2.2 billion in the next five years.

Emerging markets account for more than one third of global clean energy investments. However emerging markets still represent only one fifth of global green bond issuance. In 2019, the emerging market green bond issuances amounted to $52 billion which represented an increase of 21% compared to year 2018. By 2019, the cumulative outstanding bond issuance amounted to $168 billion. About 59% of cumulative green bond issuance were made by financial institutions. About 35 emerging markets have made green bond issuances since the year 2012. IFC have $29.4 trillion investment potential in emerging market cities. In 2019, China remained the largest issuer among emerging markets accounting for more than $30 billion.

IFC estimates cumulative climate investment potential of $29.4 trillion across six key sectors in emerging market cities through 2030. These sectors include waste, renewable energy, public transportation, climate-smart water, electric vehicles, and green buildings. IFC has estimated that climate mitigation and adaptation need in emerging markets require investment between $1.7 trillion and $3.4 trillion annually by the year 2030. IFC is a significant player in the climate business segment. IFC focusses on five strategic areas of clean energy, climate smart cities, climate start agribusiness, green buildings and green finance. IFC has committed to align 85% of its new investment projects with the objectives of the Paris Agreement starting July 1, 2023 and 100% of these investments starting July 1, 2025. IFC's Financial Institution Group (FIG) have committed $18.5 billion to climate related projects through 160 plus emerging market financial institutions. In the first quarter of 2025, the value of FIG's climate finance projects amounted to $1.75 billion across 12 projects which included $1 billion in own account volume and $750 million in core mobilization. The investment partners of FIG have reported projects which have led to an estimated reduction in GHG emissions of 24.33 million tCO_2e/year.

IFC was the pioneer for issuance of a $ 1 billion benchmark green bond in the year 2012. IFC have issued 207 green bonds valued at $13.9 billion in 21 currencies. The role of IFC's advisory services is to facilitate global client financial institutions to build climate finance portfolios to reduce annual GHG emissions. The Global Blue Bond Project of IFC had achieved a cumulative financing total of $1.6 billion by 2024 since its inception in 2020. This includes three IFC blue loans, with a combined value of $172 million. IFC had partnered with T. Rowe Price to develop a global blue bond investment strategy. This partnership received the 2024 ESG Initiative of the Year award in the Americas from Environmental Finance. For its blue themed bonds that support sustainable ocean economies, IFC was recognized as the Best Multilateral Institution for Sustainable Finance by Global Finance. In the fiscal year 2024, FIG had committed $84.4 million in own account climate adaptation and resilience finance across 15 projects in areas of climate smart agriculture, green buildings, renewable energy and biodiversity. Some of the significant deals include that of IFC's commitment of $130 million to DLL, a Rabobank subsidiary to finance sustainable equipment for agri-SMEs in Brazil, Chile and Poland. In Morocco, IFC shared risk sharing facility for up to $15.8 million to Banque Centrale Populaire to assist farmers and distributors acquire photovoltaic and drip irrigation equipment thereby enhancing renewable energy and water management in agriculture.

In India, IFC have partnered with Axis Bank to provide a $500 million loan to develop a blue finance market and scale up financing of green projects in India. This initiative is the first blue investment by IFC in India. This investment facilitates private sector investment in emerging asset class along with raising direct long-term funding for investments such as water and wastewater management, reduction of marine pollution, restoration of ecosystems and offshore renewable energy. IFC will aid Axis Bank in expanding its green buildings portfolio which includes affordable housing projects.

IFC invested $300 million in AAIB's $500 million sustainability bond, Egypt's first and Africa's largest by a private bank. Allocating 75% to green projects and 25% to social assets, the bond supports Egypt's 2030 goal to reduce greenhouse gas emissions by 37% while advancing sustainable and inclusive finance initiatives. In July 2024, IFC and BBVA Colombia launched the world's first biodiversity bond, issuing a $15 million tranche of an eventual $70 million. The bond funds projects combating biodiversity loss, including reforestation, regenerative agriculture, and wildlife habitat restoration, while establishing criteria and metrics for biodiversity-focused initiatives.

The first fund dedicated to green bonds in Latin America was launched at COP26 by German development bank KfW. KfW have committed €74 million to the fund. According to IFC estimates, green bond issuance from emerging markets are expected to amount to $100 billion by three-year period. In 2020, World Bank facilitated Egypt to develop a green bond framework to support its inaugural $750 million sovereign green bond.

Sustainable Finance Investments by African Development Bank (AfDB)

With 70% of its infrastructure still to be built and natural resources valued at over $6.2 trillion, Africa presents significant opportunities for climate action. To achieve its climate goals, the continent requires up to $2.8 trillion by 2030, while meeting the Sustainable Development Goals (SDGs) will demand around $1.3 trillion annually.

The AfDB supports the economic development and social progress of countries in Africa by promoting investment of public and private capital projects. The AFDB strategy for 2013–2022 focused on improvement of Africa's growth and transition to green growth. During the period 2011–2015, AfDB implemented five-year climate change action plan and mobilized over US$ 6.5 billion for over 80 climate - resilient projects and 90 low carbon development projects in Africa. By the end of 2015, AfDB invested US$ 9.6 billion for climate finance adaptation activities related to agriculture, water resources and forests. AfDB also focusses on gender and youth sensitive development projects. The mitigation activities focus on sustainable transport, renewable energy and sustainable land use systems. In 2023, AfDB established the Climate Action Window (CAW) under the African Development Fund (ADF) with an initial capitalization of $429 million. The bank had launched the first call for proposals for the CAW at COP28 in Dubai. CAW aims to mobilize $13 billion in future replenishments. Bank, following its Climate Change and Green Growth Strategic Framework 2021–2030, aligns its investments with climate action to support sustainable, resilient, and low-carbon development in Africa. Approximately 97% of the bank's projects have integrated climate change and green growth considerations. In 2023, the bank has effectively mobilized over $275 million of new climate finance via various modalities. Climate finance was predominantly channelled through loans (52%), guarantees (28%) and grants (12%). The establishment of the Climate Change and Green Growth Department (PECG) in the year 2016 facilitated the consolidation of the bank's climate change agenda. PECG pursues the key objective of ensuring the bank's commitment to direct at least 40% of annual project approvals from 2020 onwards towards climate finance with at least 50% of these directed towards adaptation.

The Bank's initiatives such as African Financial Alliance on Climate Change (AFAC), the African Circular Economy Alliance (ACEA), and the Africa Circular Economy Facility (ACEF) expand climate finance, while the Africa NDC Hub aim to accelerate funding, technology and capacity for Paris Agreement goals. The Africa NDC collaborates with 20 other international and regional organizations for Paris Agreement commitments. The Africa Adaptation Acceleration Program (AAAP) launched in partnership with the Global Center on Adaptation (GCA) aims to mobilize up to $25 billion for adaptation by year 2025. The platform AFAC developed by the Bank aim to bolster Africa's financial sector investments in climate action through the use of green instruments, climate risk disclosure and climate finance flows among African financial institutions which lend to the private sector. The bank actively collaborates with a group of ten other MDBs and regional development banks to develop a coordinated response to the climate emergency. In 2023, out of a total financing volume of $10.6 billion made by AfDB, approximately 55% was directed towards climate finance. In 2023, the volume of climate finance provided by the bank grew by 173% compared to the year 2020.

The bank offers financial solution to support climate action. AfDB offers partial credit guarantee to mobilize sustainable financing in Senegal. The proceeds will be used exclusively to finance eligible green and social expenditures and projects by the Government under the Plan for an Emerging Senegal 2014–2035 and the country's NDC. African Development Bank Partial Credit Guarantee (PCG) is for an amount not exceeding UA 400 million. The $140 million AfricaGoGreen Fund (AGGF) finances green mobility, appliances, housing, and energy efficiency projects, backed by CTF, AfDB, SEFA, KfW, and other investors. This project is 100% designated as mitigation finance.

The $11.5 billion Climate Investment Fund (CIF) offers low cost, long term financing to advance climate action. The AfDB being the implementing entity of the CIF funds have supported the development of 43 climate investment plans across 27 African countries. The bank has deployed $1.042 billion in CIF resources and $2.32 billion of its own co-financing. AfDB is also the implementing agency for Global Environment Facility (GEF). The GEF serves as a financial mechanism for five international conventions. It provides grants to developing countries for projects related to biodiversity, climate change, international waters, land degradation, and persistent organic pollutants. By 2023, the Bank's GEF portfolio included 39 active projects in 25 countries, with a total volume of $302 million in GEF grants and co-financing of about $2.8 billion.

The Green Climate Fund serves as the financial mechanism for the United Nations Framework Convention on Climate Change (UNFCCC). The African Development Bank signed an Accreditation Master Agreement with the GCF which allows the bank to pursue funding exceeding $250 million for projects with the highest category of environmental and social impact risk. The $106.3 million Canada-African Development Bank Climate Fund (CACF) provides concessional financing for climate projects, prioritizing women's empowerment in public and private sector investments. In 2023, AfDB provided $69.9 million of CACF resources to co-finance projects including three sovereign operations – a $5.4-million loan for the Food and Nutrition Insecurity Resilience Project in Senegal, a $15-million loan for the Abia State Infrastructure Development Project in Nigeria, and a $13.2-million loan for the Last Mile Connectivity Project in Kenya. Launched in 2021 by AfDB and GCA, Africa Adaptation Acceleration Program (AAAP) seeks to mobilize $25 billion by 2025 for climate adaptation in Africa, focusing on food security, infrastructure, youth, and finance. Launched in 2007 by the African Union, the Great Green Wall Initiative combats desertification, land degradation, and climate change by restoring land and promoting green growth in the Sahara region.

References

Climate Change and Green Growth at the African Development Bank, Annual Report 2023.

Green Bond Funds – Impact Reporting Practices 2021, Environmental Finance.

https://documents1.worldbank.org/curated/en/856781551372777380/First-Corporate-Green-Bond-in-Indonesia-SupportingIndonesia-s-Efforts-to-Fight-Climate-Change-Case-Study.pdf

https://impact.economist.com/projects/building-a-better-future/bhps-plan-to-help-power-the-energy-transition/

https://projects.worldbank.org/en/projects-operations/project-detail/P172548

https://projects.worldbank.org/en/projects-operations/project-detail/P177004

https://thedocs.worldbank.org/en/doc/21c2fb7dfb189f10a0503004757b03f4-0340012022/original/Case-Study-MalaysiaGreen-Sukuk-Market-Development.pdf

https://thedocs.worldbank.org/en/doc/242151559930961454-0340022019/original/CasestudyBlueBondSeychellesfinal6.7.2019.pdf

https://www.ifc.org/en/insights-reports/2020/em-gb-report-2019

https://www.ifc.org/en/what-we-do/sector-expertise/financial-institutions/climate-finance/green-finance

https://www.worldbank.org/en/about/annual-report/promoting-sustainable-finance-capital-markets

IFC, Amundi, Emerging Market Green Bonds Report 2019.

IFC, Financial Institutions Group (FIG), www.ifc.org | www.ifc.org/ClimateFinance, Sept 2024.

Sustainable Finance and Environmental, Social, and Governance (ESG) Advisory Innovative Sustainable Financing Solutions for Emerging Markets, The World Bank.

World Bank bonds for sustainable development, connecting investment with purpose, treasury, World Bank presentation 2023.

Chapter 10
Green Finance Initiatives by Financial Institutions

Green Finance Initiatives by BlackRock

BlackRock is a leading publicly traded investment management firm with $10.0 trillion of assets under management ("AUM") as of December 31, 2023. As of December 31, 2023, BlackRock had approximately 19,800 employees in more than 30 countries who serve clients in over 100 countries across the globe. BlackRock's role in the transition to a low-carbon economy is as a fiduciary. BlackRock incorporate environmental, social and governance information along with other information into its firmwide processes to enhance risk adjusted returns. As a fiduciary, Black Rock manages investment risks and opportunities which would impact portfolios including financially material Environmental, Social and Governance data.

BlackRock's ESG integration framework is rooted in its legacy of rigorous risk management, supported by its Aladdin platform, which combines ESG data and investment expertise to identify opportunities and manage risks effectively. The framework is structured around three core pillars—investment processes, data & analytics, and transparency—empowered by providing employees with relevant ESG data, tools, and education. The process for evaluating and managing financially material environmental, social and governance (ESG) risks in Black Rock's active funds and advisory strategies aligns with BlackRock's broader risk management approach. Each strategy outlines how financially material ESG data or information is incorporated into its investment process. Portfolio managers are responsible for managing exposures to financially material ESG risks. Investment teams must demonstrate how they integrate financially material ESG data or information into their investment processes. For index portfolios, the primary responsibility is to replicate the characteristics of a predetermined benchmark index based on the methodology defined by index providers. In the case of European-domiciled funds, as required by regulation, BlackRock evaluates financially material ESG risks. BlackRock's Aladdin platform includes advanced analytic tools like Aladdin

B. R. Kumar, *Green Finance*, Sustainable Finance,
https://doi.org/10.1007/978-3-032-03333-8_10

Climate, which enables scenario analysis to identify investment risks and opportunities linked to climate change and the transition to a low-carbon economy. In private markets, where ESG data is less standardized and accessible than in public markets, BlackRock is advancing efforts to improve the collection, aggregation, evaluation, and measurement of financially material ESG information from private companies and third parties.

BlackRock employs a robust three-lines-of-defense approach to managing material investment risks in client portfolios:

1. First Line of Defense: Investment teams and business management serve as primary risk owners, ensuring investment risks are understood and aligned with client objectives.
2. Second Line of Defense: The Risk and Quantitative Analysis (RQA) group oversees investment and enterprise risk management frameworks, including the evaluation of financially material ESG risks. RQA conducts regular risk reviews with portfolio managers and includes a dedicated Sustainability Risk group to monitor and manage sustainability risks across the platform. Legal and Compliance also form part of this defense line.
3. Third Line of Defense: The Internal Audit function provides independent assurance, assessing the adequacy and effectiveness of BlackRock's internal controls to enhance risk management, control, and governance processes.

Oversight of firm-wide investment processes, including ESG integration, is managed by the Investment Sub-Committee of BlackRock's Global Executive Committee (GEC). This committee, which includes senior leaders such as the firm's President, Head of Portfolio Management, and Chief Risk Officer, receives ESG integration updates from the RQA Sustainability Risk team at least annually. BlackRock is a member of several industry associations which are related to sustainability and the transition to a low carbon economy which include ISSB Investor Advisory Group, Taskforce on Nature related Financial Disclosures (TNFD), Net Zero Asset Managers Initiative and Glasgow Financial Alliance for Net Zero. BlackRock International is a member of Climate Action 100+. BlackRock provide clients with analytics, insights, strategies and engagement to support the energy transition, net goals and enhanced corporate governance including proxy voting options. BlackRock remain long term investors in carbon-intensive companies due to their critical role in the economy, the global low-carbon transition, and clients' financial goals. BlackRock avoid broad sector divestments, prioritizing an orderly transition to a net-zero economy while aligning with long-term financial objectives and enabling systemic economic transformation.

Currently, about 25% of BlackRock's assets under management (AUM) in corporate and sovereign issuers are invested in entities with science-based targets or equivalent. As the transition advances and issuers and asset owners adapt, BlackRock project that by 2030, at least 75% of BlackRock's corporate and sovereign AUM on behalf of clients will align with issuers meeting science-based targets or equivalent standards.

The BlackRock Investment Institute Transition Scenario (BIITS), powered by Aladdin®, provides a research-based forecast to help investors navigate low-carbon transition risks and opportunities. While it informs investment decisions, clients choose whether to incorporate BIITS into their processes, acknowledging diverse transition perspectives. The BIITS identifies transition "fast lanes," primarily in developed markets, where decarbonization is expected to accelerate by 2050, notably in global power generation. Regions and carbon-intensive sectors outside these fast lanes face uncertainty due to higher costs of capital and technology. The BIITS projects annual energy system investment to rise from $2.2 trillion in recent years to $3.5 trillion this decade and $4.5 trillion by the 2040s. By then, low-carbon investments are expected to comprise up to 80% of the total, up from approximately 60% today. While higher-carbon sectors remain relevant, they may face transition risks, which can be mitigated through prudent planning and diversification. The BIITS estimates that extreme weather and other climate-related physical damages could reduce economic growth by more than 5% by 2050. Most of these losses are expected to occur regardless of the pace of the low-carbon transition, with the transition's speed becoming a key factor in mitigating damages only after 2050.

The BIITS aims to help investors navigate the low-carbon transition. It will ultimately feed into the BlackRock Investment Institute's long-term economic and asset return expectations and BlackRock's risk management technology. The BIITS expects a gradual but uneven shift toward sustainable products, services and assets. For example, it assumes consumers will prefer electric vehicles (EVs) over gasoline-powered cars over time. The BIITS expects capital investment into the energy sector to grow to an average of US$4 trillion per year through 2050, an increase from recent average investment levels of US$2.2 trillion a year. The BIITS's overall capex estimate is equivalent to more than 2% of global GDP in 2025. BlackRock pursues a sustainability strategy that is focused on reducing GHG emissions associated with its facilities, data centres, and upstream value chain.

BlackRock's base year, for emissions reporting, is 2019, which is consistent with BlackRock's emissions reduction goals. BlackRock uses the most appropriate 100-year Global Warming Potentials ("GWP") obtained from the Intergovernmental Panel on Climate Change ("IPCC") report to convert GHG emissions into carbon dioxide equivalents ("CO_2e"). BlackRock utilizes a spend-based approach with emissions being estimated using spend multiplied by either industry- and commodity-level emissions factors or a supplier-specific emissions factor if available.

BlackRock estimates that renewable energy offers the largest infrastructure growth opportunities in the coming decade. The company suggest that there exist key climate infrastructure opportunities in clean power generation, energy efficiency in residential, commercial and/or industrial sectors, transmission, distribution and energy storage solutions, ultra-low emission or electrified transportation and mobility. The global climate team of BlackRock has more than US$5 billion assets under management and more than 250 wind and solar investment projects.

BlackRock, the world's largest asset manager, has extensive experience in renewable energy and sustainable investing. The firm is dedicated to incorporating climate and environmental risks into its investment and risk management processes, including creating new methods to assess physical climate risks and stress-testing portfolios for potential future carbon price scenarios.

The Climate Finance Partnership (CFP) aims to accelerate climate-related investments in emerging markets. It is a collaboration between BlackRock, the governments of France, Germany, and Japan, and leading U.S. impact organizations, first proposed at the One Planet Summit in New York.

By 2050, nearly half of global energy capacity will be in the form of non-OECD renewables. This requires vast sums of public and private investment estimated to be $4.8 trillion in the next 15 years. This represents one of the largest infrastructure growth opportunities over the coming decades.

In 2024, BlackRock updated climate stewardship policies and will initially apply to 83 European investment funds with $150 billion in assets under management and would prioritize sectors and companies which are critical to the clean energy transition. BlackRock's updated decarbonization policy emphasizes both financial performance and alignment with limiting global warming to 1.5 °C. It targets firms contributing to decarbonization or facing high transition risks, urging disclosures on net-zero strategies, emissions, and climate-related risks. The policy responds to client demand, adjusts voting guidelines, and may oppose directors failing climate commitments.

BlackRock and ALTÉRRA hosted a roundtable with over 20 governments, development finance institutions, philanthropies, and investors to explore scaling climate infrastructure investment in emerging markets. BlackRock plans a new blended finance strategy with key partners, including GEAPP, Shell Foundation, and G7 PGI, to mobilize capital. ALTÉRRA committed $350 million at COP28 to BlackRock's emerging markets climate infrastructure platform, including $100 million for CFP and $250 million as anchor catalytic capital for a new strategy. This investment targets ambitious funding models to support the climate transition, focusing on developing countries.

BlackRock's Investment Strategies

The four categories of BlackRock's sustainable investing platform -Screened, Uplift, Thematic and Impact adopt different strategies to facilitate investors to attain their investment objectives. In Screened category, investments are limited by excluding issuers or business activities which do not meet specific environmental, social or governance (ESG) criteria. For example, BSF BlackRock Systematic Asia Pacific Equity Absolute Return Fund is a screened category fund. In Uplift category, the focus is on investments which demonstrate better ESG characteristics compared to a defined universe or benchmark. Examples for uplift category include BGF ESG Multiple Asset Fund, BGF Sustainable Asian Bond Fund and BGF Sustainable emerging markets bond fund. In thematic strategy, investments are focussed on issuers whose business models both contribute to and benefit from long term sustainability outcomes. Examples for this category include BGF Nutrition fund, BGF Sustainable Energy Fund and BGF Sustainable Global Infrastructure Fund. Impact Fund focusses on investment commitment to generate positive, measurable and additional sustainability outcomes.

Through transition investing, BlackRock aims to contribute to the shift towards a low carbon economy. It is estimated that the average annual spend in the energy system through 2050 is expected to reach US$4 trillion per year, up from US$2.2 trillion over the last decade. Examples for BlackRock's transition investment products include BGF Brown to Green Materials Fund, BGF Circular Economy Fund, BGF Climate Action Equity Fund and BGF Future of Transport Fund. The BGF Emerging Markets Impact Bond Fund aims to invest at least 80% of its total assets in a portfolio of green, social and sustainability (GSS) bonds issued by government.

On Jan 9 2025, BlackRock had announced that it would leave the Net Zero Asset Managers Initiative.

Bank of America's Sustainable Finance Investments

Bank of America serves approximately 69 million consumer and small business clients with approximately 3700 retail financial centers, approximately 15,000 ATMs and award-winning digital banking with 58 million verified digital users.

Table 10.1 gives the major milestones of Bank of America's green initiatives.

Table 10.1 Green milestones

Year	Highlights
2007	Launched the first sustainable finance goal (Environmental Business Initiative) to mobilize $20 billion over 10 years
2013	Bank of America becomes the first major bank to issue a green bond
2015	Bank of America made an additional $125 billion commitment under its Environmental Business Initiative
2019	The bank achieved renewable electricity and carbon neutrality in its operations, one year ahead of schedule. A new 10-year, $300 billion commitment was made under the Environment Business Initiative
2020	Aims to mobilize $1.5 trillion by 2030 of which $1 trillion will be earmarked for climate projects and 0.5 trillion for social development Joined the Partnership for Carbon Accounting Financials as a core member
2021	Set a goal to achieve net zero greenhouse gas emissions before the year 2050 in its financing activities, operations and supply chain Became a founding member of the Net-Zero Banking Alliance, which serves as the banking element of the Glasgow Financial Alliance for Net-Zero
2022	Bank of America becomes the market leader for ESG debt issuance in terms of volume
2024	The bank set financed emissions targets for the maritime shipping and iron and steel sectors

Source: Bank of America website

Bank of America work within the International Sustainability Standards Board (ISSB) S2 Climate related Disclosures framework which incorporates the Task Force on Climate Related Financial Disclosures (TCFD) framework. Bank of America have diversified its sustainability coverage through inclusion of the Global Reporting Initiative (GRI) index which includes metrics on social and community support. Bank of America focusses on social development, scaling capital to community development, affordable housing, healthcare and education and activities directed to racial and gender equality. Bank of America focusses on engaging clients and communities through the fastest growing sport in the US. The US Soccer Federation and Bank of America have a long-term partnership and the bank is the first official bank partner of all 27 US National teams. Bank of America have invested $25 million to advance reskilling and upskilling of students through partnerships with employers and 21 historically Black colleges and universities.

The circular economy is based on three principles of elimination of waste and pollution, circulation of products and materials and regenerate nature. Currently the global economy is only 7.2% circular which means that more than 90% of materials extracted are either wasted, lost or unavailable. According to BofA Global Research, plastic consumption, waste, emissions and leakage could increase by 50–70% by the year 2040. Plastics which makes up 16% of global solid waste and 4% of emissions can be recycled.

Bank of America have set a target of mobilizing and deploying $1.5 trillion towards sustainable finance by the year 2030. Approximately $ one trillion is allocated for environmental transition while the rest of the fund is earmarked for inclusive social development. Bank of America have deployed $560 billion in sustainable finance with over $316 billion specifically to support the transition to a low carbon sustainable economy. In 2023, Bank of America had mobilized and deployed $150 billion against 10-year $1.5 trillion sustainable finance goal for which $81 billion was meant for environmental transition. The Global Sustainable Finance Group (GSFG) works with the management team and partners to support the company's sustainable finance objectives.

Bank of America have committed to reach Net Zero based on 20 years of climate leadership. Since 2003, the bank has been a leader in environmental reporting, reducing operational impacts and scaling climate finance.

The Retail and Preferred banking division of Bank of America serve millions of US consumers and small businesses offering digital, paperless services and 80% recycled plastic cards to support sustainability. Bank of America offer loans and leases for hybrid and fully electric vehicles, including financing for home charging stations. Since 2021, Bank of America have mobilized approximately $6.4 billion in hybrid and electric vehicle originations. Additionally, the bank provides rewards and benefits such as cash back on EV charging and support for tax credits on eligible electric vehicle leases. Bank of America educate clients of Global Wealth and Investment Management (GWIM) on sustainable investing, bridging the gap between interest and adoption, while aligning investment products related to renewable energy, clean water and water scarcity across asset classes to support their sustainability goals. Interest in sustainable investing have led to GWIM client balances rising from $25 billion in 2019 to $53 billion in 2023, alongside positive net flows.

Bank of America had led U.S. Steel's $240 million green bond issuance, supporting recycling and processing of ferrous scrap metals for electric arc furnace steel production. BofA Securities advised TenCate Grass Holding B.V. on its acquisition by a private equity firm. TenCate specializes in sustainable, fully circular artificial turf solutions. In February 2023, BofA Securities led Enlight Renewable Energy's $289 million U.S. IPO, the first U.S. listing of a Tel Aviv company since 2014.

The bank is one of the largest US corporate issuers of sustainability themed bonds. During the period 2013–2023, Bank of America had issued $14.93 billion across six green, two social and three sustainability bonds. In 2023, the Global Corporate and Investment Banking (GCIB) business segment of bank was number four globally in terms of ESG debt issuance volumes and number two globally in terms of green bond issuance volume.

The Global Sustainable Finance Group of the bank provides asset-based debt financing, tax-incentive investments, and capital solutions to scale decarbonization. It supports mature technologies like wind, solar, EVs, and battery storage, alongside emerging solutions like clean hydrogen, SAF, and carbon capture. Additionally, it facilitates sustainable investment in emerging markets through blended finance. The Community Development Financial Institutions and Global Sustainable Finance teams help clients leverage subsidies and credit enhancements to attract private capital for low-income and disadvantaged communities.

Bank of America led Gabon's $500 million debt-for-nature transaction, refinancing sovereign debt with political risk insurance from the U.S. International Development Finance Corporation. The deal attracted investors, extended tenor, and reduced interest payments. Gabon committed $163 million for conservation, aiming to protect 30% of lands and oceans by 2030.

Bank of America raised capital for firms in alternative protein and sustainable farming, deploying funds into blended finance vehicles focused on natural capital, including climate-smart agriculture. In 2023, the bank invested in the Responsibility Climate Smart Agriculture & Food Systems Fund and engaged in voluntary carbon credit markets, supporting nature-based solutions. Aligned with the Mangrove Breakthrough Initiative, the bank aim to mobilize $4 billion by 2030 to protect 15 million hectares of mangroves, enhancing economic, carbon sequestration, climate resilience, and biodiversity benefits.

Bank of America was a joint bookrunner on LG Energy Solution's $1 billion inaugural green bond, funding low-carbon transportation and energy efficiency projects. LG Energy is a leading global producer of rechargeable lithium-ion batteries for automotive, mobile, and energy storage applications. Bank of America served as a green structuring agent, joint bookrunner and billing and delivery agent for Stellantis's €1.25 billion seven-year inaugural Green Bond offering within the Green Bond framework. Stellantis is a global automaker and mobility provider. Stellantis will allocate the net proceeds from its Green Bonds, issued under the 2023 Green Bond Framework, to investments and expenditures supporting the design, development, and production of Zero Emission Vehicles, including Battery Electric

Vehicles (BEVs) and Fuel Cell Electric Vehicles (FCEVs). Bank of America acted as a joint active bookrunner and billing & delivery agent for National Grid's €1.75 billion dual-tranche bond, including €750 million in Green notes. National Grid, a major electricity and gas provider in the U.K. and U.S., aims to lead the clean energy transition. Bank of America co-led Snam's €500 million E.U. Taxonomy-aligned Transition Bond into Italgas. Proceeds will fund existing or future eligible projects under Snam's Sustainable Finance Framework. This landmark deal is the first transition-exchangeable bond and the third Italian equity-linked bond issuance since August 2023. In 2023, Bank of America became a part of the financing working group for the newly launched Methane Abatement Financing Taskforce led by Climate Bonds Initiative. Bank of America advised SkyNRG on a €175 million investment from Macquarie's MGETS Fund, supporting its growth and ambition to become a leading SAF producer. Bank of America co-led Cemex's $1 billion Green Perpetual NC5 Subordinated Notes, its first green bond. This landmark hybrid transaction in building materials will fund eligible green projects, including renewable energy, energy efficiency, pollution control, clean transportation, sustainable water management, circular economy products, and advanced production technologies.

Table 10.2 highlights the progress made by Bank of America towards sustainable finance goals.

Bank of America have set voluntary 2030 financing activity targets as part of its net zero goal for sectors such as auto manufacturing, aviation, cement, energy, power generation, iron and steel and maritime shipping. The bank uses physical unit emissions intensity metrics to manage its net zero alignment and 2030 financing activity targets.

Table 10.3 highlights the absolute financed emissions and economic intensities of Bank of America in the year 2022.

Sustainable Finance at Citigroup

Citi bank is a global leader in wealth management and the preeminent banking partner for institutions with cross border needs. Citi facilitates nearly $5 trillion financial flows and its global network allows it to move the equivalent of Germany's GDP each day across borders, currencies and asset classes. Citi serves 19,000 institutional clients of which 85% are Fortune 500 companies. Citi has presence in 180 countries. Citi has committed $1 trillion to ESG.

Citi has financed and facilitated $441.2 billion toward its $1 trillion sustainable finance 2030 goal related to environmental and social finance activity since 2020. Citi has attained or surpassed targets for five of eight goals to decrease its operational footprint by 2025 against a 2010 baseline which include goals to reduce location-based greenhouse gas emissions, renewable energy sourcing, water consumption and waste reduction. In 2023, Citi had invested $92.7 billion in green infrastructure, climate technology and social initiatives. Sustainable finance

Table 10.2 Progress toward sustainable finance goals made by Bank of America

Sustainable finance categories	Cumulative Program to date ($ Million)		
	Environmental	Social	Total
Mergers and Acquisitions: advisory associated with clients aligned to SDGs and advisory to facilitate capital flows to target companies in developing economies	110,243	19,363	129,606
Lending, Leasing and Trade Finance: Corporate and sustainability linked lending, lease and trade financing for clients/use of proceeds aligned with SDGs including in developing economies	21,528	18,717	40,245
Global Markets: capital markets advisory, underwriting and distribution for municipal and corporate clients and activity aligned with the SDGs	58,843	56,329	115,172
Asset based finance: sustainable asset-based finance	8634	0	8634
ABS/MBS: Underwriting of green-and social labelled ABS/MBS	3361	171	3532
Public Finance/Municipals: labelled municipal underwriting aligned to SDGs and financing provided to municipals	46,848	56,158	103,006
Regional Banking: lending, leasing and capital markets activity aligned with SDGs	10,912	50,640	61,552
Retail and preferred: Hybrid/EV lending, LMI lending for homeownership and small business	6382	18,638	25,020
Business Banking: Lending to clients aligned with SDGs	138	704	842
Global Commercial banking: advisory, lending, leasing and capital market activity for clients aligned with SDGs	4392	31,299	35,691
Other	2924	4739	7663
Merrill and Private Bank: net inflow/outflow to ESG AUM	7522	3761	11,283

Source: Metrics and Targets, Bank of America, Sustainability Report 2024, Page 70

Table 10.3 Absolute financed emissions and economic intensities

Sector	Utilized commercial credit loan exposure ($ million)	Percent of total utilized commercial credit loan exposure	Economic intensity (tCO_2e/million$)
Auto Manufacturing	1010	0.14%	1196
Aviation	4509	0.64%	921
Cement	625	0.09%	2847
Coal	16	0.00%	21,787
Energy	5601	0.79%	3670
Iron and Steel	1496	0.21%	1810
Power Generation	9417	1.34%	371

Source: Metrics and Targets, Bank of America, Sustainability Report 2024, Page 74

activities for environmental issues accounted for 64% ($59.3 billion), social activities accounted for 16% ($14.7 billion) of the total amount financed for sustainable activities. In 2023, renewable energy accounted for the largest single-issue finance criteria as the bank had invested $14 billion in renewable energy related activities.

The bank reported significant progress on its 2025 operational targets, achieving a 49% reduction in location based GHG emissions, surpassing its 45% goal. It has sourced 100% renewable energy annually since 2020, cut waste by over half, reduced water consumption by one-third, and secured sustainable building certifications for over 40% of its facilities, based on 2010 baselines. Citi, a member of the UN-backed Net-Zero Banking Alliance, is progressing toward its 2025 sustainability goals but has yet to fully achieve three targets. Its operations have reduced energy consumption by 35% against a 40% goal, sourced 9% of water from reclaimed or reused sources in 2023 versus a 25% target, and diverted 30% of waste from landfills, aiming for 50% by 2025. Citi has also surpassed its $1 billion financing goal for its Action for Racial Equity program.

According to Forbes study, there are $22.89 trillion in assets globally which are being professionally managed under responsible investment strategies. Citi was one of the first global institutions to adopt the UN's sustainable development goals and facilitate $100 billion towards sustainable green initiatives. Citi has already made $95 billion in green investments which included projects which had saved 4.5 million metric tons of carbon dioxide which was equivalent to the annual green house gas emissions of more than 800,000 passenger vehicles. Citi had also financed renewable energy projects with outputs which powered more than 300,000 homes along with financing water quality projects which benefitted 43.6 million people in the US. In 2023, Citi financed nearly $6.5 billion in US affordable housing. In the year 2023, the Citi Foundation's inaugural Global Innovation Challenge offered $25 million to 50 community organizations to improve food security and financial health of low-income families and communities. The Citi Impact Fund assist entrepreneurs of underserved communities. Financial inclusion innovation programs of Citi such as Citi® ATM Community Network and the Citi Start Saving® platform offers opportunities for financial access across the US. In 2023, Citi was ranked as number one US lead underwriter for global sustainable finance bonds. Citi was also the number one emerging market sustainable bond underwriter in year 2023. In the same year Citi had financed approximately $6.5 billion in affordable housing projects in the US. For the past 14 years, Citi has been the number one affordable housing lender in the US. Citi has supported the World Bank for a $50 million emission reduction linked bond issuance for funding the manufacture and distribution of water purifiers for schools in Vietnam. Citi have structured many sustainable financing frameworks for sovereign, banking, energy, chemicals, power, utilities, cement, real estate and industrial sector issuers.

First Solar, a leading U.S. solar module manufacturer, secured a $700 million tax credit transfer in December 2023, facilitated by Citi. This landmark transaction, leveraging Section 45X tax credits from the IRA, enabled First Solar to access low-cost capital while helping the buyer achieve ESG goals and maximize after-tax returns. The off grid solar energy company Sun King and Citi launched a pioneering $130 million securitization deal to expand off-grid solar financing in Kenya. Structured around Sun King's customer credit model, the transaction enables affordable solar access for unbanked communities while supporting the company's growth through investor-backed securitization of future customer payments. In 2023, Citi provided a $105 million loan to Chelsea Investment Corporation to develop Harrington Heights in San Diego, offering 273 affordable rental units, including 75 for veterans and the homeless. The LEED Gold-certified project includes on-site support services from Alpha Project, enhancing residents' job skills, education, and well-being. ThyssenKrupp Nucera, a former joint venture of Thyssenkrupp AG and De Nora SpA, went public in July to expand its green hydrogen business. Citi, as a joint global coordinator for the IPO, helped raise funds for automation, supply chain expansion, technology development, and global growth in hydrogen production.

Citi joined 28 lenders in AES' $3 billion construction loan facility to finance 3 gigawatts of new clean energy projects. Covering 40 solar, wind, and storage projects across 14 states, the facility leverages IRA provisions to support AES' renewable expansion, continuing Citi's long-standing financing partnership since 2016. Citi structured a $160 million green loan for Sungwoo Hitech to expand its hydrogen EV parts plant in Mexico, supporting growing EV demand and creating 1500 jobs. In 2023, Citi closed a €500 million financing for Kazakhstan's rail company KTZ, backed by a 95% MIGA guarantee, to fund electric locomotives, track rehabilitation, and infrastructure upgrades.

Citi and EBRD launched a sustainable supply chain finance program for Finnish Technology and Services company Metso and its Turkish suppliers, offering affordable financing and incentives for emissions reduction, supporting SMEs' green transition. Citi provided a letter of credit to EVERY Company, supporting its growth in animal-free egg protein innovation, advancing sustainable food production through precision fermentation.

Citi is a member of multiple voluntary industry groups such as The Glasgow Financial Alliance for Net Zero (GFANZ), Net Zero Banking Alliance (NZBA), The Rocky Mountain Institute (RMI) Center for Climate-Aligned Finance and the Partnership for Carbon Accounting Financials (PCAF).

The Citi Impact Fund invests in start-ups that drive both financial returns and positive social impact by addressing critical societal challenges with innovative solutions. During the period 2020–2023, the impact fund has made investments in 44 companies. The Impact fund have invested in $140 million in "double bottom line" companies and funds. Noted investment were made by the Citi Impact Fund in the digital healthcare company- Wealthy, climate resilience analytics -Vibrant Planet, and financial inclusion software provider, Prism Data. Citi also made follow-on investments in Pathstream, Clerkie, Pallet, Jetty, The Mom Project, and TailorMed.

Citi onboarded NYC-based fintech MoCaFi to its ATM Community Network via Sunrise Banks, enabling surcharge-free Citibank ATM access and supporting economic mobility through streamlined public subsidy distribution. The Citi Foundation drives economic progress through grants promoting financial inclusion, youth job opportunities, and community development, leveraging Citi's expertise and open request for approvals (RFPs) to support global initiatives. In 2023, Citi Foundation offered $86 million in grants. In 2018, Citi was the first major U.S. financial institution to publicly release the results of a pay equity review comparing its compensation of women to that of men, as well as U.S. minorities to U.S. non-minorities.

Citi has committed to achieving net zero greenhouse gas (GHG) emissions by 2050. In this direction, Citi have laid out emissions reduction plans for its financing in six sectors in loan portfolio comprising auto manufacturing, commercial real estate, energy, power, steel and thermal coal mining. Citi have incorporated sustainable finance across five core interconnected businesses consisting of services, markets, banking and international, wealth and US personal banking. The Services segment of Citi assist clients in understanding the impact of ESG factors on liquidity and working capital management decisions. The services segment covers export and agency finance, green, sustainable, and social trade and working capital loans, sustainable supply chain finance, sustainable deposit and cash management solutions, and sustainable commercial card options. The markets division supports clients and colleagues in identifying, executing, and scaling opportunities across products and asset classes. It integrates sustainability into business operations, offering solutions like infrastructure finance, sustainable securitization, contract hedging, and carbon credits trading to help clients achieve their ESG and sustainability objectives effectively. Citi's Banking and International team help clients across sectors transition to a sustainable, net-zero future by providing sector-specific advisory, capital markets, and corporate banking solutions. The Wealth business of Citi provides managed opportunities, alternative investments, and capital markets access, helping clients achieve financial and sustainable goals through socially responsible, ESG integration, thematic, and impact approaches. The US Personal Banking offers simplified banking to help customers avoid fees and access enhanced Citi benefits and services across all income levels. Citi is involved in social finance activities in emerging markets through financing activities for affordable infrastructure and housing, diversity and equity, economic inclusion, education, food security and healthcare. Citi aim to invest in opportunities for 15 million low income households globally which include 10 million women by year 2025.

Table 10.4 highlights the progress towards sustainable finance goal of $1 trillion achieved by Citi in billions of US dollars till 2023.

Table 10.5 highlights the progress achieved by Citi towards sustainable finance goal in different areas.

Table 10.6 shows the impact data for the $1 trillion sustainable finance goal of Citi.

In 2023, the Task Force for Climate-related Financial Disclosures report found that 71% of the bank's energy sector clients lack a comprehensive transition plan or have one with uncertain execution feasibility.

Green Finance Initiatives by Goldman Sachs

Goldman Sachs is a leading global financial institution offering a broad range of financial services to a large and diversified client base such as corporations, financial institutions, governments and individuals. Goldman Sachs report its activities in three business segments: Global Banking &Markets, Asset & Wealth Management and Platform Solutions. In 2023, the bank had a total net income of $46 billion.

Table 10.4 Sustainable finance goal progress achieved

Business	Total progress (in billions of USD)
Investment Banking	377.1
Mergers & Acquisitions	108
Debt Capital Markets	216.6
Thematic Bonds (Green, Social, Sustainable)	130.3
Sustainability Linked Bonds	10.1
Sustainability Linked Loans	72.4
Green, Social and other Loans	3.7
Equity Capital Markets	10.3
Municipal Underwriting	42.1
Corporate Lending	46.2
Services	
Treasury and Trade Solutions	13.6
Markets	4.1
Corporate/Other (Citi Investments)	0.2
Total	441.2

Source: 2023 Citi ESG Report

Table 10.5 Area wise progress status

Sustainable finance criteria	Total progress (in billions of USD)
Circular Economy	2.9
Clean Technology	4.7
Energy Efficiency	8.5
Green Buildings	8.6
Renewable Energy	57.9
Sustainable Agriculture and Land Use	1
Sustainable Transportation	85.2
Water Quality and Conservation	7.6
Environmental: Multiple	121.7
Total Environmental	298.2
Affordable Basic Infrastructure	1.3
Affordable Housing	37.2
Diversity and Equity	0.6
Economic Inclusion	9.1
Education	9
Food Security	0.9
Healthcare	7.4
Social: Multiple	14.8
Total Social	80.5
Environmental and Social	62.4
Total	**441.2**

Source: 2023 Citi ESG Report

Table 10.6 Impact data progress

Environmental impacts (in thousands)	Total
(1) Avoided greenhouse gas emissions ($mtCO_2e$)	5997
From renewable energy projects	5417
From green buildings and energy efficiency projects	580
(2) Renewable energy production and storage capacity added (MW)	4
From renewable energy projects	4
From battery storage projects	0.1
Social Impacts (in thousands)	
(3) Total people impacted	61,072
From microfinance lending, basic infrastructure, basic digital device, education and other social purposes	9209
Through renewable energy projects	5208
From affordable housing projects	401
From education, transit system, utility improvement and economic development projects financed by US municipal bonds	46,253
(4) Total jobs supported	2624
From microfinance lending, basic infrastructure, basic digital device, education and other social purposes	2367
Through renewable energy projects	31
Through green building projects	7
From affordable housing projects	172
From education, transit system, utility improvement and economic development projects financed by US municipal bonds	47

Source: 2023 Citi ESG Report

Goldman Sachs have established a Sustainable Finance Group (SFG) which acts as the centralized group which drives climate strategy and sustainability efforts across different segments of bank in order to advance climate transition and inclusive growth. For example, the Sustainable Banking Group within Global Banking & Markets focusses on supporting the corporate clients to reduce their direct and indirect carbon emissions. The multiple teams within the Asset & Wealth Management offers specialized services related to sustainable investing. The Sustainability & Impact Solutions team in Asset & Wealth Management facilitates the integration of insights, advisory services, and investment solutions across all asset management client segments. The Public Responsibilities Committee assists the Board in its oversight of firmwide sustainability strategy. Goldman Sachs have announced a target to deploy $750 billion in sustainable financing, investing and advisory activity by the year 2030. By December 2023, the bank has achieved approximately 75% of the targeted goal with major part dedicated to Climate Transition. With respect to Climate transition, Goldman Sachs have committed to align its financing activities with a net zero by 2050 pathway. In this context, Goldman Sachs have set an initial set of 2030 targets for energy, power and auto manufacturing portfolios. The bank focusses on investing in new commercial solutions to drive decarbonization in the real economy. Carbon neutrality is a priority for the firm operations and supply chain. The bank aims to support Inclusive

Growth through sponsored initiatives, such as One Million Black Women, 10,000 Women and 10,000 Small Businesses.

In 2005, Goldman Sachs became one of the first US banks to develop an Environmental Policy Framework. Over period the bank scaled its suite of sustainable finance capabilities and solutions to meet the growing demand of clients.

Table 10.7 highlights the sustainability milestones for Goldman Sachs.

Table 10.7 Green Finance milestones for Goldman Sachs

Year	Highlights
2001	Committed $19 billion through Urban Investment Group
2005	One of the first US banks to develop an Environmental Policy Framework
2007	Launched GS SUSTAIN, which provides research and data tools to clients explore ESG related topics
2008	Launched 10,000 Women, reaching over 200,000 women across 150 countries
2009	Launched 10,000 Small Businesses, serving over 17,000 entrepreneurs to date with 330,000 employees and $33 billion in total revenue
2012	Inaugural clean energy financing and investment target set
2014	10,000 Women and International Finance Corporation launched the Women Entrepreneurs Opportunity Facility covering more than 200,000 women entrepreneurs. Offered $7.5 billion in loans to women entrepreneurs since inception
2015	Goldman Sachs achieved carbon neutrality across operations and business travel. Acquired Imprint Capital Advisors
2019	Established the Sustainable Finance Group. The bank had announced $750 billion Sustainable Finance Commitment by 2030. The bank launched flagship research series on the economics of decarbonization
2020	Launched AWM's Sustainable Investing Group and GBM's Commodities Sustainable Solutions
2021	Launched one million Black women in partnership with Black women led organizations to invest $10 billion in investment capital and $100 million in philanthropic capital by year 2030
	Issued $800 million inaugural Goldman Sachs benchmark sustainability bond
	Announced Goldman Sachs Bloomberg Climate Finance Partnership, including the Climate Innovation and Development Fund alongside the Asian Development Bank
	Launched Carbon Portfolio Analytics for clients in Marquee
	Founder US bank member of open source data non-profit OS-Climate
2022	Established GBM's Sustainable Banking Group
	Acquired NN Investment Partners for benefits related to sustainability
2023	Sourced $500 million of blended private and public sector finance through the Climate Innovation and Development Fund
	Raised $2.6 billion for climate transition strategies
	Expanded Marquee's portfolio offering to allow clients to assess their portfolios' climate transition
	Launched 10,000 small Businesses Investment in Rural Communities to cover business education and capital access programs to 20 rural US states over the next 5 years
	Goldman Sachs Asset Management (GSAM) named Top 3 Sustainable Alternatives Manager by PEI Media

Source: Goldman Sachs 2023, Sustainability Report

Goldman Sachs had achieved a number of green finance milestones across a number of key initiatives. The bank has invested $555 billion in sustainable finance activity since the year 2019. Goldman Sachs had sustainability issuance of $2.5 billion since the year 2021. Goldman Sachs have been ranked as the world's third largest private markets impact manager with private markets impact capital of $9.4 billion. The bank has raised $2.6 billion for climate transition related Horizon strategies. The notional value of primary market climate related debt issuance in which Goldman Sachs participated amounted to $77 billion. Goldman Sach's Climate Innovation and Development Fund had unlocked private and public sector capital amounting to $500 million for some of the pioneering projects and solutions in countries such as Vietnam and India. The bank has deployed over $19 billion for inclusive growth since the launch of the Urban Investment Group in real estate projects, social enterprises and lending facilities for small businesses. The bank has committed over $2.3 billion in investment capital and $33 million in philanthropic capital since the launch of One Million Black Women which would impact the lives of over 200,000 Black women and girls. Another inclusive growth initiative was the commitment to 10,000 Small Businesses with a recent $100 million expansion of 10,000 Small Businesses Investment in Rural Communities. Goldman Sachs has also offered $3 billion in philanthropic giving worldwide which benefitted over 10,800 non-profits in 140 countries.

Sustainable Finance Strategy

Goldman Sachs leverages its investment banking, asset management, and risk expertise to help diverse clients achieve sustainability goals through a strategic, client-focused sustainable finance approach. Goldman Sachs' sustainability strategy focuses on supporting clients, managing its operations, and addressing market gaps. Through its One Goldman Sachs model, it delivers sustainable finance solutions. The firm enhances value by equipping employees and managing its footprint. Strategic partnerships and innovative solutions help bridge market gaps, addressing emerging sustainability challenges.

Global Banking & Markets segment's sustainability advisory offers M&A, IPO, and decarbonization strategies. It provides sustainable financing, ESG-focused products, and investor connectivity. Services include ESG analytics, climate transition support, and renewable energy market solutions. Additionally, it covers raw material markets, risk management, and financing for green initiatives and urban development. Asset & Wealth Management sustainability advisory supports clients with portfolio strategies, climate intelligence, and ESG analytics. It offers sustainable investment products, including climate-focused funds and private market options. Services include investor engagement, emissions disclosure guidance, and dedicated transition resources like the Value Accelerator to drive sustainable growth and accountability. Global Banking & Market segment's primary businesses drive sustainable finance by providing advisory, financing, and risk management across public and private markets. The Sustainable Banking Group supports energy transition, decarbonization, and circular economy goals through tailored capital solutions. The Commodities Sustainable Solutions team advances climate objectives via financing and trading in clean power and carbon markets.

Asset & Wealth Management segment of Goldman Sachs offers sustainability-focused investment solutions across public and private markets. AM Sustainable Client Solutions provides advisory and insights, while Public Markets Investing supports climate transition and inclusive growth. The Sustainable Investing Group and Sustainability & Impact team drive sustainable strategies, integrating ESG principles across investment platforms. Goldman Sachs Alternatives also has teams specializing in sustainable investing.

External Investing Group (XIG) identifies, researches, and selects top third-party investment managers. Within XIG, Imprint specializes in thematic research, manager selection, and co-investments in sustainable growth. In Private Wealth Management, the Sustainable Solutions Group (SSG) advises clients on sustainable investing strategies and drives innovation to meet impact investing goals.

Two research initiatives, GS SUSTAIN and Carbonomics offered by the Global Investment Research team of the bank, offer invaluable insights to address sustainable investment decisions. GS SUSTAIN offers research and data on innovation, regulation, and capital flows in sustainable investing. Carbonomics analyses decarbonization economics, exploring costs, incentives, and financing for net-zero technologies, helping clients make informed sustainable investment decisions.

In March 2023, Goldman Sachs introduced a Global Impact Corporate Bond strategy and a USD Green Bond strategy, managed by its Green, Social, and Impact Bonds team from the 2022 NN IP acquisition.

Notable Green Transactions Facilitated by Goldman Sachs

Goldman Sachs Alternatives co-led a $1 billion Series D for Redwood Materials, a leading lithium -ion battery materials manufacturer to strengthen the U.S. battery supply chain for EVs and energy storage. Goldman Sachs co-managed Amara NZero's €270 million Green Senior Secured Notes, supporting its energy transition efforts. Amara NZero is a global leading distributor of products and services used in the energy transition, directly contributing to worldwide decarbonization efforts. This high-yield green bond, aligned with ICMA principles, financed acquisitions. Goldman Sachs Alternatives invested in Grow Therapy, a platform enhancing accessible behavioral healthcare by connecting mental health professionals with patients for virtual/in-person visits and payments. Goldman Sachs led a $600 million debt management transaction for Ohio State University, part of a bond financing raising $300 million for a new hospital facility.

In 2023, Goldman Sachs Alternatives began emissions inventorying for its portfolio, helping companies measure and reduce carbon footprints. It offers GHG accounting, decarbonization planning, and Scope 1–3 analysis. In 2023, 29 companies participated in this program and thus accelerated projects to process activity-based emissions information from diligence into a detailed decarbonization analysis. Goldman Sachs supports open-source tools like OS-Climate, a Linux Foundation project, to provide transparent climate data and analytics, advancing investment in the climate transition. In 2022, Goldman Sachs helped a Caribbean island issue debt for blue economy development, including climate risk management and marine resource preservation. It also supports debt-for-nature swaps to help sovereign clients achieve environmental and financial goals. Goldman Sachs led a $1.1 billion senior secured financing for IDB Invest, the private sector financing arm of the Inter-American Development Bank to purchase MPC certificates and compensate Chile's power generation companies. This initiative supports the government's goal of stabilizing electricity prices for vulnerable consumers while providing liquidity to power companies and supporting the growth of solar energy in Chile. Goldman Sachs was the sole global coordinator, sole placement agent and joint bookrunner for the secured financing. This capital aims to improve the efficiency of the Chilean electricity sector which have seen the solar production rise by more than 100% since the year 2015. Goldman Sachs facilitated ENERGO-PRO's €300 million Senior Unsecured Guaranteed Notes issuance in July 2023, backed by a $545 million DFC credit guarantee. This enabled ENERGO-PRO to secure long-term financing at lower interest rates, scale production, and diversify energy sources in Eastern Europe, reducing reliance on Russian exports.

In 2015, Goldman Sachs Asset Management acquired Imprint Capital Advisors and formed XIG Imprint, focusing on impact investing across asset classes. XIG Imprint identifies opportunities driven by policy support, such as Germany's subsidies for renewables, investing in firms like NeXtWind, a German onshore wind repowering company. In August 2023, XIG Imprint invested $15 million alongside Sandbrook Capital in NeXtWind. The company plans to expand into solar and battery co-location, leveraging expertise from its management team and partners.

In 2021, Goldman Sachs and Bloomberg Philanthropies partnered to launch the Climate Innovation and Development Fund (CIDF) in association with the Asian Development Bank. CIDF have invested approximately $500 million of blended private and public sector across seven projects during the period 2022–2023. In September 2023, Goldman Sachs launched a $100 million Investment in Rural Communities, part of the 10,000 Small Businesses (10KSB) program. The initiative includes $75 million in lending capital, $15 million for education, and $10 million in capacity-building grants. It aims to support over 800 rural small businesses across 20 states. Goldman Sachs partnered with New York City HDC and HPD to create a $50 million guaranty facility for minority developers (MBEs) in affordable housing. The facility, with $25 million from Goldman Sachs and $25 million from the city, helps MBE developers access construction financing, supporting at least 10 projects over 5 years. In April 2023, Goldman Sachs financed the acquisition of Project Horizon, preserving 10,474 affordable housing units across 90 properties in eight states. The acquisition safeguards affordability for over 30,000 residents, preventing units from converting to market rates. Goldman Sachs provided $454 million in joint venture equity to support the preservation effort. Goldman Sachs led a Series

B financing for Ignite Reading, which provides one-on-one tutoring based on the Science of Reading. Their program has shown significant success in improving reading outcomes for diverse K–12 students. In June 2023, Goldman Sachs launched its first dedicated social impact public equity strategy with $1.3 billion in assets. The strategy invests in companies aligned with social sustainability, focusing on solutions addressing social issues through products, services, or technologies, aiming to create positive social impact globally.

Elia Group acquired a 35.1% stake in energyRe Giga for $400 million, valuing the company at $1.1 billion. The investment funds onshore wind, solar, and offshore wind projects, marking Elia's entry into the US market. Goldman Sachs served as the sole financial advisor on the transaction. Goldman Sachs acted as financial advisor for the spin-off of Nextracker, a leader in solar tracker and software solutions. Following a $638 million IPO in February 2023, Nextracker spun off from Flex Ltd. in January 2024. The spin-off accelerates clean energy production by optimizing solar performance. Goldman Sachs served as exclusive placement agent for Fervo Energy's $244 million capital raise. The funds support Fervo's growth, advancing its enhanced geothermal system (EGS) technology. With a successful first project online and ongoing drilling at Cape Station, Fervo aims to deliver clean energy by 2026. Goldman Sachs provided a $70 million loan for Carolina Renewables' RNG production facility in North Carolina, converting agricultural and industrial waste into sustainable energy. The facility helps reduce greenhouse gas emissions by substituting fossil fuels with renewable energy. Goldman Sachs advised General Motors on its $150 million investment in NMG, aimed at securing sustainably sourced EV battery materials. The investment supports NMG's Phase-2 Matawinie Mine and Bécancour Battery Material Plant in Canada, contributing to GM's EV production and strengthening its North American-focused, sustainable supply chain for electric vehicles, natural gas, supporting a circular economy and meeting local energy demand. Goldman Sachs acted as sole private placement agent for Ascend Elements' $622 million Series D round. The funding will support the construction of the Apex 1 facility in Kentucky, North America's first pCAM and CAM manufacturing plant. Ascend Elements produces sustainable battery materials using recycled inputs to reduce carbon emissions.

Northvolt, a European lithium-ion battery supplier, aims to reduce carbon footprints and source 50% of raw materials from recycled batteries by 2030. Goldman Sachs co-led a $1 billion investment in 2019 and participated in follow-on funding rounds, supporting Northvolt's expansion and sustainable battery supply chain development.

Goldman Sachs' Commodities Sustainable Solutions team is developing GS Pearl Street, a platform providing trading, route-to-market, and financing solutions for clean power technologies. Leveraging 20 years of experience, the platform supports the transition to renewable power, offering grid-scale energy storage owners long-term project financing and market access.

Goldman Sachs invested in Verdalia Bioenergy, which aims to deploy €1 billion by 2026, developing biomethane plants across Europe. Verdalia focuses on Spain and Italy, advancing Europe's decarbonization efforts through low-carbon natural gas produced from organic waste, enhancing energy security and reducing methane emissions.

The World Economic Forum estimates that $10.1 trillion in annual business value and 395 million jobs could be created by 2030 through the preservation of our ecosystems, biodiversity, and natural capital.[1] In 2021, Apple, Goldman Sachs through Imprint, and Conservation International launched The Restore Fund to invest in reforestation projects. The fund focuses on carbon sequestration, biodiversity, and local job creation, with investments in Brazil's Cerrado region supporting forest restoration and ecosystem conservation. Imprint has invested in a 35,000-hectare portfolio of properties with Timberland Investment Group and other investors. Goldman Sachs served as lead financial advisor to Evoqua Water Technologies in its $7.5 billion acquisition by Xylem Inc. in May 2023. This all-stock transaction created one of the world's largest pure-play water technology companies, combining expertise to address global water challenges and advancing sustainability efforts.

Since launching its 10-year, $750 billion sustainable finance commitment in 2019, Goldman Sachs has achieved $555 billion in commercial activity, including $302 billion in climate transition efforts. Key contributors to this include clean energy, sustainable transport, and ecosystem services. With respect to supply chain sustainability, Goldman Sachs have set a new target of $1.5 billion for the period 2023–2025 for small and diverse spenders. As of December 2023, Goldman Sachs Asset Management manages $327.6 billion in sustainability-related assets under supervision. Throughout 2023, Goldman Sachs issued the equivalent of approximately $543 million of sustainability issuances, with proceeds fully allocated to new investments and loans.

Sustainable Finance -Morgan Stanley

Morgan Stanley is a major financial services firm which employ more than 82,000 people in 41 countries. The three major business segments of Morgan Stanley are Institutional Securities, Wealth Management and Investment Management. Morgan Stanley board of directors (Board) committees have explicit oversight responsibilities for D&I, climate and sustainability. The Governance and Sustainability Committee oversees ESG initiatives. The Board Risk Committee oversees climate risks. In the year 2022, Morgan Stanley enhanced its Firmwide ESG governance by formalizing and standardizing the ESG organization structure. The Global Sustainability Office (GSO) is the main driver for the firm's sustainability strategy and innovation. GSO is organized across three areas of focus. Global Sustainable Finance have partnership with Institutional Securities, Wealth Management and Investment Management to offer innovative ESG advice, products and solution for

[1] WEF: *New Nature Economy Report II*, 2020.

clients. Morgan Stanley Sustainable Insights Lab serves as an ESG data hub for the firm. Firmwide sustainability integrate ESG considerations across business practices, operations and culture. The Morgan Stanley Institute for Sustainable Investing helps accelerate the field of sustainable investing.

In year 2022, Morgan Stanley donated $166 million for philanthropic activities. Morgan Stanley's sustainable finance target is to mobilize over 700 billion dollars in capital to be mobilized towards the goal of one trillion dollars by 2030 including over US dollar 550 billion in low carbon and green solution. Morgan Stanley was involved in the first corporate green bond issuance in 2013.

In 2020, the bank committed to achieve net zero financed emissions by year 2050. In 2022, Morgan Stanley achieved carbon neutrality across its global operations. In 2019, Morgan Stanley announced its Plastic Waste Resolution to help facilitate the prevention, reduction and removal of 50 million metric tons of discarded plastic from rivers, oceans, landscapes and landfills by 2030. Morgan Stanley have made significant progress with removal of 14 million metric tons of plastic waste by year 2022. During the period 2013–2022, Morgan Stanley have supported ESG-labelled debt transaction valued at approximately 430 billion US dollars. The firm had made investments worth $40 billion in AUM with sustainability features. The Investment Impact Platform (IIP) of Morgan Stanley serves over 328,000 clients and have invested in client assets valued at US$68 billion. The platform enables the Wealth Management clients to align portfolios based on 310 plus investment strategies across asset classes on themes such as climate action, gender lens investing, racial equity, and faith-based investing. Morgan Stanley IQ®, the proprietary application provides clients with a comprehensive menu of metrics which include nine impact themes and more than 100 social and environmental impact metrics. The tool enables the financial advisors to find investment solutions which may align clients' portfolios with top priority impact goals over time. The MSIM Emerging Markets Equity team supports a responsible energy transition by engaging with companies, promoting feasible decarbonization targets, and encouraging board-level oversight and carbon analysis. In 2022, the International Equity team engaged pharmaceutical companies on clinical trial diversity, advocating for better disclosures, accountability measures, and integration into business processes.

During the period 2010–2022, Morgan Stanley have committed US$32 billion in community development loans and investments. For small business loans, US$426 million were committed by the firm. These initiatives led to the creation or retention of 246,000 jobs. The firm launched Climate Strategy Assessment Framework (CSAF) to understand clients' transition plans and commitments. Morgan Stanley is the only major US headquartered global financial services firm on the Partnership for Carbon Accounting Financials (PCAF) Steering Committee. The firm focusses on enhancing the climate resilience of its operations. Bennington Wind Farm accounts for approximately 50% of Morgan Stanley's global energy consumption. Renewable electricity accounted for 100% of global operational electricity in the year 2022. In 2021, Morgan Stanley announced 2030 interim financed emissions targets to guide its lending activities based on credible science aligned emission pathways. These targets focussed on emission intensive lending portfolio sectors consisting of auto manufacturing, energy and power. Morgan Stanley is a member of the Center for Climate and Energy Solutions' Business Environmental Leadership Council—the largest U.S.-based group of corporations focused on addressing climate challenges and supporting climate policy. In 2022, five visionary startups each received $250,000 as grants as part of the Sustainable Solutions Collaborative. Among them was Notpla, a UK based sustainable packaging start-up which invented a seaweed-based alternative to single use plastic containers with transformative potential. Morgan Stanley Investment Management (MSIM) had introduced D&I-focused investment strategies, including the Next Level Fund for diverse entrepreneurs, Calvert Diversity Research strategies, and a liquidity fund supporting diverse broker-dealers.

In November 2022, MSIM launched 1GT, a growth oriented private equity platform to invest in companies seeking to mitigate climate change. The Morgan Stanley Inclusive Ventures Lab (the Lab) was launched to address inequities in funding of ethnically and racially diverse and women led start-ups. By 2023, 92 companies have gone through the program achieving more than $1 billion in combined valuation and raising over $200 million in funding after participating in the Lab.

The Next Level Fund established as a partnership between MSIVG and MSIM Invests in early-stage tech ventures led by women or underrepresented founders through privately negotiated equity and venture capital investments.

Morgan Stanley is a member of the Center for Climate and Energy Solutions' Business Environmental Leadership Council, the largest U.S.-based group of corporations focused on addressing climate challenges and supporting climate policy. Morgan Stanley is a member of the Partnership for Carbon Accounting Financials (PCAF) and the Net-Zero Banking Alliance (NZBA).

Key Green Investments

Recykal, a circular economy focused firm involved in digitizing the supply chain for waste and connecting waste generators directly with waste processors and recyclers, received investment from the Morgan Stanley India Infrastructure. In 2022, the company had channelized more than 100,000 metric tons of dry waste back into the circular economy and away from landfills and water bodies. Morgan Stanley served as a bookrunner for the PepsiCo's $1.25 billion 10-year green bond. Transactions that pose potential environmental and social risks are reviewed by the relevant business units and the ESRM Group.

In 2022, Morgan Stanley became the sole global coordinator and joint lead manager for EQT's €1.5 billion sustainability-linked bond issuance. EQT became the first private equity company globally to formalize science-based targets (SBTs). The bond's coupon step-up was tied to EQT Funds achieving 40% SBT-approved investments by 2025, reinforcing commitment to science-based climate targets and accountability. Morgan Stanley acted as the bookrunner for the consumer packaging firm, Novolex's $5.1 billion sustainability linked leveraged buyout financing aligning with its goal to cut emissions intensity by 20% by 2025 and 30% by 2030. Morgan Stanley served as the active bookrunner for Germany's €4 billion green bond, funding projects across five sectors under its Green Bond Framework to support sustainability and environmental initiatives. Morgan Stanley served as joint placement agent for Northvolt's $1.1 billion private convertible note, funding its European battery production expansion to meet rising demand with a lower carbon footprint. The firm also served as joint lead manager for New York City's $400 million social bond, funding reimbursements for affordable housing projects to support community development. In 2020, Morgan Stanley issued $1 billion social bond to direct capital into affordable housing projects to support vulnerable communities.

Morgan Stanley served as the joint placement agent for H2 Green Steel's €260 million equity issue, supporting its hydrogen-powered steel plant in Boden to reduce carbon emissions in heavy industries. In 2022, the firm served as joint global coordinator for New World Development's $700 million green and social bond, funding projects in green buildings, affordable housing, and socioeconomic development in Hong Kong. Morgan Stanley had also served as sole underwriter for the Family Forest Impact Foundation's $10 million green bond, funding incentives for U.S. landowners to join the Voluntary Carbon Offset market and support ESG investment. The financial institution also served as the sole financial advisor to British Petroleum for its $4.1 billion acquisition of Archaea Energy, which was meant to advance BP's bioenergy investments to support decarbonization and lower carbon intensity. Morgan Stanley was also the lead left bookrunner and stabilization agent for Hannon Armstrong's $200 million Green Exchangeable Bond, supporting investments in energy efficiency, renewable energy, and sustainable infrastructure.

Morgan served as global coordinator for Sanofi's €1.5 billion bond offering, including €650 million sustainability-linked notes targeting essential medicine access for 1.5 million patients in low-income countries by 2026. For over a decade, Morgan Stanley had been a leader in the US municipal and not for profit bond market. The bank had been underwriting senior managed green, social and sustainability bonds. The Public Finance Group had served as underwriter across thematic areas such as affordable housing, renewable energy, mass transportation, climate resiliency, carbon capture, sustainable water and wastewater, cultural and educational facilities. In 2022, the Global Capital Markets team served as Diversity and Inclusive (D&I) Coordinator for 19 large scale investment grade bond transactions for brands such as Starbucks, Amazon, American Express, PayPal and Meta. The Equities and Fixed income divisions offer a wide range of ESG focused solutions to institutional clients which span data, analytics, capital introduction, hedging solutions, carbon markets and structured products. The Securitized Products Group (SPG) collaborates with global alternative investment managers to incorporate ESG data and climate risk factors into their investment framework for managing collateralized loan obligations (CLO) transactions. Morgan Stanley actively engages in the trading of carbon credits, offsets, and renewable energy certificates, facilitating over 14 million MWh of transactions in renewable assets with renewable energy projects and sustainability-focused power consumers.

In 2023, Morgan Stanley became the joint global coordinator for renewable electricity producer Hidroelectrica's €1.9 billion IPO. In 2023, Morgan Stanley had mobilized $820 billion in capital toward the goal of $ one trillion by 2030 which included $640 billion in low carbon and green solutions. Institutional Securities have mobilized ESG labelled debt transactions valued at $97 billion in year 2023. Approximately $77 billion in client assets were invested through the Investment Impact Platform (IIP). In 2023, Morgan Stanley became the sole structuring agent and active bookrunner for telecom Company Allo's $576 million inaugural sustainability labelled securitization issuance. The firm was the joint book runner and delivery agent for Aegea's $500 million sustainability linked bond issuance. Aegea is the leading provider of basic sanitation services in Brazil. Morgan Stanley facilitated global container logistics integrator, Maersk's $750 million green bond issuance to finance clean transportation and green buildings. Morgan Stanley advised H2Green Steel for securing €1.5 billion in equity financing. Morgan Stanley advised H2 Green Steel on both the Series B1 and B2 rounds. The firm was the joint lead manager for the inaugural €1 billion sustainable bond issuance for the Republic of Cyprus. The proceeds from the issuance would be used to finance or refinance projects to promote sustainability in terms of climate change and other environmental and social purposes. JERA Green, the subsidiary of JERA, Japan's largest power generator was advised by Morgan Stanley to acquire 100% of Parkwind for €1.55 billion for enhancing its global renewables platform, particularly in offshore wind sector. Morgan Stanley was the lead manager for the $349 million financing for the Battery Park City Authority's sustainable finance projects. Morgan Stanley was the co-lead manager for $200 million tax exempt sustainability bonds issued by Freddie Mac. US banks Morgan Stanley Bank and Morgan Stanley Private Bank National Association have made over $3 billion in community development loans and investments in year 2023.

HSBC Green Finance Investments

HSBC is one of the largest banking and financial services organisations in the world. HSBC's global operations serve approximately 42 million customers across 62 countries and territories. In 2020, the bank announced its goal to become a net zero bank by the year 2050. In 2021, the bank included the transition to net zero as one of the four key pillars of the corporate strategy. During May 2021, HSBC passed a resolution on climate change which were approved by 99.71% of the shareholders. The bank has set target to provide between $750 billion to $1 trillion of sustainable finance and investment by the year 2030. During the period 2020–2022, the bank has achieved $210.7 billion of the targeted goal. Of this green and sustainable investment amounted to $183 billion and social investment amounted to $28.8 billion.

In 2020, HSBC bank had launched $100 million five-year climate solution partnership. HSBC support public sector clients in over 80 countries and territories with sustainable banking services, facilitating financing for national, regional, and city-level transitions, including capital market access. HSBC deliver investment solutions which help its institutional customers allocate capital toward a more sustainable economy. The bank provides 40 million personal and private customers with sustainable banking solutions and investment options to support their wealth management and eco-friendly lifestyles. HSBC's relationship managers and local sustainability teams help SME customers access a network of specialists who offer local and international assistance. HSBC have launched self-service tools, including an ESG Hub in its Hong Kong Mobile Banking app, connecting customers to sustainable banking, investment products, and ESG insights. HSBC have partnered with GFANZ and the Taskforce on Nature related Financial Disclosures (TNFD) on nature related risk. The bank has created a Nature Based Solutions Accelerator as part of its five-year partnership with WWF and WRI. HSBC have also become a signatory to Business for Nature's Call to Action, and through HSBC Asset Management as a signatory to the Finance for Biodiversity Pledge. HSBC provide institutional investors access to sustainable bonds, ESG derivatives, and thematic indices, along with ESG-focused securities financing, hedging, and sustainability-linked solutions. HSBC offer green mortgages and energy efficiency loans in eight markets, with preferential terms for certified green buildings and financing to enhance home energy efficiency. HSBC offer electric vehicle (EV) to finance the purchase of battery electric or plug in hybrid vehicles at preferential commercial terms compared to other standard loan products. The asset management division integrates sustainability across asset classes, while Private Banking and Insurance offer sustainable investments, including private equity co-investments for ultra-high-net-worth clients. In 2023, Climate Asset Management, a joint venture between HSBC Asset Management and Pollination, offered its natural capital strategy to ultra-high-net-worth clients, providing access to nature-based assets. In 2022, HSBC introduced a Global Biodiversity Discretionary Strategy for Global Private Banking customers in Asia, covering eight themes, including sustainable food systems, water solutions, and biomaterials. The bank aim to be the bank of choice for climate tech pioneers, leveraging its global presence to support early-stage businesses and emerging technologies. For example, the bank partnered with Univers, a leading decarbonization platform, to support their expansion and help corporate clients develop effective carbon abatement strategies. HSBC Innovation Banking, launched after acquiring SVB UK, combines innovation expertise with global teams in the US, Israel, and Hong Kong to support climate tech growth. HSBC have a $1 billion climate tech allocation offering flexible venture debt to support growth, focusing on long-term banking relationships to sustain cash flow and investments. HSBC Asset Management Climate Technology Venture Capital Fund aims to raise $200 million to support fast-growing climate tech companies in energy transition, transport, and sustainability. The $3 billion HSBC New Economy Fund, launched in 2023, supports start-ups in healthcare, life sciences, climate tech, industrials, and consumer sectors in Hong Kong and China. HSBC have plans to invest $100 million as an anchor partner to support decarbonization in high-carbon sectors through clean hydrogen, energy storage, sustainable aviation fuel, and more. HSBC help corporate customers decarbonize supply chains by offering improved financing terms to suppliers with strong sustainability performance. In 2019, the bank has collaborated with US retailer Walmart to roll out a finance programme that pegs their supplier's financing rate to sustainable outcomes. The bank has partnered with EcoVadis, which provides ratings to help companies manage sustainability practices within their supply chain.

Climate Asset Management, a joint venture between HSBC Asset Management and Pollination, accelerates natural capital investment to protect ecosystems and biodiversity. With over $650 million committed, its two strategies—Natural Capital and Nature-Based Carbon—focus on sustainable agriculture, forestry, and nature restoration in developing economies while delivering financial returns and community benefits. HSBC has partnered with iCapital to expand access to Climate Tech strategy, offering it to wholesale customers across Europe, the Middle East, and Asia. HSBC Asset Management has a range of targeted strategies and solutions as part of sustainable investment strategy. In 2022, HSBC launched the first biodiversity-screened equity index and ETF, integrating nature considerations into investment portfolios by screening companies based on biodiversity performance. The bank is targeting the purchase of 100% renewable electricity by 2030 and an interim target of 90% by the year 2025.

Table 10.8 gives the major green finance milestones achieved by HSBC.

Third-party analysis estimates $155 trillion is required to finance the transition to net zero by 2050 in the markets HSBC serves. Approximately 40–50% of corporate capital expenditure by 2030 will be directly linked to the transition, funding the new technologies and low-carbon infrastructure vital to the industries of the future. During the period 2020–2022, HSBC provided and facilitated $210.7 billion of sustainable finance and investment. The Asset Management business of HSBC and its

Table 10.8 Major Net Zero Timelines

Year	Milestones
2021	Set target to be net zero bank by year 2050 including portfolio of financed emissions. Set target to be net zero in own operations and supply chain by 2030. Set target to provide between $750 billion to $1 trillion of sustainable finance and investment by the year 2030. Launched $100 million five-year Climate Solutions Partnership
2022	Published net zero-aligned Group thermal coal phase-out policy. Became a member of the Net Zero Banking Alliance and Net Zero Asset Managers Initiative. Made the transition to net zero a key pillar of the Group corporate strategy. Published net zero-aligned Group thermal coal phase-out policy
2023	Set on-balance sheet 2030 financed emissions targets for oil and gas, and power and utilities. Published Statement on Nature. $650 million raised for natural capital funds by Climate Asset Management. Set on-balance sheet 2030 financed emissions target for thermal coal mining
2024	Set on-balance sheet 2030 financed emissions targets for key transport and heavy industry sectors. Published initial Net Zero Transition Plan. Became a founding member of the Global Climate Finance Centre and the Capacity-building Alliance of Sustainable Investment. Became a founding funder of the Just Transition Finance Lab, hosted at LSE's Grantham Research Institute

Source: HSBC Holdings plc Net Zero Transition Plan

joint venture with Pollination, Climate Asset Management are offering sustainable exchange traded funds (ETFs); alternative funds focused on climate tech, carbon markets, conservation, sustainable infrastructure and nature-based solutions. HSBC's forestry and agricultural commodities policies require customers associated with major deforestation risk commodities to obtain independent certification of sustainable business operations.

Green Investments by HSBC

HSBC have associated with Pentagreen Capital which targets $1 billion of capital investment in bankable clean energy and adaptation projects in Asia. HSBC have made provisions for $1 billion allocation of venture debt capital for climate start up. Approximately more than three quarters of HSBC oil and gas on balance sheet financed emissions come from a concentrated group of upstream and integrated energy companies. HSBC have set a target to reduce the emissions intensity of on balance sheet financed emissions of its automotive portfolio to 66 tCO_2 per million vehicle kilometres by 2030, which represents a 66% reduction versus the 2019 baseline. HSBC set a target to reduce the emissions intensity of on-balance sheet financed emissions for its cement portfolio to 0.46 tCO_2 per tonne of cement by 2030.

In the year 2022, HSBC had increased its sustainable lending transactions by over 50%. In the same year, HSBC became the sole sustainability coordinator for a GBP 103.7 million green loan to JDR Cable Systems to construct a manufacturing facility to produce the next generation of high voltage subsea power cables for offshore wind farms. HSBC also acted as sole global coordinator and joint sustainability structuring bank for a $400 million sustainable club loan to Geely Automobile for R&D related to electric and hybrid vehicles.

At COP26, HSBC launched a £500 million Green SME Fund to support renewable energy and energy efficiency investments with financial incentives. In 2022, HSBC launched a $9 billion sustainable finance allocation to support businesses transitions to low carbon operations in China's Greater Bay Area. In 2023, HSBC offered a $8 million green term loan to Ampd Energy to finance the deployment of giant batteries at construction sites. HSBC acted as mandated lead manager on the GBP 2 billion financing to support the construction and operation of the 882 MW Moray West offshore wind farm in the UK. The bank had structured green project finance facility through refinancing of existing debt for a 300 MW operational solar project owned by ReNew Power in Rajasthan, India. In collaboration with two government funds and consortium of financial institutions, HSBC provided finance for $8.4 billion facility for the world's largest green hydrogen-based ammonia production plant.

According to IEA estimates, approximately $360 billion- $450 billion of investment in mining of critical minerals will be needed by 2030, with over 60% of the capital requirements for copper for usage in renewables, grid expansion, and other innovative technologies. The mining customers include diversified majors and mid-tier firms across HSBC's markets. HSBC have set a thermal coal financing target to reduce drawn balance exposure by at least 25% by 2025 and 50% by year 2030 and will phase out all financing of thermal coal mining by 2030 in the EU and OECD and 2040 in the rest of the world. Third party analysis for 1.5 °C-aligned scenarios estimates that decarbonising residential and commercial real estate will require $29 trillion by 2050. Majority of investments are required for district heating and heat pumps. These technologies would require about $27 trillion to be applied across both residential and commercial real estate through 2050. Retrofits would require about $8 trillion in capital expenditure investment. Real estate accounts for over 80% of lending to personal customers and 20% of lending to wholesale customers. HSBC's residential real estate exposure is composed primarily of mortgages which are issued to customers in the UK and Hong Kong.

HSBC jointly structured the UK Government's first ever green bond issuance valued at GBP 10 billion to finance green projects. The bank acted as a sustainability structuring agent on Uruguay's $1.5 billion inaugural sustainability linked bond issuance. HSBC assisted the Hong Kong government for the issuance of the world's first tokenized green bond and green bonds exceed $14 billion in value in year 2023.

In 2023, HSBC became the joint bookrunner and joint lead manager for Pertamina Geothermal Energy's $400 million green bond issuance. The proceeds from the issuance would be utilized by Pertamina Group to decarbonize the energy sector as well as to support the energy security across Indonesia.

The sustainability linked solutions offered by HSBC include hedges, foreign exchange swaps and repurchase agreements. HSBC designed a $50 million sustainability linked loan for Archirodon, an international EPC contractor with significant presence in Middle East region. The bank also offered an ESG KPI linked Vanilla Interest Rate Swap to hedge the client's EUR debt from rising interest rate risk. The bank acted as a joint financial adviser and broker for Biffa, a leading waste management firm for their GBP 2.1 billion enterprise value acquisition by energy transition investor Energy Capital Partners (ECP).

HSBC launched Pentagreen Capital with Temasek, committing $150 million in seed capital to accelerate sustainable infrastructure development in Southeast Asia. The initiative aims to provide over $1 billion in loans within 5 years, focusing on clean transport, renewable energy, energy storage, and water and waste management projects. Just Energy Transition Partnerships (JETPs) are multilateral agreements promoting renewable energy and fossil fuel phase-down while investing in transition-aligned jobs. HSBC support JETPs in Indonesia and Vietnam, identifying investment barriers and facilitating at least $10 billion for Indonesia and $7.8 billion for Vietnam over the next 3–5 years. The bank partnered with FAST Infra to launch the sustainable Infrastructure Label, a universal system for certifying sustainable infrastructure assets.

HSBC Climate Asset Management's Restore Africa Programme, launched in partnership with the Global EverGreening Alliance in 2021, is the world's largest community-based land restoration project. It aims to restore 2 million hectares of degraded land, benefiting 1.5 million smallholder farmers across Kenya, Uganda, and Malawi, with expansion across six countries. In 2023, Climate Asset Management expanded Apple's Restore Fund, managing a natural capital investment vehicle that supports suppliers in incorporating nature-based carbon removal projects.

Green Finance Investments by Allianz

Allianz Group is one of the world's leading insurers and asset managers with 125 million private and corporate customers in around 70 countries. Allianz had been in the insurance and risk management business for over 134 years. Allianz is one of the world's largest asset managers, with third party assets of 1712 billion euros under management at year end 2024. In the year 2023, the Allianz Group had achieved a total business volume of approximately 162 billion euros. Allianz employs over 157,000 people globally. Allianz had a climate change strategy in place since the year 2005. Allianz published its first comprehensive Net-Zero Transition Plan in year 2023 and have committed to achieve net zero emissions by year 2050.

In the year 2023, 715 insurance transactions were assessed for sustainability risks. In 2023, Allianz invested over €736.8 billion in a wide range of asset classes and the sustainable investments totalled €167.4 billion. In 2023, sustainability themed investments amounted to €424.5 billion. The sustainable investments of Allianz grew 27% year on year from €131.5 billion in 2022 to €167.4 billion in 2023.

The two major asset management businesses of Allianz are the Allianz Global Investors and PIMCO. Allianz have EUR 560 billion in assets under management for institutional and retail investors worldwide. Allianz offer equity, fixed income, private market and multi asset strategies. Allianz offers single country and global strategies and thematic and sector portfolios.

Allianz have prioritized three of the 17 Sustainable Development Goals (SDGs) namely SDG 8-Decent work and economic growth, SDG 13-Climate action, SDG 17-Partnerships for sustainable society. Allianz paid €48.2 billion for claims in its P&C business. Allianz provide affordable insurance solutions to over 85.5 million emerging market consumers to improve access to financial services. Allianz contribute to the economic and social development of countries in which it operates with a total tax contribution of €20.0 billion. The company have paid 14.7 billion euros in wages in 2023. In 2023, Allianz funded 18 social projects through its Social Impact Fund. The Sustainability Integration Framework adopted by Allianz focusses on climate change, social impact, responsible investment and governance.

The intermediate targets and commitments for 2030 based on Allianz's Net Zero Transition Plan involve increase of climate solutions investment by at least €20 billion from current level of €37 billion as of year 2023. The aim is to showcase progress in P&C insurance portfolios and reduction of CO_2 emissions by 30% absolute in the retail motor segment and 45% with regards to the GHG intensity in the commercial insurance segment. The emission reduction target policies are applicable to nine key European markets such as Austria, Belgium, France, Italy, Germany, Netherlands, Spain, Switzerland and the UK. By 2030, Allianz aims to engage with 20 million current and potential customers to support their transition to electric mobility.

In 2019, Allianz facilitated the establishment of UN convened NZAOA consisting of 87 institutional investors as of December 2023 with USD 9.5 trillion assets under management with the commitment to transition of their investment portfolios to net zero GHG by 2050. The NZAOA members are the first in the finance industry to set intermediate targets, which include emission reduction ranges for 2025 and for 2030.

Allianz's MoveNow Future Workout is a three-week digital program teaching financial and insurance literacy, empowering youth. Subsidiaries in 70+ countries receive €500,000 grant for this project through Social Impact Fund.

Allianz Global Investors (Alliance GI) is an active investment management firm which is a part of the Allianz Group. Alliance GI manage EUR 533 billion of assets for institutions and individuals worldwide. The firm's investing approach based on sustainability KPIs aligns sustainable outcomes and financial returns. The SDG Loan Fund of the firm have raised USD 1.1 billion of investor capital on the basis of an innovative blended finance model. The firm had also launched its first socially focused equity strategy. Currently 61% of the firm's mutual fund AUM are managed according to a sustainable investment approach. Around 40 of the Allianz Global Investor funds incorporate GHG intensity as a KPI alongside seeking attractive returns. In 2023, Allianz had introduced 25 new sustainable products which included five new funds. The firm had invested EUR 2.9 million in employee development which included mandatory firm wide sustainability training. In 2023, Alliance GI engaged with 374 companies across 32 locations and participated in 9137 shareholder meetings.

Alliance GI had supported a French insurance company in assessing the climate profile and biodiversity footprint of its portfolio. AllianzGI's risklab advisory team is an integral part of its service for institutional investors. With a global team of 60 advisers, risklab provides specialized advice and tailored solutions to help clients achieve their investment objectives. Alliance GI's Socially Responsible Investment (SRI) strategy integrates ESG factors into fundamental research, selecting top performing firms within each sector. Using proprietary ESG ratings, the firm assess corporate governance, environmental impact, social responsibility, and business behavior. Portfolio construction applies negative and positive screening to enhance ESG quality while excluding high-risk industries like coal and tobacco. In 2023, Alliance GI launched its first systematic SDG-aligned global equity strategy which offered investors with the benefits of broad diversification while addressing multiple SDGs. The green bonds strategy of the company followed a sustainable investment objective to mobilize capital to support the transition to a low carbon society, preserve natural capital and adapt to climate change. The SDG Loan fund which was one of the largest blended funds in the market was jointly conceived by AllianzGI, FMO and the Dutch Development Bank.

The Emerging Market Climate Action Fund (EMCAF) had commitments from Germany's KfW, UK government. The total commitment of EMCAF is approximately EUR 385 million. The mid-market private equity, GEF South Asia Growth Fund III focusses on financing companies which are active in climate mitigation, adaptation and environmental sustainability sectors in Asia. Alliance GI is expanding impact strategies in private debt and equity across markets.

In November 2023, Brazil launched its first sustainability-linked bond with participation in the bond tender offer by AllianceGI. The firm engaged with eight utility companies using Climate Action 100+ criteria, gaining insights on diverse transition pathways, regulatory impacts, and grid investment challenges. The firm will continue monitoring their progress toward 2030 goals and coal exit plans. The company has tracked an Asian bank's climate strategy since 2022, noting progress in sustainability KPIs and decarbonization targets. In 2023, AllianzGI joined the GFANZ Asia Pacific Network, which supports the expansion of net-zero finance in Asia-Pacific region.

Vanguard's Sustainable Investments

Vanguard is a leading investment management company providing a wide range of investment options, financial advice, retirement services, and market insights to individuals, institutions, and financial professionals. Vanguard serves more than 50 million individual investors. Vanguard offer more than 30 investment products globally which have specific environmental, social and governance objectives. For investors seeking to reduce exposure to carbon-intensive industries, the ESG index funds aim to minimize such investments while maintaining broad market-like returns. Vanguard's actively managed ESG funds aim to generate excess returns by investing in companies with strong ESG practices, as determined by fund managers per each fund's mandate.

Vanguard's Investment Stewardship program is responsible for voting proxies and engaging with company boards and management teams on behalf of Vanguard-advised funds. In 2023, the Investment Steward activity saw engagement of 1334 companies and 1659 company engagements. Wellington Management, Vanguard's largest external advisor, oversees $400 billion globally. In late 2023, it engaged with rail companies, including Union Pacific, to assess decarbonization strategies and climate transition risks. Union Pacific aims for a 26% reduction in Scopes 1 and 2 emissions and a 20% low-carbon fuel target by 2030.

Union Pacific has committed to spend more than $1 billion on modernizing locomotives to reduce Scope 1 emissions by an additional 2%. Ninety-One, managing over $150 billion, oversees the Vanguard Global Environmental Opportunities Fund, investing in companies supporting a lower-carbon economy. Waste Management, the largest U.S. waste company, advances decarbonization through landfill carbon sequestration, methane capture for fuel and energy, and recycling, significantly reducing carbon emissions and raw material demand.

Vanguard Fixed Income Group (FIG) manages most of Vanguard's fixed income funds, integrating ESG considerations where appropriate. FIG assesses ESG risks alongside credit risks, tailoring its approach across sub-asset classes. Excluding money market funds, FIG refines its ESG process based on market trends, regulations, and issuer engagements to mitigate financial risks.

Vanguard prioritizes material climate-related risks in investment and stewardship, assessing their impact on portfolio companies' long-term value. It emphasizes corporate disclosures' role in price discovery and returns. As climate risk disclosure improves, security prices will better reflect these risks, benefiting all investors through more accurate risk assessments and valuations. Vanguard's actively managed ESG funds align with net zero goals, targeting under 2 °C warming. External managers set interim targets, disclosed in fund prospectuses and monitored by Vanguard.

Vanguard reports ESG index funds' asset-weighted emissions, total carbon footprint, and carbon intensity using MSCI data. MSCI sources emissions data from companies, governments, NGOs, and media but does not provide third-party assurances. Vanguard relies on MSCI's data accuracy without independent verification or third-party review of the reported information.

Vanguard had set goals in 2020 to reduce emissions and carbon footprint. By 2023, it maintained 100% renewable electricity globally in owned and leased properties. Energy comes from on-site renewables, direct utility supplies, or Green-e certified renewable energy certificates, achieved first in 2021 and continuing since. Twenty-two buildings (or 37%) of Vanguard's total square footage across its global locations were either LEED, BREEAM, or WELL certified.7 7 LEED (Leadership in Energy and Environmental Design) is administered by the U.S. Green Building Council. BREEAM (Building Research Establishment Environmental Assessment Methodology) is administered by BRE Global, a subsidiary of the U.K.-based BRE Group. WELL is administered by the International Well Building Institute (IWBI). Of the 22 buildings, four were new certifications for Vanguard in 2023.

Vanguard currently offer seven ESG products which include four exclusionary index funds and three active funds. For investors seeking to minimize exposure to industries or business activities with elevated ESG-related risks or those that conflict with their values, Vanguard provide index products designed to restrict or exclude specific sectors, including firearms, tobacco, and fossil fuels. Vanguard offer active ESG strategies where managers aim for excess returns by investing in companies with strong ESG practices, improvements, or positive social and environmental impact. The exclusionary indexed ESG products are ESG US Corporate Bond ETF (VCEB), ESG US Stock ETF (ESGV), FTSE Social Index Fund Institutional Shares (VFTNX) and ESG International Stock ETF (VSGX). The actively managed funds can be categorized as inclusionary and impact. The inclusionary funds are Global ESG Select Stock Fund Admiral Shares (VESGX) and Global Environmental Opportunities Stock Fund Admiral Shares (VEOAX). The Impact fund is Baillie Gifford Global Positive Impact Stock Fund Investor Shares (VBPIX).

Table 10.9 shows the list of Vanguard's ESG funds.

Table 10.9 Vanguard's ESG funds

Fund	Investment type	Management style	Geographic coverage
ESGV ESG US Stock ETF	ETF	Indexed (approx.1500 stocks)	US only
VFTAX FTSE Social Index Fund	Mutual Fund	Indexed (approx.500 stocks)	US only
VSGX ESG International Stock ETF	ETF	Indexed (over 6000 stocks)	International only
VBPIX, Baillie Gifford Global Positive Impact Fund	Mutual Fund	Actively Managed (approx.25–50 stocks)	US and International
VEOIX. Global Environmental Opportunities Stock Fund	Mutual Fund	Actively Managed (approx.25 stocks)	US and International
VEIGX Global ESG Select Fund	Mutual Fund	Actively Managed (40–50 stocks)	US and International

Source: https://investor.vanguard.com/investment-products/esg

Vanguard's Investment Stewardship team is responsible for voting proxies and engaging with portfolio companies on behalf of Vanguard-advised fund. The Investment Stewardship team engages with companies on material risks, including ESG risks, to assess board oversight and disclosure. Proxy votes follow clear, publicly disclosed policies and board-approved procedures for each Vanguard fund. Vanguard ensure transparency by disclosing proxy voting policies and decisions to support long-term investor interests.

In early 2020, Vanguard established goals to curb emissions and reduce the global carbon footprint of its operations. Vanguard's greenhouse gas emissions reporting follows the Greenhouse Gas Protocol corporate standard. The company aims to achieve carbon neutrality throughout its global operations by year 2025. Vanguard achieved 84% carbon neutrality by year end 2023. Vanguard achieved 100% renewable energy in year 2021. Green building criteria and certifications are integral to Vanguard's building design standards. Approximately 37% of Vanguard's total square footage across its global locations are either LEED, BREEAM or WELL certified. Vanguard is a member of the US Environmental Protection Agency's Green Power Partnership which aim to increase voluntary use of electricity produced from renewable energy resources. In 2023, Vanguard purchased over 94,000 MWh of renewable energy, which resulted in a reduction of more than 30,000 tCO_2e.

Vanguard's Sustainable Life funds are tailored for investors seeking long-term growth while integrating sustainable investment criteria into their portfolios. The Vanguard SustainableLife funds have a 2050 net zero emissions target in alignment with the Paris Agreement. The aim is to invest 60% of shares and corporate bonds in companies with net zero science-based targets (SBTs) by the year 2030. The next aim is to increase the investment to 90% by 2040 and finally by 100% in shares and bonds of companies which are net zero by year 2050. Vanguard Sustainable Life funds are highly diversified, multi-asset portfolios featuring a core large-cap equity allocation of approximately 80–110 stocks, complemented by 10–60% in bonds to manage risk. Vanguard's Oversight & Manager Search team evaluates current and potential fund managers to assess their ESG practices and approach. In 2019, Vanguard assigned full proxy voting responsibilities to external advisers, allowing them to align voting and engagement with their investment strategies while ensuring alignment with fund objectives.

Vanguard's credit research team evaluates Aurizon Holdings, a top Australian rail operator, considering its earnings diversification and decarbonization strategy. Aurizon's shift from road to rail enhances ESG credentials, with 95% lower emissions. Engagements with Aurizon provide insights into climate risks, supporting its improving ESG profile and long-term strategy.

Berkshire Hathaway Sustainability Initiatives

Berkshire Hathaway's (BHE) sustainability strategy focusses on climate mitigation and efforts to achieve net zero greenhouse gas emissions by the year 2050. Berkshire have investments in wind, solar, geothermal energy projects as well as methane leak detection programs with its pipelines. BHE sustainability strategy is focused on climate mitigation and includes efforts to achieve net-zero greenhouse gas emissions by 2050. BHE plans to transition its vehicle fleet to electric and enhance EV charging infrastructure along major highways, supporting broader EV adoption within its service area.

BHE plans to leverage its Green Financing Framework to align its financing strategy with environmental sustainability goals. Additionally, the company has collaborated with the Edison Electric Institute, the American Gas Association, and financial community members to enhance reporting on key sustainability metrics. BHE and its subsidiaries green strategy are in alignment with the Green Bond Principles (GBP) published by the International Capital Markets Association and the Loan Market Association Green Loan Principles (GLP). S&P Global Ratings has provided a second party opinion regarding Berkshire Hathaway Energy's Green Financing Framework environmental credentials and its alignment with the GBP and GLP.

By 2022, Berkshire Hathaway Energy has invested $37 billion in renewable energy generation. Through year end 2023, the company had invested nearly $40 billion in clean power generation. In early 1980s, BHE developed its first geothermal project in South California. The businesses occupy number one position among investor owned utilities with clean power in operations. BHE participate in voluntary industry ESG/Sustainability initiative advanced through Edison Electric Institute. BHE is rapidly moving to shift its power mix to wind and solar. Berkshire is expected to get 45% of its power from wind, solar, geothermal energy and hydropower. In 2022, more than 40% of BHE's owned generation capacity in 2022 came from wind and solar alone.

The Berkshire Hathaway Sustainability Leadership Council unites company representatives to champion sustainability efforts and support subsidiaries in developing and implementing their sustainability strategies. Berkshire Hathaway companies have committed to Science Based Targets, net zero emissions, emission reduction goals, sustainable fuels, water conservation etc.

Benjamin Moore the market leader in paint industry, have partnerships with non-profit and community organizations and have resulted in more than $777,000 in grant funding and over 6300 gallons of paint donated to help uplift communities. BNSF Railway Company had capital investment plan of $3.92 billion in the year 2024. Approximately $2.88 billion is devoted to maintaining BNSF's core network and related assets. BNSF along with the San Joaquin Valley Pollution Control District was awarded a $22.6 million grant from the California Air Resource Board for testing emissions reducing technologies for rail yards in BNSF. Brooks Sports Inc, the subsidiary of Berkshire Hathaway Inc headquartered in Washington was founded in year 1914 is a subsidiary of Berkshire Hathaway Inc. Brooks Sports is a sports equipment company which designs and markets high performance men's and women's sneakers, clothing, and accessories. Brooks introduced BioMoGo, the world's first biodegradable midsole, marking a major breakthrough in sustainable technology for running footwear. Brooks had total community impact investment of $6.2 million in year 2023.

Clayton is a leading single-family home builder. Over 20,000 team members build, sell, finance and insure modern manufactured homes, modular homes, CrossMod® homes, site-built homes and PMRVs. CrossMod® homes combine modern designs, energy efficiency, and high-end materials while maintaining the quality, speed, and efficiency of off-site construction. In 2023, Berkshire Hathaway subsidiary, Power utility PacificCorp sold $1.1 billion of environmentally friendly bonds dues in 2053, the longest maturity to be offered in the sustainable debt market.

Berkshire's insurance and reinsurance business activities are conducted through numerous domestic and foreign-based insurance subsidiaries. Berkshire's insurance subsidiaries provide insurance and reinsurance of property and casualty risks and reinsurance of life and health risks worldwide. Berkshire underwrite high GHG emitting activities. In 2019, Berkshire owned 12% of oil and gas assets held by insurance companies. The company also holds the second largest insurance industry stake in coal.

Green Initiatives by UBS Group

UBS Group is a multinational investment bank and financial services company based in Switzerland. UBS is the largest Swiss banking institution and the largest private bank in the world. UBS Group AG is a holding company and conducts substantially all of its operations through UBS AG and Credit Suisse AG, and subsidiaries thereof. The invested assets of more than USD 5 trillion are regionally diversified across the globe.

UBS have undertaken significant sustainability and ESG initiatives such as reduction of emissions intensity from in-scope investments. Being one of the world's largest asset managers, UBS partners with clients to support them in mobilising capital for more sustainable world. UBS is included in the Dow Jones Sustainability Index and have an AA rating from MSCI. UBS holds an A rating and is included in the Leadership band for its climate risk management and transparency by Carbon Project Disclosure. In 2023, UBS acquired Credit Suisse. This merger resulted in the first ever combination of two global systematically important financial institutions (G-SIFIs). After the merger, UBS have implemented a revised sustainability and climate risk policy framework. The bank focusses on minimizing scope 1 and scope 2 greenhouse gas (GHG) emissions. The bank aims to achieve net zero greenhouse gas emissions across its scope 1 and 2 and specified scope 3 activities by year 2050. In 2023, UBS Group had USD 292.3 billion of impact investments. UBS AG Global Wealth Management had USD 11.2 billion clients' impact investing assets in year 2023. UBS AG Asset Management had 1611 ESG resolutions voted upon. By 2023, sustainable investments account for 46.5% of assets under custody for UBS AG Personal & Corporate Banking. UBS have facilitated 102 green, social, sustainability or sustainability linked bond deals. In 2023, UBS Optimus network of foundations had raised USD 328 million which benefitted 7 million beneficiaries. UBS increased investments in sustainable investments from USD 266 billion in year 2022 to USD 293.3 billion in year 2023. Following the acquisition of Credit Suisse Group, UBS have refined the UBS Group lending sector decarbonization targets. UBS aim to align 20% of UBS AG Asset Management's total asset under management (AuM) with net zero using science-based portfolio alignment approaches by the year 2030. This included implementing revisions to fund documentation and investment management agreements in certain portfolios by the year 2030.

Decarbonization targets have been established for Swiss real estate mortgages (commercial and residential real estate) and for financing of in-scope activities in the fossil fuels (oil, gas and coal), power generation, iron and steel and cement sectors. Through ESG Advisory Group, UBS assist clients to assess ESG themes throughout the corporate lifecycle.

UBS AG Asset Management is a co-lead and collaborative investor in Climate Action 100+. UBS Group is the second largest manager of open-ended funds and ETFs by sustainable invested assets using Morningstar's classification. The sustainable investment proportion of UBS AG total amounted to 6.5% of the total assets in 2023. UBS Investment bank facilitated 102 green, social, sustainability or sustainability linked (GSSS) bond transactions globally in 2023 which amounted to USD53.7 billion. UBS Group occupied 1st Swiss franc denominated GSSS bond issuance in the home market of Switzerland with 50% market share.

Table 10.10 highlights the climate related risks and opportunities metrics of UBS.

Table 10.11 gives the highlights of sustainable invested assets by UBS Group.

UBS AG Global Wealth Management continues to drive Sustainable Investing (SI), with significant growth in impact and discretionary assets. In 2023, the impact investing assets held by UBS AG Global Wealth Management clients amounted to USD 11.2 billion. The discretionary asset allocation totalled USD 22.5 billion. UBS AG Global Wealth clients had access to seven private market impact investment

Table 10.10 Climate related risks and opportunities metrics

Year	2021	2022	2023
Risks			
Carbon Related Assets (USD billion)	36	33.6	34.2
Exposure to climate-sensitive sectors, transition risk (USD billion)	52.4	52.5	58.1
Exposure to climate-sensitive sectors, physical risk (USD billion)	36.7	38	46.2
Exposure to nature-related risks (USD billion)	67.3	64.6	72
Opportunities			
Number of green, sustainability, and sustainability-linked bond deals	98	69	93
Total deal value of green, sustainability, and sustainability-linked bond deals (USD billion)	63.3	42.4	49.3
UBS-apportioned deal value of above (USD billion)	13.2	8.8	11.6

Source: UBS Group Sustainability Report 2023

Table 10.11 Sustainable Investments (Values in billions of US dollars)

Year	2021	2022	2023
Total invested assets (UBS Group)	4614.50	3980.90	5714.10
Sustainable Investments by UBS AG			
Sustainability focus	222.7	246.9	270.4
Impact Investing	28.1	19.2	21.8
Total Sustainable Investments	250.8	266.1	292.2
SI as percent of total investment	5.4	6.7	6.5

Source: UBS Group Sustainability Report 2023

vehicles which were aligned with the United Nations Sustainable Development Goals. During 2023, UBS offered a range of voluntary learning opportunities at client events such as APAC flagship sustainable finance conferences.

For over 20 years, SI had been an integral part of UBS Asset Management business. By end 2023, UBS AG Asset Management had managed sustainable focus and impact investing assets of value USD 203 billion. UBS AG Asset management offered 35 net zero ambition portfolios for clients. UBS structured and executed WATC's inaugural AUD 1.9 billion green deal, supporting government projects for decarbonization, and secured a key structuring mandate for Australia. UBS acted as joint global coordinator, physical bookrunner, and sustainability coordinator for a EUR 270 million green bond supporting Amara Nzero's LBO, marking EMEA's first LBO-linked green bond. In August 2023, UBS also facilitated Nordea's first global senior non-preferred sustainability-linked loan (SLL) note across core currency markets.

Approximately 41.5% of net new investment products in UBS AG P&C Personal banking were sustainable. UBS entered into new partnership with the Ecole Polytechnique Fédérale Lausanne (EPFL) to support innovation in sustainability and collaboration through joint projects. UBS became the first bank to join the Swiss Green Fintech Network, which support the development of innovative and scalable technology solutions. By end 2023, Group Treasury held more than USD

8 billion of green, social and sustainability bonds in its high-quality liquid assets (HQLA) portfolios. The total exposure to transition and physical risk is estimated to be USD 477.89 for UBS.

UBS is a founding member or current signatory of groups such as the Task Force on Climate-related Financial Disclosures (the TCFD), the Net-Zero Banking Alliance (the NZBA), the Net Zero Asset Managers (the NZAM) initiative, the Glasgow Financial Alliance for Net Zero (GFANZ) and the Partnership for Carbon Accounting Financials (PCAF). As of 31st December 2023, the AuM for Credit Suisse according to SI fund (Exclusion, Integration, Thematic or Impact) amounted to USD 148.3 billion.

Green Investments by BNP Paribas

BNP Paribas is a French multinational universal bank and financial services holding company headquartered in Paris. The company was established in year 2000 by the merger of two major financial institutions, Banque Nationale de Paris (BNP) and Paribas.

The amount of financing allocated to low carbon energies by BNP Paribas amounted to 28.2-euro billions, 32-euro billions and 36.8-euro billions in the year 2022, 2023 and 2024 respectively. The 2030 target aims to invest an amount of 40 billion euros in low carbon energy financing. These funds are for hydroelectric, solar and wind-based projects. The Group aims to ensure that these projects account for 80% of its financing for energy generation by year 2028 and 90% by 2030. BNP Paribas targets a 70% reduction for its financed emissions in the oil and gas sector, to go from 27.3 million tonnes of CO_2e at the end of September 2022 to 8.2 $MtCO_2e$ in 2030. For automotive sector, BNP aim to reduce its portfolio emission intensity by 23% in year 2025. For the steel, aluminium and cement sectors, the reduction targets are 25%, 10% and 24% by the year 2030.

The Group's transaction classification principles for sustainable loans are based on external market standards such as those of the Loan Market Association and the European Taxonomy in Europe. The sustainable loan financing amounted to euro 87 billion and euro 117 billion in year 2022 and 2023 respectively. The targeted sustainable loan financing for the year 2025 was estimated to be euro 150 billion. The sustainable bond issuance arranged by BNP Paribas for corporates, financial institutions and sovereign clients amounted to euro 32 billion and euro 67 billion in year 2022 and 2023. The 2025 target sustainable bond issue was estimated to be of value euro 200 billion. The amount of assets under management for open ended funds of BNP Paribas Asset Management funds were valued at euro 223 billion and euro 254 billion in 2022 and 2023. The 2025 target was estimated at euro 300 billion.

BNP Paribas was the only French bank in the ranking Global 100 Most Sustainable Corporations in 2024. BNP Paribas joined the A list 2023 of CDP which covers the top 1.5% of companies according to the climate questionnaire rating.

BNP Paribas has structured its range of responsible funds into 3 main categories of ESG integration funds, certified funds (which have received one or more European sustainable investment labels) and funds with a sustainable investment objective, for example sustainable thematic funds. By end of 2023, BNP Paribas Asset Management managed 19 billion euros of assets in its range of open-ended funds domiciled in Europe with a sustainable investment objective according to SFDR classification in terms of Article 9. BNP Paribas manages 11 solidarity funds valued at 2.9 billion euros with 171 million euros invested in social and solidarity economy structures which promotes access to employment, housing and health. Paribas Asset Management launched its first climate focused strategy in year 2002. The firm ranks among the largest ESG passive managers in Europe and had launched the first low carbon ETF in year 2008. By end 2023, BNP Paribas Asset Management managed EUR 15.6 billion in Paris Aligned benchmarks and Climate Transition Benchmarks passive strategies. The company also launched the Climate Impact Infrastructure Debt fund. The firm facilitate clients to invest in renewable energy, clean mobility and circular economy.

BNP Paribas Asset Management offers individual and institutional investors thematic funds such as BNP Paribas Aqua, BNP Paribas Climate Impact, BNP Paribas Energy Transition and BNP Paribas Green Bond. BNP Paribas Cardif through its partners offers its clients with life insurance policies. BNP Paribas Real Estate Investment Management manages different real estate funds for different types of investors. All the open-ended funds for retail investors are classified according to Article 8 or Article 9, as per Sustainable Finance Disclosure Regulation (SFDR). Most of these funds also have a label such as Social Responsible Investment (SRI) or Finansol. BNP Paribas REIM offers a range of funds for institutional investors such as the first environmental impact real estate fund, European Property Impact Fund (EIPF), Next Estate Income Fund III which invests in buildings with positive ESG characteristics and high level of environmental certification. Healthcare Property Fund Europe (HPF Europe) focusses on the healthcare sector with ESG approach.

As a part of its own account investments, BNP Paribas has allocated 450 million euros by year 2025 for investments in startups and firms with innovative solutions for the ecological transitions. The company had allocated 200 million euros in startups and impact companies which implement innovative solutions in areas of local development and climate, social and solidarity activities and natural capital. Approximately 175 million euros were allocated in startups of the energy and ecological transition. In 2021, BNP Paribas in partnership with Solar Impulse Foundation created the BNP Paribas Solar Impulse Venture Fund with commitment of €75 million euros to finance startups of the ecological transition in Europe and North America. BNP Paribas have been a pioneer in responsible investment since the year 2006. The Group restructured its responsible approach by pooling its business lines and experts in protection, savings and investment within a single division termed Investment & Protection Services.

By 2023, 171 funds of BNP Paribas Asset Management with 139.5 billion euros in assets under management were certified with a European responsible label.

BNP Paris Asset Management acquired Danish natural resources specialist International Woodland Company (IWC) to facilitate clients to invest in sustainable forestry, agriculture, natural ecosystems, carbon credits and conservation projects.

In 2023, BNP Paribas Asset Management updated its Global Sustainability Strategy, focusing on Energy transition, Ecosystems, and Equality (3Es), while enhancing climate reporting and Net Zero commitments. In 2023, BNP Paribas Asset Management opposed 1080 resolutions at 200 companies for inadequate climate reporting and engagement. It expects major GHG emitters to commit to net zero by 2050. Supporting 85% of climate-related shareholder proposals, it also opposed 55% of say-on-climate proposals that fell short of expectations.

In early 2024, BNP Paribas Asset Management launched the Global Net Zero Transition strategy, applying the NZ:AAA framework with a just transition focus. It includes a charity fund donating fees to Electriciens sans frontières, supporting renewable projects in the Global South while expanding climate-focused investment solutions across its strategies.

Table 10.12 illustrates the initiatives undertaken by BNP Paribas to combat climate change.

By September 2023, BNP Paribas' financing of low carbon energies amounted to EUR 32 billion which represented 65% of the Group's financing to energy production and renewables and amounted to EUR 28.8 billion. It has been estimated that the annual investments in low carbon energy requirements is expected to increase from USD 1.8 trillion in year 2023 to around USD 4.5 trillion a year by the early 2030s.

BNP Paribas Cardif is cutting its investment carbon footprint, aiming for a 23% reduction in equities and corporate bonds by 2024 and a 12% cut in office property carbon intensity by 2030. It committed EUR 800 million annually to energy transition investments with cumulative investments exceeding EUR 1.1 billion in 2023. BNP Paribas Real Estate committed to reducing direct and indirect emissions from its operations and buildings. It promotes net zero solutions, emission reductions, and sustainable materials. In 2023, it partnered with Materrup to use low-carbon cement in five pilot projects, cutting construction site emissions and advancing sustainable real estate. BNP Paribas Real Estate partnered with iQspot to enhance energy efficiency, enabling 16% energy savings without renovations. Its REIM division launched the European Impact Property Fund (EIPF) in 2020, acquiring 10 assets by late 2023 and investing in climate performance improvements aligned with the Paris Agreement.

BNP Paribas Wealth Management offers climate-focused investment solutions and integrates sustainability preferences in advisory services. Since 2008, it has provided free philanthropy advisory, with growing interest in biodiversity and green tech. By 2023, it invested EUR 87.2 million in 12 companies and eight funds supporting ecological transition innovations. BNP Paribas committed EUR 75 million to the SFDR Article 9 BNP Paribas Solar Impulse Venture fund, which closed at EUR 131.2 million in 2023. That year, it invested in Hello Watt, supporting home energy renovations to help individuals reduce their carbon footprint.

Table 10.12 Climate change initiatives

Year	Initiatives
2010	First coal related restrictive financing and investment policy adopted
2016	Stopped Oil Project Financing
2017	Ceased business with shale oil and gas and tar sands specialists
2018	An agreement was signed with other European banks to implement a common methodology for alignment of credit portfolios within the framework of Paris Agreement
2019	Joined the UNEP's Principles for Responsible Banking (PRB) to share tools with other banks and align credit portfolios with the objectives of the Paris Agreement
2020	Made commitment to stop financing the thermal coal sector value chain by 2030 in the EU and OECD countries and by 2040 in the rest of the world
	Published its first Task force on Climate related Financial Disclosures (TCFD) report
	Published the first report on the application of the PACTA methodology to measure the alignment of credit portfolios
2021	Joined organizations such as net zero alliances of the Glasgow Financial Alliance for Net Zero (GFANZ), Net Zero Banking Alliance (NZBA), Net Zero Owner Alliance (NZAOA) and Net Zero Asset Managers Initiative (NZAM)
	Made commitments to reduce the bank's financing to upstream oil and gas by 10% during the period 2020–2025
2022	Published climate-related business targets strategy plan with euro 200 billion commitment for transition by corporate clients to a low carbon economy by the year 2025. Support to energy firms in Artic and Amazon regions restricted. Commitments made to reduce financing to upstream oil and gas by 12% during the period 2020–2025. Published the first Climate Analytics and Alignment report with CO_2 emission intensity reduction targets for power, oil and gas, automotive sectors. BNP Paribas Asset Management and BNP Paribas published their net zero commitments
2023	First integrated climate report published with emission intensity targets for sectors such as steel, aluminium and Cement. BNP Paribas stopped all financing for new oil and gas fields, and commits to reduce by 80% of its upstream oil exposure and by 30% of its upstream gas exposure by year 2030. Low carbon financing constituted 65% of the financed energy mix with the objective to reach 80% by the year 2030
2024	Publication of emission intensity reduction targets for aviation, shipping and commercial real estate. Decrease of at least 23% of carbon footprint (scopes 1 and 2) of equity and corporate bond portfolios held directly by BNP Paribas Cardif and achieve an emission intensity of under 125 gCO_2/kWh for the Power Generation. EUR 200 billion was committed for the transition of corporate clients to a low carbon economy
2025	EUR 200 billion was committed for the transition of corporate clients to a low carbon economy. NZBA 2025 intensity emission targets for power generation and automotive sectors. NZAM 2025 Investments 100% net zero aligned
2030	Low carbon financing to be 90% of financed energy mix. Full exit of thermal coal value chain OECD and EU countries
2040	Full exit of thermal coal value chain worldwide
2050	Net Zero target

Source: BNP Paribas 2023 Climate Report

BNP Paribas supports start-ups through strategic partnerships. TEB, the subsidiary in Türkiye collaborates with Plan A to calculate CO_2 emissions for textile and automotive clients. In Poland, BNP Paribas Bank Polska invested in Envirly for Midcap clients. It also advised ChargePoly on raising EUR 15 million for ultrafast EV charging solutions.

In 2023, BNP Paribas deployed EUR 200 million in impact investments, making 16 new investments totalling EUR 56 million. Notable among these was Ecov, a shared mobility operator promoting accessible transport and reducing CO_2 emissions through carpooling in areas with limited public transport.

BNP Paribas arranged a $1 billion loan for ReNew Power to finance 1.3 GW of wind and solar projects with battery storage, ensuring uninterrupted energy supply. This is India's largest financing for a round-the-clock renewable project, with energy sold to SECI, optimizing land use and grid infrastructure. BNP Paribas led a $2.5 billion financing for AES Corporation to develop 3 GW of solar, wind, and storage projects in the U.S. within a year. BNP Paribas-. Commercial & Personal Banking in France (CPBF) co-led financing for Kallista, enabling a corporate power purchase agreement with Lhyfe for wind-generated electricity to produce green hydrogen. This deal secures Lhyfe's energy needs for future hydrogen sites while allowing Kallista to repower a wind park, supporting long-term renewable energy growth and sustainability.

BNP Paribas played a key role in financing the €4.4 billion Baltic Power project by Orlen and Northland Power, Poland's first offshore wind farm. With 76 turbines, it will supply renewable energy to 1.5 million households from 2026, making it Europe's largest offshore wind project in 2023.

BNP Paribas supports agriculture's sustainable transition across Europe. In Italy, BNL introduced a credit policy to finance converting biogas to biomethane plants, aligning with a 2022 government decree. This initiative aims to accelerate the transition of 2000 biogas plants to produce sustainable fuel for vehicles, promoting ecological sustainability. BNP Paribas established Low Carbon Transition Group with 200 bankers in 2023 and a target of 250 by 2025 to facilitate clients to transit to a sustainable economy. The Group provides banking and non-banking solutions for decarbonization, focusing on energy, mobility, industry, and green hydrogen while supporting SMEs in key domestic markets of France, Belgium, Italy, Luxembourg and Poland.

BNP Paribas co-led Stellantis' €1.25 billion green bond placement, funding the development and production of electric vehicles and fuel cell technology. BNP Paribas, as mandated lead arranger, facilitated €800 million in financing for AESC to build a gigafactory in France. The project's first phase will produce 9 GWh of batteries annually, powering 200,000 Renault electric vehicles from 2025, supporting Europe's transition to sustainable mobility. BNP Paribas, as Exclusive Senior Debt Advisor and Lead Arranger, supported Northvolt in securing $5 billion for expanding Europe's first circular gigafactory. This largest non-recourse green financing will scale Northvolt Ett and advance battery recycling, reducing carbon footprints by 70% compared to mined materials, fostering sustainable battery production.

Arval and BNP Paribas Leasing Solutions launched a Europe-wide offering to ease EV adoption by providing leasing, charging station installation, maintenance, and recycling. Corporate clients benefit from home charging reimbursement and the "Leasing Solutions Charge & Lease" package, enabling seamless charging infrastructure rollout for businesses and individuals.

BNP Paribas Personal Finance introduced a long-term electric bike rental service in France, offering flexible subscriptions with insurance and annual servicing. Available for individuals and corporate employees through Arval's bike leasing in 14 countries, this initiative promotes low-carbon mobility for commuting and professional travel. BNP Paribas co-bookran Heidelberg Materials' €750 million Sustainability-Linked Bond, tied to CO_2 reduction targets, aiming for net zero emissions by 2050.

BNP Paribas Fortis co-coordinated a €400 million sustainability-linked loan for Renewl, with interest tied to recycling 75% of waste by 2025 and reducing carbon emissions. Commercial & Personal Banking in France (CPBF) financed a €3.3 million foundry sand regeneration project for La Fonte Ardennaise, enabling 90% sand recycling, conserving resources, reducing landfill waste, and cutting CO_2 emissions by 20,000 tonnes annually.

BNP Paribas is expanding support for customers' energy-efficient housing across Europe, offering dedicated financing and solutions to reduce energy costs, increase comfort, and decarbonize residential real estate.

BNP Paribas Polska secured up to €100 million with the European Investment Bank to support energy efficiency projects in Poland. The EIB also partnered with the bank to offer technical assistance and energy audits to housing associations under the European Local Energy Assistance Program for investment preparation. BGL BNP Paribas offers preferential mortgage rates for energy-efficient homes and supports buyers with expert advice on renovations to enhance energy performance and EPC ratings.

Green Financing by Deutsche Bank

Deutsche Bank AG is a German multinational investment bank and financial services company headquartered in Frankfurt Germany. This global financial institution has a loan book of almost euro 500 billion and assets under management of euro 518 billion. Deutsche Bank's sustainability framework follows generally accepted international standards and principles including the International Capital Market Association Green and Social Bond Principles, UN Global Compact and EU Taxonomy. Deutsche Bank (DB) actively participates in the development of green bond financing. In 2020, Deutsche Bank published its first Green Bond framework. This framework allowed the issuance of green financing instruments such as covered bonds, commercial papers, repurchase agreements and deposits. In 2022, the green financing framework was updated to include sectors such as green building, residential real estate, clean transportation, Information and Communication

Technology. In 2024, DB published ESG Investments Framework which sets out criteria and evaluation processes to report ESG investments in the context of DB Group's sustainable finance and ESG investment targets. The ESG Investments Framework complements the bank's Sustainable Finance Framework.

In 2022, the green asset pool for Deutsche Bank amounted to Euro 5.4 billion and Euro 2.9 billion in 2022 and 2023 respectively. In 2023, Deutsche Bank issued 15 Green Bonds and eight Green Structured Notes along with multiple green deposits. The bank aims to achieve cumulative sustainable financing and investment volumes of euro 500 billion during the period 2020–2025. During the period 2020–2022, the bank exceeded its euro 200 billion interim target in sustainability financing and investment with cumulative total of euro 215 billion. During the same period, the corporate bank and investment banking contributed euro 40 billion and euro 128 billion towards sustainable financing. The Private Bank had contributed euro 48 billion during the 2020–2022 period. The modelled revenues from these sustainable activities are expected to be around euro 1.4 billion by the end of 2025.

Table 10.13 shows the sustainable milestones of Deutsche Bank.

Decarbonization of residential and real estate have a key role for achieving Germany's net zero commitment. With network of 1000 branches and agencies, as well as over 7000 advisors, Deutsche Bank is well positioned to support private homeowners to reduce carbon footprint of its properties.

The bank offers customized loan products for energy efficient refurbishments at favourable rates through its subsidiary BHW KlimaDarlehen. Subsidy services are offered for gaining access to around 6000 available grants and other subsidies.

Deutsche Bank acted as mandated lead arranger, underwriter, book runner and sustainability structuring agent for A$4.6 billion sustainability linked loan (SLL)

Table 10.13 Timeline sustainable milestones

Time period	Important milestones
2015–2019	Environmental and Social Policy framework revised. Paris Pledge for Action signed. UN Principles for Responsible Banking signed. Sustainability as part of corporate strategy established. Introduction of Coal Mining Policy
2020	Green Financing Framework published. Coal Mining and Oil & Gas Policy updated. Sustainable Finance framework published. Equator Principles signed. Sustainable finance target of euro 200 billion announced
2021	Net Zero Banking Alliance commitment signed. Partnership for Carbon Accounting Financials joined. First Sustainability Deep Drive hosted
2022	Net Zero carbon buildings commitment signed. Net Zero Forum for carbon intensive transaction and transition plan assessment established. Approximately 96% of global electricity consumption renewably sourced. Net zero targets for carbon intensive sectors published. EP100 and RE 100 initiative of the Climate Group joined
2023	Financed emissions from European residential real estate loan portfolio disclosed. Initial Transition Plan for Cola Mining, Cement, Shipping published. Thermal Coal Policy updated

Source: Deutsche Bank, Initial Transition Plan, 2023

for hyper scale data center specialist, Air Trunk. This loan is a refinancing of Air Trunk's first sustainability linked loan originated in year 2021. This SLL for AirTrunk is the first of its kind wherein data center combined carbon, power and water usage effectiveness as part of loan's KPI. This SLL was also the first publicly known financing by a data center company to incorporate a gender pay equity target. In 2021, Deutsche Bank became the joint global coordinator for the first sustainability linked bond (SLB) which raised euro 300 million for Hamburg based shipping and container liner company, Hapag Lloyd. The SLB is linked to the achievement of carbon reduction targets. Hapag Lloyd has invested into twelve new Megamax vessels with LNG propulsion for reducing the fleet's carbon intensity. In early 2023, DB acted as initial mandated lead manager and sustainability coordinator on a euro 600 million amortizing term loan contract for Eesti Energia. The loan is sustainability linked with two ESG KPI's: carbon intensity of scope 1, 2, 3 emissions and yearly addition of renewable energy capacity. The loan supports Eesti Energia's goal to achieve carbon neutrality in electricity production by 2035.

DB acted as joint underwriter for Volkswagen International Finance's euro 1.75 billion dual tranche green bond offering for manufacture of battery vehicles and a euro 2 billion triple tranche inaugural green bond offering for Volkswagen Leasing GmbH. DB was also a joint ESG coordinator in financing Volkswagen's transition to low carbon transportation.

In 2022, Deutsche Bank acted as joint bookrunner for the NZ $3 billion inaugural green bond offering for the New Zealand Debt Management. DB was also involved in the coordination of structuring workstream to establish the Sovereign Green Bond Framework for climate change mitigation and adaptation. In 2023, DB acted as a joint active bookrunner and joint sustainability coordinator for Nokia's inaugural euro 500 million sustainability linked bond offering which was issued for Nokia's Science Based Target initiative (SBTi) validated reduction target for greenhouse emissions. DB acted as the bookrunner and the ESG coordinator for the inaugural euro 800 million sustainability linked transaction for IHO's green house gas emission reduction target. In 2023, DB and the European Investment Bank (EIB) entered into a new cooperation to support medium sized companies in their sustainability transformation. Medium sized firms can apply for loans through DB to finance their transaction to more sustainable business models. The EIB will provide guarantees for up to 50% of the loan amount.

Sustainable Finance at JP Morgan Chase

JP Morgan Chase is an American multinational financial services firm and is among the largest four banks of America. The bank operates in 48 states in USA and employs 309,926 employees in 65 countries. JP Morgan had assets of $3.9 trillion by December 31, 2023. The bank is a market leader in investment banking, financial services for consumers and small businesses, commercial banking, financial transaction processing and asset management.

It is estimated that over $5 trillion is required each year to scale low and zero carbon technologies. JP Morgan aims to facilitate $1 trillion to support the development and scaling of climate initiatives by year 2030. Majority of emissions in USA is accounted from electric power, transportation and industrial sectors. By 2024, the US venture investment into climate technology start-ups were expected to be $26 billion. Batteries play a significant role in the electrification of residential, commercial and industrial environments. Venture investments was expected to reach an estimated $6.5 billion by the end of year 2024. Clean mobility funding was expected to reach an estimated $5.8 billion by end of year 2024. Venture investment into food and agriculture technologies was expected to reach an estimated $9.8 billion by the end of 2024.

JP Morgan Chase developed its own methodology to calculate Energy Supply Financing Ratio (ESFR). The Energy Supply Financing Ratio (ESFR) measures financing for low-carbon versus high-carbon energy supply. While it provides insight into capital allocation, it is not tied to a specific target. The decision to disclose ESFR followed shareholder engagement, including with the New York City Comptroller. For 2023, the ESFR was 1.29×, meaning $1.29 was directed toward low-carbon energy for every $1 supporting high-carbon energy. JP Morgan have set nine net zero aligned targets for eight sectors -Oil & Gas, Electric Power, Auto Manufacturing, Aviation, Shipping, Iron & Steel, Cement and Aluminium by 2050 which are aligned with the International Energy Agency standards. The Green Economy banking (GEB) team offers subject matter expertise, banking solutions and specialized credit underwriting to companies which primarily focus on decarbonization technologies, products and services. GEB serves businesses in North America and the Europe, Middle East and Africa covering sectors such as renewable energy, sustainable finance and climate tech. JP Morgan is a market leader for sustainability themed debt issuances with over $36.7 billion investments in green, social, sustainable and sustainability linked bonds underwritten by 2023.

In 2021, the bank had set up its $1 trillion green objective as part of its broader $2.5 trillion sustainable development target. The bank has financed and facilitated $285 billion toward its $1 trillion green objectives. Approximately 41% went towards development finance, 37% towards green and 22% towards community development. Investment banking accounted for $133 billion which were used for activities including capital raising in debt and equity markets and underwriting of sustainable bonds. Corporate and Investment bank accounted for $101 billion which constituted activities for emission contracts and investments in tax credit vehicles in alternative energy. Consumer & Community banking accounted for $35 billion which were used for support for small businesses, home ownership and consumer adoption of electric vehicles. Commercial banking accounted for $15 billion which were used for affordable housing, retrofitting, rehabilitating or constructing accredited energy efficient building.

In 2023, JP Morgan financed and facilitated approximately $194 billion toward the sustainable development target. Out of this $66 billion was earmarked for green objective, $102 billion towards development finance objective and $26 billion toward the community development objective.

The bank aim to support the green and sustainable markets through own sustainable bond issuances. In 2023, the company issued one Green Bond for an aggregate total notional amount of $2 billion. In 2023, the aggregate nominal amount of all eligible projects included in the sustainable asset portfolio amounted to $3027 million.

In 2023, JP Morgan invested in the United Airlines Ventures Sustainable Flight Fund, an innovative initiative supporting early-stage companies working on Sustainable Aviation Fuels to advance decarbonization in air travel.

JP Morgan Asset Management (JPMAM)'s Global Sustainable Investing and Stewardship team provides ESG research, develops sustainable investment solutions, and leads stewardship activities, including proxy voting and company engagement on climate risk and other thematic issues. JPMAM's Global Sustainable Investing and Stewardship team provides ESG research, develops sustainable investment solutions, and leads stewardship activities, including proxy voting and company engagement on climate risk and other thematic issues. J.P. Morgan Global Private Bank expands sustainable investing, offering strategies in clean energy, transportation, and circular economy. In 2023, OpenInvest enabled personalized, values-based investments on issues like deforestation and emissions. Since 2020, the bank has achieved its target of sourcing renewable electricity for 100% of its global electric power needs annually.

As of December 31, 2023, JP Morgan had $1.6 trillion of consumer credit exposure which included residential real estate, auto loans and credit cards. The firm use catastrophe models to estimate the potential impact of hypothetical severe weather events on real estate portfolios.

Table 10.14 highlights the sustainable asset portfolio by funding year.

J.P. Morgan helped secure $1.2. billion in corporate credit facilities for Generate Capital to advance sustainable infrastructure growth. JP Morgan facilitated the acquisition of Calpine Corporation by Constellation Energy, the largest US producer of clean, emissions-free energy in a deal valued at approximately $26.6 billion. The acquisition would create the largest, cleanest coast to coast generation portfolio in the US across nuclear, natural gas and geothermal.

AtmosZero is involved in the commercialization of Boiler 2.0, a cost effective and scalable solution to decarbonize steam. JP Morgan is AtmosZero's primary operating bank and senior lender.

In the food industry, Canada's Maple Leaf Foods aims to become the most sustainable protein company in the world. JP Morgan extended an ESG linked credit facility to the company. Maple Leaf uses the credit facility to support its growth in

Table 10.14 Sustainable asset portfolio

Funding year	Green bonds
2021	1180
2022	1848
2023	3028

Source: JP Morgan Annual Sustainable Bond Report 2023

both meat and plant production. These initiatives are used to construct a $720 million technologically advanced and animal welfare focused poultry plant in Ontario. This ESG credit facility is also used to acquire and retrofit food processing plant in Indianapolis.

JPMorgan Chase is financing SB Energy (SBE), a U.S. utility-scale solar and storage platform with a 25 GW project pipeline. In 2024, it participated in a $700 million credit facility with $75 million. Additionally, JPMorgan supports SBE through tax-oriented investments and investment banking services.

JPMorgan Chase is financing Electric Hydrogen, which produces low-cost green hydrogen to decarbonize industries like steel, shipping, and aviation. With facilities in Massachusetts and California, the company scales electrolyzer plants. In 2024, JPMorgan participated in a $100 million credit facility and provides treasury and investment banking solutions.

In December 2021, JPMorgan Chase provided $66.4 million in tax equity financing for Riverstart Solar Park, a 200 MW solar project in Indiana. Operational since 2022, it supports energy security, powers 38,000 homes annually, created 500 jobs, and generated $5 million in landowner income from 2020–2023.

In 2021 JPMorgan Chase played a key role in financing the 800 MW Vineyard Wind project, the first large-scale offshore wind farm in the U.S. The bank served as Joint Lead Arranger for over $2 billion in financing, supporting the project's goal of supplying clean energy to 400,000 Massachusetts households while reducing 1.68 million metric tons of carbon emissions annually. JPMorgan provided Investment Banking services (senior secured loan arrangement), Markets products (risk hedging), and Treasury products (cash management), contributing to the U.S. transition to cleaner energy sources.

In February 2021, JPM DFI structured a $620 million corporate bond for Liquid Telecom, aimed at improving telecom access across 20+ African countries. The bond will expand broadband networks, enhancing education, healthcare, and financial inclusion, while supporting SDGs #8 and #9 related to decent work and resilient infrastructure.

In terms of community development, JP Morgan supports areas such as homeownership, affordable housing, small business, education and healthcare. In June 2021, JPMorgan Chase provided $600 million to A&E Real Estate to refinance and preserve 53 rent-regulated buildings with 3531 units across New York City.

The low carbon transition is a focus for JP Morgan's banking teams. During October 2021, JP Morgan acted as Joint Placement Agent on a $1 billion equity placement to capitalize a new passenger EV subsidiary for Tata Motors. In June 2021, JPMorgan Chase acted as Active Bookrunner for NextEra Energy's $1.5 billion green bond to fund renewable energy projects. The bond supports emissions reduction goals and includes a coupon step-up mechanism to ensure transparency if allocation and impact certification aren't provided within 2 years.

In 2023, JPMorgan Chase provided $27.6 million to support Viridi Energy and AOE in building a waste-to-energy facility in Yaphank, New York. Expected to process 210,000 metric tons of food waste annually, it will produce RNG and agricultural products, advancing circular waste management and U.S. sustainability goals.

With respect to community development objectives, in 2023, JPMorgan Chase provided a $25 million loan to Concern Housing for a 66-unit affordable housing project in Brooklyn. Expected to be EGCC-certified, it will offer stable housing and support services for homeless adults, veterans, and individuals with psychiatric disabilities, promoting sustainability and community well-being.

Launched in 2021, JPMorgan Chase's CB Green Economy Banking team specializes in sustainable finance, offering expertise, credit underwriting, and banking solutions. Focused on five key sectors, the team supports emerging and established companies in renewable energy, efficiency tech, sustainable finance, agriculture, and clean mobility, with plans for global expansion.

In 2021, JPMorgan Chase saw record inflows in sustainable investments, growing sustainable AUM by 60%. JP Morgan closed the $150 million Global Impact Fund, designed to support private investments aligned with UN SDGs, further advancing progress in sustainable finance. Launched in 2019, JPMorgan Chase's Sustainable Equity Strategy invests in equity funds prioritizing ESG factors and sustainable themes. By 2021, the strategy grew to over $1.5 billion in AUM, reflecting strong investor interest in sustainable investing. Launched in 2018, the J.P. Morgan ESG (JESG) fixed income indices integrate ESG factors into benchmarks, with $40 billion in AUM by 2021. In Q4 2021, JPM expanded the suite with JESG GCI (covering corporate bonds) and GENIE (tracking the $1 trillion green bond market), alongside new carbon analytics and footprint reports.

In August 2021, JPMorgan Chase issued a $1.25 billion green bond, funding nine U.S. renewable energy projects in wind, solar, and geothermal. These projects are expected to generate 7000 GWh annually, supplying 650,000 homes with clean electricity, reinforcing the firm's commitment to sustainable energy investment.

In 2021, JP Morgan deployed or committed over $450 million in philanthropic capital globally, of which over $345 million was in grant capital and over $105 million in loan and equity capital. JP Morgan have a commitment by 2025 to originate an incremental 40,000 home purchase loans ($8 billion) and refinance an additional 20,000 mortgages for Black, Hispanic and Latino households. The 2025 commitment also includes financing the creation and preservation of 100,000 affordable rental units through $14 billion in new loans, equity investment and other efforts. JP Morgan also target an additional $100 million in New Markets Tax Credit ("NMTC") investments with a focus on Black-owned or -led projects primarily serving Black populations.

JPMorgan Chase provided $59 million of tax equity to support Ormat Technologies Inc.'s McGinness Hills Phase 3 geothermal power plant in the Great Basin of Central Nevada, resulting in 48 MW of additional clean power to the grid.

In June 2023, JPMorgan Chase arranged a $1 billion credit facility for First Solar, enhancing liquidity for its U.S. expansion, manufacturing, and R&D. First Solar's advanced thin-film technology enables efficient, sustainable solar panel production, supporting the decarbonization of electricity generation. JPMorgan Chase advised Altor in H2 Green Steel's $1.9 billion capital raise to fund its flagship plant in Sweden. Expected to open by 2025, it will use renewable hydrogen to cut CO_2 emissions by 95%, pioneering large-scale green steel production with advanced technology and circularity-focused processes.

In 2023, JPMorgan Chase formed the Corporate Advisory and Sustainable Solutions (CASS) team to provide strategic advice, capital solutions, and green investment. The team includes Corporate Finance Advisory, the Center for Carbon Transition, Infrastructure Finance Advisory, and Sustainable Solutions, supporting clients in sustainability, decarbonization, and green financing initiatives globally. In 2023, JPMorgan Chase acted as Joint Lead Manager and Joint Bookrunner for Brazil's first $2 billion sustainable bond issuance. Proceeds will fund green and social projects under Brazil's Sovereign Sustainable Bond Framework, supporting low-carbon transition, environmental protection, and socioeconomic development. JPMorgan Chase's Global Markets Sustainability Center (GMSC) provides sustainability and climate solutions across asset classes. It offers ESG benchmarks, investable indices, and structured notes supporting sustainability initiatives. In 2023, proceeds from structured notes funded non-profit organizations tackling ocean plastic pollution and providing free tutoring for low-income U.S. students. J.P. Morgan Asset Management's Sustainable Investing team provides ESG research, climate risk insights, and investment solutions while leading stewardship activities like proxy voting and company engagement to create long-term value.

Table 10.15 discusses the environmental milestones achieved by JP Morgan Chase.

In 2023, JP Morgan spend $31 billion towards its Racial Equity Commitment. In the same year JP Morgan committed over $393 million in philanthropic capital of which $330 million was in grant capital and over $63 million in loan and equity capital. JP Morgan also invested an additional $170 million in the US Medical plan for employees and their families. The net proceeds from JP Morgan's 2021 issuance of Fixed to Floating Rate Notes were fully allocated to financing affordable housing projects. JPMorgan Chase provided nearly $9 million in loans for Cambridge Apartments in Seattle, rehabilitating a historic building and preserving 157 affordable housing units for low-income residents. JPMorgan Chase provided $3 million

Table 10.15 Environmental milestones

Year	Key milestones
2020	Announced plans to establish emissions intensity reduction targets for key sectors in financing portfolio
2021	JP Morgan became the first major U.S. bank to set 2030 interim emissions intensity reduction targets for the Oil & Gas, Electric Power, and Auto Manufacturing sectors, aligned with the IEA Sustainable Development Scenario
2022	Established 2030 interim emissions intensity reduction targets for the Iron & Steel, Cement, and Aviation sectors, aligned with the International Energy Agency's Net Zero Emissions by 2050 scenario
2023	Set 2030 emissions intensity reduction targets for Shipping and Aluminum, aligned with the IEA NZE scenario. Updated the Oil & Gas Energy Mix target and revised Oil & Gas Operational, Electric Power, and Auto Manufacturing targets to align with the IEA NZE scenario
	Published "The Methane Emissions Opportunity," highlighting the benefits of reducing methane emissions and flaring in the Oil & Gas sector and how the bank support clients' efforts

Source: 2023 JP Morgan Environmental Social and Governance Report in loans and $10 million in tax equity for 55 affordable housing units in Philadelphia, designed sustainably with Energy Star appliances and reserved for low-income residents. JPMorgan Chase provided over $18 million in tax equity for Stella and Bluewater in San Diego, offering 160 affordable units, including those for homeless individuals and veterans. JPMorgan Chase provided over $3 million in tax equity for Mason Place in Fort Collins, Colorado, a 60-unit supportive housing project for homeless individuals earning 30% or less of AMI.

References

2021 Environmental Social & Governance Report.
Allianz, Sustainability Reporting, On a joint path, Allianz SE Sustainability Reporting—short version.
Allianz Global Investors Sustainability and Stewardship Report 2023: Snapshot.
Allianz Global Investors Sustainability and Stewardship Report 2023.
Annual Sustainable Bond Report 2023.
BlackRock Investment Institute and Aladdin Sustainability Analytics, July 2023.
BNP Paribas 2023 Climate Report.
Citi, 2023 Environmental, Social and Governance Report.
Deutsche Bank, Green Financing Instruments Report 2023.
Deutsche Bank, Initial Transition Plan, 2023.
Goldman Sachs 2023 Form 10-K.
Goldman Sachs 2023, Sustainability Report.
HSBC Green Finance Bond Report 2024.
HSBC Net Zero Transition Plan 2024.
https://about.bankofamerica.com/en/topic/topics_banking-and-finance_sustainable-finance
https://corporate.vanguard.com/content/corporatesite/us/en/corp/who-we-are/sets-us-apart/corporate-sustainability.html
https://energyalliance.org/investing-in-emerging-economies/
https://group.bnpparibas/en/our-commitments/sustainable-finance-follow-our-progress-in-figures
https://group.bnpparibas/en/our-commitments/transitions/responsible-savings-and-investments
https://institutional.vanguard.com/investment/strategies/esg.html
https://www.allianz.com/en/sustainability/sustainability-hub/sustainability-at-allianz/our-approach-to-esg.html#:~:text=Sustainability%20in%20proprietary%20investments&text=We%20aim%20to%20create%20a,investments%20totaled%20%E2%82%AC%20167.4%20billion
https://www.blackrock.com/corporate/insights/our-approach-to-sustainability
https://www.blackrock.com/corporate/literature/publication/blk-esg-investment-statement-web.pdf
https://www.blackrock.com/institutions/en-us/strategies/alternatives/real-assets/infrastructure/climate-finance-partnership
https://www.blackrock.com/institutions/en-zz/literature/whitepaper/bii-investment-perspectives-sustainability-july-2023.pdf
https://www.blackrock.com/sg/en/investment-strategies/sustainable-transition-investing#uplift
https://www.citigroup.com/global/investors/esg-for-investors
https://www.esgdive.com/news/citi-441b-1t-sustainable-finance-2030-goal-esg-report/714745/
https://www.jpmorgan.com/insights/sustainability
https://www.jpmorgan.com/insights/sustainability/q1-2025-decarbonization-and-sustainability-trends

https://www.vanguard.co.uk/content/dam/intl/europe/documents/en/sustainablelife-funds-brochure.pdf
Investment perspectives Sustainable and transition investing July 2023.
J P Morgan Environmental, Social and Governance Report, 2023.
JP Morgan 2024 Climate Report.
JP Morgan & Chase Co. 2022. Social Bond Annual Report.
McKinsey & Company. (2023). *The agricultural transition: Building a sustainable future*. Available at: https://www.mckinsey.com/industries/agriculture/our-insights/the-agricultural-transitionbuilding-a-sustainable-future
Morgan Stanley ESG Report 2022.
Sustainability at Bank of America, Report, September 30, 2024.
Sustainable Financing: What does the rise of ESG mean for Trade Finance.
UBS Sustainability Report 2023.
Vanguard TCFD Report 2023.

Chapter 11
Sustainable Finance Investments by Chemical Companies

Green Investments by Bayer

Bayer is a life science company and global leader in healthcare and nutrition. The innovative products offered by Bayer prevent, alleviate and treat diseases. Bayer is also involved in ensuring that the world has a reliable supply of high-quality food, feed and plant based raw materials. The Bayer Group comprises 340 consolidated companies in 80 countries and employs over 99,000 people. The total revenues generated by Bayer Group in year 2023 amounted to €47.6 billion. Crop Science is the global leader in agricultural sales, specializing in crop protection, seeds, and traits. The company provides a diverse portfolio, including high-value seeds, enhanced plant traits, innovative chemical and biological crop protection solutions, and digital tools, all supported by comprehensive customer service to promote sustainable agriculture. Pharmaceuticals focuses on prescription drugs for cardiology and women's health, along with specialty therapeutics in oncology, hematology, and ophthalmology. It also advances cell and gene therapy through a strategic unit covering research, development, and marketing, ensuring comprehensive value creation from innovation to patient care. Bayer is a global leader in contraceptive pharmaceuticals and aim to provide modern contraception to 100 million women in LMICs, having already attained 46 million in year 2023. In 2021, the company approved capital expenditure of more than €400 million to expand the contraceptive production facility in Finland and build a new plant in Costa Rica. Consumer Health is a world leader of non-prescription medicines for self-medication and self-care. The portfolio comprises nutritional supplements, allergy, cough and cold, dermatology, pain and cardiovascular risk prevention and digestive health.

Bayer has set ambitious climate targets aiming for Net Zero GHG emissions by 2050, with interim goals for 2030. The company achieved an 11% reduction in total GHG emissions from 2019 to 2023.

B. R. Kumar, *Green Finance*, Sustainable Finance,
https://doi.org/10.1007/978-3-032-03333-8_11

Bayer fosters digital farming through partnerships, creating an ag-tech ecosystem for industry interoperability and sustainable practices. With over 100 technology agreements, it offers Climate FieldView™ to customers and 70+ industry partners, enabling integrated services, data models, and connected solutions for optimized farming. Bayer partnered with Pheasants Forever to develop a digital tool that helps farmers optimize land use by balancing agriculture, biodiversity, and renewable energy production. The company have partnered with FarmRise (India) which is a mobile app serving 100,000+ monthly users with farming advice, pest evaluation, drone rentals, carbon programs, weather updates, and commodity pricing insights. Bayer entered into a partnership with WeGrow (China) which is a digital platform combining social networking, education, and rewards to connect farmers, share agronomic expertise, and promote sustainable agricultural practices. Bayer have entered into partnership with FoodWings (Ghana), GeoPotato (Bangladesh) and Apollo Agriculture (Kenya). FoodWings provides drone-based services for pest control and farm inputs. GeoPotato uses satellite technology for early blight detection in potatoes. Apollo Agriculture leverages data, AI, and remote sensing to offer financing, insurance, and advisory services, enhancing farm profitability. In the sphere of plant breeding innovations, Bayer's PreceonTM Smart Corn System offer digital support tools and agronomic recommendations to improve the way corn is grown to make more sustainable. Bayer signed the Zero Hunger Private Sector pledge and committed US$160 million to combat hunger worldwide.

Bayer is a founding member of the Farm to Market Alliance, which supports smallholder farmers in Kenya, Rwanda, Tanzania and Zambia. Bayer's Crop Science division leads in crop protection and seeds, driving strong growth in a €100 billion plus agricultural market. With sustainable innovations, it aims to scale regenerative agriculture and expand into adjacent markets, potentially doubling its addressable market to €200 billion by 2030 through digital, scientific, and agricultural advancements.

For the development of biological crop protection solutions, Bayer entered into a licensing partnership with UK based AlphaBio Control to introduce the first ever biological insecticide designed to control pests in arable crops. Bayer holds a 15% market share in the crop protection market, yet the firm are accountable for only 2% of the overall environmental impact associated with crop protection products. Bayer's innovation and digital solutions are key enablers for scaling of its regenerative agriculture. Bayer expects to launch ten blockbuster innovators in the next decade with sales potential exceeding 500 million euros.

Bayer plan to extend its smallholder farmers reach from 53 million in year 2023 to 100 million by year 2030. Bayer aims to double its revenue to small holders' farmers by 2030. In 2021, Bayer launched its decarbonization program for agriculture in Europe. Bayer uses EcoVadis rating to assess new suppliers with high inherent sustainability risk. In 2023, over 50% of the purchasing volume amounting to €11.4 billion was attributable to suppliers with sustainability rating or subject to sustainability audit. With exclusion of seeds, approximately €2.2 billion of Bayer's procurement spend in 2023 was attributable to companies with a potentially high sustainability risk. Bayer is a member of the Pharmaceutical Supply Chain Initiative

(PSCI) and Together for Sustainability (TfS). TfS members are chemical companies who represent a global annual turnover of over €800 billion and a global spend of more than €500 billion in the chemical industry in 2023.

In 2023, the Nutrient Gap Initiative impacted more than 30 million people in underserved communities. Bayer aims to invest €500 million in renewable energies by year 2030. Bayer joined the EV100 initiative of the Climate Group and has validated its activities according to the criteria of that initiative. Bayer have aligned its capital expenditure to the goal of achieving net zero greenhouse gas emissions by year 2050. Bayer perform a voluntary ecological assessment for capital expenditure projects exceeding €10 million. In 2023, Bayer contributed €52 million to global social impact programs and partnerships, including €18 million in product donations (at book value) to non-profit organizations. The majority of the donations were prescription and over-the-counter products from Bayer's Pharmaceuticals and Consumer Health divisions. Approximately 66% of Bayer's cash and product contributions went to low- and middle-income countries. Bayer aims to reduce the ecological footprint of agriculture by closely involving with farmer community. Farming accounts for 22% of greenhouse gas emissions worldwide. Bayer have undertaken climate related and environmental initiatives for reducing the environmental impact of crop protection products by 30% by the year 2030. Bayer Foundation and Coca Cola are among four impact investors to back the US$4 million Green Catalytic Fund which support 350 projects and enterprises in Latin America and the Caribbean region. The impact fund aims to reduce 6.2 million tons of carbon emissions and restore 2.5 million hectares of land or forest over 5 years, with 40% of funded organizations led or co-led by women. This fund is a partnership between Latimpacto and IDB Lab (the Inter-American Development Bank's innovation arm), with a US$1 million investment from the IDB. Coca-Cola and the Bayer Foundation have each invested US$500,000, while the IDB's Amazon Unit contributed US$2 million.

Green Finance Investments by DowDuPont

DowDuPont (NYSE: DWDP) is a holding company comprised of The Dow Chemical Company and DuPont which are independent, publicly traded companies in agriculture, materials science and specialty products sectors. Dow conducts its worldwide operations through six business units across three operating segments: Packaging & Specialty Plastics, Industrial Intermediates & Infrastructure, and Performance Materials & Coatings.

DuPont de Nemours, Inc. (DuPont) is a publicly traded, premier multi-industrial company based in Wilmington, Delaware, United States of America. Dupont is a global innovation leader in technology-based materials and solutions which facilitate transformation of industries. DowDupont is recognized as a sustainability leader in the Materials Industry category. DowDuPont™ (NYSE: DWDP) was named to the Dow Jones Sustainability World Index (DJSI) by S&P Dow Jones

Indices and RobecoSAM, the investment specialist focused exclusively on sustainability investing. Over 80% of the DowDuPont's innovation portfolio is expected to offer solutions for meeting the challenges of sustainability. DuPont was named the Best ESG Partner by Samsung Electronics. DuPont achieved a 58% reduction of Scopes 1 and 2 emissions from the 2019 baseline which exceeded its 2030 goal of 50% ahead of schedule and exceeded its 2030 Scope 3 emissions reduction goal of 25% from the 2020 baseline. In 2023, DuPont achieved Great Place to Work® certification and was named to Forbes list of Best Employers for Diversity and Bloomberg's Gender-Equality Index, among others.

Dupont provide cutting-edge products, advanced technologies, and high-performance materials to leading manufacturers across various industries, including semiconductors, circuit boards, displays, digital and flexographic printing, healthcare, aerospace, industrial, and transportation sectors. Dupont provide technologies which help purify more than 50 million gallons of water and enable water reuse and recycling and desalination. Dupont offers a broad portfolio of water purification and separation technologies. Dupont offers a wide range of personal protection solutions. The firm also develop solutions for managing the air, water and thermal performance of buildings and residences. The innovative products also include specialty medical devices and components, silicones for healthcare and industrial applications, precision parts for aerospace, industrial and automotive applications, and specialty industrial materials for printing plates. The automotive products deliver a broad range of technology-based products and solutions for current and advanced mobility. Dupont's sustainability strategy framework is built on three pillars of Innovate, Protect and Empower.

In 2022, Dow engaged a large public accounting firm to assist with a complete refresh of its Sustainability/ environmental, social and governance materiality assessment. This assessment helped validate the sustainability priorities for Dow and its stakeholders to inform its sustainability disclosures and strategies. This Green Finance Framework is focused on two of these strategic areas: Climate Protection and Circular Economy. The green finance framework has been prepared in accordance with the 2021 Green Bond Principles, (GBP), as published by the International Capital Market Association (ICMA) and the 2023 Green Loan Principles 3 (GLP) issued by the Loan Market Association (LMA), the Asia Pacific Loan Market Association (APLMA) and the Loan Syndications and Trading Association (LSTA).

In 2023, DuPont established a sustainability network, 'Good Earth Stewards' (GES), led by its employees. Dupont's investment in innovation is approximately 4% of net sales and basically targets high growth opportunities in its eight innovation platforms. In 2023, the company had invested $6.5 million in targeted communities through cash and in-kind donations in three strategic areas: basics to thrive, STEM education and innovations for good.

By 2030, Dow aim to reduce its net annual carbon emissions by 5 million metric tons vis a vis its 2020 baseline. By 2050, Dow intends to be carbon neutral. By 2050, Dow will partner to conserve 50,000 acres of habitat and 20 water dependent sites will be water resilient. By 2030, Dow aim to transform plastic waste and other forms of alternative feedstock to commercialize 3 million metric tons of circular and renewable solutions annually. By 2035, Dow will enable 100% of Dow products sold into packaging applications to be reusable or recyclable. Dupont have impacted more than 5.7 million lives for the better since January 2020. Dupont supported more than 880 projects via charitable grants and cash donations in year 2023. In 2023, Dow realized $1.2 billion in net present value from business-driven projects which drive sustainability. In 2021, Dow achieved target to screen 100% of capital projects for potential benefits and impacts to nature, water, air, soil, land use and opportunities to utilize engineered natural technology.

In February 2024, Dow issued $1.25 billion in dual tranche Green bonds. By Dec 31 2024, Dow has allocated the full net proceeds of the Green Bond to help fund investments and expenditures toward decarbonization projects, circular economy-adapted products and process technologies, renewable energy and energy efficiency projects, in line with its Green Finance Framework. Approximately 65% of the net proceeds of the Green bond has been allocated to expenditures for the development and construction of decarbonization project in Alberta, Canada—Fort Saskatchewan Path2Zero Expansion Project. In 2023, Dow's Board of Directors approved the final investment decision for this project. The Path2Zero Project requires a total investment of approximately $6.5 billion on a gross basis, excluding governmental incentives and subsidies of around $1.5 billion which bring the net spend to around $5 billion. It converts cracker off-gas into hydrogen as a clean fuel for ethylene production. The project includes building a new ethylene cracker and increasing polyethylene capacity by 2 million metric tons per annum (MTA) as well as retrofitting the site's existing cracker to net zero Scope 1 and 2 emissions. The investment is expected to deliver approximately $1 billion of EBITDA growth per year at full run rates over the economic cycle. Over 89% of Dow's R&D innovation pipeline are aligned to sustainability focus areas of climate protection, circular economy and safer materials. The dual green bond offering was nearly 10 times oversubscribed, attracting over 200 unique investors. Notably, Dow secured more than 50 'dark green' investors among 75 first-time participants. Dow also estimated that the green label contributed to cost savings of 5 basis points on the 10-year tranche and 10 basis points on the 30-year tranche.

Dow has also invested 34 million in corporate and foundation based in kind contribution aligned to long term strategy of the company. Dow had diverse spend of $335 million in global certifications in 17 countries across five continents. This included $253 million with diverse suppliers and $82 million with small businesses. By 2030, Dow aims to reduce its net annual carbon emissions by 5 million metric tons versus its 2020 baseline. The company aims to be carbon neutral by year 2050.

Through 2050, Dow aim to systematically reduce GHG emissions footprint with a phased, site-specific approach. On average, the company plan to invest approximately $1 billion per year across the economic cycle to support both earnings growth and the decarbonization of its manufacturing assets. The strategy includes replacing end-of-life and less efficient assets with advanced technologies such as circular hydrogen, carbon capture and storage, and advanced nuclear, among others. As the company progresses in decarbonization, it is also positioned for strong earnings growth. The company aim to remain on track to achieve $3 billion in underlying EBITDA improvements while reducing Scope 1 and 2 net annual carbon emissions by 5 million metric tons by 2030, compared to its 2020 baseline. The inaugural green bond offering raised more than $1.25 billion to finance Dow's sustainability strategy of Decarbonize & Grow, Transform the waste strategies which included both expenditures and investments for the Path2Zero project in Canada. The green bond was issued at very low spreads which demonstrated the market's interest in sustainability focused growth investments. Dow have a portfolio of more than 12,000 products which support approximately 10,000 customers. The proper use and disposal of Dow's products have a large and meaningful impact on the environment. By 2025, Dow is poised to deliver $1 billion in value through projects which are suitable for business and better for ecosystems including water.

In 2023, Dow invested $2.36 billion in capital expenditures, with approximately $908 million (38.5%) dedicated to projects with direct environmental sustainability drivers and $848 million (36%) allocated to climate-aligned initiatives. These investments support Dow's climate transition plan and include (a) The development of Dow's first net-zero Scope 1 and 2 GHG emissions manufacturing facility in Fort Saskatchewan, Alberta, Canada. (b) Replacement of obsolete steam and power assets in Louisiana to reduce Scope 1 GHG emission. (c) Flare gas recovery projects at multiple U.S. Gulf Coast facilities, enabling gas recycling or reuse as an alternative fuel, lowering both Scope 1 and Scope 2 GHG emissions.

The Company expects that projects with environmental sustainability drivers will continue to increase and are anticipated to reach more than 60% of the company's annual capital spending by 2025, driven primarily by the company's Decarbonize & Grow projects.

During February 2024, the wholly owned subsidiary, The Dow Chemical Company ("TDCC"), closed its green bond offering of $600 million aggregate principal amount of 5.150% notes due 2034 and $650 million aggregate principal amount of 5.600% notes due 2054.

In 2022, Dow announced its Transform the Waste strategy which would enable the development of circular ecosystems by transforming plastic waste and alternative feedstock to commercialize 3 million metric tons per year of circular and renewable solutions by 2030.

The decarbonization goals and targets are grounded and based on more than 125 years of science, technical expertise and decades of sustainability leadership. The targets are aligned with the widely recognized IEA Net Zero Emission by 2050 Scenario (NZE), which accounts for realities of industrial sectors.

Dow is einvesting in manufacturing technology innovations, including fluidized catalytic dehydrogenation (FCDh), ethane dehydrogenation (EDH), and electric cracking (e-cracking), to transition to cleaner facilities by 2050. The final l commissioning of the FCDh unit in Louisiana is underway, offering up to 25% lower capital costs and reducing energy use and GHG emissions by up to 20%. Dow's collaborative e-cracking program with Shell remains on track for a 2025 startup, aiming to decarbonize steam cracking furnaces. EDH technology development continues, expected to lower capital intensity by 20% and carbon emissions by 40% compared to Dow's existing crackers.

By 2030, Dow will transform plastic waste and other forms of alternative feedstock to commercialize 3 million metric tons of circular and renewable solutions annually. The company is on track to launch Dow's first advanced recycling polymer in 2023.

As part of Dow's sustainability strategy to advance a circular economy, Dow acquired Circulus, a U.S.-based mechanical recycler. This acquisition enhances the company's ability to offer high-performance circular resins for industrial, consumer, and transportation applications while supporting the firm's Transform the Waste target. Dow also have an agreement with X -energy, a developer of advanced small modular nuclear reactor and fuel technology.

Green Finance -BASF

BASF is a European multinational company and the largest chemical producer in the world. Its headquarters are located in Ludwigshafen, Germany. BASF comprises subsidiaries and joint ventures in more than 80 countries, operating six integrated production sites and 390 other production sites across Europe, Asia, Australia, the Americas and Africa. The BASF Group consists of 11 operating divisions which are grouped into six segments consisting of chemicals, materials, Industrial solutions, Nutrition & Care, Surface Technologies and Agricultural solutions.

During the Covid 19 environment, BASF donated more than 100 million protective masks through the "Helping Hands" campaign. Globally, BASF offered 175,000 litres of sanitizers per week free of charge during the covid period. BASF have established a green finance framework to issue green finance instruments to finance and/or refinance sustainable products which are beneficial to environment or society. BASF'S green finance framework had been set up in line with the ICMA Green bond principles and LMA Green loan principles.

BASF is a founding member of Alliance to End Plastic Waste (AEPW) which was founded in year 2019. There are 46 members in the association. BASF have made commitments to spend US$1.5 billion over 5 years for infrastructure development, innovation, education, engagement and clean up. For example, BASF have collaborated with non-profit initiative RenewOceans in Varanasi, India to use ReFence technology to collect plastic from waterways in River Ganges. Approximately 30% of BASF Group sales are accounted from sustainable solutions. BASF is a founding member of the value balancing alliance. BASF's sustainability strategy focusses on refinancing sustainable products known as accelerators. As a part of its chemical recycling strategy, BASF invested €20 million in Quantafuel in year 2019. Quantafuel is pyrolysis of mixed plastic waste and purification of the resulting oil. BASF provided technical support in the start-up of Quanta fuel's commercial plant in Skive, Denmark.

During May 28,2020, BASF issued its inaugural green bond with a volume of €1.0 billion as the first European chemical company. This issue received a second party opinion from ISS ESG. By the end of 2021, BASF had assigned €1059 million to eligible green projects. By end 2021, sustainability analyses and assessments were conducted for more than 56,000 specific product applications which accounted for €71 billion in sales compared to greater than 57,000 products which accounted for €54.1 billion in 2020. In 2021, BASF generated sales of €24.1 billion with Accelerator products compared to €16.7 billion in 2020.

During March 2022, BASF issued its second green bond valued at €1.0 billion to finance BASF's green projects and products according to BASF's Green Finance Framework. The proceeds were meant to fund eco-efficient and circular economy products, production technologies and processes. The funds were eligible for the highest level of sustainable product solutions called "Accelerator". These products are characterized by substantial sustainability contribution in the value chain and have no negative impacts on any other relevant sustainability criteria. The carbon management strategy of BASF focusses on long term research and development program to reduce greenhouse gas emissions. The aim is to achieve the company's climate protection target and set the course for low carbon chemical production. The green strategy also aims for the development, manufacturing and acquisition of low carbon transportation components such as electric vehicle battery materials. BASF is developing innovate technologies for ChemCyling that promote recycling of plastics. This includes research and development on new materials and additives which facilitate recycling processes. Chemical recycling allows to recycle waste for which there are no recycling solutions.

By 2025, BASF plans to invest up to €1 billion to achieve its climate protection targets. Additional investments of up to €3 billion are to follow by 2030.

Table 11.1 highlights the details of the eligible projects under green finance framework of BASF during the recent times. The values are given in millions of dollars.

In 2022, within the permitted maximum lookback period of 3 years, €544 million was newly allocated to Eligible Projects, leaving €456 million unallocated. Of the allocated amount, €256 million was assigned to 2021 and €288 million to 2022. Funding for new projects constituted 53%, while refinancing of existing projects accounted for 47%. In 2021, €245 million was allocated to refinance BASF's stake

Table 11.1 Green finance projects during the period 2021–2023

	Amount allocated (euro million)		
Eligible Projects	2021	2022	2023
Eco efficient and circular economy adapted products, production technologies and processes	11	288	290
Renewable energy	245		6
Total eligible projects	256	288	296

Source: BASF Green Bond Allocation Report 2023

in the Hollandse Kust Zuid offshore wind farm, with the remaining €11 million directed toward carbon management. In 2022, €161 million funded electric vehicle battery materials and plant expansions in Germany, Finland, and China, while €127 million supported R&D, operational excellence, and carbon management initiatives.

The green funding for the projects amounted to 1000 million euros. In 2023, €296 million of the outstanding €456 million were newly assigned to Eligible Projects. Funding for new projects accounted for 100% of the allocation amount. Approximately €142 million were allocated to the electric vehicle battery materials and plants category and was used to finance the construction and further expansion of production plants in Schwarzheide, Germany and Onoda, Japan. Approximately €144 million was accounted as expenses for BASF's Carbon Management program. About €6 million were accounted as project expenses in the category of Renewable Energy. BASF's carbon management focuses on five levers to reduce greenhouse gas emissions: using renewable energy, developing low-carbon production processes, utilizing alternative raw materials, and enhancing energy and resource efficiency, especially at Verbund sites. These initiatives aim to cut emissions across electricity, steam production, and industrial process These measures have reduced the CO_2 emissions of BASF Group by around 1 million metric tons during the period 2013–2021. In 2021, 76 production sites across the world had certified energy management systems which accounted for 90% of BASF's primary energy demand. BASF is expanding its battery materials business through investments, partnerships, and innovative recycling to support the growing e-mobility market. It is building a precursor plant for cathode active materials in Harjavalta, Finland, and a production plant in Schwarzheide, Germany, to enhance sustainable battery solutions.

BASF aims to move toward a more circular economy by using recycled and renewable feedstocks and creating new business models. BASF has launched a new circular economy program. By year 2030, BASF aims to double its sales generated with Loop Solutions for the circular economy to €10 billion. WWF's One Planet Business Framework (OPBF) guides businesses toward true sustainability and long-term success. It addresses environmental (climate, freshwater, biodiversity) and social (human rights) themes, defining One Planet maturity. The framework follows a five-step process with eleven transformational levers to drive sustainable business practices. To support companies in their circular transition, the WWF has collaborated with Taival Advisory to develop a special focus module to the OPBF, putting circularity front and center: the Circular Business Assessment (CBA). During 2022, BASF participated in the pilot phase of the Circular Business Assessment.

Around 250 million metric tons of plastic waste are generated each year. Out of this, only 20% are recycled. Chemical recycling (ChemCycling®) can turn plastic waste that is not recycled mechanically for technological, economic or ecological reasons into raw materials for chemical production. In ChemCycling®, BASF uses feedstock from chemical recycling of plastic waste for its broad Ccycled® product portfolio. The recycled feedstock is attributed to the certified Ccycled® products through a mass balance approach. BASF have a portfolio of over 200 mass-balanced Ccycled® products, certified under REDcert2 or ISCC Plus.

In 2018, BASF Group's global emissions totalled 21.9 million metric tons of CO_2 equivalents, roughly half of the 1990 levels. The 2030 emissions target aims for a 60% reduction from 1990, surpassing the European Union's goal of a 55% decrease.

Green Investments by Saudi Basic Industries Corporation (SABIC)

Saudi Basic Industries Corporation (SABIC) is one of the world's largest petrochemicals manufacturer. SABIC serves customers in more than 140 countries and employs 31,000 people. Saudi Aramco have 70% ownership stake in SABIC. SABIC is the second largest public company in the Middle East and is listed in Tadawul.

SABIC Jubail building is LEED Gold certified for its smart solutions in resource management and energy efficiency. It uses more than 1500 solar panels enhanced by wind energy technology. SABIC keep track of its sustainability performance through a number of key performance indicators (KPIs). These KPIs are based on measurements such as greenhouse gas emissions, freshwater use, material loss along with energy production and consumption. SABIC is a part of Saudi Green Initiative (SGI) that addresses renewable energy, forestation, production of clean hydrogen and carbon capture and storage.

In year 2022, SABIC invested $28.9 million in Corporate Social Responsibility (CSR) programs through charitable donations, sponsorships, partnerships and volunteer service in 20 countries. Through its TRUCIRCLE™ portfolio, SABIC is developing products and solutions aimed at circularity and carbon neutrality. SABIC have committed to process at least one million metric tons of TRUCIRCLE products from bio based or recycled feedstock annually by 2030. SABIC is a regional sustainability leader. SABIC have build one of the world's largest carbon capture and utilization (CCU) plants and carbon credit issuance under the UN Clean Development Mechanism (CDM) scheme. SABIC is establishing a Carbon Capture Use and Storage (CCUS) hub in Jubail to capture a total of 4 million metric tons of CO_2 annually. In 2022, SABIC launched BLUEHERO™ to advance the circular economy, supporting EV innovation with flame-retardant materials and expertise to accelerate the global energy transition. SABIC is building its first advanced recycling demonstration unit, capable of converting 15–20 kt per year of raw pyrolysis oil into certified circular polymers.

SABIC remains committed to Saudi Energy Efficiency Program (SEEP), collaborating with EECM teams to develop a roadmap supporting the government's 2025 goals. SABIC have invested US$1.38 billion into 80 affiliate projects and 8 mega projects. SABIC commissioned the YANPET EG-II Energy Efficiency project that reduced the plant's energy intensity by 30%. SABIC invested US$28.9 million in 124 global CSR programs which targeted over 160,000 people in 20 countries. SABIC also initiated SABIC Pioneers program with 1468 retired employees.

SABIC is rated BBB by MSCI ESG rating which qualifies for the MSCI ESG indices. In 2023, Sustainalytics score was 28.8. SABIC's ESG score on the 2022 Bloomberg ESG data index increased by 39% compared to the previous year. SABIC is a member of Alliance to End Plastic Waste (AEPW). In 2023, the Low Carbon Emitting Technologies Initiative was relaunched as the Global Impact Coalition which was a CEO led effort of nine industry giants SABIC, BASF, Covestro, Clariant, LyondellBasell, Mitsubishi Chemical Group, Siemens Energy, Syensq. In 2023, along with PepsiCo, AstroLabs and others, SABIC launched Mega Green Accelerator to develop solutions to address sustainability challenges.

Green Finance Investments by Covestro

Covestro is the world leading manufacturer of high-quality polymer materials. Performance materials and Solutions & Specialties are the two major segments of Covestro. Performance Materials segment comprises Covestro's standard polycarbonates, standard urethane components and base chemicals. Solutions & Specialties sector comprises six business entities such as engineering plastics, coatings and adhesives, tailored urethanes, thermoplastic polyurethanes, specialty films and elastomers. The company was formed by the spin off of Bayer Material Science in year 2015.

The company aim to produce 100% of its products from alternative raw materials. The company expects to use raw materials sourced from biomass and recycled components. In 2022, Covestro purchased and incorporated over 55,000 tons of renewable raw materials. In the year 2020, Covestro launched its corporate strategy termed "Sustainable Future "to position Covestro optimally to drive sustainable growth, achieve climate neutrality and a circular economy.

Covestro follows a conservative approach by focussing on mechanical recyclability. The recyclable product portfolio accounts for 15% of the total resource outflows. The mechanically recyclable products made up 28.4% of the product portfolio of Covestro. The company focusses on building a future proof and sustainable product portfolio using the Portfolio Sustainability Assessment (PSA) based on the methodology developed by the World Business Council for Sustainable Development (WBCSD). Covestro have over 20 R&D projects on specific recycling solutions for its products in the area of chemical recycling. Covestro aims to achieve complete carbon neutrality by the year 2050. Covestro relies on a management system which integrates growth, value creation and sustainability within the framework of ESG criteria with a focus on greenhouse gas emissions.

In 2023, Covestro launched the global "STRONG" program to accelerate Covestro's growth and ensure long-term competitiveness. The program focuses on optimizing structures, processes, and increasing efficiency, particularly in production and administration. Through digitalization, STRONG aims to achieve annual global savings of €400 million by 2028.

By end of 2027, Encina a producer of ISCC PLUS-certified circular chemicals, will supply Covestro with chemically recycled raw materials. These materials enable the production of more sustainable products with a reduced carbon footprint. In 2024, the company spend 392 million euros on R&D. Covestro is strengthening its circular economy efforts by investing in BioBTX, a pioneer in chemical recycling. This partnership will help build the world's first BioBTX ICCP demonstration plant in the Netherlands, producing essential chemicals—benzene, toluene, and xylene—from mixed plastic and organic waste. With a million-euro investment, Covestro is developing technology which can process 20 kilotons of plastic waste annually. The technology facilitates handling of mixed waste which can turn waste into valuable raw materials for plastic production. This initiative represents a critical step toward industrial scale application and sustainable chemical industry. Covestro's investment in BioBTX supports its venture capital program, advancing innovative recycling solutions. The partnership explores new recycling options, enhances plant performance through digitalization, and aligns with Covestro's climate neutrality goals. Set to launch by 2027, the project strengthens Covestro's leadership in sustainable innovation and circular economy in Europe. Covestro's materials drive global innovation, enabling lightweight automotive solutions, energy-efficient construction, and advanced materials for renewables, supporting sustainability and growth across key industries worldwide.

In 2023 Covestro performed a physical climate risk analysis for 47 sites for the short-term time horizon through the year 2030, for the medium-term time horizon through the year 2040, and for the long-term time horizon through the year 2050. Covestro's net zero target for the year 2035 corresponds to a reduction in gross emissions by 91.1% to 94.6% compared with the baseline year of 2020. Covestro have estimated investments between €250 million and €600 million for more sustainable production processes by the year 2035 in order to achieve net zero for Scope 1 and Scope 2 emissions at all environmentally relevant sites. Covestro expects that energy efficiency is expected to cut operating expenses by €50 million to €100 million a year. By year 2035, Covestro expect to invest approximately €600 million in recycling and bio-based technologies. The installation of plant units with enhanced catalysts will enable a significant reduction of approximately 160,000 metric tons of CO_2 equivalents annually starting in 2025. In total, Covestro invested €33 million in initiatives related to the CO_2 roadmap during the year 2023. This amount accounted for 3.8% of the investments in property, plant and equipment in 2023. Out of this amount €6 million was attributable to taxonomy-eligible economic activities. At least 25% alternative non-fossil raw materials are contained in CQ products from Covestro.

Henkel and Covestro are innovating wood adhesives with bio-based raw materials, using a mass balance approach with over 60% renewable content. These adhesives enhance timber durability, lower buildings' carbon footprints, and support the circular economy, making construction more sustainable and environmentally friendly. Covestro and Deutsche Telekom used Makrolon® RE, a bio-waste-based polycarbonate, for MagentaTV One's housing and remote. This material cuts carbon emissions by 80% compared to fossil-based alternatives, proving sustainable materials can maintain high performance. Covestro provides Carlisle with biocircular MDI for insulation panels, reducing CO_2 emissions by up to 99% compared to oil-based alternatives. This enables high-performance, low-carbon insulation, supporting energy efficiency and net-zero goals in construction.

In May 2022, Covestro introduced its Green Financing Framework, enabling the issuance of green bonds and other debt instruments linked to sustainable investments. Verified by ISS ESG for alignment with ICMA's Green Bond Principles, the framework supports funding for environmentally beneficial projects. Under this initiative, Covestro issued its first green euro bond in November 2022, raising €500 million with a 4.75% fixed coupon, maturing in November 2028. The proceeds were allocated to sustainable projects promoting the circular economy, including renewable energy, energy efficiency, and sustainable building initiatives.

In fiscal 2020, Covestro AG secured a €2.5 billion syndicated revolving credit facility with a five-year term, including two one-year extension options. The first extension was exercised in March 2021, extending the term to March 2026, and the second extension was used in March 2022, prolonging it to March 2027. The facility is linked to an ESG rating, with the interest rate adjusting based on the external ESG score. As of December 31, 2024, the credit line remained unused.

On October 7, 2022, Covestro issued its first Schuldschein loans, totalling approximately €650 million, denominated in U.S. dollars and euros. Tied to an ESG rating, the loans were structured in fixed and variable interest rate tranches with three-, five-, and seven-year terms. In October 2023, Covestro repaid €260 million of these loans ahead of schedule.

Green Finance Initiatives by Clariant

Clariant is one of the world's leading specialty chemical company. Clariant offers innovative and sustainable solutions for many industries. Clariant business operations are reported in three business units: Care Chemicals, Adsorbents & Additives, and Catalysts. In 2023, Clariant made sales of 4377 CHF million. Clariant were one of the first specialty chemical companies to set emission reduction targets in line with the Paris Agreement. Under the framework of Science Based Targets initiative (SBTi), Clariant aims to reduce Scope 1 and Scope 2 greenhouse gas emissions by 40% and cut emissions in Scope 3 by 14% by 2030 compared to the year 2019.

Clariant has an innovation pipeline of high-performance solutions throughout its three business units. These solutions are strongly linked to customer-driven sustainability requirements. Sustainability-driven innovations, including bio-based and decarbonization solutions like EcoTain®, support growth by meeting the rising demand for circular and eco-friendly products.

Clariant's Portfolio Value Program (PVP) is a systematic and transparent assessment tool of the sustainability performance of products across their life cycles. PVP is aligned with the Portfolio Sustainability Assessment (PSA) of the World Business Council for Sustainable Development (WBCSD) and the European Safe and Sustainable by Design initiative.

In 2023, Clariant achieved innovation growth sales of 3.5% and these innovations helped the company to reduce carbon emissions. The innovative catalyst technologies enable about 35 million tons of carbon dioxide equivalent emission reductions for customers across various industries per year. The company is aiming for net zero emissions for scope 1 and 2 by year 2050. Clariant is among the few chemical companies which had adopted a scope 3 science-based target which help to measure suppliers' performance in terms of emission reduction. In 2013 Clariant signed the UN Global Compact.

Clariant is a member of the Dow Jones Sustainability Index (DJSI) and is considered as one of the most sustainable companies in its sector. Clariant is also a member of the S&P Sustainability Yearbook 2023. Clariant's sustainability activities are evaluated by Sustainalytics and received ESG risk rating of medium risk with score of 20.9 which corresponds to rank 40 out of 569 evaluated companies in the chemical industry. The Morgan Stanley Capital International (MSCI) ESG rating for Clariant in year 2023 was AA. The recent rating of Institutional Shareholder Services was B- for Clariant. Clariant is headquartered in Muttenz, Switzerland. S&P Global Ratings has granted Clariant's Green Bond a BBB- rating.

The recent highlighted innovations for Clariant include q new hydrogen economy catalysts which aid the energy transition, PTFE free and biodegradable coatings to prevent the formation of microplastics and low carbon biodegradable ingredients for personal and home care markets. Clariant's TexCare® Gemini SG Terra is a breakthrough soil release polymer for laundry, featuring innovative rheology control. It eliminates the need for extra thickeners, simplifying formulation. With high renewable carbon content, it enables high-performance eco-detergents, making it a sustainable and efficient choice for personal and home care applications. In 2023, Clariant launched Rootness® Mood+, a light-mimicking skin tone equalizer derived from environmentally friendly plant milking technology.

Clariant's VITA range features 100% bio-based Polyglycols (PEGs) and ethylene oxide derivatives, reducing fossil carbon in coatings. Its Dispersogen Flex 100, streamlines paint formulations by minimizing ingredients, lowering complexity, transportation, and costs, while supporting sustainable and efficient industrial applications. Clariant's contract R&D enhances metallurgical performance, cost efficiency, and sustainability in mineral processing. Clariant's launch of the world's largest e-methanol project in Kasso, Denmark, producing 32,000 tons annually using MegaMax® catalysts, marks a major step in combating climate change.

During October 2023, Clariant Additives made investment of CHF 60 million for a flame-retardant facility in Daya Bay, China. It enhances local access to sustainable Exolit OP products, supporting E-mobility and electronics growth. In June 2023, Clariant joined the EU-funded FOREST project, collaborating with 14 partners across eight countries. The project focuses on developing lightweight bio-based materials, including flame-retardant composites, to support the decarbonization of the transport sector.

Clariant Additives launched Ceridust® 8170 M, a PTFE-free solution for architectural powder coatings, addressing environmental impact while maximizing performance with polyethylene and bio-based waxes. In 2023, investments by Clariant in environmental, safety, and health initiatives rose to CHF 44.2 million, with CHF 21.0 million allocated for environmental protection. Expenditures in operational facilities decreased to CHF 99.9 million, including CHF 59.7 million for environmental protection, due to cost efficiency measures.

In 2023, Clariant Global Function Technology & Sustainability introduced structural changes to strengthen the link between innovation and sustainability. The Sustainability Transformation team manages Clariant's innovation- and sustainability-related processes, tools, and reporting. Clariant regularly reviews its innovation approach as part of its Strategic Management Process.

During August 2022, Clariant successfully priced its first green bond. The CHF 175 million green bond was issued with a coupon of 2.717% and a 2027 maturity date. The green bond issuance were under the green financing framework for sustainability. Clariant will allocate bond proceeds to finance or refinance investments in Eligible Assets under its Green Financing Framework. These funds support a low-carbon, sustainable society through capital expenditures, acquisitions, joint ventures, and R&D in circular economy products, eco-efficient technologies, renewable energy, energy efficiency, and pollution control initiatives. UBS Investment Bank and Skandinaviska Enskilda Banken (SEB) acted as joint lead managers for this green bond issue.

In 2021, Clariant conducted a thorough materiality assessment to identify key issues for the company and its stakeholders. Engaging both internal and external stakeholders, the assessment evaluated 28 topics across economic, governance, environmental, and social dimensions. Key material topics include employment opportunities, climate protection, product stewardship, and diversity, equity, and inclusion.

Clariant has implemented a globally integrated management system to drive its sustainability strategy. Adhering to international standards, it ensures compliance with ISO 9001, ISO 14001, ISO 50001, and OHSAS 18001. This certified framework enhances performance, aligning with business growth and sustainable value creation.

In 2023, Clariant streamlined its portfolio to focus on specialty chemicals. After a strategic review, it sold its North American Land Oil business to India-based Dorf Ketal in April, citing its distribution-heavy model and limited sustainability focus as misaligned with Clariant's profitability goals. In 2023, capital expenditure amounted to CHF 205 million and were directed towards growth, maintenance and sustainability investments.

Clariant is a signatory of the EU Commission-driven Circular Plastics Alliance (CPA) and actively participates in several industry collaborations such as the Alliance to End Plastic Waste (AEPW), the Polyolefin Circular Economy Platform (PCEP), and World Business Council on Sustainable Development (WBCSD) working groups on circular chemicals, circular transition indicators (CTI), and plastic pollution and accountability. Clariant is a founding member of AEPW. Clariant's

EcoCircle initiative, launched in 2019, supports the global shift to a circular economy by transitioning from a linear to a circular plastics value chain.

Green Finance Initiatives by LyondellBasell

LyondellBasell (LYB) is a leader in the global chemical industry creating solutions for everyday sustainable living. The company is the world's largest producers of polymers and a leader in polyolefin technologies. LyondellBasell manufacture high quality and innovative products for applications in sustainable transportation, food safety, clean water and quality healthcare. LYB is the largest producer of polyethylene (PE) and polypropylene (PP) in Europe. LyondellBasell have 6000 patents and patent applications worldwide. In 2023, the net income of LYB was $2.1 billion.

LyondellBasell have structured its sustainability approach centred around three global challenges of ending plastic waste, climate action and promotion of a thriving society. LYB aims to be net zero in greenhouse gas emissions from operations by the year 2050. The company aims for 42% absolute scope 1 and 2 greenhouse gas emissions reduction from operations by 2030. LYB aims for gender parity in senior leadership globally by year 2032. Currently women serve 25% of global senior leadership of the company. The company have plans to assess a minimum of 70% of key suppliers globally using sustainability criteria by the year 2025. In 2023 60 manufacturing sites achieved Goal ZERO in terms of injuries, incidents and accidents.

The sustainability goals of the company include elimination of plastic waste by production of 2+MMT1 of recycled and renewable-based polymers by year 2030. For every dollar the company invest in venture funds tackling the plastic waste challenge, the firm attract an additional five dollars from co-investors. In 2020, LyondellBasell joined the UN Global Compact to contribute towards the 17 UN Sustainable Development Goals (UN SDGs) by year 2030. LYB had strengthened its circular and low carbon solutions (CLCS) business by making significant investments to secure feedstock supply, expand recycling footprint and develop scalable technologies to reduce plastic waste.

The sustainable goal of the firm involves production and marketing of at least two million metric tons of recycled and renewable based polymers annually by 2030. Zero loss of plastic pellets to the environment from operations is envisaged. In 2018, LYB collaborated with Germany's Karlsruhe Institute of Technology (KIT) to develop proprietary MoReTec technology, which uses a catalyst to improve the breakdown of plastic waste. The company aim to accelerate the development and implementation of scalable recycling technologies with focus on advanced recycling technology such as MoReTec. The company have made investment decision to develop first of its kind, commercial scale advanced recycling plant, MoReTec–1 in Germany. LYB received a €40 million grant from the EU Innovation Fund to support development of MoReTec–1 unit.

LyondellBasell aims to grow Circulen portfolio of recycled and renewable based products. CirculenRecover transforms plastic waste into high-quality polymers through mechanical recycling, blending them with fossil-based products for diverse industrial, household, and consumer applications. CirculenRevive polymers enable recycling of hard-to-recycle plastics for high-standard applications. In partnership with Berry Global and a global food brand, LYB provide advanced recycled polymers for snack cracker packaging.

LYB is partnering with Neste, Berry Global, Pactiv Evergreen, and Dart Container to develop cold beverage cups that minimize fossil resource use and promote a circular economy. These cups, made with CirculenRenew polymers from renewable raw materials like used cooking oil, match virgin resin quality while reducing fossil feedstock use and CO_2 emissions.

In the regulated pharmaceutical sector, LYB's CirculenRenew polymers enable sustainable solutions. Partnering with Wellspect HealthCare, LYB developed LoFric Elle, a female urinary catheter made from renewable materials—one of the first such medical devices in a fossil-reliant industry.

LYB have expanded its mechanical recycling capacity globally through joint ventures and acquisitions in Europe, Asia, and North America. LYB have acquired 100% ownership in Quality Circular Polymers (QCP) based in Belgium and Netherlands. QCP is an industry leading mechanical recycling company with a production capacity of 55,000 metric tons per year and produces high-quality high-density polyethylene (HDPE) and polypropylene (PP) polymers from post-consumer plastic waste. LYB have 50% equity stake in Stiphout Industries B.V which is involved in the sourcing and processing of post-consumer plastic packaging waste. LYB invested 50% stake in Rodepa Vastgoed B.V, the holding company of Dutch recycler DPSR, which processes 50,000 metric tons of plastic waste into recycled PP and LDPE. LYB partnered with LMF Nord, GmbH to recycle post-commercial flexible packaging and build a Northern Germany plant converting LLDPE and LDPE waste into quality recycled materials. LYB acquired Mepol Group, an Italy- and Poland-based recycled compounds manufacturer, to strengthen Advanced Polymer Solutions business and accelerate growth by leveraging Mepol's expertise and LYB's scale.

By 2030, LyondellBasell intend to procure at least 50% of its electricity from renewable sources. The goal of Lyondell Basell is to assess a minimum of 70% of its key suppliers globally using sustainability criteria by 2025. The company utilizes EcoVadis assessments and joined Together for Sustainability (TfS) initiative. LYB have 25% equity stake in Cyclyx International to develop plastic waste sorting infrastructure in the US. The company had signed a final agreement to build the first Cyclyx Circularity Center (CCC). Cyclyx is a joint venture of Agilyx, Exxon Mobil and LYB. LYB have 50% equity stake in Rodepa Vastgoed, the holding company of De Paauw Sustainable Resources, a Dutch plastic waste recycling company to develop post consumer and post-industrial plastic packaging waste in Europe.

Under the 15-year agreement with Vattenfall, LYB will secure 450 gigawatt-hours (GWh) annually of offshore wind energy to support LYB's circular and low-carbon solutions in Germany, including powering the company's MoReTec-1 plant in Wesseling. Vattenfall is a European energy company that has been advancing the electrification of industry, powering homes, and modernizing lifestyles for over 100 years through innovation and collaboration. LYB is investing upstream in plastic-waste sorting and recycling operations across Europe, Asia, and North America to develop a comprehensive range of sustainable solutions across various recycling processes.

LYB signed a 10-year Power Purchase Agreement (PPA) with wpd for 79 GWh annually of onshore wind power from the Licata project in Sicily. Starting in 2026, the agreement will provide renewable, low-carbon electricity to the region, including LYB's Ferrara production site and research center, the largest for Ziegler-Natta catalyst development.

The Value Enhancement Program (VEP) of LYB boosts capacity through debottlenecking, enhances reliability, reduces costs and emissions, and improves margins via procurement, logistics, and customer service by year-end 2023, VEP delivered approximately $400 million in recurring annual EBITDA.

The company support foodbanks in the communities through monetary donations, food collection drives and employee volunteerism. In 2023, LYB gave $14 million as donations to charitable organizations, including financial and in-kind donations and the total value of employee volunteer hours.

LyondellBasell's green framework supports financing its sustainability strategy, focusing on ending plastic waste and addressing climate change. It aligns with ICMA Green Bond Principles and Green Loan Principles. LyondellBasell plan to allocate the net proceeds from LyondellBasell's Green Finance Instruments to finance and/or refinance, fully or partially, new or existing green projects that meet the eligibility criteria of the Eligible Green Project Categories.

On May 17, 2023, LyondellBasell announced the pricing of its inaugural green bond offering, raising $500 million through 5.625% Guaranteed Notes due 2033. The notes, guaranteed by LyondellBasell, will fund new and existing Eligible Green Projects in categories such as circular economy, renewable energy, pollution prevention, and energy efficiency. The offering, is part of LyondellBasell's Green Financing Framework. The company may temporarily invest unallocated proceeds in short-term investments or debt repayment. ING Financial Markets LLC and Morgan Stanley & Co. LLC are managing the offering, which is registered with the SEC. As of December 31, 2023, LYB have allocated approximately $195 million of proceeds toward eligible green projects.

In 2023, LYB invested in Lombard Odier Investment Managers' Plastic Circularity Fund, aiming to reduce plastic waste and GHG emissions, targeting $500 million. LYB also invested in Chrysalix Venture Capital's new Carbon Neutrality Fund. This fund supports emerging companies developing low-carbon technologies, with a focus on hard-to-abate sectors like the chemicals industry. Earlier LYB invested in Closed Loop Circular Plastics Fund and Infinity Recycling's Circular Plastics Fund.

Mitsubishi Chemical Group's Sustainable Finance Investments

Mitsubishi Chemical Group Corporation is a Japanese company established in year 2005 by the merger of Mitsubishi Chemical Corporation and Mitsubishi Pharma Corporation. The Mitsubishi Chemical Group operates within two core business groups: the Chemicals Business, which includes Specialty Materials, MMA & Derivatives, and Basic Materials & Polymers; and the Group Business, which includes Pharma and Industrial Gases. The Specialty Materials Business Group provides myriad products and services targeting growth markets in various fields such as mobility, life solutions, and electronics. In 2021, the company announced that it would be leaving the commodity chemical businesses by the year 2023.

Mitsubishi Corporation has more than 1700 portfolio companies in approximately 90 countries worldwide, including resource-intensive businesses such as natural gas and mineral resources.

In 2018, the Mitsubishi Chemical Group developed KAITEKI Vision 30 (KV30) by identifying social issues based on its vision for society in 2050 and working backward to shape its goals for 2030. Under KV30, the company introduced the "Forging the Future" medium-term management plan, aimed at strengthening business growth by enhancing profitability and financial stability. For the Group, with the chemical business at its core, addressing critical challenges like carbon neutrality (CN) and the circular economy (CE) is essential for achieving a more sustainable society.

Under its new Group concept, the Mitsubishi Chemical Group will set up its use of the Management of Economics (MOE), Management of Technology (MOT) and Management of Sustainability (MOS). In 2023, the percentage of sales revenues derived from sustainability related products amounted to 13%. The percentage of GHG emission reduction in year 2023 amounted to 16% compared to base year 2019. The company had a target of 29% reduction in GHG emissions by fiscal 2030.

The R&D expenditures for knowledge and technology driving business model reform amounted to Yen 121.6 billion. The Industrial gases segment participated in green hydrogen production project in Belgium. The Healthcare segment launched Mounjaro®, the world's first sustained release GIP/GLP-1 receptor agonist.

Japanese trading house Mitsubishi Corp plans to invest more than USD 690 million to build one of the world's largest green hydrogen production facilities in the Netherlands. Mitsubishi will collaborate with Eneco Diamond Hydrogen, a joint venture (JV) between Mitsubishi and Dutch major renewable energy company Eneco, for the production of green hydrogen. Mitsubishi will start construction of the electrolysis plant in 2026, with hydrogen production anticipated to commence in 2029. The projected manufacturing capacity of the plant would reach 80,000 tons annually, nearly 30 times greater than the current largest facility in operation globally.

Mitsubishi is exploring collaboration with Koura, a leading U.S. fluoroproducts producer, to enhance North America's lithium-ion battery electrolyte supply chain and strengthen advanced technology development. Matheson Tri-Gas signed an agreement to supply oxygen to 1PointFive's Texas DAC plant, set to open in mid-2025. The plant will capture 500,000 tons of CO_2 annually, with safe sequestration. Matheson will install an air separation unit to support the DAC process, enhancing carbon capture efforts in North America.

The Mitsubishi Chemical Group focuses on green transformation and advanced specialty materials to support sustainability and evolving market needs. In 2023, it restructured R&D into business and corporate functions to drive innovation, enhance technology development, and accelerate value creation through strategic execution, open innovation, and intellectual property initiatives.

Mitsubishi aim for sustainable production of MMA and PMMA through chemical recycling, a commercial plant, and plant-based materials. The Group is developing plant-based MMA via fermentation to meet growing green transformation demands while enhancing eco-friendly solutions for its customers. The Group develops, recovers, and recycles carbon fiber in Japan and Europe to reduce vehicle weight. It also explores new applications for recycled carbon fiber.

In April 2024, Mitsubishi revised its sustainability management structure to integrate sustainability into business strategies, enhance data-driven decision-making, and promote carbon neutrality. Mitsubishi analyse social trends to identify growth opportunities, strengthen competitiveness, and foster stakeholder collaboration.

Mitsubishi set targets to reduce GHG emissions, water, and waste impacts. Achieving a 29% GHG reduction in Japan since 2013, the company focus on efficiency, recycling, and life cycle assessments. The Group is evaluating the impact of climate change that is expected in the years up to 2030 through scenario analysis. Mitsubishi Chemical accelerates circular economy efforts by expanding plastic and carbon recycling, using biomass, reducing GHG emissions, and leveraging life cycle assessments to minimize environmental impact. Mitsubishi Chemical obtained ISCC PLUS certification for multiple sites and products, ensuring traceability of recycled materials across the supply chain to support sustainability efforts. At Ibaraki Plant, Mitsubishi build Japan's largest waste-to-oil facility with ENEOS, using Mura Technology's process to recycle 20,000 tons annually into petroleum and plastics.

In fiscal 2022, Mitsubishi established a system to calculate carbon footprints for all products. In 2023, the company expanded it globally, enhancing environmental efforts through digital transformation and collaborations. Mitsubishi developed a CSR Procurement Guideline to promote responsible procurement. Partners are engaged through a CSR questionnaire, providing feedback, training, and dialogue on compliance and sustainability issues.

Mitsubishi Chemical Group, a leading producer of specialty materials for industrial and medical sectors, has joined Emerald's Industrial Transformation Fund as a limited partner. This partnership will support Mitsubishi Chemical Group in advancing strategic innovations in key business areas, including specialty materials for electronics, healthcare, and life sciences.

References

BASF Green Bond Allocation Report 2022.
BASF Green Bond Allocation Report 2023.
BASF Green Bond Impact Report 2021.
BASF Green Bond Road Show, 2020.
Bayer Crop Science Sustainability Progress Report 2023.
Bayer Sustainability Report 2023.
Case Study—BASF Circular Business Assessment Pilot, 2022.
Clariant Integrated Report 2023.
Covestro Annual Report 2024.
Driving accountability and best-in-class performance, dow i 2023 progress report. https://corporate.dow.com/content/dam/corp/documents/about/066-00469-01-2023-progress-report.pdf
Dupont Sustainability Report 2024.
https://asia.nikkei.com/Business/Energy/Japan-s-Mitsubishi-eyes-massive-green-hydrogen-plant-in-Netherlands
https://corporate.dow.com/en-us/purpose-in-action/sustainability-targets.html
https://emerald.vc/mitsubishi-chemical-group-joins-emeralds-industrial-transformation-fund-as-limited-partner/
https://www.clariant.com/en/Corporate/News/2022/08/Clariant-placed-a-green-bond-in-the-amount-of-CHF-175-million
https://www.clariant.com/en/Sustainability/Environmental/Portfolio-Management#sourcing
https://www.lyondellbasell.com/492c34/globalassets/sustainability/policy/green-financing-framework.pdf
https://www.lyondellbasell.com/en/news-events/corporate%2D%2Dfinancial-news/lyondellbasell-prices-public-offering-of-inaugural-green-bond/
https://www.lyondellbasell.com/en/news-events/corporate%2D%2Dfinancial-news/lyondellbasell-takes-another-step-toward-energy-transition-with-new-power-agreements/
https://www.rbccm.com/en/story/story.page?dcr=templatedata/article/story/data/2025/02/aligning-funding-and-sustainability-strategy-through-debt-capital-markets
LyondellBasell Sustainability Report 2023.
Mitsubishi Chemical Group Corporation KAITEKI REPORT 2024.
SABIC Integrated Annual Report 2023.
SABIC Sustainability Report 2022.
Sustainable Finance Disclosure Regulation (SFDR) Index 2023.

Chapter 12
Sustainable Finance in Mining and Metal Industry

Sustainable Finance -BHP

BHP Group Ltd. is an Australian multinational mining and metals public company founded in year 1985 and headquartered in Melbourne, Australia. As of the year 2024, BHP was the world's largest mining company by market capitalization. The company focusses on mining and selling iron ore, copper and coal. The company operate globally across a range of commodities which include iron ore, copper, nickel, metallurgical and thermal coal. BHP uses technological innovation such as new flotation technology to help lower energy costs. In 2015, the company released Climate Change: Portfolio analysis report to provide investors with information regarding how climate related risk would affect portfolio and its response to climate change. In 2021, BHP published Climate Transition Action Plan which outline approaches to reduce GHG emissions and manage climate related risks for its operations. The company disclose both upstream and downstream Scope 3 GHG emissions in its Annual Report. Downstream GHG emissions disclosures cover product processing (category 10) and usage (category 11), with third-party steelmaking accounting for 76% of total Scope 3 emissions.

BHP implemented Fatality Elimination Program (FEL) in the year 2020. The FEL program requires the assets of BHP to implement fatal risk controls across their respective material safety risk profiles. In 2024, on average assets had achieved over 90% compliance for FEL program controls. The global Leadership Program encourages the workforce to provide feedback to the leaders about safety issues and concerns. In 2022, BHP launched its social value framework which focusses on the six pillars of Decarbonisation, Healthy environment, Indigenous partnership, Safe, inclusive and future ready workforce, Thriving empowered communities and Responsible supply chains. The social value scorecard of the company was also published during June 2022. During fiscal 2024, BHP's voluntary social investment totalled US$136.7 million. Of this, US$ 102.4 million were employed for directing

B. R. Kumar, *Green Finance*, Sustainable Finance,
https://doi.org/10.1007/978-3-032-03333-8_12

funding for initiatives related to social value framework. Approximately US$ 15.2 million was allocated to non-operated joint venture social investment programs and US$ 1.8 million under the BHP Matched Giving Program. The administrative costs to carry out the social investment activities amounted to US$12.5 million. About US$ 6.4 million was used to support the operations of the BHP Foundation. In 2024, the incremental capital and operating expenditure on initiatives associated with operational GHG emission reductions was US$61 million.

The company is on track to meet its medium-term goal to support 40% GHG emissions intensity reduction of BHP-chartered shipping of BHP products by year 2030 from a 2008 baseline. BHP support its customers in the steelmaking sector to develop solutions to reduce the GHG emissions intensity of steel production. This objective is achieved through a mix of collaborative partnerships and consortiums, research, investments through BHP Ventures. BHP have collaborative projects with 48 industry partners which include nine steelmaking customers accounting for 20% reported global steel production. The company engaged 78% of its top 500 suppliers to align their GHG emissions targets with its net zero goal for operational emissions by 2050. The company is on track to meet its medium-term goal to support 40% GHG emissions intensity reduction of BHP chartered shipping of BHP products by year 2030. The company aims to achieve operational GHG emissions target of at least a 30% reduction by FY 2030 against an FY 2020 baseline.

The company estimate that up to US$ 4 billion in nominal terms in spend and commitments are required over the decade to FY 2030 to execute its operational decarbonisation plans. The biggest remaining source of operational GHG emissions is diesel. The company have collaborated with Caterpillar and Komatsu to support the development of battery run electric trucks. BHP have partnered with Rio Tinto and BlueScope on an Australian electric smelting furnace pilot, a promising technology to reduce GHG emissions and process diverse iron ores.

BHP plans to achieve net zero operational GHG emissions by the year 2050. BHP's global operations focus on the resources mix which are needed to both further economic development and decarbonise. BHP offers copper which is essential for renewable energy technologies and infrastructure, nickel which is critical for electric vehicles (EVs) which are projected to comprise nearly 30% of global annual vehicle sales by the year 2035, iron ore and metallurgical coal for the steel required in global infrastructure and the energy transition. In addition, the company is expanding into potash which is a key resource for improving agricultural efficiency and alleviating pressure on limited arable land. These commodities have a significant role to play in reducing GHG emissions. According to BHP analysis, the world would require nearly twice as much steel in the next 30 years if global warming has to be capped at 1.5 °C. For accelerating the development of electric vehicles, solar energy and other renewable technologies, copper output must also double over the next three decades while nickel production has to nearly quadruple to power new battery technology over the same timeframe. In July 2019, BHP announced a 5-year, $400 million Climate Investment Program to develop GHG emission reducing technologies for its own operations, as well as those from use of its resources. In July 2022, BHP and Ford Motor signed an MOU for the multi-year supply of nickel, a metal critical to electrical batteries for the next generation vehicles. BHP makes investments in nickel from August 2022 and have spent more than A$ 140 million on exploration in Western Australia over the next 3 years. For potash, BHP had a $5.7 billion capital expenditure plan for its Jansen potash mine in Saskatchewan.

Sustainable Finance-Glencore

Glencore plc is a Anglo-Swiss multinational commodity trading and mining company with headquarters in Baar, Switzerland. The Industrial business of Glencore spans the metals and energy markets producing multiple commodities from over 60 industrial assets. In 2023, Glencore produced 113.6 million tonnes of coal, with most of it sold into the approximately 1.3 billion-tonne seaborne coal market. This market typically represents around 12–16% of the global annual coal consumption, which stands at approximately 8.3 billion tonnes, the majority of which is mined and used domestically.[1]

The company recycle key commodities to support the circular economy. The climate strategy of Glencore focus on reduction targets for Scope 1, 2 and 3 industrial emissions and long-term net zero target by the end of 2050.Glencore's first Climate Action Transition Plan was published in the year 2020. The company introduced a new interim target of reduction of industrial emissions by 25% by the end of 2030 against the 2019 baseline.

Glencore acquired a 77% stake in Teck's steelmaking coal business for $6.93 billion, aligning with its climate commitments. This strategic move enhances Glencore's portfolio with high-quality steelmaking coal, a vital resource for industries like energy transition infrastructure, transportation, and construction. The total capital expenditure on industrial assets was approximately $6.1 billion of which 48% was for copper and cobalt assets, 15% for zinc and 9% for nickel. In 2023, the industrial capital expenditure related to energy industrial assets amounted to $1.5 billion. Every 3 years, Glencore's industrial assets conduct self-assessments against internal Standards aligned with ICMM's Performance Expectations.

Glencore's Fatal Hazard Protocols (FHPs) establish mandatory measures to manage common fatal hazards at industrial assets, addressing historical fatalities and high-risk incidents. Designed to prevent repeat incidents, FHPs complement Safety Standards, which outline mandatory requirements for managing fatal and catastrophic hazards in selected industrial operations. In 2020, the Global Tailings Review, comprising ICMM, UNEP, and PRI, published the Global Industry Standard on Tailings Management (GISTM). Glencore contributed to its development through ICMM membership.

[1] IEA 2023, Coal Market Update July 2023, https://www.iea.org/reports/coal-market-update-july-2023/demand, License: CC BY 4.0

Glencore's Cerrejon coal mine is in in La Guajira, a water-deficit region in Colombia. Cerrejón is working to improve the efficiency of water use in its activities, while aiming to also preserve and protect the basins within its area of influence and seeking water solutions for neighbouring communities. In addition to the distribution of water through tankers and the water train, which adapts tank cars to supply drinking water to local communities, Cerrejón continues to work on identifying sustainable water access solutions. One such solution is the new system built to improve water supply to over 500 users in the rural areas of Papayal and Oreganal in the municipality of Barrancas. The system aims to increase frequency of water access, continuity and coverage for users connected to the aqueduct. The new system required an investment of over US$500,000, with Cerrejón contributing approximately US$440,000 and a water utility company providing the remainder. These funds are being used to repair and upgrade infrastructure such as pumps and storage tanks, improve the main pipeline, and strengthen the water network in local communities.

Glencore's Goedgevonden (GGV) coal colliery in South Africa is implementing a wetland offset strategy to compensate for habitat loss from mining. Required to rehabilitate two hectares for every one lost, GGV aims to restore 1168 hectares in the Greater Lakenvlei Protected Environment. The phased approach enhances wetland function and long-term sustainability. In 2015, Cerrejón modified a 3.6 km section of Bruno Creek for mining, relocating it 700 metre north while replicating natural conditions. Completed in 2017 with government approval and community consultation, the project is continuously monitored. Cerrejón minimizes freshwater use, supports ecosystem conservation, and enhances Ranchería River flow, benefiting biodiversity. As of December 2023, Glencore owned or leased 2.1 million hectares, with 7% affected by firm activities. In 2023, Glencore disturbed 4900 hectares and rehabilitated 2100. Of the 106,000 hectares requiring rehabilitation, 40,000 hectares have been restored. Rehabilitation efforts align with local landscapes and community needs.

In 2023, two Australian coal operations ceased production, including Liddell Coal Complex in New South Wales, which closed after 100 years. Rehabilitation began during operations, with $4.5 million spent in the final year, restoring 73 hectares for native woodland and pasture to support post-mining land use. Newlands Open Cut in Queensland closed in 2023 after 40 years of operation. Nearly $61.5 million was spent on rehabilitation, including reshaping overburden, water management, and seeding 332 hectares. Over 211 hectares have been certified by regulators. Since its operations began, Cerrejón has reclaimed over 5000 hectares of mined land and is working to offset six hectares for every hectare impacted. It has approved 2500 hectares of environmental offsets, focusing on biodiversity restoration. Its endangered species program supports wildlife like jaguars, turtles, and caimans, and strengthens ecosystems.

Cerrejón's rehabilitation efforts have increased local environmental awareness and created alternative livelihoods, benefiting over 500 community members through plant nurseries and tree planting. Women lead the nurseries, producing

600,000 native trees annually. The company is restoring eight million dry forest trees over 10 years and leads in open biodiversity data in Colombia.

Terminal 1 at Canada's Belledune Port, built in 1967 for Brunswick Mining and Smelting, supported the import/export of zinc, lead, copper, and sulphuric acid. After the smelter's closure in 2019, Glencore removed its infrastructure. During demolition, a water sampling program was initiated with local First Nations communities, ensuring minimal environmental impact. The project, completed in early 2023, included virtual stakeholder engagement and regular updates.

The Blackbird Mine in Idaho, USA, closed in the 1980s, leaving contaminated water. Remediation work began in 1995, prior to Glencore's acquisition in 2013. Ongoing efforts include water treatment, infrastructure improvements, and creek stabilization. Monitoring shows recovery in the Panther Creek watershed, with fish habitats now suitable for salmon.

Glencore's Ferroalloys department in South Africa is incorporating environmental DNA (eDNA) sampling into its biodiversity monitoring efforts. This non-invasive method efficiently detects species, including rare ones, and supports biodiversity assessments. The department is piloting eDNA at multiple sites and developing biodiversity targets in partnership with the Endangered Wildlife Trust.

JP Morgan has invested £200 million in mining giant Glencore through sustainable funds. To qualify as a sustainable fund, JP Morgan requires at least 51% of investments exhibit positive environmental and/or social characteristics. It must also exclude companies that derive more than 20% of their revenues from thermal coal extraction. Despite being the world's largest shipper of thermal coal, Glencore was included in the bank's sustainable investment funds since its coal generated revenues were below the 20% threshold. In 2024, South African renewable energy company Pele Green Energy had a financial close for a Solar Plant with Glencore's South African ferroalloys unit and its joint venture partner Merafe Resources. The deal valued at $116 million was for the development of the Sonvanger Solar PV Power Plant in the Free State province of South Africa.

Sustainable Finance Investments at Jiangxi Cooper

Jiangxi Copper is the largest copper producer in Mainland China. The company was established in year 1997 and was listed in Hong Kong and London. The operations of the company include polymetal minerals development which include copper, gold, silver, rare earth, lead and zinc. The company had diversified into trade, financial and logistics field. The company have built mining bases in China, Peru, Albania and Afghanistan. The holding listed company is Shandong Humon Smelting Co. It is one of the top ten gold smelting enterprises in China. The company had five operating smelters, five fully owned operating mines and ten modern copper processing plants. The operating income in year 2023 amounted to 521.89 billion RMB. The total investment in scientific and technological research and development amounted to 5.442 million RMB in year 2023.The total investment in ecological and environmental protection amounted to 545 million RMB. Jiangxi Copper actively aligned with the UN SDGs and national carbon goals, integrating sustainability into development. The company followed the Strategic Planning for Carbon Peaking and Carbon Neutrality of Jiangxi Copper Group. Following the 14th Five-Year Plan, the company adopted a new development philosophy, fulfilled social and corporate responsibilities, and promoted ecological and economic harmony for carbon peaking, neutrality, and sustainable growth. The company established the ESG Development Committee under the Board of Directors to oversee ESG strategy, risk management and performance. The company have incorporated ESG factors into the risk management mechanism and process. The specific risk control responsibilities for ESG factors are assumed by corresponding functional departments and relevant responsibilities are detailed in the Internal Control Manual. The company focuses on the construction of global leading green and intelligent industrial chain, supply chain and value chain to offer sustainable and strategic support. The goal of the company is to achieve carbon peaking by year 2030 and carbon neutrality by year 2060. The company's strategy is to promote low carbon technology and process throughout the industrial chain for carbon peaking and carbon neutrality. By year 2025, all mines and factories would meet the construction standards of national green mines and green factories and over two national mine parks will be established. The company aims to maximize use and recycle of water resources. The total reuse rate of industrial water is over 90%. On the basis of the disclosure requirements of GRI, SDGs, the Shanghai Stock Exchange and the Hong Kong Stock Exchange, 29 ESG related issues were identified for the year 2023 through peer benchmarking and expert judgement. Out of these, 13 were environmental issues, 8 were social and governance issues. In year 2023, the production and operation units of Jiangxi carried out more than 100 environmental inspections of different types and achieved rectification completion rate of 100%. In 2023, the total greenhouse gas emissions reached 2.2877 million tons of carbon dioxide equivalent. By end of 2023, Jiangxi had three national level green mines, 11 national level green factories and four types of green design products. Through ecological rehabilitation, Jiangxi was able to reclaim and restore 54,000 square meters of the Maple Ridge tailings ponds and Bailing Bay refuse dump.

The Guixi Smelter implemented multiple energy-saving initiatives, reducing industrial energy consumption and saving over 46,423 tons of standard coal annually. Key projects included system optimization, fuel transformation, and efficiency upgrades. Additional efforts in Dexing Copper Mine and Yinshan Mining improved motor efficiency, reduced diesel consumption, and optimized electricity usage, enhancing sustainability. To lower carbon emissions and enhance green energy consumption, the Copper Foil Company purchased and utilized 15.57 million kilowatt-hours of green power through the national green power trading platform in 2023, reducing carbon dioxide emissions by 8880 tons. Nanchang Jiangtong and Shandong Humon built photovoltaic stations, reducing carbon emissions by 55,780 tons annually. Dexing and Chengmenshan mines introduced electric vehicles, promoting green transportation and clean energy. Chengmenshan Copper Mine enhanced water recycling by upgrading pipeline networks and implementing a backwater utilization project, improving industrial water reuse and reducing dust and equipment cooling water consumption.

Dexing Copper Mine developed innovative reclamation technology, restoring landforms and suppressing acid production. In 2023, it restored 790,000 square meters, transforming wastelands into ecological parks. The total reclaimed area now exceeds 600 hectares, with over 85% of reclaimable land restored. The project won prestigious industry and scientific awards. Jiangxi Copper Co., Ltd. strengthened land management, enhancing asset efficiency and ecological restoration. In 2023, it established a land asset ledger, ensured compliance, secured 550 acres for new projects, leased 203 acres for revenue, and reclaimed land through reforestation and restoration, fulfilling environmental responsibilities and supporting sustainable land use.

In 2023, Jiangxi Copper introduced Green Procurement Guidelines, integrating sustainability into material supply, restricting high-energy consumption equipment, promoting eco-friendly procurement, and setting green assessment criteria for suppliers to ensure compliance with environmental and energy conservation standards. In 2023, Jiangxi Copper implemented an energy-efficient procurement plan, purchasing 99 high-efficiency motors and 37 transformers worth RMB eight million. The company also promoted material recycling, recovering 36,839 packaging barrels, and collaborated with suppliers to establish a sustainable green procurement supply chain. Jiangxi Copper introduced a unit-consumption contracting procurement model, focusing on service life and total consumption for agreements, avoiding price wars and promoting high-quality industry development.

In 2023, Jiangxi Copper implemented 76 new unit-consumption contracting projects, generating RMB 22 million in annual benefits, fostering supplier cooperation, and promoting new procurement practices through exchange meetings. By configuring proprietary technologies such as flotation foam imagers and fault diagnosis at Sizhou mineral processing plants, Jiangxi increased copper recovery by 1.06 percentage points and generated over RMB 4.7 million in annual economic benefits.

The independently developed photovoltaic cable by Jiangxi, using irradiation cross-linking technology, has significant energy-saving and carbon-reduction effects. Certified by TUV and PCCC, it has been successfully applied in major photovoltaic projects, generating an annual output value of over RMB 12 million and increasing economic benefits by more than RMB 1.4 million. Guixi Smelter, the world's largest copper smelting plant, integrates advanced technologies like AI, 5G, and big data for intelligent decision-making, enhancing efficiency, quality, and competitiveness.

In 2023, as part of rural revitalization, targeted assistance efforts were initiated in Yaoqian and Nanban villages focused on strengthening Party organizations, developing industries, and supporting local employment, with a total investment of RMB 5.91 million, including RMB 4.88 million for poverty alleviation. These initiatives aimed to promote economic development and enrich local communities. In 2023, RMB 1.41 million was invested in Yaoqian Village for industry development and infrastructure, while RMB 4.5 million supported infrastructure projects in Nanban Village, boosting local development.

During the "Twelfth Five Year Plan", Jaingxi Copper invested 5.6 billion RMB to build over 400 environmental protection devices which included 9 large wastewater treatment plants. Approximately 1.6 billion RMB has been invested to protect environment every year. During March 2023, Jaingxi acquired 55.3% in Jiangxi Environmental Protection Material Co Ltd. The acquisition was aimed to strengthen the ecological restoration of mining business. The purchase consideration for the acquisition was RMB166,021,000 in the form of cash environmental protection system has been implemented in all subordinated plants. During December 2023, Jiangxi Jiangtong Environmental Resources Technology Co., Ltd., a subsidiary of the Group acquired a 51% stake in Jiangxi Jiangtong Dingsheng Environmental Technology Co., Ltd. The purchase consideration for the acquisition was RMB10,408,000 in the form of cash.

Sustainable Finance Investments at Rio Tinto

Rio Tinto Group is the world's second largest metals and mining corporation which operate in 351 countries and employs 57,000 people globally. The portfolio of products includes iron ore, copper, aluminum and range of other materials. Tinto have more than 150 years of mining and processing experience. Rio Tinto generated earnings of $11.8 billion in year 2023.The net cash generated from operating activities amounted to $15.2 billion in year 2023.The portfolio of products includes iron ore, aluminum, bauxite, copper, diamonds, titanium dioxide, lithium, salt and borates. The company aims for targets of a 50% reduction in scope 1 and scope 2 emissions by 2030 and achieve net zero by 2050. Rio Tinto anticipate a total capital spend on decarbonization of $5–$6 billion by 2030.

In 2023, Rio Tinto advanced BioIron™, a breakthrough steelmaking technology that cuts CO_2 emissions by over 95%. Using biomass and microwave energy instead of coal, it reduces electricity use by 65% compared to green hydrogen. After successful small-scale tests, the company secured a site for larger trials and regulatory approvals. In 2023, the California Boron operation switched to renewable diesel, cutting CO_2 emissions by 45,000 tonnes annually. In 2024, Utah's Kennecott copper operation will follow, reducing 495,000 tonnes. The company formed a joint venture Group to acquire 50% to enhance low carbon aluminium production. This follows major North American investments, including a $1.1 billion AP60 smelter expansion in Canada and a $107 million alumina conveyor at Kitimat, to support customers' decarbonization goals. Rio Tinto have committed $150 million to create a Centre for Future Materials led by Imperial College London.

The Boron operation in California has transitioned to renewable diesel, thereby reducing CO_2 emissions by up to 45,000 tonnes annually—equivalent to removing 9600 cars from the road. The Kennecott copper operation in Utah have also entirely shifted to renewable diesel cutting emissions by approximately 495,000 tonnes per year, comparable to removing over 107,000 cars. Rio Tinto formed a joint venture with Giampaolo Group to acquire a 50% stake in Matalco, enhancing its supply of low-carbon aluminium. As aluminium production accounts for 3% of global CO_2, this partnership supports demand for sustainable solutions by offering high-quality, primary, recycled, and blended aluminium products. Rio Tinto have made $1.1 billion investment to expand its AP6O smelter equipped with low carbon technology at Complexe Jonquière in Canada, and $107 million to install a new alumina conveyor at Kitimat. In 2023, Rio Tinto have made $ 84 million in voluntary social investment. In 2023, the company have made Australian dollar investment of $725 million. The company have spent A$1 billion towards generation of local jobs for local people in Western Australia.

Following investments in Simandou high grade iron ore project in Guinea, Rio had plans to invest $6.2 billion on mine, port and rail infrastructure development. The company had approved $77 million for a pre-feasibility study for the development of the Rhodes Ridge project in Western Australia. Central costs totalled $ 1 billion which were driven by higher investments in decarbonization, research and development, and technology. In 2023, the capital expenditure of $7.1 billion consisted of $1.0 billion for growth prospects, $1.6 billion of replacement, $4.3 billion of sustaining and $0.2 billion of decarbonization capital. In 2023, provisions for close down and restoration costs and environmental clean up obligations amounted to $17.2 billion. The company had extended its climate partnership with China Baowu to speed up steel value chain decarbonization and reduce scope 3 emissions. The company had built the largest solar power plant across Canada's territories at Diavik Diamond Mine which featured over 6600 solar panels.

For climate related governance, Rio Tinto established a central team, Rio Tinto Energy and Climate (RTEC) to monitor the decarbonisation initiatives. The team is led by the Chief Decarbonization Officer who reports to the Chief Technical Officer. In 2022, Rio Tinto launched the physical resilience program which included a climate risk and resilience assessment methodology. The decarbonization investment is derived from the Group's capital allocation framework which are aligned to the firm's 2025 and 2030 Scope 1 and 2 emissions targets.

Table 12.1 highlights the decarbonization expenditure by the company during the year 2022 and 2023.

To achieve its 2030 emission reduction goals, Rio Tinto is prioritizing renewable energy for Boyne and Tomago aluminium smelters, which contribute to one-quarter of its emissions. In December 2023, the company signed a PPA to purchase all

Table 12.1 Decarbonization expenditure in millions of dollars

Expenditure Details in millions of dollars	2022	2023
Capital expenditure on abatement projects	86	94
Carbon credits and renewable energy certificates	33	61
Operational expenditure	138	234
Investments	42	36

Source: Strategic Report −2023 riotinto.com

electricity and green products from the 1.1GW Upper Calliope Solar Farm, ensuring a sustainable energy solution. In alumina processing, Rio Tinto have developed a decarbonization energy strategy for Yarwun and QAL refineries. In December 2023, Rio Tinto signed a PPA to buy all the electricity and associated green products to be generated in the future from the 1.1 GW Upper Calliope Solar Farm project. The company have completed the commercial and technical due diligence of the submissions for the supply of renewable electricity to Gladstone aluminium assets. As the world's largest iron ore producer, the company have collaborated with 40 plus partners in 10 countries to develop sustainable, economic pathways for decarbonizing steel production.

Rio Tinto have signed a multi-year agreement to supply high-grade iron ore pellets to H2 Green Steel and are exploring global opportunities to advance hydrogen-based steel production. Rio Tinto is the first major mining company to release its site by site water usage data. Rio Tinto have developed asset closure strategies to identify potential future land uses and focus on opportunities to reduce closure costs and risks over the asset lifecycle. In 2023, the company completed eight additional asset closure strategies. There are 90 plus legacy assets managed within the portfolio and 59% of active operations have asset closure strategies in place. In 2023, provisions for closure amounted to $17.2 billion compared to $15.8 billion in year 2022. The company aims to invest up to $ 3 billion per annum for growth capital expenditure which focusses on energy transition commodities such as copper, battery materials, high grade iron ore and critical minerals such as rhenium, tellurium, scandium and selenium.

Case Studies in Metal Industry

China Baowu Steel Group

China Baowu Steel Group is a state-owned iron and steel company headquartered in Baosteel, China. It is the world's largest steel producing company in the world. In 2023, China Baowu's asset amounted to RMB 1.36 trillion with steel production of 130 million tons and total operating revenue of RMB 1.11 trillion. China Baowu rank 44th on the Fortune Global 500 list in year 2024.

Baowu drives sustainable growth through high-end, intelligent, green, and efficient development. Focusing on innovation, smart manufacturing, and low-carbon technology, it collaborates with ecosystem partners to advance sustainability, support global economic progress, and contribute to human civilization and environmental well-being.

Baowu established a carbon-neutral system, integrating green initiatives into governance. In 2023, it introduced measures for carbon goals, ensuring strategic oversight and sustainable transformation. In 2021, China Baowu became the first in the steel industry to announce a timeline for carbon peaking and carbon neutrality with the aim to achieve carbon neutrality by year 2050.Baowu had incorporated the application of the extreme energy efficiency technologies into the benchmarking and evaluation system. The Three -in-one green development model encompasses "green manufacturing, green products, and green industry". In 2023, Baowu had made a total investment of 15.597 billion RMB for environmental protection. In 2023, the overall green index increased by 9.3 points. In year 2023, the comprehensive energy consumption per tonne of steel and carbon dioxide reduction rate per tonne of steel decreased by 1% and 1.3% compared to year 2022.

Bayi Iron & Steel's 2500 m^3 HyCROF low-carbon metallurgy project began operations during September 2023, marking Baowu's breakthrough in green technology. Expected to cut one million tonnes of CO_2 annually, it sets a global benchmark for low-carbon smelting, reinforcing Baowu's leadership in sustainable industrial innovation. This is equivalent to planting a forest which cover 1000 km^2 in Xinjiang, significantly contributing to environmental sustainability.

Baowu advances hydrogen metallurgy for carbon-neutral steelmaking. Using hydrogen as fuel and reducing agent, it reduces fossil fuel reliance. On December 23, 2023, Baowu completed thermal load testing for its hydrogen-based shaft furnace at Zhanjiang, a key step toward a zero-carbon plant with efficient, sustainable production processes. During December 2023, Baowu enhanced its leadership in green steelmaking through completion of China's first million tonne hydrogen-based shaft furnace. Baowu optimized HyCROF thereby achieving 96% operating rate and 40% carbon reduction for high temperature billet production, carbon dioxide resistant products and partnerships for large scale CCUS projects. Baowu introduced China's first hydrogen metallurgy pilot platform which focusses on hydrogen-based shaft furnace pelletizing, reduction gas pre-treatment and process optimization. Industrial trials and electric smelting support Baosteel's zero carbon steel plate factory. In 2021, 22 low-carbon projects were evaluated, 87 papers published, and 45 patents filed. In 2022, 16 projects received RMB 27.5 million funding. During 2023, Bayi Iron & Steel launched China's largest automated metallurgical dust and sludge utilization project, processing 600 tonnes daily. Using rotary kiln technology, it enables zero emissions, solid waste recycling, and prevents pollution, generating annual economic benefits of RMB 100 million while enhancing sustainability in steel production. During 2023, Magang Zhixin launched a scrapped vehicle recycling project, dismantling 10,000 vehicles annually to support sustainability, carbon neutrality, and circular economy development in China. In 2023, over 130 million tonnes of carbon emission allowance trading contracts were performed in the local carbon markets of Hubei, Guanedong Fujian, Chongqing and Shanghai.

In 2023, Hwabao Equity Investment Fund of partner Baowu, focused on green and low-carbon sectors, launching the RMB 10 billion Baowu Green Carbon Fund to support sustainable industrial development. Hwabao Securities launched innovative carbon finance services for cost reduction, compliance, and asset activation. It received regulatory approval for carbon trading, becoming the only industry-backed securities firm with carbon trading qualifications, strengthening its role in sustainable finance and emissions management. Hwabao WP Fund Management introduced seven public fund products supporting carbon peaking and neutrality goals, including Huabao ESG Responsible Investment and Huabao Green Energy

ETF. Baowu Group Finance introduced green credit products, including green leasing and pollutant discharge right loans, expanding green finance applications with a portfolio exceeding RMB 10 billion.

Hwabao Equity Investment Fund Management developed an ESG investment system for the Baowu Green Carbon Fund, integrating global standards such as GRI, SASB and TCFD. By 2023, the Baowu Green Carbon Fund had invested in 12 projects and had resulted in overall 5.73% reduction in emission intensity. On December 12, 2023, the Baowu Green Carbon Fund closed with over RMB 10 billion subscribed. By December end 2023, nearly RMB 3 billion was invested in green and low-carbon projects.

Sustainable Finance -Arcelor Mittal Group

Arcelor Mittal is one of the world's leading integrated steel and mining companies. ArcelorMittal is the largest steel producer in Europe and among the largest in the Americas. This Metals & Mining industry leader have manufacturing presence in 15 countries and customers in 40 countries. In 2023, the company mined 42 million tonnes of iron ore and 58.1 million tonnes of crude steel. Steel shipments of 55.6 million tonnes were made in year 2023.

ArcelorMittal produces a broad range of high-quality finished and semi-finished steel products. ArcelorMittal produces flat products, including sheet and plate, and long products, including bars, rods and structural shapes. It also produces pipes and tubes for various applications. ArcelorMittal has a net zero by 2050 target. Arcelor Mittal have a target of 25% reduction in carbon dioxide emissions intensity by year 2030(scope 1 and 2) respectively. Arcelor Mittal aims to build the first full scale carbon emissions steel plant in Sestao, Spain by year 2025. Arcelor expects $10 billion total investment to achieve 2030 Group decarbonisation target. Arcelor Mittal expect that public funding would cover 50% of the total cost of decarbonization. Arcelor aims to offer customers with net zero equivalent steel through an audited certification scheme. ArcelorMittal launched the first products under its new XCarb™ brand. XCarb™ green steel certificates and XCarb™ recycled and renewably-produced steel attracted a premium price. XCarb™ certified tonnes first sold in 2020, expanded to 120,000 tonnes in 2021 and is expected to reach 600,000 tonnes in year 2022.

ArcelorMittal was ranked best steel company for low carbon innovations by CDP's Melting Point. ArcelorMittal was ranked first in five categories relating to steel companies' readiness for a low carbon transition. ArcelorMittal signed a Memorandum of Understanding with international energy firm Equinor to develop value chains in carbon capture and storage. ArcelorMittal commissioned Midrex Technologies to design a Hamburg plant producing 100,000 tons of direct reduced iron yearly, transitioning from grey to green hydrogen. ArcelorMittal had plans to reduce CO2e emissions by 30% by 2030.CDP had recognized ArcelorMittal for its leadership on climate change from among over 8000 companies worldwide that were scored on their 2019 disclosures.

The European Investment Bank, backed by the European Commission, granted ArcelorMittal a €75 million loan for its Ghent projects, Carbalyst and Torero, which will reduce CO2 emissions by 350,000 tonnes through waste conversion. In 2020, ArcelorMittal Europe unveiled its CO2e emissions technology strategy to introduce green steel solutions, increasing production from 30,000 tonnes in 2020 to 600,000 tonnes by 2022. ArcelorMittal made its first XCarb™ innovation fund investment, committing $10 million to Heliogen, whose solar technology concentrates on sunlight to replace fossil fuels.

ArcelorMittal have plans to establish a large-scale DRI and EAF steel plant in Bremen and a DRI pilot plant in Eisenhüttenstadt, aligning with Germany's hydrogen expansion. Using green hydrogen, both sites aim to produce 3.5 million tonnes of low-emission steel by 2030, significantly reducing CO2 emissions. By 2025 the Sestao plant aim to produce 1.6 million tonnes of zero carbon emissions steel. ArcelorMittal completed its second XCarb™ innovation fund investment, leading Form Energy's $200 million Series D round with a $25 million equity contribution.

Hydrogen DRI technology is progressing, but at current green hydrogen costs ($3.5–5/kg), steel production could be $150–$250 per tonne more expensive than natural gas-based DRI. Arcelor Mittal Europe is implementing projects in almost all its flat products sites to use gases from different sources for blast furnace injection. ArcelorMittal Asturias has the most advanced coke oven gas project. The use of this innovative technology will result in a reduction in CO2 emissions of 125,000 tonnes a year. In 2021, ArcelorMittal had launched its $500 million innovation fund with awards of up to $100 million a year to innovative businesses and technologies. An initial award of $10 million was made to Heliogen, a technology company which focused on development of heat, electricity and fuels from concentrated solar energy. The Heliogen technology is capable of creating 100% green hydrogen. ArcelorMittal had invested $25 million in Form Energy, a company developing innovative low-cost energy storage technology for a reliable, renewable electric grid. The Energy Transitions Commission estimates that additional investments to achieve zero carbon emissions will amount to US$ 1 trillion to US$ 2 trillion per year. According to estimates, ArcelorMittal's 2030 global target of 25% requires the gross capital cost of approximately US$ 10 billion of which 35% of capex would be deployed by 2025 and rest beyond 2025.

In July 2021, the European Commission introduced the "Fit for 55" package, a set of proposals aimed at aligning the EU's climate, energy, land use, transport, and taxation policies to reduce net greenhouse gas emissions by at least 55% by 2030. Public funding supports large-scale CO2e reduction technologies through grants, favorable loans, or equity investments, often involving multiple government levels to drive decarbonization projects. The EU Innovation Fund launched in 2020 is one of the world's largest programmes and will invest up to €10 billion between 2020–2030 to support the commercial demonstration of innovative low-carbon technologies.

Carbon Contracts for Differences (CCfDs) incentivize zero-emissions steelmaking by covering the cost gap between emissions allowances and contract prices. Investors receive payouts when carbon prices are low but must compensate if prices exceed the strike price. CCfDs reduce financing costs, encouraging climate-friendly investments and supporting steel industry decarbonization. A consumer carbon charge on steel could fund low-carbon technologies and incentivize sustainable choices. Compared to power and transport, steel offers a higher CO2e reduction per dollar invested. Introducing a charge at purchase, such as $75 per car, could accelerate the transition to low-emission steel production.

For the US$ 5.5 billion Revolving Credit Facility (the RCF), ArcelorMittal have linked the calculation of loan margins to key indicators to meet sustainability goals and emissions reduction goals. The margin payable can be increased or decreased based on certain metrics related to its environmental and sustainability performance. The metrics measured include the carbon dioxide intensity of ArcelorMittal's European operations and other ArcelorMittal facilities which are certified by ResponsibleSteel™ by the end of each year. The company uses two breakthrough carbon neutral strategies namely Smart Carbon initiatives, Carbalyst® which is a carbon capture and reuse project and Torero which converts waste wood into bio-coal. In its Hamburg, Germany plant, the company is developing an industrial scale project to use hydrogen instead of natural gas for the reduction of iron ore. ArcelorMittal is a founding member of ResponsibleSteel™ which is the founding member of the global steel industry's only global multi stakeholder certification initiative which covers over 200 requirements for ESG standards. Crédit Agricole Corporate and Investment Bank acted as ESG coordinator.

Sustainability Initiatives at Ansteel

Ansteel Group Corporation was the first largescale integrated iron and steel enterprise established in China. It was formed by the merger of Anshan Iron and Steel Group Company and Pangang Group Ltd. In 2023, Ansteel was ranked 283rd in the Fortune Global list. The company produce 53 million tons of iron, 64 million tons of steel, 40,000 tons of vanadium products and 500,000 tons of titanium products. Ansteel is the world's largest vanadium producer and China's largest titanium raw material producer. The products of Ansteel are sold to more than 70 countries. The company have 29 subsidiaries and organizations. The company made revenues of RMB 288.016 billion in year 2023. The total assets of the company amounted to RMB 482.67 billion in year 2023. The R&D investment intensity amounted to 3.88%. The year on year decrease of comprehensive energy consumption per RMB 10,000 of output value was 0.51%. The company have 4000 plus greened and reclaimed land. The year on year decrease of particulate matter/smoke and dust emissions was 11.94%. The number of national green mines was 16. The company added innovation platforms such as the Liaoning Academy of Materials, Ansteel Group Corporation Ltd., Advanced Metal Materials Industry Innovation Center and

Ansteel Technology Innovation Center. By end of 2023, Ansteel had accumulated 12,347 valid patents which included 6946 effective invention patents and 168 valid overseas patents. The company focus on AI to digitalize industrial upgrading to foster industrial ecology and shape new model of digitalized green and low carbon development. In 2023, Ansteel digitalized 55 production lines and 53 intelligent manufacturing achievements. The company have built the only hydrogen refuelling station for iron and steel enterprises in the Northeast region. The company have signed key projects at the 2023 State owned Central Enterprises Symposium on Assisting Northeast China's Revitalization. The annual iron ore concentrate output amounted to 53.28 million. There were 54 raw material suppliers certified for environmental management systems. In 2023, the company invested RMB 258,000 in environmental protection training. In 2023, Ansteel invested around RMB 16.1 billion in environmental protection. In 2023, the company invested RMB 258,000 in environmental protection training. With the investment of RMB 1.6 billion, Xichang Steel & Vanadium have implemented 80 projects which included ultra-low emission transformation for high sulfur sintering gas. Pangang Group Vanadium & Titanium Resources Co Ltd. have successfully raised RMB 2.28 billion and have secured funding for seven key ongoing projects for development of the vanadium and titanium industry. The consumption driven assistance fund amounted to RMB 81.84 million. The investment in R&D amounted to RMB 2.852 billion. In 2023, the company had announced 122 projects for the second technology leadership plan. The company have invested RMB 16.4 million in offering aid and implemented seven assistance programs.

Green Finance Initiatives at Nippon Steel

Nippon Steel Corporation is Japan's largest steelmaker and one of the world's leading steel producers. Nippon Steel Group does business in the core segment of Steel making and Steel Fabrication which consist of engineering and construction, chemicals, and materials and system solutions. Nippon have manufacturing bases in Japan and 15 other countries.

Nippon Steel have adopted "Nippon Steel Carbon Neutral Vision 2050" as part of its widespread efforts towards a decarbonized society. Nippon Steel has obtained the EcoLeaf, an ecolabel certified by the Sustainable Management Promotion Organization in compliance with ISO 14025 international standards for 47 products. The Ecoleaf is an EPD3 certification program in use in Japan which aim to disclose quantitative environmental information about the entire life cycle of a product from resource mining and manufacturing to disposal and recycling. The Nippon Steel Group's main business is in steelmaking with annual crude steel production capacity of approximately 47 million in Japan and 19 million tons overseas with annual steel processing capacity of 37 million.

The Nippon Steel Group has established a global supply network of 37 million tons in steel processing mainly for use in automobiles, infrastructure, electric appliances and containers, resources and energy. Nippon Steel developed Tran Tixxii Eco, the world's first pure titanium eco friendly material. This ecoproduct made from over 50% recycled titanium reduces carbondioxide emissions and conserves resources without comprising design. Nippon Steel and Anglo-American PLC agreed to collaborate on reducing CO2 emissions by optimizing high-grade iron ore use in blast furnace and direct reduction steelmaking. R&D expenses in year 2023 amounted to ¥70.5 billion. Nippon Steel held approximately 30,000 patents in Japan. In accordance with the international standard ISO 14001, Nippon Steel has built an environmental management system with each steelworks manager who serves as the responsible person. Nippon Steel uses environmental accounting to track the environmental costs and effects. Environmental conservation costs combine the costs of capital investment associated with environmental measures, energy saving and recycling measures and expenses.

Nippon Steel has adopted environmental accounting to be used as guidelines for corporate activities, and to accurately track the environmental costs and effects. Environmental conservation costs combine the costs of capital investment associated with environmental measures, energy-saving and recycling measures. The environmental costs amounted to ¥185.0 billion in fiscal 2022. This consisted of ¥17.4 billion for capital investment and ¥167.6 billion for environmental conservation. The Carbon Neutral Vision 2050 of Nippon Steel aims to achieve carbon neutrality using three breakthrough technologies: "Reduction with hydrogen in BFs," "Hydrogen direct reduction of iron," and "high-grade steel production in large size EAFs."

During the period 2008–2021, Nippon Steel developed technologies to lower CO2 emissions by 30%. Nippon Steel is involved in development under the Super Course50 subsidized by the Green Innovation Fund project wherein social infrastructure for hydrogen supply is available toward realizing the Carbon Neutral Vision. Nippon Steel along with Japan CCS, ENAA, and ITOCHU, have launched an R&D and demonstration project on integrated CO2 ship transportation under a NEDO-commissioned initiative.

Nippon Steel's NSCarbolex™ Solution provides high-performance products that help reduce CO2 emissions, including NSafe™-AutoConcept, which lowers emissions during automobile manufacturing and driving. Nippon Steel recycle 100% of waste plastics collected from households through chemical recycling by using a coke oven in accordance with the Containers and Packaging Recycling. Nippon Steel processes approximately 200,000 tons annually, or about 30% of the volume of waste plastics collected nationwide. The cumulative amount processed during fiscal 2000–2022 was approximately 3.91 million tons which is equivalent to 12.50 million tons in terms of reduction in CO2 emission.

Table 12.2 shows the environmental costs incurred by Nippon Steel during the period 2022.

In 2023, Nippon decided to increase the manufacturing capacity of non-oriented electrical steel sheets. The total accumulated investment amount was approximately 213 billion yen. In 2023, Nippon issued a green bond totalling 50 billion-yen in order to finance production facilities, research and development and other related

Table 12.2 Environmental costs in billions of yen

Costs	Capital Expenditure	Capital Expenditure	Total Expenses
Pollution prevention costs	Air pollution control (including measures against dust), et	8.2	35.1
	Water and soil pollution prevention, noise and vibration prevention	6.8	10.6
Global warming prevention costs	Energy saving measures	2.4	7.4
Cost of recycling resources	Recycling of resources and generated materials		50.3
	Industrial waste treatment (including PCB, coal ash, etc.)		12.5
	Business-related general waste treatment, etc.		0.5
Environmental management activities cost	Construction of EMS and acquisition of ISO14001 certification		0
	Monitoring and measurement of environmental loads		1.2
	Personnel expenditures related to environmental measures, etc		3.1
Research and development costs	Development of Ecoproducts		6.8
	Development of products which have low environmental impact during manufacture, etc		34.1
Social activity costs	Beautification and greening of offices		1.3
	Supporting environmental organizations, etc.		0.7
Other environmental costs	Environmental fines		4.1
Total		17.4	167.7

Source: Nippon Steel Sustainability Report 2023

expenditures for non-directional electrical steel sheets used in eco-friendly car-driving motor. Nippon Steel aims to position the issuance of green bonds to ensure the steady progress towards Carbon Neutral Vision 2050. Caron neutrality in steel industry requires huge R&D expenditures and capital expenditures. Nippon Steel is expected to incur ¥0.5 trillion in R&D expenses and ¥4–5 trillion in capital expenditures.

During November 2021, Nippon Steel invested a total of ¥123 billion in facilities to improve the capacity and quality of electrical steel sheets in Japan.

As part of its Steel Carbon Neutral Vision 2050, Nippon Steel have issued the following green finance bonds (Table 12.3).

Table 12.3 Green bond issuance by Nippon Steel

Date of issue	Type of finance	Issuance amount	Maturity of issuance
March 9 2023	Green bond	30 billion JPY	5 year
March 92,023	Green bond	20 billion JPY	10 year

To achieve carbon neutrality by 2050, Nippon Steel aim to reduce CO2 emissions in the supply chain by providing two values: Advanced products and technical solutions that contribute to reducing CO2 emissions in society (NSCarbolexTM Solution) and steel products certified as reducing CO2 emissions in the steelmaking process (NSCarbolexTM Neutral). By 2021, Nippon Steel decided to invest a total of 123 billion in facilities to improve the capacity and quality of electrical steel sheets in the Hirohata Area of Setouchi Works and the Yawat.

During March 2023, Nippon steel decided to issue a green bond in the Japanese market through a public offering. The 7th series of unsecured straight bonds amounted to JPY 30 billion with denomination of JPY 100 million. The interest rate for the issue is 0.564% per annum. The maturity date for the issue is March 2028. The 8th series of unsecured straight bonds for Nippon Steel Corporation for issuance of JPY 20 billion had interest rate of 1.150% per annum.

The bond will be issued to procure part of the funds required to finance production facilities, research and development expenses and other related expenditures for non-directional electrical sheets to be used in eco-friendly car motors. The lead managing underwriters for the issuance were Mizhuho Securities Co Ltd., SMBC Nikko Securities Inc., Mitsubishi Morgan Stanley Securities Co Ltd., Nomura Securities Co Ltd. and Daiwa Securities Co Ltd. A part of the proceeds was allocated to replenish cash reserves previously used to fund the construction of the cited production facilities.

References

Ansteel Group 2023, Sustainability Report.
ArcelorMittal, Climate Action Report July 2021.
BHP Annual Report 2024.
BHP's Climate Transition Action Plan (CTAP) 2024.
China Baowu Steel Group Corporation Lt, Green and Low Carbon Development Report 2023.
Glencore Annual Report 2023.
Glencore Sustainability Report 2023.
https://www.bhp.com/sustainability/climate-change
Jiangxi Copper Company Environmental, Social and Governance Report 2023
Nippon Steel Sustainability Report 2023.
Rio Tinto Annual Report 2023-Strategic Report.

Chapter 13
Sustainable Finance Initiatives in Equipment Manufacturing and Automobile Segment

Equipment Manufacturing Segment

Green Finance -Komatsu

Komatsu is a leading manufacturer of construction, mining, forestry and industrial heavy equipment. The construction, mining and utility equipment segment develops, manufacturers, sells and services construction and mining equipment. The construction equipment includes small and medium sized hydraulic excavators, bulldozers, wheel loaders which are used mainly in construction and civil engineering work, forklifts and forestry machinery. Komatsu business consists of three main business segments of (a) construction, mining and utility equipment, (b) retail finance and (c) industrial machinery and others. In 2023, the construction, mining and utility equipment sales amounted to ¥3615.2 billion. In the same year, retail finance and industrial machinery sales amounted to ¥103.5 billion and ¥195.6 billion respectively. In 2023, sales ratio outside of Japan amounted to 91% of total sales. The sales composition is led by the large markets in North and Latin America.

Komatsu offer solutions which optimize customers' operation processes through digitalization, along with eco friendly and highly efficient products. Komatsu is a participant in the United Nations Global Compact (UNGC). Komatsu had launched the world's first hybrid hydraulic excavator which reduces fuel consumption by approximately 25%. Komatsu became the first in the industry to introduce hydraulic excavators to the Japanese market which standardize the installation of in-house Kom Vision Human Detection & Collision Mitigation System. In 2023, Komatsu received GX construction equipment certification for seven models of electrified construction equipment. In 1995, Komatsu started the business to recycle and supply components collected from customers. In 2008, Komatsu introduced the world's first commercial AHS. By 2024, over 700 units were installed between 23 mines in five countries around the world with a cumulative total of 7.5 billion tons. Komatsu

B. R. Kumar, *Green Finance*, Sustainable Finance,
https://doi.org/10.1007/978-3-032-03333-8_13

pioneered Smart Construction, integrating KomVision for safety and digital technologies for site visualization, enhancing safety, productivity, and environmental adaptability in the construction industry. For past 18 years, Komatsu was selected for the Dow Jones Sustainability World Index. The aftermarket business accounts for about 50% of Komatsu construction equipment and vehicle sales and 60% of profits. Currently 770,000 units of Komatsu equipment are in operation worldwide. Komatsu have a target of achieving carbon neutrality by 2050. Komatsu have a joint development agreement with General Motors Company for the development of hydrogen fuel cell modules to be used in ultra class mining dump trucks.

R&D investments in 2023 amounted to Yen 103.4 billion which accounted for 2.7% of net sales. Komatsu offer forest management solutions which combine information on machine operation with forest resource management using drones and satellites. Smart Construction is a digital solution that centralizes 3D terrain data from drones and ICT equipment, enabling real-time site monitoring and high-quality construction. It enhances process management, inspection efficiency, and machine guidance. With over 10,000 installations annually, Komatsu is expanding its global presence in North America, Europe, and Australia. In 2019, Komatsu endorsed the recommendations of the Task Force on Climate related Financial Disclosures. During 2023, Komatsu acquired American Battery Solutions to accelerate the development and production of batteries optimized for Komatsu's construction and mining equipment. In 2024, Komatsu in alliance with Denyo Co Ltd. developed a concept machine for generator using a hydrogen mixed combustion engine as a power feeder for electric mini excavators. Komatsu Group along with EARTHBRAIN jointly developed the Smart Construction Teleoperation system for construction equipment. Komatsu is developing the forestry equipment business which aims for recycling-oriented forestry and the component remanufacturing business.

Approximately 90% of CO2 emissions in the lifecycle of construction equipment is generated by machines in use. Accordingly, Komatsu is working to not only make its products fuel efficient by developing high-efficiency engines, hybrid systems and electric models, but also reduce total CO2 emissions from construction sites by automating construction or promoting autonomous operation of construction equipment to make the entire process of construction efficient.

Komatsu issued a green bond through a public offering on the Japanese market. Under the 3-year midterm management plan, "DANTOTSU Value-Together, to "The Next" for sustainable growth is to be completed by March 2025. Komatsu is upholding three pillars of growth strategies, namely, "Value Creation by Means of Innovation", "Growth Strategies Based on Business Reforms", and "Structural Reforms for Growth." Komatsu aims to accelerate its efforts to create a decarbonized society by reducing environmental impact and provide high quality efficient products, services and solutions. The issue amount was JPY 10 billion with bond maturity period of 5 years and interest rate of 0.13%. Initiatives were designed to help reduce carbondioxide emissions from products in use to 50% by 2030 compared to 2010. The proceeds from the bond issuance will be used to find solutions for environment problems due to use of products and manufacturing. Investments will focus on hybrid hydraulic excavators, eligible for Japan's Ministry of Land, Infrastructure, Transport, and Tourism's low-carbon construction equipment certification, as well as electric construction equipment. The proceeds will be utilized for supporting fuel economy machine operations by using IoT.The focus will also be for development of solutions for wide use of ICT intensive construction equipment. Komatsu aim to cut CO2 emissions from manufacturing by 50% and raise renewable energy usage to 50% of total consumption by 2030. The focus is on energy savings for factories and equipment in plants, power generation by using solar panels, biomass production and purchase of renewable energies. The lead manager for the project was Nomura Securities Co Ltd. and the issuance received AA- rating.

In 2020, Yen 10,000 million worth of bond were raised and utilized for investments in rental assets to promote use of ICT intensive construction equipment and for projects meant for energy savings of factories and equipment in plants and power generation by using biomass.

Komatsu had issued sustainability linked USD denominated senior unsecured straight bonds with issuance value of amount USD 600 million. The issuer was Komatsu Finance America Inc. and guarantor was Komatsu Ltd. The interest rate is 5.499% per year from October 6, 2022, to October 5, 2025. Starting October 6, 2025, it will increase by 10 bps if SPT 1.1 is unmet and by 15 bps if SPT 2.1 is unmet as of March 31, 2025. The offerings in overseas markets was primarily made in US, Europe and Asia. Moody's gave a rating of A2 and S&P gave a rating of A for sustainability linked bond issue. The issuance amount targeted a 45% reduction in Scope 1 and 2 CO2 emissions intensity (KPI1) from production by March 31, 2025, based on the 2010 baseline.

Sustainable Finance Investment at Caterpillar Inc

Caterpillar is the world's leading manufacturer of construction and mining equipment, off-highway diesel and natural gas engines, industrial gas turbines and diesel electric locomotives. The company operates through three primary segments of Construction Industries, Resource Industries and Energy &Transportation. The company also provides financing and related services through its Financial Products segment. Caterpillar is also a leading US exporter. In 2024, Caterpillar had sales revenues of $64.809 billion. The Construction Industries segment is primarily responsible for supporting customers using machinery in infrastructure and building construction applications. The Resource Industries segment is primarily responsible for supporting customers using machinery in mining, heavy construction and quarry and aggregates. The energy & transportation segment focus on customers in oil and gas, power generation, marine, rail and industrial applications, including Caterpillar machines.

The Sustainability and Public Policy Committee (SPPC) at Caterpillar oversees climate, environmental, and social policies at Caterpillar. It recommends sustainability strategies, monitors progress, and reviews shareholder proposals on climate risk and public policy. The Chief Sustainability Officer and enterprise sustainability team engage with the SPPC bimonthly to discuss key initiatives. In 2022, Caterpillar conducted a climate opportunity and risk assessment, including scenario analysis, to better understand climate change's potential impacts on its business and strengthen its preparedness for the energy transition. Caterpillar estimated the percentage of key Caterpillar manufacturing sites and facilities exposed to relevant physical climate hazards under different future scenarios. Caterpillar estimated the percentage of manufacturing sites and facilities exposed to relevant physical climate hazards under different future scenarios.

The mining equipment of Caterpillar supports the growing demand for critical materials essential to advancing energy technologies, including copper, lithium, nickel, and aluminum for electric vehicles, battery storage, renewable energy, and grid modernization. The construction equipment helps build the infrastructure required for the energy transition to improve fuel efficiency and productivity of machines. Caterpillar offer machines and engines which are capable of operating on alternative fuels such as biodiesel, biogas, hydrogen, hydrotreated vegetable oil and methanol. The Cat® 980 XE Wheel Loader features a Caterpillar-designed continuous variable transmission, enhancing fuel efficiency by up to 35% and reducing GHG emissions by 17% compared to its predecessor. The Cat R2900 XE, Caterpillar's first diesel electric underground LHD loader, delivers larger payloads, faster loading and reduced emissions. Caterpillar has significantly expanded its portfolio of generator sets that operate on natural gas blended with up to 25% hydrogen by volume. The lineup now includes the Cat CG132B, Cat CG170B generator sets, and the G3500H series platform. Caterpillar-designed lithium-ion batteries power various industrial applications with a modular design for flexible configurations. Built on proven technology, they are scalable to industry and customer needs while maximizing sustainability through recycling and reuse at the end of their life cycle. In 2022, Caterpillar unveiled the first battery-electric 793 Large Mining Truck prototype, supported by key mining customers through its Early Learner program.

Caterpillar has long invested in autonomous development and the team reached a milestone of 10 years of autonomous operations in 2023. Through the end of 2023, this fleet comprised more than 630 large mining trucks, which has moved a cumulative 7.5 billion metric tons of materials. Over the past 20 years, Caterpillar had invested over $30 billion in R&D to offer innovation in autonomy, alternative fuels, connectivity and digital, electrification etc. In 2023, Caterpillar launched Pathways to Sustainability a 4-year training program for enrolled customer groups. Caterpillar and Albemarle have entered into a collaboration to strengthen the lithium supply chain and enhance the sustainability of lithium mining. The Cat Energy Storage System (ESS) supports energy storage, grid stabilization, and renewable integration. The new Cat Compact ESS enhances mobile power solutions, reducing noise and enabling renewables.

Remanufactured products offered through Cat Reman, Solar Turbines, Progress Rail, Caterpillar Energy Solutions and Cat Defense have resulted in reduced GHG emissions compared to manufacturing new products. Cat Certified Rebuilds by trained professionals extend equipment lifespan while incorporating updates.

Innovation models such as failure models predict issues before they occur, reducing maintenance costs and extending component life. Condition monitoring & remote diagnostics minimize service calls and emissions. Advanced analytics optimize productivity, reducing fuel consumption and emissions. Digital tools like VisionLink enhance fuel efficiency, reduce idle time and improve profitability. Battery replacement management supports recharging and end of life solutions. The San Luis Potosi Mexico facility operates entirely on on-site renewable solar electricity through energy conservation initiatives. Caterpillar's enterprise energy team promotes energy efficiency and renewable power through procurement and on-site solutions like photovoltaics, microgrids, and CHP systems. They evaluate opportunities to expand these initiatives, enhancing sustainability and facility efficiency. Caterpillar upholds high EHS standards through a global management system. Facilities conduct annual compliance assessments, while an EHS team reviews self-assessments and audits select locations. Remanufactured parts lower ownership costs, support the circular economy, and align with Caterpillar's goal to increase remanufacturing sales and revenue by 25% by 2030. From 2018 period, there has been 31% increase in sales and revenues from remanufacturing offerings. Approximately 147 million pounds of materials were taken back for remanufacturing through Cat Reman. During 2018–2023, Cat Reman have introduced 29% more remanufacturing offerings to support sustainability and total cost of ownership initiatives. Remanufacturing produces 65–87% less GHG process emissions compared to manufacturing new parts. Cat Reman product line meets the needs of the industries served by Caterpillar, including construction, mining, energy and transportation, as well as on-highway truck engines. Cat Certified Rebuild programs extend equipment life by offering cost-effective updates, enhancing material longevity. Each rebuild includes 350+ tests, reconditioning or replacing about 7000 parts, and comes with a like-new warranty.

Since 1985, Cat dealers have completed more than 50,000 Cat Certified Rebuilds on machines, powertrains and components. In 2023, Caterpillar reduced its total energy use by 23% from the 2018 baseline. In 2023, more than 27% of electrical energy was obtained from renewable sources. In the year 2023, Caterpillar reduced its SCOPE 1(direct) emissions by 27% from its baseline year 2018. Since 1981, Cat Financial has supported Caterpillar, Cat® dealers, and customers with tailored financial solutions. It offers retail and wholesale financing, extended protection, and coverage for Cat machinery, engines, Solar® gas turbines, related equipment, and marine vessels. All Caterpillar diesel engines can operate on 100% HVO.

Caterpillar have made investments in tech start-up Nth Cycle to boost recycling. The investment comes as part of a $44 million Series B round of financing in privately held Nth Cycle which commercialise recycling methods for green energy transition. Caterpillar have made investments of more than $30 billion in R&D over the past 20 years. Cat dealers have completed more than 50,000 Cat Certified Rebuilds on machines, powertrains and components. Caterpillar Foundation contributed $935 million since the year 1952. Caterpillar have set science-based Scope 1 and 2 goal to reduce absolute greenhouse gas (GHG) emissions from its operations by 30% by 2030 compared to the baseline year 2018.

Sustainable Finance -John Deere

John Deere and its subsidiaries manufacture and distribute various equipment worldwide. The company operates through four segments of production and precision agriculture, small agriculture and turf, construction and forestry and financial services. John Deere is the world's largest agricultural equipment manufacturer which sells in more than 100 countries.

John Deere's corporate sustainability function is part of the Accounting & Finance organization and serves to drive the enterprise's sustainability strategy and governance. Deere's centralized sustainability team drives, measures, and reports on sustainability strategies, including Leap Ambitions. They coordinate enterprise-wide efforts, track progress, enhance core processes, and engage external stakeholders to communicate the Smart Industrial Operating Model and sustainability initiatives. John Deere's Smart Industrial Operating Model, introduced in fiscal year 2020, aims to transform agriculture and construction by delivering innovative technologies that create economic and sustainable value for customers. Launched in 2022, the Leap Ambitions serve as key benchmarks for measuring progress toward these strategic goals.

In 2021, John Deere conducted an inaugural materiality assessment to identify sustainability topics that are the most relevant to its business and its stakeholders and to inform its future goals. John Deere has announced a set of focused goals, known as "Leap Ambitions", to measure its strategy across these high priority areas.

During April 2022, Deere & Company issued a Sustainability Linked Bond tied to Sustainability Performance Target of achievement of at least a 20% reduction in absolute Scope 1 and Scope 2 GHG emissions by fiscal year end 2025 compared to a 2021 baseline. This was equivalent of reducing 648,800 metric tons CO2 emissions by fiscal year-end 2025. The company made $51.72 billion in net sales during the year 2024.

John Deere aim to demonstrate low/no carbon alternative power solutions by year 2026. The aim is to achieve 95% recyclable product content by year 2030 and ensure that 65% of product content is based on sustainable material. The company had 50% growth in remanufacturing revenue. John Deere aims to reduce environmental footprint by year 2030. The aim is for 50% operational CO2 e emissions (Scope 1 & 2) reduction. John Deere has an agreement with SpaceX to bring satellite communications through its Starlink network to farmers who experience rural connectivity challenges. This facilitates countries such as Brazil to fully leverage the company's precision agriculture technologies. Contractor farmers in India rely on small tractors outfitted with Deere Modular Telematics Gateway (MTG) for their businesses. John Deere's "2026 Leap Ambition goal" aims to ensure 100% new small agriculture equipment enabled connectivity for growers for data collection and digitalization of their businesses. The leap ambition goal is to engage 75% of the acres to be sustainably engaged by the year 2030.The John Deere Operations Center™ supports agronomic decision-making and promotes sustainable practices by tracking input reductions—such as fuel and herbicides—that can contribute to cost savings.

John Deere advances its Solutions as a Service model to enhance profitability and sustainability by making precision technology more affordable, accessible, and adaptable. Innovations like See & Spray™ and ExactShot™ integrate with foundational tools and upgrade kits, helping farmers of all sizes maximize efficiency and reduce costs.

John Deere's See & Spray™ Ultimate and ExactApply™ reduce herbicide use by targeting weeds precisely, improving efficiency and sustainability. ExactShot™ minimizes fertilizer waste by dosing directly on seeds, cutting usage by over 60%. ExactEmerge™ enables high-speed planting, doubling efficiency while maintaining accuracy, optimizing crop growth and cost savings. Precision ag technology is an example of innovative practices which are capable of producing sustainable results. For example, throughout the production cycle, a Deere customer farming 6500 acres of corn and soybeans evenly split with these technologies would result in sustainable outcomes such as herbicide cost savings of $63,000, fertilizer cost savings of $178,500, time and labor cost savings of $4000, fuel cost savings of $8500, seed cost savings of $58,500 respectively. The estimated total cost savings was estimated to be approximately $312,500 on account of total economic and sustainable outcomes from this model farm initiatives.

John Deere collaborates with farmers to tackle common challenges like rising costs, labor shortages, and data needs. In Sonoma County, a 2024 pilot program with winegrowers showcased Smart Apply, a LiDAR-based system that optimizes spraying by adjusting to foliage size, improving efficiency, reducing inputs, and enhancing sustainable farming. John Deere's precision technology, including SmartGrade™, enhances construction efficiency by improving grading accuracy, reducing rework, and addressing labor shortages. A site study showed 37% faster project completion, 53% better accuracy, and 58% higher productivity. SmartGrade's next generation offers enhanced control, flexibility, and remote support, maximizing jobsite performance and profitability.

John Deere enhances jobsite safety with its "show me, tell me, assist me" strategy. SmartDetect™ uses machine learning and cameras for hazard alerts, while SmartDetect Assist™ helps slow or stop equipment to prevent collisions. Advanced vision systems provide operators with a 280-degree view, improving awareness and accident prevention. Launched in February 2024, the WRC 240i streamlines soil stabilization by crushing, mixing, and screening stony ground in one pass at up to 600 tons/hour. It enhances efficiency by adding binding agents and water, reducing construction time and conserving resources compared to traditional material removal and replacement methods. For over 20 years, Deere has integrated electrification into its products, enhancing efficiency. The next step is full battery-electric solutions, offering numerous benefits. Customers in high-value crop farming, turf care, and construction are increasingly seeking this option to improve sustainability and operational performance.

The 850 X-Tier Dozer's E-Drive system enhances responsiveness, power, and fuel efficiency. Wirtgen Group advances roadbuilding with the Kleemann MR 100i NEOe impact crusher, designed for urban mining. It operates on grid power for zero emissions or in diesel mode for reduced noise and fuel consumption.

The John Deere Foundation strengthens the food chain through grants and partnerships, uniting Farmlink and Feeding America® to distribute rescued food. With a $6.6 million, 3-year commitment, Deere continues its decades-long support of local food banks, enhancing food access across its home communities and beyond. During 2024, John Deere invited shareholders with more than 40% of outstanding share ownership to engage in conversations related to sustainability topics.

Hitachi Construction Machinery-Green Finance

The Hitachi Construction Machinery Group is a construction machinery manufacturer which focusses on hydraulic excavator, wheel loader and mining machinery fields. Hitachi Construction Machinery offers Solution Linkage, a suite of ICT and IoT solutions which are designed to enhance operational efficiency. ConSite, a proprietary technology of Hitachi Construction Machinery, utilizes big data to analyse and deliver valuable insights on construction equipment operations. Launched in 2013, it enhances efficiency through automated data analysis. In 2017, Hitachi introduced an industry-first oil condition monitoring service using sensors. Moving forward, the company aims to further integrate sensing and AI technologies to predict equipment failures and improve performance.

Build on the foundation of the ConSite service solution, the autonomous haulage system, fleet management system and ICT construction solutions, Solution Linkages delivers comprehensive data driven insights. By leveraging open innovation and collaborating with expert technology partners, it enables smarter, more effective construction and mining operations. The Fleet Management System monitors each dump truck on a real time basis and dispatches trucks optimally.

Hitachi Construction Machinery Group developed ZCORE, an advanced system platform that enables equipment to "recognize, analyze, and act"—tasks traditionally performed by operators at construction sites. Hitachi Construction Machinery Group focus on analysis that uses digital twin technology to recreate real phenomena in cyberspace. In 2024, Hitachi established the concept called "LANDCROS" for delivering innovative solutions.

In 2021, the Hitachi Construction Machinery Group reassessed its material issues, considering social trends like SDGs and ESG, as well as external environmental factors affecting corporate value. This review identified four key material issues with significant business impact, shaping the company's long-term strategy. The Hitachi Construction Machinery Group aims to be the world's leading solution provider, offering innovative, technology-driven solutions alongside its construction machinery and service systems.

By prioritizing customer needs through Customer Interest First (CIF) activities, the company continuously identifies and addresses evolving challenges. This approach emphasizes rapid adaptation, hypothesis testing, and learning from failures to drive innovation. Through close collaboration with customers and partners, Hitachi fosters a cycle of continuous improvement, embodying the "Kenkijin Spirit" to deliver reliable, value-added solutions in a rapidly changing industry. Hitachi Construction is working to reduce carbon dioxide from its product development and manufacturing processes to achieve carbon neutrality by 2050. Since 2020, Hitachi have been evaluating climate change related risks and opportunities. The Financial Investment Committee has set aside budget for investment in carbon neutrality and prioritizes investment in its screening process for capital and R&D investment project. Following the conclusion of the first agreement related to Positive Impact Finance loan in year 2022, Hitachi issued its first green bond in March 2024 to raise funds of 10 billion yen. The funds will be used to develop products in order to solve environmental issues such as fully electric truck without engine. The Research & Development Group advances machine performance through regular updates but now focuses on digital and communication technologies. With software challenges increasing, the Open Innovation Promotion Office leads collaborations to enhance AI-driven obstacle detection and machine control, ensuring faster development and adaptation to industry changes.

Hitachi developed a battery-powered dump truck, tested since 2024 in Zambia, using trolley dynamic charging for net-zero emissions. The RBT series of remotely operated hydraulic excavators launched in May 2024, integrating advanced low-latency communication. Additionally, autonomous excavation trials using the ZCORE system demonstrated progress in self-driving technology. In May 2023, Hitachi partnered with aptpod, Inc., a Japanese IoT startup, to develop a remote control and automation system for construction machinery. Utilizing aptpod's high-speed IoT platform and digital twin technology, the collaboration aims to enhance efficiency and operational capabilities. In 2023, R&D investment accounted for 2.2% of sales.

Important sustainability-related issues are discussed at the CSR Promotion Managers Meeting and the Environmental Promotion Managers Meeting, and then reported to the Sustainability Promotion Committee which meets twice a year comprising executive officers and presidents of major Group companies. Hitachi have set the goal of reducing CO2 emissions by 22% and 33% by FY2025 and FY2030, respectively. Hitachi aim to achieve carbon neutrality by year 2050.

The Hitachi Construction Machinery Group promotes the use of zero-emission machines to reduce waste from various angles through its value chain businesses, including parts, service, remanufacturing, rentals, and used equipment. With the above focus, Hitachi promotes the 4Rs (Reduce, Reuse, Recycle, and Renewable) throughout the Group. Hitachi Construction Machinery Group has formulated a "Biodiversity Policy" that serves as the basis for the Group's biodiversity initiatives. Hitachi was selected for inclusion in the Asia Pacific Index of the Dow Jones Sustainability Indices (DJ).

During 2024, Hitachi issued green bond with maturity of 5 years. The issue amount was JPY 10 billion. The coupon rate was 0.667%. The issue received a credit rating of A. The fiscal agent was MUFG Bank, Ltd. The lead managers were Daiwa Securities Co Ltd., Nomura Securities Co Ltd., SMBC Nikko Securities Inc. The proceeds will be allocated for financing capital investments and R&D and refinancing existing investments for projects established by Hitachi Construction

Machinery. The projects were R&D related to development of battery-powered/wired electric construction machinery, hydrogen engine/fuel cell drive construction machinery and associated products/services. The projects also involve those related to the installation of energy efficient equipment and facilities which contribute to the improvement of energy efficiency. The structuring agent for the deal was Daiwa Securities Co. Ltd.

Green Finance Investments in Volvo Construction Equipment

Volvo Construction Equipment (CE) is a leading international company which develops, manufactures and markets equipment for construction and related industries. The company offer a broad range of products, efficient worldwide services and complete customer solutions.

Volvo CE as part of its Science Based Targets (SBTi) aim to achieve net zero value chain emissions by 2040 with significant reduction as early as 2030. Volvo Group have made commitments to achieve net-zero value chain greenhouse gas emissions across all business areas by 2040—10 years ahead of the SBTi commitment. This accelerated target accounts for the average lifespan of Volvo products, which is approximately 10 years in the customer use phase. To ensure the entire rolling fleet reaches net-zero emissions by 2050, all products delivered after 2040 must be emissions-free.

Volvo CE has set interim targets for 2030, including reducing emissions from its own operations, facilities, and manufacturing processes by 50%. Additionally, it aims to achieve a 30% absolute reduction in emissions from product use, which represents the largest share of the company's carbon footprint. In the construction equipment industry, the majority of emissions come from indirect sources—specifically, the emissions generated when machines are in operation after leaving the factory. Volvo is associated with climate change initiatives such as the Construction Climate Challenge (CCC) and the WWF Climate Savers Program. The company have adopted three streams of electromobility such as battery electric machines, hydrogen fuel cell powered equipment and improved internal combustion engine solutions. Volvo have broad range of over 55,000 supply chain partners around the globe.

Volvo Group and Daimler Truck have signed a non-binding agreement to form a 50/50 joint venture in Gothenburg, Sweden, to develop a software-defined vehicle platform for trucks and buses. The partnership aims to drive digital transformation, enhance sustainability, accelerate development, increase production volumes, and share costs. Volvo Group, Renault Group, and CMA CGM have formed a joint venture, Flexis SAS, to develop battery-electric commercial vehicles on a software-defined platform using Google Android OS. The first model, set for production in 2026, will support last-mile deliveries and complement Volvo's heavy and medium-duty trucks.

Volvo Group and SSAB have entered into a collaboration agreement to research, develop, mass-produce, and commercialize the world's first vehicles made with both fossil-free and scrap-based near-zero-emission steel. Volvo Group is partnering with H2 Green Steel to source near-zero-emission steel for creation of a net-zero greenhouse gas value chain by 2040. Starting in 2026, Volvo will receive steel from H2 Green Steel's new plant in Boden, Sweden, where coal is replaced with green hydrogen, resulting in water and heat as the primary emissions. In 2024, Volvo Group and Westport Fuel Systems formed Cespira to commercialize HPDI fuel technology for long-haul and off-road applications, enabling compliance with Euro 7 and EPA standards using carbon-neutral and renewable fuels. Additionally, Volvo and Ovako launched Sweden's largest fossil-free hydrogen plant to support sustainable transportation solutions. Volvo Autonomous Solutions is partnering up with industry pioneer Aurora to develop and scale safe and efficient autonomous transport solutions with the Aurora Driver and Volvo's on-highway truck offering. The partnership's initial focus is a hub-to-hub applications for North America. Volvo Group and Samsung SDI have a strategic alliance to develop battery packs for Volvo Group's electric trucks. Working with Samsung SDI, Volvo Group aims to accelerate the speed of development, and strengthen the long-term capabilities and assets within electromobility across truck segments and markets.

Volvo Group is collaborating with SEEL to advance electromobility and develop a sustainable, competitive battery value chain in Sweden and Europe. The partnership will enhance knowledge-building and cooperation, with SEEL's testing facilities supporting energy storage, powertrain development, and safety-critical battery testing. Volvo Group has joined the Clean Energy Partnership, a cross-industry alliance promoting green mobility with hydrogen and fuel cells. Bringing together energy, automotive, and gas sectors, the partnership sets standards across transport modes to drive impact and reduce CO_2 emissions from road transportation. Electricity is a collaboration of Volvo to advance sustainable, electrified transport. Volvo also have societal partnerships with organizations such as the First Moves Coalition, the Alliance of CEO Climate leaders, the Road Freight Zero coalition, CALSTART's Drive to Zero Campaign etc.

In 2016, Volvo A60H, the world's largest articulated hauler was introduced. In the same year, Volvo CE introduced a range of futuristic concepts such as serial hybrid wheel loader, an autonomous battery electric load carrier and a cable electric excavator. In 2020, two electric compact machines, the ECR25 Electric and L25 Electric were introduced. In 2021, Volvo CE introduced Fuel Cell Test Lab to develop hydrogen fuel cell technology. Volvo CE leads sustainable change by disclosing industry's most extensive catalogue of Product Carbon Footprint (PCF) reports as part of the Life Cycle Assessment program. Volvo CE experts have developed a detailed in-house methodology to analyze the carbon footprint of every stage in a product's lifecycle, covering both traditional and electric machines. From raw material extraction to end-of-life recycling, it follows global ISO Life Cycle Assessment standards and the Greenhouse Gas Protocol.

Green Investments by Cummins Inc

Cummins is a leader in global power solutions. Cummins Inc's complementary business segments design, manufacture, distribute and service a broad portfolio of power solutions which include diesel, natural gas, electric and hybrid powertrains and powertrain related components. As of 2023, Cummins received fortune 500 ranking of 146. The Engine Segment manufactures and markets engines for trucks, buses, recreational vehicles, construction and farm equipment, mining, marine, rail etc. Power Systems manufacturers and markets standby and prime power generators and large industrial engines for use in mining, rail, marine and defense applications. The Component segment supplies products which complement the engine and power segments which include turbochargers and transmissions. Accelera segment manufactures and markets battery, fuel cell and electric powertrain technologies as well as electrolyzers which are critical to no carbon hydrogen production. Distribution segment sells, services and supports Cummins products through a worldwide network of wholly owned, joined venture and independent locations. Over one million Cummins engines were built in year 2020. The R& D expenditure in 2023 amounted to $1.4 billion. The company has filed 791 patents.

Cummins had been a leader in the commercial vehicles industry. Destination Zero is Cummin's customer-driven decarbonization strategy, combining advanced engine solutions with innovation in zero-emissions technology. This multi-solution approach addresses current needs while developing future sustainable solutions for diverse applications. Cummin's Destination Zero strategy aligns with PLANET 2050, Cummin's long term sustainability initiative to drive product decarbonization and growth. As part of its sustainability initiative in its core business, the company launched the industry's first fuel agnostic platform, the Cummins HELM™ to target higher efficiency, lower emissions and multiple fuels. This include the B, X10 and X15 engine platforms. The platform is supported by more than $1 billion investment across the company's U.S., engine manufacturing network. Included in the Cummins HELM™ platform is the X15N natural gas engine that now has more than 35,000 global production engines running outside North America.

The integrated powertrain is a key outcome of Cummins' acquisition of Meritor in August 2022. By combining technologies and expertise, Cummins-Meritor delivers solutions across combustion and electric applications worldwide. In 2023, the company achieved over $100 million in new global business, with growth spanning North America, South America, India, Europe, Australia (aftermarket), and China's off-highway sector.

Cummins have a joint venture with Daimler Trucks & Buses US Holding LLC, PACCAR and EVE Energy to accelerate and localize battery cell production and the battery supply chain in the U.S. Cummins have received ESG rating of AAA assigned by Morgan Stanley Capital International. Since 2014, Cummins have reduced greenhouse gas (GHG) emissions by 34 million metric tons and is on track to achieve reduction of 55 million metric tons by 2030.This would be equivalent of removing 245,000 new class 8 semitrucks off the highway for 12 months. Cummins have completed 24 onsite solar projects to enhance the use of renewable energy. The completed projects reduce over 14,486 metric tons of carbon dioxide equivalent annually. The company have 66 global sites with solar arrays. Cummins have a memorandum of understanding with Chevron to leverage complementary positioning in hydrogen, natural gas and other lower carbon fuel value chains. In 2021, Cummins introduced $13 million new global community program called Cummins Water Works to address global water crisis, improve water quality and access sanitation supplies. Cummins Water Works was formed in partnership with global non-profits such as the Nature Conservancy, Water.org and WaterAid. It has generated approximately 6.9 billion gallons in annual water benefits since its 2021 launch. The program has helped more than 1.2 million people. Cummins is featured on the S&P Dow Jones Sustainability Index. Cummins was ranked as one of the top 150 large public companies for environmental performance in JUST Capital's 2024 rankings of American's Most Just Companies.

Cummins introduced the B6.7H hydrogen engine, designed for agricultural tractors and machinery, delivering 290 hp. and 1200 Nm of peak torque. Additionally, Cummins and Versatile signed a letter of intent to integrate 15 L hydrogen engines into Versatile's equipment, driving the decarbonization of the agricultural industry. Cummins have partnered with the Eclipse Foundation, Microsoft, Bosch and other industry leaders to revolutionize an industry standard for telematics and the next generation of commercial vehicles. The acquisitions of Meritor and Siemens Commercial Vehicles strengthen Accelera's eMobility business, enhancing capabilities in batteries, e-axles, traction systems, auxiliary controls, and electric powertrain integration.

Cummin's joint venture with Daimler Trucks & Buses US Holding LCC and Amplify Cell Technologies aim to localize battery cell production for commercial electric vehicles and is expected to create more than 2000 US jobs. Cummins projects a $1 to $2.5 billion revenue decline in its diesel engine business as customers shift toward low-carbon and zero-emission technologies, depending on adoption rates.

Cummins is investing in zero-emission technologies, expecting rising demand to offset declining internal combustion engine sales, with $6–$13 billion in revenue from battery electric, hydrogen fuel cells, and electrolyzers by 2030.

By the end of 2021, Cummins produced 6200+ battery modules and deployed 2000+ hydrogen fuel cells, including for the world's first hydrogen-powered passenger train with Alstom. To support Accelera's growth, Cummins anticipates a $1.3 billion cash outflow from 2022–2027 for operations, R&D, production, and maintenance. Cummins have a 50:50 joint venture with Sinopec to form Cummins Enze in order to accelerate the affordability and availability of green hydrogen in China. Cummins also entered into an agreement with Sion Power Corporation to design and supply battery cells based on their proprietary lithium metal technology for commercial vehicle applications. Cummins also have partnership with energy major Iberdrola, to build the world's largest electrolyzer plants for the production of green hydrogen in Spain.

Over 75% of Cummins' inbound packaging is single use, generating 140 million pounds of annual waste. Reduction efforts cut only 10–14 million pounds per year. Additionally, packaging waste is directly linked to revenue growth, meaning increased production leads to higher waste levels, posing a significant sustainability challenge. Cummins plans a $122 million investment over 5 years to expand returnable packaging, aiming for 75% usage of domestic inbound materials, supported by tracking, logistics, and warehousing. The PLANET 2050 strategy have a 2030 goal to reduce absolute greenhouse gas (GHG) emissions from facilities and operations by 50%. In 2022, Cummins completed more than 183 projects reducing GHGs, investing approximately $18.2 million. As a result of these projects, the company achieved GHG savings of 18,256 metric tons of CO2e (Carbon dioxide equivalent). Cummins implemented 219 emission reduction initiatives in 2022, resulting in an estimated CO2e savings of 25,508 metric tons. Cummins plans a $122 million investment over 5 years to expand returnable packaging, aiming for 75% usage of domestic inbound materials, supported by tracking, logistics, and warehousing.

Automobile Segment

Green Investments by Toyota Motor Corporation

Toyota Motor Corporation is a Japanese multinational automotive manufacturer. It is the one of the largest automobile manufacturer in the world producing about ten million vehicles per year. Toyota's major business segments are automotive operations, financial services operations and other operations. Toyota's automotive operations include the design, manufacture, assembly and sale of passenger vehicles, minivans and commercial vehicles such as trucks and related parts and accessories. Toyota's financial services business consists primarily of providing financing to dealers and their customers for the purchase or lease of Toyota vehicles. Toyota's financial services business also provides mainly retail installment credit and leasing through the purchase of installment and lease contracts originated by Toyota dealers. Toyota sells its vehicles in approximately 200 countries and regions. Toyota's primary markets for its automobiles are Japan, North America, Europe and Asia.

Toyota offer over 100 passenger and commercial models. In 2024, Toyota had sales revenues of ¥45,095.3 billion and net income ¥5071.4 billion. Toyota is aiming to achieve carbon neutrality by the year 2050.Driven by CASE innovations (Connected, Autonomous, Shared, and Electric), the automotive industry is undergoing a once-in-a-century transformation. Embracing this shift, Toyota is evolving from a traditional automobile manufacturer into a mobility company.

Toyota is integrating Toyota Safety Sense across most passenger vehicles in Japan, the U.S., and Europe, featuring collision mitigation braking. Additionally, it is expanding Intelligent Clearance Sonar (ICS) to prevent pedal misapplication accidents and introducing a sudden acceleration suppression system for obstacle-free roads in future models. Toyota's ICS has reduced pedal misapplication accidents by 70%, while combining ICS with Toyota Safety Sense has lowered rear-end collisions by 90% in Japan. Since 1995, Toyota's Global Outstanding Assessment (GOA) has set stringent passive safety goals, continuously enhancing collision safety and passenger protection to improve real-world accident performance.

Toyota has sold a cumulative total of over 23.15 million electrified vehicles worldwide reducing 160 million tons of CO_2.Since 2022, it has introduced a full line up of electric vehicles such as dedicated-platform battery electric vehicles (BEVs) while promoting hybrid electric vehicles (HEVs), plug- in hybrid vehicles (PHEVs), and fuel cell electric vehicles (FCEVs) based on regional energy conditions.

Since the 1990s, Toyota's Mobility Teammate Concept has focused on fostering a collaborative relationship between people and vehicles, enhancing mutual communication and improvement. This philosophy drives Toyota's vision of safe, accessible mobility for all, including the elderly and physically challenged. Lexus Teammate embody this approach through advanced driving support technologies.

In 2020, Toyota unveiled the Connected City project, transforming its Higashi-Fuji Factory site into a real-world testbed for autonomous driving, MaaS, robotics, AI, smart homes, and personal mobility. In 2023, Toyota announced plans to introduce 10 BEV models and had a target to produce 1.5 million units by year 2026 in order to achieve carbon neutrality by year 2050. The company aims to release next generation BEVs by year 2026. Toyota achieved 100% renewable electricity introduction rate at all plants in Europe and South America and installed wind power generators at the Tahara Plant.

Toyota Motor Corporation (Toyota) has collectively named bonds whose proceeds are to be used for projects which contribute towards solving environmental and social issues as "Woven Planet Bonds". In 2021, Toyota has developed the Woven Planet Bond Framework to issue the sustainability bonds. Moody's ESG Solutions has provided the second party opinion for the framework with respect to alignment with Green Bond Principles (GBP) 2018, Social Bond Principles (SBP) 2020, and Sustainability Bond Guidelines (SBG) 2018 which are administered by the International Capital Market Association (ICMA). Toyota will allocate Woven Planet Bond proceeds to new or existing projects meeting Green or Social eligibility criteria, including projects financed up to 36 months before issuance. The eligible projects are related to safety technology, assisted mobility vehicles and clean transportation. The bond proceeds are also eligible for research and development, investments in property plant and equipment, manufacturing cost for the development/manufacturing of vehicle and components for Battery Electric Vehicle and components for Fuel Cell Vehicle (FCEV), renewable energy etc. The proceeds will be allocated within 24 months.

The total proceeds from the Woven Planet Bonds amounted to 308 billion yen of which 114.9 billion yen was allocated for safe mobility and mobility opportunities for vulnerable groups. An amount of 189 billion yen was allocated for reduction of vehicle CO2 emissions. Approximately 4.1 billion yen was apportioned for reduction of CO2 emissions from factories and offices. The proceeds of the issuance have been allocated to finance eligible projects within the fiscal year March 2022.

Table 13.1 shows the details of the total proceeds from the bond issuance.

Table 13.2 shows the impact of eligible social projects.

Green Investments by Ford Corporation

Ford Motor Company was incorporated in year 1919 to produce and sell automobiles designed and engineered by Henry Ford. Ford employs 177,000 people worldwide. The company sells automobiles and commercial vehicles under the Ford brand and luxury cars under its Lincoln brand. The company is listed on the New York Stock Exchange and is controlled by the Ford family. Ford Company conducts business through the segments-Ford Blue, Ford Model e, Ford Pro (previously represented by Automotive segment), Ford Next (previously the Mobility segment) and Ford Credit. Ford Blue primarily includes the sale of Ford and Lincoln internal combustion engine ("ICE") and hybrid vehicles, service parts, accessories, and digital services for retail customers. This segment focuses on developing Ford and Lincoln ICE and hybrid vehicles. Ford Model e primarily includes the sale of electric vehicles, service parts, accessories, and digital services for retail customers. This segment focuses on developing EV and digital vehicle technologies, as well as software development. Ford Pro primarily includes the sale of Ford and Lincoln vehicles, service parts, accessories, and services for commercial, government, and

Table 13.1 Woven Planet Bond details

Woven Planet Bond					
Item	Yen denominated bond		Dollar denominated bond		
Term	5 years	10 years	3 years	5 years	10 years
Amount of issue	50 billion yen	50 billion yen	500 million dollar	500 million dollar	500 million dollar
Cash in date	June 1 2023	June 12,023	July 13,2023	July 13, 2023	July 13, 2023
Maturity date	June 1 2028	June 1 2033	July 13,2026	July 13, 2028	July 13, 2033

Source: Woven Planet Bonds Report 2024

Table 13.2 Impact of social projects in year 2023

Number of vehicles produced with TSS (TOYOTA Safety Sense)	7,221,962
Number of vehicles sold with Advanced Park	122,347
Number of assisted mobility vehicles sold for the elderly and people with disabilities (Welcab) sold	10,337
Green projects	
Number of BEV sold	37,624
Number of FCEV	3440

Source: Woven Planet Bonds Report 2024

rental customers. Included in this segment are sales of all core Ford Pro vehicles, such as Super Duty and the Transit range of vans in North America and Europe and all sales of Ranger in Europe. The Ford Credit segment is comprised of the Ford Credit business on a consolidated basis, which is primarily vehicle related financing and leasing activities. Basically, the vehicle brands are Ford and Lincoln. In 2023, Ford Motor sold approximately 4413,000 vehicles at wholesale throughout the world. Ford Credit offers a wide variety of automotive financing products to and through automotive dealers throughout the world. The net income attributable to Ford Motor Company was $4347 million in 2023.

In 2024, Ford Motor published its 25th annual sustainability report and maintains its leadership position in sustainability reporting. In 2004, Ford launched the Escape Hybrid, the world's first hybrid SUV. In 2015, Ford developed the Ford Mobility Plan for advancing connectivity, mobility, self-driving vehicles and big data. In 2020, Ford had set target to be carbon neutral by no later than 2050. In 2020 Ford produced a new powered air purifying respirator and new ventilators. Ford contributed over $1.13 million to worldwide COVID relief. Ford also offered $ three million to community organizations. In 2007, Ford joined the United States Climate Action Partnership and UN Global Compact. In 2008, Ford launched Ford Mustang with the first soy foam-based seats and headrests. In 2009, Ford launched the EcoBoost engine which optimizes power and efficiency using turbocharging and direct gasoline injection. In 2011, Ford launched the full electric Focus EV. In 2016, Ford became a signatory to the UN Sustainable Development Goals (SDGs) and became the first OEM to join the Responsible Business Alliance (RBA). In 2021, Ford became the first automaker to use 100% recycled ocean plastics to produce automotive parts. In 2023, Ford generated revenues of $176 billion. In North America, Ford sell gas, hybrid and electric versions of its Flagship F-150 pickup truck all at high volumes.

During the period 2017–2023, Ford Motor had reduced its overall carbon foot print in both manufacturing and non-manufacturing sector by 47%. The US department of energy have acknowledged Ford achievement of sustained energy and greenhouse gas savings at 31 locations in the US. In 2024, the philanthropic arm, the Ford Fund have invested more than $73.7 million in charitable contribution across key areas of impact such as essential services, education of work, entrepreneurship and mobility. The company have invested $2 billion in the Cologne Electric Vehicle Center to make it carbon neutral. In 2021, Ford had made $11.4 billion planned investment in BlueOval City and BlueOval SK Battery Park. In 2021, Ford became the first American auto firm to introduce the Sustainable Financing framework to support the financing of clean transportation projects. Ford aims to use 20% recycled or renewable plastics in North America and Europe by 2025, 10% in China, and maximize aluminium recycling for sustainability.

Ford is proud to be one of the first U.S. automakers to align with the international community to limit global warming as part of the Paris Climate Agreement. Globally Ford aim to reach carbon neutrality no later than 2050.

Ford has achieved a 6% reduction in its Scope 3 GHG emissions per vehicle kilometre since 2019. In 2023, Ford was the number two EV brand and number 1

EV truck in the US. Ford also had the number one internal combustion engine vehicle and hybrid in the US. EcoBoost engines were deployed across nearly 100% of the portfolio for improved fuel economy. In 2023, Ford sold 270,000 hybrids globally. Ford had introduced lithium iron phosphate batteries on Mustang Mach E vehicles. In the year 2023, the company have sold 4.413 million wholesale vehicles globally. The number of EVs sold globally was 130,905.

In 2023, approximately 51 of Ford's global manufacturing operations used renewable electricity and 70.5% used carbon free electricity. Ford's manufacturing facilities in Europe, Mexico and Ohio had equivalent of 100% carbon free electric sourcing. Over 85% of Ford's vehicle parts and materials are recycled and reused at the end of the life. Ford established an interim target of 20% renewable and recycled plastics by 2025 in new vehicle designs for North America, Europe, Turkey, and 10% in China. Ford also had recovered up to 20 million of high strength, military grade, aluminum alloy per month through the closed loop recycling system to build F series. Ford used nine industry and world's first plant-based materials in its production vehicles since year 2000. In 2023, Ford facilities had sent approximately 16,300 metric tons of waste to landfill. Ford conducted RSC Global and Initiative for Responsible Mining Assurance (IRMA) EV Battery Material supply chain audits and supported suppliers to develop corrective action plans as needed. The company use 100% carbon free electricity in all manufacturing by year 2035. The company aims to eliminate single-use plastics from its operations by 2030. The interim goals are backed by science-based targets approved by the Science Based Target initiative (SBTi). The company have interim goals to reduce scope 1 and scope 2 GHG emissions from its operations by 76% by 2035 from a 2017 baseline. The company also aims to reduce scope 3 GHG emissions from the use of sold products by 50 per vehicle km by 2035 from a 2019 baseline. In 2021, Ford joined RouteZero, a global coalition, to sign the ZEV Declaration, pledging to work towards making sales of all new cars and vans zero-emissions by 2040 globally.

Ford has established a holistic Ford Credit Sustainable Financing Framework to obtain financing through green, social and sustainability transactions. These transactions include senior unsecured notes, securitizations, loans, commercial paper, retail deposits, convertible notes. The framework has been developed in alignment with the International Capital Market Association (ICMA) Green Bond Principles, the ICMA Social Bond Principles, the ICMA Sustainability Bond Guidelines and the Loan Market Association Green Loan Principles. An amount equal to the net proceeds from each sustainable financing will be used to finance ore refinance in whole or in part new or existing green or social projects, assets or activities undertaken by Ford. The eligible green categories include projects in clean transportation sector and clean manufacturing. This include renewable energy projects related to wind, solar, geothermal, hydropower and biomass. The other projects are related to water conservation and sustainable water management in industrial processes.

Ford has established a Sustainable Finance Committee (the "Committee") to oversee the project evaluation and selection process in order to ensure that selected projects comply with the eligibility criteria defined in the Use of Proceeds section of the sustainability framework. The Committee will be made up of senior leadership and other representatives from each of Ford's Treasury, Sustainability, Corporate Finance and Investor Relations.

In 2021, Ford issued $2.5 billion inaugural green bond, the largest non-financial corporate green bond to date. In 2022, Ford issued the second green bond issuance valued at $1.75 billion and released the inaugural sustainable financing report. During the period between January 1, 2021 and June 30, 2023, $4.21 billion, the total of the net proceeds of the first and second Green Bonds, were allocated. The total of the net proceeds of the two bonds had been fully allocated to the design, development and manufacture of the company's current EV lineup — the Mustang Mach-E, F-150 Lightning, and E-Transit — and EVs to be unveiled in the future, as well as other development activities. Ford also has over $17 billion in revolving corporate credit facilities, which include key sustainability metrics. During 2023, Ford announced a $5 million investment in mobility solutions for addressing transportation insecurity in Ford's hometown communities. Ford Motor Company is undertaking a $7 billion planned investment by Ford through the creation of BlueOval City as the largest ever one-time investment in electrification by an auto company in the US.

The top priority of Ford is to build an EV business with a highly competitive cost structure which balances growth and profitability. The company currently focusses on its first generation EVs consisting of Mustang Mach-E, F-150 Lightning and E-Transit. The Sustainable framework received highest advanced rating from second opinion provider VE of Moody. In 2022, Ford's Green Bond Issuance won the Green Debt Instruments Category award at the seventh Annual Climate Bond Awards.

On a combined basis, approximately 86% of the spending has been allocated to investments into specific products in Ford's EV lineup. Rest of the 14% have been allocated to development activities which benefitted the entire EV portfolio. These investments include the development of eDrive motors which would power its existing and future EV lineup and unique tech stack architecture which are required for electric vehicles. Ford has also allocated about $100 million of spending to Ion Park, the battery R&D Center in Michigan.

Table 13.3 shows the green bond issuance of Ford Motor Company.

Green Investments by General Motors Corporation

General Motors Company (GM) is an American multinational automotive manufacturing company headquartered in Detroit, United States. General Motors design, build and sell trucks, crossovers, cars and automobile parts and provide software enabled services and subscriptions worldwide. The Vehicles are developed, manufactured and/or marketed under the Buick, Cadillac, Chevrolet and GMC brands. Cruise is the global segment which is responsible for the development of autonomous vehicle technology. General Motors provide automotive financing services through the General Motors Financial Company.

Table 13.3 Green bond issuance

Issue	CUSIP	Issuance type	Currency	Notional	Coupon	Issue date	Maturity date
Ford Motor Company	345370DA5	Senior unsecured notes	USD	$2.5 billion	3.25%	Nov 12, 2021	Feb 12, 2032
Ford Motor Company	345370DB3	Senior unsecured notes	USD	$1.75 billion	6.10%	Aug 19, 2022	Aug 19, 2032

Source: Ford Sustainable Financing Report Nov 2023

General Motors have joined the ZEROgrid Initiative along with other leading companies and RMI to create a reliable and affordable grid. General Motors was named as the only original equipment manufacturer automaker on Ethisphere's World's Most Ethical Companies list consecutively for the fifth time. The company aims to achieve carbon neutrality in global products and operations by year 2040. The company aims to reduce Scope 1 and Scope 2 GHG emissions from its operations by 72% by 2035 against a 2018 baseline. The company aims to source 100% renewable electricity globally by year 2035. The company have the target goal of reducing Scope 3 GHG emissions from the use of sold products by 51% per vehicle kilometer by 2035 against a 2018 baseline.

General Motors aims to eliminate tailpipe emissions from new US light duty vehicles by year 2035. The company also have the target of reducing water intensity by 35% by 2035 against a 2010 baseline. General Motors aim to source 100% renewable electricity from US sites by end of 2025. GM aims to achieve approved Science Based Target initiative (SBTi) targets for operations and products.

The company aim to source 100% renewable electricity globally by 2035. The company aim to reduce Scope 1 and 2 GHG emissions from its operations by 72% against a 2018 baseline. The Company have membership of the First Movers Coalition which demonstrate commitments to low carbon steel, aluminum, concrete and cement. General Motors have implemented the Department of Energy's DOE 50001 Ready Program across its businesses. 50,001 is a voluntary global standard for energy management systems in industrial, commercial and institutional facilities. GM has received the ENERGY STAR Sustained Excellence Award for the past 12 years. General Motors have industry leadership in sustainable energy among all manufacturing companies as it is the leading buyer of renewable energy through power purchase agreements. The aim of the company is to reduce Scope 1 and Scope 2 GHG emissions from its operations by 72% by 2035 against a 2018 baseline. GM plan to achieve sales of 40–50% of annual US volumes of EVs by year 2030.

GM is building a diverse EV portfolio by leveraging the affordable Chevrolet Bolt models and the proprietary Ultium platform for next-generation electric vehicles. By end 2025, the company plans to increase capacity to build one million EVs annually in North America. In 2021, GM launched Ultium Charge 360, integrating charging networks, mobile apps, and services to streamline the EV charging experience for customers. The GM start-up BrightDrop helps decarbonize last-mile deliveries with electric products, software, and services, supporting major fleet customers in achieving efficiency and sustainability. In June 2022, Cruise became the first to operate a commercial driverless ride-hail service in a major U.S. city. GM Financial supports the growth of Cruise by extending a $5 billion line of credit which will be used to finance the purchase of Cruise Origins. GM participates in programs such as Responsible Business Alliance ("RBA"), Responsible Minerals Initiative ("RMI") and the Initiative for Responsible Mining Assurance ("IRMA").

General Motors is a founding member of the Clean Energy Buyers Alliance (CEBA), a business association of more than 400 energy customers and partners working towards deployment of market and policy solutions for a carbon free energy system. General Motors is also a part of Emissions First Partnership which promotes greenhouse gas accounting framework that prioritizes emissions impact and encourages actions which reduce carbon. General Motors joined the ZEROgrid Initiative in year 2023 to advance grid decarbonization, enhance reliability and develop a framework for impactful clean energy procurement and corporate engagement.

GM aims for carbon neutrality by year 2040 and eliminate tailpipe emissions from its new light duty vehicles by year 2035. For the period 2020–2025, GM have estimated to spend $35 billion in electric vehicles, fuel cells and autonomous vehicles which include capital, engineering expenses and other development costs.

The sustainable finance framework of GM has been developed in alignment with the Green Bond Principles 2021, Social Bond Principles, 2021, Sustainability Bond Guidelines 2021 and Green Loan Principles 2021. GM green eligibility criteria include investments (including equity investments in joint ventures) and expenditures for the design, development or manufacture of clean transportation technology. This includes zero emission vehicles, battery technology, battery storage and battery management system. Investments, capital, and operating expenditures related to new manufacturing facilities, upgrades and modifications to existing manufacturing facilities to produce clean transportation solutions are also included in the criteria. Projects related to clean transportation solutions which include new and upgraded manufacturing facilities, ICE-to-EV conversions, renewable energy, waste reduction, water efficiency, and R&D to enhance sustainability are eligible for green bond issuances. GM Social eligibility criteria is applicable for projects which strengthen communities by supporting diverse suppliers, dealerships, and workforce development through training, resources, loans, and economic opportunities for underrepresented groups.

GM Financial supports Clean Transportation adoption through loans, leases, and financing for zero-emission vehicles, future propulsion solutions, and clean transportation infrastructure, including charging equipment.GM have established a Sustainable Financing Council consisting of senior representatives from Treasury, Sustainability, Controllership, product development finance, investor relations and legal aspects.

The GM Financial Working Group will be responsible for tracking an internal register of the Eligible Assets allocated to the Eligible Portfolio, under the oversight of GM Financials' Global Asset-Liability Committee ("ALCO") of GM Financial. Moody's ESG provide a Second Party Opinion ("SPO") on the environmental and social benefits of GM Framework as well as the alignment with the Principles.

General Motors have made $2.25 billion of investment grade green bonds as part of its sustainable finance framework in year 2022. In 2023, over 39 million pounds of recycled plastics were used in General Motor vehicles.

Table 13.4 shows details of green investments made in North American manufacturing region.

General Motors engage with aluminium and steel suppliers to identify, develop and acquire lower GHG intensity materials and products. By 2030, General Motors aims for at least 10% of crude steel and primary aluminium used in U.S., Canada, and Mexico manufacturing to be near-zero emissions or low carbon, within a 20% price increase. General Motors also develops recycled textiles, targeting 50% recycled seat inserts and 100% recycled overhead fabrics, carpets, and mats. GM is developing plant-based leather alternatives, recycled polyester backing, and low-VOC silicone materials while co-developing Fine Mycelium™ with MycoWorks for durable, renewable, and premium interior materials. GM's CarBravo enhances the used-car buying experience with extensive inventory, online and dealership

Table 13.4 Green investments by general motors

Details	Amount
Build electric trucks and SUVs, Factory Zero Detroit Hamtramck Assembly Centre, Michigan	$2.2 billion
Renovation of Orion Assembly, Michigan to initiate production of new electric trucks	$ 4 billion
Assistance for future EV production, Pontiac Metal Center	$ 40 million
Production of Cadillac CELESTIQ, Global Technical Centre, Michigan	$ 81 million
New technology to prepare facility for EV readiness, Davison Road Processing Centre, Michigan	$100 million
Support future EV and ICE vehicle production, Marion Metal Centre, Indiana	$491 million
Support drive unit castings, Bedford Indiana	$51 million
Production of Cadillac LYRIQ, Spring Hill Manufacturing, Tennessee	$2 billion
New equipment installation to support electric motor production, Lockport Components, New York	$154 million
Battery pack cooling lines for EV products, Rochester Operations, New York	$56 million
Electric drive units for EVs, Toledo Propulsion Systems, Ohio	$760 million
Production of BrightDrop Zevo 600 and BrightDrop Zevo 400,CAMI Assembly, Ontario	$800 million
Production of electric drive units for EVs, St Catharines Propulsion Plant, Ontario, Canada	$500 million
New Paint shop, support for production to produce EVs, batteries and EV components, Ramos Arizpe Mexico	$ 1 billion

Source Sustainability Report, 2023

shopping, standard warranties, nationwide service, and flexible ownership benefits through GM's dealer network.

GM's Customer Care and Aftersales (CCA) remanufacturing program supports a circular economy by reducing raw material use and landfill waste through part reuse. In 2023, CCA sold over 700,000 remanufactured units, including engines and transmissions. Additionally, GM recycled 40 million pounds of non-remanufacturable parts like fascias and aluminum wheels. GM collaborates with recycling companies and the U.S. Advanced Battery Consortium to develop recycling and reuse solutions for new battery cells. GM has partnered with North American battery recyclers for years to dismantle and recycle EV batteries. In 2022, GM Ventures invested in Lithion, a Québec-based battery recycling company. Lithion's advanced technology enables efficient recovery of raw materials, supporting sustainable manufacturing and reducing environmental impact in GM's product development and operations.

GM's Global Purchasing and Supply Chain manages a vast supplier network, ensuring quality, affordability, and sustainability while enhancing competitiveness, mitigating risks, and optimizing efficiency. GM have spent approximately $105 billion for supply chain initiatives. About 87% of approximately 4000 supplier locations are third party certified to the IATF 16949 Quality Standard. In 2023, GM and POSCO Future M expanded their Ultium CAM Joint Venture, strengthening North America's EV battery supply chain to support 360,000 annual EV productions by 2025–2030.

In January 2023, GM invested $650 million in Lithium Americas to develop North America's largest lithium resource at Thacker Pass, securing battery raw materials. GM's GPSC Sustainability Team integrates sustainability into the supply chain, focusing on logistics, materials, and packaging while encouraging suppliers to set bold emissions reduction goals. GM's HYDROTEC fuel cells extend electrification to various industries. In 2024, GM and Honda began joint production, supporting trucks and SuperTruck 3 for reduced emissions and efficiency. GM is developing HYDROTEC solutions with Komatsu for mining trucks, Autocar for zero-emission vocational vehicles, Liebherr for aircraft power, and Nel Hydrogen for renewable hydrogen production.

Chevrolet, Cadillac, GMC and Buick brands are strategically building an EV portfolio in the luxury, SUV and truck segments. In 2021, GM began production at Factory ZERO, GM's first fully dedicated electric vehicle assembly plant. In January 2022, GM made announcement regarding conversion of assembly plant in Michigan to fully dedicated EV truck production plant.GM have allocated $2.24 billion of net proceeds from its inaugural green bond issuance to capital expenditure disbursements which occurred between August 1,2021 and March 31,2023.

Table 13.5 shows the issuance statistics of GM's bond issues.

Table 13.6 shows the allocation statistics of net proceeds.

Table 13.5 GM bond issuance

Issuer	CUSIP	Issuance Type	Currency	Net Proceeds $ million	Coupon	Issue Date	Maturity Date
General Motors Co	37045VAY6	Senior Unsecured Note	Dollar	$995	5.40%	08/02/2022	15/10/2029
General Motors Co	37045VAZ3	Senior Unsecured Note	Dollar	$1241	5.60%	08/02/2022	15/10/2032

Source: General Motors 2023 Sustainable Finance Report

Table 13.6 Allocation of net proceeds

ICMA Category Clean Transportation	Refinancing	Financing	Total
Allocation period	Aug 21-July 22	Aug 22-march 23	Aug 21-march 23
Proceed allocation to capital expenditure on electric vehicle manufacturing facilities ($ million)	$1018	$1218	$2236
Percent of net proceeds allocated	46%	54%	100%

Source: General Motors 2023, Sustainable Finance Report

Green Investments by Volvo Group

AB Volvo, the parent company of the Volvo Group, is a Swedish limited liability company, with its shares admitted to trading on Nasdaq Stockholm. Volvo employs 102,000 people with customers in 180 markets. In 2024, the net sales amounted to EUR 46 billion. The Volvo group was established in 1927. Volvo Group is the world's leading manufacturer of trucks, buses and construction equipment, marine and industrial engines. The Volvo Group sells majority of its products under the Volvo, Volvo Penta, Rokbak, Renault Trucks, Prevost, Nova Bus and Mack brands. The company also have ownership in SDLG, Milence, Eicher, Dongfeng, cellcentric, Flexis and Cespira among other companies. Volvo Group operates manufacturing and assembly plants in 17 countries on 5 continents. Volvo Group's supply network is made up of more than 50,000 suppliers globally. During the past 10 years, the company have manufactured 2.1 million trucks and 70,000 buses. Volvo have produced over 700,000 construction equipment over the past 10 years. By end of 2024, Volvo Trucks had delivered 4991 electric trucks to customers in 46 countries since the launch of its first electric trucks in year 2019. These trucks have driven more than 141 million kilometres or 3535 laps around the world.

Volvo Group is a leading force towards the electrification of the transportation, mobility and equipment sectors. The Volvo Group has developed a strategy to address range of sustainability issues. Volvo Group conducted a double materiality assessment (DMA) to evaluate the impacts and risks. The Volvo Group has included sustainability targets in its incentive program since 2022. The company aim to achieve net zero greenhouse gas emissions by 2040. Volvo focusses on a three-pronged approach for the decarbonization of the product offer and customers' fleets of vehicles and machines. The main long-term solutions to decarbonization are electrification in combination with the adoption of other low emission technologies. This include battery electric, fuel cell electric and internal combustion engines which are running on lower carbon fuels such as green hydrogen, biogas and HVO. The total investments in R&D amounted to SEK 31.9 billion in year 2024.The total GHG emission from own operations were 30% lower in 2024 compared to 2019.

In 2021, a complete range of electric Volvo trucks were launched. In the same year Volvo Group and SSAB unveiled the world's first vehicle created using fossil free steel. In 2022 serial production of Volvo's heavy-duty electric trucks began. Approximately 35% of all vehicles sold by Volvo Group will be electrical by year 2030.Volvo Dynamic Steering has helped prevent accidents and made truck drivers' day-to-day work safer.

Volvo Group has launched a Green Finance Framework for financing of investments and projects in the area of clean transportation. This framework is classified as Dark Green by the Center for International Climate and Environmental Research. Volvo Group's green financing is a way for the Volvo Group to connect its sustainable transport product and solution strategy with its funding strategy. Volvo Group has implemented its code of conduct which are based on international conventions and standards such as the OECD Guidelines for Multinational Enterprises, the International Bill of Human Rights and the International Labour Organization's fundamental principles and rights at work. The Volvo Group participated in the WWF Climate Savers program 2010–2020.

The Volvo Group has committed to the Science-Based Targets initiative (SBTi) call for action campaign Business Ambition for 1.5 °C. The campaign requires greenhouse gas emissions to be net-zero across the Group's value chain by 2050. As part of climate initiatives, Volvo Group focus on three main technologies. Volvo focusses on the introduction of battery electric technology to enable zero tailpipe emissions. Bus segment accounts for major part of adoption of battery electric technology. Volvo also focusses on development of fuel cell technology for heavy transports which enable zero tailpipe emissions for transport segments where battery electric solutions are not suitable. Volvo also focusses on more efficient combustion technology in combination with lower carbon fuels.

Green financing is a way for the Volvo Group to connect its sustainable transport product and solutions strategy with its funding strategy. The structure of the green finance framework is in line with the key pillars of the ICMA Green Bond Principles, LMA and APLMA Green Loan Principles. Eligible categories and asset description of clean transportation include the development, production and customer finance of vehicles, machines and engines with zero tailpipe emissions such as battery electric vehicles and fuel cell electric vehicles. Investments in clean transportation falls into three categories such as GBP & GLP Category and Eligible Assets. For R&D, capital and operating expenditure are considered as eligible assets. For production, capital expenditure for sourcing, tooling, testing concepts, manufacturing, production processes and production facilities are considered as eligible assets. Customer finance for zero tailpipe emission battery electric and fuel cell electric vehicles, machines and engines are considered as eligible assets.

The Volvo Group has established a Green Finance Committee ("GFC") to evaluate and select Eligible Assets and to allocate Green Financing to such assets and to make sure they align with the EU Taxonomy. The Green Finance Committee will also evaluate potential environmental and societal risk as identified in Volvo Groups sustainability policy. The Green Finance Committee consists of senior representatives from Group Finance; Group Trucks Technology; Corporate Responsibility; Corporate Legal and The Group's Environmental Director. All green customer finance loans will be identified electronically in the Volvo Group's internal systems.

Nissan's Green Investments

Nissan Motor Company was founded as a full-fledged automaker which manufacture competitive, high quality low priced domestic cars. In 2023, the net sales of Nissan amounted to 12,685 billion yen.

In 2002, the Nissan Green Program was introduced to address environmental issues. In 2023, Nissan launched the fifth generation, Nissan Green Program 2030 along with the Nissan Social Program 2030. In November 2021, Nissan introduced Nissan Ambition 2030 with the Nissan NEXT business transformation plan to achieve sustainable goals. By fiscal 2030, Nissan aim to introduce a total of 34 electric vehicles and increase model mix of electrified vehicles to over 60% globally. By 2026, Nissan aims for an investment in electrification amounting to Yen 2 trillion. By fiscal 2027, Nissan aim to introduce next generation ProPILOT with door to door autonomous driving technology. Nissan is advancing the in-house development of all solid-state batteries (ASSBs) to enhance EV safety, efficiency and affordability. The aim is to introduce Nissan EVs powered by ASSBs to the market by fiscal 2028.Nissan plan to introduce new mobility services including an on demand automated vehicle dispatch service by fiscal 2027. Nissan's exclusive EV production hub, EV36Zero aim to expand in key regions.

Nissan's exclusive EV production hub, EV36Zero, will be expanded to key regions, including Japan, China, and the United States.4R Energy is a joint venture between Nissan and Sumitomo to develop end of life solutions for electric vehicle batteries. The joint venture focuses on initiatives for reuse, refabrication, resale and recycle of lithium-ion batteries.

Nissan is developing a distributed energy model to enhance EV appeal and support grid stability. Building on its Blue Switch program, the company launched Nissan Energy Share in 2024, enabling EVs to supply power to homes and communities. By Fiscal 2026, Nissan aims to introduce 16 electrified models such as battery electric vehicles (BEVs), e-POWER system vehicles and plug-in hybrid electric vehicles and 14 new ICE models. During the period 2024–2030, Nissan aim to introduce 34 EV models which would cover all market segments. The global electric vehicle model mix is expected to increase to 40% in fiscal 2026 and 60% by fiscal 2030. In 2024, Nissan had 1.2 million e-POWER vehicle sales. Nissan plan to invest more than Yen 400 billion in battery facilities. Nissan will manage R&D investments and Capex to maintain in the range of 7–8% of net revenue.

In 2023, Nissan launched the fifth generation NGP2030. NGP2030 is a concrete action plan for implementing the environmental aspects of Nissan Ambition 2030. In 2021, Nissan announced its goal of achieving carbon neutrality across the entire life cycle of its products by 2050.Under the Nissan Green Program 2030(NGP2030), Nissan had set its first lifecycle carbon dioxide reduction target.

Nissan has formulated the Nissan Social Program 2030 (NSP2030). As part of NSP2030, Nissan advances initiatives in six key areas of safety, quality, intellectual property, responsible sourcing, community engagement, and employee empowerment which are guided by materiality assessments.

Nissan sustainable finance framework received Moody's second part opinion and were aligned with Green Bond Principle 2021, Social Bond Principle 2023, Sustainability Bond Principle 2021, Green Loan Principle 2021 and Social Loan Principle 2023. The funds raised under Nissan's Sustainable Finance Framework were first represented by the "Sakura" bonds issued in November 2022. The second tranche of funds, issued in January and February 2023 for both institutional and retail investors, was fully allocated to four eligible green and sustainability projects as defined in the framework. These include development and production of electrified vehicles and batteries as well as technology development and infrastructure development for the creation of the EV ecosystems and smart cities and the development of safer and more sustainable mobility.

During March 2024, Nissan have completed its procurement of funds through the issuance of green bonds worth 10 billion yen for domestic institutional investors. The green bonds represent the first issuance of fundraising for finance sales group of Nissan following the adoption of sustainable finance framework by Nissan. They will be utilized as capital for sales finance receivables for zero emission vehicles thereby facilitating the development of Nissan group's EV through sales finance operations. Nissan Motor Co Ltd. developed its Sustainable Finance Framework in July 2022 and has issued sustainability bonds to the amount of 200 billion yen in January and February 2023.

Table 13.7 shows the summary statistics of sustainability bonds.

100 billion yen of the net proceeds from the issuance have been allocated to existing eligible projects in the fiscal year ended March 2021, March 2022, and March 2023. 100 billion yen of the net proceeds from the issuance have been allocated to new eligible projects between April 2023 to June 2023.

Tables 13.8 and 13.9 show the allocation of proceeds.

The total green allocation amounted to 168 billion yen.

The sustainability total amounted to 32 billion yen. Nissan have been a member of UN Global Impact.

Table 13.7 Summary of sustainability bonds

Issue	66 unsecured bonds (with inter-bond pari passu clause) (sustainability bonds) Nickname: Sakura Bond	#67 unsecured bonds (with specific inter-bond pari passu clause) (sustainability bonds)	#68 unsecured bonds (with specific inter-bond pari passu clause) (sustainability bonds)
Investor	Retail	Wholesale	Wholsesale
Payment date	February 6, 2023	January 27, 2023	January 27, 2023
Redemption date	January 20, 2026	January 20, 2026	January 20, 2028
Total issue amount	140 billion yen	50 billion yen	10 billion yen

Source: Nissan Sustainability Bonds Report 2024

Table 13.8 Eligible Green Projects for Nissan

Eligibility categories	Eligibility criteria	Allocated amount
Clean transportation	Research & development, investments and expenditures for the design, development, and manufacturing of zero emission vehicles and components	164 billion yen
Scope 1 and 2 CO2 emission reduction	Expenditures related to the purchase of renewable energy	4 billion yen

Source: Nissan Sustainability Bonds Report 2024

Table 13.9 Eligible sustainability (Green/Social) projects for Nissan

Eligibility categories	Eligibility criteria	Allocated amount
Installation of basic infrastructure toward the realization of an EV society	Clean transportation (research & development and investments and expenditures for BEV charging ports)	2 billion yen
Autonomous driving technologies	Autonomous driving technologies (research & development for Nissan's ProPILOT1, new technology to enhance collision avoidance with next generation LiDAR or other future technologies toward zero fatalities from traffic accidents)	28 billion yen
Mobility as a Service (MaaS)	Research & development, investments and expenditures related to services using zero-emission and low carbon vehicles and the services in specified area where access to public transport is limited, such as depopulated and devastated areas.	2 billion yen

Green Finance Investments- Honda Motor Co, Ltd

Honda Motor Co, Ltd. is a Japanese multinational conglomerate automotive manufacturer headquartered in Japan. Honda has been the world's largest motorcycle manufacturer since 1959. Honda has been the world's largest manufacturer of internal combustion engines with production of more than 14 million internal combustion engines each year.

Honda is the world's largest manufacturer of power units, with combined annual production volume of 30 million units of motorcycles, automobiles, power products, outboard motors and aircraft.

The Honda Philosophy encompasses Fundamental Beliefs—such as "Respect for the Individual" and "The Three Joys"—along with the Company Principle and Management Policies. These core values are shared across all Honda Group companies and their associates, guiding corporate management, business activities, and individual decision-making.

In December 2023, Honda was selected for the seventh consecutive year as a component of the Dow Jones Sustainability World Index after being ranked within the top four in the global automobile sector in the annual review of the Dow Jones Sustainability Indices (DJSI).

The DJSI are investment indices run by U.S.-based S&P Dow Jones Indices LLC. Honda has been recognized as a "Top 10%" company in the 2024 Sustainability Yearbook by S&P Global Inc. In February 2024, Honda was selected by CDP, an international non-profit environmental information disclosure organization, as a "A-List" company in the area of climate change for 2023. Honda's existing global vehicle assembly and product assembly plants have acquired ISO 14001, an international certification for environmental management systems. Honda aims to achieve "zero" industrial water intake and industrial waste by 2050.

Honda has set the target of electrifying 15% of motorcycles, 30% of automobiles and 36% of power products respectively in 2030. Emissions from the use of products account for approximately 80% of carbon dioxide. On account of certification of products which were launched in 2024, 18 motorcycle models, 36 automobile models and 3 power products models were HEPS certified.

Honda was the world's first automaker to comply with the US Clean Air Act through the development of low pollution CVCC engine which successfully reduced carbon monoxide, hydrocarbon and nitrogen oxide emissions. Honda Environmental and Safety Vision was established in year 2011. In 2024, the application rate of Honda SENSING in emerging countries was 60%. Honda aims to roll out HONDA SENSING 360 to all automobile models by year 2030. For motorcycles, Honda focusses to equip more models with its advanced braking systems such as ABS and CBS with high visibility for both riders and other road users. Honda aims to achieve carbon neutrality by year 2050 and is working to apply and deploy fuel cell systems as one of the technologies to achieve the goal of carbon neutrality. In Japan, Honda is collaborating with Isuzu Motors Ltd. to develop fuel cells for heavy duty trucks and to establish basic technology platforms such as vehicle control. Honda North

America Inc., Honda's U.S. subsidiary, participates in working groups established by the Automotive Industry Action Group (AIAG) to strengthen sustainability in the supply chain.

Honda will develop the eMaaS concept to enhance mobility freedom and promote renewable energy use. The initiative focuses on three key areas: expanding the use of Honda Mobile Power Packs, utilizing large-capacity batteries for electrified vehicles, and advancing fuel cell system applications.

Honda aims to lower costs and advance a hydrogen society by expanding its fuel cell vehicle (FCV) lineup and utilizing fuel cell systems in commercial trucks, stationary power sources, and mobile applications.

Honda targets a 1.8% annual waste reduction per unit of production (vs. FY2019) across all corporate activities, aiming for sustainable waste management by FY2031. Honda has developed the sustainable finance framework and had obtained second party opinion from Vigeo Eiris. The framework is aligned with the Green Bond Principles 2021, the Social Bond Principles 2021, the Sustainability Bond Guidelines 2021 as administered by the International Capital Market Association. Honda will aim for zero traffic collision fatalities involving Honda motorcycles and automobiles globally by year 2050. Honda plans to develop Honda Mobile Power Pack, swappable batteries and expand the utilization of renewable energy by enabling infrastructure linked smart power operations for recharging.

Honda will allocate an amount equal to the net proceeds from the issuance of green bonds, social bonds, sustainability bonds, to new projects that meet at least one of the Eligibility Criteria. In Clean Transportation category, the eligible criteria include investments including R&D in electric automobiles and electric motorcycles. The investments are for the development and manufacturing of vehicles and components including batteries for zero emission vehicles. Investments can also be made for recharging facilities for electrical automobiles and electric motorcycles. Under environment friendly production technologies and processes, the eligibility criteria include investments and other related expenditures for the promotion of reuse and recycling of used vehicle parts such as batteries and bumpers. In sustainable water management category, eligibility criteria consist of investments and other related expenditures for conservation of water resources. Investments and other related expenditures are also eligible for the development and manufacturing of advanced safety and driver assistance systems and automated driving technologies for the realization of zero traffic collision fatalities and provisions of various means for vulnerable groups.

The eligibility criteria for eligible projects are decided by departments such as finance, sustainability planning, environment, safety, accounting and other departments.

In 2022, Honda issued US dollar denominated green bonds totalling US$ 2.75 billion for environmental initiatives. Honda Motor have issued US$ 1000 million senior notes due 2025, US$1000 million senior notes due 2027 and US$ 750 million senior notes due 2032.

Table 13.10 shows green bond issues as of year 2024.

Table 13.11 highlights the allocation for green bonds.

Table 13.10 Green bond Issues

Description	Issue date	Maturity date	Amount issued (USD)	Maturity in years	Interest rate
USD-denominated Green Bond Due 2025(Unsecured Straight Bond)	March10,2022	March 10,2025	1000	3	2.271% per annum
USD-denominated Green Bond Due 2027(Unsecured Straight Bond	March10,2022	March 10,2027	1000	5	2.534% per annum
USD-denominated Green Bond Due 2032(Unsecured Straight Bond)	March 10,2022	March 10, 2032	750	10	2.967% per annum

Source: Honda Motor Co., Ltd Green Bond Report 2024

Table 13.11 Allocation for Green bonds

Section	Amount in billion yen
Proceeds raised	317.4
Balance as of April 1,2023	199
Proceeds used (FY2024)	199
New projects	199

Source: Honda Motor Co., Ltd. Green Bond Report 2024

Green Investments by Volkswagen

The Volkswagen Group is one of the leading multi brand groups in the automotive industry. Volkswagen Group consists of two divisions-the Automotive Division and the Financial Services Division. The automotive division comprises passenger cars, commercial vehicles and power engineering business areas. The activities of the automotive division comprise development of vehicles, engines and motors, vehicle software and batteries, the production and sale of passenger cars, light commercial vehicles, trucks, buses and motorcycles. Volkswagen delivered nine million vehicles in year 2024. The annual turnover for Volkswagen amounted to Euro 325 billion in 2024.

Decarbonization is a key element of the new auto strategy of Volkswagen Group. The new auto strategy of Volkswagen has established clearly defined Group initiatives across the brand groups with focus on central technology platforms such as "Architecture", "Software", "Battery, Charging & Energy", and "Volkswagen Group Mobility". By year 2030, Volkswagen Group aims to reduce its passenger cars' and light commercial vehicles' production-related CO_2 emissions by 50%. By 2030, the Group aim to reduce 30% less CO_2 on average per vehicle over the entire life cycle than in 2018.Volkswagen have the target to reduce greenhouse gas emissions in production by 50.4% in absolute terms compared to year 2018 by 2030. The top priority goal of Volkswagen is to implement measures to avoid or reduce carbondioxide emissions. The next efforts focus on gradually transitioning the energy supply across the value chain to renewable sources. The unavoidable CO2 emissions are offset through high-standard climate protection projects, such as voluntary carbon offsetting for net carbon-neutral delivery of electric vehicles. The company already operate eight production sites on a net carbon neutral basis. By 2026, Volkswagen plan to invest around €52 billion in electric mobility across the Group. The Group also increased the planned shares of electric vehicles in the core markets of EU, the US and China. The new electric vehicles are manufactured at eight sites in Europe, China and the US. By 2023 all EU sites are to be supplied with 100% electricity from renewable sources. By 2030, the same target is planned for global sites outside China. Volkswagen had the goal of generating 1.2 million MWh of power from renewable energies by 2030. The Volkswagen Group is the first automotive manufacturer to support the expansion of renewable energy on an industrial scale. New wind farms and solar parks are being constructed in several regions of Europe.For example, Volkswagen supported the construction of a solar plant with a total capacity of 170 million kWh per year. Volkswagen, in partnership with other OEMs, established the joint venture IONITY, which had deployed 430 fast-charging stations on major European highways by 2022. By 2025, the Group and its partners aim to operate around 18,000 public fast-charging points across Europe. BP aims to construct around 8000 fast-charging points across Europe together with Volkswagen. In North America, Volkswagen's Electrify America's charging infrastructure is to be doubled to more than 1800 locations and expanded by 10,000 fast chargers by 2026. In China, Volkswagen is planning a total of 17,000 fast-charging points by 2025 through the CAMS joint venture. By 2025, Volkswagen and its partners aim to establish around 45,000 fast-charging points across Europe, China, and the USA, with Volkswagen investing approximately €400 million in the European program. Volkswagen intends to develop the electric vehicle as a mobile power bank, thus helping electric vehicles to become an active part of the energy system in the future as storage devices. In 2022, Volkswagen became the first automotive manufacturer to join the LEAF Coalition (Lowering Emissions by Accelerating Forest finance). The Volkswagen Group was among the first automobile manufacturers to commit itself to the goals of the Paris Agreement. By 2030, Volkswagen aims for fully electric vehicles to account for 70% of sales in Europe and over 50% in North America and China.

Volkswagen AG is a participant in the UN Global Compact. In 2022, Volkswagen had issued €3.5 billion in green bonds based on the new Green Finance framework. Since 2020, the Volkswagen Group has issued a total of €10.5 billion in green bonds to refinance capital expenditure for all-electric vehicles (BEVs). The funds raised under the Green Finance Framework are specifically used to refinance environmentally friendly projects such as e-mobility which satisfies the clean transportation category of the Green Bond Principles of the International Capital Market Association. During the period 2022–2026, the shift from a carmaker to a software driven mobility provider requires massive investments amounting to an estimated €89 billion. In 2021, the EU taxonomy aligned capital expenditures for the manufacturing of low carbon technologies for transport amounted to €14.2 billion. In

2021, EU taxonomy aligned capital expenditures for the 'manufacturing of low-carbon technologies for transport' amounted to €14.2 billion.

In 2024, the share of BEVs in Volkswagen Group was 8.3% and the global share was expected to reach 50% by 2030. Through Man Energy Solutions, Volkswagen offer technologies which play a key role in the decarbonization of critical industries. Since 2023 Volkswagen has been investing in decarbonization efforts both internally and externally through a venture capital fund. With an initial investment of USD 300 million, the fund aims to accelerate the development of innovative decarbonization technologies. By 2030, the Volkswagen Group aims to finance at least 30% of its outstanding bond volume through green bonds with the aim to increase it to 50% by 2040. For the achievement of this target, the majority of the annual euro annual bond issues are already structured as green bonds or comply with the EU taxonomy classification system. The funds raised under the green finance framework are specifically used to refinance environmentally friendly projects such as e-mobility. Volkswagen have plans to invest EUR 52 billion in electric mobility by 2026 and offer 75 fully battery electric car models worldwide by year 2029. Volkswagen expects to increase its share of electric vehicles in the core markets of EU, China and US to more than 50% by the year 2030.Volkswagen have established a green finance committee which consists of fixed senior management representatives from the Group's treasury, sustainability, accounting, controlling and legal department.

References

Association Climate Review 2023, Volkswagen Group.
Business Impact Report, John Deere 2024.
Caterpillar Sustainability Report.
Caterpillar TCFD Report.
Cummins Inc. – Climate Change 2023 CDP Climate Report.
Cummins Sustainability Progress Report 2023–2024.
Ford, Integrated Sustainability and Financial Report, 2024, sustainabilityford.com
Ford and Ford Credit Sustainable Financing Framework June 2021.
Ford Sustainable Financing Report 2023.
General Motors 2022 Sustainable Finance Framework.
General Motors Sustainability Report 2023.
Honda ESG Data Book 2024.
Honda Motor Co, Sustainable Finance Framework, 2022.
Honda Motor Co., Ltd Green Bond Report.
https://corporate.ford.com/social-impact/sustainability.html
https://economictimes.indiatimes.com/tech/funding/caterpillar-invests-in-tech-startup-nth-cycle-to-boost-recycling/articleshow/105742154.cms?utm_source=contentofinterest&utm_medium=text&utm_campaign=cppst
https://www.hitachicm.com/global/en/sustainability/sustainable-finance/green-bond/
https://www.komatsu.jp/en/sustainability
https://www.volvoce.com/
Integrated Report 2024, Sustainability.

Komatsu Green bond reporting 2022.
Komatsu Report 2024.
Nissan Motor Corporation, Integrated Report 2024.
Nissan Sustainability Bonds Report 2024.
Sustainable Financing Report 2023.
Toyota, Woven Planet Bonds Report Jan 2024.
Toyota Integrated Report 2024.
Toyota Motor Corporation Woven Planet Bond Framework, May 2023.
Volkswagen Group-Green Finance Framework 2022.
Volvo Group Integrated Annual Report 2023.

Chapter 14
Case Study Sustainable Finance in Energy Sector

Saudi Aramco's Green Investments

Aramco is one of the world's largest integrated energy and chemicals companies in the world. Aramco and its affiliate, S-Oil had initiated the $ 7 billion Shaheen project in South Korea to develop one of the world's largest refinery integrated petrochemical stream crackers. In 2023, the total capital expenditures amounted to $42 billion and net cash amounted to $27 billion.

Aramco had completed the $2.76 billion acquisition of Valvoline Inc.'s global products business. Aramco entered the global LNG business through a definitive agreement to acquire a minority stake in MidOcean which would enable Aramco to tap into international LNG opportunities. Aramco's liquids to chemicals strategy focusses on a $3.4 billion deal to increase its presence in China. In MENA region, Aramco, TotalEnergies and SABIC had converted oil derived from plastic waste into International Sustainability and Carbon Certification (ISCC+) certified circular polymers. Through Aramco and Stellantis collaboration, Aramco provided synthetic fuel compatible with 24 engine families in Europe. Saudi Aramco entered into a shareholder agreement to develop two photovoltaic solar projects in Al Shuaibah with a planned combined capacity of 2.7 GW. Aramco and ENOWA developed first of its kind synthetic fuel demonstration plant. Aramco aims to provide affordable, reliable energy with low upstream carbon intensity while targeting net-zero Scope 1 and 2 emissions across wholly-owned operations by 2050. Saudi Aramco played a key role in Oil and Gas Decarbonization Charter, a global industry charter established at COP28 and signed by more than 50 oil and natural gas companies. Aramco is the largest buyer of carbon credits in the Regional Voluntary Carbon Market Company's second auction in Nairobi, Kenya during June 2023.Aramco achieved 100% ISO 14001 certification at 52 upstream and downstream asset-based organizations enrolled in Aramco' Environmental Management System (EMS). In 2023, Aramco continued upgrading Sulfur Recovery Units (SRU) with tail gas treatment

B. R. Kumar, *Green Finance*, Sustainable Finance,
https://doi.org/10.1007/978-3-032-03333-8_14

units. Aramco had planted approximately 6.5 million mangroves and an additional 1.1. million native trees. In 2023, Aramco have made social investments of $475 million in Saudi Arabia and abroad.

Aramco aims to achieve net zero scope 1 and scope 2 GHG emissions across wholly owned operating assets by year 2050. Aramco's Hawiyah carbon capture utilization and storage pilot have the capacity to capture 800,000 tons CO_2 per annum. In 2017, Aramco installed Aramco's first wind turbine at the Turaif Bulk Plant. In 2019, Aramco inaugurated Saudi's first hydrogen fueling station. In 2020, Aramco shipped world's first Blue ammonia. Aramco aims to achieve net positive biodiversity by expanding work in over 985 km2 of protected areas. To address climate challenges, Aramco established a new $ 1.5 billion Sustainability Fund to invest in technologies to address climate challenges. Aramco signed an agreement to construct one of the world's largest planned carbon capture and storage hubs. Aramco was granted the first certification for blue ammonia and blue hydrogen for SASREF/SABIC AN. In 2023, Aramco set targets to invest in the Al Shuaibah 1 and Al Shuaibah 2 photovoltaic solar projects which are expected to have a combined capacity of 2.7 GW. For circular economy, Aramco, Total Energies and SABIC completed MENA region's first processing of oil from plastic waste at scale to make certified circular polymers.

Aramco has more than doubled funding for its global venture capital arm, adding $4 billion. Half of this amount is allocated to Aramco Ventures for investing in late-stage sustainability and digital ventures. In 2023, an integrated steel plate manufacturing complex was established in Ras al Khair Industrial City.

Aramco and King Abdullah University piloted a carbon sequestration method using situ mineralization, converting CO2 into carbonate rocks, enhancing efficiency, and reducing costs through innovative technologies. Approximately 63% of R&D spend for Aramco is attributed towards sustainability issues.

By 2035, Aramco aims to reduce its carbon intensity by 15% against the 2018 baseline. In 2023, Aramco established the new Energies organization to achieve low carbon solutions and meet its GHG emissions. For the next 10 years, Aramco have allocated 10% of its capital investments in New Energies. Launched in 1975, the Master Gas System is one of Aramco's largest projects, playing a key role in transforming the Kingdom's energy mix. By utilizing produced gas instead of flaring, it has helped avoid approximately 100 million metric tons of CO2 equivalent emissions annually. Aramco have deployed an array of digital solutions to optimize energy efficiency which include technologies of Fourth Industrial Revolution(4IR) such as cloud computing, AI and Big Data. The Leak Detection and Repair (LDAR) is a robust program aimed at proactively monitoring and repairing methane leaks. The carbon intensity of upstream operations of Aramco is among the lowest relative to major crude oil producers per barrel of oil equivalent. Aramco has a target to invest in up to 12 GW of solar and wind energy by year 2030. Aramco continues to assess opportunities to expand in mangrove planting within the Kingdom. Since 2000, Aramco have improved its energy management performance by 13.4%. Aramco's jet fuel production in Saudi Arabia has a lower carbon intensity (CI) than conventional jet fuel. Aramco is involved in the development of hydrogen market. The Open Hydrogen Initiative, led by GTI Energy and partners, develops open-source tools to measure hydrogen production's carbon intensity, supporting transparent and reliable hydrogen markets. Aramco, alongside 40 plus organizations from industry, academia, NGOs, and government, is developing a unique framework to reduce carbon emissions and support a transparent, credible, and unified hydrogen market. The Saudi government has introduced a National Renewable Energy Program in year 2016. Aramco plays a pivotal role in energy transition through the company's gas expansion plans and equity participation in Public Investment Fund's renewable energy transition. Aramco received the World Economic Forum Global Lighthouse Network recognition under WEF's Shaping the Future of Advanced Manufacturing and Production Platform.

Aramco has established a Digital Sustainability Flagship Program to streamline all the digital efforts across the company related to climate and sustainability. Strategic technologies are developed to enable emissions mitigation or displacement which include renewables and energy storage, hydrogen production technologies, non-metallic applications development, thermal crude to chemicals deployment and lower carbon fuels. Aramco is a member of OGCI which contribute financially to Climate Investment.

In 2023, sustainability related R&D amounted to $540 million. In 2023, 20% of new patents filed were in sustainability technologies. The ongoing R&D initiatives include CO2 mineralization to calcium and magnesium, carbonates which utilize cement and steel waste materials. Initiatives such as Power Sense conserves and reduces energy by measuring the amount of electrical flow of each component at the rig.

Table 14.1 shows the R&D spend in millions of dollars.

Table 14.1 R&D Spend in million dollars

R&D focus area	2022	2023
CCS	41.5	40
Renewable energy	6.4	7.5
Energy efficiency	64.8	71
Waste management & recycling	32.3	16.3
Water management	32.2	50.1
Gas treatment	40.5	42.8
Lower-carbon hydrogen production	26.4	57.8
Sustainable mobility	136.6	208.9
Crude-to-chemicals	30.3	16.4
Nonmetallic applications	24.2	29.6
Total R&D for sustainability technologies	435	540
Total Aramco R&D	737	861
Percent of sustainability-related R&D	59%	63%

Source: ARAMCO I Sustainability Report 2023

Aramco uses market mechanisms to address climate change and sustainable development. In 2023, Aramco retired approximately 500,000 carbon credits. The use of carbon offsets is a significant part of Aramco's net zero planning as it enables mitigation of hard to abate emissions. In 2023, Aramco developed its Internal Guidelines for Carbon Offsets and Crediting in order to commit to sourcing high intensity carbon credits. Aramco supports the development of Regional Voluntary Carbon Market Company (RVCMC) in Saudi Arabia. Aramco took part in RVCMC's second auction, the world's largest, acquiring one million of the over two million CORSIA-eligible and Verra-registered carbon credits auctioned.

During October 2022, Aramco launched the $1.5 billion Sustainability Fund through the global venture capital arm, Aramco Ventures. The portfolio of the Sustainability Fund includes 27 investments with a total committed amount of $349 million. In year 2023, the Sustainability Fund made commitments of $239 million and completed investments in 17 companies. Investments are directed towards innovative areas such as carbon capture, synthetic fuels and energy efficiency. Aramco's Sustainability Fund is among the largest sustainability focused venture capital funds in the industry. Aramco Ventures manages five funds. These include a digital /industrial fund which supports investments in technologies of strategic importance, the Prosperity 7 funds I and II investing in disruptive technology, the Sustainability Fund and Late Stage Venturing Fund. The five funds under three venturing programs were valued at $ 7 billion. Digital funds had assets of value $0.5 billion, the prosperity 7 fund I &II had assets of value $1 billion and $2 billion respectively. The late stage venturing fund had assets of value $2 billion.

Aramco entered into an engineering agreement with Topsoe to construct a lower carbon hydrogen production demonstration plant. Aramco had plans to invest in 12 GW of solar and wind energy by year 2030. Aramco aims to cut greenhouse gas emissions by 50% by 2030 and reach net-zero by 2050. It plans to invest in 100 GW of non-fossil fuel capacity, contributing 10% of Saudi Arabia's energy generation by 2030.

Exxon Mobil's Green Investments

Exxon Mobil is an American multinational oil and gas corporation. The company operations include exploration and production of oil and gas, electric power generation, and coal and minerals operations. Exxon Mobil's primary businesses provide products related to energy, chemicals, lubricants and lower emission technologies. Exxon Mobil is one of the largest integrated fuels, lubricants and chemical companies in the world. ExxonMobil focusses on conducting business which is compatible with the environmental and economic needs of the communities. These policies are put into practice through a disciplined management framework called the Operations Integrity Management System (OIMS).

The focus areas of sustainability for Exxon Mobil are given in the following table (Table 14.2).

Table 14.2 Focus areas of sustainability

Delivering economic benefits	Respecting human rights	Advancing climate solutions
Caring for land and biodiversity	Expanding the plastics life cycle	Minimizing operational waste
Enhancing process safety	Evaluating product benefits with life cycle assessments	Managing socioeconomic impacts
Conserving water resources	Investing in people	Expanding the plastics life cycle
Progressing product safety		

Source: Exxon Mobil website

During the period 2022–2027, Exxon Mobil had made commitments of $17 billion as part of low carbon emission initiatives. Of the total investment, approximately 60% is focused on reducing own emissions and 40% is directed toward building lower emissions business with third party customers.

Exxon Mobil had achieved highest refinery throughput since 2007. Exxon Mobil introduced an additional 250,000 barrels per day of refining capacity in 2022. Exxon Mobil had deployed new technology to measure and mitigate methane emissions and had achieved methane emission reduction from operating assets by more than 40% by year 2021 compared to year 2016. As part of its 2030 greenhouse gas emission reduction plans, Exxon Mobil reduced its Scope 1 and Scope 2 emissions intensity by 9%.

The 2030 emission reduction plans focus on absolute reduction in corporate wide greenhouse gas emissions by 20% and absolute reduction in upstream greenhouse gas emissions of approximately 30%. The emission reduction plan also has aims for absolute reduction in methane emissions by 70% and absolute flaring reduction of approximately 60%. Biofuels, hydrogen-based fuels and carbon capture and storage offer lower emission solutions for hard to decarbonize sectors. Exxon Mobil have announced leading plans to achieve net Zero Scope 1 and 2 emissions by 2030 through the Permian Basin unconventional operations. Exxon Mobil's 2030 greenhouse gas emission plans are expected to result in a 20–30% reduction in corporate wide greenhouse gas intensity which include reductions of 40–50% in upstream intensity,70–80% in corporate wide methane intensity and 60–70% in corporate wide flaring intensity.

To support net-zero goal, Exxon Mobil have plans over 100 emission-reducing upgrades, including carbon capture, electrification, and equipment replacements across global upstream operations. ExxonMobil is developing approximately 12 million metric tons per year of low cost, high efficiency liquefaction capacity to meet expected global demand growth for LNG. In 2021, the Gulf Coast Growth Venture was launched and it features a 1.8 million metric ton ethane steam cracker, two polyethylene units producing 1.3 million metric tons annually and a monoethylene glycol unit with a 1.1 million metric ton capacity. The Baton Rouge Louisiana polypropylene project had expanded the production capacity along the Gulf Coast by 450,000 metric tons per year.

Exxon Mobil has an equity share of about one-fifth of the world's carbon capture at about nine million metric tons per year which is the equivalent of approximately two million gasoline powered passenger vehicles per year. Exxon Mobil produce about 1.3 million metric tons of hydrogen annually. Exxon Mobil had announced a blue hydrogen production plant at Baytown, Texas which can produce nearly one million metric tons per year of hydrogen. Exxon Mobil also signed a memorandum of understanding with SGN and Macquarie's Green Investment Group to explore the use of hydrogen and carbon capture to reduce CO_2 emissions in England's Southampton industrial cluster. Exxon Mobil is a sponsor of the Open Hydrogen Initiative which support the development of a globally traded hydrogen market. This initiative is led by GTI Energy, S&P Global Commodity Insights, and the U.S. Department of Energy's National Energy Technology Laboratory. Exxon Mobil aims to supply approximately 40,000 barrels per day of lower emission fuel by year 2025 and have a further goal of 200,000 barrels per day by 2030. This strategy would reduce more than 25 million metric tons CO_2-equivalent emissions per year from the transportation sector.

Imperial Oil, ExxonMobil's Canadian affiliate, secured a long-term contract for low-carbon hydrogen at Strathcona refinery. Using hydrogen, canola oil, and a proprietary catalyst, the project will produce 20,000 barrels of renewable diesel daily, cutting transportation emissions by approximately three million metric tons of CO_2 annually. Exxon Mobil is piloting native grassland restoration in the Permian as a method to increase carbon sequestration in soil in degraded lands. Exxon Mobil is a founding signatory to the Aiming for Zero Methane Emissions Initiative which was announced in year 2022. Exxon Mobil have also partnered with Scepter to develop satellite-based technology to improve global methane detection and quantification.

ExxonMobil's plastics packaging reduces life-cycle emissions, avoiding 13 million metric tons annually in the U.S. and potentially 40 million metric tons globally by 2030. ExxonMobil have been working with the MIT Energy Initiative to develop a new life cycle approach tool which covers pathways of multiple technologies which represent most sources of greenhouse gas emissions.

Table 14.3 shows the environmental expenditures incurred by Exxon Mobil during the period 2019–2023.

Table 14.3 Environmental expenditures

Year	2019	2020	2021	2022	2023
Environmental expenditures in billions of dollars	5.2	4.5	4.6	5.7	7.1

Source: https://corporate.exxonmobil.com/sustainability-and-reports/metrics-and-data#Sustainabilityperformancedata

Green Investments by Chevron

Chevron is one of the world's leading integrated energy companies. Chevron produces crude oil and natural gas; manufactures transportation fuels, lubricants, petrochemicals and additives; and develops technologies that enhance its business. Chevron focuses on developing scalable lower-carbon businesses, including hydrogen, carbon capture and storage, carbon offsets, and emerging technologies like geothermal. Chevron have 11.1 billion barrels net oil equivalent proved reserves. In 2023, Chevron had total assets valued at $261.6 billion and operating revenues valued at $196.9 billion.

Chevron invests in oil and gas business to lower the carbon intensity of its operations and pursue new lower carbon businesses. The company have set targets to lower carbon emission intensities by 2028. The lower carbon investments are projected to be $ 8 billion through 2021–2028. The carbon reduction projects during the period 2021–2028 is valued at $ 2 billion. Chevron aims to reduce carbon intensity by high grading the portfolio, improve operations and use the MACC process to drive emissions reductions on existing facilities. Chevron evaluate emission reduction opportunities in energy management, methane reduction (venting, fugitives, flaring), carbon capture, utilization, storage and offsets to enhance sustainability.

Chevron is advancing over 120 GHG abatement projects, investing $350 million in 2023 and $2 billion through 2028, targeting four million tonnes of annual emissions reductions. By 2030, Chevron's natural gas sales could help avoid up to 100 million tonnes of CO_2e emissions annually compared to coal. Chevron is working on over 100 energy management projects forecasted to reduce emissions by more than 1.5 million tonnes of CO_2e per year once fully implemented. Chevron and Algonquin Power are co-developing renewable power projects to supply 500 MW of electricity, investing up to $250 million by 2025. Chevron and TotalEnergies Renewables USA completed the solar power project in Lost Hills production facilities in California which will provide more than 1.4 billion kilowatt hours of solar energy over the 20-year term of the agreement.

Chevron's methane intensity has reduced by more than 50% since the year 2016. Approximately 95% of Chevron's methane emissions originate from the production of oil and natural gas. Chevron has adopted an Upstream methane-intensity target of 2.0 kg CO_2e/boe by 2028, which represents a 53% reduction from 2016 baseline. Chevron have invested in Malta Inc., a start-up firm which develops a long duration energy storage system for grid scale applications.

Chevron aims to produce capacity of roughly 100 mbd of renewable fuels which includes renewable diesel, sustainable aviation fuel, biodiesel and other biofuels by year 2030.Chevron Renewable Energy Group and Bunge acquired Chacraservicios which cultivates novel oil seeds. Chevron and Brightmark LLC have formed the joint venture fund Brightmark RNG Holdings LLC to fund the construction of infrastructure and the commercial operation of diary biomethane projects in multiple states in USA. With the acquisition of Beyond6, LLC and its network of 56 CNG stations across the United States, Chevron could market the RNG which it produces or procure through a nationwide network of CNG locations. Chevron focusses on development and deployment of carbon capture, utilization and storage (CCUS) technologies. Chevron have 50% ownership interest in the Bayou Bend joint venture with TotalEnergies and Equinor. Bayou Bend is a carbon capture and storage (CSS) project along the Texas Gulf Coast.

Chevron is exploring commercial opportunities through collaborations that enhance supply chains and technology advancements. The company holds or has applied for patents on about 20 hydrogen-related inventions. Chevron has majority interest in ACES Delta LLC, a joint venture involved in the development of the Advanced Clean Energy Storage project in Delta.

Chevron has invested in Baseload Capital, a private investment firm specializing in low- and medium-temperature geothermal and heat power assets. Additionally, Chevron have a joint venture with Baseload's U.S. subsidiary to develop geothermal projects, with the first initiative launching in Nevada. Chevron U.S.A. Inc. is a co-owner of Chevron Phillips Chemical Company LLC (CPChem), a 50–50 joint venture which advances plastics circularity. Chevron funds and support the Pecos Watershed Conservation Initiative, a public private partnership which aim to sustain the health of the Pecos River and its tributaries in the Permian Basin.

Chevron have made social investments of over 1.2 billion since 2016. Chevron Technology Ventures have invested in 140 plus novel technology companies since 1999. Recent investments include initiatives for industrial decarbonization, emerging mobility, operational enhancement and digitalization. For industrial decarbonization, Chevron have made investments in Immaterial, a developer of proprietary, bespoke monolith structured metal organic framework absorbents. Chevron have made investments in Ardent Process Technologies which develops modular membrane-based carbon capture solutions designed to reduce the carbon intensity of industrial processes through efficient gas separation. For real time optimization and increased reliability, Chevron have made investments in Electric Era, a company which commercializes fast charging solution for electric vehicles. Chevron invested in Flyability, a developer of aerial drones for confined-space inspections in challenging industrial environments, enhancing safety by reducing worker risk in hazardous areas. Chevron have invested in Oxford Quantum Circuits, the developer of novel, commercially available quantum computer for enabling new forms of information processing.

Chevron supported the Miller Centre for Social Entrepreneurship to help Asia-Pacific enterprises expand and enhance their social and economic impact. Chevron had upgraded the diesel hydrotreater at the El Segundo Refinery, California to process either 100% renewable or traditional feedstocks. Chevron have made a majority stake acquisition in ACES Delta, LCC to develop a green hydrogen storage project in Utah. Chevron had allocated $10 billion in carbon investments to reduce the carbon intensity of Chevron for the period 2021–2028. Chevron is a member of Clean Hydrogen Future Coalition (CHFC) which promote clean hydrogen as a critical pathway to achieve global decarbonization objectives. Chevron engages with American Petroleum Institute (API) to support the development of policies which advance market-based approaches and innovation to support the goals of the Paris

Agreement. Chevron joined Oil and Gas Climate Initiative (OGCI) in year 2018 and committed $100 million to the $1 billion plus OGCI Climate Investments fund which supports technologies which aim at reducing GHG emissions across the oil and gas value chain and hard to abate sectors. Chevron collaborates with US Chamber of Commerce to promote market-based climate policies, support breakthrough technologies, and advocate for streamlined regulations. Chevron have invested over USD one billion in carbon capture, utilization and storage projects in Canada and Australia. This included the Gorgon Carbon Dioxide Injection project which is one of the world's largest integrated carbon capture and storage projects.

Chevron's focus is on creation of a portfolio of renewable fuel options, like renewable diesel and biodiesel, in policy-enabled markets. Chevron develops compressed natural gas (CNG), renewable e natural gas (RNG), hydrogen, renewable diesel (RD) and biodiesel (BD). Sixty percent of US terminals of Chevron are capable of renewable or biodiesel distribution. Chevron and Brightmark LLC have formed a joint venture Brightmark RNG Holdings LLC to develop projects across the United States to produce RNG. Chevron became part of Getting to Zero Coalition, 160 companies led industry led platform for collaboration initiatives across the maritime and fuels value chains within the financial sector. The coalition aims to get commercially viable deep sea zero emissions vessels powered by zero emission fuels into operation by year 2030 and aim towards full carbonization by year 2050. Chevron had partnered with CalBio and dairy farmers to form CalBioGas LLC to produce and market diary based biomethane as an RNG transportation fuel in California.

Chevron and Bunge North America, Inc. have formed a 50–50 joint venture, Bunge Chevron Ag Renewables LLC, combining Bunge's oilseed processing expertise and farmer relationships with Chevron's fuel manufacturing and marketing strengths. The venture aims to meet the growing demand for lower-carbon fuels and develop renewable fuel feedstocks. Chevron is a member of Airports of Tomorrow (AoT), supporting aviation's energy transition through hydrogen propulsion, biofuels, SAF, and innovation to advance lower-carbon fuels in hard-to-abate sectors.

Chevron is working to develop and deploy CCUS technologies. Chevron, with Talos Energy and Equinor, co-owns Bayou Bend, a Texas Gulf Coast CCS project. Expanded in 2023, it offers 1 billion tonnes CO_2 storage for industrial emitters. Chevron, in three joint ventures, holds offshore GHG assessment permits covering 7.8 million acres to explore potential carbon storage and injection sites. Chevron invested in Carbon Sync to develop soil carbon sequestration projects in Western Australia, promoting regenerative farming to improve soil health and capture carbon while gaining commercial and technical insights. Chevron have invested in Carbon Clean, a carbon capture company providing solutions for hard to abate industries. Chevron is a member of IETA, supporting the development of a global GHG emissions trading framework.

Chevron is developing a lower-carbon hydrogen and ammonia business, targeting heavy transport, power, and hard-to-abate sectors, with supply focus in the U.S. West, Gulf Coast, and Asia-Pacific. Chevron previously held patents on nearly 70 inventions relevant to future plans and currently has around 20 patents or applications. It produces one million tonnes of hydrogen annually for refining. Chevron has a majority interest in the Advanced Clean Energy Storage Delta (ACES Delta) electrolytic hydrogen production and storage project in Delta. Chevron has an agreement with Iwatani to co-develop and construct up to 30 hydrogen fuelling sites in California by 2026. Chevron has invested in Aurora Hydrogen, a developer of hydrogen production technology that uses microwave energy without generating any CO_2 emissions or consuming water. Chevron and Caterpillar are collaborating on hydrogen demonstration projects and stationary power applications. Chevron works with Solar Turbines to develop a low-emissions turbine blending hydrogen with traditional fuels to reduce GHG emissions.

Chevron have invested in Baseload Capital, a private investment company which focusses on development and operations of geothermal and heat power assets. Chevron have invested in Eavor Technologies that provide a closed loop geothermal technology for power and heat markets. Chevron have a joint collaboration with Mitsui Oil Exploration Company (MOECO) to explore the technical and commercial feasibility of advanced geothermal power generation in Japan. Chevron has invested in Zap energy, a start-up which develops next generation modular fusion energy system. Chevron have a memorandum of understanding with KazMunaiGas in Kazakhstan to explore low carbon projects in sectors such as CCUS, hydrogen, energy efficiency, methane management and carbon financial disclosure methodology. Chevron and JERA have collaboration for the production of lower carbon fuels, CCUS and new technology commercialization. Chevron has collaborated with PT Pertamina to explore potential lower carbon business opportunities in Indonesia.

Chevron collaborates on multiple initiatives to advance decarbonization. It partnered with 123Carbon to pilot blockchain-based insetting for biofuel bunkering in Singapore and with Smart Freight Centre (SFC) to develop market-based approaches for reducing freight emissions. Chevron also worked with Xpansiv and CMS to ensure traceability for lower-carbon fuel oil transactions. Through the Open Footprint Forum, it helps create standardized emissions data models. Additionally, Chevron contributed to developing ISO 6338: 2023, a method for calculating GHG emissions from LNG plants via IOGP and ISO.

Chevron collaborates on GHG emissions transparency initiatives. It co-developed the Statement of Greenhouse Gas Emissions (SGE) Methodology with Pavilion Energy and QatarEnergy to quantify LNG cargo emissions. Through PACT and WBCSD, Chevron helped create the Pathfinder Framework and Pathfinder Network to standardize carbon footprint data exchange. Additionally, it partners with the E-liability Institute to pilot a carbon-accounting approach for accurate, auditable emissions tracking.

In 2018, Chevron Technology Ventures, the venture capital arm of Chevron had set up the Future Energy Fund I with investment commitments of $100 million. The Future Energy Fund II was later introduced. In 2024, Chevron Venture Capital announced the launch of its third venture capital fund, the Future Energy Fund III with commitments of $500 million. The Future Energy Fund focus on innovations in industrial decarbonization, emerging mobility, energy decentralization and circular carbon economy.

Green Investments by Shell plc

Shell plc is a British multinational oil and gas company headquartered in London, England. Shell aims to become a net zero emissions energy business by 2050. By 2024, scope 1 and 2 emissions were down by 30% compared to 2016 reference year for Shell. By end 2024, Shell had achieved 60% of the reduction required to halve the emissions from its operations by 2030 compared to year 2016. Shell's energy transition strategy aims to reduce the carbon intensity of energy products by 6–8% by 2023, 20% by 2030, 45% by 2035 and 100% by 2050. In 2021, 89% of shareholders voted in support of Energy Transition Strategy.

Shell sells around 4.6% of final energy consumed in the world and produce around 1.4% of total primary energy. In the road freight sector, Shell works with transport companies, truck manufacturers and policymakers to identify pathways to decarbonisation. Shell focus on increasing production of low carbon biofuels. Shell aim to associate with H2Accelerate consortium to create infrastructure to generate and supply clean hydrogen across Europe. Shell is launching sector-based business to drive decarbonization in aviation, road transport, passenger transport, shipping, technology, and industry, ensuring accountability for emissions reduction in each sector.

By end of 2023, Shell had achieved more than 60% of its target to halve emissions from its operations by 2030 compared to 2016. In 2023, approximately 23% of capital spending of Shell amounting to $5.6 billion was invested in low carbon solutions. Shell have investment plans of $10 to $15 billion on low carbon solutions during the period 2023–2025. In 2023, Shell spent approximately $628 million on decarbonization R&D projects, an increase from $440 million in 2022. Approximately 45–50% of cash capital expenditure will be accounted by the renewable and energy solutions sector during the period 2025–2030.

In Netherlands, Shell have entered into an agreement to offer renewable power to Amazon from an offshore wind farm being constructed off the coast of the Netherlands. Amazon's guaranteed demand enables Shell to invest in green hydrogen and CCS, creating a green energy hub in Rotterdam, using wind power to decarbonize fuel production at Pernis refinery. Amazon's air cargo fleet is expanding, and Shell, with its extensive refueling network, will supply six million gallons of blended sustainable aviation fuel made from agricultural waste. In 2020, Shell and Amazon made minority investments in US based ZeroAvia, for decarbonising aviation with hydrogen-powered planes. Shell and Microsoft have formed a strategic alliance to develop digital technologies for carbon footprint reduction. Shell supplies Microsoft with low-carbon energy and renewable energy solutions. Shell and Rolls-Royce, partners for over 100 years, are now collaborating to test Rolls-Royce engines running on 100% sustainable aviation fuel (SAF) for cleaner aviation. Shell is a founding partner of the Clean Skies for Tomorrow Coalition, part of the Mission Possible Platform, working toward net-zero aviation emissions by mid-century. Shell is reducing emissions by installing eight efficient cracker furnaces at Moerdijk, cutting energy use by 10 per cent, and building a 250 MW co-generation plant at its Pennsylvania chemicals facility.

Shell expect to offer its customers nature-based solutions to offset 120 million tonnes per annum of its Scope 3 emissions by year 2030. Shell provides carbon-neutral driving in seven countries and carbon-neutral LNG cargoes, using nature-based carbon offsets to compensate for full life-cycle emissions, including methane.

In 2020, Shell invested around $90 million for the purchase of nature-based offsets and expect to invest around $100 million a year. In the same year, Shell acquired Select Carbon in Australia which operates 70 carbon farming projects spread across ten million hectares. Shell collaborates with project developers for projects based on reforestation, agroforestry and mangroves. In 2020, Shell purchased more than four million tonnes of credits on behalf of customers sourced from projects around the world. Shell is part of seven of the 51 large scale carbon capture and storage projects globally listed in 2019 by the Global CCS Institute. In 2020, Shell invested around $70 million in carbon capture and storage (CCS) projects. Shell focus on selective investments in competitive LNG assets to deliver more than seven million tonnes per annum of new capacity. Shell offers carbon neutral LNG, which uses nature-based carbon credits to offset full life cycle emissions including methane. Shell has plans to reduce the number of refineries from 13 sites to six high value chemicals and energy parks and reduce the production of tradition fuels by 55% by 2030. Shell will produce chemicals from recycled waste and by 2025, aim to process one million tonnes a year of plastic waste.

Shell is expanding electric vehicle charging points worldwide to 500,000 by year 2025 and 2.5 million by 2030 serving homeowners, businesses, and forecourts. Shell had opened the largest electric vehicle charging station in the world in China. In March 2023, Shell acquired Volta Inc., expanding its U.S. EV charging network to 3000+ charge points across 31 states, with 3400 more in development. Shell is developing utility scale battery storage systems in select markets. During 2023, Shell entered into a partnership to deliver battery storage system in Australia. Shell is building Holland Hydrogen 1 in the Netherlands, a 200 MW renewable hydrogen plant powered by offshore wind, set to decarbonize fuel production, transport, and industry by late 2020s.

Shell has leadership position for the development of integrated hydrogen hubs to serve industry and heavy-duty transport. Shell focuses on producing premium biofuels such as sustainable aviation fuel, renewable diesel and renewable natural gas (RNG). Shell have acquired a 35% stake in Green Energy, Oman to produce hydrogen from seawater which is powered by up to 25 GW of solar and wind energy. At Shell's Energy and Chemicals Park Rotterdam in Netherlands, Shell is integrating biofuels, hydrogen and CCS into its existing facilities.

As part of strategy for the decarbonisation of transport, Shell have set a target to reduce emissions from the use of oil products by 15–20% by year 2030. In 2023, Shell acquired Nature Energy, one of the largest producers of renewable natural gas in Europe. Shell's Timi platform in Malaysia have started operations mainly powered by solar and wind energy. In 2022, Shell completed the acquisition of renewable power company SPRING Energy and decided on the investment on Holland Hydrogen and LNG expansion projects in Qatar. Shell aims to increase its liquified natural gas (LNG) business by 20–30% by the year 2030.

In 2024, Shells decided to convert the hydrocracker of the Wesseling site at the Energy and Chemicals Park Rheinland into a production unit for Group III base oils to produce high quality engine and transmission oils. Shell is one of the world's largest traders and blenders of biofuels meeting approximately 6% of global demand. Raizen, the joint venture of Shell in Brazil is one of the world's biggest ethanol producers which deliver lowest carbon intensity biofuels. In 2023, Raizen produced approximately 3.12 billion litres of ethanol. During February 2023, Shells completed nearly $2 billion acquisition of Nature Energy making Shell one of the largest producers of renewable natural gas (RNG) in Europe.

Shell select projects which are certified under credible and independent carbon credit standards. These include the Verified Carbon Standard, Gold Standard and the American Carbon Registry. In 2023, Shell's net carbon intensity accounted for 20 million carbon credits of which four million were linked to the sale of energy product.

Shell Ventures invests in start-ups and bigger companies that seek to electrify energy systems, decarbonise transport, gain data-based insights and provide innovative customer solutions. In 2023, Shell invested in German company, Kraftblock, which has created energy storage systems to help the industry sector switch from fossil fuels to renewable energies. Shell Ventures have partnered with Corvus Energy to provide battery storage systems for maritime use, replacing diesel and reducing emissions on Shell-operated vessels in the Gulf of Mexico. Shell supported the Fit for 55 package which included targets for the use of renewable hydrogen and advanced biofuels. In 2024, Shell and ExxonMobil were chosen by the Singapore government as lead developers for a cross-border CCS project, aiming to store 2.5 million tonnes of CO_2 annually by 2030.

Green Investments by PetroChina

PetroChina Company Ltd. is joint stock limited company incorporated during 1999 upon restructuring of the former China National Petroleum Corporation. PetroChina is one of the major oil and gas producers and distributors in China and a significant player in the global oil and gas industry. The company engages in a wide range of activities related to oil, natural gas and new energy and materials. The Company is rapidly advancing its green transformation by integrating oil, gas, and new energy. It aims to develop a diversified energy mix—combining oil, gas, geothermal, electricity, and hydrogen to become a comprehensive energy provider. The company have established five international oil and gas cooperation zones in Central Asia, the Middle East, Africa, Latin America and Asia Pacific. In 2024, PetroChina's crude output amounted to 941.8 million barrels and marketable natural gas output amounted to 5133 billion cubic feet. The company focusses on the development of its new energy business which include geothermal, heating, wind and photovoltaic power generation, hydrogen, carbon capture, utilization and storage (CCUS). In 2024, the company's investment in new energy businesses amounted to RMB 24.05

billion. In 2024, the company processed 1378.4 million barrels of crude oil and produced 119.867 million tonnes of refined oil products. The company manufactures thousands of trademarked chemical products across six major categories with top ranked production capacities in China for ethylene, synthetic resin and synthetic rubber. The Company advances refining, chemicals, and new materials upgrades, aiming for high-quality, green, low-carbon products and moving up the industrial value chain. In 2024, PetroChina's production of chemical new materials amounted to 2.045 million tonnes with significant growth in the production of functional synthetic resins, synthetic rubber, specialty fibers and high-end carbon materials. PetroChina operates 22,441 gas stations, 19,700 Smile convenience stores, 26 hydrogen refueling stations, and 3803 battery charging (swapping) stations. By year 2025, the proportion of natural gas in PetroChina's total domestic oil and gas equivalent production was expected to be increased by 55%.

The Company launched the Green and Low-carbon Development Action Plan 3.0, promoting a circular carbon economy through innovative projects in clean energy, hydrogen, and CCUS. It also introduced three key initiatives—Green Enterprise, Clean Energy Contributor, and Carbon Economy Pioneer—supported by ten major projects to drive sustainable transformation. By 2035, methane emissions intensity is expected to decrease by 20% as compared to year 2025.PetroChina aims to implements four key measures -carbon reduction, utilisation, substitution, and storage—to minimize and offset emissions, advancing steadily toward carbon peak and neutrality goals. In March 2025, the Company fully utilized its own carbon sink resources and obtained the 2024 "PetroChina Headquarters Carbon Neutrality Certificate" through self-declaration and certification by the Beijing Sanxing 9000 Certification Body. PetroChina's Xinli Oil Extraction Plant Sector III, Jilin Oilfield's first zero-carbon demonstration zone, was recognized as a "zero-carbon factory standard demonstration zone" in 2024. It is China's only oil and gas production site showcasing innovative, space-efficient, centralized operations for oil extraction, water injection, and transmission. Cumulative green electricity produced by this zero-carbon demonstration zone as of the end of 2024 has reached 58 million kWh, saving 410,000 m3 of natural gas and replacing all regional energy consumption with 100% clean energy.

PetroChina Yunnan Petrochemical, based in Anning Industrial Park, Kunming, is PetroChina's first refinery to pilot an ESG system. Recognized as a "National Green Factory," "Green Factory in the Oil and Petrochemical Industry," and "PetroChina's Green Enterprise," it serves as a model for sustainable industrial development. Yunnan Petrochemical has invested more than RMB 4.5 billion in environmental protection in total. In 2024, the Company enhanced carbon management by aligning with national GHG standards, establishing a GHG Accounting Centre, and upgrading its carbon asset platform. Emission accounting shifted from quarterly enterprise-level to monthly equipment-level analysis, improving accuracy in carbon assessment, trading, and reporting for better emissions control and supervision. In 2024, PetroChina Karamay Petrochemical improved carbon footprint management for gasoline and diesel, earning a Product Carbon Label Evaluation Certificate through detailed life cycle analysis. The Company has built a robust carbon asset management system, implementing key policies and establishing a Carbon Asset Trading Centre. It ensures standardized carbon trading practices and manages a diverse portfolio of carbon assets, including China Emission Allowance (CEA), China Certified Emission Reduction (CCER), and European Union Allowances (EUA), to strengthen compliance, control, and centralised management in carbon markets. PetroChina is actively involved in the establishment of China's carbon market and are one of the first ten companies to participate in national carbon market transactions. In 2021, PetroChina entered into the world's first five-year carbon neutral LNG trade agreement with Shell to conduct full lifecycle GHG emission. By end December 2024, 19 shipments have been delivered under the long-term carbon neutral LNG trade agreement thereby completing approximately USD 800 million in carbon neutral LNG transactions. In March 2024, the Company signed its first Australian green electricity deal, securing 60 MW wind power via a two-year agreement with Pacific Blue.

In 2024, the Company completed the world's first physical sustainable aviation fuel(SAF) trade and RMB-settled SAF transaction, expanding its presence in Europe's biofuel and carbon markets. PetroChina formulated the 14th Five-Year Plan for Green Development, the PetroChina's Carbon Neutrality Guidebook, and the PetroChina's Guidebook for Carbon Sequestration Forest Construction. PetroChina actively participated in CNPC's "Tree Planting for Carbon Neutrality" campaign. Since its launch in 2022, the initiative has raised RMB 47 million through contributions from employees and the public. Over 300 hectares of carbon sequestration forests have been planted, generating around 100,000 tonnes of forest carbon sinks. In 2024, the Company advanced CCUS projects across various oil fields, enhancing CO_2 storage technologies and injecting 1.899 million tonnes of CO_2 annually. Jilin Oilfield of PetroChina has independently developed core technologies for carbon dioxide capture, storage, and enhanced oil recovery (CCUS-EOR), establishing China's first and Asia's largest full-process, full-industry-chain CCUS-EOR demonstration project. In 2024, PetroChina became a signatory of Oil and Gas Decarbonization Charter (OGDC) joining more than 50 oil and gas companies to stay committed in reducing carbon emissions. In August 2024, Daqing Oilfield of PetroChina acquired CNPC Electric Power Co Ltd. to develop new energy and electricity sales businesses of PetroChina.

The environmental protection expenditure of PetroChina amounted to RMB 2.99 billion. The compliance disposal rate of general solid waste was 100%. PetroChina actively support global initiatives and international agreements, including the 2030 Agenda for Sustainable Development, the Convention on Biological Diversity, and the UN's Kunming-Montreal Global Biodiversity Framework. In 2024, PetroChina had invested RMB 902 million in upgrading energy saving and water saving technologies. In 2024, the Company launched the Energy Conservation and Carbon Reduction Action Plan, executing 11 key tasks to boost efficiency, clean energy use, and electrification. PetroChina build photovoltaic and wind power projects to improve its clean energy sufficiency.

The year on year increase in the proportion of non-fossil energy in total energy consumption is 2.5 percentage points. PetroChina has formulated the Green and

Low-carbon Development Action Plan 3.0, centred around four principles: carbon reduction, carbon reuse, carbon recycling and carbon removal. In 2024, the global investment in public welfare by PetroChina amounted to RMB 566.71 million. PetroChina spend an amount of RMB 244.65 million for rural revitalisation and an amount of RMB 48.36 was spend for environmental protection in year 2024. In 2024, PetroChina effectively utilized targeted assistance funds, investing RMB ten million to support the Henan Taiqian County Down Garment Industrial Park—National Down Garment Quality Inspection Centre project, which generated over RMB two million in income from inspection services alone. PetroChina practice responsible procurement, incorporating green and low carbon development into all stages of material supply chain management. PetroChina aims to establish a green supply chain across the entire operational life cycle from supplier selection and project design to procurement, logistics and material disposal while promoting green procurement practices. The company holds a total of 21,754 valid patents. PetroChina's first smart e-commerce service platform for the energy and chemical industry— the Yunmengze Smart Platform was launched for trial operation in year 2024. PetroChina had announced plans to spend about $1.49 billion annually for the five-year period 2021–2025 for low carbon emission transitions.

Green Investments by TotalEnergies

TotalEnergies is a French based global integrated energy company. TotalEnergies produce and market oil and biofuels, natural gas, green gases, renewables and electricity. The company employs over 100,000 employees in nearly 120 countries. The company is world's third largest producer of liquefied natural gas. TotalEnergies have 31.6 GW of gross installed electricity capacity. The company has more than 13,000 service stations and nearly 78,000 charge points worldwide. TotalEnergies have produced 292,000 tons of biofuels. TotalEnergies have made green investments valued at 17.8 billion dollars which included 27% for low carbon energy. The company aims to lead the energy transition and achieve carbon neutrality by 2050. The company have net electricity production target of 100 TWh in 2030. The company had 26 GW of gross installed renewable electricity capacity. The company aims for 40% net emissions reduction target from its operated facilities by 2030 compared to year 2015. The company have 25% target for reducing the lifecycle carbon intensity of energy products sold by 2030 compared to year 2015. The sustainable development approach focuses on four key areas of energy and climate, employee safety and well-being, environment and positive impact on stakeholders.

In 2024, TotalEnergies attained and even exceeded its 2025 methane emissions reduction target of 55% against 50% in year 2020. The company have a billion-dollar energy efficiency plan for the period 2023–2025 and in 2024 launched a new billion-dollar plan to cover its projects for 2026–2028. By end of year 2024, these investments amounted to USD 750 million and resulted in emissions reduction by around 1.5 Mt. CO2e/year and generated energy savings of more than USD 100 million/year.

In 2024, more than 170 projects were implemented to reduce emissions by more than 2 Mt. CO2. In 2024, net electricity production reached 41TWh which represented an increase of 23% compared to previous year. In 2024, TotalEnergies distributed 990 kt of bottled LPG in Africa and Asia serving 15 million households and 60 million people. The company aim to distribute bottled LPG to 100 million people by 2030 in Africa and India. In 2024, TotalEnergies had made $ 4.8 billion investments in low carbon energies. The company have made over one billion dollars of investment in R&D and digital development in year 2024 with 68% devoted to low carbon and decarbonization solutions. The company have more than 3500 researchers in its 18 R&D centers. TotalEnergies aim to produce 1.5 Mt./year of Sustainable Aviation Fuel by year 2030. The company aims to supply clean cooking energy to over 100 million people.

TotalEnergies focusses on integrated multi energy strategy built on two core pillars of Oil & Gas particularly LNG and electricity. The company aims to grow its overall energy production by an average of 4% annually between 2024 and 2030. TotalEnergies plans to grow its Oil & Gas production by around 3% per year over the next five years, predominantly from LNG.TotalEnergies focusses on replication of its integrated Oil & Gas business model into electricity value chain to achieve a profitability of 12% for the integrated power segment. TotalEnergies is building a cost-effective portfolio combining renewable (solar, onshore wind, offshore wind) and flexible assets (CCGT, storage) in order to deliver low carbon electricity. TotalEnergies' portfolio in Brazil has steadily grown since 2015 and currently comprises 11 licenses, 4 of which are operated. TotalEnergies had acquired 34% stake in a joint venture with Casa dos Ventos, one of Brazil's leading renewable energy companies. This joint venture aims to develop a renewable energy portfolio which include onshore wind, photovoltaic and battery storage targeting a capacity of 12 GW by 2030. In 2024, TotalEnergies acquired the 1.3 GW West Burton B gas plant in UK with battery storage, then sold a 50% stake to EPH. In January 2025, TotalEnergies and STMicroelectronics signed a 15-year agreement for the supply of 1.5 TWh of renewable electricity in France. In 2024, TotalEnergies commissioned two solar power plants in southeast Texas—Danish Fields (720 MW) and Cottonwood (455 MW)—both featuring co-located battery storage. TotalEnergies has acquired majority stakes in the Jammerland Bugt (240 MW) and Lillebaelt South (165 MW) offshore wind projects located in Denmark. TotalEnergies signed an agreement with Scatec to acquire interests in renewable hydroelectricity projects in Africa, notably in the Bujagali hydroelectric power station in Uganda. The consortium composed of TotalEnergies and the Saudi developer AEW has signed an electricity sales contract of 25 years with Saudi Power Procurement Company for the 300 MW Rabigh 2 solar power plant. Through the Go Green project in Europe, TotalEnergies aim to provide a 100% low carbon electricity supply from 2025 in its refining and chemicals sector. In April 2024, TotalEnergies launched the Marsa LNG project, a 1 Mt/y LNG 2 liquefaction plant in Oman. Marsa LNG will be one of the lowest carbon intensity LNG plants in the world. In 2024, the final investment decision was taken for the GranMorgu project, a new oil exploration and production development in Suriname. This project incorporates the best technologies for reducing greenhouse gas emissions.

TotalEnergies aims to cut CO_2 emissions by up to three million tons annually by 2030 by using low-carbon hydrogen to decarbonize its European refineries. TotalEnergies is launching four project types to support Europe's low-carbon hydrogen market: biohydrogen from biomass for SAF, electrolysers using its renewable power (via joint ventures or tolling contracts), and long-term green hydrogen purchases from local electrolysers or imports. With the aim to produce renewable hydrogen in TotalEnergies' biorefineries, a new unit with a capacity to produce 25,000 tonnes per year is to be built and operated by Air Liquide. In 2024, TotalEnergies acquired a 50% stake in the OranjeWind offshore farm with a total capacity of 795 MW in Netherlands to leverage its position as an integrated electricity player. In the Netherlands, TotalEnergies and Air Liquide have set up a 50/50 joint venture to build and operate a 250 MW electrolyser at the Zeeland refinery. In France, TotalEnergies, in partnership with Engie, is advancing the Masshylia project to reduce emissions at the La Mède biorefinery and for customers in the Fos-Berre industrial port area.

TotalEnergies has signed long-term tolling agreements with Air Liquide to supply renewable electricity to dedicated electrolysis capacity operated by partners, who in turn supply the company with green hydrogen. During June 2024, TotalEnergies and Air Products had announced an agreement for the annual supply of 70,000 tonnes of green hydrogen to the refining & chemicals sites in Europe for a period of 15 years from 2030. In Germany, TotalEnergies and VNG, a German natural gas distribution company, signed an agreement in June 2023 to supply green hydrogen to the TotalEnergies Leuna refinery. About 80% of TotalEnergies' non-operated production is operated by partners who are members of initiatives such as OGDC and OGMP 2.0. Established in year 2022, TotalEnergies OneB2B Solutions supports major companies across 35 industries with customized low-carbon solutions, including renewables, BESS, biogas, biofuels, truck charging, and CCS. TotalEnergies is expanding a network of high-power electric charging stations across European motorways, major roads, and urban hubs, aiming to equip 1500 sites by 2030. The company is also developing its charging network in a number of large cities around the world, with a portfolio of over 30,000 charging points in Paris, Amsterdam, London, Brussels and Singapore. TotalEnergies and Vanguard Renewables have entered into an agreement to create a 50/50 joint venture to initially develop, construct and operate ten biomethane projects with a combined annual capacity of 0.8 TWh. TotalEnergies intends to become a major player in the production of SAF (Sustainable Aviation Fuel), with a target of 1.5 Mt/ year in 2030. In 2024, TotalEnergies signed a $100 million agreement with Anew Climate and Aurora Sustainable Lands to support forest conservation, promote sustainable management, and enhance carbon storage in the U.S.

Each year TotalEnergies spend more than USD one billion on R&D and innovation. In 2024, 68% of the company's R&D budget was devoted to new energies in sectors such as renewable electricity, batteries and for reduction of environmental foot print. TotalEnergies has launched a floating wind farm pilot project to supply renewable electricity to an offshore oil and gas platform in the North Sea.

To prepare for Corporate Sustainability Reporting Directive (CSRD) compliance, TotalEnergies mapped nature-related Dependencies, Impacts, Risks, and

Opportunities (DIRO) with key business units and a third party, considering global benchmarks and stakeholder concerns. In 2022, Total Energies joined the CEO Water Mandate, part of the United Nations Global Compact, joining a platform of over 400 companies committed to advancing water management. In 2025, Total Energies and its partner Plastic Energy will start a new plastic waste recycling facility on the Grandpuits platform.

TotalEnergies have invested \$17.8 billion in year 2024 which included \$4.8 billion for low carbon energy mainly in power. In 2025, TotalEnergies plan to invest between \$17 and \$17.5 billion, with \$4.5 billion allocated to low-carbon energies, primarily within Integrated Power. TotalEnergies plan to maintain an annual capital expenditure target of \$16–\$18 billion per year over the next five years.

Green Finance Investments by ConocoPhilips

ConocoPhilips is one of the world's leading exploration and production companies in the world. ConocoPhillips has a 60-year history of leadership in LNG and LNG technology. In 2024, ConocoPhilips produced 1987 thousand barrels of oil equivalent per day (MBOED) globally. In 2024, the company's reserve replacement ratio was 244%. In 2024, ConocoPhilips generated earnings of \$9.2 billion and returned \$9.1 billion of capital to shareholders. With the acquisition of Marathon Oil, ConocoPhilips had added approximately two million tonnes per annum of net LNG capacity in Equatorial Guinea to its global portfolio. The acquisition is expected to deliver over \$ one billion of run rate synergies by the end of year 2025. The total assets in year 2024 amounted to \$123 billion dollars.

ConocoPhilips is a member of the Oil and Gas Methane Partnership (OGMP) 2 initiative for improvement in methane measurement and reporting. The company was awarded the OGMP 2.0 Gold Standard Pathway designation. ConocoPhilips had spent approximately \$350 million on Scope 1 and Scope 2 emissions reductions and low carbon opportunities in year 2023. This investment resulted in emission reductions of approximately 0.8 million tonnes per annum. An additional amount in the range of \$300 to \$ 400 million was allocated for year 2024.ConocoPhilips had accelerated its Scope 1 and Scope 2 GHG emissions intensity reduction target through 2030 from 40–50% to 50–60% using a 2016 baseline for both gross operated and net equity emissions. ConocoPhilips works with World Bank's Carbon Pricing Leadership Coalition as a private sector partner for effective carbon pricing. In 2020, ConocoPhilips adopted a climate related risk framework to reduce its operational greenhouse gas (GHG) emissions to net zero by year 2050. The aim is to reduce GHG emissions intensity to 50–60% by 2030 on both a gross operated and net equity basis from a 2016 baseline. The company also aims to achieve near zero methane emissions intensity by year 2030. ConocoPhilips aims to achieve a target of zero routine flaring by the end of 2025. In 2023, the total gross operated GHG emissions were approximately 17.4 million tonnes. In 2021, ConocoPhilips had joined the Oil Sands Pathways to Net Zero Alliance alongside major companies representing about 95% of Canada's oil sands production. The Alliance aims to reduce Scope 1 and Scope 2 greenhouse gas emissions from oil sands operations thereby supporting Canada's climate goals through carbon capture and storage technologies. ConocoPhillips supports technology development through its annual Marginal Abatement Cost Curve (MACC) process, which identifies and prioritizes emissions reduction opportunities based on the breakeven cost of carbon ($ per tonne of CO_2e reduced). Since 2018, ConocoPhilips have spent approximately $750 million on research and development, equipment, products and services and projects to reduce GHG emissions through the MACC process., ConocoPhillips is a founding member of the Climate Leadership Council (CLC), an international policy institute founded in collaboration with business and environmental interests to promote a carbon dividends framework in the U.S.

In 2023, ConocoPhilips supplied Asian markets with approximately 0.34 trillion cubic feet of natural gas and LNG.In early 2021, ConocoPhillips created a multidisciplinary Low Carbon Technologies organization to support its net-zero goals for Scope 1 and 2 emissions, assess the low-carbon energy landscape, and prioritize future investment opportunities. In 2022, ConocoPhilips made an investment to support the development of a novel turquoise hydrogen production technology from Ekona Power Inc., a Vancouver based hydrogen technology venture. ConocoPhilips invested in LongPath Technologies, a scalable laser based continuous emissions monitoring solution with the potential to cover targeted assets or provide basin wide multi operator coverage. In 2023, ConocoPhilips made social investments of $63.2 million. In 2023, ConocoPhilips raised $2.7 billion from a three-tranche deal to buy out Total's 50% stake in the Surmont oil facility, a Canadian oil sands field it co owns with the French major oil company.

References

Aramco/Sustainability Report 2023.

Chevron Corporation 2023 Climate Change Resilience Report.

ConocoPhilips, Building a Resilient Strategy for the Energy Transition Managing Climate Related Risks 2023.

ConocoPhillips Sustainability Report 2023.

ConocoPhillips 2024 10-K.

2023, Corporate Sustainability Report Chevron.

ExxonMobil | Advancing Climate Solutions | 2023 Progress Report.

https://corporate.exxonmobil.com/sustainability-and-reports/sustainability#Aboutthereport

https://www.chevron.com/-/media/chevron/sustainability/documents/addressing-climate-change-pdf-download.pdf

https://www.chevron.com/sustainability

PetroChina Company Limited 2024 Environmental, Social and Governance Report.

Shell Energy Transition Strategy 2021.

Shell Energy Transition Strategy 2024.

TotalEnergies, Sustainability & Climate 2025 Progress Report.

Chapter 15
Green Investments in Pharmaceutical Industry

Green Investments by Pfizer

Pfizer Inc. is a research-based, global biopharmaceutical company. Pfizer is one of the world's most innovative health companies with 175 years of operations. Most of the revenues for Pfizer comes from the manufacture and sale of biopharmaceutical products. Pfizer manages its commercial operations through a global structure consisting of three operating segments. Biopharma, the innovative science-based biopharmaceutical business engages in the discovery, development, manufacture, marketing, sale and distribution of biopharmaceutical products worldwide. PC1 is the contract development and manufacturing organization and leading supplier of specialty active pharmaceutical ingredients. Pfizer Ignite offers strategic guidance and end to end R&D services to select innovative biotech companies. The company had total revenues of $63.6 billion in year 2024.

Pfizer had set its first formal greenhouse gas emission reduction (GHG) goal in the year 2001. During the period 2001–2020, Pfizer have reduced its GHG emissions by more than 60%. In 2015, Pfizer became one of the first companies to receive validation of its GHG reduction goal by the Science Based Target Initiative. Pfizer aim to reduce its Scope 1& 2 emissions by 46% by 2030 compared to a 2019 baseline. The company have targets to reduce emissions by 95% by year 2040. As a near term target toward this longer-term goal, by 2025, Pfizer aim for 64% of its purchased goods and services suppliers by spend to set their own science based GHG reduction targets. Pfizer also aim to reduce emissions, from a 2019 baseline, for upstream logistics by 10% and business travel by 25%. Pfizer intends to allocate amounts equivalent to the net proceeds of potential issuances of GSS Bonds to finance and/or refinance, in whole or in part, new and/or existing Green and/or Social Projects. Pfizer aims to achieve the voluntary Net Zero standard by 2040, 10 years earlier than the timeline described in the standard.

B. R. Kumar, *Green Finance*, Sustainable Finance,
https://doi.org/10.1007/978-3-032-03333-8_15

In March 2020, Pfizer launched the $12.5 billion sustainability bond, the first to be issued by a biopharmaceutical company. In 2021, Pfizer priced its $1 billion sustainability bond in aggregate principal amount of 1.75% senior notes due 2031. Pfizer intended to use the net proceeds to finance or refinance in whole or in part for research and development of COVID-19 vaccines and other projects of Pfizer which had environmental or social benefits. Citigroup Global Markets Inc., Goldman Sachs & Co. LLC, J.P. Morgan Securities LLC and Morgan Stanley & Co. LLC acted as joint book-running managers for the offering. The Pfizer Sustainability bond aligned with the Green Bond Principles, Social bond principles and the International Capital Market Association's sustainability bond guidelines. The net proceeds from the sustainability bond issuance have been allocated to environmental projects which support green design and construction of new office and manufacturing facilities.

Pfizer focuses on development of sustainable medicines by reducing the environmental impact of medicines throughout the product life cycle addressing areas such as GHG emissions, water scarcity and discharge. Pfizer aims for conservation of resources towards a circular economy and integration of green chemistry/biotechnology principles throughout its process lifecycles. As part of its waste and recycling goals, Pfizer apply green chemistry principles in research, development and manufacturing processes. The company also explore means to reuse, recover or recycle solvents. Pfizer support waste reduction and recycling efforts across its supply chain and conduct preselection waste vendor audits. The manufacturing and R&D sites have long term environmental sustainability masterplans outlining planned actions to reduce impact. Pfizer currently sources around 6% of electricity from renewables for worldwide operation. The aim is to purchase 100% electricity from renewable energy sources by year 2030. In 2021, Pfizer entered into a 15-year virtual power purchase agreement with Vesper Energy to receive 310 MW of renewable energy from Vesper Energy's 500 MW Hornet Solar project in West Texas. Pfizer is a part of Energize, a unique initiative by 10 global pharma companies to support suppliers in decarbonizing operations through renewable energy with guidance from Schneider Electric.

In 2020 through an ESG priority assessment, Pfizer identified its ESG priorities. The company identified 30 key topics which were mapped into six priority areas. These priority areas were aligned with Pfizer's blueprint strategy and were incorporated into its Enterprise Risk Management (ERM) process. In December 2023, Pfizer completed its acquisition of Seagen Inc., a global biotechnology leader in Antibody -Drug Conjugates (ADC) technology for transformative cancer treatment. With the addition of Seagen's four in line medicines, Pfizer's industry leading Oncology portfolio includes over 25 approved medicines and biosimilars across more than 40 indications including nine medicines which are either blockbuster or have the potential to be blockbuster.

Pfizer is at the forefront of applying AI in pharmacovigilance-the science of monitoring the safety of medicines and vaccines. For example, Pfizer is exploring how AI can evaluate and classify reports submitted by individuals regarding potential safety concerns. ESG at Pfizer is governed by the Sustainability Steering Committee chaired by the Chief Sustainability Officer.

The Compensation Committee oversees the executive compensation program, which incorporates an 'ESG Scorecard' to help align the funding of its annual short-term incentive plan. This plan, covering over 40,000 eligible colleagues and leaders worldwide, is partially tied to specific social and environmental key performance indicators (KPIs).

Pfizer was one of the initial signatories to the US Department of Health and Human Services (HHS) climate pledge. The pledge calls on stakeholders in the US Healthcare system to reduce GHG emissions and build a more climate resilient healthcare infrastructure. Approximately 51% of Pfizer's suppliers by spend have commitments to develop science based GHG emissions reduction targets. Emissions related to upstream transportation and distribution were 31% lower than in year 2022. In 2023, Pfizer adopted the My Green Labs (MGL) Certification program at its Cambridge, Massachusetts, site to facilitate engagement of laboratory-based colleagues in environmental stewardship. For the promotion of sustainable medicines, Pfizer follows the best practices in the AMR Industry Alliance's (AMRIA) Antibiotic Manufacturing Standard. A core pillar of Pfizer's product innovation work is its efforts to help slow the spread of antimicrobial resistance (AMR). In 2022, Pfizer initiated life cycle assessments for small molecules, large molecules, vaccines, and devices to identify key development stages with the greatest potential for reducing environmental impact.

Pfizer apply an internal performance metric grounded in the hierarchy of control principles—avoid, reduce, reuse, recycle, and dispose—to guide waste management decisions and encourage minimization. In 2023, Pfizer launched an initiative focused on reducing landfill waste from its manufacturing sites. As part of this effort, Pfizer diverted approximately 8.6 million kilograms of waste generated by the July 2023 tornado at its Rocky Mount, North Carolina facility to waste-to-energy facilities. Since 2019, Pfizer have reduced landfill-bound waste from routine operations by more than 5.4 million kilograms.

Through the Accord for a Healthier World, Pfizer aims to provide access to the full portfolio of medicines and vaccines to 1.2 billion people living in 45 lower-income countries around the world. Pfizer's digital solution, offers a standardized and secure platform to streamline processes for third parties managing Pfizer support programs, combined with a mobile app for patient.

In 1998, Pfizer and the Edna McConnell Clark Foundation co-founded the International Trachoma Initiative (ITI), a non-profit dedicated to helping eliminate trachoma, the leading infectious cause of blindness worldwide. Pfizer, The Bill & Melinda Gates Foundation, Children's Investment Fund Foundation (CIFF), and Becton, Dickinson & Company (BD) have expanded their collaboration to provide millions of women in low- and lower-middle income countries with greater access to injectable contraceptives.

Green Investments in J&J

Johnson & Johnson(J&J) and its subsidiaries (the Company) is engaged in the research and development, manufacture and sale of a broad range of products in the healthcare field. The company have approximately 138,100 employees worldwide. The Company is organized into two business segments: Innovative Medicine and MedTech. The Innovative Medicine segment is focused on the therapeutic areas of Immunology, Infectious diseases, Neuroscience, Oncology, Cardiovascular and Metabolism, Pulmonary Hypertension. The MedTech segment includes a broad portfolio of products used in the cardiovascular, orthopaedics, surgery, and vision categories.

In 2024, J&J had $88.8 billion in consolidated sales. Innovative medicine had reported $57 billion in sales. J&J have 26 products/platforms which generate $1 plus billion in annual sales. The company have donated 2.6 plus billion doses of Vermox to facilitate treatment of intestinal worm. The company have spent $17.2 billion in R&D during 2024. In 2023, the total spend with small and diverse suppliers amounted to $4.9 billion. Hospitals in 11 countries have partnered with Johnson and Johnson for recycling program for single use medical devices. In 2023, 40,000 operating room and hospital staff were trained in resource limited settings.

Approximately 87% of Johnson & Johnson's global electricity requirements were sourced from renewable sources which include 100% of its operations in Europe, the US and Canada. The company have achieved 23% reduction in its absolute Scope 1 & 2 GHG emission reduction since 2021. In 2022 according to Access to Medicine Index, J&J was ranked number 2 and featured as an index top three performer for the sixth consecutive year. J&J was included in the FTSE4Good Index Series for the 23rd year, which measures the performance of publicly traded companies with ESG practices. In 2022, J&J was ranked number one in the pharmaceuticals and biotechnology sector in North America for Moody's ESG scorecard. J&J achieved an MSCI "A" rating in year 2023.

As a part of J&J Health for Humanity Goal, J&J supported more than 1.3 million health workers. Overall more than 2.28 million healthcare workers were supported since the year 2021. J&J spent 10 years developing the first new MDR-TB treatment in more than 40 years and the last 10 years advancing access to this treatment. In 2012, J&J introduced SIRTURO, the first targeted TB medicine with a novel mechanism of action.

J&J and the Lions Club International Foundation's Sight for Kids (SFK) program offers comprehensive eye health services to more than three million children annually in low income schools in several countries. In 2023, SFK offered almost 2.5 million eye screenings for children and issued spectacles for more than half million children. J&J have a 20-year legacy of accelerating the fight against NTDs. In 2023, J&J products valued at $four million were provided to communities impacted by natural disasters around the world. Approximately $5.3 million funding was provided as response to natural disasters in year 2023. In 2020, J&J launched "Our Race to Health Equity" (ORTHE) which is a multiyear initiative which focusses on closing the racial health gap in US. In 2023, the investments made by J&J totalled $80 million to community led organizations and programs. J&J provided $38 million to the Business Matching Fund to support more than 50 programs. J&J's corporate venture arm JJDC supports a portfolio of more than 100 companies and have invested over $3.5 billion in capital since 2014. J&J empowers physicians with simplified surgical experiences through its VIRUTUGUIDE AI Patient Matched Platform.

Since 2021, the absolute Scope 1 and Scope 2 GHG emissions have reduced 23%. In 2023, J&J received A-score for leadership in environmental transparency and climate change performance. Currently 87% of global electricity is sourced from renewables. Since 2005, J&J have allocated up to $40 million per year in capital relief through carbon dioxide capital relief program for energy projects which offer scope for carbon dioxide savings and financial return. During the period 2005–2023, the carbon dioxide capital relief program has resulted in annual energy savings of $69 million and the total spent on completed projects amounted to $387 million. The annual energy savings amounted to 2016 TJ. The total number of J&J sites which were LEED certified or equivalent was 62. J&J sites achieved "My Green Lab" certification for implementing sustainability best practices. As part of improved packaging sustainability, J&J uses fibre-based pulp injection molding (PIM) for secondary packaging of immunology self-injectable devices. Currently 30% of self injectable device product lines uses PIM trays. Through the Supplier Sustainability Program, J&J monitor, engage and collaborate with suppliers on environmental, social and ethical obligations. The global supplier diversity spend and impact in year 2023 for J&J amounted to $4.9 billion. The total US spend with Tier 1 diverse and small businesses amounted to $3.9 billion in year 2023. Since its induction in the Billion Dollar Roundtable, J&J have spent more than $20 billion with Tier 1 diverse suppliers. This initiative comprises companies which advance best practices for supplier diversity and spend at least $ 1 billion annually with diverse owned suppliers.

Green Investments by Astra Zeneca

AstraZeneca is a global science led patient focused pharmaceutical company. The company employs 89,900 employees worldwide. The company had revenues of $54.1 billion in year 2024. In 2024, the company invested $13.6 billion in R&D. The pharma company has a portfolio of products for major diseases in areas such as oncology, cardiovascular, gastrointestinal, infection, neuroscience, respiratory and inflammation. The company was founded in year 1999 through the merger of the Swedish Astra AB and the British Zeneca Group.

Healthcare sector is estimated to account for 5% of global emissions. AstraZeneca focusses on decarbonisation across its value chain through the flagship Ambition Zero Carbon strategy program. The company is investing $ 1 billion to reduce emissions from the lab to the patient and promotes more circular approaches for discovery, development and delivery of medicines with latest digital technologies and innovation. The AZ Forest programme is a $400 million initiative to plant and maintain 200 million trees by year 2030. By 2023, Astra Zeneca have planted 19.9 million trees under this initiative. The Sustainable Markets Initiative Health Systems Task Force is a public private partnership promoted by Astra Zeneca for the transition to net zero health systems. In 2023, Astra Zeneca launched joint environmental targets for suppliers. Through the Young Health Program in 40 countries, Astra Zeneca have directly engaged over 15 million young people on non-communicable disease risk factors since 2010. Astra Zeneca is a member of Dow Jones Sustainability Indices. The patient access programmes promoted by Astra Zeneca have reached 13.6 million people. Approximately 66.4 million people had accessed healthcare programmes of AstraZeneca such as Healthy Heart Africa (HHA), Young Health Programme (YHP) and Healthy Lung Programmes (HLP). Since 2015, AstraZeneca have achieved 67.6% reduction in Scope 1 and 2 greenhouse gas (GHG) emissions. Since 2015, Astra Zeneca have achieved 13.2% reduction in waste. Since 2010, 127,384 healthcare works were trained by AstraZeneca. AstraZeneca Board has 46% female representation and 31% ethnic minority representation.

AstraZeneca have disease area-focused R&D organisations which have responsibility for discovery through to late-stage development for Oncology, BioPharmaceuticals and Rare Disease. Two commercial units, one for Oncology and one for BioPharmaceuticals, align product strategy and commercial delivery across its US and Europe-Canada regions.

AstraZeneca does not file patent applications in any low-income countries (LICs) or least developed countries (LDCs). The total community investment amounted to $115.4 million. The company have invested $4778.8 million in product donations through the patient assistance programmes. Hearty Health Africa (HHA) program aims to treat ten million people with hypertension and cardiovascular disease across Africa by year 2025. By 2023, the program had conducted more than 47.9 million blood pressure screening and trained over 11,300 healthcare workers since its launch in 2014. About 1516 healthcare facilities were activated through the HHA program. The Young Health Programme (YHP) is youth led advocacy movement which is active in 40 countries worldwide supporting community programmes, research for vulnerable and under resourced communities.

Since its launch in 2010, the YHP has partnered with over 60 non-profit organizations worldwide, including UNICEF, to directly reach more than 15 million young people and train over 580,000 youth as Peer Educators. In 2023 alone, the YHP impacted more than five million young people through its prevention and education programmes. In 2023, Astra Zeneca contributed $115.4 million in financial and non-financial donations to more than 810 non-profit partners across 76 countries. AstraZeneca have offered $4.7 billion of medicines through patient assistance programmes throughout the world. The largest patient assistance programme is AZ&Me Prescription Savings program in the US. In 2023, approximately 97.6% of paper-based product packaging materials used were supplied from sustainable sources. In 2021, AstraZeneca partnered with the Association of Community Cancer Centers for cancer screening and treatment programmes to underserved communities across Kentucky. AstraZeneca is engineering next-generation vaccines utilising innovations such as mRNA, virus-like particles and bioconjugates.

Since 2020, AstraZeneca have applied the Task Force on Climate related Financial Disclosures (TCFD) framework. In 2023, the company invested $33.7 million in energy efficiency and on-site renewable energy. The company have achieved a 17.5% absolute reduction in total energy consumption from its 2015 baseline. In 2021, AstraZeneca obtained 100% imported electricity from certified renewable sources by purchasing energy certificates that matched both the country and the year of consumption.

AstraZeneca have spent $19.4 million during 2022–2023 for on site solar photovoltaic (PV) installations at nine locations in seven countries. AstraZeneca have entered into a 10-year PPA agreement with StatKraft, Europe's largest renewable energy producer to source electricity from wind farm in Sweden. In 2023, AstraZeneca entered into a collaboration with Vanguard Renewables to facilitate delivery of renewable natural gas (RNG-biomethane) to sites in US by end of 2026. In 2023, the company entered into a 15-year agreement with Future Biogas to establish the first unsubsidized industrial scale supply of biomethane in the UK.

Through the SMI Health Systems Task Force, AstraZeneca is collaborating across the healthcare sector to fast-track the transition to net-zero health systems with the focus on supply chain decarbonisation, sustainable patient care pathways, and leveraging digital innovation in clinical research. The Life Cycle Assessment (LCA) programme determines the type and magnitude of environmental impacts across the product value chains and is in line with ISO standards 14,040 and 14,044. AstraZeneca is part of the Horizon Eternal consortium consisting of 17 EU organizations which advance sustainable pharmaceutical manufacturing, usage and disposal practices. With respect to product sustainability, 64% of total syntheses had met resource efficiency target at launch. The company aims to ensure that 100% of AstraZeneca site discharges and greater than 90% of supplier site discharges are in compliance with safe API discharge concentrations. The company aims to reduce waste by 10% below the 2015 baseline by year 2025.

Table 15.1 highlights the details of green investments made by AstraZeneca during the period 2021–2023.

The company aims to reduce Scope 1 and 2 greenhouse gas (GHG) emissions by 98% from 2015 base year.

Table 15.1 Green Investments by AstraZeneca

Year	2021	2022	2023
Total dollar amount given in grants (in millions)	25.74	26.49	26.49
Participants tracked for progress	70,081	71,732	73,091
US based non profits funded	58	58	58
People reached by patient access programmes (cumulative, million)	11.55	12.83	13.69
Product donation through patient access programmes (USD, million)	2351.5	3100.2	4778.9
Total community investment (USD, million)	112.9	108.06	115.44

Source: AstraZeneca Sustainability Report 2023

Green Investments by Merck

Merck is a premier research-intensive biopharmaceutical company. This global healthcare company focusses on delivering innovative health solutions through its medicines, vaccines, biologic therapies and animal health products. The company is known as Merck& Co in the US and Canada. In the rest of the world, the company is known as MSD. Pharmaceutical and Animal Health are the two operating segments though which Merck manage business. The Pharmaceutical segment constitute human health pharmaceuticals and vaccine products. Human health pharmaceutical products consist of therapeutic and preventive agents. Human health vaccine products consist of preventive paediatric, adolescent and adult vaccines. The Animal Health segment discovers, develops, manufactures and markets a wide range of veterinary pharmaceutical and vaccine products. The annual revenue in year 2023 amounted to $60.1 billion. In 2023, over 550 million people received Merck's medicines and vaccines. The R&D spend in year 2023 amounted to $30.5 billion. In 2023, approximately 240 million people had access to Merck's innovative medicines and vaccines through access solutions. About 83% of the top 20 global burdens of disease were addressed by Merck's pipeline and products. The company aim to enable 350 million people to access its medicines and vaccines by year 2025.

Merck have committed to a net zero target for its greenhouse gas (GHG) emissions across its global operations by 2045 aligned with the guidelines of the Science Based Targets initiative (SBTi). Merck have increased its spend with small and diverse Tier 1 and 2 suppliers from $3.2 billion in 2022 to $3.6 billion in 2023. In 2024, Merck achieved rank 34 in Barron's Top 100 Most Sustainable US Companies. In 2023, Merck added sustainability metrics to its company scorecard which would affect the pay-out under its annual incentives.

In 2021, Merck launched sustainability financing framework to raise and direct funds to critical projects to meet its sustainability goals and advance UN Sustainable Development Goals (SDGs). The sustainability financing framework of Merck is aligned with the International Capital Markets Association (ICMA) 2021, Green Bond Principles, the 2021 Social Bond Principles and the 2021 Sustainability Bond Guidelines. In 2021, Merck issued inaugural offering of $ 1 billion sustainability bond. The bonds net proceeds support projects to increase access to essential health care services and reduce environmental footprint. By September 2023, Merck have fully allocated the $994 million of its net proceeds from its 2021 sustainability bond.

Access to Health is a priority sustainability focus area for Merck. Approximately 81% of the funds were allocated to projects completed or in progress during the 3-year lookback period, while the remaining 19% went to projects completed or underway between the bond issuance and time period September 30, 2023. The bond proceeds were allocated to investments in partnerships which addressed barriers to healthcare for underserved populations and to expenditures in research and development.

Table 15.2 shows the green investment of Merck during 2023.

Table 15.2 Green investments by Merck

Sector	Value in millions of dollars
Healthcare	579
Socio economic advancement and empowerment	100
Green buildings	286
Sustainable water and waste water management	29

Source: Merck Sustainability Report 2023

Table 15.3 R&D investments

Year	2019	2020	2021	2022	2023
R&D expenses in billions of dollars	9.7	13.4	12.2	13.5	30.5
Top 20 global burdens of disease addressed by products and pipeline	100%	88%	71%	83%	83%
Established significant external licenses and collaborations	78	123	92	97	76

Source: Merck Impact Report 2023–2024

The proceeds from the sustainability bond were utilized by Merck Foundation to address systemic barriers to health equity, pregnancy and childbirth care, enterprise health equity initiatives and partnerships for the Advancing Health Online (AHO) initiatives. In 2021–2022, these social investments were accessed by over 20.8 million people. By 2022, over 33 million people received social investments from Merck. The health equity goal of the company is to reach over 50 million people by year 2025.

Merck is in the process of building a range of partnership to strengthen cancer prevention, care and support systems. In the US, Merck support the American Cancer Society's Get Screened campaign. In 2022, Merck launched a $ one million Health Equity Catalyst Fund to create solutions to promote equitable health outcomes and care experiences for underserved sections of society. The Health Equity Catalyst Fund supports 15 community level efforts in 13 countries. In June 2021, Merck and Meta launched Advancing Health Online (AHO) to explore how social media can enhance global community health and resilience. The AHO Fund has awarded over 40 global grants to support research on using behavioural science and digital platforms to boost vaccine confidence and access. Merck is part of the Billion Dollar Roundtable, recognizing corporations that annually spend $ one billion plus with women and minority owned suppliers to promote global supplier diversity. In 2022, Merck spent $2.3 billion in the US with more than 640 diverse suppliers with nearly $5 billion in economic impact and sustained over 30,000 jobs. Over $100 million of sustainability bond proceeds were allocated to diverse supplier spend. Approximately 3.7 million square feet of "green" floor space were either completed or are in construction stage. Projects funded by sustainability bond proceeds encompassed over 900 thousand square feet of space. The company had reduced water usage by 17% since year 2015.The Micro Lab Extension at Carlow, Ireland facility has achieved LEED Gold certification.

Table 15.3 shows the R&D Investments by Merck.

R&D expenses include a $2.7 billion charge in 2020 related to the acquisition of VelosBio, Inc., a $1.7 billion charge in 2021 related to the acquisition of Pandion Therapeutics, Inc., $1.7 billion of intangible asset impairment charges in 2022, and charges of $17.1 billion in 2023 for the acquisitions of Prometheus Biosciences, Inc., and Imago BioSciences, Inc., and the formation of collaborations with Daiichi Sankyo and Kelun Biotech.

Over a decade ago, Merck co-founded Hilleman Laboratories with Wellcome Trust to expand affordable access to vaccines and biologics in low- and middle-income countries. In 2022, Merck licensed two preclinical TB treatment candidates to Gates MRI, aiming to support combination therapies for a leading cause of death in LMICs.

The company aim to reach at least 75% of countries worldwide annually with human health medicines and vaccines. In 2023, Merck products reached 79% of countries. The company achieved a 100% security risk completion rate for all new logistics partners during the logistics procurement process. In Canada, Merck had partnered with Ministry of Health and a pharmacy chain to promote new supply chain initiative which introduces a block chain based secure network for real time tracking of vaccine doses.

Table 15.4 highlights the details of product donations made by Merck.

The MECTIZAN Donation Program is the longest-running drug donation program for neglected tropical diseases. The MMOP is the primary program through which Merck donates medicines and vaccines for global disaster relief and humanitarian assistance in LMICs. In 2023, Merck reached 42,000 people through the MMOP.

During the period 2021–2023, over 54 million people received social investments to address health equity. In 2023, Merck made $44 million in social investments to address health equity through philanthropy, strategic collaborations and impact investing. Merck for Mothers is a $650 million global initiative to protect pregnant mothers. By 2023 since inception, Merck for Mothers Initiative has reached more than 30 million women to improve maternal health outcomes. Merck

Table 15.4 Product donations by Merck

Product donations	2019	2020	2021	2022	2023
Product donations through U.S. patient assistance program (U.S. dollars in millions)	1460	1603	1455	1685	1570
Product donations for ex-U.S. programs and U.S. disaster relief (U.S. dollars in millions)	1550	1280	284	97	483
Total estimated number of people reached through product donation programs (millions)	403.7	268.3	197.3	359.2	385.2
Estimated number of people reached through the MECTIZAN donation program (millions)	403	267.8	197	358.9	385
Patients utilizing U.S. patient assistance program (millions)	0.239	0.19	0.13	0.113	0.129
Estimated number of people reached through the MMOP (millions)	0.458	0.283	0.139	0.119	0.042

Source: Merck 2023/2024 Impact Report

Foundation established the Alliance for Equity in Cancer Care for underserved communities with $20 million commitment over 5-year period 2022–2026. The Foundation is investing $11 million over 6 years (2023–2028) to support Project ECHO® at the University of New Mexico Health. This initiative aims to improve cancer care delivery in low- and middle-income countries (LMICs) by expanding access to best-practice care through knowledge sharing.

Merck have net zero target for its greenhouse gas (GHG) emissions across its global operations by 2045. Merck have a dedicated Sustainable Capital Fund which allocated $12 million annually to support sustainability initiatives at its sites. The company have committed to sourcing 100% of its purchased electricity from renewable energy by 2025. The company achieved 31% reduction in total waste generation in its largest hazardous waste generating site in 2023. In 2023, approximately 55% of Merck's facilities sent zero operational waste to landfill. The company had $3.6 billion spending with small and diverse Tier 1 and 2 suppliers globally in 2023. The economic impact of this spending amounted to $5.6 billion.

Green Investments by Novartis

Novartis is a global innovative medicines company which is engaged in the research, development, manufacturing, distribution, marketing and sale of a broad range of innovative pharmaceutical medicines. The medicines of Novartis treat serious diseases from cancer and heart disease to neurological conditions and rare genetic illnesses. The core therapeutic areas of Novartis include cardiovascular, renal and metabolic immunology, neuroscience and oncology. In 2024, Novartis reached nearly 300 million patients with innovative therapies. Novartis have built legacy in areas such as breast cancer and chronic myeloid leukemia with medicines such as Kisqali and Scembix developed by researcher in Novartis lab. The company prioritize platforms such as RLT and RNA therapeutics and increasingly integrate artificial intelligence and data science through its R&D activities. By means of a combination of in-house R&D and targeted acquisitions and licensing agreements, Novartis has more than 30 potential new high value medicines in its pipeline. Novartis operates more than 33 manufacturing sites globally. Novartis sell its medicines in approximately 120 countries worldwide.

The company focus on exploratory research work on core therapeutic areas. The company is investing in technology platforms to deliver high value medicines. Novartis focus on two established platforms (chemistry and biotherapeutics) plus three advanced Technology platforms (radioligand therapy (RLT), xRNA, and gene and cell therapy) to develop transformative new medicines. Novartis have 5582 full-time equivalent scientists, physicians and business professionals at Biomedical Research sites. The company has 12,773 full-time employees worldwide. In 2021, Novartis conducted materiality assessment with input of more than 500 external and 12,000 internal stakeholders. In 2024, the net sales of Novartis amounted to USD 50.3 billion.

ESG-related performance, including climate and nature targets, was one of four equally weighted strategic goals forming 40% of the Executive Committee's 2024 incentive system. Novartis have incorporated the recommendations of the Task Force on Climate-related Financial Disclosures (TCFD) to strengthen climate governance, strategy and risk management processes. The company have a transition plan to become net zero by 2040. As part of near-term target, Novartis have committed to using 100% renewable electricity across its operations by 2025. The company is also transitioning its fleet to electric vehicles by year 2030. The company systematically integrate life-cycle assessment (LCA) methods in its R&D pipeline to calculate and improve the environmental impact of its products. Novartis work closely with organizations such as World Business Council for Sustainable Development (WBCSD), the Sustainable Markets Initiative (SMI), the Pharmaceutical Environmental Group (PEG), and the Pharmaceutical Supply Chain Initiative (PSCI) to reduce the effects of climate change and nature loss. Novartis apply a shadow carbon price of USD 100/tCO2e in decisions on strategic capital expenditure over USD 20 million. Novartis estimate the planned investment needed for implementing its net-zero transition plan based on three-time horizons: medium term (up to 2030), aligned with its near-term target; long term (up to 2040), transitioning to net zero across its value chain; and maintaining net zero up to 2050, in line with the Paris Agreement. In 2024, the company had deployed capital expenditure of USD 40 million on environmental projects to improve energy efficiency and adopt renewable energy solutions.

In line with SBTi-approved target boundary, Novartis have reduced its Scope 1 emissions by 22% and its Scope 2 emissions by 72% from a 2022 base year. In 2024, globally 96% of purchased electricity consumption by Novartis was renewable, compared with 92% in 2022. The company use 100% renewable electricity in North America (US and Canada) and Europe through its virtual power purchase agreements. In 2024, the capital expenditure deployed towards environmental sustainability amounted to USD 40 million.

Table 15.5 shows expected investment for Novartis's transition plan. The values are given in millions of US dollars.

Operating expenditure is calculated by multiplying the volume of credits required per year by forecast offset prices considering multiple variables.

Table 15.6 shows the anticipated effects from Novartis's climate-related transition risks and opportunities.

The upstream value chain analysis of the company for assessing the current economic exposure levels to physical risk events found that 427 first tier supplier constituting 9% of the company's total third party spend are exposed to significant climate risk. Such suppliers represented USD 119 million of revenue to be at risk. Novartis have a target to reduce the amount of waste sent for disposal by half by 2025, compared with a 2016 baseline. The company have target to eliminate polyvinyl chloride (PVC), a long-lasting plastic in secondary and tertiary packaging at Novartis sites by year 2025. By end 2024, 97% of Novartis manufacturing sites met internal water quality standards.

Table 15.5 Green Investments for transition plan (Millions of dollars)

		2024–2030	2031–2040	2041–2050
Emission reduction scope 1 and 2	Operating expenditure	150	15	20
	Capital expenditure	330	10	
Carbon certificates	Operating expenditure	8–19	58–203	289–936

Source: Novartis in Society, Integrated Report 2024

Table 15.6 Impact of climate risks and opportunities (Millions of dollars)

		2024–2030	2031–2040	2041–2050
Carbon pricing risk	Operating expenditure	70–184	117–311	72–213
Electricity cost opportunity	Potential savings in operating expenditures	133–228	281–504	187–384

Source: Novartis in Society, Integrated Report 2024

Novartis is a member of the International Labour Organization Global Business and Disability Network and the Valuable 500, promoting inclusion for people.

Green Investments by Bristol Myers Squibb

Bristol Myers Squibb (BMS) is a global biopharmaceutical company. From tuberculosis vaccines to wartime penicillin, HIV treatments, and ground-breaking cancer research, BMS has continually advanced to meet patient needs and adapt to the evolving world of science. The focus areas of BMS are Oncology, hematology, immunology, neuroscience and cardiovascular diseases. In 2023, the company invested $9.3 billion in R&D. The total revenues in 2024 amounted to $48.3 billion. Bristol Myers continually paid dividends to shareholders for 93rd consecutive year in 2025. Bristol Myers have an initiative to drive operational efficiencies and increase productivity with the aim of achieving $1.5 billion in cost savings by the end of 2025.

Bristol Myers Squibb Foundation is an independent charitable organization which supports community-based programs that promote disease awareness, screening, care and support among high risk populations. BMS have created tailored programs to expand access to innovative treatments. BMS have made available 12 transformative products in 80 plus low- and middle-income countries (LMICs) which include 40 plus low-income countries at equitable pricing. The company is positioned to drive continued innovation and expand treatment options across therapeutic areas based on differentiated research platforms which include cell therapy and targeted protein degradation. During the past 3 years, BMS have received more than 50 global regulatory approvals. By 2023, 58% of clinical trial sites were located in racially and ethnically diverse metro areas of the US. In 2023, BMS published its inaugural Task Force on Climate related Financial Disclosures

(TCFD) Report and submitted its science-based targets to the Science Based Targets initiative (SBTi) for external validation. BMS have delivered 10 new medicines since 2019 and have a growing registrational portfolio. During the period 2020–2023, over 12 million people were benefitted from the BMS health equity grants. BMS have 30 plus assets in early stage clinical development. Approximately 47.4% of BMS employees at executive level are female. BMS have a 15-year Virtual Power Purchasing Agreement (VPPA) with National Grid Renewables for 145 megawatts of solar energy. The company aims to provide one million healthcare providers with educational programs by year 2033.BMS have offered 7.8 million patients with medicines in high income countries. By 2024, 73% of all late stage assets have access plans. The company targets to provide access to 208 plus patients in LMICs by year 2033. During the 2023, Bristol Myers provided $26.9 billion in discounts, rebates, price concessions and fees to commercial insurers, government programs, providers, intermediaries and others. It was estimated that approximately 46 cents of each dollar of company's gross sales went back into the healthcare system. Of the total amount, approximately half went to Medicare and Medicaid and 15% to the Veteran Affairs and the US Department of Defense. When developing prices, BMS considers costs across the span of a medicine's life cycle.

LMICs, home to 84% of the global population, face rising non-communicable diseases (NCDs) with increasing life expectancy. BMS addresses health system challenges by expanding access through tailored, innovative healthcare programs. In countries where BMS medicines are not registered, healthcare professionals (HCPs) can request medicines for individual patients through Direct Import pathway in accordance with local laws and regulations. In 2022, BMS launched a 2-year tailored tiered pricing access program for Opdivo, an immunotherapy treatment for cancers in six lower and upper middle-income countries. Through the direct import and DTI imports pathways, BMS have expanded access to 12 medicines in 80 plus LMICs using tiered pricing mechanism. BMS has been a longstanding leader in health equity, partnering in initiatives like Access Accelerated to reduce chronic NCD care inequities in low- and middle-income countries (LMICs). BMS had cofounded Access Accelerated in year 2017. Since 2020, Access Accelerated's partnership with the World Bank Healthy Lives Fund has enabled dozens of LMICs to mobilize over $3.7 billion in new investments to enhance NCD care access. In 2023, Bristol Myers Squibb had provided $19.4 million through 277 grants and donations to organizations to support patients to address health equity.

During the period 2020–2023, over 12 million patients received services and programs as result of health equity grants. During the same period, 1211 educational resources and platforms were created and 2229 live/virtual events were held by BMS. Through partnerships such as the Forum for the Future's Climate and Health Coalition, BMS is raising awareness and driving action to address the complex public health impacts of climate change. The Bristol Myers Squibb Foundation, an independent charitable organization, works to advance health equity in underserved communities. The Winn Awards, launched by the BMS Foundation in 2020, aim to boost clinical trial diversity, reduce health disparities, and train future clinical researchers. In 2023, BMS Foundation had invested $51.4 million as health equity grants. Launched in 2017 with a $50 million BMS Foundation investment, the

HOPE program expands access to cancer and blood disorder care for children in sub-Saharan Africa. The BMS Foundation provided $3.3 million in grants to 11 organizations through an initiative called New Jersey Safety Net Innovation Program. BMS have delivered 10 new products since 2019. BMS has over 100 active strategic collaborations and an extensive network of more than 200 active research alliances to build on its internal R&D strengths. Bristol Myers Squibb has a robust and innovative pipeline of transformational new medicines in all phases of development. The company have a number of programs in discovery to address high unmet needs in treating amyotrophic lateral sclerosis (ALS), Alzheimer's disease, Huntington's disease, multiple sclerosis (MS) and Parkinson's disease. BMS developed a study optimization and digital protocol solution (DPS) capability, which has been deployed against all full development studies since 2021. This DPS capability has avoided over $120 million in study costs and reduced patient and site burdens by an average 7% per trial.

BMS has developed a toolkit, the Digitally Accelerated Clinical Trial (DACT) model, which spans the full clinical trial pathway from early protocol development to study execution. The BMS Foundation provides a matching donation of $2 for every $1 donated by employees based in the continental U.S. and Puerto Rico to designated organizations focused on social justice and diversity.

By 2030, BMS aims to purchase 100% of purchased electricity from renewable sources. BMS have targets to reach equitable water use, zero waste to landfill and 100% electric vehicles in its commercial fleet by year 2040. The company aims to achieve net zero emissions in Scopes 1, 2 and 3 by year 2050. During 2023, BMS implemented more than 70 projects to reduce energy use and greenhouse gas (GHG) emissions across its operations. The company aim to reduce absolute Scope 1, 2 and 3 GHG emissions from fuel and energy related activities by 55% by 2033 compared to 2022 base year. The adoption of Automatic Fault Detection and Diagnostics System is expected to have carbon savings cost of 5–10%. Through the "Greener by Design" approach, BMS significantly reduced waste across its small molecule development portfolio eliminating approximately 650,000 kg of waste across seven projects in 2022 and 2023. BMS co-founded the M2030 Activate program to reduce API-related emissions by supporting suppliers in adopting science-based targets and improving sustainability, efficiency, and procurement practices. For nearly a decade, BMS has offered an internal Green Lab certification program, empowering scientists to reduce environmental impact by minimizing energy use, water consumption, and waste in their workspaces.

References

AstraZeneca Sustainability Impact Report 2024.
AstraZeneca Sustainability Report 2023.
Bristol Myers Annual Report 2024.
Bristol Myers ESG Report 2023.
https://www.pfizer.com/about/responsibility/environmental-sustainability
J&J 2023 Health for Humanity Report.

J&J Annual Report 2024.
Merck 2023, Sustainability Bond Report.
Merck Impact Report 2023–2024.
Novartis in Society, Integrated Report 2024.
Pfizer 2023 Impact Report.
Sustainability Bond Framework 2021.

Chapter 16
Green Investments by Airlines Industry

Green Investments by Delta Airlines

Delta Airlines is a global airline based in United States. In 2024, Delta served over 200 million customers. In 2025, Delta was awarded for the fourth consecutive year with the Cirium Platinum Award for global operational excellence and named the most on time airline in North America. In 2024, Delta Airlines rewarded employees with $1.4 billion in profit sharing payments. Delta and its alliance partners collectively serve over 120 countries and territories and over 800 destinations around the world. By end 2024, Delta offered up to 5000 peak day flights to more than 290 destinations on six continents. Delta leverage its coastal gateways and strategic relationships with international airline partners to expand its international service. By December 2024, Delta's global network was supported by a fleet of 1292 aircraft. In 2024, Delta's operating income amounted to $6 billion. In 2024, Delta celebrated its 100th anniversary. Delta focusses on updating its fleet with fuel efficient aircraft offering more premium seating and cargo space while upgrading existing cabins to enhance premium options and interior consistency.

It is estimated that the global aviation sector currently contributes 2–3% of the total greenhouse gas emissions. The global aviation industry is a hard to abate sector and jet fuel is the number one contributor to airline industry's carbon footprint. Sustainable Aviation Fuel (SAF) is a significant lever to decarbonize flight and reduce lifecycle emissions from jet fuel by up to 80%.

Delta works to replace a portion of traditional jet fuel with sustainable aviation fuel (SAF) and partnering with innovators to transform the future of flight. Delta aim to replace 10% of its jet fuel refined from fossil fuel with sustainable aviation fuel by the end of 2030. To achieve this goal, Delta aim to procure over 400 million gallons of SAF annually till end of 2030. Delta have industry leading sustainable fuel agreements with corporate customers for sustainable air travel. With the focus on building a more efficient fleet, Delta retired more than 200 aircraft and replaced

B. R. Kumar, *Green Finance*, Sustainable Finance,
https://doi.org/10.1007/978-3-032-03333-8_16

them with aircraft which are 25% more fuel efficient. In 2023, Delta took delivery of 43 aircraft which were on average 28% more fuel efficient per seat mile than aircraft retired since 2019. In 2023, Delta saved a cumulative 21 million gallons of fuel compared to 2019 through measures such as enhanced flight routing, aircraft enhancements and onboard efficiencies.

In 2023, 3.5 million gallons of sustainable aviation fuel were delivered for Delta. Approximately 31% of critical ground service equipment (GSE) fleet were electrified due to deployment of 1647 new electric units since 2020. In 2017, Delta was among the first airlines to receive US Federal Aviation Administration (FAA) validation for its Safety Management System. In 2023, Delta signed the International Air Transport Association (IATA) Safety Leadership Charter.

Delta is committed to net zero carbon emissions by 2050. In 2020, Delta announced a $ 1 billion commitment over 10 years towards carbon neutrality. Launched in January 2023, the Delta Sustainable Skies Lab is an innovative airline research hub dedicated to advancing climate goals. It focuses on research, design, and testing to drive industry innovation and scale proven technologies and actions, supporting Delta's goal of achieving net-zero emissions by 2050.

In 2021, Delta proposed medium- and long-term targets for validation by the Science Based Targets initiative (SBTi) and joined the United Nations Race to Zero – Business Ambition for 1.5 °C campaign. In 2022, SBTi validated Delta's medium-term target, which is aligned with holding warming to well below 2 °C. Delta had 45 million gallons or 1% fuel burn savings from operational improvements in 2025. By 2035, Delta targets 1.1 billion gallons or 3% operational fuel savings. By 2050, Delta aims for 5% operational fuel savings.

Delta have short-term offtake agreements with industry leaders, including Shell and Neste, and had more than doubled SAF deliveries in 2023 compared to 2022. To reduce fuel burn, Delta is limiting APU use by installing GPUs and PCA units at hubs, including major upgrades in Detroit and Boston with Federal Aviation Administration (FAA) grant support. Delta is pioneering one of the first U.S. trials of TaxiBot®—a pilot-operated tow vehicle that allows aircraft to taxi without using their engines. Delta is expanding its sustainable aviation fuel (SAF) efforts through cross-industry partnerships, policy advocacy, and value chain optimization, through the launch of the Minnesota SAF Hub in year 2023. In September 2023, Delta joined MIT and key partners in forming the Zero Impact Aviation Alliance to explore sustainable aviation solutions through research-driven collaboration and action planning.

Through the GREATER MSP Partnership, Bank of America, Delta, Ecolab and Xcel Energy established the Minnesota SAF Hub – the first large-scale SAF Hub in the United States. The partnership uses a phased strategy to boost SAF production in Minnesota, leveraging policy support, agriculture, renewable energy, R&D, infrastructure, and strong jet fuel demand at MSP.

In 2023, Delta began testing new paper cups onboard as part of its effort to reduce plastic waste, targeting the elimination of nearly seven million pounds of single-use plastics annually once fully implemented. In 2023, Delta provided $60 million in charitable giving in line with the commitment to contribute 1% of company's net income to communities worldwide. In 2023, Delta employees and customers raised $18 million for major fundraisers such as American Cancer Society, American Heart Association, Breast Cancer Research Foundation, Children's Healthcare of Atlanta, Covenant House, Delta Care and Scholarship Fund and United Way.

Delta took delivery of 43 next generation aircrafts in year 2023. There had been improved fleet wide fuel efficiency of 5.5%. In 2023, Delta carried more than 189,000 wheelchairs, scooters and mobility devices across its domestic network. In 2023, Delta spent $ 2 billion with Tier 1 diverse suppliers and $79 million in Tier II diverse spend involving subcontractors who work with Tier 1 suppliers.

Since 2020, Delta have retired 3574 gas- and diesel-powered GSE units from its core fleet and introduced 1647 zero-emission eGSE units, achieving a total of 31% electrification of its critical GSE fleet. The Delta Air Lines Foundation have contributed $14 million to support Global Citizen's efforts to deliver the 2030 United Nations Sustainable Development Goals to end extreme poverty and combat the global climate crisis.

Green Investments by United Airlines Holding

United Airlines Holdings, Inc. (together with its consolidated subsidiaries, "UAL" or the "Company") is a holding company and its wholly-owned subsidiary is United Airlines. The Company transports people and cargo throughout North America and to destinations in Asia, Europe, Africa, the Pacific, the Middle East and Latin America. United Airlines Holdings (UAL) through United and its regional carriers, operates across six continents. UAL is a member of Star Alliance, a global integrated airline network. In 2024, Star Alliance carriers served more than 1200 airports in 195 countries and territories with over 17,000 average daily departures.

By end of 2020, United Airlines had pledged a net zero goal to reduce its greenhouse gas (GHG) emissions by 100% by 2050 without relying on the use of voluntary, traditional carbon offsets. The Company also have a mid-term target of reducing its carbon emissions intensity by 50% by 2035 compared to 2019. The Company's sustainability strategy focuses on four pathways: reducing greenhouse gas emissions, using sustainable alternatives to conventional jet fuel, enhancing non-flight operations, and collaborating with stakeholders—including employees, customers, suppliers, and policymakers—to accelerate action and commercialize sustainable technologies across the aviation industry. In 2015, UAL made its first investment in a company which focusses on commercializing SAF production. In 2016, UAL became the first airline globally to start using SAF in its regular operations on an ongoing basis at various airports. In 2021, UAL launched the Eco-Skies Alliance to partner with corporations in funding the premium cost of sustainable aviation fuel (SAF). It also created UAV, a corporate venture arm, to invest in innovative sustainable aviation technologies shaping the future of air travel. In 2022, UAL became the first U.S. airline to sign an international SAF purchase agreement, securing up to

52.5 million gallons from Neste. In 2023, UAL launched the United Airlines Ventures Sustainable Flight Fund to support startups developing technologies for decarbonizing aviation, energy supply chains, and SAF production. In 2024, UAL became the first airline to procure SAF for use at ORD, signing agreements with two suppliers. UAL focuses on strategic electrification of ground service equipment (GSE) across its hubs and stations. By 2024, over 5070 units of UAL'S GSE were electric which accounted for 38% of its GSE fleet. In 2022, the Company collaborated with federal policymakers to support new SAF tax incentives, promoting increased sustainable aviation fuel production across the United States. UAL led efforts to enact Illinois' Sustainable Aviation Fuel Purchase Credit in 2023, reducing SAF costs, and became the first airline to use it in 2024. In the same year, UAL co-founded the SAF Coalition to unite aviation fuel stakeholders and advocate for federal policies boosting domestic SAF production.

The International Civil Aviation Organization's ("ICAO") Carbon Offsetting and Reduction Scheme for International Aviation ("CORSIA"), adopted in October 2016, aims for carbon-neutral growth in international aviation by requiring airlines to buy carbon offsets or use eligible sustainable fuels.

UAL was the first airline to use SAF blend at ORD. The 2024 GHG footprint incorporates the emissions from both conventional jet fuel production and combustion. This methodology captures the full lifecycle emissions of jet fuel usage and facilitate UAL to chart both Scope 1 and Scope 3 emissions reductions from the replacement of conventional jet fuel with SAF. As of December 2024, the total volume of SAF used in UAL operations represented approximately 0.3% of the total aviation fuel usage. United replaced plastic mini wine bottles with canned wine in economy class, eliminating an estimated 4.7 million single-use plastic bottles annually across its flights. United replaced plastic mini wine bottles with canned wine in economy class, eliminating an estimated 4.7 million single-use plastic bottles annually across its flights. In 2024, United launched its first reusable cup and mug pilot program at its club located at Raleigh Durham International Airport. In 2023, United collaborated with the Port Authority of New York and New Jersey to implement a food waste recycling pilot program at the United Club and terminal concessionaries. In 2024, this resulted in approximately 120 tons of organic waste being diverted from landfills.

United enabled customers to contribute $1–$7 toward its Sustainable Flight Account for SAF purchases. Since 2023, over $800,000 was raised from 264,000 ticket purchases. United received over $one million in grant funding in 2024 to help procure 12 electric mobile ground power units (eGPUs). United partners with non-profit organizations to create meaningful impact in the communities. The company offered corporate contributions valued at $23.9 million to charitable causes. United is an investor in alternate fuels, advanced propulsion technologies and carbon capture and utilization technologies. In 2023, United launched Sustainable Flight Fund with over $200 million in capital commitments from 22 corporate partners.

Green Investments by American Airlines Group

American Airlines Group Inc. was established in 2013 through the merger between American Airlines and US Airways Group. The company is listed on NASDAQ Global Select Market. American Airlines offers thousands of flights per day to more than 350 destinations in more than 60 countries. The airline is a founding member of the oneworld® alliance, whose members serve more than 900 destinations around the globe. By December 2024, American Airlines operated 977 mainline aircraft supported by its wholly owned regional airline subsidiaries and third-party regional carriers. The regional carriers of American Airlines provide scheduled air transportation under the brand name "American Eagle". In 2024,54 million passengers travelled through the regional flights of American Airlines. In 2024, American Airlines served approximately 21,000 unique origin and destination pairs, transporting over 1 billion pounds of time sensitive freight and mail across its network. In 2022, American Airlines transported more than 199 million passengers.

In 2024, American Airlines was included in the Dow Jones Sustainability World Index (DJSI) for the second consecutive year and to the Dow Jones Sustainability North America Index for the fourth consecutive year. Only two airlines were included in the DJSI. American Airlines aim to achieve net zero GHG emissions by 2050 and have set an intermediate target to reduce GHG emissions intensity by 45% by 2035 relative to a 2019 baseline. This includes both direct emissions (Scope 1) primarily from the combustion of jet fuel used in flight and the indirect emissions (Scope 3) from the production of the jet fuel which the Airlines use and the consumption of jet fuel which is used by the contracted regional carriers of American Airlines. In 2023, American Airlines have achieved 3% reduction in GHG emissions intensity since 2019. The airlines have also achieved 54% reduction in Scope 2 emissions since 2019. In 2023, American Airlines have achieved 9.8% improvement in fuel efficiency compared to year 2013, thereby avoiding nearly 22.9 million metric tons of CO2 e. Over 25,000 tons of CO2 were avoided through use of renewable fuels.

American Airlines have received validation from the Science Based Targets initiative (SBTi) for its 2035 GHG reduction target. American Airlines have entered into agreements to purchase SAF as part of its target to replace 10% of its conventional jet fuel with SAF in year 2030. In 2023, American Airlines used 2.7 million gallons of SAF.

American Airlines evaluate and invest in innovations for low and no carbon fuel sources over the long term. American Airlines have made direct investments in companies which engage in the development of hydrogen electric propulsion technology and green hydrogen distribution. American Airlines is also an anchor partner of Breakthrough Energy Catalyst, which aims to make investments to speed up the development of new clean energy technologies including SAF.

In 2023, the EU enacted the ReFuelEU Aviation initiative to create a SAF blending mandate for aviation fuel suppliers. This requires fuel suppliers to, over the course of each year, blend minimum shares of SAF with petroleum jet fuel prior to the fuel's delivery to aircraft operators at EU airports, starting from January 1, 2025. In January 2021, the EPA adopted GHG emission standards for new aircraft engines, aligning with the 2017 ICAO aircraft engine GHG emission standards. For climate related governance, the Board has formally assigned its CEO the responsibility for the management of climate change strategy.

With respect to flight operations and efficiency, American Airlines aim to achieve absolute reduction of 50 million gallons of jet fuel from fuel efficiency initiatives by 2025. American Airlines adopted Expanded Smart Gating technology, which was expected to save 1.4 million gallons of fuel and reduce CO_2 emissions by 13,400 metric tons annually by minimizing gate conflicts, taxiing times, and airport congestion. The airlines also saved eight million gallons of fuel by using interactive inflight software.

With level to strategy lever of flight renewal, American Airlines aim to fly 30% of its available seat miles (ASMs) with latest generation more fuel-efficient aircraft in 2025. American Airlines operated 25.7% of Available Seat Miles (ASMs) using latest generation aircraft, generating approximately $10.6 billion which was over 20% of annual revenue from passengers flying on these more efficient jets. American Airlines entered into an agreement to purchase 10 Airbus A321neos from Alaska Airlines.

American Airlines is also investing in Next generation aircraft to advance the development of low and no carbon aircraft. The airlines aim to introduce hydrogen powered zero emission aircraft into its fleet by 2032 or earlier. In 2023, American Airlines signed an MoU with Embraer to support the development of the Energia concept aircraft, exploring electric, hydrogen and hybrid propulsion technologies. American Airlines also made strategic investments in ZeroAvia to advance hydrogen powered flight. The airlines placed a conditional order in 2024 for hydrogen retrofit kits for 65 seat regional jets from ZeroAvia. American Airline signed a firm offtake agreement for Infinium's Power-to-Liquids (PtL) eSAF, supporting project financing and enabling development of the PtL production facility.

American Airlines engages with key jet fuel providers to understand climate and sustainability strategies to identify potential opportunities for partnership. American Airlines participate in the voluntary carbon market to neutralize aviation's residual emissions. American Airlines utilize offsets and removals after exploring in sector decarbonization tools. In 2023, American Airlines signed a carbon removal purchase agreement with Graphyte to purchase 10,000 tons of permanent carbon removal thereby becoming the inaugural customer of the carbon removal start-up.

Approximately 70% of American Airlines total capital expenditures in 2022 and 2023 were allocated for decarbonization benefits. American Airlines is funding the development of next generation, low carbon aircraft technologies and making substantial new commitments to Sustainable Aviation Fuel (SAF) such as premium payment to facilitate SAF partners to secure additional investment and scale production. As part of decarbonization efforts, American Airlines purchases and put into services new, more fuel-efficient aircraft and engines. For example, in year 2022, American Airlines invested in 24 new Airbus A321neo and three Embraer E175 aircraft and leased nine new Boeing 787–8 aircraft. American Airlines also retrofit existing aircraft with measures to improve efficiency. In 2022, American Airlines retrofitted 30 aircraft to complete a multiyear retrofitting project for 468 aircrafts. American Airlines initiated and advanced multiple aircraft retrofit projects, including carbon brake upgrades for the Boeing 737 fleet, reactivation of 28 stored 737 s with similar retrofits, and early design planning for Boeing 777 and Airbus A321 subfleet modifications. In year 2022, 62 electric units were added to American's GSE fleet which included 47 bag tractors and 15 belt loaders.

For Airspace modernization, the airline focusses on Airspace system improvements which increase efficiency. American Airlines have initiated ADS-B In installations on Airbus A321s and collaborated with the FAA on trial programs as part of a multiyear implementation project. American Airlines also focuses on SAF technology advancements. American Airlines is an anchor partner of Breakthrough Energy Catalyst, with a $100 million commitment to advance Sustainable Aviation Fuel (SAF) and other low-carbon technologies. The airline has agreement to purchase SAF. The company have finalized 500 million-gallon SAF offtake agreement with Gevo thus bringing total SAF commitments to 620 million gallons. By 2022, American's mainline fleet averaged 12.2 years old which was the youngest mainline fleet among the US network carriers.

American donated $1.5 million in 2022 to the Organization of Black Aerospace Professionals (OBAP). Founded in 1976, this non-profit is dedicated to the encouragement and advancement of minorities in all aviation and aerospace careers.

In 2023, Breakthrough Energy Catalyst announced its commitment to invest $75 million in Infinium's PtL project. Through partnership with Cool Effect, American Airlines offers customers the option to purchase carbon offsets. Over 90% of each dollar supports carbon projects focused on protecting and conserving the planet's natural resources.

Opened in 2023, American's new catering kitchen which is largest in USA supports sustainability by composting food waste, contributing over 419,000 pounds of preconsumer compost in 2023. American Airlines continues recycling onboard waste and is working to reduce single-use plastics. In 2024, it relaunched soft goods using recycled materials for bedding. In 2023, Cargo expanded use of BioNatur Plastics™, a recyclable, biodegradable alternative to traditional plastics, significantly reducing long-term landfill impact. In 2022, American became the first U.S. airline to join the Transport Taskforce of United for Wildlife. In 2022, American became the first carrier in the United States to adopt CEFA Aviation Mobile Services, a cloud-based application that allows pilots to recreate their flights on their company tablet.

Green Investments by Lufthansa Group

The Lufthansa Group is a global aviation with leading presence in Europe. The company employees 101,709 people. In 2024, the Lufthansa Group generated revenues of EUR 37,581 million. The Lufthansa Group consists of the business segments Passenger Airlines, Logistics, MRO and Additional Businesses. The Passenger Airlines segment consists of Lufthansa Airlines, SWISS, Austrian Airlines and Brussels Airlines. The intermodal network of Lufthansa covers more than 40 destinations in five countries with more than 3000 connections per week.

Lufthansa have adopted innovative measures to halve its net carbon emissions by 2030 compared to 2019 and achieve neutral CO2 balance by year 2050. The Lufthansa Group was the first airline group in Europe with a science-based CO2 reduction target in line with the goals of the 2015 Paris Climate Agreement. Compensation measures and innovative technologies for capturing and storing CO_2 directly from the air (Direct Air Carbon Capture and Storage – DACCS) serve as complementary tools in the Lufthansa Group's sustainability strategy.

New generation aircraft require up to 30% less fuel than the predecessor aircrafts and emit less carbon dioxide. The Lufthansa Group continuously invests in modern and particularly fuel-efficient fleet. The Lufthansa Group currently has approximately 250 fuel-efficient aircraft on order, including 100 state-of-the-art long-haul jets. In the medium term, these highly efficient twin-engine aircraft are set to replace older four-engine models, such as the Boeing 747-400, Airbus A340-600, and Airbus A340-300, which are being gradually phased out. In 2023, The Lufthansa Group had signed a Memorandum of Understanding with Lilium to explore a potential strategic partnership for the deployment of electric vertical take-off and landing (eVTOL) aircraft in Europe. The Lufthansa Group is actively involved in a range of initiatives and research projects. For instance, Lufthansa Technik is collaborating with partners in Hamburg to convert a decommissioned Lufthansa Airbus A320 into a 'field laboratory' for testing maintenance and ground handling processes for future hydrogen-powered aircraft. Lufthansa Group along with German Aerospace Center, the ZAL Center for Applied Aeronautical Research and Hamburg Airport have partnered to design and test maintenance and develop ground-based processes for hydrogen technology. The SAF used by the Lufthansa Group is produced from biogenic residues such as from used cooking oils. Over its entire life cycle, SAF made from biogenic residues has a reduced CO2 footprint of around 80% compared to conventional kerosene made from fossil crude oil. The Sun-to-Liquid (StL) process is an innovative technology for producing SAF from high-temperature solar heat, water and CO2 (for example from the atmosphere). In 2022, the Lufthansa Group and the Group airline SWISS have agreed a strategic partnership with the Swiss-based company Synhelion for the market launch of Sun-to-liquid fuel.

The Lufthansa Group is the first to use AeroSHARK film, mimicking sharkskin to reduce drag, cutting fuel use and CO_2 emissions. The Lufthansa Group aims to reduce resource consumption by replacing single-use items with sustainable alternatives. The airlines have replaced over 200 onboard products out of 600 items since 2022 which include reusable cups, paper outer packaging and post-flight packaging recycling. The Lufthansa Group is reducing food waste through initiatives like a discounted "to go" offer on fresh onboard items, saving nearly three tonnes in 2023. By October 2023, 99.6% of the Lufthansa Group's fleet met or exceeded ICAO Chapter 4's strict minus-10-decibel aircraft noise standard. The Lufthansa Group steadily advances the implementation of environmental management systems according to ISO 14001 or EMAS at the Group companies. The Lufthansa Group supports IAGOS through its sub-projects CORE and CARIBIC, contributing valuable atmospheric data to advance global climate research.

In a globally unique project, the Lufthansa Group and the Karlsruhe Institute of Technology (KIT) are currently converting the Lufthansa Airbus A350-900 "Erfurt" (registration D-AIXJ) into a flying research laboratory for climate research.

In January 2023, the Supervisory Board established an ESG Committee to advise the Supervisory Board, its committees and the Executive Board on environmental, social and governance issues that are essential to the sustainable economic development of Lufthansa Group. The Chief Sustainability Officer (CSO)—is responsible for the Company's environmental, climate and social impact at Executive Board level. In 2023–2024 a climate scenario analysis (CSA) was used by Lufthansa Group to identify and assess climate related risks and opportunities and helps to understand the potential business implications of climate change (physical risk) and climate policy, regulation and technology (transition risk). In 2023, the Lufthansa Group extended its transition to carbon-neutral drive systems to include smaller locations—Berlin, Düsseldorf, Cologne, and Stuttgart—alongside its major operational sites.

In 2023, the Lufthansa Group became the first airline group to offer Green Fares, a separate fare including full compensation for flight-related carbon emissions. This offering is available on the global route network. Green fares can be booked on more than 850,000 flights a year and in all travel classes as of December 2024. In March 2024, SWISS and the Lufthansa Group formed a strategic partnership with Swiss company Climeworks to collaboratively scale up innovative CO_2 removal technology.

The Lufthansa Group has introduced a new Environmental Cost Surcharge to help cover the rising costs of complying with environmental regulations. Effective January 1, 2025, the surcharge will apply to all flights operated and sold by the Lufthansa Group departing from EU countries, the UK, Norway, and Switzerland, for tickets booked from June 26, 2024. The surcharge will range from €1 to €72, depending on the route and fare.

Green Investments by Air France KLM

Air France is the flag carrier of France. The airline is a subsidiary of the Air France KLM Group and one of the founding members of the SkyTeam airline alliance. Air France aims to reduce carbondioxide emissions by 30% by 2030. Air France is replacing its old planes with new aircraft designed to consume 25% less fuel. The airline also aims to reduce noise footprint by more than a third. In 2025, these aircrafts would account for 45% of its fleet and 70% by 2030. Air France aim to incorporate at least 10% of SAF globally by 2030. Air France have used 43,953 tonnes of SAF in 2024, thereby reducing CO_2 emissions by over 150,000 tonnes—the equivalent of 496 round trips between Paris and New York. Air France focusses on eco friendly piloting and operational measures to reduce fuel consumption on the ground and air by 4–5%. Air France aims to adopt different practices such as weight reduction onboard, usage of a single engine during taxing, adapting flight paths or employing a continuous descent approach. On board, children's menus are made exclusively with ingredients from organic farming. Air France prioritizes local and seasonal products on flights to Paris. Business class passengers on long-haul flights can pre-select meals, reducing waste, lowering aircraft weight, and saving fuel. In 2023, this initiative avoided loading over 52,000 unused hot meals.

Air France aircraft consume an average of 3.3 litres of fuel per passenger per 100 km. The aim is to achieve less than 3 litres by 2030. In 2022, Air France recycled 20 tons of plastic bottles, bricks, and cans and 530 tons of glass bottles. Since 2018, Air France have eliminated 90% of single-use plastic items on board. Air France recover and recycle the textile waste of its uniforms, work clothes and foams of used chairs. Air France is ramping up the use of bio-sourced materials both in flight and on the ground. Between 2018 and 2023, the airline eliminated or replaced 90% of single-use plastic items on board—such as cups, cutlery, and bowls—resulting in 316 million items processed and 2233 tonnes of plastic avoided.

Pilots use innovative tools which allow them to adapt their flight paths to optimize fuel consumption. These tools were offered by startups such as the French company Openairlines and its SkyBreathe solution or the company SafetyLine with its OptiDirect application.

Air France invest more than €1 billion annually in acquiring new-generation aircraft. By 2025, Air France will add 38 Airbus A350s to its long-haul fleet, and 60 Airbus A220s will join its short- and medium-haul fleet. Air France's "Train + Air" service lets customers combine train and flight bookings with guaranteed connections. Over 160,000 travellers use it yearly via Paris airports.

Green Investments by Emirates Group

Emirates Group is a major air transport and travel services powerhouse. The Group's global footprint extends to 277 cities across continents, making Dubai one of the world's most connected cities. By end 2024, Emirates was flying to 151 destinations in 79 countries and territories. In 2024, Emirates Group had passenger revenue of over AED 100 billion and a cash balance of AED 47.1 billion. In 2023–2024, Emirates Group had made investment commitments of AED 111 billion for aircraft fleet and cabin renewal programme. Emirates made net profit of AED 17.2 billion in year 2023–2024. At Dubai Airshow 2023, Emirates made investment worth $58 billion for 110 additional widebody aircraft from Airbus and Boeing. Emirates began constructing a new US$ 950 million engineering complex at Dubai World Central to support its fleet into the 2040s, and signed contracts worth US$ 2.7 billion for new aircraft seats, galleys, landing systems, inflight connectivity solutions, and MRO services.

In 2023–24, Emirates added 16 more fully refurbished A380 aircraft to its fleet as part of its ongoing US$2 billion retrofit programme. These aircraft feature the latest cabin interiors and have expanded the availability of the popular Emirates Premium Economy experience to even more customers globally. Additionally, Emirates invested over AED 30 million in enhancing its dedicated Emirates Lounges, reopening eight upgraded facilities in Brisbane, Düsseldorf, Frankfurt, Hamburg, Hong Kong, Johannesburg, Manchester, and Munich. In 2023–2024, Emirates SkyCargo had carried 2.2 million tonnes of goods around the world.

Emirates work closely with stakeholders across the sustainable aviation fuel (SAF) ecosystem. Emirates signed new supply agreements which enabled Emirates to uplift Sustainable Aviation Fuel (SAF) at its Dubai hub. Emirates also operated the first A380 demonstration flight powered by 100% SAF in one engine. Emirates founded a US $200 million fund to support R&D projects to reduce the impact of fossil fuels in commercial aviation. Emirates is a founding member of Air-CRAFT, a UAE-based research consortium for renewable and advanced aviation fuels. Emirates also became a member of The Solent Cluster, a UK initiative focused on producing low-carbon fuels for a variety of sectors, including aviation. Emirates also converted and refurbished diesel-powered ground support equipment (GSE) in its Italy operations to run on hydrotreated vegetable oil and electric power. Emirates 's UAE businesses such as dnata logistics, Arabian Adventures, Alpha Flight Services and City Sightseeing Worldwide had transitioned to biofuel for its landside fleet of vehicles. Dnata became the first combined air services provider to receive the International Air Transport Association's (IATA) environmental management certification.

Emirates Group's Environmental Sustainability Framework is based on three pillars of strategy involving reduction of emissions, responsible consumption and preservation of wildlife and habitats. Emirates' pilots follow Green Standard Operating Procedures (Green SOPs), developed through a comprehensive approach that combines education, awareness, data analytics, and advanced technology. In 2023–24, the implementation of Green SOPs and other operational initiatives led to a reduction of over 48,000 tonnes in fuel consumption and more than 151,000 tonnes in carbon emissions. Dnata actively monitors fuel consumption across its GSE fleet using Vehicle Tracking Management Systems. The company conduct logistics mapping to minimize airside travel distances, optimize shift planning and allocate parking slots to reduce unnecessary fuel burn. The group foster responsible driving through targeted education, awareness initiatives and comprehensive training programmes.

Dnata completed the United Nations Global Compact Climate Ambition Accelerator Programme. Emirates entered into an agreement with Shell Aviation to get over 300,000 gallons of blended SAF at DXB airport. Emirates Flight Catering acquired Bustanica, the world's largest indoor vertical farm, supporting the UAE's efforts to enhance food, water and agricultural security. Emirates also have collaboration with Neste for the supply of SAF in year 2024 and 2025. Emirates follows a strategy to improve fuel efficiency, investment in sustainable aviation fuels(SAF) and electrify its GSE and vehicle fleets. Dnata Green Fleet Strategy focuses on phasing out diesel operated engines and switching to hybrid, electric or hydrogen-based energy system. Emirates have allocated US$ 200 million to progress advanced fuel and energy solutions for aviation. Emirates usage of SAF contributed to emissions reductions of about 4700 tonnes of CO2 e (carbon dioxide equivalent) over the lifecycle of the fuel. Emirates transition to biofuel has contributed to emissions reductions of about 2200 tonnes of CO2 e over the lifecycle of the fuel. Emirates have invested in solar power systems to generate clean electricity at its major facilities. Emirates investments in renewable electricity in the UK and Ireland generate approximately 19,200 MWh, which saved over 4000 tonnes of CO2 e annually. Emirates has committed to implementing the Carbon Offsetting and Reduction Scheme for International Aviation (CORSIA). The Emirates Group supports IATA's goal of achieving net-zero carbon emissions across airline industry by 2050. Emirates actively contributes to the United for Wildlife Transport Taskforce. The ground handling staff at dnata are trained in IATA's live animal regulations and internal policies on carrying wildlife.

With reference to environmental performance reporting, the Emirates Group reports it emissions in CO2 equivalent (CO2e), which includes the climate impact of nitrous oxide (N20) and methane (CH4) greenhouse emissions.

References

American Airlines Sustainability Report 2023.
American Airlines Sustainability Report 2022.
Corporate Impact Report 2024, United Airlines.
Delta Annual Report 2025.
Delta ESG Report 2023.
Form 10-K for American Airlines Group, 2025.
https://content.delta.com/content/www/us/en/about-delta/sustainability.smt-platinum.html
https://corporate.airfrance.com/fr/une-restauration-plus-responsable
https://www.esgtoday.com/lufthansa-raises-fares-to-cover-costs-of-new-climate-regulations/
https://www.lufthansagroup.com/en/company.html
https://www.lufthansagroup.com/en/responsibility/climate-environment/
LUFTHANSA GROUP Taskforce on Climate-related Financial Disclosures (TCFD) Report 2023.
The Emirates Group Annual Report | 2023–2024.
United Airlines Holdings, Inc. Annual Report 2024.

Chapter 17
Green Investments in Technology Sector

Green Investments by Apple

Apple company designs, manufactures and markets smartphones, personal computers, tablets, wearables and accessories. Apple also sells a variety of related services. iPhone is the Company's line of smartphones based on its iOS operating system. The iPhone line includes iPhone 16 Pro, iPhone 16, iPhone 15, iPhone 14 and iPhone SE. Mac is the Company's line of personal computers based on its mac OS operating system. The Mac line includes laptops MacBook Air and MacBook Pro, as well as desktops iMac, Mac mini, Mac Studio and Mac Pro. iPad is the Company's line of multipurpose tablets based on its iPad OS operating system. Wearables, Home and Accessories Wearables includes smartwatches, wireless headphones and spatial computers. Apple's advertising services include third party licensing arrangements and the company's own advertising platforms. Apple offers a portfolio of fee-based service and support products under the AppleCare brand. Apple's reportable segments consists of Americas, Europe, Greater China, Japan and Rest of Asia Pacific.

Apple have reduced its overall greenhouse gas emissions across scopes 1, 2, and 3 by more than 55 percent in comparison to its baseline year 2015. During the same period, revenue increased by 64 percent. Apple have avoided 31 million metric tons of emissions through initiatives such as transitioning its supply chain to renewable electricity and sourcing recycled content. Apple aim to achieve carbon neutrality for its entire carbon footprint by year 2030. Apple aim to transition its entire value chain which include manufacturing and product use to100 percent clean electricity by year 2030. By March 2024, over 320 suppliers have committed to use 100 percent renewable energy for their Apple Production. These Apple suppliers account for 95 percent of Apple's direct spend for materials, manufacturing and assembly of its products worldwide. In 2023, 22 percent of materials shipped by Apple were produced from recycled or renewable sources. Titanium was added to Apple's

B. R. Kumar, *Green Finance*, Sustainable Finance,
https://doi.org/10.1007/978-3-032-03333-8_17

priority materials list in year 2023. In year 2023, 56 percent of the cobalt shipped in Apple designed batteries came from recycled sources.

Apple aims to completely remove plastics from its packaging by year 2025. The product packaging shipped by Apple in 2023 contains only 3 percent plastic which was down from 21 percent in year 2015. Apple focusses on transition to 100 percent recycled cobalt, tin, gold and rare earth elements in select components and applications by year 2025. In 2023, approximately 56 percent of the cobalt shipped in Apple designed batteries came from recycled sources. Apple aims to replenish all its corporate freshwater withdrawals in high stress locations by year 2030. Apple have partnerships for freshwater replenishment projects which has resulted in 31.2 million gallons of volumetric water benefits. Apple aims to certify all Apple owned data centers to the Alliance for Water Stewardship (AWS) by year 2025. The company have certified five data centers and 20 suppliers according to AWS standard. Through the Supplier Clean Water Program, Apple have supported an average 42 percent reuse rate across its 242 participating supplier facilities. In 2023, 100 percent of established final assembly sites maintained zero waste to landfill operations.

Manufacturing products accounted for 59 percent of Apple's gross carbon footprint. Transportation of products account for 9 percent of Apple's gross carbon footprint. To reduce transportation-related emissions, Apple is transitioning more of its product shipments to lower-carbon alternatives to air freight, such as ocean and rail. According to company's carbon footprint methodology, transporting the same Apple product by ocean produces 95 percent fewer emissions compared to air transport. Apple product iMac uses 58 percent less energy than the ENERGY STAR requirement.

Apple Watch Series 9, Apple Watch SE, iPad, MacBook Air, Mac mini, the Siri Remote, MacBook Pro and Mac Studio uses 100 percent recycled aluminium in its enclosure. For iPhone 15, Apple have increased recycled content by using 75 percent recycled aluminum in the enclosure. Apple have introduced 100 percent certified recycled cobalt for battery of Apple Watch and iPhone. The company has also increased the content of certified recycled gold across all product lines from 4 percent in 2022 to approximately 25 percent in 2023. By 2025, Apple aim to use 100 percent recycled cobalt in all Apple designed batteries. In 2023, Apple redesigned all packaging for Apple Watch Series 9 and Apple Watch SE models to introduce a new compact design which allowed for 25 percent or more devices per shipment. Apple's product energy use accounts for 29 percent of Apple's gross carbon footprint. Apple have cut overall product energy use across all major product lines by more than 70 percent since 2008. Apple aim to transit to 100 percent fibre-based packaging by 2025. Since 2017, all the wood fiber used in its packaging comes from either certified recycled sources or responsibly managed forests. Through its partnerships with the Conservation Fund and World Wildlife Fund, Apple have protected and enhanced the management of over one million acres of forests in US and China. In 2021, Apple had deployed a proprietary server design focused on energy and computing efficiency which added an additional 36 million kilowatt hours. Over 100 suppliers' facilities had participated in its energy efficiency program and had achieved more than 2 billion kilowatt-hours of electricity savings and over

2,200,000 MMBtu in additional energy savings which resulted in nearly 1.7 million metric tons of CO2e. In 2023, Apple's energy efficiency program eliminated 41 million kilowatt hours of electricity. Self Service Repair supports 40 Apple products in 33 countries. Apple have sent nearly 12.8 million devices and accessories to new users for reuse from programs such as Apple Trade In and AppleCare. Apple had directed 40,000 metric tons of electronic scrap to recycling facilities globally with the help of customer and employee programs. Apple have partnered with an industry leading automotive filtration and technology company to design a sustainable air filtration solution. By 2023, 108 corporate offices, data centres, and retail stores of Apple across the world—totalling more than 18 million square feet of green building space—were certified under the Leadership in Energy and Environmental Design (LEED) or the Building Research Establishment Environmental Assessment Method (BREEAM).

Through Apple's partnerships with The Conservation Fund and World Wildlife Fund, Apple have protected and enhanced the management of over one million acres of working forests in the U.S. and China.

Green Bonds

In 2016, Apple issued its first $1.5 billion green bond and second $1 billion green bond in 2017. In 2019, Apple had its third green bond issuance which raised $2.2 billion across two tranches. The 2019 Green bond aims to reach carbon neutrality across Apple's entire carbon foot print which included the full product life cycle by 2030. In total Apple had issued $4.7 billion green bonds with over $3.2 billion allocated by 2022. The 2019 Green bond cumulative allocation covered 70 projects with 39 percent allocation amounting to $864.2 million.

Table 17.1 shows the project allocation by eligible category for the 2019 Green bond issuance. Apple has allocated USD 157.7 million to eligible projects in year 2023.

Table 17.1 Allocation by Eligibility Criteria (USD millions)

Use of proceeds category	Net Proceeds Allocation, FY 2023	Net Proceeds Allocation Cumulative
Low Carbon Design	30.7	87.9
Energy Efficiency	0.5	5.5
Carbon Mitigation	1.6	8.9
Renewable Energy	93.7	683.4
Carbon Sequestration	31	78.5
Total allocation	157.5	864.2
Net Proceeds raised		2192.9
Percentage allocation		39%

Source: Apple Green Bond Report 2023

The 70 projects to which Apple allocated Green bond funds since issuance are estimated to result in direct environmental benefits of lifetime greenhouse gas emission mitigation of 13,800,000 metric tons CO2e and 707 MW installed renewable energy capacity. In year 2023, Apple introduced 11 new projects which focusses on long term environmental initiatives. In fiscal year 2023, Apple allocated green bond proceeds to its investment in the 320-megawatt 2300-acre IP Radian Solar project in Brown County. Green bond funds were allocated to research initiatives for improving the purity of recovered materials to be reused in Apple products. Green bond proceeds were allocated to supply chain programs such as Supplier Clean Energy Program and the Supplier Energy Efficiency Program. Launched in 2015, the Supplier Energy Efficiency Program aims to facilitate suppliers optimize energy use in their facilities by focusing on methods to reduce energy use and avoid energy waste. Apple's Supplier Clean Energy Program supports suppliers in transitioning to clean, renewable electricity by providing policy advocacy, guidance on renewable energy procurement, data-driven insights, and opportunities to engage with renewable energy experts. As of September 2023, over 300 manufacturers have committed to using 100 percent clean energy for their Apple production by 2030, covering more than 90 percent of the company's direct manufacturing spend. The company have invested in providing education and training across its supply chain through platforms such as Clean Energy Academy. Apple have allocated green bond proceeds to China Clean Energy Fund for investment in clean energy. To achieve carbon neutrality by 2030, Apple have made investment in certified forestry projects through the Restore Fund to remove one million metric tons of CO_2. Apple aim to certify these projects under the Verified Carbon Standard (VCS) and the Climate, Community & Biodiversity Standards (CCBS). In Fiscal 2023, Apple announced a Restore Fund expansion, committing up to an additional \$200 million, to be managed by Climate Asset Management.

Green Investments by Google

Alphabet is a collection of business of which Google is the largest. The core products and platforms of Google are Android, Chrome, Gmail, Google Drive, Google Maps, Google Play, Search and YouTube. Google products are reported in two segments, Google Services and Google Cloud. All non-Google businesses are collectively reported as Other Bets. Google have centralized certain AI-related research and development which is reported in Alphabet level activities. Google Search facilitate people to search information with trillions of searches on Google every year. Google Cloud helps customers to solve business challenges, improve productivity, reduce costs and focus on new growth engines. The company focus on innovation and building of new products and features. During the past five years, Google have invested more than \$150 billion in research and development. Google's world class infrastructure spans more than 200 countries and territories connected by more than two million miles of terrestrial and subsea cables thereby creating a super AI powered products. Google is a pioneer in the development of AI and since 2016, an AI -first company. The multimodal Google AI, Gemini is used across all of its 15 products with half a billion users. In 2024, Google launched Gemini 2.0 which combine different types of information which include text, code, audio, image and video. Google Maps have about 2 billion users. Today, all seven of two billion user products -Android, Chrome, Gmail, Maps, Play Store, Search and You Tube uses Gemini. In Search, AI Overviews reach one billion people. In 2025, Google plan to invest approximately $75 billion in capital expenditures and launch a first ever project to power data centers using small modular reactors. Google AI aim to expand training through its $120 million AI Opportunity Fund. YouTube Music and Premium have exceeded 125 million subscriptions and YouTube hit one billion monthly podcast users and is the most watched streaming service in the US. Android is the world's most popular operating system with more than 3 billion active devices worldwide. Collectively Google One and YouTube have amassed over 200 million subscribers. Google have offices and data centers on six continents, in over 200 cities, across nearly 60 countries.

Google Cloud generates revenues primarily from consumption-based fees and subscriptions for infrastructure, platform, applications and other cloud services. In 2021, Google have set goal to reach net zero emissions across all of its operations and value chain by 2030. The company aim to reduce 50 percent of its combined Scope 1, Scope 2 and Scope 3 absolute emissions compared to 2019 base year by 2030. In 2023, the total GHG emissions were approximately 14.3 million metric tons of carbon dioxide equivalent (tCO2e), which represents its Scope 1, Scope 2 (market-based), and Scope 3 emissions.

Google have built the world leading efficient infrastructure for the AI era which include its sixth generation Tensor Processing Unit, Trillium. A Google owned and operated data center is on average, approximately 1.8 times as energy efficient as a typical enterprise data center. Google have introduced a water risk framework to further identify climate conscious cooling solutions which consider carbon free energy availability. AI has the potential to help mitigate 5–10 percent of global greenhouse gas (GHG) emissions by 2030. In 2017, Google became the first major company to match 100 percent of its annual electricity consumption on a global basis with renewable energy. Through its products, Google aim to facilitate individuals, cities and other partners to reduce one gigaton of carbon equivalent emissions annually by year 2030. The water stewardship initiatives of Google had replenished an estimated one billion gallons of water in year 2023. The packaging for new Google products was at least 99 percent plastic free. Pixel 8 and Pixel 8 Pro uses 100 percent plastic free materials. For past two years, Google has provided information to over one billion users to help them make more sustainable choices annually through its products. Google product Flood Hub displayed forecasts for over 80 countries on five continents covering more than 460 million people globally. Google launched fuel efficient routing which has enabled 2.9 million metric tons of GHG emissions which was equivalent to taking approximately 650,000 fuel-based cars off the road for a year. Google has achieved seven consecutive years of 100 percent renewable energy matching on a global and annual basis. Google have nearly doubled its water replenishment portfolio with 74 projects in year 2023. Google maintained a global average of approximately 64 percent carbon free energy across its data centers and offices. In 2023, Google diverted 78 percent of operational waste from disposal across its global fleet of Google owned and operated data centers. Google have implemented innovations such as advanced geothermal, carbon-intelligent computing, and demand response, while collaborating with partners like Microsoft and Nucor to drive clean electricity adoption and participating in Frontier to support emerging climate technologies. Google's AI tool for optimizing traffic signals -Green Light were implemented in 12 cities across four continents. Google's Solar API facilitate solar development and covers over 472 million buildings across 40 countries which include 95 percent of all buildings in the United States. Nest thermostats use algorithms powered by AI and machine learning to optimize residential heating and cooling systems and reduce energy consumption. Google had introduced a new generative design feature in Google Earth which facilitate planners to determine the best building designs and solar options for urban areas. Google introduced Tapestry, which is a part of X, Alphabet's moonshot factory which aim to offer access to clean, reliable and affordable electricity worldwide. Google Cloud have partnered with companies such as mCloud, ElectricityMaps and Flexidao which build solutions to decarbonize the energy sector. Google's predictive analytics offer innovative ways to promote clean energy. For example, Engie collaborated with Atlas AI to leverage its analytics platform—powered by Google Cloud—to effectively identify potential off-grid solar customers in Kenya. Google empower people with information on a wider range of transit and urban mobility option. Google Maps offers bus, train, subway, and ferry directions via its transit icon, delivering over 3 billion kilometres of public transit results daily. Google have created the Travel Impact Model (TIM), a public model for predicting the per-passenger CO_2e emissions produced by a flight. Google, Breakthrough Energy, and American Airlines developed AI to predict and avoid contrails, which cause 35 percent of aviation's warming impact, helping reduce emissions. YouTube highlights authoritative climate voices and adds contextual information panels to search results and videos, especially during major environmental events or climate-related searches. Google's monetization policy bans advertisement and revenue generation for content that denies the well-established scientific consensus on climate change and its causes.

It is estimated that the world loses around ten million hectares of forest every year. Google's geospatial tools empower innovative solutions to protect forests and avoid deforestation. Google is a founding partner of the Forest Data Partnership which aims to stop deforestation caused by commodity production. The UN Food and Agriculture Organization uses Google Earth tools to support countries with Measurement, Reporting and Verification (MRV) systems for tracking forest change, helping them measure emissions reductions and earn payments. Google Cloud and partners like Airbus and UP42 use satellite data to boost agricultural productivity, optimize resources, and support food security in vulnerable regions. Global Fishing Watch, founded by Oceana, SkyTruth, and Google, uses satellite data and AI to monitor fisheries. This initiative received $60 million from TED

Audacious Project in 2023. MethaneSAT, developed by the Environmental Defense Fund (EDF) with Google Cloud, uses satellite data and algorithms to track methane emissions from oil and gas globally. This partnership aims to create a global map of infrastructure, helping identify key emission sources and inform mitigation efforts. BlueSky Resources uses Google Earth Engine to combine sensor data and satellite imagery, helping organizations identify methane emission sources and create effective mitigation strategies. Google's AI technology, CircularNet, drives Recykal's waste management platform—Asia's largest circular economy marketplace—enabling precise identification of recyclable materials. Google's AI Crisis Alerts provided timely wildfire information to over 30 million users across 180 wildfire events around the world. Google's MetNet-3 and DeepMind's GraphCast provide advanced weather forecasts with high accuracy, while WeatherBench 2 supports research and innovation in global weather models. Google Research, in collaboration with CliMA, is improving climate model accuracy by simulating stratocumulus clouds using TPUs and high-performance computing to enhance predictions. Google's Tree Canopy tool uses AI and aerial imagery to help cities plan tree planting. It expanded to 2000 cities, partnering with American Forests for equitable shade distribution.

In year 2022, Google announced a $30 million Google.org Impact Challenge for non-profit organizations to submit big ideas for climate action. In 2023, Google.org awarded a $5 million grant to the World Resources Institute (WRI) to use sensors, satellite imagery, and AI for climate data modelling. Google's new Pollen API shows current pollen information for the most common allergens in over 65 countries. In 2023, Google launched the first street-by-street air quality data for Bengaluru in India.

In 2023, Google joined the Avelia Sustainable Aviation Fuel program, offering SAF credits to corporate customers. In 2024, Google also joined the United Airlines Ventures Sustainable Flight Fund, a pioneering initiative to boost SAF production through catalytic investment. Google aim to neutralize its residual emissions with high-quality carbon removal credits by 2030.

Google is advancing both technology- and nature-based carbon removal solutions, pledging $200 million to Frontier in 2022 to scale carbon removal technologies. In 2023, Google finalized its first carbon credit deals with Charm Industrial, Carbon Capture, and Lithos Carbon, contributing to the growth of the carbon removal field. Google is a member of the First Movers Coalition and a champion for their Carbon Dioxide Removal sector.

In March 2024, Google pledged to match the U.S. Department of Energy's Carbon Dioxide Removal Purchase program, committing at least $35 million to carbon removal credits within 12 months. By the end of 2023, Google.org had contributed over $7 million to strengthen carbon markets, including a $1 million grant to ICVCM to promote high-integrity solutions.

In 2023, Google launched the Carbon Removal Research Awards, granting over $3 million to universities for studies on ocean alkalinity, enhanced weathering, and other carbon removal methods. In 2023, Google joined the Avelia Sustainable Aviation Fuel program which offered SAF credits to corporate customers. In 2024,

Google joined the United Airlines Ventures Sustainable Flight Fund to invest for SAF production. The water stewardship projects replenished an estimated one billion gallons of water which represented approximately 18 percent of 2023 freshwater consumption of Google's data centers and offices. By 2023, Google supported 74 water stewardship projects spanning 46 watersheds. Google aim to became a circular Google by maximizing the reuse of finite resources across its operations, products and supply chains. Google diverted 78 percent of its global data centres and offices operational waste from disposal. In 2023, Google reduced food waste per Googler by 38 percent compared to the year 2019. Since 2015, Google have resold more than 44 million hardware components from its data centers into the secondary market for reuse by other organizations. Google aims to include recycled materials in 100 percent of Google consumer hardware products. In 2020, Google achieved this goal for its Nest, Pixel and Chromecast devices. Google have set a target to use recycled or renewable material in at least 50 percent of plastics used across its consumer hardware product portfolio by 2025. In 2023, Google achieved UL 2799 validation for waste diversion at all final assembly manufacturing sites for its consumer hardware products.

Google Cloud offers organizations solutions to drive impact for their business and sustainability. Scientists, researchers, and developers have been using Google Earth Engine—Google's planetary-scale platform for Earth science data and analysis—to detect changes, map trends, and quantify differences on the Earth's surface.

Google.org began supporting the Asia Venture Philanthropy Network's (AVPN) APAC Sustainability Seed Fund in 2022 with a $3 million grant, benefiting 13 local organizations dedicated to underserved communities across the region. Google offered an additional $5 million grant for the launch of the APAC Sustainability Seed Fund 2.0. This initiative is also backed by the Asian Development Bank (ADB), which serves as the fund's strategic and outreach partner.

Sustainability Bonds

In 2020, Google issued $5.75 billion in sustainability bonds which was the largest sustainability bonds issued by any company in history at that time. The net proceeds funded new and ongoing projects which are environmentally or socially responsible. The total allocation as of date amounted to $5.69 billion. The eligible projects for energy efficiency relate to expenditures related to design, construction, operation and maintenance of energy efficient facilities and infrastructure. The clean transportation projects involve expenditures related to procurement, maintenance and operation of electric vehicles (EV), bicycles and associated infrastructure. The circular economy and design projects involve expenditures related to projects which are designed to increase waste diversion from landfill and design out waste. A committee consisting of representatives from Alphabet's Sustainability, Treasury, and Finance teams evaluates a broad array of projects from across the company to identify Eligible Projects.

Table 17.2 shows the detailed bond allocation of the sustainability bond issuances made by Google.

Google have offered 3700 loans to small and medium sized businesses focused on Black community. Google have offered 46,950 loans to small and medium sized businesses which amounted to $185 million. In 2019, Google had announced a $ 1 billion Bay Area housing commitment to support the development of at least 20,000 homes at a range of income levels throughout the region. In 2022, Google launched a $100 million Google Career Certificates Fund to target over 20,000 American workers and drive $ 1 billion in wage gains. Google aim to spend $2.5 billion for increasing its spending with diverse suppliers which include historically underrepresented groups.

The net proceeds from the bond issuance have been fully allocated to expenditures, contractual and capital commitments in Eligible projects as defined by Alphabet's sustainability bond framework.

Table 17.3 highlights the bond details by notes.

In 2021, Google allocated net proceeds from its sustainability bond to data center campuses and resulted in cumulative total allocation of $1.02 billion in capital. Google have allotted sustainable bond proceeds to 45 power purchase agreements (PPAs) with total cumulative allocation of $1.75 billion in expenditures and contractual commitments to purchase electricity from renewable energy sources which had combined capacity of approximately 5.3 gigawatts. In 2021, Google allocated net proceeds from its sustainability bond to buildings which resulted in cumulative total allocation of $2.47 billion in capital expenditures related to the design,

Table 17.2 Allocation details (in USD millions)

	2025 notes		2030 notes		2050 notes		
Eligible Categories							
Reporting Year	2021	2022	2021	2022	2021	2022	Cumulative Total
Environmental							
Energy Efficiency	$112	$66	$252	$148	$277	$163	$1018
Clean Energy	$224	$83	$502	$187	$552	$205	$1753
Green Buildings	$218	$215	$490	$481	$538	$529	$2471
Clean Transportation	$3	$1	$6	$3	$6	$3	$22
Circular economy and design	$1	$1	$2	$1	$2	$1	$ 8
Social							
Affordable housing	$12	$2	$27	$5	$30	$7	$83
Commitment to racial equity	$14	$12	$32	$26	$35	$29	$148
Support for small businesses and Covid 19 crisis responses	$23	$9	$52	$21	$584	$22	$185
Total allocation of net proceeds	$607	$389	$1363	$872	$1498	$959	$5688
Net proceeds allocated by tranche(%)	61%	39%	61%	39%	61%	39%	100%

Source: Alphabet Sustainability Bond Impact Report 2022

Table 17.3 Bond details

Notes	Coupon	Issued amount ($ million)	Net proceeds ($ million)
2025 Notes	0.45%	$1000	$996
2030 Notes	1.10%	$2250	$2235
2050 Notes	2.05%	$2500	$2457
Total		$5750	$5688

Source: Alphabet Sustainability Bond Impact Report 2022

construction and improvement of 14 green buildings. The cumulative total allocation for seven circular economy and design projects amounted to $8 million which included a software system for usage in kitchen to track and reduce pre-consumer food waste. This software system has assisted Google to prevent over 1.4 million kilograms of food going into the waste stream. Google have supported affordable housing projects with total commitments of $83 million across 21 projects enabling 3050 affordable units. Sustainability bond issuances have also been allocated for advancement of economic opportunity for Black community. This includes investment in Black led capital firms, start ups and organizations which support Black entrepreneurs and investment firms. Google have made cumulative total allocation of $148 million across 15 racial equity initiatives.

Google work with suppliers in 85 countries. Alphabet's Conflict Minerals Policy directs suppliers to perform due diligence on the source and chain of custody of minerals used to manufacture products for Google.

Green Investments by Microsoft

Microsoft was founded in year 1975. Microsoft develop and support software, services, devices and solutions. The company offer an array of services which include cloud-based solutions that provide customers with software, services, platforms and content. Microsoft's products include operating systems, cross device productivity and collaboration applications, server applications, business solution applications, desktop and server management tools, software development tools and video games. Microsoft also design and sell devices which include PCs, tablets, gaming and entertainment consoles, intelligent devices and related accessories.

Microsoft 365 is an AI-first platform that integrates Office, Windows, Copilot, and security tools to empower employees through productivity, collaboration, and employee experience solutions. Dynamics 365 is a portfolio of intelligent business applications which deliver operational efficiency and breakthrough customer experiences. Microsoft Power Platform boosts productivity with low-code tools and automation, while Copilot Pro enhances AI assistance, and LinkedIn leverages AI to empower professionals. The Microsoft Cloud delivers seamless integration, openness, and efficiency, with Azure providing hybrid consistency, strong AI and data tools, and trusted security and compliance.

Microsoft's carbon negative commitment focusses on primary areas of reduction of carbon emissions, increasing use of carbon free electricity and carbon removal. In 2020, Microsoft established $ 1 billion Climate Innovation Fund (CIF) to advance innovation. The CIF fund till date have allocated $761 million toward innovative climate technologies including commercial direct air capture technologies, sustainable aviation fuel (SAF) and industrial decarbonization. In 2023, the CIF has invested $45 million in scaling innovative water solutions which included $25 million in WaterEquity's water and climate resilience strategy. CIF have made investments in 55 companies. Through CIF, Microsoft have made investments in companies such as H2 Green Steel, FlexiDAO and Heirloom Technologies. H2 Green Steel aims to produce five million tons of near-zero emissions steel by 2030, using renewable electricity and green hydrogen to cut CO_2 by 95 percent. FlexiDAO, the carbon free energy analytics platform helps Microsoft track and certify clean energy for its 100/100/0 goal, supporting digital solutions across 37 percent of its global Scope 2 portfolio. Heirloom Technologies, a direct air capture company will deliver up to 315,000 tons of permanent carbon removal via America's first commercial direct air capture facility. The CIF has made investments in companies such as Mitiga Solutions, Linevision, KOKO Networks, Cross Boundary Energy Access, EverEnviro and Solstice. Mitiga Solutions uses AI, science, and HPC to help businesses assess and manage climate risk through its self-serve EarthScan™ platform and advanced risk models. LineVision uses AI and real-time sensor data to provide dynamic line ratings, helping transmission owners increase capacity from existing infrastructure by factoring in local weather conditions. KOKO Networks provides clean bioethanol cooking fuel in Kenya, helping households shift from charcoal. It reached one million customers and is expanding across East Africa. CrossBoundary Energy Access funded solar mini grids in Nigeria with ENGIE, bringing first-time electricity to 28,000 people and supporting income-generating activities like grain milling. EverEnviro, a top renewable natural gas producer in India, supports farmers, creates rural jobs, improves waste management, and supplies clean fuel through Agri-residue collection. Solstice, a CIF portfolio alum, is developing two Illinois community solar projects with ENGIE to serve underserved communities and cut residents' electricity costs by up to 60 percent.

The company aim to be a carbon-negative, water-positive, zero-waste company that protects ecosystems by 2030. Since 2020, Microsoft's Scope 1 and 2 emissions have decreased by 6 percent. Scope 3 accounts for over 96 percent of its total emissions which includes emissions from its supply chain, life cycle of hardware and devices and other indirect sources. By 2030, Microsoft aims to match 100 percent of its electricity consumption by zero carbon energy purchases 100 percent of the time. By 2030, Microsoft aim to remove more carbon than it emits. By 2050, Microsoft aim to remove an amount of carbon equivalent to all its historical operational emissions. In 2023, 76.5 percent of the total emissions of Microsoft originated from its suppliers. Microsoft plans to construct an Electric Vehicle Fleet Facility to operate a 100 percent electric fleet by 2030. In 2023, Microsoft's Cloud Logistics team reduced emissions through a three-pillar strategy: advanced emissions tracking, optimized supply chain operations avoiding 90,000+ mtCO2e, and promoting low-carbon logistics solutions. In FY23, Microsoft contracted 5,015,019 metric tons of carbon removal to be retired over the next 15 years. In 2023, Microsoft signed a long-term offtake with Mombak for carbon removal from reforestation in the Brazilian Amazon. In 2023, Microsoft signed a 10-year agreement with World Energy for sustainable aviation fuel (SAF) certificates, targeting the replacement of 43.7 million gallons of fossil jet fuel and co-funding a major global SAF project.

In 2023, 18.5 K metric tons of waste was diverted from landfills and incinerator. Approximately five million metric tons of carbon removal were contracted in fiscal year 2023. Microsoft has adopted a first-mover strategy in advancing carbon-free electricity infrastructure, making long-term investments to add more clean energy to the grids where the company operate on. Microsoft have contracted portfolio of renewable energy assets to more than 19.8 gigawatts which included projects in 21 countries. In 2023, Microsoft achieved its water access target by providing more than 1.5 million people with access to clean water and sanitation solutions. Microsoft drive innovation in water through first of its kind replenishment projects like FIDO which leverages AI enabled acoustic analysis to reduce water loss from leakage. In 2023, Microsoft achieved a reuse and recycle rate of 89.4 percent for its servers and components across all cloud hardware. In 2023, Microsoft diverted over 18,500 metric tons of waste from landfills across datacenters and campuses and cut single-use plastics in product packaging to just 2.7 percent. In 2023, the total renewable electricity use amounted to 23.6 million MWh which was estimated to power Paris with renewable electricity for about two years. The total contracted water replenishment made by Microsoft since 2020 amounted to 61.7 million m3. Microsoft have invested more than $3 million to improve water access in Brazil, India, Indonesia, Mexico and Chile. Microsoft aims for 75 percent construction and demolition waste diversion for all projects by year 2030. As of FY 2023, 15,849 acres of land have been legally designated as permanently protected. Microsoft has exceeded its land protection target of 11,000 by more than 40 percent. Microsoft is a key partner of Sustainable Packaging Coalition (SPC), the initiative which advances sustainable packaging through education, collaboration and action. Microsoft supports sustainable software through the Green Software Foundation, promoting carbon-aware computing, industry standards, education, open-source tools, and climate-conscious development practices. Microsoft is a member of the secretariat, Carbon Trust which focusses on decarbonizing the use phase of connected devices. The Global Carbon budget project which Microsoft aims to develop with Tsinghua University aims to develop the world's first near real time global carbon budget assessment framework driven by AI and data science techniques. Microsoft has provided over $25 million in resources to 18 disasters in 16 countries.

Green Investments by Oracle

Oracle Corporation is an American multinational computer technology company headquartered in Texas. Oracle sells database software such as Oracle Database and Cloud Computing. Oracle's core application software is a suite of enterprise software products such as enterprise resource planning (ERP) software, human capital management (HCM) software, customer relationship management (CRM), enterprise performance management (EPM) software, Customer Experience Commerce (CX Commerce) and supply chain management (SCM) software.

Oracle has set a target to achieve net zero emissions by 2050 and halve its greenhouse gas emissions by 2030 relative to a 2020 baseline. The Enact platform, built on Oracle Blockchain, simplifies solar ownership, certifies energy and carbon benefits, and enables customer participation in the growing Renewable Energy Certificate market. Oracle Fusion Cloud Sustainability streamlines ESG data collection by integrating and automating it across Fusion Applications, enhancing reporting accuracy, transparency, compliance, and enabling informed, data-driven decisions. Oracle Fusion Cloud Enterprise Performance Management (EPM) helps in the integration of financial and non-financial data so that organizations can fulfil more than reporting requirements. Oracle Fusion SCM Analytics supports supply chain professionals by analysing supplier performance, ensuring compliance, and minimizing risk and supply chain disruptions. Oracle Cloud Infrastructure (OCI) is a high-performance green cloud solution which runs on renewable energy and uses principles of circular economy to consolidate and optimize IT infrastructure.

The 2025 sustainable goals for Oracle include renewable energy use across all operations including Oracle Cloud. Oracle aims to have an environmental program in place for 100 percent of key suppliers. The company aims to have 33 per cent reduction in potable water use per square foot. 100 percent of OCI data centers in Europe are supported by renewable energy. Oracle's multifaceted renewable energy strategy focusses on a range of contract mechanisms and technologies such as renewable power purchase agreements, onsite renewable and carbon free generation, use of renewable energy credits and diversification of energy sources. Oracle also work closely with colocation suppliers to improve data transparency and drive renewable energy adoption. Customers are using Oracle technologies like AI and blockchain to advance sustainability, from ensuring ethical supply chains to improving crop yields with machine learning, driving positive environmental impact across industries. Oracle supports the circular economy by offering hardware take-back programs to reduce e-waste, extending product life through spare parts recovery, energy-efficient design, and remanufactured components, while managing the full lifecycle of its data center equipment. About 99.8 percent of Oracle's processed hardware are recycled or reused. Approximately 10.9 million pounds of retired customer hardware assets are collected for recycling or reuse. All technology recycling partners of Oracle are ISO 14001 certified. 100 percent renewable energy is used at 92 offices globally. There are 33 Oracle owned buildings which are ENERGY

STAR certified. About 88 percent of key direct suppliers of Oracle have an environmental program in place.

Established in 2008, the Environmental Steering Committee (ESC) is led by Oracle's Chief Sustainability Officer and includes senior directors and executives from key lines of business such as finance, risk management, social impact, procurement, operations, and manufacturing.

Oracle Fusion Cloud Applications support sustainability by helping businesses efficiently manage ESG data, reduce waste, and assess environmental impacts across operations. Oracle Fusion Cloud Enterprise Performance Management (EPM) aids in ESG tracking and reporting; Oracle Fusion Cloud Supply Chain & Manufacturing (SCM) supports responsible sourcing and product lifecycle analysis; HCM promotes workforce diversity and sustainability engagement; and OCI provides energy-efficient, high-performance computing. Oracle Cloud Infrastructure (OCI) offers high-performance computing powered by renewable energy, helping organizations lower carbon emissions and reduce energy costs. Oracle Financial Services Climate Change Analytics Cloud Service is a climate risk processing, reporting, and analytics solution for financial institutions that provides data sourcing and storage, computation of climate risk metrics, and analytics for internal, statutory, and management reporting.

Norwegian forestry research organization is using Oracle Autonomous Database and AI on Oracle Cloud Infrastructure to understand the forest value chain and improve long term sustainability.

Green Investments by IBM

International Business Machines Corporation (IBM) is an American multinational technology company with presence in over 175 countries and employs over 282,000 people. It is one of the 30 companies represented in the Dow Jones Industrial Average. IBM is the largest industrial research organization in the world. IBM is addressing the hybrid cloud and artificial intelligence (AI) opportunity with a platform-centric approach, focused on providing client value through a combination of technology and business expertise. Approximately 75 percent of IBM mix is in the software and consulting segment. The strategic focus of IBM is on hybrid cloud and artificial intelligence.

The Software segment offers software solutions which address client needs for a hybrid cloud platform, data and AI automation. The software segment has two business areas-Hybrid Platform & Solutions and Transaction Processing. Hybrid Platform & Solutions comprises Red Hat, Automation, Data &AI and Security. Transaction Processing supports clients' mission critical on-premise workloads in industries such as banking, airlines and retail. Consulting offers deep domain, technical, and industry expertise and market-leading capabilities in business transformation, technology implementation and managed services, including cloud managed and application services. Consulting comprises three business areas of Business Transformation, Technology Consulting and Application Operations.

In 2024, IBM generated $62.8 billion in revenues and $12.7 billion in free cash flow. In 2024, IBM allocated more than $7 billion to research and development. Over 90 percent of Fortune 500 companies are using IBM's hybrid cloud products and solutions.

As part of responsible scaling and deployment strategies for AI, IBM released watsonx. Governance™, an end-to-end toolkit for AI governance that enables responsible, transparent and explainable AI workflows. IBM aims to train two million learners in AI skills by 2026 through expanded education efforts, building on the 11 million already engaged, as part of its broader goal to train 30 million people by 2030.

In 2023, IBM promoted a risk-based approach to AI regulation and a skills-first strategy for addressing tech talent gaps by publishing a policymaker's guide on responsible AI foundation models and backing two bipartisan workforce development bills in the U.S. Since 2022, IBM have invested $100.3 million towards apprenticeships and new-collar programs.

Since 2021, IBM have completed 2130 energy conservation projects which avoided an estimated 256,000 MWh of energy consumption. IBM aims to procure 75 percent of the electricity from renewable sources by 2025 and 90 percent by 2030. IBM have plans to divert 90 percent (by weight) of IBM's total non-hazardous waste from landfill and incineration by 2025 through reuse, recycling, composting and waste to energy processes.

First tier suppliers of hardware, software and services of IBM are required to adhere to the Responsible Business Alliance (RBA) Code of Conduct which outlines requirements for labour, health, safety, environmental, ethics and management systems. IBM led the formation of AI Alliance, to build an open community which promotes responsible AI innovation. By 2025, IBM aim to contribute $30 million in cash, technology, and services through the IBM Sustainability Accelerator program to support organizations aiding communities vulnerable to environmental risks. In 2024, IBM committed up to an additional $45 million over the following five years. Since 2021, IBM have invested nearly $11.7 million towards the IBM Sustainability Accelerator program. In 2023, the total charity contribution of IBM amounted to $386.9 million.

In 2023, IBM conducted 82 full audits and 48 re-audits of first-tier suppliers in 22 high-risk countries to assess compliance with the RBA Code. A total of 664 nonconformances were identified, and corrective action plans were implemented and monitored through follow-up audits to ensure progress toward full compliance.

In 1971, IBM formalized its corporate environmental policy to provide the strategic framework for its global environmental management system (EMS). IBM have currently 21 environmental sustainability goals which address energy and climate change, conservation and biodiversity, pollution prevention and waste management, supply chain and EMS.

IBM's Flex Platform was chosen by the EGDC to help assess digital solutions' environmental impact across six sectors. In 2023, IBM and NASA expanded their

AI collaboration by open-sourcing geospatial and language models using NASA data, enabling applications like natural hazard detection, climate forecasting, and supporting reforestation and renewable energy efforts. IBM and Technip Energies partnered to scale VolCat Technology, a sustainable PET recycling method. In 2023, TEN launched Reju to industrialize this regeneration process. Since 2007, IBM has contributed technical expertise and leadership to The Green Grid (TGG), supporting global energy efficiency standards and regulations for data centers across the U.S., EU, China, and India. IBM has long championed climate action, co-founding ENERGY STAR in 1992, disclosing CO2 emissions since 1994, and supporting renewable energy and global agreements like the Paris Agreement. In 2019, it joined the Climate Leadership Council, backing a bipartisan carbon tax with dividends returned to citizens.

In 2023, IBM implemented 675 energy conservation projects globally thereby avoided an estimated 95,000 MWh of energy consumption which have resulted in savings of $11 million approximately. Since 1990, IBM have conserved an estimated 10.1 million MWh of energy consumption which was equivalent to four times its current annual energy consumption and had a savings of approximately $691 million and have avoided an estimated 4.66 million mtCO2e emissions. In 2023, IBM reduced its operational GHG emissions by 68.5 percent against base year 2010. IBM aims to source all directly procured paper and packaging from sustainably managed forests. In 2023, 99.8% (by spend) met this standard through certified suppliers.

In 2023, IBM generated 16,500 metric tons of non-hazardous waste, up 12% from 2022 due to construction and office returns. Despite this, IBM met its 2025 goals by diverting 94.2 percent of waste from landfill/incineration and limiting waste-to-energy use to 10 percent. Efforts included recycling, reuse programs, and waste segregation improvements. Since the late 1980s, IBM has prioritized environmentally responsible packaging by minimizing materials, using recyclable content, and collaborating with suppliers. In 2021, IBM set a goal to eliminate nonessential plastic packaging by end of 2024. By 2023, it completed 13 of 21 plastic reduction projects, including replacing PU foam with recyclable wood-based inserts—earning a WorldStar Award.

In 2023, IBM completed packaging redesigns and plastic reduction projects that eliminated an estimated 99.7 metric tons of virgin plastic annually. Initiatives included replacing plastic materials with recycled or plant-based alternatives and redesigning packaging for IBM Spectrum Fusion and IBM Power, which collectively removed 73.5 metric tons of packaging waste. IBM designs products for serviceability, upgradability, and recyclability, aiming to limit landfill or incineration waste to under 3 percent. In 2023, 96.8 percent of 12,400 metric tons of end-of-life products were reused, resold, or recycled. Since 1995, IBM has processed 1.14 million metric tons of product waste globally. IBM designs products for serviceability, upgradability, and recyclability, aiming to limit landfill or incineration waste to under 3 percent. In 2023, 96.8 percent of 12,400 metric tons of end-of-life products were reused, resold, or recycled. Since 1995, IBM has processed 1.14 million metric tons of product waste globally.

IBM set a 2021 goal to document 100 client engagements by 2025 demonstrating environmental benefits through its technology. By 2023, 72 projects were documented. IBM's sustainability solutions, powered by AI and automation, help clients track energy use, GHG emissions, and goals, driving business transformation and reducing costs, waste, and emissions.

IBM helps companies accelerate their business and sustainability goals across five key areas:

1. Energy Transition & Climate Resilience: IBM uses AI, IoT, and blockchain to support energy grid resilience and utility operations.
2. Intelligent Assets & Infrastructure: AI-powered solutions improve asset lifecycle management, boosting productivity and reducing waste.
3. Sustainable Supply Chains: IBM optimizes supply chain transparency and resilience with AI and blockchain.
4. Responsible Computing & Green IT: IBM modernizes IT infrastructure with energy-efficient solutions, AI-driven automation, and hardware recycling.
5. Sustainability Strategy, Data & Reporting: IBM Consulting guides clients through sustainable transformations, integrating ESG data and reporting solutions.

These services support clients like Neste, Transport for London, Antonello Produce, and BanFast in achieving their sustainability objectives.

Green Investments by Nvidia

Nvidia is a multinational technology company which specializes in in GPU-accelerated computing and artificial intelligence (AI). GPU are used in gaming, professional visualization, data centers and autonomous vehicles. Researchers and developers use computing solutions to focus on important applications from simulating molecular dynamics to climate forecasting. Nvidia have a platform strategy which brings together hardware, software, algorithms, libraries and services to create value for markets served by Nvidia. Nvidia computing powers breakthroughs across key scientific fields—from climate modelling and materials science to wind tunnel simulations and genomics—by combining advanced GPUs with high-performance networking technologies. Nvidia powers over 75 percent of the supercomputers on the global TOP500 list, including 24 of the top 30 systems on the Green500 list.

The company have invested over $45.3 billion in research and development since its inception. Nvidia's invention of GPU in year 1999 sparked the growth of the PC gaming market and redefined computer graphics. In 2024, Nvidia had revenues of $60.9 billion.

Nvidia's accelerated computing ecosystem is powering AI adoption across enterprises. With nearly five million developers and 40,000 companies in its network, over 1600 generative AI companies are building on Nvidia's platform. Since its

2006 launch, CUDA® has delivered 300+ libraries, 600 AI models, numerous SDKs, and 3500 GPU-accelerated applications—surpassing 48 million downloads. NVIDIA's Earth-2 platform uses AI to create a digital twin of the planet, enabling highly detailed weather predictions at a two-kilometer scale. Nvidia report its business results in two segments. The Compute & Networking segment comprises data center accelerated computing platforms and end to end networking platforms. The Graphics segment includes GeForce GPUs for gaming and PCs. Nvidia platforms incorporate processors, interconnects, software, algorithms, systems and services. These platforms focus on four large markets of data center, gaming, professional visualization and automotive.

NVIDIA accelerated Spark delivers up to 5 times faster data processing, cuts computing costs by up to 4 times and can reduce carbon footprint by as much as 80 percent. Pandas is the world's leading data analytics library, used by nearly ten million data scientists. Nvidia's new Blackwell platform empowers organizations to build and deploy real time generative AI powered by large trillion parameter language models. NVIDIA Blackwell GPUs are generally 20 times more energy efficient than traditional CPUs for certain AI and high-performance computing (HPC) workloads. The NVIDA GB200 Grace Blackwell Superchip is estimated to offer 25 times better energy efficiency over the prior Hopper generation for massive LLMs.

By 2025, Nvidia aim to maintain 100 percent renewable electricity for offices and data centers under operational control. In Fiscal 2024, Nvidia launched a Corporate Sustainability Steering Committee which is responsible for overseeing and providing input for sustainability strategy and program. NVIDIA introduced over 24 new microservices enabling global healthcare enterprises to harness generative AI for imaging, language, and biological simulations across any cloud. In FY24, over 90 percent of NVIDIA GPU systems packaging was recyclable materials. NVidia's new ALCHEMI NIM microservice accelerates chemical and materials research using AI, enabling faster, energy-efficient simulations to discover sustainable materials supporting the renewable energy transition. It dramatically reduces discovery time and costs, offering up to 100 times speedups in evaluating chemical stability using advanced GPU-powered simulations.

Green Investments by Samsung Electronics

Samsung Electronics is a South Korean multinational major appliance and consumer electronics corporation. Samsung Electronics is one of the largest technology company in the world. The group consists of numerous affiliated businesses which operate under the Samsung brand. Samsung Electronics consists of two divisions-Device eXperience (DX) and Device Solutions (DS). The DX Division produces and sells finished products such as TVs, refrigerators, washing machines, air conditioners, smartphones, network systems, and computers. The DS Division consists of the Memory Semiconductor Business, Foundry Business, and System LSI Business which produce and sell semiconductor components such as DRAM, NAND Flash, and mobile APs.

The Sustainability Committee under the Board of Directors oversees sustainability management of the company. The CEO presides over the company's Sustainability Council with Business Unit heads and operative department heads. The company aims to achieve net zero Scope 1, 2 emissions for DX division by 2030. The company aims to improve power consumption of major models in seven product categories by 30 percent. Samsung aims to cumulatively collect 25 million tonnes of e waste by 2050. During the period 2009–2023, Samsung have recovered a total of 6.297 million of e-waste. The DX division aim to replenish 100 percent of water used globally by 2030. The DX division aim to apply recycled resin to all plastic parts by year 2050. Samsung operate e-waste recovery programs in approximately 70 countries globally. Samsung obtained Platinum Zero Waste-to-Landfill certification in 2 Korean, 12 global manufacturing sites world-wide.

In 2023, Samsung secured a total of 250,000 tonnes of carbon credits through agroforestry and mangrove projects in India and Indonesia. The company also have plans to transition to 100 percent zero-emission vehicles (electric and hydrogen cars) in Korea by 2027. The US subsidiaries achieved 100 percent renewable energy transition in 2020. Samsung aim to reduce power consumption in major product models such as smartphones, TVs, refrigerators, washing machines, air conditioners, PCs, and monitors by an average of 30 percent by 2030 compared to 2019 models with similar performance. As of 2023, Samsung already achieved a 25 percent reduction. Samsung aim to expand e-Waste collection system to approximately 180 countries by year 2030. Samsung aims to use recycled resin in 100 percent of the plastic components in products procured by the DX division by year 2050. Samsung Electronics focusses on environmental impact reduction by replacing plastics and vinyl used in several products' packaging with recycled materials while reducing GHG emissions in its product transportation through miniaturizing and light weighting its packaging. The Galaxy S24 series launched by Samsung Electronics in year 2024 used 100 percent recycled paper in package boxes. Samsung aim to restore 100 percent of globally used water for DX division by year 2030.

The DS Division developed RCS, the semiconductor industry's first large-scale rooftop gas treatment system, using catalysts to collectively treat emissions from all facility outlets. In 2019, Samsung signed a 75 MW wind PPA with partners, enabling its U.S. sites to achieve 100 percent renewable energy and win a U.S. EPA award. The DS Division secured 76.2 GWh/year solar PPAs starting 2025, installed 2.8 MW solar and geothermal systems, and plans further renewable energy expansion. The DS Division implemented a Life Cycle Assessment process for semiconductor products, with third-party verification to ISO standards to ensure accurate carbon footprint data. The DS Division aims for a 99.9 percent recycling rate by 2030 through waste recycling, developing new recycling technologies, and reducing disposable product usage. Samsung aim to achieve highest level certification (Platinum) for all DX division manufacturing sites by year 2025.

Samsung Electronics aims to invest over KRW 7 trillion in environmental management activities by 2030. In 2021, Samsung Securities issued ESG-rated bonds to fund eco-friendly investments valued at KRW 100 billion. The bonds received the highest-grade Green 1 among green bonds from NICE Credit rating. Samsung Energy Transition Fund was launched in year 2021. The fund invests in energy infrastructure-related companies such as renewable energy production, eco-friendly buildings, energy technology and efficiency improvement.

Green Investments by Cisco Systems

Cisco Systems is an American multinational digital communications technology conglomerate. Cisco is a worldwide leader in technology that powers the internet. Cisco develops, manufactures and sells networking hardware, software, telecommunications equipment and other high technology services and products which includes artificial intelligence (AI) networking and cybersecurity solutions. Cisco specializes in specific tech markets such as Internet of things, domain security, videoconferencing. Cisco offers an industry leading portfolio of technology innovations in networking, security, collaboration and cloud management to connect industries and communities. The products and technologies of Cisco are grouped into Networking, Security Collaboration and Observability.

In 2024, Cisco had made nearly $54 billion in revenues. The company employs 90,400 employees in 95 countries. In fiscal 2024, Cisco launched a $1 billion global AI investment fund to bolster the start-up ecosystem. Cisco have surpassed $ 1 billion in AI orders from webscale customers and expect an additional $ 1 billion in AI product orders in fiscal 2025.

Cisco aims to achieve net zero by year 2040. Cisco was one of the first technology hardware and equipment companies to have its net zero goal validated under the SBTi Net-Zero Standard. By year 2025, Cisco aim to have 90 percent reduction in absolute Scope 1 and 2 GHG emissions compared to year 2019. By year 2030, Cisco aims for 30 percent reduction in absolute Scope 3 emissions from purchased goods and services, upstream transportation and distribution. In 2006, Cisco had set its first GHG emissions reduction goal and since then have been setting and achieving a series of five-year goals to reduce its absolute scope 1 and 2 GHGs. During the period 2023–2025, Cisco would invest approximately US$ 39 million in renewable energy, energy efficiency, building and fleet electrification projects. In fiscal 2024, Cisco implemented 27 energy efficiency projects which avoided 1.3 gigawatt-hours of energy consumption and 850 metric tonne carbon dioxide equivalent each year.

In 2024, Cisco entered into a 15-year Virtual Purchase Power Agreement (VPPA) in Europe to pursue clean energy strategy. Cisco had launched a multiyear, multimillion-dollar partnership with Mercy Corps to develop scalable tech driven climate solutions for drought affected communities in Kenya. The Cisco Foundation is investing $100 million over ten years to strengthen ecosystems through non-profit grants and impact investments in early-stage climate start-ups. By 2024, Cisco Foundation has approved $35 million for climate solutions in six key priority areas.

Backed by $300 million, Cisco's Social Justice Actions promote diversity, equity, fair pay, advocacy, and investment in underserved communities and diverse-led start-ups. In 2016, Cisco had set a 10-year goal to positively impact one billion people by 2025 through its social impact grants and signature programs. Cisco Networking Academy has reached 24 million learners in 191 countries since 1997 and aims to train 25 million more in digital and cybersecurity skills by 2032. Cisco have set target to have 70 percent of Cisco component and manufacturing suppliers (by spend) to achieve a zero-waste diversion rate at one or more sites by fiscal 2025. By fiscal 2025, 100 percent of new Cisco products and packaging will follow circular design principles. By 2025, approximately 50 percent of plastics used by weight in Cisco products will be used of recycled content. Approximately 96 percent of electricity for Cisco facilities came from renewable sources. By Fiscal 2025, approximately 80 percent of Cisco component, manufacturing and logistics suppliers by spend have a public absolute GHG emissions reduction target.

Over the next 10 years, Cisco plan to engage, support and invest in 40 communities around the globe. Approximately US $ 556 million in cash and in-kind contributions were provided by Cisco and the Cisco Foundation. Since 2021, Cisco Foundation have approved US$ 35 million to fund climate solutions. Since 2015, Cisco had 1600 Country digital acceleration projects in 50 countries. In 2018, Cisco made commitments to respect human rights in AI design, development and use. In 2022, Cisco formalized its commitment with its Responsible AI Principles and Framework. Cisco have collaborated with Dell, Microsoft and other technology companies to launch OpenEoX, a global initiative to standardize the exchange of end of life and end of support information within the software and hardware industries.

Cisco does not source minerals directly but works with suppliers to prevent links to conflict or environmental harm. In 2024, Cisco joined the Initiative for Responsible Mining Assurance and expanded due diligence to cover key minerals. As of 2023, 70 percent of 3TG smelters and 64 percent of cobalt refiners in its supply chain met third-party standards. Cisco is a founder and active member of the Responsible Business Alliance (RBA) and the company have adopted RBA Code of Conduct as its Supplier Code of Conduct. Cisco assess its suppliers' conformance to the Code for labor, health and safety, environment, and ethics by requesting self-assessments and conducting third-party audits. In fiscal 2024, Cisco conducted more than 160 RBA audits of supplier sites to assess working conditions for approximately 490,000 workers in its supply chain. In fiscal 2024, several Cisco Catalyst 9000 switches earned ENERGY STAR certification, helping customers reduce environmental impact while maintaining performance.

The Cisco Foundation supports ecosystem restoration and community climate adaptation through its US$100 million climate commitment. Since 2021, $17 million in grants and US$ 18 million in investments were made by Cisco Foundation for development of climate solutions. The Cisco Foundation's clean energy impact investments include support for Jaza Energy, which integrates solar-powered hubs with telecom towers, and Aikido Technologies which, develop floating offshore wind turbines. Cisco Foundation have supported partners to develop and apply AI to bridge digital and data gaps. Partners like Bridges to Prosperity maps optimal bridge sites. Charity water's AI powered algorithm uses data from rural water pump sensors to predict failure of water pumps and CareerVillage scales career coaching based on AI. Cisco Crisis Response (CCR) leads private-sector efforts in humanitarian aid, partnering with governments, relief organizations, and affected communities during crises. In 2024, CCR have provided US$ 6.9 million in cash grants, US$3.4 million in product donations and US$ 1.2 million in disaster campaigns. During the past 10 years, Splunk acquired by Cisco in 2024 had invested more than US$62 million in grants, donations, product offerings and technology training. Cisco offers customers Splunk's free Sustainability Toolkit to help them track and improve their environmental performance.

Green Investments by General Electric

General Electric (GE) Company is a high tech global industrial company which operates through three segments -Aerospace, Renewable Energy and Power. GE was incorporated in year 1892. The products of GE include commercial and military aircraft engines and systems, renewable energy generation equipment and grid solutions, gas, steam, nuclear and other power generation equipment. In 2023, GE had announced spinoff of the company into three global investment grade public companies -GE Aerospace, GE Vernova consisting of Renewable Energy and Power and GE Healthcare. GE serve customers in over 160 countries. Manufacturing and service operations are carried out at 59 manufacturing plants located in 24 states in United States and at 102 manufacturing plants located in 25 other countries. By December end 2023, GE and consolidated affiliates employed approximately 125,000 people.

The Sustainability framework and sustainability management aim to provide the policies, procedures, governance and KPIs to mitigate highest priority risk areas. The 4R circularity framework aims to accelerate GE's transition to more sustainable use of natural resources, minimize waste and lower the footprint of manufacturing operations.

In 2023, GE invested $ one billion in R&D across its three business segments. GE Vernova's sustainability framework comprises four pillars -Electrify, Decarbonize, Conserve and Thrive. GE's advanced 6 MW onshore wind platform featuring two-piece blade has reached 6.1 MW with nearly 11 GW in firm orders by end of 2023. GE Vernova and Sembcorp Marine are partnering on three HVDC contracts for TenneT's 2GW Program, supporting Europe's goal to be climate-neutral by 2050. GE's first SF6-free 420 kV gas-insulated line was installed at the UK's Sellindge substation, cutting global warming potential by 99 percent.

GE Vernova's sustainability programs focus on electrifying and decarbonizing the planet. Approximately 25 percent of the world's electricity is generated with the help of GE Vernova's technology base. Electrification is one of the most important enablers for global decarbonization at scale thereby providing opportunities to install renewable energy or low carbon generation technologies. GE Vernova develops and delivers a wide range of products and solutions to generate and convert electricity from wind, hydro, solar, nuclear, natural gas, and steam sources. In 2023, GE Vernova added an additional 29 GW of new generating capacity online of which 42 percent were in developing countries. GE is investing in advanced nuclear technologies to provide lower carbon, dispatchable electricity. GE aim to decarbonize gas turbines by catalysing hydrogen in the marketplace and fostering installation of CCS. GE Vernova's Hydro Power business provides advanced, sustainable hydropower technologies and services—from individual equipment to turnkey solutions—for both new and existing plants worldwide. GE Vernova's onshore wind business is a world leader in onshore wind technology with an installed base of approximately 55,000 turbines around the world. GE Vernova's Solar & Storage Solutions business offers solar, battery storage, and control technologies to support a reliable, dispatchable, and renewable energy future. GE Vernova's Electrification Software, including GridOS®, provides smart tools to accelerate electrification and decarbonization, helping utilities build a reliable, sustainable, and affordable energy grid. GE Vernova's Power & Energy Resources Software business boosts energy efficiency, safety, and sustainability with Proficy® software, supporting industries from manufacturing to utilities.

GE aims for net zero by year 2050. By 2023, GE achieved 46 percent reduction in gross Scope 3 emissions from the use of its sold products relative to year 2019. GE aim for carbon neutrality for Scope 1 and 2 GHG emissions by year 2030. GE aims to cover approximately 90 percent of GE's top products in terms of 4R circularity framework by year 2030. During 2019–2023, GE Vernova achieved 39 percent reduction in Scope 1 and 2 market-based emissions.

GE Vernova's advanced research business is an innovation powerhouse with 150+ current research R&D projects. GE Vernova is investing in decarbonizing gas turbines through hydrogen fuel and carbon capture. With 120+ turbines using hydrogen globally, GE is advancing toward 100 percent hydrogen capability. Carbon Capture and Storage (CCS) captures CO2 from power generation and industrial processes for underground storage. GE is developing solid sorbent-based technology and exploring CO2 utilization to lower emissions. GE Vernova has developed a unique Direct Air Capture (DAC) system combining thermal management and advanced sorbent materials, optimizing CO2 removal from the air.

In 2023, GE Vernova received three U.S. Department of Energy projects to develop sustainable aviation fuels from captured CO2. This includes a $3.3 million study for a DAC hub in Houston, TX, aiming to capture one million tons of CO2 annually. GE Vernova's Nuclear Power business, in partnership with Hitachi, develops advanced reactors like the BWRX-300, a flexible, 300 MW small modular reactor for electricity, steam, and hydrogen production.

GE Vernova's Financial Services business provides financing for energy projects globally through project financing, equity investments, and capital raising from financial institutions. GE Vernova's Financial Services has developed over 7 GW of renewable projects globally, including wind, solar, and storage, and has partnered with Alfanar Energia España to develop a 334 MW renewable energy portfolio in Spain. GE Vernova's Financial Services and KUKE, Poland's Export Credit Agency, formed a €1 billion agreement to support global energy decarbonization and electrification through capital investment in renewable and gas power projects. GE Vernova's Consulting Services offers energy expertise, solving power system challenges, enabling technology integration, and guiding decarbonization pathways to accelerate the Energy Transition. GE Vernova's Consulting Services, in partnership with the Natural Resources Defense Council, studied the benefits of interregional transmission in the Eastern U.S., showing enhanced affordability, reliability, and resiliency.

GE Vernova launched a Product Stewardship and Circularity program in 2023, focusing on resource scarcity, life cycle impact, eco-design, and meeting regulatory and customer expectations for lower-carbon products. In December 2023, the ZEBRA consortium announced a successful completion of full-scale validation testing of the first 100 percent recyclable blade.

Green Investments by Intel

Intel is a global designer and manufacturer of semiconductor products. Intel design, manufacture and sell semiconductor products including CPUs which are used globally in devices and services across consumer, enterprise, government and education sectors. Intel's customers include OEMs, ODMs, cloud service providers, and others. Intel also develop and produce semiconductor technologies at a worldwide network of facilities. The company had revenues of $54.2 billion in year 2023.

Intel has set long-term commitments to achieve net-zero Scope 1 and 2 GHG emissions by 2040 and net-zero upstream Scope 3 GHG emissions by 2050. Intel invest in GHG reductions including chemical substitution, abatement, energy conservation, process optimization and renewable and alternative electricity. As a result, Intel have avoided approximately 82 percent of its cumulative Scope 1 and 2 GHG emissions over the last decade and have reduced its absolute operational GHG emissions by 78 percent from its peak of year 2006. In 2023, Intel achieved 99 percent renewable electricity globally. In 2023, upstream Scope 3 GHG emissions accounted for 37 percent of its total value chain. Intel supported collective action on industry wide emissions reductions as a founding member of the Semiconductor Climate Consortium (SCC). Intel aims to reduce Scope 3 supply chain emissions to at least 30 percent lower by 2030. Intel through collaboration with its supply chain ecosystem aim to reach net zero upstream Scope 3 GHG emissions by year 2050. Intel aims to achieve 100 percent renewable electricity across its global operations. During 2020, 5 percent of Intel's total waste went to landfill and the company had implemented circular economy strategies for 65 percent of manufacturing waste. In 2023, Intel upcycled 76,000 tons, or approximately 63 percent, of its manufacturing waste.

In 2024, for the 14th year, Ethisphere Institute named Intel to its annual list of the World's Most Ethical Companies. Intel and other tech companies support the Digital Climate Alliance, which promotes policies enabling digital solutions to drive climate action, efficiency, transparency, and resiliency. Intel is a founding member of the Responsible Business Alliance (RBA). In 2023, Intel introduced Intel® Core™ Ultra mobile processors that deliver reimagined power efficiency, world-class compute and graphics performance, and the best AI PC experience10 to mobile platforms.

In the U.S., Intel is expanding operations in Arizona, New Mexico, and Oregon, and building two state-of-the-art chip factories in Ohio. Backed by a proposed $8.5 billion in CHIPS and Science Act funding from the U.S. Department of Commerce, these projects are expected to drive more than $100 billion in U.S. manufacturing and research investments over the next five years. Intel plans to invest over $33 billion in Germany to build a wafer fabrication mega site and up to $4.6 billion in an assembly and test facility in Poland.

In 2023, Intel spent $1.6 billion with diverse-owned suppliers. In 2023, Intel conserved approximately 10.2 billion gallons of water internally and through community collaborations, and enabled restoration of 3.1 billion gallons through investments in watershed restoration projects. Intel has been a founding member of The Semiconductor Research Corporation since its inception. Intel and European public and private sector collaborators are investing $13 million over four years to launch six research centers for sustainable semiconductor manufacturing. Intel is making a $7 billion investment at its site in Penang to build Intel's largest advanced packaging facility for 3D packaging technology. Intel launched the 5th Gen Intel® Xeon® Scalable processors, which deliver improvements in performance and efficiency compared to the previous generation.

Intel's Green bond

During August 2022, Intel issued its first Green Bond, a 10-year, USD 1.25 billion senior notes offering with a fixed coupon rate of 4.15 percent per annum. By end 2022, Intel allocated $ 0.425 billion. The net proceeds of the green bond offering were used to fund eligible projects in six key areas as detailed in the Intel Green Financing Framework adopted during August 2022. This framework is aligned with the Green Bond Principles, Social Bond Principles and Sustainability Bond Guidelines. The six eligible project areas are Green Buildings, Circular Economy and Waste Management, Energy Efficiency, Pollution Prevention and Control, Water Stewardship and Renewal Energy. A committee consisting of representatives from Corporate Sustainability, Corporate Responsibility, Legal, Treasury, Finance and other Intel teams is responsible for the evaluation, selection and assessment of the performance of eligible spending and projects, on an annual basis, to ensure alignment with the Green Financing Framework.

Table 17.4 Green bond cumulative allocation

Category	Amount
Circular Economy and Waste Management	$21 million
Renewable Energy	$39 million
Energy Efficiency	$51 million
Water Stewardship	$99 million
Pollution Prevention and Control	$215 million
Total	$425 million

Source: Intel Annual Green Bond Report 2023

Table 17.5 Environmental impact

GHG reduced (as CO2e)	5.3 million
Energy saving	59 million Kwh
Water Saved	4.5 billion gallons
Waste diverted from landfill	56,000
Waste reduction	1900 tons

Source: Intel Green Bond Report 2023

Table 17.4 shows the green bond cumulative allocation for the period 2021–2022. The total net proceeds were $1.245 billion and the outstanding net proceeds was $820 million.

Table 17.5 shows the environmental benefits received for the $425 million spending to which Intel allocated green bond funds during 2021 and 2022.

Intel has established a goal to conserve 4 billion kWh of energy from its 2020 baseline by 2030. Intel have allocated Green Bond funds to various energy conservation projects in 2021 and 2022 and in total the company had plans to invest approximately $300 million in energy conservation projects. Intel invested in new energy conservation projects that saved approximately 162 million kWh in 2021 and approximately 160 million kWh in 2022, of electricity. Intel have identified strategic investment areas in efficient lighting, chilled water cooling, compressed air and heat recovery and electrification. To reduce energy usage in operations, Intel is investing in HVAC upgrades and heat recovery projects. For new factory construction projects, Intel is incorporating energy efficiency into design and equipment selections. Intel is uniquely positioned, as both an Integrated Device Manufacturer (IDM) and a foundry, to collaborate across its entire value chain to achieve emission goals.

Intel uses high global warming potential gases in semiconductor manufacturing, but through abatement technologies, renewables, and efficiency measures, it has avoided 80 percent of Scope 1 and 2 emissions over the past decade. Intel invests heavily in advanced abatement technology to limit emissions and have allocated Green Bond funds to the purchase of these Point of Use abatement systems in 2021 and 2022.

References

Alphabet Annual Report 2024.
Alphabet Sustainability Bond Impact Report 2022.
Apple Environmental Progress Report, 2024.
Apple Green Bond Report 2023.
Cisco FY 2024 Purpose Report.
Cisco Systems Annual Report 2024.
GE VERNOVA, Sustainability Report 2023.
Google 2024 Environmental Progress Report.
https://www.oracle.com/social-impact/planet/
IBM Annual Report 2024.
IBM Impact, ESG Report 2023.
Intel Annual Green Bond Report 2023.
Microsoft Annual Report 2024.
Microsoft Environmental Sustainability Report 2024.
Nvidia Annual Report 2024.
Nvidia Sustainability Report 2024.
Oracle Environmental and Social Impact Datasheet 2024.
Samsung Electronics Sustainability Report 2024.
Sustainable // 2023-24 Intel Corporate Responsibility Report.

Chapter 18
Green Investments in Telecom/ Communication Services Sector

Green Investments by AT&T

AT&T, formerly known as SBC Communications Inc. (SBC) was formed as one of several regional holding companies which was created to hold AT&T Corp's (ATTC) local telephone companies. In 1984 AT&T were spun off from ATTC pursuant to an anti-trust consent decree and became an independent publicly traded telecommunications services provider. AT&T is a leading provider of telecommunications and technology services globally. The Communications segment provides wireless and wireline telecom and broadband services to consumers. The Communication segment consists of business units such as Mobility, Business Wireline and Consumer Wireline. Mobility offers wireless service and equipment. Business Wireline offers ethernet-based fiber services, fixed wireless services, IP Voice and managed professional services, as well as legacy voice and data services and related equipment, to business customers. Consumer Wireline offers broadband services to residential customers in select areas, including high-speed fiber connections and AT&T Internet Air (AIA), a fixed wireless service delivered over its 5G network. Consumer Wireline offers legacy telephony voice communication services.

Over the decade, AT&T has committed $5 billion to connect 25 million people to affordable, high speed internet access and digital literacy resources. AT&T Connected Climate Initiative and Equinix have a joint collaboration to enable customers reduce one billion metric tons of greenhouse gas (GHG) emissions by year 2035.

By end of 2024, AT&T invested $2.87 billion to reach 12.1 million people.AT&T is expanding its networks, reduce its cost barriers for low income customers. AT&T is expanding its fiber network to cover 29 million consumer and business locations in parts of more than 100 US metros. To stimulate economic development at community level, AT&T have spent more than $4.1 billion for small and local suppliers to leverage the scale of AT&T's supply chain and network investments.AT&T also

B. R. Kumar, *Green Finance*, Sustainable Finance,
https://doi.org/10.1007/978-3-032-03333-8_18

opened 28 new AT&T Connected Learning Centers™ in communities in 2024 and targets to open 100 by the end of 2027. AT&T is deploying 5G and fiber networks to connect communities.

AT&T aim to reduce its absolute Scope 1 and 2 greenhouse gas (GHG) emissions by 63% by end of year 2030 compared to 2015 base year. AT&T aim to achieve Scope 1 and 2 emissions carbon neutrality by end of year 2035. By 2023, AT&T had 81% attainment towards its Scope 1 and 2 science-based target. Approximately 8.8 million metric tons of CO2e were reduced by 2023 compared to 2015 base year. AT&T aim to deliver connectivity solutions which would enable business customers to reduce one billion metric tons of GHG emissions during the period 2018–2035.AT&T aim to integrate sustainability performance metrics into its sourcing for 80% of the spend by end of 2025. AT&T aim to reduce its carbon footprint by approximately 740,000 metric tons of CO2e between 2024 and 2028.

In 2022, AT&T invested over $118 million to implement approximately 7000 energy efficiency and reduction projects which drove annual energy savings of 1680 MWh and gross annualized energy cost savings of $144 million. During 2015-2022, AT&T implemented approximately 161,000 energy efficiency projects such as integration of EBMS and decommissioning obsolete portions of its network operations. This initiative has resulted in 7,053,000 MWh of annual energy savings and annualized energy cost savings of approximately $663 million. AT&T's large-scale renewable energy projects have delivered more than 2.8 million renewable energy credits to offset its greenhouse gas emissions. Over $61 million of investment was made for real estate decommissioning projects. More than $42 million was invested in network projects for decommissioning, process optimization and smart control initiatives. Approximately $ 14 million was invested to upgrade and repair building infrastructure and system. AT&T have included over 250,000 assets across AT&T's mobility, wireline and retail portfolio to calculate the financial impact of its physical climate risks using IPCC climate data. During 2018–2022 period, AT&T have identified 24 Smart Carbon Solutions which have enabled emissions reduction of 149.2 million MT of CO_2e.

During 2021–2024 period, AT&T worked with more than 100 non-profit organizations to distribute more than 138,000 hot spots and devices to 385,000 plus people. During November 2023, AT&T was awarded $55 million in Broadband Equity, Access, and Deployment (BEAD) funding to help expand AT&T Fiber in Louisiana. This funding was part of a 4-year, $205 million public-private initiative aimed at bringing high-speed internet to over 20,000 unserved and underserved locations across the state. During 2024, AT&T Foundation contributed $72.5 million in cash and $2.6 million in in-kind giving. AT&T have conserved 9.5 MWh of energy and more than $867 million were saved from energy projects since 2015.By end 2024, 31 smart climate solutions were implemented by AT&T. AT&T aim to reduce the amount of US waste send to landfill by 30% by 2030 compared to base year 2019. By 2024, land waste was reduced by 11%.

AT&T implements thousands of innovative energy efficiency projects across its network and operations to reduce electricity consumption costs and emissions. By transitioning its network from copper DSL to fiber, AT&T offers faster network and reduces energy consumption by 70% in the region. Since 2020, the total energy consumption decreased by 14.5% and renewable energy procurement has increased by 21.5%. The company aims to reduce the amount of US waste send to landfill by 30% by the end of 2030. Approximately 12.5 million consumer devices were recovered by AT&T in 2024, which included 5.7 million devices through the Mobility trade in program. In 2024, about 89% of shipping cartons were transitioned to recycled content in certain US regions such as Texas, York, Pennsylvania and California. AT&T through Network Disaster Recovery Program have established disaster response procedures to monitor and respond to weather related events which could impact infrastructure. AT&T have invested over $ 1 billion over past three decades for its Network Disaster Recovery Program. AT&T screens 80 K+ network locations using risk scores based on climate data. AT&T has one of the largest and most advanced recovery programs in the world with more than 750 pieces of specialized response equipment which covers land, sea and air.

FirstNet®, built with AT&T, is the only nationwide, high-speed broadband communications platform exclusively designed for America's first responders and public safety personnel. FirstNet was developed and maintained through a public-private partnership with the First Responder Network Authority. AT&T has been a pioneer in AI for nearly 70 years.AT&T have integrated sustainability performance metrics into its sourcing for 80% of its spend by the end of 2025. AT&T focuses on a multi-layered approach to monitor, prevent and offer rapid response to security threat by the end of 2025.

Green Investments by Verizon

Verizon Communications is one of the world's leading providers of communications, technology, information and streaming products and services to consumers, businesses and government entities. Verizon offer data, video and voice services and solution on its networks and platforms. Verizon operate and manage two strategic business units-Verizon Consumer Group and Verizon Business Group. The consumer segment provides consumer focused wireless and wireline communications services and products. In 2024, the consumer segment's revenues amounted to $102.9 billion accounting for approximately 76% of Verizon's consolidated revenues. By December 2024, Consumer segment had approximately 115 million wireless retail connections of which 83% were post-paid connections. Consumer division had approximately ten million total broadband connections. The Business segment offers wireless and wireline communication solutions, including fixed wireless access (FWA) broadband, data, video, voice, IoT services, corporate networking, security, and managed network services. In 2024, business segment revenues amounted to $29.5 billion. By December 2024, the Business segment had approximately 31 million wireless retail post-paid connections.

Verizon aim to achieve net zero operational emissions by year 2035. During 2019–2022, Verizon had 23.3% reduction in scopes 1 and 2 emissions and 15.1%

reduction in scope 3 emissions. By February 2024, 3.6 GW of renewable energy contracts were put in place by Verizon. By 2030, Verizon aims to achieve 53% reduction in its scope 1 and 2 operational emissions to limit global warming. Verizon have committed to set a Science based Targets Initiative (SBTi) target to reach net zero emissions across its value chain by 2050. Verizon also have set targets to source renewable energy equivalent to 50% of its annual electricity usage by year end 2025 and 100% by 2030.

Since 2019, Verizon has issued six green bonds totalling approximately $6 billion. In 2019, Verizon became the first US telecom to issue a green bond. In 2019, Verizon raised $1 billion in net proceeds. By 2019, approximately $500 million of net proceeds were allocated. Verizon have allocated approximately $5 billion of the net proceeds to renewable energy projects. Verizon is one of the leading corporate buyers of renewable energy in US and member of the Clean Energy Buyers Association. By 2025, Verizon had in place 28 long term renewable energy purchase agreements (REPAs) for solar and wind power. With total of approximately 3.6 gigawatts renewable energy generating capacity. The renewable energy capacity which Verizon had contracted is expected to avoid over 4.7 million metric tons of CO_2e annually. These agreements do not require physical delivery of energy and can reduce Verizon's exposure to energy price volatility. Verizon's Renewable Energy Purchase Agreements (REPAs) are expected to help avoid about 4.5 million metric tons of greenhouse gas emissions annually which is equivalent of removing over one million cars from the road—and support the development of new wind and solar projects across 16 states, creating local jobs. By February 2025, 19 projects related to REPAs are in commercial operation to generate renewable energy to support to a greener grid. The operational projects are expected to produce approximately 7.7 million megawatt-hours (MWh) annually. The online portfolio of the company consists of ten solar and nine wind projects located in 13 states in USA. Verizon have signed a REPA with Deriva Energy for 70 MW of renewable energy capacity at North Allegheny. The company has also signed a REPA with Leeward Renewable Energy for 179 MW of renewable energy capacity at the White Wing Ranch Solar Project.

By February 2025, Verizon has allocated nearly $700 million of the $979 million net proceeds of its sixth green bond entirely to REPAs for renewable energy projects. These REPAs support 475 MW of new renewable energy capacity, with approximately 76% coming from solar energy and 24% from wind energy. By February 2025, Verizon had allocated $5.65 billion of the nearly $6 billion in net proceeds from the green bonds issued under its green bond program.

Table 18.1 shows Verizon's cumulative bond program summary.

Table 18.2 shows the green bond structure issued by Verizon.

Verizon focusses on sustainable paper sourcing and ensures that at least 50% of the paper used annually contains a minimum of 10% recovered fiber and/or post-consumer waste content. Verizon's device trade-in program promotes a circular economy by allowing consumers to return used devices for credit. These devices are repaired, repurposed, or resold, with recycling as a last step. Home internet devices are also refurbished and reused for 4G, 5G, and Fios services. Verizon partners with

Table 18.1 Cumulative allocation of green bond in millions of dollars

Year of issuance	Renewable energy	Green building	Energy efficiency	Biodiversity & conservation	Total net proceeds
2019	636.9	319.3	36.7	0.8	993.7
2020	994.1				994.1
2021	991.1				991.1
2022	981.4				981.4
2023	994.1				994.1
2024	699.9				699.9

Source: Green Bond Impact Report 2025

Table 18.2 Green bond structure

Year	Green bond
2020	3.875% notes due 2029
2021	1.5% notes due 2030
2022	2.85% notes due 2041
2023	3.875% notes due 2052
2024	5.05% notes due 2033
2025	5.50% notes due 2054

Source: https://www.verizon.com/about/investors/green-bond-reports

the Carbon Trust to measure the CO_2 emissions avoided by customers using its products and services. In 2023, a refined model showed that Verizon solutions helped avoid over 20.1 million metric tons of CO_2e. In 2023, Verizon awarded a total of $500,000 to four winners leveraging advanced technology, including 5G, to develop climate resilience solution.

Verizon aims to provide ten million youths with digital skills training by year 2030.Verizon Innovative Learning Initiative have provided over seven million students nationwide with digital tools and resources. Verizon have invested $173.8 million in learning and development initiatives for its employees. Verizon Innovative Learning has invested nearly $1.2 billion to support digital equity and inclusion in education since 2012. In 2023, Verizon have invested nearly $116 million in Verizon Innovative Learning. Verizon is deploying 5G technology to over 100 Verizon Innovative Learning Labs across US.

Verizon have invested $2.6 billion in healthcare benefits and services. The company uses EcoVadis assessment tool to evaluate the suppliers' responsible performance. Since 2013, 728 suppliers were assessed through EcoVadis. During the past 10 years, Verizon had $54.3 billion spend for diverse suppliers. In 2023, Verizon spent $6.1 billion in goods and services directly and indirectly with diverse suppliers. Since 2009, Verizon has planted over 20 million trees. Since 2019, over 45,000 plus individuals were prepared for jobs of the future. Since 2021, over 273,000 small businesses were provided with resources to enhance digital economy. The company have a target to source 100% of the energy from renewables by year 2030. In 2023, Verizon partnered with a third-party consultant to revive its prioritization assessment. Verizon is a member of the Joint Alliance for CSR (JAC), an association of telecommunications operators who audits common suppliers.JAC audits are based on a common verification, assessment and development methodology which include the generation of corrective action plans. Since JAC's inception in 2010, 1060 supplier audits have been completed. Verizon's conflict minerals due diligence framework was designed to align with the Organization for Economic Cooperation and Development's Due Diligence Guidance for Responsible Supply Chains of Minerals from Conflict Affected and High-Risk Areas. Verizon's strategic decarbonization audit program was designed to identify and implement cost effective energy conservation initiatives across its real estate portfolio. Each year, sites are selected for a comprehensive energy improvement program based on factors such as fuel usage, building age and size, energy performance, and compliance with local standards. These sites undergo a detailed year-long audit focused on HVAC electrification and tailored solutions for technical challenges. The most effective electrification, energy-saving, and retro-commissioning measures are then implemented over a one- to two-year project cycle. Verizon reduces fleet emissions through several strategies, including replacing older bucket trucks with hybrid models that use battery-powered lifts, developing electric battery systems to replace gas generators in fiber splicing vans, recalibrating engines in legacy Fios vans to lower emissions, and using vehicle dispatching technology to reduce mileage.

Verizon partnered with the US Environmental Protection Agency (EPA) Energy Star program for certification of its 100% of eligible facilities. In 2023, Verizon joined the renewable energy initiative RE100. Verizon have set targets to source renewable energy equivalent to 50% of its annual electricity usage by 2025 and 100% by 2030.

Green Investments by Vodafone Group

Vodafone Group business comprises infrastructure assets, shared operations, growth platforms, retail and service operations. The retail and service operations are split into three broad business lines-Vodafone Business, Europe Consumer and Africa Consumer. Vodafone offers a range of market leading mobile and fixed line connectivity services in its European markets. Vodafone operate mobile and fixed networks in 15 countries and have stakes in further seven countries through its joint ventures and associates. Vodafone also partner with mobile networks in 43 countries. Vodafone's portfolio also includes core connectivity business such as digital services, the Internet of Things (IoT) and financial services. Vodafone is the largest mobile and fixed network operator in Europe and a leading global IoT connectivity provider. With 85% 4G population coverage, Vodafone aim to extend network access to rural communities across Europe and Africa. Vodafone have connected 66.2 million customers to its financial inclusion services. The company aim to connect 75 million customers to mobile money and financial inclusion services. To support micro, small and medium enterprises across Europe and Africa, Vodafone

Business offers digital advice service V-Hub. V-Hub have supported 3.3 million micro, small and medium sized enterprises for digitalisation. Since 2021, 100% of the electricity that Vodafone use in Europe has been matched with renewable sources thereby achieving its 2025 goal 4 years ahead of schedule. Fintech services in Africa connect more than 66.2 million people to facilitate entrepreneurship and economic development. Vodafone aim to drive digital inclusion to the hardest-to-connect communities by bringing 4G to an additional 70 million people in sub-Saharan Africa through participation in the UN Partner2Connect digital coalition. Vodafone aim to connect 75 million people and their families to mobile money services by March 2026.

In Africa, device-financing options are expanding to increase smartphone access. In South Africa, the Easy2Own plan offers flexible payment options, with over 3700 customers enrolled. In Kenya, the Lipa Mdogo program—launched in 2020 by Safaricom, Google, and Meta—provides smartphones for as little as KSh20 a day and supports farmers through DigiFarm. To date, 1.2 million 4G devices have been connected through the program. Through Vodafone Business, Vodafone provide products and services that were specifically tailored for MSME and, small-office home-office, ('SOHO') businesses to guide them through technology choices to improve their digital readiness.

Through Vodacom's subsidiary Mezzanine, the eVuna platform is helping digitalize small-scale agriculture in Sub-Saharan Africa. eVuna offers SaaS tools and a marketplace for farmers, including dairy management and evouchering systems. In Kenya, Safaricom used eVuna to help the government distribute fertilizer subsidies to over 5.9 million farmers. The platform also supports dairy cooperatives by digitally tracking milk deliveries and sending daily summaries to farmers via SMS, replacing manual record-keeping. In South Africa, Mezzanine supports the Department of Agriculture by issuing over 270,000 vouchers to smallholder farmers, totalling more than ZAR 1.6 billion in value.

The Vodafone Foundation, in partnership with UNHCR, is expanding access to quality digital education for refugee and host community students through the Instant Network Schools program in six African countries. Since 2013, the initiative has transformed 118 classrooms into connected, solar-powered multimedia hubs, benefiting over 274,000 students and 4700 teachers.

Vodafone's M-Pesa and other mobile money platforms, designed to enable financial inclusion, has 66.2 million active customers and generated €351 million in revenues in 2024.Energy use by Vodafone's mobile access network, fixed line network and technology centres accounted for 93% of total global energy consumption.

Vodafone have achieved 59% reduction in Scope 1 and 2 GHG emissions since 2020. The company aims for net zero operations in Europe by 2028 and in Africa by 2035. In FY24, Vodafone advanced Scope 3 GHG emissions reduction by integrating climate action into its procurement process, assigning 20% weight to ESG criteria—including 5% for climate performance—in supplier selection. Vodafone also collaborates with the Joint Alliance for CSR (JAC) to streamline and standardize supplier engagement across the telecom industry. In 2024, Vodafone solutions have enabled the avoidance of 32.8 million tonnes of CO_2e—approximately 75 times the

Table 18.3 Eligible green project portfolio

Segment	Amount in € millions
Energy efficiency	1281.44
Renewable energy	2.89
Green building	61.33
Total	1345.66

Source: Vodafone Green Bond Report 2020

emissions from its operations (Scope 1 and 2) in FY24. Since setting its enablement target in 2020, Vodafone's customers avoided a total of 78.3 million tonnes of CO_2e.

Vodafone Group Plc has designed a sustainable and sustainability linked framework under which Vodafone can issue green, social, sustainability and sustainability linked funding instruments to finance or refinance projects which enable the company to meet its environmental and social objectives. In May 2020, Vodafone released its first Green Bond Report. Vodafone plans to use Green Bond proceeds to fund eligible green projects, focusing on energy efficiency through IoT technologies. These include smart metering, lighting, logistics, fleet management, and EV charging. Investments will support IoT networks like NB-IoT and URLLC to enhance energy efficiency and enable smart city solutions.

Vodafone will invest in energy-efficient network upgrades, hardware, software, and storage to decouple data growth from environmental impact. Initiatives include AI-driven energy management, legacy system modernization, onsite renewable energy, and green buildings certified to high efficiency standards. Vodafone's Green Bond Committee includes representatives from Treasury, Sustainable Business and Energy performance. In 2019, Vodafone issued its first green bond and raised € 750 million. The green bond issuance was issued during May 2019 with due date November 2026.

Table 18.3 shows the details of the eligible green project portfolio.

In 2024, Vodafone issued its second green bond raising EUR 575 million to support the company's sustainable strategy. Under its Green Bond Framework, Vodafone will allocate proceeds to green projects within 36 months in alignment with the company's climate and environmental objectives. The offering consisted of €575 million 6.125% Senior Notes due 2032. The proceeds of this green bond would be used to refinance $625 million 6.0% Senior Notes due January 2027.

Green Investment by Comcast

Comcast Corporation is a global media and technology company with three primary businesses: Comcast Cable, NBCUniversal, and Sky. Comcast Cable is a leading provider of broadband, video, voice, wireless and other services. NBCUniversal consists primarily of NBCUniversal's television and streaming platforms which include national, regional and international cable networks. Sky is one of Europe's leading entertainment companies which includes a direct to consumer business, providing video, broadband, voice and wireless phone services and content business. During the past 5 years, Comcast have invested $20 billion to grow its network.

Comcast have invested $one million to bring high-speed broadband services to Biola, a rural farming community. Comcast supported 258 organizations by offering $13.6 million in grants for connectivity and adoption. Lift Zones offer free Internet access and also offer essential digital services in neighbourhood locations like community centres and recreation facilities. By the end of 2023, Comcast had installed more than 1250 Lift Zones. In 2023, Comcast Corporation awarded more than $25 million to hundreds of community organizations nationwide to specifically support digital skills programs. Since 2021, Comcast support has helped 5686 learners get jobs and created $320 million in economic impact. Comcast Rise supported 13,500 entrepreneurs and offered $125 million in monetary, marketing and technology grants. In 2023, NBCUniversal purchased 227 EVs. Comcast have saved 11 million gallons of fuel and avoided 95,000 metric tons of greenhouse gas emissions by 2023.

Comcast aim to be carbon neutral for Scope 1 and 2 greenhouse gas (GHG) emissions by 2035. The company have reduced market based, enterprise wide Scope 1 and 2 GHG emissions by 31% in 2023 compared to year 2019. In 2023, Comcast sourced approximately 1.1 million megawatt hours of clean and renewable energy which accounted approximately 25% of the company's enterprise electricity load.

During February 2023, Comcast had issued its inaugural $ 1 billion green bond to support environmental initiatives. By 2024, Comcast have fully allocated the $995 million in net proceeds in accordance with its green financing framework which focusses on renewable energy, energy efficiency, green building, clean transportation and circular economy. For renewable energy, expenditures are directed towards the construction, development, acquisition, operation, or maintenance of renewable energy generation, such as solar and wind energy, that are long-term and new to the grid, as well as renewable energy storage projects. For energy efficiency, criteria for expenditures are related to the design, construction, manufacture, installation, or operation of systems, products, and technologies intended to reduce energy consumption or greenhouse gas emissions. For clean transportation, expenditures are related to the acquisition, design, development, construction, maintenance, or operation of electric and alternative vehicles and related infrastructure. In the case of circular economy, expenditures are related to designing out waste in Comcast's products and services, projects for waste prevention, reduction, and recycling for Comcast's facilities, operations, and supply chain.

Table 18.4 highlights the project allocation and impact of Comcast's green bond issuance.

One of the key sustainability projects completed in 2023 include Sky Studios Elstree, a cutting-edge UK film and TV studio recognized as 'Outstanding' by BAFTA's Albert for sustainability. It uses 100% renewable electricity, with 25% from rooftop solar, and includes features like rainwater harvesting, LED lighting, EV charging, and an all-electric vehicle fleet.

Comcast reduced fleet emissions by piloting electric and hybrid vehicles, using telematics and fuel efficiency technology, and providing digital support tools, resulting in savings of millions of gallons of fuel. Comcast allocated $19.3 million in green bond net proceeds to clean transportation initiatives, including electric vans and pickups for Xfinity service technicians, and a substantial fleet of electric and solar-powered golf carts for production and operations teams at the Universal

Table 18.4 Project allocation and impact

Categories	Amount	Impact
Green building	$742.6 million	New or expected certified green real estate was 1.2 million square feet
Circular economy	$211.5 million	Amount of waste diverted from landfills amounted to 84,000 metric tons
Clean transportation	$19.3 million	Annual GHG emissions reduced by 1200 mtCO2e
Energy efficiency	$19.2 million	Annual reduction in energy consumption amounted to13,600 MWh
Renewable energy	$2.4 million	Annual GHG emissions reduced by 300 mtCO2e

Source: Comcast Corporation | 2024 Green Bond Report

Studios Lot. Electric vehicle deployments include select Xfinity service vehicles and electric and solar-powered golf carts for crews at the Universal Studios Lot. Comcast operates long-standing refurbishing programs that minimize waste by extending the life of devices through testing, repair, and reuse of returned equipment. Additionally, its National Recycling Program focuses on recycling or diverting cable equipment waste from landfills by recovering and redistributing valuable materials.

Comcast introduced sustainable packaging like the Handshake Box, made from recyclable materials with minimal ink and sourced domestically to eliminate overseas shipping. Its flat-pack design reduces waste, emissions, and costs by cutting carbon from transportation and improving warehouse storage efficiency.

Green Investment by T Mobile

T Mobile provide wireless communications services through a variety of service plan options in USA. T-Mobile offers customers a wide selection of wireless devices, including smartphones, wearables, tablets, home broadband routers and other mobile communication devices that are manufactured by various suppliers. The company also provide products and services that are complementary to its wireless communications services, including device protection, financial services and advertising. By 2024, the company provided wireless communication services to 129.5 million postpaid and prepaid customers. In 2024, the company made 6.1 million post-paid net customer additions. In 2024, T-Mobile received $52.3 billion revenues for post-paid services. Approximately 98% of the US population is covered by its 5G network. T-Mobile's 5G Home internet was available to over 50 million US households. T-Mobile has the first and largest nationwide 5G network.

T Mobile flagship Project 10 Million program aims to provide resources to ten million underprivileged school aged children. T Mobile have invested $6.4 billion in products and services and connected nearly six million student households with free or highly reduced connectivity. T-Mobile network is powered by 100% renewable electricity. T Mobile aims to achieve a 95% reduction in energy consumption (MWh) per petabyte (PB) of data traffic by 2030 from a 2019 baseline. T Mobile had $ 3.1 billion spent with suppliers from traditionally underrepresented backgrounds in 2023. T Mobile had total diverse supplier spend of $14 billion since 2020. Approximately 66% of suppliers completed environmental and social assessments through Eco Vadis. T Mobile distributed $1.7 million worth of in-kind products and services to impacted communities in 2023. T Mobile's partnership with Pano AI won the 2023 GTI Innovative Mobile Service and Application award. Approximately 56% of suppliers had set science-based emissions target by the end of 2023. T Mobile is a member of the Billion Dollar Roundtable who have committed to a supply chain spend of $ 1 billion annually with small and diverse owned businesses. T Mobile have granted $11.3 million to 250 small town communities across 43 states in USA. T-Mobile offers 5G Home internet services to over 50 million US households, a third of which are in rural areas. T-Mobile is addressing the digital divide among older adults in rural areas through a multi-year sponsorship with AARP's Older Adult Technology Services (OATS). In 2023, with T-Mobile's support, OATS partnered with 100 community organizations to provide vital tech training across rural southern communities. In 2023, T-Mobile partnered with Kai XR, an all in one immersive learning platform to support young adults at Harris County Juvenile Detention Centre in Texas. T-Mobile had made $25 million commitment to fund community development projects in small towns and rural markets across the US.T-Mobile was ranked as number 1 out of 400 companies on USA Today's first ever America's Climate Leaders list for 2023.

T-Mobile have a set a goal to reach net zero emissions for its net zero emissions for its entire carbon footprint by 2040.T Mobile had 30% reduction in total Scope 1, 2 and 3 emissions since 2020. In 2023, the total carbon footprint had decreased by approximately 14%. The company aim to reduce absolute Scope 1, 2 and 3 GHG emissions by 55% by 2030. T-Mobile externally report on carbon emissions annually through its Pathway to Net-Zero report, CDP Climate change response, GRI and SASB indices.

T-Mobile had 62% reduction in energy (MWh) per PB of data since 2019. T-Mobile's purchased electricity constituted 100% from renewable energy sources. Approximately 93% of T Mobile's wireless handset models are certified through UL ECOLOGO or EPEAT. T-Mobile have collected and processed over 100 million customer devices for reuse, resale or recycle. The year over year emissions associated with purchasing goods, services and capital goods decreased by over 940,000 MT CO_2e. T-Mobile reduced transportation and shipping emissions by over 200,000 metric tons of CO_2e by cutting costs, decommissioning parts of its network, and improving efficiency, which removed over 1000 trucks and expedited vans from operation. To develop renewable energy portfolio, T-Mobile invested in longer term renewable energy projects like Virtual Power Purchase Agreements (VPPAs) for on-site solar and renewable back power initiatives. By 2023, the solar portfolio of the company had grown over to 100 projects across nine states in USA.T-Mobile have collected 19 K metric tons of network e-waste in year 2023.

References

AT&T Annual Report 2024.

AT&T Sustainable Report 2024.

Comcast Green Bond Report 2024.

Comcast Impact Report 2024.

https://sustainability.att.com/reports/reporting-frameworks/tcfd

https://www.vodafoneziggo.nl/en/nieuws/vodafoneziggo-successfully-launches-2nd-green-bond-to-support-its-sustainability-strategy/

T-Mobile 2023 Corporate Responsibility Report.

Verizon Annual Report 2023.

Verizon Annual Report 2024.

Vodafone Annual Report 2024.

Vodafone Bond Report 2020.

Vodafone Sustainability Framework 2022.

Chapter 19
Green Investment in Food & Consumer Packaged Goods Sector

Green Investments by Cargill

Cargill with a history of 159 years, is a family owned company which provide food, ingredients, agricultural solutions and industrial products to nourish the world. Cargill connect farmers with markets, customers with ingredients and family with daily essentials. Cargill partner with farmers and ranchers growing crops and raising animals. Cargill originate, source, store and trade commodities. Cargill make and transport craft meat, egg and alternative protein products, salts, oils, starches, cocoa and sweeteners. In 2024, Cargill made $160 billion in revenues. In 2024, Cargill contributed $130 million to contribute towards a more resilient food system.

Through She Thrives Initiative with CARE, Cargill provided educational opportunities to over 1000 women small holder farmers in Vietnam. With LadyAgri initiative, Cargill provided women in Cameroon with climate smart food processing equipment such as solar dryers to support market accessibility. Through En Pro de la Mujer with Educampo, Cargill empowered 200 women farmers in Mexico.

To support healthier food choices, the company has led efforts to eliminate industrially produced trans-fatty acids (iTFAs) from the global food supply. As the first global edible oils supplier to meet WHO's best practice standards, it has removed over 1.5 billion pounds of iTFA-containing products serving major clients like PepsiCo.

Cargill focusses on innovation across industries for Asia Pacific customers. In 2024 Cargill opened a new Cocoa Development Center in Indonesia for sustainable cocoa products. Cargill had launched a first of its kind pet food plant in China which produces fresh meat pet food for its PetMaster® brand. Cargill had opened a new global innovation centre to serve swine customers and the livestock industry in China and across Asia. Cargill also sources cocoa ingredients to meet high traceability standards for Nestle's KitKat through an innovative program to support cocoa farmers. Cargill have supported farmers to adopt regenerative agriculture

B. R. Kumar, *Green Finance*, Sustainable Finance,
https://doi.org/10.1007/978-3-032-03333-8_19

practices to reduce greenhouse gas footprint of Nestle's Purina's US pet food supply chain.

Cargill aims to reduce emissions by 50% by 2030 and achieve net zero by 2050. Cargill have entered into partnership with Ocean Breeze Energy's Bard Offshore Wind Farm in Germany for renewable energy initiatives. As McDonald's egg supplier, Cargill partnered with the company and US egg producers to create a supply of cage free eggs. By 2023, all McDonald's US restaurants serve 100% cage free eggs.

To meet evolving consumer demand for better protein options, the company is leveraging its food and innovation expertise. At the new Protein Innovation Hub in France, customers can co-create customized chicken products. Investments in advanced technology in this hub enhance safety and efficiency, while exploration of alternative proteins supports emerging consumer preferences.

Most of the world's food is transported by sea. Ocean shipping accounts for 3% of global greenhouse gas (GHG) emissions. As a charterer, Cargill is driving industry transformation through innovative solutions like the *Pyxis Ocean*—the first bulk carrier retrofitted with WindWings®, airplane-style wings developed with BAR Technologies and MC Shipping. This technology reduces fuel use and emissions by harnessing wind power. Early voyages have delivered strong results, making it the most efficient Kamsarmax vessel per RightShip's GHG rating. Cargill is supporting the global ruminant industry in cutting methane emissions by improving feed and animal nutrition. It developed the first Gold Standard-approved method to measure reductions from feed supplements, including SilvAir™, which can lower methane emissions in cattle by up to 10% without affecting milk or meat production. Cargill's partnership platform with Global Water Challenge spanning across programs in Brazil, India and West Africa have benefitted over 150,000 people with improved water access in Cargill's priority communities.

Cargill is making investments to improve farmers' livelihoods. Cargill RegenConnect™ program has covered ten million acres of North American farmland and engaged farmers in 24 US states to improve farm productivity. In 2024, Cargill contributed $130 million to enable a more resilient food system. Approximately $100 million have been invested in efficiency and sustainability capital projects. Approximately 38 billion litres of water were restored in water stressed regions. Since 2017, the company have offered 7.2 million farmer training. Cargill aims to provide ten million farmer trainings in sustainable agricultural practices by 2030.

Since 2020, Cargill facilitated transition of approximately 1.1 million acres to regenerative agriculture practices across North America. Cargill have offered 34 million meals globally through its corporate giving effort. Since 2015, Cargill has partnered with the World Resources Institute (WRI) to advance global sustainability. By combining WRI's tools with Cargill's agricultural expertise, Cargill promote standardized accounting, science-based methods, and open-source solutions to drive industry-wide progress on sustainability goals. Cargill and Solidaridad have partnered for over a decade to promote sustainable, climate-smart agriculture and improve farmer livelihoods. In 2023, the partnership launched a new 3-year, $4.6

million initiative to support 2000 farmers in five countries, focusing on palm oil producers in Colombia and Malaysia and soybean farmers in Argentina, Bolivia, and Paraguay. Cargill and Heifer International co-founded the Hatching Hope Global Initiative to improve nutrition and smallholder farmer livelihoods through poultry production and consumption. Aiming to reach 100 million people by 2030, the initiative has impacted 26.9 million lives since 2018 through global partnerships with non-profits, governments, and industry. Costco partners with Cargill's regenerative agriculture program, RegenConnect®, to advance its climate goals while helping farmers improve soil health, build resilience, and drive positive environmental outcomes. As a global ingredient supplier, Cargill partners with Nestlé to promote sustainable farming, protect natural resources, and reduce emissions. Joint projects include improving cocoa supply chain transparency in Côte d'Ivoire and Ghana, and converting cocoa shells into low-emission fertilizer. Cargill aim to improve nutrition and economic livelihoods by reaching 100 million people by year 2030 through the production, promotion and consumption of poultry. The company has reached 26.9 million people with this objective by 2018.

By 2024, the company have reduced Scope 1 and Scope 2 emissions by 15.8% compared to 2017 baseline. Cargill aims to reduce Scope 1 and Scope 2 absolute operational greenhouse gas (GHG) emissions by 10% in 2025.The company aims to reduce global GHG emissions from its global supply chain by 30% by 2030 measured per ton of product. Cargill's Scope 1 and 2 target was set and approved by the Science Based Targets initiative (SBTi) in 2019 against a 2017 baseline.

The company had increased its contracted renewable energy capacity by 42% since 2023. Globally Cargill's portfolio of power purchase agreements, green tariffs, and onsite renewable electricity consisted of more than 60 projects covering 20 countries. These renewable energy solutions include wind, solar, hydro and geothermal. In 2023, Cargill's renewable electricity mix resulted in emission reductions of 908,000 metric tons CO2 equivalent.

Cargill is advancing maritime decarbonization by partnering to develop wind-assisted propulsion. In 2023, it chartered the Pyxis Ocean, the first vessel retrofitted with WindWings® to harness wind power. Early voyages show strong results, positioning it as the most efficient Kamsarmax ship and informing future scale-up across the fleet.

The Coalition for Climate-Smart Agriculture Policy is a group of food and agriculture companies and environmental NGOs dedicated to scaling climatesmart agriculture through public-private partnerships. Current coalition members include Cargill, Danone, Environmental Defense Fund (EDF), JBS, McDonald's, PepsiCo, The Nature Conservancy (TNC), and Unilever.

Cargill joined the MIT Climate & Sustainability Consortium in 2021 to help accelerate real-world climate solutions. Through cross-industry collaboration, it has contributed to projects on clean transport, biofuels, and carbon capture. Cargill also launched MCSC's first Sponsored Research Consortium focused on soil carbon science in agriculture and forestry. Cargill is partnering with Conservation Science Partners (CSP) to develop a biodiversity baseline for soybean-producing landscapes within Brazil's Cerrado biome.

Cargill has committed $2.1 million in funding to Water.org, a global non-profit which focusses on providing access to safe water. Since 2018, approximately 26.9 million people have gained nutrition and economic livelihood through Hatching Hope program. Since 2001, Cargill has partnered with the World Food Program USA and the U.N. World Food Programme, contributing over $30 million to support school meals, improve farmer livelihoods, and provide emergency food aid across Asia, Africa, and Latin America. Cargill's aqua nutrition business provides species-specific, sustainable fish and shrimp feeds that support environmental goals while addressing diverse market and environmental needs. In 2023, aqua nutrition had sold 1.85 million metric tons of feed and have 18 dedicated aquafeed mills.

In 2023, Cargill partnered with World Wild Fund(WWF), Finance Earth, and others to launch the Fisheries Improvement Fund, aiming to mobilize $100 million by 2030 to support sustainable fisheries through innovative tools and local partnerships. Cargill supported a pilot project in Chile by applying its supply chain and marine expertise, leading to the March 2024 launch of a new approved FIP for anchoveta and sardine. The FIP is now active, and Cargill has begun purchasing fish oil from it. The new FIP is the first backed by the Fisheries Improvement Fund, using repayable financing. A levy on each metric ton purchased helps fund the FIP and repay the initial investment. Cargill's Land Innovation Fund supports sustainable, deforestation-free soy production in South America's Amazon, Cerrado, and Chaco biomes. Over 3 years, it has driven transformation through innovative projects, policy development, and technology. It has impacted 2.5 million hectares, with 2.2 million under environmental monitoring and 41,000 hectares of native vegetation protected. Cargill's 3S program, formerly Triple S, links farmers with downstream soy customers who prioritize sustainability in their supply chains.

In 2023, in North America, Cargill provided $17 million in financing to US corn and soybean farmers and partnered with Farm Credit Canada to provide financing to Canadian farmers for crop inputs. For over 60 years, Cargill and CARE have collaborated to improve agricultural productivity and market access. During the past 15 years, the partnership has reached more than 4.6 million people through 34 projects in 12 countries. Cargill will invest $14 million in this program over the next 3 years with the target to reach more than 1.6 million people. Since 2010, Cargill and Earthworm Foundation have partnered to promote sustainable, community-based solutions across supply chains. Cargill also launched 27 Village Savings and Loan Association (VSLA) groups to strengthen the economic development of oil palm families.

Green Investments by Coca Cola

The Coca Cola is a total beverage company and sold in more than 200 countries and territories. Coca Cola own or license and market numerous beverage brands. The beverages offered by company account for 2.2 billion of the estimated 65 billion servings of all beverages consumed worldwide every day. Coca Cola own 30 billion-dollar brands across several beverage categories worldwide. Coca Cola's global portfolio of beverage brands include soft drinks such as Coca-Cola, Diet Coke, Coca Cola Zero Sugar. Coca Cola also offers water, sports, coffee and tea. Coca cola also offers juice, value added dairy and plant-based products.

In 2022, Coca Cola launched 246 low or no sugar beverages. The Coca Cola Zero Sugar beverage is available in more than 170 markets. The 2030 Water Security Strategy focuses on increasing water security by collaborating with partners to provide a steady supply of clean water for people and ecosystems in sectors where the company operate and source ingredient. Since 2015, Coca Cola replenished water used in its finished beverages to nature and communities. Approximately 68% of the products in its beverage portfolio have less than 100 calories per 12 ounce serves. The company aims to use at least 50% recycled content in its packaging by 2030. During the 5-year period 2020–2025, Coca Cola aims to reduce the use of its virgin plastic derived from non-renewable sources by a cumulative three million metric tons. In 2023, Coca Cola have reduced the absolute use of virgin plastic by more than 75,000 metric tons. Approximately 62% of Coca cola's packaging was collected for recycling in year 2023. In 2023, sales of finished products served in reusable packaging increased by more than 100 million-unit cases. The systemwide renewable electricity usage increased from 21% in 2021 to 24% in 2023.

Coca Cola aim to use 35–40% recycled materials in its primary packaging by 2035. Coca Cola have targets to collect 70–75% of the bottles and cans which the company introduce into the market each year by 2035. The company have returned 148% of the water used in its finished beverages to nature and communities in 2023. Since 2015, Coca Cola have reduced its water use ratio by 10%. In 2023, the water use ratio was decreased to 1.78 litres of water use per litre of beverage.

By 2023, Coca Cola had awarded more than $1.6 billion in grants to support initiatives for sustainable access to water and circular economy. Coca Cola have collaborated with tech partners to create bottle prototype made from 100% plant-based sources. Coca Cola reduces packaging waste by expanding reusable packaging and dispensing solutions, adopting Returnable Glass Bottles (RGB) and replacing secondary plastic with KeelClip™ paperboard packaging in most of its markets.

Coca Cola aims to achieve net zero by 2040.Coca Cola have achieved a 7% decline in absolute emissions since year 2015 towards a 25% science-based reduction target by 2030. In 2016, Coca Cola were one of the first companies to adopt the Science Based Targets.

Table 19.1 highlights the sustainability goals of Coca Cola.

Green Bonds

The company aims to increase the allocation of annual capital expenditure to investments aligned with its sustainable strategy to reach 50% of Capex by 2030. The company had added value across its value chain which amounted to €10.8 billion.

Table 19.1 Sustainability goals of Coca Cola

Areas	Goals
Water leadership	Achieve 100% regenerative water use across 175 facilities identified as facing high levels of water stress by 2030. Work with partners to help improve the health of 60 watersheds identified as most critical for the system's operations and agricultural supply chains by 2030. During the period 2021–2030, the company aim to return a cumulative total of 2 trillion litres of water to nature and communities globally.
Company's portfolio	Target to offer drinks with reduced added sugar.
Climate	The company aim to achieve net zero emissions by 2050. The company aim to reduce absolute emissions by 25% by 2030 against a 2015 baseline.
Sustainable agriculture	Sustainably source 100% of priority agricultural ingredients over time.
People & communities	Aspire to be 50% led by women globally

Source: The Coca Cola Company 2022 Business & Sustainability Report

In September 2022, Coca Cola published its Green finance framework which was aligned with the ICMA GBP and LMA GLP standards. The framework specifies five eligible green categories under which projects can be considered eligible green projects.

The inaugural green bond of €500 million was issued in September 2022 under the EMTN programme and has a tenor of 3 years and coupon of 2.75%. The green element of the bond has attracted an elevated interest from both existing and new sustainability-oriented investors. The net green bond proceeds of €496 million were used to refinance or finance, in part or in full, existing or new Eligible Green Projects. Every newly issued green instrument will be immediately and fully allocated to the portfolio. Any unallocated part of green instrument would be allocated to the portfolio within 36 months of its issuance.

By December 2022, the portfolio included €573 million out of total Coca-Cola HBC green projects' spend in years 2019–2022 with 61% falling into Circular Economy category and 39% into Energy Efficiency.

Table 19.2 shows details of the outstanding green instruments in € millions.

Table 19.3 shows the details of eligible green project portfolio in € millions.

As part of circular economy initiatives, Coca Cola is eliminating hard to recycle plastic film from can multipacks using KeelClip™, a minimalist paperboard solution now available in 22 countries, including all EU markets. Alongside the QFlex carton in Ireland, these efforts removed about 2600 tonnes of plastic film from the company's supply chain in 2022. Additional plastic reduction innovations are also being piloted. Coca Cola is also investing in energy efficient coolers to help reduce carbon emissions. Coca Cola have invested over €50 million in in-house rPET facilities to date to achieve rPET goals.

Table 19.2 Outstanding green instruments

ISIN	Issuance Date	Due date	Notional amount	Net proceeds
XS2533012790	23rd September 2022	23rd September 2025	500	496

Source: Green Finance Report 2022

Table 19.3 Eligible Green Project Portfolio (in € million)

Eligible green category	2019	2020	2021	2022	2019–2022	Share of portfolio
Circular economy	49	71	104	126	350	61%
Energy efficiency	68	41	47	67	223	39%
Total portfolio	117	112	152	193	574	100%

Source: Coca Cola Green Finance Report 2022

Green Investments by PepsiCo

PepsiCo is a leading global beverage and convenient food company with a complementary portfolio of brands, including Lay's, Doritos, Cheetos, Gatorade, Pepsi-Cola, Mountain Dew, Quaker and SodaStream. The company make, market, distribute and sell a wide variety of beverages and foods in more than 200 countries and territories. In 2024, the revenues of PepsiCo amounted to $92 billion.

In 2021, PepsiCo introduced a new North Star to guide at PepsiCo: pep + ("PEP Positive") strategy which aims to deliver sustainable growth. Pepsi's products are transported over 1.2 billion miles globally by the company owned fleet using gas, biofuel and electric vehicles with additional miles covered by third party providers. In 2023, PepsiCo products were sold in over 200 countries and territories. The company have more than 290 manufacturing facilities. Pepsi have spent more than $800 million on R&D in year 2023.

Table 19.4 highlights the sustainability milestones of Pepsi.

There are over seven million acres of farmland in PepsiCo's agricultural footprint. Over 1.8 million acres were farmed with regenerative farming. Over 90% of the company's grower sourced crops are sustainably sourced globally. Over 60 countries supply agricultural crops and ingredients for many of the iconic brands of PepsiCo. In 2023, PepsiCo doubled its regenerative farming footprint year on year to more than 1.8 million acres globally. PepsiCo sustainably sources 58% of its key ingredients.

PepsiCo is helping drive public-private partnership funding in the U.S. by supporting grant submissions to the USDA's Climate Smart Commodities Program. As a result, its partners Field to Market and SWOF were awarded grants totalling up to $165 million for their projects.

PepsiCo and ADM launched a 7.5-year partnership to reduce carbon intensity by promoting regenerative agriculture on up to two million acres, with over 440,000 acres impacted in 2023. In 2023, PepsiCo extended the Positive Agriculture Outcomes Accelerator to support innovative, scalable projects advancing its 2030

Table 19.4 Sustainability milestones

Year	Milestones
2006	PepsiCo integrates sustainability into its daily business operations
2010	PepsiCo introduces first all electric delivery truck
2012	PepsiCo wins Stockholm Industry Water Award
2013	PepsiCo launches Sustainable Farming Program. By 2023, over 90% of grower sourced crops are sustainably sourced worldwide through this initiative
2017	PepsiCo launches first demonstration farm in India. By 2023 83 farms were tested.
2019	PepsiCo receives climate leadership awards for organizational leadership and supply chain
2020	PepsiCo achieved its safe water access goal five years ahead of schedule, reaching over 91 million people with access to safe water since 2006, as of 2023.PepsiCo has successfully transitioned to 100% renewable electricity across its U.S. direct operations.
2021	PepsiCo introduces pep+, a strategic end to end transformation to create growth and value for company.
	PepsiCo sets an ambitious new target to achieve net-zero emissions by 2040.
	PepsiCo has set a 2030 goal to implement regenerative agriculture practices on seven million acres, aiming to reduce greenhouse gas emissions by at least three million tons.
2022	PepsiCo announces a global packaging goal to deliver 20% of beverage servings sold through reusable models by 2030
	PepsiCo marks the 40th anniversary of its supplier diversity program with a commitment to spend over $400 million annually with black- and Hispanic-owned suppliers.
	PepsiCo issues a new $1.25 billion 10-year green bond
	PepsiCo and N-drip enters into partnership to help farmers globally adopt advanced water-efficient irrigation technology.
2023	PepsiCo achieved its 2025 goal of improving operational water-use efficiency by 25% in high water-risk areas 2 years early, based on a 2015 baseline.
	PepsiCo and Walmart launched a seven-year collaboration to support U.S. and Canadian farmers in enhancing soil health and water quality.
	PepsiCo announced a $216 million multi-year investment in strategic partnerships with three farmer-focused organizations to advance regenerative agriculture.

Source: PepsiCo ESG Summary 2023

goals through financial and technical co-investment. PepsiCo plan to catalyse more than $30 million in investments through 2028 in over 30 different projects across sectors and supply chains. PepsiCo and CIAT launched the Climate Resilience Platform to provide actionable insights on climate impacts and promote resilience through regenerative agriculture, seeking partners to scale its impact. PepsiCo launched climate action strategy in 2021 and set three interim science-based targets for reducing greenhouse gas emissions by 2030 from a 2015 baseline. These targets include reducing absolute greenhouse gas emissions across its entire value chain by over 40% by 2030, including a 75% cut in direct operations and a 40% reduction in indirect emissions. In 2023, PepsiCo's total GHG emissions across Scopes 1, 2 and 3 were approximately 58 million metric tons, which represents a 4% decrease from the 2015 baseline and a 5% reduction from 2022.

PepsiCo is helping remove decarbonization barriers for suppliers by incentivizing ESG performance through a financing program with Citi, offering better rates for meeting sustainability goals. The company aims to reduce the use of absolute virgin plastic from non-renewable sources by 20% by 2030.PepsiCo facilitated the launch of the first packaging producer responsibility organization (PRO) in the US, Circular Action Alliance (CAA).

Green Bonds

In October 2019, PepsiCo issued its first green bond, a 30 year $ 1 billion senior notes offering with a fixed rate coupon of 2.875% per annum. Proceeds of $464 million was allocated for decarbonization efforts, $437 million for waste package reduction and $73 million to improve water sustainability. By December 2021, PepsiCo had fully allocated the net proceeds of $$974 million from this green bond issuance.

In July 2022, PepsiCo issued its second Green Bond, a 10- year, $1.25 billion senior notes offering, with a fixed coupon rate of 3.90% per annum. By December 2023, PepsiCo had allocated $859 million, approximately 70% of net proceeds. The individual investments ranged between $45,000 to approximately $40 million. In total the allocation has funded over 250 projects.

PepsiCo has allocated $474 million of the 2022 Green bond net proceeds to support sustainable plastics and packaging basically through the procurement of rPET in North America. PepsiCo have used green bond net proceeds to advance its water goals, allocating approximately $16 million to replenishment and $70 million to operational efficiency in high water-risk areas. Since 2022, $26 million from the green bond issuance have supported regenerative agriculture projects reaching over 5300 farmers and two million acres, helping sequester over one million metric tons of GHGs and reduce emissions by 110,000 metric tons. PepsiCo have allocated $27 million of net proceeds to climate focused projects which included fleet efficiency, renewable energy expansion and energy efficiency improvements.

Table 19.5 shows the details of the green bond spend by year in millions of dollars.

Table 19.5 Green bond spend

Year	Amount in millions of dollars
2017	193
2018	257
2019	256
2020	81
2021	155
2022	294
2023	329

Source: PepsiCo 2022/2024 Green Bond Report

Table 19.6 shows details of the green bond allocation by category as of December 2021.

Table 19.7 shows details of the green bond allocation by category as of December 2023.

Green Investments by McDonald

McDonald's is a leading global foodservice retailer, with more than 41,000 restaurants in over 100 countries. By year end 2025, approximately 95% of McDonald's restaurants were franchised. By year end 2023, McDonald's company owned and operated restaurants totalled over 150,000 worldwide of which approximately 70% were based outside of the US. More than two million individuals work in McDonald's franchised restaurants. In 2020, McDonald announced Impact Strategy which were centered around four impact areas of planet, food quality and sourcing, jobs, inclusion and empowerment and community collection. McDonald have committed to source chickens raised with improved welfare outcomes. The company have outlined eight specific commitments for in scope markets which are expected to be fully implemented by 2024. By 2023, McDonald has achieved its commitment of sourcing 100% cage free eggs for items served on its breakfast menus. As of 2023, more than 96% of pork purchased in the US comes from suppliers that have phased out the use of gestation stalls for housing pregnant sows. McDonald is committed to eliminate WHO designated Highest Priority Critically Important Antibiotics (HPCIAs) in chicken across key markets.

In 2023, the Science Based Targets initiative (SBTi) validated McDonald's global 2050 net zero emissions reduction target. By 2023, scope 1, scope 2 and

Table 19.6 Green bond allocation

Category	Amount in millions of dollars
Packaging	437
Decarbonization	464
Total net proceeds	974

Source: PepsiCo 2022 Green Bond Report

Table 19.7 Green bond allocation

Category	Amount in millions of dollars
Packaging	474
Decarbonization	272
Water	87
Regenerative agriculture	26
Unallocated net proceeds	381
Total net proceeds	1240

Source: PepsiCo 2024 Green Bond Report

scope 3 emissions were reduced by 6%, 38% and 4% compared to 2018 base year. By end 2023, the US systemwide spend with diverse owned suppliers were 26.2% which resulted in McDonald's reaching its 25% diverse owned supplier aspirational goal. By 2023, approximately 97.9% of its primary fibre-based guest packaging globally was sourced from recycled or certified sources. By end 2023, 99.5% of its guest packaging items did not contain intentionally added fluorinated compounds. In 2023, about 88.3% of restaurants in markets with advanced infrastructure provided guests the option to recycle and/or compost packaging materials. By 2023, McDonald reduced virgin fossil fuel-based plastic in Happy Meal toys by 63.7%.

In Sweden, 55 McDonald's locations offer EV charging. Updated signposts combine classic gas station styles with Big Mac and Happy Meal pricing to attract customers. In São Paulo, Brazil, a 24-hour McDonald's is being built using wood and recycled materials, featuring innovative, low-energy construction techniques for sustainability. In December 2023, McDonald's piloted circular décor in two French restaurants using recyclable materials, energy-efficient lighting, and innovative design. Investing in renewable energy is central to McDonald's climate strategy. Since 2019, McDonald have signed multiple VPPAs to support solar and wind projects across four U.S. states. These initiatives are already operational in Texas, Illinois, Oklahoma, and Louisiana, with more projects planned to come online in the near future. In 2023, 86.7% of primary guest packaging was made from renewable, recycled or certified sources. McDonald aim to source 100% of its primary guest packaging from renewable, recycled or certified materials by end of year 2025. The company aims to drastically reduce plastics in Happy Meal toys around the globe and transition to more sustainable materials by end of 2025. Fiber, wooden and pressed paper cutlery were deployed across 50 markets. The company aims to eliminate deforestation from its global supply chains by end of year 2030. In 2022, McDonald joined the Forest Positive Coalition to combat deforestation.

McDonald's prioritizes product traceability for food safety, partnering with suppliers through standards like Good Agricultural Practices (GAP) certification, the Supplier Quality Management System (SQMS) and Distributor Quality Management Process (DQMP)and conducting unannounced third-party restaurant audits. McDonald's has been on the Fruits and Vegetable Technical Committee with the Global Good Agriculture Program (GLOBALG.A.P.) since 2017.

100% of soy sourced for the feed of chicken used in McDonald's products supported deforestation-free supply chains globally. 100% of the palm oil used in McDonald's restaurants and as an ingredient in McDonald's products supported the production of sustainable palm oil. Approximately 93.8% of fish for McDonald's Filet-O-Fish® comes from sustainably managed wild-caught fisheries, verified annually by the Sustainable Fisheries Partnership.

McDonald had teamed up with McCain Foods to launch the Sustainable Fries to launch the Sustainable Fries Fund, a £1 million joint investment to help U.K. potato growers adopt more sustainable practices. The company also have associated with McCain through a $1 million Future of Potato Farming Fund to incentivize Canadian growers. McDonald have established market specific targets for responsible antibiotic use in its beef supply chain scope markets.

By end of 2025, McDonald announced an investment of approximately $600 million to open new restaurants. In 2023, McDonald's and its U.S.-based Franchisees contributed over $25 million in tuition assistance for Restaurant Staff in the U.S. McDonald contributed over $5.9 million to Ronald McDonald House Charities (RMHC) by donating one cent from each Happy Meal sold in participating U.S. locations. Additionally, the company donated $1 million to Operation HOPE's Founder's Circle, supporting financial education and empowerment programs in underserved communities. McDonald had donated $20 million to Ronald McDonald House Charities as part of its 5-year $100 million commitment. Over $13 million was raised for RMHC Canada through in-restaurant giving efforts, including McHappy Day, special product promotions.

McDonald engages and invests in projects that focus on supply chain impact. McDonald's partnered with FFAR and committed up to $4.5 million with Arizona State University to study natural versus continuous grazing practices on 10 southeastern U.S. ranches. As part of a 5-year pilot initiative with Cargill, the Walmart Foundation, and WWF, McDonald's has invested $1.6 million since 2020 to support Northern Great Plains ranchers through the Ranch Systems and Viability Planning (RSVP) network. McDonald's is a member of the Clean Energy Buyers Association (CEBA), working alongside energy buyers, providers, and service partners to address market complexities and advance clean energy solutions. McDonald had joined the Consumer Goods Forum's Forest Positive Coalition, a multi-company initiative to stop commodity-driven deforestation.

Arcos Dorados, the franchise that operates the McDonald's brand in 20 markets in Latin America issued sustainability linked bond and became the first company in the restaurant industry to sell a financial instrument with environmental objectives. The company issued $350 million sustainability linked senior notes with a coupon of 6.125% which matures in 2029. The transaction was five times oversubscribed and raised funds for $1.8 billion. McDonald USA has partnered with AgMission™, a global collaboration to reduce greenhouse gas (GHG) emissions in agriculture to develop and implement climate smart farming solution with a $ 5 million commitment over the next 5 years.

Green Investments by Unilever

Established over 100 years ago, Unilever is one of the world's largest consumer goods companies. The company fulfil 24 million customer orders annually. Unilever have around 400 brands meeting consumers' daily needs. Products of Unilever are used by 3.4 billion people every day. Unilever products are sold in 190 countries. In 2024, turnover of Unilever amounted to €60.8 billion. In 2024, the R&D investment amounted to € 987 million. Since 2015, Unilever had reduced Scope 1 and 2 greenhouse gas emissions by 72%. Unilever have assisted 2.58 million SMEs to grow their retail value chain.

The company aims to reduce absolute operational GHG emissions (Scope 1 &2) by 100% by 2030 from a 2015 baseline. Unilever have a target to reduce absolute Scope 3 energy and industrial GHG emissions by 42% by 2030 from a 2021 baseline. Against the 2021 baseline, Unilever have reduced its absolute Scope 3 Forest, Land and Agriculture (FLAG) emissions by 14% and by 8% for energy and industrial emissions.

The company have a target to have 95% volume of key crops to be verified as sustainable sourced by 2030. Another target is to implement regenerative agricultural practices on one million hectares of agricultural land by 2030.Unilever aims to protect and restore one million hectares of natural ecosystems by 2030. Unilever aim to implement water stewardship programmes in 100 locations in water stressed areas by 2030.Unilever focusses on controlling plastic pollution through reduction, circulation and collaboration. Unilever aims to reduce virgin plastic footprint by 30% by 2026 and 40% by 2028 from a 2019 baseline. The company aims for 1005 of its plastic packaging to be reusable, recyclable or compostable by 2030(for rigids) and 2035(for flexibles). Approximately 57% of plastic packaging can be recycled, reused or composted. By packaging type, this means that 76% of Unilever's rigid plastic packaging and 13% of its flexible plastic packaging can be recycled, reused or composted.

Unilever aims to help 250,000 smallholder farmers in its supply chain access livelihoods programmes by 2026.Around a quarter of its emissions in scope of its net zero goal come from forests, land and agriculture. In 2024, 97% of Unilever's supply chain for palm oil, paper and board, tea, soy and coca were deforestation free. Since 2021, Unilever had made investments of € 218 million to directly source deforestation free palm oil. The company had 130,000 hectares of land covered by regenerative agricultural projects. One of the major priorities of Unilever is to develop alternatives to fossil fuel based chemical ingredients in its laundry and cleaning products. The company have made $120 million joint investment in biotechnology to develop an alternative plant-based ingredient to lather and lift dirt.

The deforestation programmes of Unilever cover a total area of nine million hectares across Latin America, South East Asia and Africa. Within this region, Unilever aim to protect and restore over 200,000 hectares of forests. In 2021, Unilever published its Regenerative Agriculture Principles. The primary objective is to reduce emissions at the farmer level. Unilever in collaboration with suppliers have 46 projects covering 270,000 hectares of land transitioning to regenerative systems. In its nutrition business, Unilever aims to cover 650,000 hectares by 2027 which represents approximately 50% of its land footprint in Nutrition. It is estimated that regenerative agriculture projects will cost €140 million by 2030. Unilever aim for a significant portion of its global diary volume to be sourced from farms implementing regenerative agricultural practices predominantly across the US, Europe, India and Turkey. Unilever's continued use of post-consumer recycled (PCR) plastic increased from 18% in 2021 to 22% in 2023, thereby reducing its reliance on virgin, fossil fuel derived plastics. Unilever have piloted a supplier climate program in year 2021 and aim to onboard 300 suppliers by end 2024, covering 44% of Scope 3 emissions from materials.

Over the period 2021–2024, Unilever has improved transport efficiency by optimizing routes and increasing load utilization. By 2026, the company aim to cut upstream transport emissions by 16% through operational improvements. Post-2026, further reductions will come from scaling electric and alternative fuel vehicles in key markets like the US and China.

Launched in 2020 Climate & Nature Fund is an impact-led investment platform of Unilever which aims to contribute to a net zero world through investment of and positively impact nature, livelihoods, and resource efficiency. Unilever aim to invest €1 billion in stand alone climate and nature projects during the period 2020–2030. In 2022, the company had created the private equity impact fund with AXA and Tikehau Capital as partners and focusses to mobilise an equal amount in co-financing from these partners. By end 2023, the Climate & Nature Fund had spent and committed €286 million. The company have a joint venture investment with Genomatica, a leader in biotech and sustainability to scale and commercialise alternatives to palm oil and fossil fuel derived cleansing ingredient. Unilever have entered into a partnership with USAID to foster the growth of small and medium sized enterprises to build a circular economy for packaging.

During March 2014, Unilever issued a £250 million Green Sustainability Bond with the proceeds being used for projects linked to greenhouse gases, water and waste targets in the Unilever Sustainable Living Plan. This 4-year corporate bond has a coupon of 2%. The deal was priced at G+ 67 bps. The bond was more than three times oversubscribed and had more than 100 investors mainly fund managers, pension funds and insurers. The bookrunners for the deal were Citi, Deutsche Bank, Morgan Stanley and Santander. Morgan Stanley was the green sustainability bond adviser to Unilever.

Green Investments by Starbucks

Starbucks Corporation is an American multinational chain of coffeehouses and roastery reserves headquartered in Seattle Washington. By November 2022, Starbucks had 35,711 stores in 80 countries of which 15,873 were located in the United States. The brand portfolio of the company includes Starbucks Coffee, Seattle's Best Coffee, Teavana, Evolution Fresh and Ethos Water. Starbucks offer more than 30 blends and single origin premium coffees.

In many of Starbucks stores, at least one type of waste is commercially recycled. Energy use in its stores roughly make up 80% of its entire carbon footprint. In 2008, Starbucks have set a goal to reduce water consumption by 25% in company operated stores by 2015. The water saving initiatives of the company include installing efficient fixtures; monitoring consumption to identify spikes in water usage and targeting leak repairs; and upgrading the water filtration systems in its stores. The company have completed the installation of Energy Management Systems in approximately 4000 stores.

Starbucks support coffee-growing communities by improving water use, protecting local water sources, and expanding access to clean drinking water through farmer training, support centers, and partnerships with non-profits focused on sanitation and hygiene. The company had been one of the Environmental Protection Agency's top ten purchasers of renewable energy in the US. The Green-E certified Renewable Energy Certificates (RECs) purchased facilitates the development of new clean-energy sources by providing wind-farm owners with additional revenue. This, in turn, helps the wind farmers sell electricity at prices competitive with power plants that use fossil fuels. The company had purchased RECs equivalent to 100% of the energy used in US and Canada operated stores by end of 2015.

The company offer a 10% discount in US and Canada to use their own reusable mugs or tumblers for their beverages. Over years Starbucks had launched several initiatives to decrease the environmental impact of its disposable cups. In 1997, Starbucks developed its recycled content cup sleeve to protect customers from hot beverages and avoid the waste of "double cupping". In 2006, Starbucks launched the industry's first hot beverage paper cup with 10% post-consumer recycled fibre. In 2008, the company rolled out a new plastic cup that has less environmental impact than the original plastic cups. In 1995 Starbucks introduced Grounds for Your Garden initiative which offers customers complimentary five-pound (2.27-kilogram) bags of used coffee grounds to enrich garden soil. Through commercial compositing many stores were able to divert other food waste and coffee grounds from the landfill.

Green Investments by Danone

Danone is a world leading food and beverage company with presence in over 120 countries. The products offered by Danone range from yogurts and plant-based products to water and specialized nutrition products. Danone focus on three key lines: Dairy and Plant based products, Water and Specialized Nutrition. The portfolio offered by Danone include leading international brands as well as brands tailored to specific regions. In 2023, Danone generated €27.6 billion in sales. Globally, the company holds the number one position in fresh dairy products, as well as in plant-based foods and beverages. It ranks second in packaged waters and early life nutrition, and fourth in adult medical nutrition. In the Essential Dairy Products category, over 60% of Danone's revenue comes from high value-added functional segments, including immunity, gut health, indulgence, and performance. Danone is a leader in specialized nutrition, offering a wide range of baby formula tailored to infants' needs. Backed by over 50 years of research and expertise in biotics, Danone leverages its deep understanding of breastmilk to develop innovative, science-based products.

In 2020, Danone became the first publicly listed company to adopt the Société à Mission status created by the French Pacte law in 2019 which covers objectives across health, environment, social topics and inclusiveness in its bylaws. Since 2015, Danone has partnered with B Lab to accelerate the growth of the B Corp movement around the globe. Around 92.8% of global net sales were covered by B Corp certification. Manufacturing and plant operations in Europe were 100% certified.

To achieve the goal of offering tastier and healthier food and drinks, the company has set the following KPIs:

By 2025, more than 85% of the volume of dairy, plant-based, water, and aqua drinks should be rated above 3.5 stars by the Health Star Rating system.

By 2025, more than 95% of the volume of kids' dairy and plant-based products should contain less than 10 grams of total sugars per 100 grams.

To promote healthier choices, the company also aims to ensure that, by 2025, more than 95% of the volume sold of dairy, plant-based, and aqua drinks includes interpretative nutritional information on the packaging or online.

To provide positive nutrition and hydration for healthier life, Danone aims to offer greater than 85% volume kids diary fortified with relevant vitamins and minerals by 2025.There are five projects initiated by Danone to address iron deficiency in children by 2025. Danone aims to provide 20 million people with access to safe drinking water by 2025. The company also invest in nutrition and hydration science and research. In 2023, Danone became the first company to set a methane reduction target for its fresh milk supply.

The company aims to achieve net zero by 2050.The company also have the KPI of 30% in methane emissions from fresh milk by 2030. The company aims for 36% reduction on Scope 1&2 emissions by 2025. Approximately 30% of key ingredients which Danone source from farms have began to transit to regenerative farming methods by year 2025.The company also have watershed preservation and restoration plans in operational site located in highly water stressed areas by 2030. For circular economy and low carbon packaging goals, the company aims to have 100% reusable, recyclable compostable by 2030.The company aims to halve the use of virgin fossil-based packaging by 2040 with 30% reduction by 2030. The company aims to cut waste across the value chain. Danone aims to reduce all food waste by half by 2030 compared to 2020 baseline.

The company earned a Triple A CDP rating for the fifth consecutive year—an achievement shared by only 10 out of 21,000 companies. Danone is included in several leading sustainability indices, such as those managed by Moody's and Sustainalytics, as well as the Ethibel Sustainability Index, MSCI ESG Indexes, FTSE4Good Index Series, Bloomberg Gender Equality Index, and the Access to Nutrition Index.

Danone prioritizes local sourcing of raw milk from over 58,000 farms across approximately 16 countries, both directly and indirectly. The majority of this milk comes from family farms, with around 90% of partner producers operating small-scale family-owned farms.

Since 2017, Danone has been a strategic partner of the Ellen MacArthur Foundation (EMF), collaborating primarily through the New Plastics Economy Initiative. In 2018, this partnership was further strengthened with Danone's signing of the Global Commitment on Plastics.

Danone issued its inaugural social bond, raising $368.5 million. The bond matures in year 2025 with 1% coupon rate and is listed on the Euronext Paris stock exchange. The bond proceeds would be used for responsible farming and agriculture, research & innovation for advanced medical nutrition and social inclusiveness. In 2025, Danone issued a €800 million bond with a 8-year maturity and a 3.438% coupon. This issuance was to enhance the funding flexibility of Danone.

Green Investments by Nestle

Nestle is a global nutrition, health and wellness company with presence in over 185 countries. Nestlé provides a wide range of products and services across various categories, including Powdered and Liquid Beverages, PetCare, Nutrition and Health Science, Prepared Dishes and Cooking Aids, Milk Products and Ice Cream, Confectionery, and Water. In 2024, Nestle offered 132 billion servings of micronutrient fortified affordable nutrition.

Nestlé has a net zero commitment by 2050 which includes SBTi-approved Forest, Land and Agriculture (FLAG) targets and Energy/Industry targets. The company aims to reduce its greenhouse gas (GHG) emissions by 20% by 2025 and 50% by 2030 from 2018 levels. Nestle aims to reduce absolute Scope 3 FLAG GHG emissions by 50% by 2030 and 75% by 2050. Nestle aims to achieve and maintain 100% assessed deforestation free primary supply chains for meat, palm oil, pulp and paper, soy, sugar, cocoa and coffee. By 2030, Nestle aims for 100% of key ingredient volumes to be responsibly sourced. By 2025, Nestlé aims for 20% of key ingredients to be sourced from farmers adopting regenerative agriculture practices, and 50% by 2030. By 2025, Nestle aims to design above 95% of its plastic packaging for recycling. By the same period, the focus is to reduce the use of virgin plastic in packaging by one third against a 2018 baseline. By 2025, Nestlé aims to source 100% renewable electricity in all its manufacturing sites.

As part of its Net Zero Roadmap, Nestlé is launching and reformulating products to align with consumer trends, focusing on lower carbon footprints and balanced diets, including more plant-based options. Nestlé's Manufacturing Masterplan Zero (MMZero) Carbon Program, launched in Europe in 2022, targets up to 50% energy reduction and 100% carbon reduction (Scope 1 and 2) in its factories. The initiative has driven operational changes, including more efficient manufacturing, energy recycling, and the use of heat pumps over fuel-based boilers. By 2024, eight industrial heat pumps replaced 100 million kWh of natural gas annually, cutting 20,000 tons of CO_2 emissions. Currently, 50 out of 96 factories in Zone Europe are part of the MMZero program. By 2023, Nestle shifted half of its global shipping to green fuels. Nestlé has signed agreements with major logistics companies—Hapag-Lloyd, Maersk, and CMA CGM—to use green fuels, such as those derived from waste, for cargo shipping. This shift is expected to cut greenhouse gas emissions by approximately 200,000 tonnes per year and eliminate the need for around 500,000 barrels of crude oil.

By 2025, Nestlé aims to design above 95% of its plastic packaging for recycling systems. By 2025, Nestlé aims to reduce its use of virgin plastics by one third, versus 2018 baseline. Nestlé has partnered with local and global organizations to improve access to water, sanitation, and hygiene (WASH), benefiting over 1.4 million people in communities surrounding its facilities.

Currently Nestle maintain 93.5% assessed deforestation free primary supply chains for meat, palm oil, pulp and paper, soy, sugar, cocoa and coffee. The company aims to grow 200 million trees by 2030.Nestlé is collaborating with farmers—either directly or through fuel providers—to produce biogas from manure and agricultural waste. This renewable biogas is then used as fuel for heavy-duty vehicles. In 2024, over 1500 tonnes of biogas were used in Europe, replacing an equivalent amount of fossil-based fuels. In 2024, Nestlé achieved 21.3% of its key ingredients sourced from farmers adopting regenerative agriculture practices.

Nestlé has been consistently included in the FTSE4Good Index since 2011 and was the first company in the breast-milk substitute sector to achieve this recognition. In 2024, Nestlé received an A rating from MSCI ESG Research for its performance on environmental, social, and governance (ESG) issues. The company remained in the Carbon Disclosure Project (CDP) leadership band for climate change, earning a B for water security, an A- for palm oil, and a B for other forest-related commodities. Nestlé was ranked 9th out of 30 global food and beverage manufacturers in the Access to Nutrition Initiative (ATNI) Global Index 2024. Nestlé was ranked second in the 2023 Nature benchmark and the Food and Agriculture benchmark from the World Benchmarking Alliance.

Nestlé is focused on reducing water use in water-stressed areas, supporting farmers with water-saving practices, and improving community access to clean water. In year 2024, the company had reduced water usage in its facilities by 2.72 million tonnes. Nestlé Purina PetCare Europe launched the Ocean Restoration Program to protect marine habitats vital to global food and livelihoods. By 2030, the program aims to restore 1500 hectares of marine ecosystems.

As part of its Net Zero Roadmap, Nestlé launched a Dairy Climate Plan to reduce emissions from feed production, enteric methane, and manure. Working with over 200 suppliers in 27 countries, the plan takes a farmer-centric approach, recognizing that solutions must be tailored to each farm. In 2020, Nestle have made commitment to invest at least CHF 3.2 billion by 2025 to support net zero roadmap. Of this investment CHF 1.2 billion was allocated for adoption of regenerative agricultural practices.

By 2030, Nestle aim to assist ten million young people with access to economic opportunities through the Nestlé Needs Youth Initiative.

References

Cargill 2024 Impact Report.
Cargill Annual Report 2024.
Creating Shared Value at Nestle, 2024.
Danone Integrated Annual Report 2023.pdf.
https://www.climatebonds.net/2014/05/unilever-opens-sterling-green-bonds-4-yr-%C2%A3250m-411m-sustainability-bond-co2-water
https://www.danone.com/sustainability/our-approach/danone-impact-journey.html
McDonald's Corporation Purpose & Impact Report 2023–2024.
McDonald's Corporation Climate Resiliency Summary 2023–2024.
Nestle Non-Financial Statement 2024.
PepsiCo ESG Summary 2023.
PepsiCo Green Bond Report 2022/2024.
The Coca Cola Company 2022, Business & Sustainability Report.
The Coca Cola Green Finance Report 2022.
The Coca-Cola Company 2023 Environmental Update.
Unilever Climate Transition Action Plan updated 2024.

Chapter 20
Green Investments in Retail Sector

Green Investments by Walmart

Walmart is a technology powered global omni channel retailer. Each week, the company serve approximately 270 million customers who visit more than 10,750 stores and numerous eCommerce websites in 19 countries. During fiscal 2025, the company generated total revenues of $681 billion. In 2007, Walmart.com launched its Site-to-Store service which enabled customers to make purchases online and pick up merchandise in stores. Walmart have over 8000 pickup and delivery locations globally. Walmart is engaged in global operations of retail, wholesale and other units, as well as eCommerce located throughout US, Africa, Canada, Central America, Chile, China, India and Mexico. Walmart serves around 2.1 million associates around the world with approximately 1.6 million associates in the US.

Walmart is listed on the 2023 Bloomberg Gender Equality Index. In 2023, for the eighth-consecutive year, Walmart was ranked as number one in National Truck Safety by the American Trucking Association. Walmart was also ranked as number one retailer in the EPA's Green Power Partnership ranking. During the period 2021–2023, the cumulative total purchases supporting American jobs amounted to $47 billion. Over $13 billion was sourced from 2400 diverse suppliers to US businesses. In 2023, Walmart had allocated $58 million as part of its $100 million commitment to the Center for Racial Equity for addressing disparities in the US criminal justice, education, financial and healthcare systems. Additionally, $7 million was contributed to support racial solidarity initiatives.

Walmart launched Project Gigaton in 2017 to drive decarbonization across its product value chains by engaging suppliers, NGOs, and other stakeholders. The initiative aims to reduce or avoid one billion metric tons of greenhouse gas emissions by 2030 by encouraging supplier action across six key areas of impact. As part of Project Gigaton, Walmart partnered with Schneider Electric to offer suppliers access to initiatives like the Gigaton PPA accelerator, enabling them to participate

B. R. Kumar, *Green Finance*, Sustainable Finance,
https://doi.org/10.1007/978-3-032-03333-8_20

in aggregated, utility-scale power purchase agreements. Walmart had partnered with CDP and HSBC to launch the Sustainable Supply Chain Finance Program—an early-payment initiative for suppliers that set science-based targets through Project Gigaton or meet specific CDP score thresholds. Over 5200 suppliers have signed up for Project Gigaton.

In 2016, Walmart became the first retailer to announce a science-based emissions target designed to achieve emissions reduction in its operations and supply chains. Walmart have reduced or avoided by suppliers over 750 million MT CO2 emissions since 2017. By 2021, Walmart have reduced Scope 1&2 emissions by 23.2% compared to 2015 baseline. Since 2005, two million acres of land were conserved by Walmart. Walmart have set goals for over 400 suppliers on responsible recruitment through Walmart's Supplier Leadership program on people. In 2016, Walmart announced "20x25" goal to source at least 20 agricultural commodities more sustainably by 2025. In 2023, Walmart achieved at least 95% "more sustainable" certification for several commodities such as fresh and frozen seafood, bananas, coffee, and tea. By 2021, Walmart had increased percentage of electricity supplied by renewable sources to 46%. Walmart through sustainable initiatives aims to manage or restore at least 50 million acres of land and one million square miles of ocean by 2030. Since 2005, Walmart have conserved over two million acres through the Acres for America program.

Walmart supports place-based and jurisdictional initiatives that create shared value for producers, suppliers, and communities. Examples include partnerships to source sustainably certified tuna in the Marshall Islands and rice from conservation-focused farms in Arkansas. These efforts promote environmental stewardship, community resilience, and sustainable farming practices.

In 2022, Walmart launched the Circular Connector to link innovative packaging companies with its private brand merchants and suppliers. Through the Walmart Sustainability Hub, over 200 sustainable packaging solutions have been submitted, resulting in more than 4000 connections to support packaging sustainability goals. In 2023, Walmart achieved 12% reduction in food waste compared to year 2016 which resulted in diversion of over 900 million pounds through composting and other methods. Approximately 63% of global private brand packaging was recyclable, reusable, or compostable. The company eliminated plastic bags at checkout in Mexico, Canada, and over 420 U.S. stores, launched the Walmart Restored marketplace for refurbished products, and globally diverted 78% of operational waste.

Walmart reviewed approximately 13,100 third-party responsible sourcing audit reports, with over 90% rated green or yellow and fewer than 2% receiving successive orange ratings. Additionally, 99% of fresh produce and floral sales in Walmart U.S. and Sam's Club U.S. came from suppliers endorsing the Ethical Charter. Walmart also continued investing in responsible recruitment and dignified working conditions through grants to organizations such as IREX, Global Fishing Watch, The Nature Conservancy, Polaris, and the Wilson Center. Walmart have donated over 665 million pounds of food in US to help fight hunger.

In 2023, Walmart supported local economies by employing approximately 2.1 million people, paying $3.31 billion in income-based taxes globally, and investing

$4.99 billion in U.S. store and club remodels. Over two-thirds of Walmart U.S.'s product spend went to items made, grown, or assembled in the U.S. The company also donated more than $1.7 billion in cash and in-kind globally and launched Spark Good, a community engagement platform in the U.S.

Walmart supports initiatives that foster in-person connections and build trust among diverse communities. Through the Walmart Foundation, it funded efforts like The Trust for Public Land's "On Common Ground" initiative with a $one million grant to strengthen community bonds through shared spaces and programs in U.S. city parks.

Walmart strengthened food safety by conducting around 71,000 independent audits and training approximately 1.2 million associates. It expanded access to healthier food by enabling SNAP benefits at all stores and online in 49 states and updated its Great for You nutrition criteria. Additionally, it reduced the use of priority chemicals in formulated consumables by 20% compared to a 2017 baseline. Walmart offers $ 16 million globally in cash and in-kind donations for disaster recovery and preparedness. Walmart, Sam's Club, and the Walmart Foundation donated over $6 million in grants and supplies to support non-profits in providing food, shelter, disaster clean-up, and relief to underserved communities.

In 2021, Walmart announced $2 billion inaugural green bond offering to advance its sustainable goals. These goals include achieving 100% renewable energy by 2035 and zero emissions in its operations by 2040. Walmart had published its green financing framework in year 2021. Walmart intend to allocate the net proceeds towards eligible green investments within the eligible green categories such as renewable energy projects, sustainable transport projects, zero waste and circular economy projects, water stewardship projects and habitat restoration. The green bond is part of $7 billion of new senior unsecured notes which the company had successfully closed across 5, 7, 10, 20 and 30-year tranches.

Citigroup Global Markets Inc. and Morgan Stanley & Co. LLC also served as active bookrunners on the green bond. BofA Securities, Inc. was the Green Structuring Agent, while Citigroup Global Markets Inc. served as Diversity and Inclusion Coordinator. The first Green Bond Impact report points that the company has allocated $1.1 billion in green bond proceeds with top investment in areas such as renewable energy, sustainable buildings, waste reduction and circular economy initiatives. During February 2020–January 2022, Walmart had allocated $378 million to renewable energy which include solar and wind power purchase agreements, virtual purchase power agreements and onsite solar and wind projects. Walmart had set an interim goal to power 50% of global operations with renewable sources by 2025. High-performance buildings received the second highest allocation of green bond proceeds of over $338 million. Walmart had allocated over $307 million to "zero waste and circular economy" projects. Additional allocations included $66 million to test new sustainable transportation solutions such as hydrogen-powered forklifts, $7 million to habitat restoration and conservation, and $3 million for water stewardship projects.

Green Investments by Amazon

Amazon is an American multinational technology company engaged in e commerce, cloud computing, online advertising, digital streaming, and artificial intelligence. Amazon serve its primary customer sets, consisting of consumers, sellers, developers, enterprises, content creators, advertisers, and employees. Walmart serves customers through both online and physical stores. Its platforms support millions of product categories accessible via websites, mobile apps, voice assistants like Alexa, streaming devices, and in-store visits. Amazon has organized its segments across three segments of North America, International and Amazon Web Services. Amazon also manufacture and sell electronic devices such as Kindle, Fire tablet, Fire TV, Echo, Ring, Blink, and eero.

The Climate Pledge Fund is a $2 billion venture investment program through which amazon aims to achieve net zero carbon emissions by 2040. The company aim to deliver at least 100,000 electric delivery vans by 2030 from Rivian and other manufacturers.

In 2023, Amazon matched 100% of the electricity used across its global operations with renewable energy sources. In 2023, the company completed over 500 solar and wind projects globally. As part of its initiatives to decarbonize its transportation and delivery fleet, amazon added 24,000 electric vehicles to its fleet. In 2023, 680 million packages were delivered by EVs.The company have replaced 95% of its plastic air pillows in delivery packaging with paper filler. Through the Climate Pledge Fund program, Amazon have invested in 26 emerging climate start-ups and helped over 500 companies in 45 countries to join the Climate Pledge. Amazon had been the largest corporate purchaser of renewable energy for over 4 years. Amazon launched the Amazon Sustainability Exchange which offer free resources to suppliers to build sustainability into their operations. Since 2015, Amazon have reduced the average per shipment packaging weight by 43% and avoided more than three million metric tons of packaging. In Europe, amazon had replaced its single use plastic delivery packaging with 100% recyclable paper and cardboard packaging. Amazon has replaced 95% of the plastic air pillows from delivery packaging in North America with paper filler.

Amazon restructured its U.S. operations into eight regions, integrating fulfilment centers, sort centers, delivery hubs, and transportation fleets to bring products closer to customers, speed up delivery, and cut nearly 16 million miles in travel, reducing vehicle emissions.

Amazon Web Services (AWS) designs its data centers for maximum efficiency, resiliency, and low carbon impact. It is estimated that AWS infrastructure is up to 4.1 times more efficient than traditional on-premises setups. The Climate Pledge Friendly program highlights products with trusted sustainability certifications. In 2023, over 1.4 million products offered by Amazon were available for purchase from its Climate Pledge Friendly program. Over 1.16 billion items sold by amazon were recognized by certifications in climate pledge programs. In 2023, Amazon set new standards for construction design in the US to reduce indoor water use by 40%.

Amazon had invested in 15 water replenishment projects which returned 3.5 billion litres to local communities in year 2023. Amazon have distributed over $32 million as cloud computing credits to 229 organizations since 2021.

Amazon Day delivery a shipping option whereby prime members choose a specific day of the week to receive orders helped avoid 200 million boxes and 226,000 metric tons of CO2e in 2023. In 2023, Amazon co-founded the Zero Emission Maritime Buyers Alliance (ZEMBA) to promote zero-emission shipping, scale adoption, and cut maritime emissions. Amazon is also a founding member of the Sustainable Aviation Buyers Alliance (SABA) and played a critical role in launching the sustainable aviation fuel certificate. Amazon is decarbonizing middle mile transportation—moving packages between facilities—by regionalizing routes, expanding EV use, adopting lower-carbon fuels, and partnering on industry solutions.

In 2023, Amazon delivered more than 125 million packages via e-cargo bikes and on foot from micro mobility hubs around the world. In the same year amazon delivered 50 million amazon packages and 1.6 million grocery orders via micro mobility solutions. In 2023, amazon piloted the use of hydrogen fuel cell vehicles in Europe and Japan.

By 2024, Amazon had announced 513 global renewable energy projects, 243 utility scale wind and solar projects and 270 solar rooftop projects at its facilities and stores. Amazon aims to reduce food waste by 50% across US and Europe operations by year 2030.

In 2024, Amazon spent $4.3 billion with over 500 certified U.S. Tier 1 diverse suppliers, while more than 200 of Amazon's U.S. suppliers reported $1.5 billion in Tier 2 certified diverse spend. The company aim to invest $1.2 billion to provide access to skills training and education to over 300,000 US employees by 2025.

In May 2021, Amazon released sustainable bond framework and issued a $ 1 billion sustainability bond. Under the sustainable bond framework, "Eligible Projects" include investments and expenditures—such as private equity investments, loans, and other financing structures—made by Amazon or its subsidiaries from the date of issuance of any Green, Social, or Sustainability Bonds, including those made within the 24 months prior. These projects must meet the eligibility criteria in one or more of the following categories: Clean Transportation, Renewable Energy, Sustainable Buildings, Affordable Housing, and Socioeconomic Advancement and Empowerment.

The company allocated 100% of the net proceeds from its 2021 sustainability bond to eligible projects in the clean transportation category. The funds were allocated to private equity investments in electric vehicle manufacturer Rivian. The project aims to support research and development for piloting and testing Rivian electric delivery vehicles. Additional uses include the purchase and installation of electric vehicle charging infrastructure across North America and Europe, as well as the acquisition of electric yard holsters, day cabs, and box trucks from multiple manufacturers. The net proceeds from Amazon's first Sustainability Bond support key decarbonization efforts, including achieving net-zero carbon by 2040, deploying 100,000 electric delivery vehicles by 2030, and making 50% of shipments net-zero carbon through the Shipment Zero initiative.

Green Investments by Costco Wholesale

Costco Wholesale Corporation operates an international chain of membership warehouses, mainly under the "Costco Wholesale" name. Costco warehouses offers one of the largest and most exclusive product category selections. Costco offers groceries, candy, appliances, television and media, automotive supplies, tires, toys, hardware, sporting goods, jewellery, watches, cameras, books, housewares, apparel, health and beauty aids, furniture, office supplies and office equipment. Costco Wholesale Industries, a division of the Company, operates manufacturing businesses, including special food packaging, optical laboratories, meat processing and jewelry distribution. Costco is open only to members and offers three types of membership: Executive, Business and Gold Star. Costco operate membership warehouses and e-commerce sites based on the concept of offering members low prices on a limited selection of nationally branded and private label products in a wide range of categories. Costco's e-commerce operations ship merchandise through its depots and logistics operations as well as through drop ship and other delivery arrangements with its suppliers. The warehouses on average operate on a seven-day,70-hour week. By end of 2024, Costco employed 333,000 employees worldwide.

Costco have committed to reduce Scope 1 and Scope 2 emissions by 39% by 2030 compared to 2020 base year. Costco aim to operate with 100% clean energy sources by 2035. Since 2020, Costco have been using a portfolio wide approach to procure, generate and use electricity from clean sources in its operations. Costco is implementing programs to improve the efficiency of heating, ventilation, air conditioning (HVAC) and refrigeration systems, light fixtures and other aspects of warehouse operations. The company aims to accelerate the phase out of HFCs. The company aims to increase its investment in refrigeration retrofits to reduce refrigerant emission Global Warming Potential (GWP) by 30% by 2030 as compared to its 2020 baseline.

Costco focusses on building its STAR (Sustainability Technical Assistance Review) program to minimize waste, waste energy and emissions in its warehouses and to meet environmental compliance obligations. In 2024, Costco donated over $84 million to local charities and over 177 million meals. The company have replaced over seven million gallons of diesel with renewable diesel and installed 13 additional CO_2-based refrigeration systems.

Costco offer over 200 EV charging stations which include locations in Canada, China, France, Korea, Spain, Taiwan, United Kingdom and the US. The Costco Auto Program offers members more than 50 different EV models through the program's approved dealer network.

In FY24, Costco engaged suppliers for action and target-setting via platforms like CDP, piloting regenerative agriculture initiatives, prioritizing human rights through partnerships with Equitable Food Initiative (EFI), CIERTO, and Seafood Task Force (STF). Costco's emissions footprint across all three scopes for fiscal 2023 totalled 186 million MT CO2e. The company aims to operate with 100% clean energy sources by 2035.Costco's comprehensive Scope 3 emissions program, "STEP", focusses on four key pillars of Supplier Targets, Transition Agriculture, Energy Solutions, and Packaging Solutions. The STEP plan will lead to a 20% reduction in its Scope 3 emissions by 2030 compared to its baseline year of FY20 excluding fuel. Emissions from Costco's fuel business comprise 40% of the company's total emissions which are largely scope 3 emissions. Costco estimate that 20% of fuel related Scope 3 emissions stem from Costco's fuel supply and could be reduced by purchasing from refineries which prioritize clean procurement and production.Costco procure only from refineries which are compliant with EPA Tier-3 regulations. Costco offer R99 consisting of 99% renewable diesel and 1% USLD at all California fuel retail sites.

Approximately 35% of fuel deliveries occur after warehouse closing hours, reducing delivery times and emissions. In 2023, over 40,000 deliveries were made by carriers using 90% or more renewable diesel. The company uses dripless and spitless fuel nozzles which yields a 90% reduction in spills. The company sell multiple eBike models and eScooter models in the warehouse and on Costco.com.

Green Investments by Alibaba Group

Alibaba Group Holding Ltd. branded as Alibaba is a Chinese multinational technology company specializing in e-commerce, retail, internet and technology. The company provides consumer to consumer (C2C), business to consumer (B2C) and business to business (B2B) sales services through global marketplaces, consumer, digital media, entertainment, logistics and cloud computing services.

Alibaba.com offers one-stop B2B trading solutions for global small and medium sized businesses. Alibaba is one of the largest retail commerce business in the world in terms of gross merchandise value (GMV). China's commerce retail business consisting of Taobao and Tsmall derives the majority of its revenues from customer management services.

Ali baba have reduced its carbon emissions by 22.907 million tons. Alibaba is transforming its cloud infrastructure to support a green low carbon circular economy by focusing on three areas of building a clean cloud; replacing traditional IT with efficient cloud computing and enabling intelligent transformations.

Alibaba aims to achieve carbon neutrality by 2030. The company aims to cut 1.5 gigatons of carbon emissions by 2035. In 2021, Alibaba had set targets of achieving carbon neutrality in its operations and halving the energy intensity across its value chain by 2030. The aim is to reduce emission by 1.5 gigatons over 15 years. Alibaba have reduced emissions by 0.40 million MtCO2e through efficiency, clean energy, and low-carbon travel, lowering carbon intensity from 9.2 to 8.7 MtCO2e/ RMB. Through Alibaba's Carbon88 platform and low carbon friendly products program, 409 brands, 1.91 million products and 187 million consumers had participated in emission reduction efforts. Energy Expert, launched by Alibaba Cloud, is an energy consumption and carbon management platform to assist enterprise clients in saving energy and improving efficiency.

In FY2023, Alibaba expanded e-commerce in rural China, generating over RMB130 billion from 832 counties and RMB4.3 billion from 160 key revitalization counties. In FY2023, Alibaba offered free e-commerce courses for MSMEs with over 17 million attendances and launched Cloud Classroom, reaching over six million corporate learners. According to researchers from Renmin University of China, the Alibaba ecosystem created or supported, directly or indirectly, a total of more than 70 million jobs in 2022. By March 2023, Alibaba had built 77 regional digital talent training bases jointly with regional governments, enterprises, and specialized industrial parks, offering over 1200 classes attended by over 190,000 attendances. In FY2023, Alibaba Group donated a total of RMB399 million to the Alibaba Foundation, mainly to philanthropic programs for COVID-19 relief, education, and environmental protection. On Alibaba.com, more than 200,000 sellers from 190 countries and regions connected with over 47 million buyers to explore business opportunities and complete transactions.

Counties formerly classified as impoverished under China's national standards achieved over RMB130 billion in sales on Ali baba's platforms. The logistics arm of Alibaba, Cainiao has enhanced rural logistics efficiency and built over 1460 country-level smart logistics centers, along with nearly 50,000 posts in villages or towns. Alibaba have enabled the Scope 3+ ecosystem to reduce 22.907 million MtCO2e of total emission. For achieving the goal of circularity in packaging, over 23.82 million cartons were recycled and reused in Cainiao Post. In FY2023, the clean energy consumption of self-operated campus of Alibaba totalled 27.858 million kWh and reduced 18,543.2 MtCO2e of emissions. Launched in October 2022, the Low-carbon Friendly Products Program established certification and measurement standards, leading to 1.91 million products from 409 brands on Taobao and Tmall by March 2023, promoting low-carbon practices across product lifecycles. The Taobao and Tmall APPs of Alibaba have served over 320,000 visually impaired users.

Alibaba has developed the sustainable finance framework for sustainable finance transactions such as issuance of green, social and sustainability bonds, loans, and other debt-like financing instruments, and use the net proceeds to finance and/or refinance projects in green eligible categories of green buildings, energy efficiency, renewable energy and circular economy and design.

Alibaba's sustainable finance framework sets out eligible uses of proceeds for funds from sustainable finance transactions which include green, social and sustainability bonds and loans. Alibaba's sustainable finance framework has received a second party opinion from Sustainalytics, and the notes have been assigned an 'A+' rating from Fitch Ratings.

Alibaba Group has allocated net proceeds of US$986.9 million from its inaugural sustainability bonds to 12 projects. The sustainability bonds issued in 2021 were used to fund areas such as energy efficiency, green buildings, covid 19 crisis response, renewable energy and circular economy and design. Alibaba allocated the largest share of the proceeds approximately 45.7% (US$ 451 million) towards building energy efficient data centres. These facilities incorporate technologies such as hot air cycling, wastewater recovery and advanced recycling systems to low energy consumption and manage the heat produced by critical hardware. Approximately 35.7% of bond proceeds were spent on building and refurbishing green buildings while the rest of the funds were used for the purchases of solar and wind power and recycling and waste management programmes.

Green Investments by Schwarz Group

Schwarz Group is an international leader in the retail industry with about 13,900 stores and 575,000 employees in 32 countries. In 2024, the Schwarz Group had total sales of 175.4 billion euros. The two retail divisions of the group, Lidl and Kaufland are major pillars in the food retail market. The other major divisions include Schwarz Produktion(food manufacturing), PreZero(environmental services) and Schwarz Digits(IT). As of fiscal 2023, the Schwarz Group comprised 1195 companies. The food discounter national companies of the Lidl retail division are food retailers in the discount sector with operations consisting of 12,350 stores and more than 220 goods distribution and logistics centres in 31 countries. The national companies of Kaufland Group are large scale food retailers with around 1550 stores and around 155,000 employees in eight European countries. Kaufland offers a wide assortment of food and everyday products with 30,000 items per store on average in Germany and 17,000 in other countries. PreZero Group is an international environmental service provider which manages the disposal, sorting, treatment, and recycling of approximately 23.9 million tons of waste and recyclables each year. Schwarz Digits provides the IT infrastructure and solutions for the companies of the Schwarz Group.

The companies of Schwarz Group continually set binding group wide targets covering focus areas of people, product quality, circular systems, and ecosystem. Lidl and Kaufland aim to achieve 100% certification through selected sustainability seals. By 2025, Lidl and Kaufland aims to use on average 25% recycled material in their private label packaging made of plastic. By 2030, the companies of Schwarz Group aim to reduce food waste by 50% at group level compared to year 2018. The companies of Schwarz group are committed to reduce all green house gases emitted to net zero by 2050. The responsibility for sustainability lies with the Chief Executive Officers of the respective companies of Schwarz Group. Since 2022, the companies of Schwarz Group have been completing an annual ESG rating assessment in partnership with Sustainalytics.

Lidl offers an e-learning course on recyclable materials management as part of in-depth training for logistics personnel. Since 2022, the companies of Schwarz Group have been systematically carrying out an annual risk analysis of all direct business partners. Lidl aimed to achieve 100% raw material certification by RSPO for procured items containing palm oil by 2022. The companies of Schwarz Group focus on sustainable product design. Circular economy is a core part of the corporate strategies of Schwarz group of companies. Since 2021, all single use PET deposit bottles produced by companies of Schwarz Produktion for Lidl and Kaufland private labels in Germany have been made of 100% recycled materials. Almost 100% of electricity purchased by the companies of Schwarz Group comes from renewable sources. During the period 2018–2025, Schwarz Produktion has set itself the target of saving at least 33 million kilowatt hours of energy through different measures.

By the end of the 2025 fiscal year, all fruit and vegetable growers supplying Lidl and Kaufland in high water-risk countries will be certified under recognized water standards. These countries include Spain, Portugal, Italy, Greece, Egypt, South Africa, Morocco, Israel, and Chile.

Green Investments by Home Depot

Home Depot is one of the largest home improvement retailers in the world, with more than 2300 stores across North America. Home Depot offer a wide assortment of building materials, home improvement products, lawn and garden products, décor products and MRO products. The company also provide a number of services such as home improvement installation services and tool and equipment rental. The company had sales revenues of $152.7 billion and $159.5 billion in year 2023 and 2024 respectively.

The company have plans to reduce absolute Scopes 1, 2 and 3 emissions by 42% by 2030 compared to a 2020 base year. The company aims to hydrogen power 90% of forklifts in its major U.S. distribution centres by 2029. The company aim to produce or procure 100% renewable electricity equivalent for all Home Depot facilities worldwide by year 2030.

By 2028, 85% of all U.S. and Canadian sales—both in-store and online—of push mowers and handheld outdoor lawn equipment will utilize rechargeable battery technology. Through the purchase and proper use of Energy Star products, Home Depot aims to save $600 million in energy costs by 2026. By 2028, Home Depot plan to reduce or convert more than 200 million pounds of plastic to sustainable materials.

In January 2025, Home Depot partnered with Georgia Power's Customer Renewable Supply Procurement program to secure the equivalent of approximately 70% of the annual electricity required for its office buildings. The Home Depot have integrated its climate related risk assessment into its companywide ERM process.

The Home Depot Foundation have granted more than $86 million to serve veterans and support communities impacted by natural disasters. The Home Depot Foundation have plans to invest $50 million to train skilled tradespeople, including veterans by 2028. In 2023, Home Depot recycled over 13,400 metric tons of cardboard,400 metric tons of plastic and 33 metric tons of EPS from its stores and distribution centers. The company have collected over 461,900 pounds of single use and rechargeable batteries for responsible recycling through customer take back program. The company have provided over 210,000 pounds of shredded paper for recycling in year 2023, which have led to preservation of over 2500 trees and saving over 200,000 gallons of water.

By 2016, Home Depot removed ortho phthalates from vinyl flooring and reduced formaldehyde levels in laminate/engineered flooring.

By end 2024, Home Depot operated 2347 stores located throughout the US, Canada and Mexico. In fiscal 2024, Home Depot invested $3.5 billion in capital expenditures to support the business operations of Home Depot.

In 2023, Home Depot announced an approximately $ 1 billion investment in increased annualized compensation for its frontline hourly associates. The program has granted awards totalling more than $1.3 billion to associates over the period 2020–2022. Since 1999, the Homer Fund had awarded more than 184,600 grants totalling more than $267 million to assist associates and families to face hardships. The company had adopted its first wood purchasing policy to focus on selling wood and products containing wood sourced from responsibly managed forests. The Home Depot uses the GHG Protocol Corporate Accounting and Reporting Standard for calculating metric tons of greenhouse gas emissions.

Home Depot have joined the U.S. Environmental Protection Agency's (EPA) Green Power Partnership (GPP), an EPA-led program that aims to advance the U.S. market for renewable electricity. Home Depot have purchase agreements to generate enough electricity to power the equivalent of approximately 800 Home Depot stores. By end 2023, Home Depot have expanded its rooftop solar installations to 99 facilities.

In 2023, hydrogen fuel cells were installed at four additional supply chain facilities, bringing the total to 35 locations using emissions-free fuel for forklifts and material-handling equipment. This is expected to reduce annual electricity consumption by approximately 39.9 million kilowatt-hours. The Home Depot promotes energy-efficient products, partners with ENERGY STAR, and aims to help customers save $600 million in energy costs by 2026. In 2023, Home Depot facilitated US customers save $1 billion in terms of utility bills through the purchase of energy efficient products. In 2023, Home Depot offered approximately 45,000 energy-saving products in stores and online, including approximately 16,000 ENERGY STAR products. Since 1992, more than $500 billion in energy costs were avoided through sustainable green initiatives by Home Depot. Home Depot helped households achieve 4 billion metric tons of carbon reduction which is equivalent to removal of more than 950 million cars from road.

Table 20.1 highlights the timelines of the sustainable forestry practices adopted by Home Depot.

Approximately 61.6% of wood products were third party certified. Home Depot source most of its wood from leading North American forestry companies that participate in sustainable forestry certifications like FSC, SFI, PEFC, and American Tree Farm. In 2023, Home Depot attained its goal to exclude EPS foam and PVC film from new private brand packaging. By 2027, all private brand fibre packaging for new SKUs in the U.S. and Canada will be compostable, recyclable, or made from recycled content. Additionally, 200 million pounds of virgin plastic will be

Table 20.1 Sustainable forestry timelines

Year	Milestones
1994	Certified sustainable wood shelving products offered to customers.
1999	First wood purchasing policy adopted.
2018	Wood from endangered regions like the Amazon, Congo Basin, Papua New Guinea, or Solomon Islands to be Forest Stewardship Council (FSC)®-certified.
2023	Made responses to CDP's forests questionnaire for the first time.
2024	Published a comprehensive assessment of Home Depot's sustainable forestry program and policies.

Source: The Home Depot ESG Report | Fiscal 2023

replaced with recycled or alternative materials by 2028. On account of private brand packaging initiatives, approximately 1.5 million pounds of damaged products were kept out of landfills. During the period 2017–2023, the packaging innovations allowed Home Depot to redesign more than 1280 packages to reduce size and materials. By the end of 2023, EPS foam and PVC film were eliminated from new private-brand packaging in U.S. and Canada stores and online. In 2023, partners of Home Depot recycled approximately five% of its hazardous waste. Since 2019, smart irrigation systems have been installed in over 500 U.S. stores, reducing landscape water use by an average of 29% compared to traditional systems. Home Depot support and actively participate in the Green Chemistry & Commerce Council (GC3) as a member and through the Retail Leadership Council. In 2023, Home Depot offered solar panel and home battery storage sales and installation services from its stores. Since 2009, the campus improvement grants program of Home Depot had helped fund more than 200 projects which have benefitted approximately 72% of the nation's Historically Black Colleges and Universities (HBCUs). In 2023, Home Depot have paid $3.74 billion as federal income tax.

Green Investments by Carrefour

Carrefour is one of the world's leading food retailers with 15,244 stores and e-commerce sites. The company have 80 million customers every year. Carrefour have presence in more than 40 countries worldwide. Carrefour have operations in eight countries in Europe (France, Spain, Italy, Belgium, Romania and Poland) and Latin America (Brazil and Argentina). France, Spain and Brazil account for 81% of consolidated gross sales. Carrefour have 324,750 employees in eight countries. In Asia, the Middle East, Africa and other geographies, the Group works with local partners who are managing and expanding a network of stores under Carrefour banners. In 2024, the Group had 15,244 Carrefour-banner stores worldwide. The Carrefour group offers services to its customers through a full range of retail formats, from hypermarkets and supermarkets to convenience stores, cash & carry outlets and the "club" format with the banner Sam's Club. Carrefour aims to become a global leader in digital retail by 2026, driven by a data-centric and digital-first strategy.

With the mission to make reading accessible to all from an early age, Carrefour has set the target of selling 30 million one-euro books by 2030.As early as 2015, Carrefour had taken a pioneering step towards de-plastification in its stores beginning notably with fruits and vegetables. These efforts have collectively led to the elimination of over 20,000 tons of packaging with significant reduction in plastic use. Carrefour has set a target to remove 15,000 tonnes of virgin plastic from own brand product packaging by 2030 which is equivalent to a 10% reduction in the quantity of virgin plastic used in its single use packaging.

Carrefour has identified 10 key product categories where plastic remains prevalent, including items like shampoo, toilet paper, and pasta. To address this, the company will introduce alternative packaging solutions focused on reducing unnecessary packaging and using materials like paper, cardboard, or recycled plastic—for instance, replacing Carrefour Bio pasta's plastic packaging with 100% cardboard. Carrefour is collaborating with nine leading suppliers—including L'Oréal, Unilever, and Nestlé—to develop eco-designed packaging solutions tailored to each product. Carrefour is introducing a de-plastification index to measure progress in reducing plastic use across key product categories and the entire store. Rated on a scale of 1–10, the index reflects transformation efforts—for instance, the fruit and vegetable section, which began de-plastification in 2015 and eliminated 5500 tons of plastic, scores 8/10. Carrefour's overall strategy is to develop the circularity of packaging. In addition to elimination of plastic, Carrefour is developing reuse solutions through the deployment of bulk and deposit systems. Carrefour has 350 stores equipped with deposit systems in France, Europe and South America.

Carrefour had signed four direct power purchase agreements in France to strengthen its renewable energy performance. Carrefour had teamed up with Bee Friendly, a non-profit organization to protect pollinating insects for its Quality Lines. Carrefour France partnered with Ademe to support the Group's SME suppliers on decarbonization pathways.

Carrefour Brazil and Coca Cola have collaborated to sell drinks in returnable packaging in the chain's hypermarkets. Carrefour and GreenYellow had launched a partnership to produce photovoltaic energy in France. Carrefour Brazil had invested 28 million reals in forest conservation projects through its Brazil Forest Fund. Carrefour Spain had signed a 10-year renewable power purchase agreement with Engie.

The company aim to halve the 2016 levels of food waste by 2025. The company aim to generate 8 billion euros in sales from products certified as sustainable. The company aim to package 100% of Carrefour brand products using reusable, recyclable or compostable material by 2025. By 2025, the company focusses on recovery of 100% of waste from its stores. By 2026, the company aim to increase the number of partner producers to 50,000.

Carrefour aim to halve greenhouse gas emissions by 2030 and achieve a 70% reduction by 2040 compared to year 2019. By 2030, the company aim to cut greenhouse gas emissions generated by products sold in stores by 20 megatonnes compared to year 2019. The company have plans to double the proportion of fruits and vegetables sourced through ultra-short supply chains in Europe. The company also have plans to expand sales of bulk products to 300 million euros by 2026. The company have the requirement that the group's top suppliers align with a 1.5 °C trajectory by 2026, failing which they will be removed from the list of referenced suppliers.

In 2024, Carrefour partnered with Danone to launch France's first rail freight delivery channel to a logistics site, supplying over 130 stores daily in the Aix-en-Provence region.

Since 2021, Carrefour stopped automatically printing checkout receipts in 2021. As part of its environmental efforts, customers can access digital receipts, promotions, and rewards through the Carrefour app or online account, supporting the Group's broader anti-deforestation strategy.

Carrefour established an anti-deforestation fund with a €10 million investment to support biodiversity projects. In 2024, its Brazil Forest Fund allocated 28 million reals to six initiatives—led by groups like The Nature Conservancy and Imaflora—benefiting 230,000 farms and protecting 1.2 million hectares in the Amazon. During the 2018–2023 period, the Carrefour Foundation assisted four million people eat healthier foods and, in 2024, began tackling food insecurity through 111 projects.

Bond Issuance

Carrefour is the sixth largest issuer of SLBs and the only retailer in the top ten. In total the French company have priced six sustainability linked bond (SLBs). All Carrefour debt issued since Mar 2022 has been in SLB format.

In 2023, Carrefour successfully placed a sustainability linked bond issue, indexed to two objectives linked to greenhouse gas emissions within the framework of the Group's Euro medium term note (EMTN) programme for a total amount of €500 million. The bond with a coupon of 3.625% per year and a maturity date of 2030, was oversubscribed almost six times. The proceeds were used to finance the group's working capital requirements and to refinance existing debt. The bond was rated BBB by Standard & Poor's.

In 2024, Carrefour successfully placed a 750-million-euro mandatory Sustainability-Linked Bond, indexed to the Group's greenhouse gas emission reduction targets and food waste reduction goals. With a coupon of 3.625% per year and maturity date of 2032, the bond was almost four times oversubscribed. The proceeds will be used to finance the Group's working capital requirements and to refinance existing debt. The bond is rated BBB by Standard & Poor's. Carrefour refinanced its two credit lines with a new 4-billion-euro facility incorporating KPIs on decarbonisation and food waste. This facility, maturing in 2029, secures the Group's financing with no specific allocation of the funds raised.

Green Investments by IKEA

Ikea operate in over 60 markets around the world. In 2023, Ikea stores had 899 million visits and had sales amounted to EUR 47.6 billion. The company had around 800 home furnishing suppliers in more than 50 markets and over 140 global food suppliers. In fiscal 2024, Ikea launched an affordable plant rice and vegetable mix dish and hybrid options. In Fiscal 2024, Inter IKEA Group invested in a Toronto-based start-up focused on creating plant-based alternatives that mimic the texture, quality, and experience of whole-cut meat and seafood. In Fiscal 2024, the total emissions of Ikea were 28% lower as compared to fiscal 2016.

IKEA aims to halve value chain emissions by fiscal 2030 compared to fiscal 2016 and reach net-zero by FY50 by reducing absolute emissions by at least 90%. In fiscal 2024, the Ikea climate footprint was estimated to be 21.3 million tonnes CO2 equivalent (eq) in absolute terms. By fiscal 2030, Ikea aims to reduce absolute GHG emissions from food ingredients and materials by at least 50% compared to fiscal 2016 baseline.

Ikea launched a new feature in its Home Smart application, now piloting in Sweden to enable users save energy and reduce costs. Ikea is a founding member of the 50 L Home Coalition which focusses on driving innovative solutions for sustainable water use and energy efficiency. The IKEA Foundation have partnered with the Aspen Network of Development Entrepreneurs (ANDE) in developing the waste management sector in India and Kenya as to support green enterprises.

In Sweden, Ikea have collaborated with Research Institute of Sweden (RISE) to reduce household water consumption by combining technical innovations with positive behavioural changes. The primary focus of Ikea is to halve emissions across the IKEA value chain by fiscal 2030 compared to baseline year 2016 and achieve net zero emissions by fiscal 2050. In fiscal 2024, the Ikea climate footprint was estimated to be 21.3 million tonnes CO2 equivalent (eq) in absolute terms. Materials used in IKEA products account for the largest part of its climate footprint. In 2019, Ikea allocated EUR 100 million to invest in carbon storage and removal projects. In 2021, Ikea launched renewable electricity programme for suppliers in China, India and Poland. In Fiscal 2024, Ikea began using thin, hot-rolled steel for products like drawer slides, streamlining production and reducing greenhouse gas emissions. In 2024, Ikea avoided 49,164 tonnes of CO2 in ocean shipping by using biofuels. In the same year, Inter KEA Group invested in New School Foods, a Canadian start-up developing plant-based fish and meat alternatives to support a more sustainable food system. Ikea supports industry movements like the We Mean Business Coalition's Mission 2025, Global Diversity Framework implementation and global events, partnering with key organizations to promote climate action, biodiversity and collective environmental responsibility. Wood is the most commonly used material in the IKEA product range. Ikea aims for at least one third of its wood-based range which include 80% of particle board to be made from recycled wood.

Metals are vital to IKEA products. Though 100% recycled metals remain challenging, IKEA increases recycled content and reduces emissions through smarter design and low-emission material choices. IKEA is increasing recycled content in textiles like bed linens and curtains, reducing textile waste through innovations in cotton reuse, synthetic recycling, and circular design pilots. In March 2024, IKEA began identifying bio-based foam alternatives, shortlisted 18 companies from 300+, and plans to collaborate on testing and piloting innovative solutions. In 2023, Ikea joined the Business Coalition for a global plastics treaty. IKEA collaborates with partners to recycle glass waste into new products, using 100% recycled glass in items like MYRMOSAIK, KRONKLEMATIS, and HÄNGBJÖRK decorations. IKEA aims for zero waste to landfill by integrating waste reduction across design, production, and supply chains, optimizing materials, tracking data, and developing a performance framework. IKEA Industry prioritizes waste reduction and recycling, achieving a 76% recycling rate in FY24, down from 81% due to limited bio ash reuse options.

Green Investments by Tesco

Tesco is a leading multinational grocery retailer which provide affordable, healthy and sustainable food. The company was established in year 1919. The Group has nearly 6700 stores across the UK, Ireland and Central Europe. Tesco operates across multiple formats, including large extra stores, supermarkets, convenience and neighbourhood outlets, along with a comprehensive online retail business. Along with its core food retail business, Tesco sells clothing and general merchandise, provides financial and telecommunication services and runs petrol filling stations. The company employs over 350,000 people globally. Tesco had reduced its emissions in 2019–2020 by 37% as compared to its 2015 baseline. As a leading retailer, Tesco serves millions of customers every week, in stores and online.

The Group is a signatory to the Taskforce on Climate-related Financial Disclosures (TCFD) and RE100. It partners with leading sustainable food organisations, including the Sustainable Fisheries Partnership, and has established key initiatives such as the Tesco Sustainable Farming Group (2007) and the Global Tuna Alliance (2019). The Group is also a member of the Palm Oil Transparency Coalition and the Informal Working Group of the Taskforce for Nature-related Financial Disclosures (TNFD).

The company have reduced its scope 1 and 2 greenhouse gas emissions (GHG) across the group by 65%. The company aim to be carbon neutral in its operations by 2035 and net zero across its supply chain by 2050.The company had power purchase agreements (PPAs) with five wind and solar farms across UK. Till date, the company have removed over 2.5 billion pieces of plastic from its own brand products in the UK. The company have reduced food waste in its operations across the group. The company have donated £4 million worth of fruit and veg to over 400 schools across the UK as part of its Stronger Starts programme. The company aim to fully recycle own brand packaging by December 2025. Tesco aim to halve food waste in its own operations by 2025 against 2016 baseline. Tesco aim to procure group electricity via Power Purchase Agreements (PPAs) and onsite generation at 45% of its electricity usage by December 2025 and 60% by December 2030. Tesco aim to have fully electric Tesco home delivery fleet by year 2030. Till date, Tesco have deployed 720 electric home delivery vans. In 2023, Tesco became one of the first global companies to set a SBTI aligned net zero target across its full group value chain by 2050 which included its Forests, Land and Agriculture emissions (FLAG). Tesco's 2022–2023 emissions within SBTi scope were estimated at 58.9 million tCO2e per year.

In its distribution fleet, Tesco have four electric large good vehicles which avoided around 30,000 diesel fuelled road miles every year. Tesco have introduced its first electric heavy goods vehicle in the Booker business, along with over 140 electric generator units that power fridge trailers while on the road. Additionally, Booker plans to replace 170 diesel-powered refrigeration units with electric alternatives. Tesco is undertaking trialling HVO fuel, shifting freight to rail, improving transport efficiency, and replacing diesel trucks with lower emission alternatives like biomethane and electric vehicles. During October 2024, Tesco signed the UK's largest corporate solar PPA for 15 years period thereby securing 65% of power from Cleve Hill Solar Park and met up to 10% of its UK electricity needs. This site would feature more than 560,000 solar panels and energy storage infrastructure.

By November 2024, Tesco had moved its finest range of dried pasta into paper packaging thereby saving more than ten million pieces of plastic a year which weighed more than 30 tonnes. The company have reduced 918 tonnes of glass from finest prosecco bottles and reduced 150 tonnes of cartons from stone baked pizza. Tesco Ireland has invested over €15 million in Reverse Vending Machines (RVMs) to support the rollout of the national Deposit Return Scheme (DRS), launched in February 2024. Tesco is committed to reduce food waste across the supply chain. Edible surplus is redistributed, while remaining waste is used for animal feed or energy recovery. Tesco have reduced its food waste across its group by 14% compared to 2016/2017 baseline. Tesco's aim is to reduce food waste from farm to fork to ensure surplus food fit for consumption is redistributed.

Across Central Europe, Tesco have achieved the UN Sustainable Development goal target to halve food waste by 2030.Since 2016, Tesco have donated over 177 million meals to charities. Tesco has resumed surplus food processing for animal and pet feed. New facilities in Daventry and Northamptonshire will handle 1000 tonnes weekly, with potential to support other retailers. Tesco aim to source 50% of UK's fresh food and drink from areas of sustainable water management by 2030. In marine environments, the company aim to source 100% MSC certified seafood by 2030. The company aim to eliminate deforestation and conversion from its supply chain.

Tesco are founding contributors to the Responsible Commodities Facility (RCF), which offers financial incentives to Brazilian farmers committed to deforestation- and conversion-free soy cultivation. Co-funded by Tesco and other UK retailers, the initiative provides low-interest loans to farms producing 180,221 tonnes of soy annually. Tesco's marine strategy ensures sustainable fish sourcing by assessing fishery health, bycatch impact, and ecosystem effects in partnership with Sustainable

Fisheries Partnership (SFP) and supply chain collaborators. With respect to farming goals, Tesco requires all key suppliers to report animal health and welfare outcome measures across the group.

By December 2025, all shell eggs and ingredient eggs for Tesco UK and ROI (excluding Booker) will be sourced from cage-free hens. Additionally, all global growers supplying the UK will be LEAF Marque certified.

Tesco's Sustainable Farming Groups (SFGs) promote knowledge sharing, innovation, emission reduction, biodiversity protection, and animal welfare across key farming sectors, while ensuring fair, transparent pricing. All 400 British dairy farmers in the Tesco Sustainable Dairy Group were paid using a cost-of-production-plus model, with over £10 million paid above market price. All 115 Tesco Sustainable Lamb Group farmers received a bonus above factory price for meeting key environmental and animal welfare standards. In 2024–2025, Tesco paid nearly £2.64 million in bonuses to farmers in its Tesco Sustainable Beef Group. Tesco is on track to source 100% cage free shell eggs across the group and 100% cage free ingredient eggs across the UK. Since 2018, Tesco removed more than 100 billion calories through product reformulation and focused on reducing fat, salt and sugar from its products. Tesco's Kids Eat Free programme provided 375,000 free meals, and the company invested £4 million to improve children's access to fresh fruit and vegetables across the UK. Since 2016, Tesco have redistributed the equivalent of more than 450 million meals to charities, community groups and colleagues.

Through its charity partners in the UK, FareShare and the Trussell Trust, Tesco donate two million meals a month to 7000 charities and community groups and have collected over 72 million meals from customer donations. Tesco became signatories of RE100 pledging to become 100% renewable by 2030.

Tesco issues sustainability linked bonds (SLB) under its EMTN programme. Tesco have linked its bank facility margins to sustainability performance, tying rates to KPIs on emissions reduction, renewable energy sourcing, and food waste redistribution. In 2020, Tesco's Revolving Credit Facility was aligned to the Sustainability-Linked Loan Principles1 ("SLLP 2020") published by the Loan Market Association (LMA).

Green Investments by Nike

Nike Inc. was incorporated in year 1967. The basic business activity of Nike involves the design, development and worldwide marketing and selling of athletic footwear, apparel, equipment, accessories, and services. Nike is the largest seller of athletic footwear and apparel in the world. The company sell its products to consumers through Nike owned retail stores and digital platforms. Nike brand products are offered in six categories of Running, Nike Basketball, the Jordan brand, football, training, and sportswear. Nike also market products which are designed for kids, as well as for other athletic and recreational uses. Sportswear, Training and Running are the top selling apparel categories. Nike offer a range of nike branded performance equipment and accessories which include bags, socks, sports balls, eyewear, watches, digital devices, protective gear and other sports related items. Nike get supplies from 122 footwear factories located in 12 countries. Almost all the footwear of Nike is manufactured outside of the United States by over 15 independent contract manufacturers with multiple factories.

In 2023, the company had made $ten million investment in Historically Black Colleges and Universities (HBCUs) and Hispanic Serving Institutions (HSIs). In 2023, the company had $ one billion cumulative spend on diverse suppliers. The fiscal 2023 representation of women in Nike's global corporate workforce remained steady at 51%. By 2023, Nike had surpassed its 2025 goal of spending $1 billion with diverse owned suppliers two years ahead of schedule. The total economic impact of diverse spend amounted to $847 million in year 2023. In 2025, Nike expanded its compliance program to include Tier 2 suppliers and distribution centres, adopting industry tools like SLCP, Higg FEM, and ZDHC testing to improve transparency. In fiscal 2023, Nike had completed the rollout of industry tools to 96% of in scope facilities. Approximately 5.2 billion litres of water were restored in extended cotton supply chain. In 2019, Nike had set an ambitious Science based target (SBT) 47 to reduce its carbon footprint by 2030 which included a 65% absolute reduction across Scope 1 and 2 emissions and 30% across Scope 3 emissions compared from a 2015 baseline. In 2023, Nike achieved a 69% absolute reduction in greenhouse gases (GHGs) from owned and operated facilities as well as 100% waste diverted from landfills in Tier 1 manufacturing. In fiscal 2023, Nike had cut manufacturing and transport emissions 19% from 2020, driven by reduced air freight use, regional centres, faster processing, and "no rush" shipping. In 2023, a key driver of Nike's carbon reduction efforts was a 50% increase in renewable energy use by manufacturers thereby reaching 20% of total energy across Tier 1 and Tier 2. Tier 1 suppliers have phased out direct coal use. About 13% of Nike's inbound ocean shipping volume were covered by certified sustainable biodiesel fuels. In fiscal 2023, Nike expanded its ocean freight alternative fuel program using sustainable biodiesel for 13% of inbound shipping and avoided over 21,000 metric tons of emissions. Nike aims to scale this further through investments in renewable fuels and partnerships like the Zero Emission Maritime Buyers Alliance to address cost and demand challenges. Renewable electricity use, primarily via U.S. and EU virtual power purchase agreements, drove a 93% reduction in NIKE's Scope 2 emissions. There are many teams at Nike which aim to achieve its environmental targets. The Responsible Supply Chain and Global Procurement team at Nike achieved 100% renewable electricity coverage for most owned or operated Nike facilities worldwide. Nike is a founding member of the Clean Energy Procurement Academy which is a new cross industry collaboration to leverage clean energy opportunities.

NIKE's Energy Minimum Program supports suppliers with data-driven energy management. In fiscal 2023, it helped Tier 2 materials suppliers reduce energy use per unit by 9%. Nike aims to eliminate coal in manufacturing by 2030, reducing coal use by 20% through adoption of cleaner fuels and collaboration across industries to support thermal decarbonization. Since 2020, Nike's Supplier Climate Action Program (SCAP) has united key suppliers to set science-based climate targets. By FY23, it covered over 65% of strategic supplier emissions, resulting in a 10-year action plan to support shared decarbonization goals. In fiscal 2023, Nike advanced its transportation decarbonization strategy by reducing air freight, investing in alternative fuels, and collaborating industry wide.

Nike is addressing water security by targeting the restoration of 13 billion litres by 2025, focusing on its cotton supply chain, which accounts for 80% of its water footprint. Partnering with The Nature Conservancy and WWF, Nike supports projects in five major sourcing countries—Australia, Brazil, India, Pakistan, and the U.S.—to restore water, improve access, and enhance long-term resilience in water-stressed regions.

Nike has incorporated sustainability goals and initiatives into its operating budget. Nike's shoe factories had reduced energy consumption by 10% year over year since 2015 with 100% renewable energy being used across its US and Canada factories. Move to Zero is Nike's initiative focused on getting the company to a "zero-carbon, zero-waste future".

References

Alibaba Carbon Neutrality Report 2021.
Alibaba Environmental, Social and Governance Report, 2023.
Amazon Sustainability Bond Allocation Report 2022.
2023 Amazon Sustainability Report.
Costco Climate Action Plan 2024.
FY23 NIKE, Inc. Impact Report.
Home Depot ESG Report 2024.
https://finance.yahoo.com/news/alibabas-sustainability-bonds-fund-green-093000281.html
IKEA Sustainability Report FY 2024a.
IKEA Climate Report 2024b.
Sustainability Report FY 22/23 of the Companies of Schwarz Group.
Tesco PLC Sustainability Report 2024/25.
Tesco sustainability linked bond framework.pdf.
Universal Registration Document 2024/CARREFOUR.
Walmart ESG Report 2023.

MIX
Papier aus verantwortungsvollen Quellen
Paper from responsible sources
FSC® C105338

If you have any concerns about our products,
you can contact us on
ProductSafety@springernature.com

In case Publisher is established outside the EU,
the EU authorized representative is:
Springer Nature Customer Service Center GmbH
Europaplatz 3, 69115 Heidelberg, Germany

Printed by Libri Plureos GmbH
in Hamburg, Germany